Auschwitz

NAZI DEATH CAMP

Translation by
Douglas SELVAGE

Edited by
Franciszek PIPER
Teresa ŚWIEBOCKA

Authors
Danuta CZECH
Tadeusz IWASZKO
Barbara JAROSZ
Helena KUBICA
Aleksander LASIK
Franciszek PIPER
Kazimierz SMOLEŃ
Irena STRZELECKA
Andrzej STRZELECKI
Henryk ŚWIEBOCKI

Auschwitz

NAZI DEATH CAMP

The Auschwitz-Birkenau State Museum in Oświęcim
2005

Cover design
Piotr KUTRYBA

Photographs and documents: Archives of the Auschwitz-Birkenau State Museum,
The United States Holocaust Memorial Museum, Polish Underground Movement in London
as well as: Lidia Foryciarz, Tadeusz Iwaszko, Adam Kaczkowski, Tadeusz Kinowski,
Zofia Łoboda, Stanisław Mucha, Günter Schindler

Index
Richard BACHINGER (GEDENKDIENST, Austria)

Corrections
Piotr SETKIEWICZ, Regina CANETTI, Richard BACHINGER, Martin MAYR
and Philippe GLATZ (GEDENKDIENST, Austria)

Third Edition

© Copyright: 1996, 2002, 2004
by Auschwitz-Birkenau State Museum and Douglas Selvage

ISBN 83-88526-27-8

TABLE OF CONTENTS

THE PROSECUTION OF SS MEN FROM THE STAFF AT KL AUSCHWITZ

From the editors

Auschwitz, the largest and best-known Nazi concentration and death camp, has become a universally recognized symbol of genocide. Crimes unprecedented in human history were committed there. Auschwitz was above all else the place where the Nazis carried out their program for the mass extermination of European Jews, the so-called "Final Solution", along with their plans for the annihilation of Poles, Gypsies, and other nationalities. The SS murdered hundreds of thousands of people in the gas chambers and by mass execution. Prisoners died from lethal injections, torture, starvation, slave labor, and the lack of basic sanitary conditions. Some were the victims of criminal medical experiments.

In all of human history, there has never been a tragedy that has inspired such multi-faceted and extensive reflection upon the morality of mankind as the tragedy that took place at Auschwitz. The basis for such contemplation lies not only in the realization of the extreme scale and form of the crimes committed there, but also in the conviction that the evil symbolizied by Auschwitz neither began when the gates to the camp opened nor ended when the last crematoria were shut down.

The crimes committed at Auschwitz unmasked the darker aspects of contemporary civilization. It opened the eyes of humanity to the fact that if genocide could take place on such a mass, industrialized and bureaucratized scale in one location, then it could happen anywhere, because it lies within the capabilities of mankind. This disturbing fact alone prevents us from forgetting Auschwitz or relativizing its significance.

One can look at the concentration and death camp Auschwitz from a number of perspectives: psychological, sociological, legal, and theological. This publication is written from the point of view of the historian. It is based on the documents currently available, survivors' testimonies, and the vast scolarship on the topic from around the world. The book is meant to fill, at least in part, a gap that has existed for years on the book market — namely, the lack of a synthetic work devoted to the history of the camp at Auschwitz. The articles that make up the book reflect the latest research upon the most crucial questions related to the history of the camp, as written mainly by scholars employed at the Auschwitz-Birkenau State Museum. The book deals with topics that up to now have only been touched upon in the existing literature, mainly in terms of random examples: the distribution of the camp's victims in terms of nationality, the plundering of the personal effects of murdered Jews, the fate of children at the camp, medical experiments upon prisoners, and aspects of the camp resistance that are little-known outside of Poland. They show the camp at Auschwitz to be a point of confrontation between violence and humanitarian impulses, between self-preservation and charity, between hope and faith, despondency and despair.

Although the existing scholarship has already dealt with many of the matters examined below, it has not always taken into consideration the full range of topics and research questions related to the camp. Polish historiography, for example, has long ignored the exceptional role of Auschwitz in the Nazis' plans for the "Final Solution of the Jewish Question". At the same time, scholarship outside of Poland has taken little notice of the fact that Poles were the second-largest group of victims at the camp after the Jews and that Auschwitz was originally planned as a concentration camp for Poles. That Gypsies were also annihilated at KL Auschwitz was rarely mentioned in the literature until a few years ago and has hardly become public knowledge.

No one, however, is capable of fully understanding the camp or formulating a complete picture of the living conditions and the tragedy that the more than one million deportees to the camp had to face. Even if one were to examine all the extensive knowledge on the subject preserved in the world's archives and libraries, it would not suffice; for the tragedy of Auschwitz is the sum total of everything that transpired at the camp — not only that which is perceptible, but also the imperceptible changes in the consciousness of the victims, the results of their physical and mental anguish.

This publication is dedicated to all the victims of Auschwitz; to those who perished and to those who were able to survive — the men, women, and children who fell victim to the terror and racial hatred of the Nazis.

Franciszek Piper,
Teresa Świebocka

Oświęcim, 1993

Translator's note

Throughout the book, I have generally used Polish place names when referring to cities and villages that are part of Poland today — in keeping with the original, Polish manuscript — and German names when referring to Auschwitz-affiliated and other German camps. In most — but not all — cases, the German name for a given camp corresponds to the German place name for the town or village where the camp was located. At times, I have honored these conventions in the breach — e.g., "the camp at Auschwitz" instead of "the camp at Oświęcim" or simply "Auschwitz".

I would like to thank my fiancèe, Helen, for her help and patience while I translated this book, and my friend Jonathan Huener, who alerted me to this opportunity. I would also like to thank the staff of the Publications Division of the State Museum at Oświęcim for the confidence that they have placed in me.

Warsaw, 1995   Douglas Selvage

THE ESTABLISHMENT
OF KL AUSCHWITZ

FRANCISZEK PIPER

THE POLITICAL AND RACIST PRINCIPLES OF THE NAZI POLICY OF EXTERMINATION AND THEIR REALIZATION AT KL AUSCHWITZ

Of the circa 50 million people who died during World War II, around twenty million [1] were victims of the unprecedented policy of extermination of the Third Reich. Until that point in time, never in the history of human civilization had anyone planned or carried out atrocities on such a massive scale, never had anyone applied industrial methods to the mass extermination of people.

The Nazi policy of expansion and extermination was rooted not only in a desire to achieve political domination of Europe and the world, but in plans for effecting wide-ranging demographic changes in areas that, according to Nazi racial doctrine, were German *Lebensraum* or "living space". Nazi doctrine proclaimed the biological inequality of different nationalities and the right of "superior" (i.e., Germanic) nationalities to dominate "inferior" ones: Jews, Gypsies, Slavs and others. [2]

Many documents from the Nazi [3] movement delineated the concept of German "living space" and the character of demographic changes to be achieved in such areas. As early as February 24, 1920, the program of the *Deutsche Arbeiter Partei* (German Workers' Party, DAP) — later renamed *Nationalsozialistische Deutsche Arbeiter Partei* (National Socialist German Workers' Party, or NSDAP) — stated the following: "We demand earth and soil (colonies) for the survival of our nation and for the settlement of our surplus population." [4] Adolf Hitler clarified the direction of the desired expansion several years later in *Mein Kampf*:

We are finally breaking away from the colonial and trade policies of the prewar period and are moving toward the territorial policy of the future. When we speak

---

[1] According to Czesław Pilichowski, a total of 19.2 million people died in both occupied and German-allied territories as a result of the Nazi terror. Czesław Pilichowski, *No Time-Limit for these Crimes* (Warsaw, 1980), pp. 12, 147.

[2] Czesław Madajczyk, *Faszyzm i okupacje 1938-1945* [Fascism and Occupation, 1938-1945]: (Poznań, 1983), vol. I, pp. 28-30, 242-51; idem., *Polityka III Rzeszy w okupowanej Polsce* [The Policies of the Third Reich in Occupied Poland], (Warszawa, 1970), vol. 1, p. 135.

[3] Translator's note: In a number of cases throughout the book , I have translated "Hitlerian" as "Nazi". This is in keeping with contemporary English usage; the term "Hitlerian" has fallen out of use in English since the end of World War II.

[4] Gottfried Feder, *Das Programm der NSDAP und seine weltanschaulichen Grundgedanken* [The Program of the NSDAP and the Basic Tenets of its *Weltanschauung*], (Munich, 1932), pp. 19-22 (as cited in Jakub Banaszkiewicz, *Powstanie partii hitlerowskiej, 1918-1923* [The Origins of the Hitlerite Party, 1918-1923], (Poznań, 1968), p. 502.

today of new lands on the European continent, we are thinking above all else of Russia and the neighboring territories under her control. [5]

In order that there would be no doubt as to the ultimate goal behind these aspirations, Hitler declared on November 5, 1937, at a secret conference attended by military officials and the foreign minister: "In our case, it is not a question of conquering peoples but exclusively our aim is the conquering of territory suitable for agricultural goals." [6] Heinrich Himmler expanded upon and completed Hitler's thought in July 1942:

Our goal is not the complete Germanization of the East in the old sense of the term — i.e., by teaching the population living there German language and law; rather, we are striving for the goal that only people of purely German race will live there. [7]

The first stage of the far-reaching demographic changes planned by the National Socialists was the transformation of the German Reich into a state composed of one nation. The propaganda slogan, *"Ein Reich, ein Volk, ein Führer"* — One state, one nation, one Führer — expressed this idea in its most concise form.

The Jews were the first to fall victim to this doctrine. With the help of an entire series of discriminatory laws, regulations, chicanery and terror, including imprisonment in concentration camps, Jews were compelled to leave Germany. As a result, the number of Jews living in Germany fell from 550,000 in January 1933 to 200,000 [8] at the outbreak of war in September 1939. All the Jews were not able, however, to leave Germany. Many countries maintained laws that prevented their immigration. Some Jews believed that they were merely witnessing yet another historical wave of antisemitism, which would eventually taper off — as it had in the past — and that the social and political situation would eventually return to normal. On a smaller scale, other minorities also faced various forms of discrimination in Germany, particularly Gypsies and Poles.

Shortly after the war broke out, the Nazis began deporting Jews and Gypsies from Germany to occupied Polish territory. Since this area was considered German "living space", intended for future German settlement, the idea was put forth of driving the Jews out of Europe to the French island-colony of Madagascar, and the Slavs, to Siberia, with the exception of a small group of individuals who bore some German blood and were considered fit for assimilation. Another proposed solution to the problem of de-populating Eastern Europe was to sterilize the people living there. In the period following Germany's greatest military successes, when the Nazis believed that the final conquest of Europe and the world was only a question of time, the highest authorities of the Third Reich became ever more inclined toward what, in their opinion, was the most radical solution — the liquidation of entire nationalities.

---

[5] Adolf Hitler, *Mein Kampf* (München, 1942), p. 742.

[6] *Das Urteil von Nürnberg* (München, 1946), p. 30. Nuremberg Document 386-PS.

[7] Ibid, p. 77. Nuremberg Document 2915-PS.

[8] Arnold Paucker, *Jewish Resistance in Germany. The Facts and Problems* (Berlin, 1991), p. 11.

Such a liquidation could take numerous forms: anything from "re-Germanization" of a certain portion of the population with a German, background through various measures to decrease the birth rate and raise the death rate, to acts of immediate, physical extermination.

Many of these concepts remained a mere subject of research or were simply being contemplated and discussed within leading circles of the Third Reich. No one could foresee what direction these ideas might take in the future; in the thoughts of the Nazi leadership, the concept of exploiting conquered nationalities for slave labor appeared side-by-side in a rather unclear relationship with ideas for their extermination. One should remember that the Nazis moved rather easily from one concept to the other, depending on existing conditions and possibilities. The idea of exterminating Jews exemplifies this fact, having been preceded not long before by the idea of resettling them to Madagascar. Thus, the actual decisions made, based on formal or informal regulations, orders, and their practical realization, will be the most important subjects for our analysis.

The policies of the Third Reich toward different nationalities in occupied Europe varied. Jews and Gypsies found themselves in the worst situation: they were condemned to extermination regardless of their age, sex, or attitude toward Nazi ideology and the governing apparatus. Starvation in ghettos, executions and, in the end, murder on an industrial scale inside gas chambers, were the means used for exterminating these two peoples.

The liquidation of other nationalities residing in areas considered German "living space" — mainly Poles — assumed a wide variety of forms, depending on their number, economic conditions, and Nazi propaganda goals. Of this group, only those who violated occupation statutes or actively participated in the struggle against the occupier were officially subject to physical extermination. In practice, however, the occupation authorities — especially in Poland and the former Soviet Union — went beyond these repressive goals and the immediate circle of individuals subject to them in order to undermine the resistance movement. Individuals merely considered suspicious — especially those whose social standing made them a potential threat to the occupier — were also subject to extermination. Hence, the Nazis killed off Poles whom they considered part of the nation's leadership strata, particularly the intelligentsia. This activity, which took the form of premeditated acts of extermination, bore all the marks of genocide. Although an effort was sometimes made to give these acts a preventive-repressive character, they were based in fact — as reflected in the Nazi leadership's comments — on a much larger goal: to degrade the Polish nation culturally and intellectually by depriving it of its intelligentsia. Every terroristic and repressive act justified under the rubric of collective responsibility — pacifications, street arrests, execution of hostages — had a genocidal character as well. The goal was not merely to exhaust the Poles psychologically, but to decimate the entire nation.

One of the most effective methods used by the Nazis for realizing their extermination policies — more effective than execution and emaciation in prisons, camps and ghettoes — was mass murder in death camps. Centers of immediate extermination were intended mainly for Jews. They differed from concentration camps in that beyond a small group of prisoners needed for maintaining the extermination facilities and for sorting out the dead's possessions, the victims were never imprisoned in them, so a large number of barracks or other living quarters were unnecessary. Jews delivered to these camps were simply rushed from the unloading platform to the gas chambers and murdered. There were four such centers: the first, at Chełmno on the Ner, was founded in December 1941, and the next three — Bełżec, Treblinka and Sobibór, were established in 1942.[9] In addition to these four, there were two other extermination centers of a different character, linked organizationally and topographically with the Auschwitz and Majdanek concentration camps.

Concentration camps for prisoners of various nationalities, differed from centers of mass extermination above all in the method of mass murder, although the goal of physically annihilating the victims remained the same. Hunger, coupled with physical exhaustion, was the basic method of extermination at the concentration camps. Other factors related to living conditions at the camp increased the prisoners' death toll: poor clothing, lack of rest and medical attention, and unsuitable living quarters. The Nazis tried to confer the character of punishment for violations of camp discipline upon executions at the camps, mainly by shooting. In contrast to the victims of extermination centers, who were murdered immediately upon arrival, concentration-camp prisoners spent a longer or shorter period of time at the camps.

An alternative to mass execution as a means of mass murder, concentration camps also served to camouflage the murders being committed. Formally linked by their name and organization to prewar camps in Germany that had been used for imprisoning Hitler's opponents, they harkened back to a concept to which public opinion in Germany and other countries had, to a certain extent, become accustomed. In other words, concentration camps, which up to that point had been a synonym for illegality and violence, became to a certain extent a screen for concealing mass murder.

The concentration camp at Auschwitz (Oświęcim), founded in 1940, also — and mainly — served as a center for the immediate extermination of Jews beginning in 1942. Taking into account the camp's two functions and the numerical predominance of Jews and Poles among its victims, one can divide the camp's history into two periods:

— a "Polish" period (1940 to mid-1942), when the majority of deportees and victims were Poles, and

— a "Jewish" period (mid-1942 to 1945), when Jews represented the majority of deportees and victims.

We should note from the very beginning, however, that the rate of extermination in the second period was several times greater than in the first; measured across the entire period of the camp's existence, Jews accounted for 85% of the deportees to the camp and 90% of its victims.

---

[9] Yitzhak Arad, *Belzec, Sobibór, Treblinka. The Operation Reinhard Death Camps* (Bloomington and Indianapolis, 1987), passim.

Poles

The decided majority of Poles held at Auschwitz had been sent there for political reasons: in revenge for participation in the resistance movement or for preventive purposes in the case of other "undesirable" elements, known for patriotism or social activism before the war or considered part of the leadership class on the basis of their education or social standing. On the same basis, local police units would send hostages to the camp for execution in revenge for the resistance movement's activities in a given area. People were also sometimes arrested at random during various terroristic-preventive campaigns (traps, round-ups, pacifications) and sent to the camp as political prisoners. The camp also provided an execution site for individuals condemned to death by the German court-martial (*Standgericht*) in Katowice or singled out for "special treatment" (*Sonderbehandlung*) during various police actions. [10]

A separate category of prisoners, almost exclusively Poles, were the so-called "reformatory prisoners" (*Erziehungshäftlinge*), sent to the camp for violating Nazi labor laws. Such prisoners were supposed to be released after six to eight weeks, but some perished before their date of release or had their sentences extended long beyond the original term. [11]

After the Warsaw Uprising had broken out, more than 13,000 Varsovians — men, women, and children — were deported to the camp in the space of two months, August and September 1944. [12]

The planned deportation to the camp of tens of thousands of men, women, and children from the Zamość region — foreseen as one of the first bridgeheads for Germanization in eastern Poland — demonstrated the Nazis' goal of exterminating the Poles, which they only achieved to a small degree. Plans had been approved to the effect that beginning in November 1942, three trains were to leave Zamość each week for Auschwitz, each carrying 1000 men, women, and children who were deemed part of the "worst" racial category (Wertungsgruppe IV according to the RuS[HA], the Main Office for Racial and Settlement Questions).

The Poles from the Zamość region were first interned at a transit camp in Zamość. They were registered, "racially evaluated" and sent to the employment office, where their ability to work was established. The Polish families of "higher racial worth" (*RuS — Wertungsgruppe I* and *II*) from the Lublin district (Zamość) were to be send to Litzmannstadt (Łódź) for potential Germanization. The Poles of *RuS — Wertungsgruppe III* and *IV* — including

---

[10] On the role of the KL Auschwitz in the extermination of Poles (intelligentsia, hostages, individuals condemned by court-martial): Autobiography of Rudolf Höss, Kommandant of Auschwitz, pp. 40-6, and of Pery Broad, SS Man from the Political Division of the Concentration Camp Auschwitz, *KL Auschwitz seen by the SS* (Oświęcim, 1994).

[11] Tadeusz Iwaszko, "Więźniowie Oświęcimia z literą 'E' [Auschwitz Prisoners with the Letter 'E']", *Biuletyn Informacyjny, Comité Intern. d'Auschwitz* 9/10 (1977), p. 4; nr 2 (1978), p. 4.

[12] Danuta Czech, *Kalendarium der Ereignisse im Konzentrationslager Auschwitz-Birkenau* [Calendar of Events in the Concentration Camp Auschwitz-Birkenau]. Reinbek, 1989, pp. 847, 868, 876, 880.

children under 14, older people over 60, and "Poles under 60, unfit to work, sick or frail" — were to be sent to "old-age communities" or "Polish reservations". Poles (14-60) considered fit for work were to be shipped to the "Third Reich" for labor without their dependents. Some Poles from *Wertungs-gruppe IV* were sent to "Birkenau as laborers" from mid-December 1942 to the beginning of 1943. In the end, the Nazis did not carry out their Germanization plan for Zamość and eventually abandoned it. Nevertheless, a total of 1300 men, women, and children were deported from the region to Auschwitz. [13]

Representatives of Poland's intellectual elite — renowned artists and scholars, politicians, clergy, doctors, teachers, lawyers, engineers, and officers — would continue to perish at Auschwitz until the end of the war. Based on fragmentary evidence, 377 transports carrying at least 38,596 people arrived at the camp from two cities alone — Warsaw and Cracow — which had played a leading role in Poland's past and present. [14] The total number of Poles deported to the camp lay somewhere between 140,000 — 150,000.

Thus, for the Poles, who perished during six long years of occupation in thousands of camps, prisons, execution sites, and penal institutions, [15] at forced labor, on the front, and in the partisan struggle, the camp Auschwitz--Birkenau became a symbol of martyrdom for the Polish nation.

Jews

As of 1942, having served up to that point as a place for deporting Poles and other nationalities (as noted above), the concentration camp at Auschwitz became above all else a center for the mass extermination of Jews. The decision to use KL Auschwitz for this goal shortly followed Hitler's order in spring or summer 1941 to murder all Jews living in Germany's sphere of influence. [16] The former commandant at Auschwitz, Rudolf Höss, wrote as follows regarding the decisions undertaken that time:

In the summer of 1941 — I cannot remember the exact date at this point — I was hastily summoned before the *Reichsführer-SS* in Berlin, directly by his adjutant. Himmler, breaking with his usual custom, explained the following to me without the presence of his assistant: The *Führer* had ordered the final solution of the Jewish question. We, the SS, were to execute the order. The existing extermination centers in the East would not suffice for activity on such a large scale. Thus, I have designated

---

[13] "Wysiedlenia w Zamojszczyźnie [Deportations from the Zamość Region]", *Biuletyn Głównej Komisji Badania Zbrodni Hitlerowskich w Polsce* XIII (1960), pp. 5-58, 3F-26F, selection of documents.

[14] Archiwum Państwowego Muzeum w Oświęcimiu-Brzezince [Archive of the Auschwitz-Birkenau State Museum at Oświęcim, henceforth APMO]. Höss Trial (*Proces Hössa*), file 13, specifications about the transports taken from partial registers of new arrivals at the camp (*Zugangsliste*).

[15] The list of various camps, prisons, detention centers and ghettos in occupied Poland published in 1979 by Główna Komisja Badania Zbrodni Hitlerowskich w Polsce (The Central Commission for the Study of Hitlerite Atrocities in Poland) catalogs 5,877 such places. *Obozy hitlerowskie na ziemiach polskich 1939-1945. Informator Encyklopedyczny* [Hitlerite Camps on Polish Territory, 1939-1945. Encyclopedic Index.] Warszawa, 1979.

[16] Gerald Reitlinger, *The Final Solution* (London, 1971), pp. 82-6.

Auschwitz for this goal, given its suitable location in terms of transportation and because the area can be easily isolated and concealed. At first, I wanted to entrust this assignment to one of the higher SS officers, but I changed my mind, because I wanted to avoid from the very start any difficulties that might arise from a division of responsibilities. I am now entrusting you with the execution of this assignment. It is a hard and difficult task, demanding total dedication, no matter what difficulties might arise. You will learn further details from *Sturmbannführer* Eichmann at RSHA [17], who will contact you in the near future... After you speak with Eichmann, you will immediately send me the plans for the projected facilities. The Jews are the eternal enemies of the German nation and must be extirpated. All Jews that come into our hands during the war will be exterminated without exception. If we are unable to destroy the biological forces of Judaism, then the Jews will one day destroy the German nation. [18]

Since a number of other sites existed with similar features, the deciding factor in Auschwitz's selection as a site for mass extermination seems to have been the concentration camp already established there — at the time, the only one in occupied Poland with the necessary administrative and technical apparatus for carrying out the Nazis' plans.

We do not know the exact date when the mass extermination of Jews began at Auschwitz. The former camp commandant, Höss, claimed in his testimony after the war that he could not give an exact date; in his memoirs, he writes that it might have been in December 1941 or January 1942, or, in another place, before the establishment of the women's camp in the spring of 1942 — i.e., before March 26, 1942. [19]

Most likely, however, the decision to include KL Auschwitz in plans for exterminating the Jews was made at the Berlin Wannsee Conference on January 20, 1942. At the conference, the head of the Main Office for *Reich* Security, Reinhard Heydrich [20], introduced a plan for "combing" all of Europe from West to East to find all the Jews and exterminate them ("evacuation to the East"). Because the planned operation would require cooperation on the part of numerous institutions, the conference was attended by representatives from a number of state ministries, including representatives from Internal Affairs (Wilhelm Stuckart), Foreign Affairs (Martin Luther), Justice (Roland Freisler), and Eastern Lands (Alfred Meyer and Georg Leibbrandt). Representatives from other state and party organs also took part in the conference: Ernst Neumann from the Plenipotentiary for the Four-Year Plan, Josef Bühler from the General Government [21], Gerhard Klopfer from the Party chancellory, and Friedrich Kritzinger

---

[17] Translator's note: *Reichsicherheitshauptamt*, or Headquarters for State Security.

[18] *Wspomnienia Rudolfa Hössa* ..., p. 193. For earlier, complete translation see "Reminiscences of Rudolf Höss" in *KL Auschwitz seen by the SS* (Oświęcim, 1972).

[19] Ibid., pp. 152, 196, 199.

[20] Heydrich was fatally wounded a few months later by Czech partisans.

[21] Transl. note: The "General Government" was that portion of occupied Poland not directly annexed to Germany and set aside — at least temporarily — for the Poles. All Poles who could not qualify as "Germans" based on their family background were to be resettled from the annexed territories to inside the General Government, which would serve as a reservoir of slave labor. The name "General Government" was in keeping with the Nazi goal of wiping the very name "Poland" off the map of Europe. It was ruled by a German administration, headed by Hans Frank, but it was also subordinated to the German army and police.

from the *Reich's* Chancellory. Also in attendance were representatives from the SS central administration: Henrich Müller and Adolf Eichmann from RSHA; Otto Hofmann from the Central Administration for Race and Settlement Policy; and security-police representatives from both the General Government and the *Reichskommisariat* "Ostland". The planned extermination was to encompass the over 11 million Jews living in Europe at the time, not only in occupied territories and dependencies, but also in neutral countries and countries to be occupied in the future, such as Great Britain, with its 330,000 Jews. [22]

The first transport known to arrive at Auschwitz came on February 15, 1942, with several hundred Jews from Bytom (part of Germany at the time). [23] The first registered transport, arrived, however on March 26, 1942, from Slovakia, carrying 999 Jewish women. Then came transports from France (March 30, 1942), Poland (May 5, 1942), Holland (July 17, 1942), Belgium (August 5, 1942), Jugoslavia (August 18, 1942), Bohemia and Moravia (Theresienstadt — October 7, 1942), Norway (December 1, 1942), Greece (March 20, 1943), Italy (October 23, 1943) and Hungary (May 2, 1944). [24] According to the protocol from the January 1942 conference in Berlin-Wannsee, all five million Jews living in these states were potential victims of Auschwitz.

The area of Europe encompassed by the plan for exterminating Jews can be divided into four parts:

— territories East of the river Bug (area of operations for so-called *Einsatzgruppen*); [25]

— the General Government (area of operations for the extermination centers Treblinka, Sobibór, Bełżec, Majdanek);

— the northwest area of Poland annexed to the *Reich*, the so-called "Wartheland" region (area of operations for the extermination center at Chełmno);

— the remaining areas of Central, Western, Northern and Southern Europe (area of operations for Auschwitz).

This division of responsibilities did not result from any rigid principles imposed from above; rather, it reflected actual practice and was subject to numerous exceptions. For example, most Austrian, German, and Slovakian Jews were deported either to the Soviet Union (Minsk, Kowno, Riga), to the ghetto at Łódź, or to various localities in the Lublin region. [26] On the other hand, while the camp at Auschwitz served mainly as a location for exterminating foreign Jews, numerous Jews from Poland — from the central (so-called General

---

[22] Raul Hilberg, *Die Vernichtung der europäischen Juden* (Berlin, 1982), pp. 285-86; Reimund Schnabel, *Macht ohne Moral* (Frankfurt, 1957), pp. 496-506.

[23] *Kommandant in Auschwitz, autobiographische Aufzeichnungen von Rudolf Höss* (Stuttgart, 1961), p. 123.

[24] D. Czech, op. cit. passim.

[25] Transl. note: The so-called *Einsatzgruppen* or "quick-response groups" were mobile squads of German policemen assigned to round up Jews and other "enemies" of the German state for immediate execution. They operated east of the river Bug in the former Soviet Union and part of what had been Poland before World War II.

[26] Klaus Drobisch, "Die Endlösung der Judenfrage — Massenmord als Element des faschistischen Weltherrrschaftsstrebens (1941-1942)", in *Juden unterm Hakenkreuz* (Berlin, 1973), pp. 286-318; R. Hilberg, pp. 490-505.

Government), western (Upper Silesia), and northern (around Ciechanów and Białystok) regions of occupied Poland — perished there as well.

KL Auschwitz took an ever greater role in the genocide after the extermination centers at Chełmno (April), Bełżec (June), Treblinka (September) and Sobibór (October) ceased operations in 1943. After the last mass execution at Majdanek on November 3, 1943 (codename *"Erntefest"* or "harvest festival"), Auschwitz remained the only center in operation for the mass extermination of Jews. (The death camp at Chełmno returned to operations for a brief period of three weeks.) It should be kept in mind that until the spring of 1944, concentration camps inside the *Reich* proper did not take part in the mass extermination of Jews. On Himmler's orders, these camps had shipped all their Jewish prisoners in October 1942 to either Auschwitz or Majdanek so that the camps inside the *Reich* would henceforth be "free of Jews" (*Judenfrei*).

In the spring of 1944, as a result of the *Reich's* deteriorating economic situation, especially in terms of manpower, the Nazis retreated from their principle of a *"Judenfreies Reich"* to make greater use of Jewish labor in German industry. Henceforth, KL Auschwitz would serve not only as a site of extermination, but also as the main transfer point for Jewish laborers being evacuated in advance of the Red Army's offensive. At Auschwitz, a gigantic sifting of human material now took place; people needed for their labor were kept alive and dispatched to various subcamps, linked to German industrial concerns, and the rest were killed and burned. More than 400,000 Jews from Hungary, 60,000-70,000 Jews from Łódź, and Jewish prisoners from Majdanek, Płaszów and other labor camps in the General Government passed through KL Auschwitz under these conditions. Among the transports arriving at KL Auschwitz, one could find Jewish residents from practically every country in Europe, and even from areas outside Europe. The total number of Jews deported to the camp numbered at least 1.1 million.

Gypsies

The third largest group of prisoners deported to KL Auschwitz were the Gypsies. As was the case with the Jews, the Nazis called for the total annihilation of the Gypsies. The only exception were two Gypsy clans: the Sinte and Lalleri. In the Soviet Union, *Einsatzgruppen* killed the Gypsies by firing squad. Inside Poland, around 50,000 Gypsies perished, either executed on the spot or murdered along with the Jews at the Nazi death camps. Gypsies were deported to the extermination centers and ghettoes from Western Europe, Germany, Austria, Bohemia, and Moravia. The largest number were imprisoned at the Auschwitz concentration camp. An order from Himmler, dated December 16, 1942, and regulations from RSHA from January 29, 1943, provided the necessary basis for deporting Gypsies to KL Auschwitz. Between February 1943 and August 1944, a total of around 23,000 Gypsies — men, women and children — were imprisoned at KL Auschwitz II-Birkenau in a so-called "family camp". They had been deported to Auschwitz from Germany, Austria, the Protectorate of Bohemia and Moravia, and lands annexed directly to the Reich. Most of them died from hunger, disease and emaciation. On August 2, 1944, after the last group of around 3000 men, women and children had been gassed, the Gypsy camp at Birkenau was liquidated. [27]

Soviet Prisoners of War

In violation of international law, prisoners of war were also held at the Auschwitz concentration camp. Only at the very beginning, for the sake of appearance, they were held in a separate area of the main camp called the "Workcamp for Soviet Prisoners of War". During the first five months, between October 1941 and March 1942, more than 9,000 of the 10,000 Soviet POWs being held there either died from starvation or were executed. Another 2,000 Soviet prisoners would be deported to the camp before its liquidation. The camp also served as a site for executing Soviet prisoners from other POW camps. These individuals, who were never registered, were either shot upon arrival or sent to their death in the gas chambers. [28] A total of at least 15,000 Soviet POWs were sent to Auschwitz.

Other Nationalities

On a lesser scale, KL Auschwitz was also an extermination center for prisoners of other nationalities: Czechs (e.g., members of the *Sokól* patriotic organization), Byelorussians (more than 5,000 men, women, and children were deported to the camp from the Minsk and Vitebsk regions alone in the course of anti-partisan campaigns), Jugoslavians, French, Germans and Austrians (among them political prisoners — e.g., members of the international brigades during the Spanish Civil War), and others. It is estimated that in addition to the Jews, Poles, Gypsies and Soviet POWs a total of around 25,000 prisoners of other nationalities were imprisoned at the camp. Thus, a total of at least 1.3 million people were deported to Auschwitz.

* * *

From a technical point of view, KL Auschwitz was an amalgamation of a concentration camp (along the lines of Dachau or Gross-Rosen) and a Nazi death camps for Jews (along the lines of Treblinka or Sobibór). In practice, the two functions were so closely linked at KL Auschwitz, that one can speak of the creation of a new, third category of death camp, where immediate killing, mainly in gas chambers, and indirect extermination, through starvation and forced labor occurred simultaneously.

The camp's basic function during its entire existence was the killing of individuals deported to it. Other functions — in particular, the exploitation of the labor force imprisoned there — were goals of only secondary importance.

---

[27] On the fate of the Gypsies, see: Autobiography of Rudolf Höss, pp. 49-53, and Reminiscences of Pery Broad, pp. 139-41, in *KL Auschwitz seen by the SS* (Oświęcim 1994); Hans Joachim Döring, *Die Zigeuner im NS-Staat* (Hamburg, 1964), pp. 153-164.

[28] Jerzy Adam Brandhuber, "Jeńcy radzieccy w obozie koncentracyjnym w Oświęcimiu [Soviet Prisoners at the Concentration Camp at Oświęcim]", *Zeszyty Oświęcimskie* 4 (1960), pp. 3-62.

DANUTA CZECH

ORIGINS OF THE CAMP, ITS CONSTRUCTION AND EXPANSION

1. Origins of the Camp

In the police-state administration of the Third Reich, the camp at Auschwitz served two functions:

1. as a concentration camp, where prisoners of various nationalities (Jews, Poles, Gypsies, Russians and others) faced progressive annihilation;

2. as a death camp, where (beginning in 1942) hundreds of thousands of Jews were put to death immediately upon arrival.

The authorities at KL Auschwitz, its administrators and armed personnel, were a criminal organization, selected to carry out Hitler's program of subjugation, physical and moral degradation, and progressive biological destruction of conquered nationalities, to the point of their complete extermination. With this goal in mind, the machinery of mass murder was added on to the concentration camp at Auschwitz, and the prisoners were subjected to a system of terror, refined torture and total exploitation.

The proposal to locate a concentration camp at Auschwitz originated in the office of the Superior SS and Police Commander for the Southeast (*der Höhere SS-und Polizeiführer Südost*) in Wrocław (Breslau), *SS-Gruppenführer* Erich von dem Bach-Zelewski. His subordinate, the Inspector for the Security Police and the Security Service (*Inspekteur der Sicherheitspolizei und des Sicherheitsdienstes — Sipo u. SD*), *SS-Oberführer* Arpad Wigand, came forward with such a project at the end of 1939, under pressure from reports of overcrowded prisons in Upper Silesia and the Dąbrowski Basin. The situation was hindering the security police in the application of terror and repression against the Polish population. *SS-Oberführer* Wigand stressed in his proposal that the resistance movement was growing in Silesia and the General Government, that mass arrests would be needed to counter it, and that the existing concentration camps would not suffice for holding everyone arrested.

Wigand indicated Auschwitz (Oświęcim) as a suitable location for a future concentration camp. He thought that the existing barracks could be put to immediate use for confining prisoners. The barracks, located near the confluence of the Vistula and Soła Rivers in the town's Zasole district, would allow the camp to expand in the future and also enable its isolation from the outside world. The convenient train connections to Oświęcim from both Silesia and the General Government were an additional argument in favor of the location.

In the first days of January 1940, the Inspector for Concentration Camps, *SS-Oberführer* Richard Glücks, sent a commission to Auschwitz, led by *SS-Sturmbannführer* Walter Eisfeld, then camp supervisor (*Schutzhaftlagerführer*) at Sachsenhausen. The commission decided based on its inspection, that the barracks at Oświęcim were not a suitable site for a concentration camp. [1]

The Office of the Superior SS and Police Commander in Wrocław (Breslau) was apparently of a different opinion. On January 25, 1940, the chief of the SS Central Office (*SS-Hauptamt*) informed *Reichsführer-SS* Heinrich Himmler that according to a report from *SS-Gruppenführer* von dem Bach-Zelewski, "in the near future a camp will be set up near Auschwitz, which has been conceived of as a type of state concentration camp". [2]

On February 1, 1940, *Reichsführer-SS* Himmler ordered that the following facilities be inspected in order to determine, among other things, where the planned camp should be located: the police prison at Welzheim and the transit camp at Kislau (both within the jurisdiction of the *Höheren SS-und Polizeiführer* Southwest), the camp in Frauenberg near Admont (under the jurisdiction of the *Höheren SS-und Polizeiführer* Alpenland), the camp at Sosnowiec and the former barracks at Oświęcim (Auschwitz) (both under the jurisdiction of the *Höheren SS-Polizeiführer* Southeast). [3] On February 21, 1940, *SS-Oberführer* Glücks informed Himmler that as a result of the inspection, it had been decided that the former Polish artillery barracks in Oświęcim (Auschwitz) would provide a suitable site for a quarantine camp (*als Quarantänelager geeignet*) once sanitary facilities were installed and several architectural changes were made. As soon as the negotiations that the chief of security police had demanded with the *Wehrmacht* reached a conclusion, the quarantine camp could be put into operation immediately. [4]

As a result of the negotiations, on April 8, 1940, the general in charge of the *Luftwaffe*, Halm, consented to the SS's rental of the Auschwitz barracks and prepared an agreement for their transfer. [5]

During the final negotiations between the *Wehrmacht* and the SS, a second commision, led by *SS-Hauptsturmführer* Rudolf Höss [6] — who had taken over, after Eisfeld, as supervisor of the Sachsenhausen concentration camp — arrived at the camp on April 18-19, 1940. On its way through Wrocław (Breslau), the commission had met with Wigand and acquainted itself with the outlines

---

[1] APMO, Höss Trial, vol. 21, card 26.

[2] APMO, D-RF-3/RSHA/117a. Collection: *Allgemeine Erlässe des Reichssicherheitshauptamtes* (henceforth: *Allgemeine Erlässe RSHA*), card 59.

[3] Ibid, card 55.

[4] Ibid, cards 55-7.

[5] WAP Katowice, Collection Rejencja Katowice, 2905, fol. 119.

[6] Rudolf Höss was called to service in the concentration camps on December 1, 1934. In the course of four years, he advanced successively from the rank of *SS-Unterscharführer* to the rank of *SS-Hauptsturmführer*. On May 4, 1940, he received the nomination to become commandant of KL Auschwitz. After November 10, 1943, he performed the commissarial duties of the head of the DI Office in Office Group D of the SS-WVHA, and was formally appointed to that post on May 1, 1944. The Supreme National Tribunal in Warsaw passed judgment and sentenced him to death on April 2, 1947.

of his project for organizing a temporary quarantine camp for Polish prisoners, who were to be resettled later to concentration camps in the *Reich* proper. According to Wigand's proposal, Auschwitz would hold 10,000 prisoners. [7]

Based on Höss's report to Glücks, *Reichsführer-SS* Heinrich Himmler ordered on April 27, 1940, the establishment of a concentration camp at Oświęcim (Auschwitz) and its subsequent expansion through the forced labor of prisoners. Höss, whom Glücks had reassigned to Auschwitz, arrived on April 30, 1940, with five SS men to oversee preparations. On May 4, 1940, Höss was officially appointed Commandant of the Auschwitz Concentration Camp. [8]

Höss began his work by informing the *starostwo* [9] in Bielsko, in whose district Oświęcim fell, of the need to resettle around 1,200 people living in barracks near the camp. The camp, he wrote, had annexed the land in question. [10] In order to prepare the future site, he requisitioned from the mayor of Oświęcim around 300 local Jews, who worked from May through to mid-June. For renovation work at the camp site, he hired 10-20 local Polish workers.

On May 20, 1940, *Rapportführer* Gerhard Palitzsch [11] brought thirty prisoners to Auschwitz, convicted criminals of German nationality, selected for Höss from among the prisoners at the Sachsenhausen concentration camp. The prisoners were assigned numbers from one to thirty and housed in Block Nr. 1. They were made into "prisoner-functionaries": the immediate, brutal supervisors to other prisoners, both inside and outside the camp (i.e., as part of work details). Around the same time, fifteen members of the SS cavalry unit in Cracow arrived to work as guards at the camp.

On May 29, 1940, a group of prisoners from the concentration camp at Dachau — a so-called "outside commando" (*Aussenkommando*), led by *SS-Unterscharführer* Beck — arrived at Auschwitz. The commando consisted of one German prisoner, a capo, and 39 Polish prisoners — mainly male high-school students from Łódź. The commando brought with it a wagon of barbed wire to fence in the future camp. The new prisoners were housed in the kitchen barrack of the former military barracks and employed in constructing

---

[7] APMO Höss Trial vol. 21 p. 27; APMO, D-RF-3 /RSHA/117a. Collection: *Allgemeine Erlässe RSHA*, cards 55-7.

[8] Jan Sehn, "Wstęp" in *Wspomnienia Rudolfa Hössa, komendanta obozu oświęcimskiego.* Warszawa, 1965, p. 16. Henceforth, *Wspomnienia Rudolfa Hössa.*

[9] Transl. note: The *starostwo* was a regional administrator in Poland.

[10] WAP Katowice, Collection Rejencja Katowice, 2910, fol.

[11] Gerhard Palitzsch led the guard staff at KL Lichtenburg, KL Buchenwald and KL Sachsenhausen, where he had begun as a *Blockführer* and later become a *Rapportführer.* In May 1940, he was transferred to KL Auschwitz. He was distinguished by his general sadism; he personally executed prisoners with a low-caliber weapon at the "Execution Wall" in the courtyard to Block 11. After the creation of the family camp for Gypsies (camp BIIe at Birkenau), he served as *Lagerführer* of that camp. He appropriated a large amount of money, valuables, clothes, etc. from people sentenced to extermination. After he was reassigned to the post of *Lagerführer* at the Brünn sub-camp, he was arrested and brought before an SS court. His subsequent fate is unknown.

the camp's first provisional fence. Each day, they were led through the square of the former garrison (once a training area for horses), behind the barracks, and to the side of the road leading from Oświęcim to Rajsko. There they erected a barbed-wire fence. The prisoners did not have freedom of movement and were forbidden to make contact with either the Jews or the civilian personnel working there, although the latter did secretly leave them some food.

The prisoners were allowed to make purchases at the canteen for SS men. They asked Beck, their *Kommandoführer*, to try to arrange the transfer of money that they had previously deposited at Dachau to the camp. They also requested to stay at Auschwitz for good. The money arrived in the second half of June, but the prisoners had already been returned to the concentration camp at Dachau. Before they left, they had found out from a German criminal whom they had known at KL Sachsenhausen that a transport of Polish prisoners from Tarnów would be arriving at the camp. When they departed on June 14, they saw the transport at the side-track next to the camp. The prisoners from Dachau regretted leaving Auschwitz. At Auschwitz, they could hope for assistance from their relatives; in Oświęcim, they were at home, in their own country. [12]

On June 14, 1940, the first transport of 728 Polish political prisoners from the prison in Tarnów — which also contained several Polish Jews — arrived at the concentration camp Auschwitz. The Commander of the Sipo and SD in Cracow had sent the transport to the camp. The prisoners were numbered 31 to 758 and housed during a quarantine period in a building of the former Polish Tobacco Monopoly, located near the side-track at the camp. It was fenced off from the remaining facilities by barbed wire.

At the same time, an additional 100 SS men arrived at the camp to strengthen the staff. They were accompanied by SS officers of various ranks, who would fill positions in the camp's administration. *SS-Obersturmführer* Josef Kramer [13], commandeered from KL Mauthausen, took over the office of Adjutant to the Camp Commandant. The position of *1. Lagerführer* was filled by *SS-Obersturmführer* Karl Fritzsch, transferred from KL Dachau, and the position of *2. Lagerführer*, by *SS-Untersturmführer* Franz Xavier Maier from the SS *Totenkopf* Division. *SS-Untersturmführer* Max Meyer, originally from the Inspectorate for Concentration Camps, became the economic and administrative supervisor (*Leiter der Verwaltung*); *SS-Oberscharführer* Herbert Minkos, recruited from KL Buchenwald, Account Supervisor (Kassenleiter): *SS-Untersturmführer* Willi Rieck, commandeered from KL Dachau, supervisor

---

[12] APMO, Collection of Testimonies, vol. 113, cards 141-2; information from former Dachau prisoner Edward Flakiewicz. This fact has not been verified by other sources (editor's note).

[13] Josef Kramer served in the office of adjutant until November 1940, when he became *Lagerführer* at KL Dachau. In April 1941 he took over the office of *Lagerführer*, and in October 1942, commandant of KL Natzweiler. From May 5 to November 25, 1944, he was commandant of KL Auschwitz II, and then of KL Bergen-Belsen. In the trial of former SS staff members from the camp at Bergen-Belsen, the British military tribunal at Lüneburg, sentenced him to death. The sentence was carried out on December 13, 1945, in Hameln.

for provisions (*Sachbearbeiter für Verpflegung*). *SS-Hauptscharführer* Otto Reinicke, commandeered from KL Flossenbürg, took over responsiblity for SS quarters and uniforms, along with prisoners' clothing (*Unterkunftsverwaltung*). *SS-Hauptsturmführer* Max Popiersch and *SS-Obersturmführer* Robert Neumann were to serve as camp doctors.[14] *SS-Untersturmführer* Maximilian Grabner became Head of the Politic Division (the camp Gestapo), having been assigned to the post by the Gestapo office in Katowice.[15]

Five days after the first Polish prisoners had arrived from Tarnów, the resettlement of the population living in the near and more-distant neighborhood of the barracks began. The first to be resettled were the residents of a barracks-colony along the side-track of a Polish Tobacco Monopoly because some had already fled. They had heard about the plans for liquidating the settlement and arresting its inhabitants. By June 18, thirty-eight families had destroyed several of the barracks where they had been living and left.

The resettlement action took place on June 19, 1940. The area employment office, supported by local police, took part in the action. 500 people were arrested, of whom 250 were sent to Germany for forced labor. The following were allowed to remain at the settlement on a temporary basis: 30 people unable to work, children below 14, the family members of eight people employed by the camp SS, and 15 families of workers from the nearby coal mine in Brzeszcze. These remaining individuals were assigned for resettlement beyond the area of the camp.[16] Some of the people arrested were shipped to the police camp at Sosnowiec subsequently shipped back to the concentration camp at Auschwitz.

On July 8, 1940, around twenty families living in the most beautiful houses in the Zasole district — on Legionów, Krótka and Polna Streets — were driven out of their homes by the local administration and the camp SS. The expellees were shipped to the Sudeten Mountains for forced labor, and their homes, along with all the furnishings, were transferred to the camp commandant's office for distribution to SS officers and their families. In November 1940, a second resettlement action took place in the Zasole district. Some of the houses were allocated to the families of SS guards from the camp. The SS settlement (*SS-Siedlung*) that arose around the camp formed a barrier that isolated the grounds of the camp from the local Polish population. In order to simplify pursuit by the police whenever prisoners escaped, 123 houses were demolished. The prisoners employed at demolishing the houses, the so-called "commando for house-demolition" (*Abbruchkommando*), were ordered to save all materials recovered from their work in warehouses at the camp. These materials were later used for expanding the camp.

Further resettlements of the Polish population in the Auschwitz area would be closely linked to specific projects:

---

[14] APMO, D-RF-3/RSHA/117/2. Collection *Allgemeine Erlässe RSHA*, cards 166. The family names of all the above-named individuals were listed in a register from the commandant's office at KL Auschwitz from July 1, 1940.

[15] Maximilian Grabner served in the office of Head of the Political Division until December 1943. Then he was removed from office, arrested, and condemned to 12 years in prison by a special SS court in 1944. On December 22, 1947, he was condemned to death.

[16] WAP Katowice, Collection Rejencja Katowice, 2910, vol. 11 and 12.

1) the plans of *Reichsführer-SS* Himmler to create a "manorial region" (*Gutsbezirk*) around the camp, where the land was to be developed into an agricultural region for raising crops, livestock, and fish, and for conducting experiments;

2) the plans of *SS-Obergruppenführer* Reinhard Heydrich, head of the *Reichssicherheitshauptamt* (RSHA),[17] to create a second concentration camp at Auschwitz for exceptionally difficult prisoners;

3) the proposal of *Reichsmarshall* Hermann Göring, Hitler's Plenipotentiary for the Four-Year Plan, that the German concern *IG Farbenindustrie* construct production facilities for synthetic rubber and gasoline at Auschwitz.[18]

Himmler had already decided to establish a manorial region around the camp in November 1940 on the basis of research and reports by Commandant Höss.[19]

In a January 2, 1941 order, the Chief of the RSHA, Reinhard Heydrich, informed the camp that *Reichsführer-SS* Himmler had approved the classification of concentration camps into three categories, depending on the type of prisoners to be held and the degree of threat that they represented to the state. Heydrich ranked the camp at Auschwitz (Oświęcim), "concentration camp Auschwitz I", along with the camps at Dachau and Sachsenhausen, as belonging to category I, intended for prisoners "less burdensome and clearly able to reform". Category II camps were intended for prisoners who were "more burdensome, but still suited for training and reform". Among the camps in this category he named — along with Buchenwald, Flossenbürg, and Neuengamme — "Auschwitz II", which, up to that point, did not exist. Commandant Höss allegedly did not know that the construction of a second camp was being considered. The order demonstrates, however, that as early as 1940, plans did exist for creating a second camp at Auschwitz, Auschwitz II. (The only camp which Heydrich ranked as category III, intended for "very burdensome" — e.g., antisocial and previously-convicted prisoners, was the camp at Mauthausen.)

On February 10, 1941, a special Commission arrived at Auschwitz. Chaired by Commandant Höss, the Commission developed a basic idea of how much territory the camp should take up and how many people would have to be resettled.

On March 8, 1941, within fifteen minutes, the entire population of the Pławy village was expelled. At the end of February and beginning of March, more than 6,000 Jews were resettled from the town of Oświęcim to Sosnowiec,

---

[17] Reinhard Heydrich was at the same time "Protector" for Bohemia and Moravia, the Czech portion of the former Czechoslovakia. After his assassination in Prague on June 5, 1942, by the Czech resistance movement, *SS-Obergruppenführer* Ernst Kaltenbrunner was named to the post of Chief of the RSHA in January 1943. The latter was condemned to death by the International Military Tribunal at Nuremberg and hung on October 16, 1946.

[18] Already in December 1940, Dr. Otto Abros, a member of the board of IG Farbenindustrie, had acquainted himself with maps of the local terrain at the Office for Planning in Katowice and identified Auschwitz (Oświęcim) as the most useful location for constructing new chemical facilities.

[19] APMO, Höss Trial, vol. 21, cards 31, 32.

Będzin and Chrzanów. On April 1, the remaining people living on Legionów, Krótka, Polna and Kolejowa Streets in Oświęcim were expelled, and the vacant apartments were given to the families of SS men and German specialists sent to work at the newly-constructed factory for synthetic rubber and fuel — the Buna-Werke — situated in Dwory, near Oświęcim. From April 7-12, the Polish population living in the villages of Babice, Broszkowice, Brzezinka (Birkenau), Budy, Harmęże and Rajsko were also resettled.

After the expulsions, workers employed in the coal mines in Brzeszcze and Jawiszowice were resettled in the houses, along with their families. 1,600 Poles were expelled to the General Government. The expellees lost practically all of their possessions.

The depopulated region of around 40 square kilometers was named the camp's "area of interest" (*Interessengebiet*). The zone consisted of the land located at the confluence of the Vistula and Soła Rivers, with its border running from Broszkowice along the Soła to the village of Bielany, and from that point through the villages of Łęki, Skidzin, and Wilczkowice, around Brzeszcze to the Vistula, and subsequently to the mouth of the Soła above Broszkowice. SS men constantly patrolled this area.

The designation of such a large area as the camp's "area of interest" was justified in terms of security and economics. As Höss explained in a letter to the Inspector for Concentration Camps, Glücks: "The local population is fanatically Polish, prepared for every possible action against the despised SS men, and every prisoner who escapes will receive immediate help as soon as he reaches the first Polish farm." [20]

Upon its establishment, the concentration camp at Auschwitz consisted of twenty brick buildings, fourteen of which were only one story high. Between May 20, 1940, and March 1, 1941, 10,900 prisoners were held at the camp, mainly Poles.

Reichsführer-SS Himmler came to Auschwitz for the first time on March 1, 1941. Accompanying him were: *Gauleiter* and Vice-President of Upper Silesia, *SS-Brigadeführer* Fritz Bracht; the Supreme Commander of SS and Police in Wrocław (Breslau), *SS-Obergruppenführer* Ernst Schmauser; *SS-Oberführer* Glücks, regional presidents, and leading figures from IG Farbenindustrie. After he conducted a general inspection of the camp and toured its various subdivisions, Himmler ordered Camp Commandant Höss to

1) expand the camp at Auschwitz so that it could hold up to 30,000 prisoners;

2) build a camp for 100,000 prisoners of war on the territory of the village of Brzezinka (Birkenau);

3) supply the chemical combine IG Farbenidustrie with 10,000 prisoners to build a plant in Dwory, near Auschwitz;

4) cultivate the entire area for agricultural purposes;

5) expand the camp's handicraft facilities.

---

[20] APMO, Höss Trial, vol. 12, card 10.

He further declared that a large armaments industry (*Rüstungsindustrie*) should be established near the camp as part of an attempt to provide the SS with a leading role in the field of armaments for the German army.

In a post-inspection regulation of March 5, 1941, Glücks informed the concentration-camp commandants of Himmler's order that even as the war continued, they were to requisition from SS military formations all the commissioned and non-commissioned SS officers needed for service at the camps. At the same time, Glücks informed them of Himmler's desire that settlements for SS men be constructed near the concentration camps. [21]

2. Construction, Expansion and Evolution of the Camp and Its Branches

The first draft of a general plan for expanding the original camp at Auschwitz, known as *Stammlager*, or "main camp", was ready in outline form in June 1941. The Main Economic-Administrative Office of the SS (*Wirtschaftsverwaltungshauptamt*, WVHA) approved a final, detailed plan in December 1942 and forwarded it to the camp commandant for realization. The actual work, however, had already begun. [22]

The area foreseen for the expansion was bordered to the south by the road from Oświęcim to Rajsko along the Soła River and to the north by the railroad track between Oświęcim and Jawiszowice. The general plan for expansion foresaw the establishment of four zones. In the first zone, to the west of the camp, an SS settlement was planned. It would include green areas, a sports field, and a riding area for horses. The second zone would contain the camp commandant's office, along with an extension composed of warehouses, the camp waterworks, workshops, and so forth, to be used for economic production. In the third zone, adjoining the commandant's office and its economic production area, the actual concentration camp would be located. In the fourth zone, bordering the camp to the west, barracks for the SS garrison would be established.

The camp itself occupied an area 1,000 m wide and 400 m long. The buildings intended for prisoners were divided by a square into two compounds. The first complex was composed of the existing structures at the main camp, which were slated for expansion. It was to contain 33 blocks for housing prisoners. A large roll-call square was planned between the first and second complex, to be erected after the workshops and other production barracks were demolished. Both complexes contained a total of 78 two-story buildings for housing prisoners.

The implementation of the plan for renovating the main camp began in 1941. Using prisoner labor and building materials gathered from demolished houses in the Zasole district, construction began on eight two-story buildings in the assembly square (at the former training ground for horses), a floor was

[21] APMO, D-RF-3/RSHA/117/1. Collection *Allgemeine Erlässe RSHA*, card 91.

[22] APMO, BW2/3/22, Collection *Zentralbauleitung*. The "General Plan of Expansion for KL Auschwitz" (*Konzentrationslager Auschwitz Generalbebauungsplan*) from November 12, 1942, was approved on December 12, 1942, and transmitted to KL Auschwitz on January 18, 1943.

added on to each of 14 larger buildings, and a camp kitchen was built. Beyond the barbed-wire fence, an SS administrative building was also erected.

By the fall of 1944, a bridge had been built across the Soła, along with two roads — one leading to the highway from Oświęcim to Kęty and Bielsko, and the other to the railway station in Oświęcim. A sewage system had been installed for the proposed expansion area, and construction had begun on a pumping station, waterwork facilities, and a heating plant. At the planned second complex, 20 two-story buildings were erected in the area of the so-called "camp extension" (*Schutzhaftlagererweiterung*) to house prisoners. Already in the spring of 1944, warehouses and clothing workshops had been established in five buildings there. Two buildings at the extension were placed at the disposal of the SS doctor, Professor Carl Clauberg. At May 26, his experiment station was transferred from Block 10 at the main camp to the new location, along with female Jewish prisoners to be used in sterilization experiments. In October, 6,000 female prisoners were transferred from the women's camp at Birkenau to several other blocks at the extension. A building for receiving prisoners (*Aufnahmegebäude*) was also erected. In the summer of 1944, it was equipped with showers and disinfection chambers.

Both the plan for expanding the camp and its partial realization demonstrate that the main camp at Oświęcim was established as a permanent facility, to be used for imprisoning and annihilating opponents of Hitler's *Reich* for many years to come. Plans were also made to renovate the town of Oświęcim in order to lend it the greatest German character possible.

The decision to locate a plant for IG Farbenindustrie in Dwory (near Oświęcim) was based on the protection that the area afforded against Allied air strikes and bombing, the proximity of coal mines, and — most importantly — the existence of the concentration camp at Auschwitz, which offered possibilities for future expansion and an enormous potential work force.

Negotiations between IG Farbenindustrie, WVHA and the camp commandant's office over supplying cheap labor from the camp for the construction of proposed synthetic rubber and fuel facilities resulted in an agreement stipulating that KL Auschwitz would provide 1,000 prisoners for skilled and unskilled labor in 1941; another 3,000 in 1942, to increase to 8,000, if necessary; and an even larger number in subsequent years. It was agreed that the prisoners would be delivered to work by train. (To this end, the camp authorities oversaw the construction of a railroad bridge across the Soła). The agreement set the prisoners' work day at 10-11 hours (nine hours in winter). IG Farbenindustrie agreed to pay the commandant's office at KL Auschwitz four marks per day for the labor of each skilled worker, and three marks per day for each unskilled worker.

In keeping with these arrangements, prisoners from Auschwitz began construction on the Buna Werke in Dwory, near Oświęcim, in April 1941. At first, the prisoners had to walk to work each day — seven kilometers each way — but were eventually delivered to work by train. The prisoners arrived at work only after significant delays because military transports had priority on the railways. In August 1942 [23], a typhoid epidemic disrupted the daily delivery of prisoners.

The difficulties involved in transporting the prisoners to work and their physical exhaustion (which affected productivity) led IG Farbenindustrie to construct a sub-camp for them near the Buna-Werke, in the depopulated village of Monowice. By the end of October 1942, prisoners were being housed there. Until November 1943, the new camp was called *"Lager Buna"* and remained part of KL Auschwitz as an affiliated camp.

Beginning in 1940, a work detail of prisoners for agricultural work was established at KL Auschwitz. Its assignment was to harvest the crops — hay, wheat, and vegetables — planted by local farmers before their resettlement beyond the camp's "area of interest". Subsequently, the camp began to organize large farms for both livestock and crops. *SS-Obersturmbannführer* Joachim Caesar was assigned to the camp by the head of SS-WVHA in February 1942 to assume the post of Director for Agricultural Enterprises at KL Auschwitz.

In keeping with Himmler's orders the camp administration oversaw in 1941-43 the establishment of large plots for crops and livestock in the evacuated and demolished farms and villages located inside the camp's "area of interest" — in Babice, Budy, Harmęże, Pławy. In Rajsko, a research station for plants (*Pflanzenzuchtstation*) was founded; most of its research focused on cultivating the plant kok-saghyz, whose roots yielded a substance that could be used to produce rubber. Barracks were erected at the farms and other agricultural facilities, and the existing buildings were adapted to house male and female prisoners. In this fashion, satellite-camps were founded at Babice, Budy, Harmęże, Pławy, and Rajsko.

During 1941, the camp's existing workshops were expanded, as was the SS enterprise "German Equipment Works" (*Deutsche-Ausrüstungswerke*, DAW), which later received orders for repairs from the army.

Construction of the camp at Brzezinka (Birkenau) began in October 1941. By that time, the population of the camp at Auschwitz had reached more than 20,000 prisoners. An additional 10,000 Soviet prisoners of war (approximately) arrived between October 7 and 25 from the prison camps at Neuhammer (today, Świętoszów) and Lamsdorf (today, Łambinowice) and were imprisoned in a separate section of the main camp. Village buildings began to be demolished in Brzezinka (Birkenau), and any building materials that could be salvaged were saved for construction of the future camp. The SS exploited forced labor from the POWs and other prisoners for this work. They would walk on foot each day to Brzezinka (Birkenau), which was around three kilometers away from the main camp. Given the enormous overcrowding at the main camp, the camp at Birkenau — foreseen for 100,000 prisoners of war — was built rapidly, without any sanitary or other facilities.

To oversee the construction of the prisoner-of-war camp, *SS-Sturmbannführer* Karl Bischoff, plenipotentiary of the Special Administration for Construction

---

[23] Editor's note: Disruptions might have occurred already in July 1942.

of the Waffen SS, was brought in from the Main Office for Budget and Construction in Berlin. The proposed plan for the POW camp at Brzezinka dated October 14, 1941, was approved the very next day by Bischoff and signed by Commandant Höss of KL Auschwitz. The plan foresaw the division of the camp into two sections by a main road that would run through it. It also called for the construction of train tracks next to the main road. A quarantine camp was to be situated to the left of the main road and the train tracks, and to their right, two new camps (I and II). The entire area encompassed an enclosed rectangle, surrounded by a barbed-wire fence and overlooked by guard towers. The sides of the rectangle measured 720 m and 1130 m. According to the plan, a total of 174 brick barracks were to be situated in each of the three camps.

Construction began with the leveling and draining of swampy terrain. Then the POWs and other prisoners were assigned to build a road from the bridge below the railroad tracks to the main gate of the future camp; to excavate sand from a gravel-pit; to unload materials sent to the site; and to lay foundations for the barracks.

The costs for undertaking — almost simultaneously — the expansion of the main camp and its workshops; the cultivation of the land lying within its interest area; and the construction of the Buna-Werke, along with the camp at Brzezinka (Birkenau) was extremely high. In the course of the construction and expansion of all these facilities between March 1941 and February 1942, thousands of Polish prisoners and Soviet POWs lost their lives.

From the preserved camp documents, one learns that for the period May 20, 1940 to January 31, 1942, a total of 36,285 prisoners were held at the camp — 26,288 mainly Polish prisoners and 9,997 Soviet POWs. During the same period, 2,435 prisoners were transferred to other concentration camps; 76 were freed; five escaped; and 1,755 Soviet POWs and other prisoners were shot, murdered with injections of phenol, or gassed with Zyklon-B. Thus, the total number of prisoners lost through transfers, escapes, and executions totaled 4,271. (The figures for the prisoners, including Soviet POWs, were taken from the surviving evidence — the successive camp numbers assigned to new arrivals at the camp.) According to these figures, at the end of January 1942, there should have been a total of 32,014 Polish prisoners and Soviet POWs left at the camp, but the actual number was only 11,449. [24] What happened to the remaining 20,565 captives?

Cases are known in which *Schutzhaftlagerführer* Fritzsch greeted new prisoners at the main camp with the words: "You have arrived here not at a sanatorium, but at a German concentration camp, from which the only exit is through the chimney of its crematorium." [25] These words provide the answer to our question. In the initial period of the camp's existence, between July 1940 and March 1941, the SS annihilated around 2,500 prisoners through chicanery

[24] APMO, D-Aul-3/1. *Stärkebuch* [Daily Situation Book], card 25.
[25] APMO, Files of the Camp Resistance vol. VII, card 464.

and starvation. From March 1, 1941, to January 31, 1942, during the expansion of the main camp, the construction of the Buna-Werke facilities and of the camp at Brzezinka (Birkenau), around 18,000 POWs and other prisoners died from hunger, maltreatment, and exhaustion from hard labor.

The special camp for Soviet POWs at the main camp was liquidated on March 1, 1942, and the surviving 945 POWs, [26] along with some other prisoners, were resettled to the camp Birkenau, which remained under construction. During March, several thousand prisoners were transferred there. At the main camp, ten blocks were fenced off from the rest; the so-called "women's division" (*Frauenabteilung*) was thus established. Although the new division was initially under the jurisdiction of the camp commandant at the women's concentration camp in Ravensbrück, the camp was subsequently subordinated to the commandant of KL Auschwitz in July 1942.

On March 26, 1942, 999 female German prisoners, transferred from KL Ravensbrück, were settled in the newly-created women's division, along with 999 Jewish women from Poprad in Slovakia. The new prisoners received the numbers 1-1998. Within a month, there were more than 6,000 prisoners in the women's division. The first 127 Polish women — political prisoners — arrived at the camp on April 27, 1942, from prisons in Cracow (Montelupich) and Tarnów. They received the numbers 6784-6910.

On July 17-18, 1942, Himmler visited Auschwitz for the second time. He was accompanied by Bracht, Schmauser, and *SS-Gruppenführer* Heinz Kammler, head of Administrative Group C at WVHA, responsible for construction on behalf of the army, SS, and police, including the construction of concentration camps and facilities for the armaments industry. They toured the agricultural facilities, the livestock farms, the station for plant--cultivation research in Rajsko, the laboratories, the drainage works, and the camp at Birkenau, including two bunkers that had been prepared for gassing people with Cyclon-B. (Two buildings in the forest, once the property of the resettled farmers Harmata and Wichaj, had been converted into the two "bunkers".) The group also toured the Buna-Werke, the main camp for men, the "women's division", the workshop facilities, the slaughter--house, bakery, the storage area for building materials, the warehouses for seized goods (dubbed "Canada" by the prisoners), the warehouses for the SS divisions, and other structures. After inspection, Himmler ordered Höss to speed up the expansion of the camp at Birkenau, to liquidate all Jewish prisoners unable to work, and to expand the camp's armament works.

By August 1942, at the planned site for the quarantine camp, two lesser sub-divisions had come into being: *Bauabschnitte* ("construction sites") Ia and Ib, or BIa and BIb. (At Auschwitz, the numbering of construction sites was often used to identify specific camps on the grounds

---

[26] APMO, D-Aul-3/1. *Stärkebuch*, card 91.

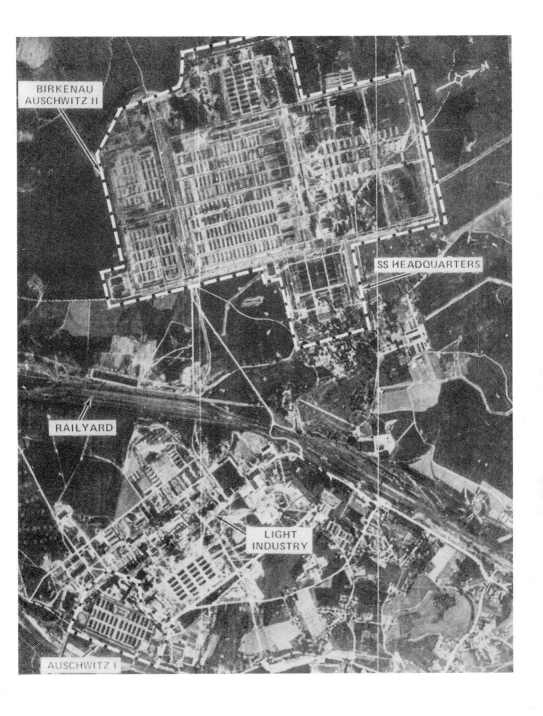

KL Auschwitz I and KL Auschwitz II-Birkenau. Aerial photograph taken by the Allies on June 26, 1944, labelled by American researchers Dino A. Brugioni and Robert G. Poirier.

A Nazi map of the camp's so-called *"Interessensgebiet"* (area of interest).

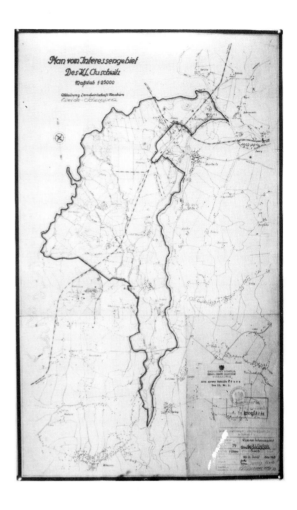

Most of the Poles who lived close to KL Auschwitz or in nearby villages were expelled in order to create the camp's so-called Interessengebiet which embraced 40 km² of land.

Auschwitz. The camp staff, several thousand strong, consisted mainly of members of the criminal organization, the *SS-Totenkopfverbände* ("Order of the Death's Head"), who were specially trained for service in the concentration camps.

Dwory near Auschwitz. *Reichsführer SS* Heinrich Himmler (first from the left) during a 1942 inspection of the Buna-Werke, the plants for producing synthetic rubber and gasoline that belonged to the German chemical combine, IG Farbenindustrie. First from the right is Rudolf Höss, the Commandant of KL Auschwitz.

KL Auschwitz I. Main gate bearing the inscription, "Work will set you free."

KL Auschwitz I. The electric fence and guard turrets surrounding the camp served to isolate it and make escape nearly impossible.

KL Auschwitz I. The SS established the camp at the site of former Polish barracks before the war.

KL Auschwitz I. The first crematorium, in which the corpses of prisoners who perished or were killed at the camp were burned. In operation from 1940 to 1943, it was partially reconstructed after the war.

KL Auschwitz II-Birkenau. The main gate to the camp, the so-called "Death Gate".

KL Auschwitz II-Birkenau. The Nazis built most of the facilities for mass extermination of Jews on the grounds of this camp — gas chambers and ovens for burning the victims' corpses. The photograph shows the last stage of work before the installation of gas chamber and ovens at Crematorium Nr. III.

KL Auschwitz II-Birkenau. The portion of the camp that contained barracks made of brick.

KL Auschwitz II-Birkenau. The second construction site (BII) contained wooden barracks and was divided into several smaller sections, where camps were established that differed in their character and assignments.

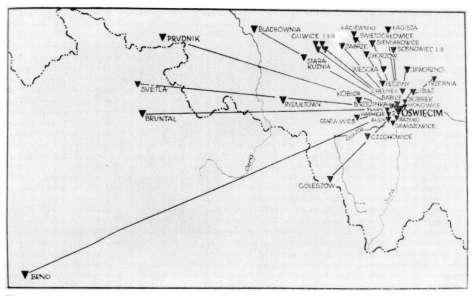

The camp at Auschwitz and its sub-camps.

Blachownia Śląska-Sławięcice. Crematorium at the Blechhammer sub-camp.

Tarnów, 1940. The Nazis sent to KL Auschwitz the first transport of political prisoners — 728 Poles, including a few Polish Jews.

The registration cards of Polish political prisoners, which list the various reasons for their arrest and imprisonment at KL Auschwitz, including, for example, participating in the Polish resistance movement, listening to foreign radio stations, and assisting Jews.

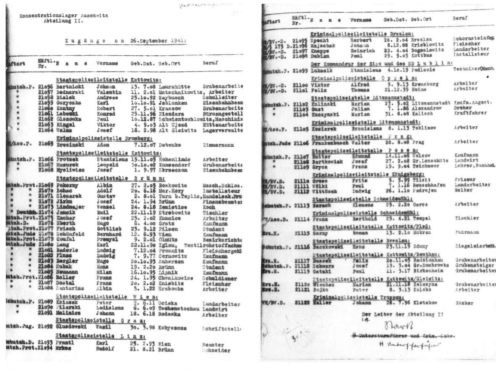

The lists of newly-arrived prisoners *(Zugangsliste)* contained basic information about every prisoner held at the camp.

The individual cards for each prisoner registered at the camp contained specific information, including a description of the prisoners' outer appearance.

New arrivals at the camp were given a camp number, entered into the camp records, and photographed in three poses.

The train platform situated between Auschwitz I and Auschwitz II-Birkenau, where trains arrived up to May 1944 with deportees to the camp. Selections were conducted among the Jews at the platform, immediately upon their arrival.

The registration cards of two Jewish prisoners, found fit to work during a selection conducted by the Nazis. They were subsequently sent to the camp.

of the larger camp.) In area BIb, a men's camp had been established and begun functioning in March as a branch of KL Auschwitz. In the first half of August, the women's division had been transferred to section BIa from the main camp; a women's concentration camp (*Frauenkonzentrationslager*) was subsequently established there as a branch of KL Auschwitz.

The partially-realized plan for building the camp at Birkenau from October 14, 1941, had to be changed because Himmler had already chosen Auschwitz in the summer of 1941 as a site for the mass extermination of Jews. Camp Commandant Höss recognized that the camp at Birkenau would best lend itself to this goal.

The mass murder of Jews began at Birkenau in the first months of 1942. During a tour of the camp, Himmler observed the entire process for liquidation the Jews. He watched the unloading of a group of Jews from a train, their "selection", their murder in the bunker by gassing, and the removal of their corpses from the bunker. The observations and results from that single act of mass murder were most likely the subject of a final discussion during Himmler's visit. The SS would seek thereafter a technical solution that would allow them not only to conduct mass murder, but also to obliterate all traces of the crime by rapidly destroying all corpses. In the Nazis' plans for exterminating millions of Jews, the camp was assigned a special role, which would require significant changes in its character and the original principles associated with its construction.

A new plan, completed on August 15, 1942 and approved by Bischoff, provided for the construction of a camp complex at Birkenau that would hold 200,000 captives and contain extermination facilities. From the previous plan, only construction site I with camps BIa and BIb remained. To the right side of the main road and the train tracks, a construction site II (BII) was planned, and next to it, construction site III (BIII), later named "Mexico" by the prisoners. Construction site IV (BIV) would be situated to the left of construction site I. The construction sites, in succession from left to right, were as follows: BIV, BI, BII, BIII. Site IV was intended for 60,000 people; site I (ie, camps BIa and BIb), for 20,000; site II, for 60,000, and site III, for 60,000.

Each construction site — except BI, which was already completed — was to be fenced off into six smaller camps, each having a separate entrance gate. At each gate, a guard house for SS men (*Blockführerstube*) was to be located. The living quarters of the entire camp would take up the area of a regular rectangle with sides measuring 720 and 2340 meters. At the end of the railroad tracks, the construction of two crematoria was planned. In fact, four crematoria were eventually built, along with gas chambers. The construction of yet another was planned, but there was not enough time to build it.

The name "prisoner-of-war camp" (*Kriegsgefangenenlager-KGL*) was used in construction documents and in correspondence intended for the camp at Birkenau. This name remained in use up to March 31, 1944.

Work had begun on realizing the new construction plan on August 15, 1942, even before it had been approved. In July, the Construction Office, for Auschwitz and Birkenau reorganized as the "Central Construction Office for the SS Military Formations and Police at Auschwitz", had already begun negotiating with several firms over the construction of four — not two — large crematoria with gas chambers. On July 13, the building firm *Hoch- und Tiefbau A.G.* of Katowice submitted a bid of 133,756.65 marks for the construction of one crematorium (without ovens). The firm *J.A. Topf und Söhne* of Erfurt would supply ovens for the crematoria and eventually install them in the gas chambers.

The camp commandant's office received payments from both the Central Construction Office and civilian building firms for the prisoners' forced labor. In 1942, around 8,000 prisoners worked each day on the camp's expansion. Several hundred engineers and technicians from among the prisoners even worked alongside civilian employees and several hundred SS men in planning.

The pace of construction was rapid. Between March and June 1943, four enormous crematoria with gas chambers were erected at Birkenau. They were approved for use after an initial test by the commandant's office at KL Auschwitz. In 1943, the work at construction site II (BII) was completed. Six residential camps were built there (BIIa, BIIb, BIIc, BIId, BIIe, BIIf), along with a warehouse (*Effektenlager*) for items seized from Jews before their extermination. The warehouse was known as camp BIIg. Camps BIIb, BIIc, BIId, and BIIe each contained 32 barracks for prisoners. In camp BIIa, 16 prisoner barracks of the "horse-stable" type (*Pferdestallbaracken*, OKH type 260/9) were built. The camp administration planned to fill each of these barracks, originally intended for 52 horses, with more than 400 prisoners.

Site BIIe was the first of the new camps to be used. In February 1943, a family camp (*Familienzigeunerlager*) for Gypsies was established there. A total of 20,967 men, women, and children would pass through this camp between February 26, 1943, and July 21, 1944. Around 1,700 Gypsies never received a camp identification number; they were sent directly to the gas chambers as suspected carriers of spotted fever. On August 2, 1944, the camp administration liquidated the Gypsy camp by sending the remaining 2,897 men, women, and children to the gas chambers.

In July 1943, the camps at sites BIId and BIIf were put into operation. Camp BIId was intended for healthy prisoners employed in certain work details. The prisoners held there had been transferred from what had been up to that point the men's camp at site BIb. The average population of the men's camp BIId (*Männerlager* BIId) from 1943-44 was around 13,000 prisoners.

A infirmary for male prisoners was founded at site BIIf. Ill prisoners from camp BIb were transferred there on July 23, 1943. It was called *Häftlingkrankenbau*, Lager BIIf. Poorly-equipped, always full, the prisoners called it the "vestibule to the crematorium". At first, it provided space for around 2,000 ill prisoners; later, around 2,500. SS doctors would conduct "selections" at the camp infirmary to liquidate excess prisoners who did not heal in the gas chambers.

In August 1943, a quarantine camp (*Quarantänelager*) was built for newly-arrived prisoners. The quarantine, which lasted several weeks, was a test of physical endurance. The population of the quarantine camp ranged, on average, between 4000-6000 prisoners.

At site BIIb, a family camp was established for Jews from the ghetto-camp Terezin (Theresienstadt) in Czechoslovakia. The camp was called *Familienlager Theresienstadt* or *Familienlager* BIIb. On September 9, 1943, 5,006 men, women, and children arrived from Theresienstadt further transports arrived on December 16 and December 20 with an additional 4,964 prisoners. By March 1944, around 1.100 Jews from the September transport had perished from hunger, illness, and the poor sanitary conditions. On March 9, 1944, 3,791 men, women, and children from the same transport were sent to death in the gas chambers. Only 75 people from the original transport survived: prisoner-doctors and twins to be used by camp doctor *SS-Hauptsturmführer* Josef Mengele in his criminal experiments (see p. 90).

Three more transports arrived from Theresienstadt between May 16-19, 1944, carrying 7,449 men, women, and children; they were also sent to *Familienlager* BIIb. At the time, camp BIIb held around 11,000 prisoners. In the first days of July 1944, after a "selection" by Mengele, 3,080 of the prisoners — young and healthy men and women — were transferred to other concentration camps. The remaining prisoners, around 7,000 men, women, and children, were exterminated between July 10-12 in the gas chambers. *Familienlager* BIIb was then liquidated.

The barracks at camp BIIc initially served as a warehouse for property seized from Jews who had been brought to KL Auschwitz for extermination.

In December 1943, at the extension to construction site II, between crematorium III and IV, a delousing station and showers (called "the sauna" by prisoners) and a warehouse-camp for stolen goods (an *Effektenlager* called "Canada II") were built. The *Effektenlager* at site BIIg contained thirty barracks. All personal items seized from extermination victims were temporarily stored here. The goods were inspected, sorted, packed, and shipped to various Nazi outposts. Gold, valuables, precious stones, and hard currency were sent to the Main Economic-Administrative Office (WVHA) of the SS and, from there, to the Bank of the Third Reich. The barracks were always filled to the brim, and unsorted baggage quickly piled up between barracks. The SS assigned more than 2,000 male and female prisoners to work in the warehouse.

In mid-May 1944, the Central Construction Office finished building railroad tracks and an unloading ramp inside the camp. The tracks and unloading ramp were situated alongside the main road through the camp, between camps BIa, BIb on one side, and camps BIIa, BIIb, BIIc, BIId, BIIe, and BIIf on the other. There were three railway tracks inside the camp.

In May or June 1944, a transit camp (*Durchgangslager*) was established for Jewish women, mainly from Hungary, on the grounds of camp BIIc and on the terrain of the uncompleted, third construction site (BIII, called "Mexico" by the prisoners). Those who were young, healthy, and able to work were sent to camp BIIc after the "selection" at the unloading ramp. Jewish women were sent to camp BIII, the "Mexico" area, when there was no time to conduct a selection. The Jewish women sent to camps BIIc and BIII were not registered or given camp identification numbers. They remained at Birkenau for weeks, under inhuman conditions, as a "deposit", awaiting a final decision from the SS regarding their fate. To the extent that their labor was needed, a few healthy Jewish women were sent to camps inside the *Reich*. Sick, weak, and exhausted women awaited death in the gas chambers. Every week, the SS doctors Josef Mengele and Heinz Thilo carried out a selection among the female residents of camps BIIc and BIII. When smaller groups (around 100 women) were selected, they were executed at gunpoint near the ovens of crematoria II and III. The population of the two *Durchgangslager*, constantly rising from newly-arrived transports of Jews, could reach as high as 30,000 women.

At the end of September 1944, the SS began liquidating camps BIIc and BIII. On October 10, only 17,202 Jewish women survived from those who had been shipped as a "deposit" to the two camps. On October 6, camp BIII was liquidated, and 12,799 women and 961 girls, mainly Hungarian Jews, were relocated to camp BIIc.

Having been a men's camp up to that point, camp BIb was chosen — after the transfer of prisoners in July 1943 to camps BIId and BIIf (men's hospital) and the creation of BIIa (for quarantine) — to become an extension of the women's concentration camp at Birkenau. It mainly housed women prisoners who worked outside the camp.

Intended for 20,000 prisoners, camps BIa and BIb housed more than 27,000 women in January 1944. Despite the high death rate a result of the inhuman conditions and constant selections, the population in the women's camp numbered 31,406 on July 12, 1944, and 39,234 on August 22. On October 3, after 17,202 Jewish women from the temporary camp were added to the population, the women's camp at Auschwitz II held a total of 43,462 female prisoners.

The Nazi concentration camps, including the camp at Auschwitz, represented a colossal reserve for cheap labor. In carrying out the policies of its superiors, who demanded that prisoners also be employed outside the concentration camps, the commandant's office at KL Auschwitz established around 40 affiliated camps or "sub-camps". They had a wide range of names: *Arbeitslager, Nebenlager, Aussenlager, Zweiglager, Arbeitskommando, Aussenkommando*. Despite their different names, all the sub-camps had the same organizational structure. They either served the SS economy directly (e.g., the farms for livestock and crops in the camp's "area of interest") or, as was normally the case, supplied labor for the factories, mines, and metalworks of such great German concerns as IG Farbenindustrie, Berghütte, Oberschlesische Hydrierwerke AG, Energieversorgung Oberschlesien AG,

Hermann Göring-Werke, Siemens-Schuckert, Rheinmetall-Borsig, and even the German state railway.

Of the 40 sub-camps affiliated with Auschwitz, 28 were located next to industrial facilities linked either directly or indirectly with the German armaments industry. Of these 28, nine were organized as part of the metallurgical industry; six were linked with coal mines; six were attached to factories for the chemical industry; three were connected to light-industrial facilities; two were engaged in building generators; one was affiliated with the building-materials industry; and one was involved in the food-products industry. In the other sub-camps, prisoners worked at constructing and renovating buildings, in forestry, with livestock and crops, and at research stations, among other things.

In 1942, sub-camps were established next to various industrial facilities: in Goleszów (cement), in Jawiszowice (coal mines), in Monowice (construction of the Buna-Werke), in Chełmek (shoe factory). In 1943, five additional sub-camps were founded next to industrial facilities: in Świętochłowice (iron works), in Jaworzno (coal mines and construction of a power station), in Libiąż (coal mines), in Wesoła by Mysłowice (coal mines), in Łagisza (construction of a power plant), and in Brno, in Czech territory (construction of the headquarters for the Technical Academy for the SS and Police).

Thus, between 1941-43, all the projects and requests from *Reichsführer-SS* Himmler, the Main Security Office of the Reich (RSHA), and Hitler's Plenipotentiary for the Four-Year Plan had been realized or were nearing realization: the establishment of a manorial region around the camp for the SS; expansion of the main camp and construction of a second concentration camp and extermination center at Birkenau; exploitation of forced labor from the prisoners for construction work at the camp and at the Buna-Werke facilities in Dwory; the establishment of war industries near the camp; and finally, the creation of affiliated camps near industrial centers in Silesia and Czechoslovakia, to exploit the forced labor of male and female prisoners from KL Auschwitz.

3. Division of the Camp at Auschwitz

Under the direction of Commandant Höss, KL Auschwitz had expanded by November 1943 into a colossal enterprise, composed of: the men's camp at the main camp in Auschwitz; the men's camp BIId, the quarantine camp for men (BIIa) and the men's infirmary (BIIf) at Birkenau; the women's camp (BIa and BIb) at Birkenau; the family camp for Gypsies (BIIe) at Birkenau; the family camp for Jews from Theresienstadt (BIIb) at Birkenau; the extermination center at Birkenau, composed of four crematoria and gas chambers; the sub-camps associated with agriculture and livestock-breeding at Babice, Budy, Harmęże, and Rajsko; the sub-camps affiliated with industrial concerns in Monowice, Jaworzno, Świętochłowice, Łagisza, Wesoła, Goleszów, Libiąż, Sosnowiec, and Brno.

Höss administered the entire Auschwitz complex through individual camp supervisors, who answered directly to him. His superiors considered him a fine organizer and agriculturalist, a model German pioneer for the territories in the East. He had behind him nine years of experience at the concentration camps. Thus, when Höss was removed from the post of camp commandant at KL Auschwitz, the leadership at SS-WVHA had to decentralize administration at the camp.

In the fall of 1943, on the orders of the head of SS-WVHA, Oswald Pohl, [27] Auschwitz was divided into three camps, under a new leadership. *SS--Obersturmbannführer* Arthur Liebehenschel [28], former chief of Administration DI at SS-WVHA, took over Höss' post on November 11, 1943. On November 22, he ordered (Garrison Order number 53/43) that the camp be divided into three parts:

Konzentrationslager Auschwitz I-*Stammlager* (the main camp in Oświęcim),
Konzentrationslager Auschwitz II-Birkenau (in Brzezinka),
Konzentrationslager Auschwitz III-*Aussenlager* (sub-camps).

KL Auschwitz I consisted of the main camp. KL Auschwitz II was composed of all the camps at Birkenau (Brzezinka), along with the sub-camps engaged in agriculture and livestock-breeding. KL Auschwitz III was composed of ten sub-camps: the camps at Monowice, Jaworzno, Jawiszowice, Świętochłowice, Łagisza, Wesoła by Mysłowice, Goleszów, Libiąż, Sosnowiec, and Brno.

On January 20, 1944, the total population of all the camps at Auschwitz numbered 80,839 prisoners, of whom 18,437 were at Auschwitz I; 49,114 at Auschwitz II (men's camp — 22,061, women's camp — 27,053); 13,288 at Auschwitz III (of whom 6,571 were at Monowice) [29]. A month later, the population at the Auschwitz camps totalled 73,669 male and female prisoners. [30]

The number of prisoners at the Auschwitz camps was subject to constant fluctuations. It decreased in response to the high death rate — the result of constant hunger, work beyond one's strength, and the ensuing destruction of the human organism. It increased with the arrival of large transports carrying new prisoners. For example, between August 12 and September 17, 1944, 13,000 Poles arrived in four transports from the transit camp at

---

[27] By judgment of the American Military Tribunal at Nüremburg, Oswald Pohl was sentenced to death on November 3, 1947, during a trial against former functionaries from SS-WVHA. The sentence was carried out on June 8, 1951, in Landsberg.

[28] Arthur Liebehenschel had served in 1934 as an adjutant at KL Lichtenburg and was transferred in 1936 to work at the Inspectorate for Concentration Camps. At first he worked in the Political Division, and then became chief of that division (future Administration DI in the SS-WVHA). In November 1943, he took over the post of commandant at KL Auschwitz I and commander of the SS garrison. On May 8, 1944, he was transferred to the post of commandant at KL Lublin (Majdanek), and after the evacuation of that camp in July 1944, transferred to the Office of the Supreme Commander of SS and Police in Trieste, Odilo Globocnik. By judgment of the Supreme National Tribunal at Cracow on December 22, 1947, he was condemned to death.

[29] APMO, Files of the Camp Resistance, vol. I, card 60.

[30] Ibid., vol. VII, card 175.

Pruszków — men, women, and children who had been arrested during the Warsaw Uprising.

On July 12, 1944, the total population of male and female prisoners at the Auschwitz camps reached 92,208. On August 22, they numbered 105,168. In addition to the prisoners listed in the camp records, a "deposit" of around 30,000 male and female Jewish prisoners had been sent to the temporary camps BIIc, BIIe, and BIII at Birkenau. [31] Thus, in August 1944, the total number of prisoners at the Auschwitz camps surpassed the 135,000 mark.

---

[31] Ibid., vol. II, card 94.

THE ORGANIZATION
OF KL AUSCHWITZ
AND THE PRISONERS'
LIVING CONDITIONS

ALEKSANDER LASIK

STRUCTURE AND CHARACTER OF THE CAMP SS ADMINISTRATION

1. The Organizational Structure of Nazi Concentration Camps

The Nazi concentration camps, whose origins dated back to 1933, retained the same basic organizational structure from an administrative point of view. Over time, however, the camps had been subject to certain reorganizations and modifications. Himmler's order of March 3, 1942, brought such re-organizations to an end with the establishment of the Main Economic--Administrative Office of the SS (*SS-Wirtschaftsverwaltungshauptamt, SS--WVHA*) and the attachment to it of the Inspectorate for Concentration Camps (*Inspektion der Konzentrationslager*, IKL) in the form of Office Group D (*Amtsgruppe D*).

SS-WVHA consisted of five administrative or "office" groups (*Amtsgruppen*), designated by the letters A, B, C, D, and W, of which Administrative Group D — Concentration Camps (*Amtsgruppe D — Konzentrationslager*) played the most important role with regard to the concentration camps. Its director simultaneously held the title of Inspector for Concentration Camps (*Inspekteur der Konzentrationslager*).

Administrative Group D was divided into four offices (*Ämter*):

DI — Central Office (*Amt DI — Zentralamt*), composed of five departments, responsible for general prisoner affairs, camp security, technical facilities, and training for SS personnel assigned to the camps.

DII — Office for Prisoner Employment Affairs (*Amt DII — Arbeitseinsatz der Häftlinge*), composed of three departments, responsible for exploiting the prisoners' labor, training them and bookkeeping.

DIII — Office for Sanitation and Camp Hygiene (*Amt DIII-Sanitätswesen und Lagerhygiene*), composed of three departments, responsible for medical care for the prisoners and SS men, for sanitation, and for hygiene.

DIV — Office for Administrative Affairs (*Amt DIV-Verwaltung*), composed of five departments, responsible for clothing, provisions, accommodations and warehouses, as well as financial administration and legal questions related to the functioning of the camps.

In addition to Office Group D, Office Group W — Economic Enterprises (*Amtsgruppe W — Wirtschaftliche Unternehmungen*) also played a limited role in the functioning of the camps. Under the personal direction of the head of SS-WVHA, *SS-Obergruppenführer* Oswald Pohl, Office Group W directed the economic activities of the entire SS organization. Its responsibilities included supervising firms and affiliates of firms that belonged to the SS and were in operation at the concentration camps. [1]

The SS personnel at KL Auschwitz — just like the staff at other camps — can be divided into three basic groups, responsible for specific tasks. From largest to smallest, they were (1) the guard division (*SS-Wachtruppen*), (2) the camp administration, and (3) the SS men employed at lower-level branches of the central SS administration or at firms established at the Auschwitz camp. All these groups formed — regardless of their different assignments and areas of competence — a community, whom we shall call "the SS staff at KL Auschwitz", or more accurately, the SS staff at the Auschwitz camp-complex.

2. The Guard Staff at KL Auschwitz

Just as the entire organizational system of the Nazi concentration camps was subject to change, so was the organization of the guard staff. After a number of reorganizations, a certain organizational model for guard divisions had been established by the outbreak of the war. The basic unit stationed at the camp was the guard battalion (*SS-Wachbataillon, SS-Totenkopfsturmbann*). Normally, an older SS officer with the title of battalion leader (*Führer des SS-Wachbataillon*) stood at the head of the organization. Organizationally, he answered to the camp commandant, who also held the office of head of the camp SS garrison.

From June 1940 to November 1943, the battalion represented the main organizational unit of the camp's guard staff. Its successive commanders at KL Auschwitz were *SS-Hauptsturmführer* Arthur Plorin (June 1940 — summer 1942), *SS-Sturmbannführer* Gebhard (summer 1942 — August 1942), and *SS-Sturmbannführer* Friedrich Hartjenstein (September 1942 — November 1943). During the battalion's existence, it was composed of a total of fourteen guard companies (*SS-Wachkompanie*). These fourteen companies included two headquarters or staff companies (*Stabskompanie*), composed of functionaries from the camp administration; one company of dog-trainers (*SS-Hundestaffel*); several companies composed of new SS men, temporarily considered training companies (*Ausbildungskompanien*), and the normal guard companies for the camp.

After the reorganization of the Auschwitz camp-complex in November 1943 and its resulting division into three camps (Auschwitz I — main camp; Auschwitz II-Birkenau; and Auschwitz III-Sub-camps), the guard battalion was liquidated, and subdivisions answering to the commandants of each of the three camps took its place.

By most estimates, the guard staff represented around 75% of all the SS men assigned to KL Auschwitz.

---

[1] In the case of KL Auschwitz, these were *Deutsche Erd- und Steinwerke GmbH, Deutsche Lebensmittel GmbH, Deutsche Ausrüstungswerke GmbH, Deutsche Versuchsanstalt für Ernährung und Verpflegung GmbH,* und *Golleschauer Portland-Zement AG.*

3. Administration of the Camp

Like all other concentration camps, the administration at KL Auschwitz consisted of five divisions (*Abteilungen*), designated by Roman numerals: Division I - Commandant's Office (*Abteilung I - Kommandantur*); Division II - Political Division (*Abteilung II - Politische Abteilung*); Division III - Prisoners Camp (*Abteilung III - Schutzhaftlager*); Division IV - Administration (*Abteilung IV - Verwaltung*); Division V - Chief Garrison Doctor (*Abteilung V - Standortarzt*).

After several reorganizations — linked, in part, to the creation of the Main Economic-Administrative Office of the SS — an additional division, Division VI - Welfare and Education of SS Units (*Abteilung VI - Fürsorge-, Schulung und Truppenbetreuung*), arose out of Division I. The size of the Auschwitz camp-complex also presented the need to create an autonomous division within Division III for prisoner employment: Division IIIa (*Abteilung IIIa - Arbeitseinsatz*).[2]

The most important post in the internal administrative hierarchy of every Nazi concentration camp was that of camp commandant (*Lagerkommandant*). In those cases in which the camp SS personnel represented an independent garrison, he also served as its commander (*Standortälteste*).[3] Every SS man on the camp staff answered to the commandant. He was formally responsible for all matters connected with the functioning of the camp under his control. Beginning in 1942, the camp commandant also served as manager for all the SS-affiliated industries operating on the grounds of the camp. His immediate superiors were the Inspector of Concentration Camps and, through him, the head of SS-WVHA.

The founder and first commandant of KL Auschwitz was *SS-Obersturmbannführer* Rudolf Franz Ferdinand Höss. He held this office until November 1943, when he was promoted to the office of Director of Administration DI — the Central Administration of SS-WVHA. He was succeeded by *SS-Obersturmbannführer* Arthur Liebehenschel, who was brought in from outside the camp to become commandant of KL Auschwitz. From May 1944 until the camp's liquidation, *SS-Sturmbannführer* Richard Baer held the post of commandant.

During the period of its existence as an independent camp, from November 1943 to November 1944, the post of commandant at KL Auschwitz II was held in succession by *SS-Sturmbannführer* Friedrich Hartjenstein (formerly one of the commanders of the Auschwitz guard battalion) and from May 1944 by *SS-Hauptsturmführer* Josef Kramer, former adjutant to the camp commandant at KL Auschwitz in 1940.

---

[2] Division IIIa existed at other camps as well, but only as an integral part of Division III. In these other cases, its director was a Deputy *Schutzhaftlagerführer* for Prisoner-Employment Affairs.

[3] One exception at KL Auschwitz was the period May-July 1944, when *SS-Obersturmbannführer* Rudolf Höss, in conjunction with the extermination of the Hungarian Jews, temporarily held the office of *Standortälteste*.

At KL Auschwitz III (Monowitz and the sub-camps), *SS-Hauptsturmführer* Heinrich Schwarz, former supervisor of Division III at the main camp, held the office of commandant from November 1943 to January 1945.

The commandant at Auschwitz I (the main camp), in his capacities as commander of the SS garrison at Auschwitz, was the immediate superior to the commandants of KL Auschwitz II-Birkenau and KL Auschwitz III (Monowitz, along with its sub-camps).

Division I — Commandant's Office

This division, which served in practice as a sub-unit of the camp administration, was responsible for SS personnel affairs and camp maintenance (including roads, communication, and transportation to the camp). It was composed of two sections: Ia and Ib.

The responsibilities of Section Ia, the Office of the SS Judicial Officer (*SS-Gerichtsführer*) included initiating and conducting legal proceedings against staff members who had committed crimes and transgressions at the camp. In this office, the SS officer responsible for camp security (*Führer für die Sicherheit*) also worked, to whom the camp police (*Lagerpolizei*), among others, answered. Given the lack of trained cadres, the responsibilities of both offices were sometimes assumed by the adjutant to the camp commandant.

Section Ib maintained camp security by providing the technical necessities for its functioning and by controlling the movement of SS men on duty. At its head stood an SS officer with the title of Adjutant to the Camp Commandant (*Adjutant*), whose responsibilities included making certain that the commandant's orders were swiftly carried out and controlling the flow of correspondence to and from the commandant. He simultaneously held the post of Assistant for SS Garrison Affairs.

The following men served at one point or the other as adjutant to the camp commandant: at KL Auschwitz I, *SS-Untersturmführer* Josef Kramer (May--October 1940), *SS-Obersturmführer* Erich Frommhagen (November 1940--spring 1941), *SS-Obersturmführer* Edmund Bräuning (spring 1941-June 1942), *SS-Obersturmführer* Robert Mulka (July 1942-March 1943), *SS-Obersturmführer* Ludwig Baumgärtner (April 1943-November 1943), *SS-Hauptsturmführer* Viktor Zoller (November 1943-May 1944), and *SS-Oberstürmführer* Karl Höcker (May 1944-January 1945); at KL Auschwitz II-Birkenau, *SS-Untersturmführer* Johannes Schindler, and at KL Auschwitz III, *SS-Untersturmführer* Rudolf Orlich.

Section Ib contained the following departments (*Referate*): the Commandant's Office, run by the Staff Sergeant for Division I (*Stabsscharführer der Kommandantur*), who coordinated the administrative tasks of that division; the Office for Weapons and Equipment (*Abteilung Waffen und Geräte*), which supplied the staff with weapons and military equipment; a vehicle-transportation unit (*Fahrbereitschaft der Kommandantur*), which secured means of transportation for the camp; the communications division (*Nachrichtenstelle*), which kept the radio, telephones, and telegraphs in working order; the post office (*Poststelle*), which received and sent correspondence outside the camp and included a censorship unit; the camp engineer (*Lageringenieur*), who operated in section Ib until 1942 and was responsible for keeping camp facilities running efficiently. A separate sub-unit within Section Ib, subordinate to the camp commandant, was the so called "Arrest Command" (*Kommandantur Arrest*), where SS men were held during disciplinary proceedings initiated by the SS judicial officer and where they then served their sentences. Most often, however, SS men were held in a special jail based on decisions made by Divisions II and III.

The commandant's office employed several dozen SS men, the largest group of which were the functionaries in the vehicle-transportation unit.

Division II — Political Division

In addition to the oversight carried out by the SS administrative organs, Division II-Political — which was basically composed of a unit of Security Police (*Sicherheitspolizei,* Sipo) and the SS Security Service (*SS-Sicherheitsdienst, SD*) — also helped to maintain control over the concentration camps. Officially, its staff was subordinate to the camp commandant at KL Auschwitz, but in substantive matters, it answered directly to the Sipo and SD post in Katowice (*Polizeistelle Sipo und SD*). The autonomy of this division was reflected, for example, in the fact that the commandant at Auschwitz had no influence over the composition of its leadership and did not have the authority to make changes because it was directly subordinate to the Main Security Office of the Reich (*Reichssicherheitshauptamt, RSHA*), and not to SS-WVHA.

From 1940-45, the post of head of the Political Division (*Leiter der Politischen Abteilung*) was held by two SS officers: *SS-Untersturmführer und Kriminal-Sekretär* Maximilian Grabner, and from December 1943, by *SS-Untersturmführer und Kriminal-Sekretär* Hans Schurz. They were assisted by deputies (*Stellvertreter des Leiters der Politischen Abteilung*), whose responsiblities included supervising the work of the Division Director's Office (*Büro des Leiters der Politischen Abteilung*). Among the officers who held this post during KL Auschwitz's existence were *SS-Hauptscharführer* Anton Brose, *SS-Obersturmführer* Wolfgang Güssgen, *SS-Haupscharführer* Helmut Westphal, and *SS-Untersturmführer* Erich Wosnitza.

Division II consisted of the following sections: the Legal-Welfare Section (*Rechts- und Fürsorgeabteilung*), responsible for questions related to the lawful functioning of the camp, including procedures for the imprisonment and release of prisoners; the Reception and Discharge Office (*Aufnahme- und Entlassungsbüro*), which received incoming prisoners and prepared the necessary documents whenever prisoners were released; the Section for Registration, Organisation, and Documentation (*Registratur, Organisation und Karteiführung*), which maintained the personal records of prisoners; the Civil Affairs Office (*Standesamt*), which provided the civilian administration with death certificates for deceased prisoners and which, as a result, exercised control over the camp's crematoria, including oversight over the disposal of corpses and destruction of evidence related to the crimes being committed[4]; the Identification Service (*Erkennungsdienst*), which kept fingerprints and photographs of the prisoners; the Investigation and Interrogation Unit (*Ermittlungen und Vernehmungen*), which undertook investigations against prisoners upon recommendation of Gestapo and Kripo authorities outside the camp or on grounds related to their stay at the camp; and the Investigation Section (*Fahndung*), which developed a spy network among the prisoners and conducted other intelligence activities.

The broad jurisdiction of Division II and its independence from the direct control of the camp administration allowed its functionaries to conduct an independent reign of terror. Since they did not need to explain or justify themselves, they could torture and kill prisoners with impunity; every summons to the Political Division was considered a death sentence. Furthermore, every SS man in the camp's police organs took part in the process of mass extermination, from verifying prisoners lists when transports arrived through destroying all leftover evidence of the crimes that they and others had committed.

Thus, more than any others, the names of the most brutal executioners from Division II remain engraved in the memories of former prisoners: *SS--Oberscharführer* Wilhelm Boger, *SS-Oberscharführer* Josef Houstek-Erber, *SS-Oberscharführer* Walter Quakernack and *SS-Unterscharführer* Gerhard Lachmann.

Division III — Prisoners' Camp

The organ established for directing prisoners affairs in their entirety was Division III — Prisoners' Camp. Although its internal organizational structure was not complicated, Division III was vast and powerful, due to the size of the Auschwitz camp complex and the number of prisoners that it held. These same factors ultimately led to the creation of Division IIIa, detached from Division III in 1942 to become an independent structure responsible for prisoner employment.

At the head of Division III stood an SS officer with the title of *Schutzhaftlagerführer* or *Lagerführer*. During the commandant's absence from the camp, he simultaneously held the offices of standing and permanent second-in-command to the commandant. His basic duties included: "providing for order and discipline" in the camp, proposing punishments for prisoners to the camp commandant, receiving reports about the number of prisoners at the camp and coordinating efforts related to prisoners' provisions and quarters with other units of the camp administration.

The size of the Auschwitz camp complex, as mentioned above, led to the establishment of the post of Camp Supervisor at Birkenau (both at the men's

---

⁴ The crematoria at KL Auschwitz I and KL Auschwitz II represented — along with their respective gas chambers — separate administrative units, controlled by the *Standesamt*. Their SS cadres were composed of individuals selected for their extreme depravity and brutality, such as: *SS-Hauptscharführer* Otto Moll, *SS-Oberscharführer* Hubert Busch, *SS--Unterscharführer* Ewald Kelm, *SS-Oberscharführer* Erich Muhsfeldt, *SS-Oberscharführer* Walter Quakernack, *SS-Unterscharführer* Robert Seitz, *SS-Unterscharführer* Karl Steinberg and *SS--Oberscharführer* Peter Voss.

and women's camps) and at Monowitz. At the women's camp, initially situated at KL Auschwitz I, but later transferred to KL Auschwitz II, an additional post, that of Head SS Overseer (*SS-Oberaufseherin*) was established in 1942. Held by a woman, the new office duplicated the office of male superviser at the women's camp.

In the years 1940-1945, the following individuals held the office of *Lagerführer* at KL Auschwitz: at the main camp, *SS-Hauptsturmführer* Karl Fritzsch (May 1940-January 1942), *SS-Hauptsturmführer* Hans Aumeier (January 1942-September 1943), *SS-Hauptsturmführer* Heinrich Schwarz (October-November 1943), *SS-Hauptsturmführer* Franz Johann Hofmann (November 1943-May 1944), and *SS-Hauptsturmführer* Franz Hössler (May 1944-January 1945). At the women's camp, founded in March 1942, *SS-Obersturmführer* Paul Heinrich Müller and *SS-Oberaufseherin* Johanna Langefeld served as its supervisors until August 1942. Subsequently, at Birkenau, *Lagerführer* included: *SS-Untersturmführer* Johann Schwarzhuber, responsible for the male portion of the camp (November 1943-September 1944), and at the women's camp, *SS-Hauptsturmführer* Franz Hössler (August 1942-May 1944, along with the *SS-Oberaufseherinnen*: Johanna Langefeld (August-October 1942), Maria Mandel (October 1942-November 1944), and Elisabeth Volkenrath (November 1944-January 1945). During its entire existence, the Camp Supervisor at KL Auschwitz III-Monowitz was *SS-Obersturmführer* Vinzenz Schöttl.

The *Lagerführer* of the main camp also received assistance from two permanent, immediate subordinates (the Second and Third Assistant *Lagerführer*), his office staff (*Büro des Schutzhaftlagerführers*), and lower-ranking, enlisted officers — the *Rapportführer* and their assistants (Second and Third Deputy *Rapportführer*). Among the duties assigned to the latter was preparing reports on the number of prisoners during roll-calls, overseeing prisoners in their quarters, and carrying out executions when called upon. At the women's camp at Auschwitz I and later at Auschwitz II, each male *Rapportführer* had a female-overseer counterpart, or *Rapportführerin*.

The lowest office occupied by SS men in the hierarchy of Division III was that of *Blockführer*, assigned to oversee prisoners in their residential blocks. Their counterparts at the women's camp held the title of *Blockführerin*, who, in this case, carried out their duties by themselves. Their basic duty was to supervise male and female prisoners in their barracks.

Division III is etched in the memories of prisoners who survived as being just as bloodthirsty as the Political Division because it bore direct responsibility for the implementation of the camp's criminal activities. The name of one of the greatest war criminals of all time, *Rapportführer* and *SS-Hauptscharführer* Gerhard Palitzsch of Division III, will forever remain part of the history of KL Auschwitz.

Division IIIa — Prisoner Employment

On April 15, 1942, an independent organizational unit, Division IIIa, split off from Division III. Such an administrative unit did not exist in other, similar camps. Its head, the *Arbeitseinsatzführer*, was responsible for arranging prisoner employment, overseeing prisoners at their work sites, and completing other duties assigned to his organization in a timely and thorough fashion.

The office of *Arbeitseinsatzführer* ("employment supervisor") at the main camp was held, in succession, by *SS-Hauptsturmführer* Heinrich Schwarz (April 1942-August 1943) and *SS-Obersturmführer* Max Sell (August 1943-January 1945). SS men and — at the women's camp — female SS overseers held the office of "employment-service supervisors" (*Arbeitsdienstführer* and *Arbeitsdienstführerinnen*) and answered to the head of Division IIIa. Beneath the overseers served the supervisors of the individual work details, the *Kommandoführer* and *Kommandoführerinnen*. All administrative matters were handled by the Office of the *Arbeitseinsatzführer*.

Just like Division III, Division IIIa carried out a repressive function with regard to the prisoners, given that forced labor represented one of the basic elements in the process of indirect murder at the camp, and also given the direct, daily contact of its personnel with the prisoners, whose persecution and maltreatment they enjoyed.

Division IV — Administration

Within the camp administration, Division IV had the most complex organizational structure. This resulted, on the one hand, from the numerous and varied responsibilities assigned to it and, on the other, from the bureaucratic way in which the camp was administrated.

At the head of Division IV at KL Auschwitz always stood an SS officer with the title of Head of the Administrative Division (*Leiter der Abteilung Verwaltung*). From 1940-45, the following officers held the post: *SS-Untersturmführer* Max Meyer (summer 1940), *SS-Hauptsturmführer* Rudolf Wagner (fall 1940-July 1942), *SS-Sturmbannführer* Wilhelm Burger (July 1942-March 1943), and *SS-Obersturmbannführer* Karl Möckel (April 1943-January 1945). The chief of Division IV, assisted by his second-in-command (among others, *SS-Hauptsturmführer* Stocker and *SS-Hauptsturmführer* Walter Polenz) and his office staff (*Büro des Leiters der Abteilung Verwaltung*), administered the entire economic system of the camp.

Besides the head's office (divided into four sections — a secretariat and three other units: personal affairs, legal affairs, and arbitration), Division IV was composed of the following sections: Provisions (*Abteilung Verpflegung*), which included the camp kitchens; Clothing (*Abteilung Bekleidung*); the Administration for Prisoners' Possessions (*Gefangenen-Eigentumsverwaltung*); *Abteilung Unterkunft*, responsible for warehouses, accommodations, and services; and, beginning in 1942, a Technical Division (*Technische Abteilung*) and the garrison's pay office (*Standortkasse*). Until 1942, the Agricultural Division (*Abteilung Landwirtschaft*) was also part of Division IV.

One unique aspect of the administration of Division IV was that several of its sections (Provisions, Clothing, and Accommodations) were divided in two, with one part exclusively responsible for the prisoners, and the other part responsible for the camp SS personnel. The administrative unit responsible for the prisoners — composed of the warehouses for the personal effects of murdered prisoners (*Effektenlager*), the "Valuables Section" (*Wertsachenab-*

teilung), and the unit responsible for prisoners' financial deposits (*Häftlings-geldverwaltung*) — mainly served to plunder the prisoners' property.

Division IV also represented the most extensive administrative unit in terms of personnel within the camp administration. In comparison with other camps, its administrative network was the most complicated. This reflects the fact that Auschwitz was also the largest death camp.

Division V — Chief Garrison Doctor

The establishment of units for medical care at the camps originated in the concerns of the SS leadership regarding the health of their staff members. The concentration of tens of thousands of people in such a small area, along with the lack of basic sanitary facilities, aroused fears about the real risk of an epidemic of diseases, against which there were no effective preventive measures. The existence of medical units also made it possible to conduct experiments upon living human beings — the prisoners.

At the head of the health service at Auschwitz, there always stood a recognized doctor of medicine, an SS officer, who received the title of Chief Garrison Doctor (*SS-Standortarzt*). This office was held, respectively, by: *SS-Hauptsturmführer* Max Popiersch (June 1940-October 1941), *SS-Obersturm-führer* Oskar Dienstbach (November 1941-March 1942), *SS-Hauptsturmführer* Siegfried Schwela (March-May 1942), *SS-Obersturmführer* Franz von Bod-mann (May-August 1942), *SS-Hauptsturmführer* Kurt Uhlenbroock (August--September 1942), and *SS-Sturmbannführer* Eduard Wirths (September 1942--January 1945).

As was the case with several sections of Division IV, Division V was administratively divided into units serving the SS personnel and units responsible for the prisoners. In terms of its internal organizational structure, it consisted of three departments: general medicine, dental, and pharmaceutical. The Office of the SS Garrison Doctor (*Büro des SS-Standortarztes*) administered the SS health service at the camp in its entirety.

In the Department for General Medicine, doctors from the SS units (*SS-Truppenärzte*) worked alongside camp doctors (*Lagerärzte*). Immediately subordinate to the doctors were the SS Sanitation Staff (*SS-Sanitär-Staffel*) at the camp hospitals for SS men and the SS sanitarians (*Sanitätsdienstgrade*), who worked among the prisoners.

At the head of the Dental Department stood the Dental-Station Supervisor (*Leiter der Zahnstation*), who directed the work of the camp dentists and dental technicians. The latter assisted the dentists, for example, by registering which prisoners had dental work made of precious metals and later melting them down.

The leader of the Pharmaceutical Division (*Leiter der Apotheke*) administered the camp warehouse that held pharmaceuticals received from the central SS medical administration and stolen from Jews sent to KL Auschwitz for extermination. The repositories for Zyklon B also lay under his jurisdiction. Several SS men were assigned to help him with administrative duties.

To the extent that Division V carried out medical assignments for the camp SS staff, its activities with respect to the prisoners were criminal. Doctors with

SS badges carried out systematic selections at the infirmaries assigned to the prisoners, during which they effectively sentenced prisoners whom they considered incapable of recovery to a rapid death. Some of the victims selected in this fashion were put to death by SS sanitarians, who, in compliance with the doctors, would administer fatal injections of phenol into the hearts of their victims.

Among the other basic duties of the SS doctors were conducting selections among the transports of Jews delivered to the camp for annihilation and later confirming the victims' deaths in the gas chambers. A portion of the SS Sanitation Staff and SS sanitarians who had been schooled in the use of airborne poisons formed a "disinfection detail" (*Desinfektionskommando*), whose duties included releasing Zyklon B into the gas chambers.

The majority of the doctors employed in Division V also took part in various criminal experiments, whose results claimed the lives of many prisoners or left them crippled for life.

It is thus not surprising that contact with SS doctors aroused among the prisoners the same reaction as contact with functionaries from the Political Division. There existed between Division II and V a peculiar, criminal, symbiotic relationship: the staff of both divisions took direct part in the process of extermination; together, they falsified the causes of death for many prisoners; and together, they obliterated the evidence of genocide.

Such doctors as *SS-Hauptsturmführer* Josef Mengele, *SS-Obersturmführer* Friedrich Entress, *SS-Hauptsturmführer* Erwin von Helmersen, *SS-Hauptsturmführer* Werner Rhode, *SS-Obersturmführer* Heinz Thilo, and such sanitarians as *SS-Oberscharführer* Josef Klehr, *SS-Unterscharführer* Hans Nierzwicki, *SS-Oberscharführer* Herbert Scherpe, and *SS-Unterscharführer* Adolf Theuer, were also known at the camp as butchers, although they never personally took part in torturing the prisoners.

Division VI — Welfare and Schooling for the SS Staff

This division split off from Division I in 1942. Up to that time, a staff sergeant from the commandant's office had carried out the same functions. The basic duty of Division VI was to organize cultural events for the camp SS personnel, such as concerts and excursions to plays and theatres. It also ran the camp library and provided the SS men with newspapers and magazines. It also provided ideological training for the staff and organized sport competitions at which staff members could win commendations for their physical fitness.

A director (throughout KL Auschwitz's existence, *SS-Oberscharführer* Kurt Knittel) headed this unit of several persons. Theoretically, Division VI had important responsibilities, but, in fact, its activities had little impact on the functioning of the camp.

3. Evolution and Characteristics of the SS Staff at KL Auschwitz, 1940-1945

The growth of the cadre of SS administrative staff at Auschwitz proceeded gradually, and its tempo reflected the progressive stages in KL Auschwitz's expansion. In 1940, the camp's personnel numbered around 700 SS men; in June 1942, already around 2,000; in April 1944, 2950, but by August of the same year, 3,342. The largest number of personnel was reached in mid-January 1945, in connection with the camp's evacuation: 4,481 SS men and 71 female SS overseers. In general, however, the SS strived to maintain a level of staffing at KL Auschwitz in keeping with the ratio of one SS man for every 30-40 prisoners. Altogether, throughout the camp's entire existence, around 7,000 SS men passed through the camp. [5]

Beyond the quantitative evolution of the staff, no less important was its qualitative change in sociological and demographic terms. In 1940, the staff at KL Auschwitz had been recruited from among personnel at other concentration camps, mainly from KL Dachau, Buchenwald, and Sachsenhausen. In the later period, the number of staff members originating from frontline *Waffen-SS* formations (mainly from the lst Armoured Division *Leibstandarte--SS* "Adolf Hitler" and the Sixth Mountain Division SS "North") and from SS reserve commands steadily grew. Gradually, the percentage of *Volksdeutsche* among the staff — from Poland, Romania, Hungary, and Croatia — increased as well. In 1943, they reached their highest level — 47,9% in relation to the total number of *Reichsdeutsche* and Austrians working on the staff. The search for staff reserves resulted in the arrival of female SS overseers at KL Auschwitz (after the establishment of the women's camp in 1942), and in the creation in March 1943 of a training company composed of Ukrainians, which never became part of the camp staff. Then, in 1944, soldiers from the *Wehrmacht* and the German National Guard (*Landschutz*) began flocking to the camp. After a brief period of training, they were given SS uniforms and assigned guard duties.

The staff was also not uniform from a sociological point of view. Its members differed in their level of education. Only 5,5% had a higher education — in this case, mainly doctors; 73% had completed their basic eduction in full or in part. Religion also divided the staff: 42,4% declared themselves to be members of the Catholic Church; 36,5% as Protestants; and the remainig individuals were dissenters, some of whom had left the church (i.e., *Gottgläubig* or agnostics).

Nonetheless, this socially dissimilar group was able to evolve rapidly — with the assistance of various social and technical measures — into an efficient apparatus for extermination, whose crimes left an enduring mark upon 20th century humanity.

---

[5] This figure comes from a card file of members of the Auschwitz SS staff, currently in the author's possession.

TADEUSZ IWASZKO

DEPORTATION TO THE CAMP AND REGISTRATION OF PRISONERS

1. Arrest and Imprisonment at the Camp

The reign of terror that the Nazis carried out against their political opponents after their seizure of power in Germany necessitated the creation of some semblance of legal sanction to justify mass arrests and detainment of prisoners in concentration camps. The institution of so-called "protective custody" (*Schutzhaft*), established by the February 28, 1933 decree, "For the Protection of the Nation and State", became the necessary sanction for illegality. A circular of January 25, 1938,[1] from the Ministry of Internal Affairs outlined the general principles according to which "protective custody" would be applied. It declared that "temporary arrest is a means of coercion for the Secret State Police to protect the nation and the state before all potential enemies and will apply to individuals who through their behavior threaten the property or security of the nation and state". People taken into "protective custody" were to be sent to concentration camps. "Protective custody", it should be emphasized, was in fact of unlimited duration. Although the order mentioned the possibility of release, it could only take place after "the method achieves its goal". This phrasing, which did not specify the conditions for release, allowed those who were arrested to be incarcerated indefinitely.

In subsequent years, the original order underwent a number of modifications that simplified the procedure for applying "protective custody", particularly with respect to Poles and inhabitants of other occupied lands. An August 27, 1941 order from the RSHA (published in connection with the aggression against the Soviet Union) serves as an example of these changes. The new order postponed the release of all prisoners from the camps and cited Himmler's orders, that "all shaveling-clerical instigators, Czech and Polish enemies of Germany, as well as communists and similar rabble, should be locked up in a camp, on principle, for a long period of time".[2] An order from May 9, 1944, greatly simplified the procedure for deporting prisoners from Eastern Europe (*Ostvolksangehörige*) in mass transports to the camps. According to the order, prisoners only had to be registered after their arrival at the concentration camps.[3]

---

[1] APMO, D-RF-32/RSHA/118/9. Collection *Erlass-Sammlung RKPA*, card 626.
[2] Ibid., card 629.
[3] APMO, D-RF-9/WVHA/8/2. Collection of orders published by the *SS-WVHA* (henceforth: Collection *Sammlung von Erlässen*), card 51.

A formal — but often ignored — prerequisite for carrying out "protective arrests" and subsequently holding prisoners at KL Auschwitz was a written "Order for Protective Custody" (*Schutzhaftbefehl*), to be issued by Office Group IV or V of the *Reichsicherheitshauptamt* or Main Office for Reich Security. Beginning in May 1943, this right, at least with regard to Poles, was transferred to the local Gestapo posts in occupied Poland.

Office Group IV, mentioned above, published decisions regarding the application of "protective custody" to political prisoners, homosexuals, Jehovah's Witnesses, individuals arrested "for betterment and conditioning" (*Besserungshäftlinge*), and returnees to Germany who could eventually be deported to another country based on their citizenship. Imprisonment for "preventive custody" (Vorbengungshaft), however, lay within the compentency of Office Group V. It was applied against common criminals, Gypsies, so-called „antisocial" prisoners, and prisoners being held in "preventive arrest" (*Sicherungsverwahrte*). "Preventive-custody" prisoners were held at concentration camps following their release from prison, where they had served a sentence based on the verdict of a court.

The form itself — "Order for Protective Custody" (*Schutzhaftbefehl*) — contained, along with details about the person to be arrested, a short justification (*Gründe*) for his or her arrest. In the case of the Polish prisoner Stanisława Olewnik, for example, the justification read as follows:

The results of her interrogation by the state police demonstrate that the arrested individual threatened the existence and security of the state by her behavior [standard formulation — TI] by providing shelter to numerous Jewish refugees and thus preventing their arrest by the police.[4]

Prisoners held in concentration camps on the basis of an "Order for Protective Custody" were called "protective prisoners" (*Schutzhäftlinge*). Regulations for preparing and presenting arrested individuals with their respective "Orders for Protective Custody" normally applied only to individuals born within the *Reich* proper or the lands annexed to it. Individuals from other areas were usually not presented with the order, or it was sent to the camp after a long period of time, often after the prisoner had already died.

The imprisonment of Soviet prisoners-of-war and their mass extermination at KL Auschwitz was carried out on the basis of special orders from the leadership of the German armed forces and regulations from RSHA. The head of the Security Police and Security Services (*Sicherheitspolizei und Sicherheitsdienst* — Sipo u. SD) ordered on August 27, 1941, that "executions should be carried out only at the nearest concentration camps. The necessary instructions will be given to the commandants. Secured facilities are to be provided for the Soviet prisoners to be liquidated, and their transport should be organized in such a way that precludes any possibility of escape.[5]

---

[4] APMO, IZ-11/1. Photocopies of the personal documents of prisoner Stanisława Olewnik (perished at the camp on 21 IV 1944), card 16.

[5] *Biuletyn Głównej Komisji Zbrodni Niemieckiech w Polsce* (Bulletin of the Main Commission for the Investigation of German Crimes in Poland), Vol. V (1949), p. 133.

Another institution, the so-called "reformatory work camp" (*Arbeitserzie-hungslager* — AEL), evolved under the supervision of the Gestapo on the basis of separate, repressive regulations promulgated in 1940-41 and supplemented in subsequent years. According to a December 12, 1941 regulation, "Only those individuals may be sent to reformatory work camps who shun labor or violate contracts, as well as elements unwilling to work or whose behavior is the equivalent of sabotage or violates general work ethics, and who for that reason should be arrested by the police". [6] This regulation was applied against untold thousands of workers, forced into slave labor for the needs of the German war economy. On the basis of the regulations mentioned above, as early as July 1941, local police units began sending to KL Auschwitz [7] "reformatory prisoners" (*Erziehungshäftlinge* — EH) for a "reformatory" sentence (up to 56 days), after which they were to be released from the camp. More than 10 percent of the prisoners (men and women) sent to KL Auschwitz for "reform" died before their release from the camp.

In 1942, prisoners designated with the cryptonym "night and fog" (*Nacht und Nebel*) — on the basis of a December 7, 1941 order from Hitler and the German High Command (signed by *Wehrmacht* Chief-of-Staff Wilhelm Keitel) — began to arrive at the concentration camp at Auschwitz. The December 1941 order proclaimed:

> From the very beginning of the Russian campaign, communist elements and other anti-German circles have increased their activities against the *Reich* and the occupation forces in occupied areas [...] Thus, the need exists for the most severe prosecution of such offenses. If the offender is not a person of German nationality, there is only one possible punishment — the death penalty. [8]

Of the 1, 170 French prisoners designated with this cryptonym who were deported from France and arrived at KL Auschitz on July 8, 1942, a majority met the same fate. [9]

Before the period of their mass extermination began, Jews were deported to KL Auschwitz under existing regulations — through the application of "protective arrest". In 1942, the RSHA began to issue special regulations that paved the way for subsequent operations under the rubric of "the final solution of the Jewish question" (*Endlösung der Judenfrage*). Using these regulations, the Nazis began to send mass transports of Jews to Auschwitz from every occupied and dependent area.

A January 29, 1943 order from Office Group V of RSHA provided for the creation of a special camp for Gypsies (*Zigeunerlager*) at KL Auschwitz to accommodate nearly 21,000 people [10].

---

[6] APMO, D-RF-3/141a. Document collection from various organs of the Third Reich, card 164.

[7] Editor's note: Particular buildings or parts of KL Auschwitz served the function of a reformatory work camp for the region of Katowice.

[8] *Der Prozess gegen die Hauptkriegsverbrecher vor dem Internationalen Militärgerichtshof* (henceforth: *Der Prozess...*), Nürnberg, 1949, vol. XXXVII, p. 572.

[9] Editor's note: The assertion that French prisoners were assigned the cryptonym "NN" is based on the testimony of two former prisoners and is not confirmed in the records of the camp.

[10] Hans Joachim Döring, *Die Zigeuner im NS-Staat*, Hamburg 1964, pp. 214-18.

2. Transport

The first transport of 30 prisoners arrived at KL Auschwitz on May 20, 1940. The prisoners were professional criminals (*Berufsverbrecher*) of German nationality, transferred to Auschwitz from KL Sachsenhausen. In accordance with a long-standing practice at Nazi concentration camps, they received auxiliary functions at the newly-founded camp. With regard to their future role, the SS men informed them that there would be Polish "criminals" to be dealt with at KL Auschwitz. This was a cynical provocation, planned in advance. Every account and memoir of former prisoners held at the camp during this period is replete with descriptions of the persecution and atrocities carried out by both the SS staff and "green" (see p. 64) prisoner-functionaries against Polish prisoners. After a certain period of time — thanks to the engagement of the camp resistance movement — the "green" prisoners' hegemony was broken, and political prisoners subsequently had a greater chance of taking over their functions.

On June 14, 1940, with the arrival of 728 political prisoners, prisoners began to arrive at KL Auschwitz either individually in so-called *Einzeltransporte* or in groups of several dozen people in *Sammeltransporte* ("collective" transports). In transit, a number of prisoners (especially Poles) were handcuffed or had their hands tied, which worsened the already harsh conditions of the journey. Only prisoners from the nearest localities arrived in trucks; all others arrived, as a rule, by train, in locked cattle cars.

The crowded railway cars carried around 80 persons apiece, who had to endure a journey of hours or days in locked, unventilated wagons, full of smells and stench, exhausted from thirst. This was only an introduction to what awaited the prisoners upon their disembarkation at the camp's railway platform. The deportees' suffering was multiplied exponentially in those cases in which the journey lasted several days, as was the case with transports of Jews to KL Auschwitz from such distant, Nazi-occupied countries as France, Belgium, Holland, Greece, and Italy.

A strong escort accompanied all transports, whose duty was to prevent prisoners from escaping. Despite the extraordinary security precautions, the occasional brave individual was able to escape from a transport.

The prisoners sent to KL Auschwitz had often already been held in other concentration camps, prisons, transit camps (*Durchganslager — Dulag*), or ghettoes. This naturally had a great impact upon their physical and psychological state. Some of the prisoners had been subjected to interrogation and torture by the Gestapo. This applied mainly to persons suspected of membership in the resistance movement, who had been arrested for treason or other provocations; partisans or activitists in the resistance movement, captured with weapons in hand or with materials providing circumstantial evidence of their anti-Nazi activities. Such prisoners were held for months in crowded prison cells, where movement was practically impossible, rations were poor, and prisoners were tortured to the breaking point.

Surviving fragments of correspondence regarding a transport of 1500 prisoners from Majdanek on July 8, 1943 — sent to Auschwitz for forced labor

— illustrate the tragic state in which prisoners arrived at KL Auschwitz from other concentration camps. After the transport came in, the camp doctor, *SS-Lagerarzt* Dr Bruno Kitt, examined the new arrivals and determined that of the 750 men, only 425 could be sent to work after a four-week quarantine; the remaining 326 were considered unsuitable for work in any form. Of the 750 women prisoners in the same transport, five died immediately upon arrival. The surviving women prisoners were in the same condition as the men and they were also afflicted with scabies.

In discussing how prisoners were transported, we should recall the conditions under which the final evacuation of prisoners — both male and female — from KL Auschwitz to concentration camps in the *Reich* proper took place in January 1945. The majority of the prisoners had to traverse almost 60 kilometers on foot before reaching the designated area where they were loaded into open coal cars. A fragment of one prisoner's testimony recalls the tragic consequences of these transports, dispatched in winter in below-freezing conditions:

> The railway cars were terribly crowded. None of the prisoners could even move or change their original position .... It is difficult for me to describe today what began to occur during the journey. Those prisoners unprotected from the cold lost consciousness. Dantesque scenes unfolded. Everybody fought for the space that he occupied. Weaker and emaciated prisoners perished and fell to the floor of the railway car .... The ear-splitting groans of the dying blended with the screams of other prisoners who were going insane. Biting, kicking, and scratching, they represented a danger to their nearest neighbors. [11]

3. Reception and Registration of Transports

Prisoners were unloaded from the rail transports at a ramp that belonged to the camp, located near the housing blocks of KL Auschwitz I. In 1942, a second unloading ramp was installed (*Judenrampe*), where mainly transports of Jews condemned to extermination were unloaded. (Only a small portion of these Jews were ever sent to the camp and registered). Beginning in May 1944, rail transports were unloaded at a special ramp, located on the grounds of KL Birkenau (between divisions BI and BII).

As mentioned above, prisoners were also brought to the camp in trucks, which were normally received at the gates of the camp, where the prisoners were unloaded and handed over to the SS authorities. Transports arrived at various times of day, sometimes at night. On the latter occasions, the light of the reflectors, beatings with machine-gun butts, the yelling and cursing of SS men, and the barking dogs that were set upon the prisoners intensified the terrifying impression that the prisoner's first contact with camp realities had upon him.

After being herded onto the grounds of the camps, the new arrivals (*"Zugang"*) were directed to buildings that housed showers. At Auschwitz I,

---

[11] APMO, Collection of Testimonies, vol. 44, card 62, account of former prisoner Józef Tabaczyński.

the main camp, this was Block Nr 26; at Birkenau, special brick buildings, commonly called the "sauna", had been constructed on the grounds of divisions BIa and BIb. If a transport arrived at night, the prisoners spent the remainder of the night either in these facilities or — occasionally — in some other barracks. The process of receiving and identifying the prisoners would not begin until the following morning.

First, new arrivals had to relinquish all underwear and civilian clothes, all valuables in their possession, identification papers, and all other goods. Prisoners could only keep a handkerchief and, in the men's case, a belt for their pants. All remaining goods were packaged in paper bags and transferred for deposit in special warehouses (*Effektenkammer*), where they remained throughout the entire period of a prisoner's stay at the camp. Naturally, no receipt was given, even if the prisoner's deposit contained valuables, suchas gold, watches, or large amounts of money.

The prisoners were then driven into the next chamber, where the next formalities took place. First, the barbers went to work and shaved all hair from the bodies of the new arrivals. This was an unpleasant operation, both in terms of the haste in which it was conducted and in terms of the blunt instruments that were used. A rag soaked in liquid disinfectant was applied to shaved areas to disinfect them.

After they disrobed and were shaved, the new arrivals were driven into the shower room. This represented the first possibility in a long time to quench one's thirst. But even this hygienic procedure, which the majority of the new arrivals awaited with impatience after the hardships of the transport, was accompanied by various chicaneries. Quite often, for example, the showers would spray scalding hot or ice-cold water on the prisoners. Anyone who ran away from the showerheads was driven back by the blows of the SS guards.

The non-stop pushing, hitting, and cursing shocked the prisoners. The women and young girls, who had to undress in the presence of sneering and derisive SS men, had a particularly difficult time. The following is a fragment from the memoirs of one female prisoner:

We, the "*Zugang*" entered the gate to the "Sauna" Female German prisoners — professional prostitutes — provided the "sauna's" administration .... All of them were old, fat, and ugly, with disheveled mops of hair on their head, nothing like the witches we know from children's tales, something whose very sight arouses horror and disgust. So these "black triangles", also known at the camp as 'Puff-Mama" [12], greeted us with vulgar curses and mocking, pushing us to quickly undress. Inside the "sauna", a young SS man with a stupid look paced back and forth; he was the so-called "*Unterscharführer*" — supervisor of the "Sauna" .... After we had stripped naked, this "Uscha" was pacing [...] and no one had any desire to leave. Up to that point, I still did not know about the practices at the camp. We stood there embarassed, staring at one another, waiting to see who would be first to disrobe .... I also disrobed, but bent down and picked up a blanket lying next to me on the

---

[12] Translator's note: *"Asoziale"* or antisocial prisoners wore a black triangle on their camp uniforms. "Puff" is a vulgar German term for a brothel, and a "Puff-Mama" was the woman who ran such a brothel.

ground and wrapped myself up in it. A female "Kapo" leapt upon me, tore the blanket from my shoulders, struck me hard in the face, and shouted: "*Heilige Madonna*", which meant, "Look, Holy Madonna!" The SS man started to laugh loudly, she added something vulgar, and all the German women broke out laughing .... almost everyone was amused by the fact that she had called me "*Heilige Madonna*" .... A German man came unexpectedly closer and hit me with a stick above my bare buttocks. He laughed helplessly, like an idiot, about his 'heroic act'. [13]

The next step after the showers was the distribution of camp uniforms, which required that prisoners enter the next chamber. Given the rush and customarily large number of new arrivals, the individual parts of the camp uniform were thrown out to the prisoners as they ran out of the showers. At the end, in less than an hour, a group of prisoners clothed in poorly-fitting, often dirty and louse-infested camp uniforms came into being. The wooden clogs distributed as a substitute for shoes made it difficult to move, especially on the icy roads in winter.

During all these exertions — which naturally took place in unheated, drafty buildings (at KL Auschwitz I, the prisoners had to change clothes and wait for the distribution of uniforms under the open sky) — the prisoners, who most often did not understand the orders and instructions given in German, were showered with the most vulgar curses and repeatedly hit by the SS men and prisoner-functionaries who were present. The prisoners, terrified by their brutal treatment, had difficulties identifying their relatives, friends and colleagues, who were now shorn of their hair and clothed in ill-fitting uniforms.

The registration procedure for new arrivals, which took place immediately after the showers and distribution of uniforms, consisted of filling out a blank form (*Häftlings-Personalbogen*). Besides their personal data, prisoners were required to give the address of their nearest relatives. The forms, kept by the camp's Political Division, were used in preparing a list of new arrivals (*Zugangsliste*) in 10-20 copies, which were distributed to all the camp's administrative divisions (*Abteilungen*), where they served as the basic source of information regarding the prisoners. A card file, established on the basis of the lists, made it easier to maintain the prisoners' records and to prepare daily and longer-term reports. After the forms were filled out, the new prisoners received successive camp numbers, which would replace their names throughout their entire stay at KL Auschwitz. At the end of the registration procedure, the prisoner's camp identification number was tattooed onto his or her left forearm.

The concentration camp at Auschwitz was the only one to tattoo prisoners for identification. The underlying cause was the high death rate among the prisoners, which sometimes surpassed several hundred in a single day. With such a large number of deaths, there were difficulties in identifying all the corpses. If the clothes with the camp number were removed from a corpse, one could no longer establish what the number of the deceased had been. At the camp hospital (*Häftlingskrankenbau*, HKB), where many prisoners died, the staff began to write ill prisoners' camp numbers on their chests with indelible

---

[13] APMO, Collection of Reminiscences, vol. 63, card 28, memoirs of the former prisoner Maria Oyrzyńska (registered at the camp under the family name Slisz).

ink. Difficulties in identifying corpses increased in spring 1941, when the mass extermination of Soviet prisoners-of-war began. It was then that the camp administration decided to adopt tattooing, which was first used with several thousand Soviet prisoners-of-war. They were tattooed with a special metal stamp that held interchangeable numbers composed of needles around 1 cm long. This stamp — when applied to the upper portion of the left breast — allowed the entire 1 number to be tattoed on at once. Next, ink was rubbed into the bleeding wounds. The POWs to be tattooed were so weak that they had to be propped up against the wall so that they would not fall down while the number was being applied. In March 1942, the staff began to tattoo in a similar fashion emaciated prisoners at KL Birkenau, whose state of health pointed to a rapid death. (Only several Poles with numbers tattooed their chests during this period survived the camp).

Since the metal stamp turned out to be impractical, tattooing was later carried out by puncturing the skin on the left forearm with individual needles. The puncture marks would form the individual digits of the camp number. Jewish prisoners began to be tattooed in this fashion at Birkenau as early as 1942. In spring 1943, the camp administration ordered that all prisoners — both previously-registered prisoners and new arrivals — be tattooed with camp numbers. A number of German prisoners and so-called "reformatory prisoners" (Erziehungshäftlinge) received no tattoo. [14] Several categories of prisoners were tattooed with an additional symbol before the number — e.g., Jews (but not all of them) with a triangular symbol; Gypsies, with the letter "Z" (the first letter of the German word Zigeuner or "Gypsy"); and beginning in May 1944, Jews received an additional letter, "A" or "B", which signified the particular series of numbers being used at the time. For unknown reasons, prisoners from several transports in 1943 were tattooed with camp numbers on the inside of their left shoulder.

Once they were tattooed, prisoners were identified by the camp number on their forearms. At Birkenau, the corpses of deceased prisoners were laid in front of the housing blocks in such a fashion that the prisoners's left hands and tattooed camp numbers were visible.

Besides being tattooed, another element in the registration process for new arrivals was being photographed in three poses. In the first photograph, a profile, the camp number was visible as well as letter symbols for the category and nationality of the prisoner. Jewish prisoners, who began to arrive in mass transports in 1942, were not photographed. [15] Beginning in 1943, due to difficulties in obtaining photographic materials, the number of pictures taken was limited, and in accordance with the orders of higher authorities, photographs were taken mainly of Germans and only sporadically of other prisoners. The photographs and negatives of the photos taken at KL Auschwitz were kept in separate locations. The SS Identification Service

---

[14] Editor's Note: A number of Polizeihäftlinge or "police prisoners" sent to the camp during the Warsaw Uprising in August-September 1944, and some Jews who arrived at the camp beginning in May 1944, were also not tattooed with camp numbers.

[15] Editor's note: There were certain exceptions to this general rule.

(*Erkennungsdienst*), one section of the camp Gestapo, was responsible for organizing and maintaining the photos.

New arrivals were subject to various chicaneries even during this simple process. The prisoner being photographed sat in a special rotating chair turned by a lever, which was violently released after the the third picture was taken. As a result, to the delight of the administrative personnel, the prisoner sitting in the chair fell to the floor.

4. Identification of Prisoners

All prisoners registered at KL Auschwitz received camp numbers which they had to wear on their uniforms in a very specific place. Printed on a small patch of cloth, the number was attached both to the shirt at the level of the left breast and to the oustside seam of the right pants leg. Each of the series of numbers at KL Auschwitz began with the number one.

The first series of numbers, given to male prisoners, came into use in May 1940 and continued to be used until January 1945, when it reached a total of 202,499 numbers. This series of numbers was also applied to Jewish prisoners from mid-May 1944. [16]

In October 1941, the next series of numbers was introduced (used until 1944), which was applied to around 12,000 Soviet prisoners-of-war. (A portion of the Soviet POWs exterminated at Auschwitz, however, were never registered and never received a camp number).

In February 1942, a separate series of numbers was introduced for "reformatory prisoners" (*Erziehungshäftlinge*), who had received numbers from the general male series up to that point. Once the new series of numbers was introduced, it was retroactively applied to previously-deceased or released prisoners from this category; on the other hand, their numbers were subsequently reassigned to incoming prisoners. This was one of the rare cases in the history of Auschwitz in which numbers were reused. In general, around 9,000 prisoners were registered with the series of numbers reserved for "reformatory" prisoners. Beginning in 1943, female prisoners in the same category were assigned their own series of numbers, beginning with the number one. Around 2000 women were registered in this series.

On March 26, 1942, the first female prisoners brought to Auschwitz received numbers from a new series that remained in use until the end of the camp's existence. Around 90,000 women were registered in this series, including Jewish women (up to mid-May 1944).

The Gypsies held at Auschwitz began to receive in February 1943 numbers from two different series — for men, 10,094 numbers were distributed through August 1944; for women, 10,888 numbers.

In mid-May 1944, a special series was introduced for newly-arrived and registered prisoners of Jewish nationality, in order to prevent the distribution of such high numbers in the general series. The new numbers were preceded by

---

[16] *Editor's note:* As of May 1944, Jews were registered only sporadically in the general series of numbers.

the letter "A" and ran from one to 20,000. After the "A" series was exhausted, it was planned to introduce subsequent series based on the letters of the alphabet. This happened with male Jewish prisoners, who received numbers from the "B" series (from one to ca. 15,000), but the "A" series for women, due to an oversight, ran beyond 20,000; a total of around 30,000 numbers were distributed.

Because the SS staff destroyed the camp's records, it is now impossible to establish with any accuracy the last number given out in each series. Altogether, more than 400,000 numbers were distributed in the different series mentioned above, which did not include around 3,000 numbers distributed to *Polizeihäftlinge* or „police prisoners". Their numbers were not included in the daily reports on the camp's population (*Stärkemeldungen*).

As noted above, the camp numbers that were distributed to prisoners allowed the SS authorities to identify prisoners, and the tattoo enabled them to identify the corpses of executed or deceased prisoners or, in the case of an apprehension, to recognize an escapee. Thus, the information sent from KL Auschwitz regarding escaped prisoners came to include the camp number as a "distinguishing mark" in 1944.

On the basis of the number displayed on a camp uniform, one could determine the length of a prisoner's stay at the camp. Over the years, only a few prisoners remained with the lower numbers distributed in 1940, 1941 or 1942. A low number meant that a prisoner had lived through a great deal and accumulated the necessary experiences that had enabled him (if he was also lucky) to survive at the camp for several years. It is not surprising that the SS authorities rid themselves of such prisoners by attaching them to transports being sent to camps inside the *Reich*; when they arrived, they had to go through the "*Zugang*" procedure once more.

In the Nazi concentration camps, various categories of prisoners existed. The category of a given prisoner could be recognized by the color of the triangle on his or her camp uniform. At first, the triangles were sewn on separately, and later (at KL Auschwitz) they were painted on next to the camp number on a separate piece of square cloth.

A red triangle designated a political prisoner, who had been placed under "protective arrest" (*Schutzhaft*). These prisoners were thus called "protective prisoners" (*Schutzhäftlinge*) in camp records. Until 1942, this was the most numerous category of prisoners at KL Auschwitz — mainly Polish prisoners, who had been arrested for actual anti-Nazi activity (members of resistance-movement organizations) or who had simply been taken prisoner during various campaigns of repression. This category included, for example, Poles arrested on the streets of Warsaw in 1940 against whom no anti-German activity had been proved or had tried to be proved. The case of the Poles deported to KL Auschwitz from the Zamość region at the end of 1942 and beginning of 1943 had a similar history. It should be emphasized that these rural Poles deported from the Zamość region also included children, who were put to death with phenol injections to the heart. 13.000 men, women and children deported from Warsaw after the Warsaw Uprising broke out in August 1944 belonged to the same category. They were Polish civilians, evacuated from Warsaw and shipped in mass transports to Nazi concentration camps.

In 1943, women and children from occupied areas of the Soviet Union (from the Minsk and Vitebsk regions) were imprisoned at KL Auschwitz. They were also registered as *Schutzhäftlinge*. In a word, the number of prisoners in this category depended upon the situation at a given time in the various occupied areas. As the Nazis intensified their campaign of repression against civilians, numerous transports of individuals classified as political prisoners would arrive at the camp and be designated with a red triangle.

Jews, the largest group at KL Auschwitz as of 1943, were listed in camp statistics as a separate category of prisoners. They were identified with a six-sided star, composed of two triangles of different colors. The first triangle, a yellow triangle, designated their Jewish nationality, while the second triangle, of a different color, would correspond to one of the categories mentioned above. In mid-1944, Jews began to be identified by the same method as the other prisoners, except that a yellow square patch would be positioned above the single triangle.

A green triangle designated the next category of prisoners, so-called "professional criminals" (*Berufsverbrecher* — BV). A relatively small group, it was filled at the beginning of the camp's existence in 1940 almost exclusively by German prisoners. The camp authorities would select prisoners from this group to fill auxiliary functions arising from routine tasks at the camp, such as overseeing the prisoners in their residential blocks and on work-details. Corrupted by their long years of survival in the Nazi prisons and camps, the "green" prisoner-functionaries would terrorize the other prisoners. The majority of prisoners at KL Auschwitz thus came to define "functionaries" as immoral individuals with violent tendencies, who exploited the offices entrusted to them to "adjust" comfortably to life at the camp. They would steal, for example, other prisoners' hunger rations and force them into submission through beatings and terror. Some of the German prisoner--functionaries maintained close contacts with SS men holding higher offices in the camp's administration (such as *Rapportführer* Gerhard Palitzsch). This was particularly the case for the group of 30 German prisoners-criminals men-tioned above, who were transferred to the camp from KL Sachsenhausen on May 20, 1940, and the subsequent group of 100, who arrived from the same camp on August 29, 1940. These prisoners formed a closed group, favored by the camp administration, that zealously carried out its assigned duties and became a tool for the SS men's criminal activities.

Another category of prisoners at the Nazi concentration camps were the so-called "antisocial prisoners" (*Asoziale* — *Asos*), who wore a black triangle. "*Asozial*" was an imprecise term, interpreted in different ways by Nazi authorities. At KL Auschwitz, prostitutes (mainly of German origin), as well as 20, 000 Gypsies, belonged to this category. Among the Gypsies, it should be noted, were many settled families, who had worked to support themselves and led normal lives. Male Gypsies who had served in the German army before their arrest and deportation to KL Auschwitz received the same black triangle as all the others.

A rather small group at KL Auschwitz were Jehovah's Witnesses and clergymen. Jehovah's Witnesses were identified with a violet triangle. Catholic clergymen received a red triangle because most of them were Polish priests and monks, imprisoned by the Nazis at the camp as part of their campaign of repression against Poland's intelligentsia. A significant number of these priests and monks perished at KL Auschwitz, and the remainder were transferred to KL Dachau (only a few individual clergymen would remain at Auschwitz).

Another small group of prisoners, identified with a pink triangle, were individuals arrested on the charge of being homosexuals. In practice, the number of homosexuals at the camp was much larger, since homosexuality was common among the long-term prisoners, particularly among the German "professional criminals" (BV), who, in carrying out their offices, would force other prisoners to submit to their will through violence or promises of improved treatment.

In July 1941, a new category of prisoners appeared at KL Auschwitz: *Erziehungshäftlinge* or "reformatory prisoners". Instead of a triangle, they had to wear a single letter "E" before their camp number. According to the official regulations, *Erziehungshäftlinge* were supposed to be sent to special "educational work camps" (*Arbeitserziehungslager*, AEL). This was not the case at KL Auschwitz, where prisoners from this category were merely quartered in a special section inside one of the blocks. During the initial phase of their presence at KL Auschwitz, *Erzeihungshäftlinge* would be disfigured during registration by leaving a strand of hair at the tip of their shaved heads. As a result, the nickname "rooster" came into almost universal usage. Quartered on the grounds of the camp, guarded by the SS staff, assigned the most strenuous jobs, and subjected to all the rigors associated with the Nazi concentration camps, their lot did not differ from that of the other prisoners.

Particularly tragic was the fate of the *Erziehungshäftlinge* deported to KL Auschwitz in 1941-42. The primitive living conditions at the camp, the hunger rations, and the spread of a typhus epidemic caused a significant number of these prisoners to die from disease and exhaustion within 56 days of their arrival, after which they were supposed to be released from the camp. In January 1943, four barracks on the grounds of the camp at Monowice (later Auschwitz III-Monowitz) were assigned to male *Erziehungshäftlinge*, while female prisoners in this category — who began to arrive at the camp in 1943 — were held at the women's division of KL Auschwitz II-Birkenau.

A special category were Soviet prisoners-of-war (*Russische Kriegsgefangenen*, RKG), the first transports of whom were registered at the camp in October 1941. Nine blocks were assigned to the Soviet POWs at the mother camp, separated from the rest of the camp by an entry gate bearing the inscription: *Russisches Kriegsgefangenen Arbeitslager* (Work-Camp for Russian Prisoners-of-War). The inscription, of course, served only as a camouflage; the Soviet POWs were subject to the same camp authorities as the other prisoners and were not treated in accordance with international conventions on prisoners-of-war. They did retain their uniforms, which were marked with stripes of oil paint and the abbreviation "SU" for "Soviet Union", but all this was meaningless; their treatment proved that they had been brought to Auschwitz for rapid annihilation. In March 1942, the surviving Soviet POWs were transferred to KL Birkenau and the fictitious "prisoner-of-war camp" was liquidated, although the daily reports on the camp's population (*Lagerstärke*) and other camp documents continued to list them separately, under the category "Soviet prisoners-of-war".

In 1944, a new category of prisoners was established at the Nazi concentration camps: so-called "civilian workers" (*Zivilarbeiter*, ZA). An order from February 14, 1944, provided for the inclusion of Russians and Poles who were unfit for Germanization (*"Russen und nichteindeutschungsfähige Polen"*) in this category. In the few surviving documents from the Auschwitz camp — particularly in the comprehensive lists — there is no evidence that such a category was ever introduced at Auschwitz, although it was certainly used at other Nazi concentration camps (KL Mauthausen, KL Flossenbürg, etc.). The order provides a likely explanation for why prisoners transferred out of KL Auschwitz to other camps later experienced a change in categories. For example, a Pole identified at KL Auschwitz as a political prisoner would be considered a *Zivilarbeiter* after his transfer to KL Mauthausen, despite the fact that he retained his uniform with its original markings: a red triangle with the letter "P". On the same basis, a prisoner's nationality might change along with this category. Prisoners originally from the territories annexed directly to the Reich (e.g., Silesia and Poznania) were registered — against their will — as "Germans". Many of them had survived several years of imprisonment at KL Auschwitz, and despite the pressures applied them, had refused to declare themselves German by signing the German *Volksliste*. Given this fact, the statistical data from the other concentration camps (e.g., KL Mauthausen) regarding prisoners' nationalities and categories should be considered false and not reflective of reality.

On February 12, 1943, "police prisoners" (*Polizeihäftlinge* — PH) began to be imprisoned at KL Auschwitz. The overcrowding at the criminal prison in Mysłowice led to their being transferred to the camp. Initially held on the ground floor of Block Nr 2, they were subsequently transferred to the ground floor of Block Nr 11, where they were not allowed to leave their assigned quarters. For them, the concentration camp served as a substitute for a criminal prison. The police prisoners kept their civilian clothes and were not tattooed with camp numbers. They received paper cards with numbers, which they kept in their pockets, but did not attach them to their uniforms in any way. After an investigation and "trial" before the Police Court-Martial (*Polizei Standgericht*) — which scarcely lasted several minutes — a death sentence was carried out on the spot. Only several prisoners from this category were entered into the camp's records, and only in those isolated cases in which the Police Court-Martial passed judgement at the concentration camp. In such cases, the prisoner went through the entire procedure associated with arrival at the camp: relinquishment of civilian clothes, issuance of a camp uniform, etc.

At KL Auschwitz, there also existed a category of so-called "privileged prisoners" (*Bevorzugte Häftlinge*). In theory, any prisoner held for a longer period of time at a concentration camp who behaved irreproachably and in accordance with camp regulations could become "privileged". In practice, the SS authorities eased the camp's regime only for a small circle of prisoner-functionaries, mainly Germans, who were allowed to grow long hair, possess a watch, and even go on Sunday walks in civilian clothes outside the camp (naturally, under the supervision of an SS guard). Among these privileged prisoners at KL Auschwitz was the long-term prisoner-functionary and German criminal Bruno Brodniewicz, who held the office of "Camp Senior" (*Lagerältester*) for several years. [17]

At the end of 1943 or beginning of 1944, a *Lageraufsicht* or "Camp Guard" was established from among the several dozen German prisoners. These prisoners were housed separately and received a special yellow armband with the inscription *Lageraufsicht*. Their duty was to oversee prisoners on their work-details. In practice, they could not play their foreseen role thanks to their armbands, which were easy to recognize; whenever they approched, the other prisoners would simulate "productive" work.

At the Nazi concentration camps, prisoners attached to punishment battalions (*Strafkompanie* — SK) had to wear an additional symbol — a small cloth circle dyed black, attached to the blouse of the camp uniform. Prisoners considered dangerous or suspected of wanting to escape received a red circle with the inscription "IL" for *Im Lager* ("in camp"), which meant that they were to be closely observed and not allowed to leave the enclosed portion of the camp. Such a designation had tragic consequences at KL Auschwitz, particularly during the first years of the camp's existence. In 1942, a large number of Polish political prisoners shipped to Birkenau and attached to the punishment company received such a designation. After the company rebelled on June 10, 1942, the SS authorities liquidated more than 300 Polish prisoners wearing the red circle in the camp's gas chambers. [18]

The first letter of a prisoner's nationality in German (e.g., "P" for *Pole*) was written or drawn in ink on the triangle that designated his or her category. German prisoners did not wear such a letter.

The daily summaries and reports from the camp staff took into account the prisoners' division into various categories. Thanks to the camp resistance movement, several such lists have survived, including: one from January 20, 1944, relating to the prisoners at KL Auschwitz I, and three that deal with the entire camp complex, from August 21, 22 and September 2, 1944. [19]

Based on these reports and other statistical lists from 1943, the largest category of prisoners at KL Auschwitz were the Jewish prisoners, and the second largest were the political prisoners of other nationalities. Earlier, the situation had been different. Before the mass extermination of Jews began, the largest category of prisoners at the camp had been the political prisoners (mainly Poles). The number of prisoners in the remaining categories constantly fluctuated, depending in large part on the policies of the Nazi authorities during a given period. Unfortunately, the destruction of most camp documents by the SS in January 1945 has prevented any detailed analysis of the camp's population structure for the entire period of its existence.

---

[17] APMO, Collection of Testimonies, vol. 72, card 135, account of former prisoner Erwin Olszówka.

[18] Ibid, vol. 4, card 591-595, account of former prisoner Józef Kret.

[19] APMO, Files of the camp resistance, vol. II, cards 60, 94-96, 116, 133.

5. Structure of the Prisoner Community

The prisoners at KL Auschwitz were of various nationalities, whose numbers underwent constant change. In the first years of the camp's existence, Poles — for whom the camp was originally founded — represented the majority. By mid-1942, due to an influx of transports bearing Jewish prisoners (the first mass-transport of Jews was recorded on March 26, 1942), the number of Poles and Jews balanced out. Thereafter, the number of Jewish prisoners grew exponentially. By the second half of 1942, Jews represented about 50% of the prisoner population, and as of 1943, the majority.

Factors that influenced the composition of the prisoner population at KL Auschwitz included the mass transfers of prisoners from other concentration camps; the high "natural" mortality rate; and selections, which resulted in prisoners being murdered in the gas chambers. In 1943, during the so-called "*Polenaktion*", several thousand Poles were transferred to other concentration camps.

The mortality rate was particularly high during the first years of the camp's existence (after two months or so, more than 80% of the new arrivals at the camp would perish), but the situation improved very little in subsequent years. For example, of the 12,757 male and female Jewish prisoners deported from Greece and registered at the camp between March 20, 1943, and August 16, 1944, only 1,838 survived until August 21, 1944 [20].

All the factors mentioned above led to constant fluctuations in the composition of the prisoner population at KL Auschwitz in terms of nationality. Unfortunately, the lack of documents prevents a more precise analysis of the changes that occurred in the nationality-structure of the camp's population. The few surviving data can only give a general outline of this phenomenon based on a few, coincidental dates.

REGISTERED PRISONERS AT KL AUSCHWITZ
BY NATIONALITY [21]

Nationality	1 VI 42		1 XII 42		1 VIII 44	
	No.	%	No.	%	No.	%
Jews	10,575	45.84	14,477	47.28	71,441	68.12
Poles	9,393	40.71	8,725	28.49	18,672	17.80
Czechs	740	3.21	3,216	10.50	136	0.13
Germans	1,585	6.87	1,018	3.32	2,327	2.22
Others	777	3.37	3,187	10.41	12,302	11.73
TOTAL	23,070	100	30,633	100	104,878	100

[20] Ibid, vol. IV, cards 262-271.
[21] Source: *Obóz koncentracyjny Oświęcim w świetle akt Delegatury Rządu RP na Kraj* [The Concentration Camp at Auschwitz in the Light of Documents of the *Delegatura* of the Polish Government at Home], *Zeszyty Oświęcimskie* 1968: I (Special issue), pp. 32, 75; APMO, Files of the camp resistance, vol. II, card 116 (paper by T. Iwaszko and Franciszek Piper).

In the transports sent to KL Auschwitz and registered at the camp, one could find prisoners of all ages: children, youths, adults, and old people. In keeping with regulations from higher authorities, Division III — Camp Supervision (*Abteilung III — Schutzhaftlagerführung*), would prepare monthly reports including the prisoners' distribution according to age groups (*Unterteilung in Altersstufen*): 20 and below, 20-30, 30-40, 40-50, 50-60, 60-70, 70-80, and 80 and above. Such reports were based on the number of prisoners remaining at the camp on the last day of a given month. A separate monthly report would relate the number of deaths according to the same age categories.

The partially-preserved lists of new arrivals (*Zugangsliste*) prove that both young and old were sent to KL Auschwitz. For example, a transport of 525 Polish prisoners from Lublin, registered at the camp on January 9, 1941 (prisoner numbers 8608-9132), included youths of around 17 years of age, as well as older prisoners, aged 70-80. The transport also brought to the camp Szczepan Cyrulski (camp number 8806), age 83.

TADEUSZ IWASZKO

THE DAILY LIFE OF PRISONERS

1. Quarantine

The isolation of newly-arrived prisoners in a so-called quarantine area was meant to prevent the spread of contagious diseases. At least that was the theory. Several types of living spaces could be used for quarantine, depending on the need at a given time: blocks, barracks, or even tents designed to hold hundreds of people (two such tents were used for quarantine at KL Auschwitz III-Monowitz). In 1943, one of the building sites at KL Birkenau, BIIa, was designated as a quarantine area for several thousand prisoners, to be held in sixteen stable-type wooden barracks. A separate quarantine area was also maintained for new arrivals at the women's camp.

Quarantine was a terrifying ordeal for every prisoner. It was here that new arrivals normally gained their first insights into the laws governing prisoner life at the Nazi concentration camps. They learned, for example, that the SS-man responsible for a given block, the *Blockführer* — assisted by prisoner-functionaries, the *Blockältester* ("block senior") and the *Stubendienst* (senior prisoners) — wielded unlimited power.

The rigorous observance of a daily routine; the brutal morning wakeup in which prisoners were driven from their quarters; endless hours of exercise, called "sport"; learning how to stand at roll-call; taking off and putting on one's cap upon command; "instruction" in singing various German songs and in the correct pronunciation of several typical German phrases (e.g., how to report to the SS-men) — such activities filled the days of prisoners in quarantine.

The primitive facilities, overcrowded living quarters, the impossibility of maintaining personal hygiene, and the terror that reigned throughout the camp had a destructive impact upon the prisoners' psyche. This was particularly true for those who went through quarantine at Birkenau, where the machinery for mass extermination was located. The notes and documents saved from destruction by Dr. Otto Wolken, a prisoner who had worked as a doctor at the outpatient infirmary, bear witness to the fatal effects of spending quarantine in section BIIa. [1]

---

[1] APMO, Höss Trial, vol. 6, card 5 and appendices, protocol of the testimony of former prisoner Otto Wolken on April 24, 1945.

The number of prisoners quarantined in camp BIIa numbered 4,000-6,000 on average. Between September 1943 and November 1944, a total of 4,023 prisoners had to be transferred from quarantine to the camp hospital because they were ill and in critical condition. In the same period, 1,902 deaths were reported. A total of 6,717 prisoners were so emaciated that the SS authorities considered them unfit for work; they were "selected" out and murdered in the gas chambers.

Prisoners eventually allowed to leave KL Auschwitz had to pass through quarantine once more before their departure. This mainly applied to so-called "reformatory" prisoners (*Erziehungshäftlinge*), since the number of prisoners released from other categories was insubstantial. Prisoners who were being held in quarantine before their release had to submit to medical examinations conducted by SS doctors. Advanced emaciation, an inability to move properly, ulcerations, tumors, bloating from hunger, or symptoms of a contagious disease would prevent prisoners from receiving permission to leave the camp. If their state of health did not improve, such individuals would be kept at the camp, and many of them would never live to see their release.

Prisoners who left the camp, given their emaciation and general appearance, met with spontaneous displays of sympathy and assistance from Polish civilians. Antonin Čenek, a Czech prisoner released from KL Auschwitz on June 2, 1942, writes:

As we stood alone at the train station, little girls came up to us and gave us bread and even milk to those of us who looked weakest. We were surprised and moved by this assistance organized by the Poles... In the train that we took home, we encountered similar touching scenes. The Poles who were travelling with us gave us everything that they had with them [2].

2. Living Conditions, Sanitation and Hygiene

One cause of the frequent epidemics at KL Auschwitz were the fatal living conditions, which differed according to the particular period of the camp's existence and varied across each of its three divisions.

In 1940, twenty brick barracks — six with two floors and fourteen with only one floor — were designated as living quarters for prisoners at the main camp, Auschwitz I. Normally, these buildings, which measured 45.38 × 17.75 m and lacked any sanitation, should not have been used to hold several hundred prisoners apiece. Nevertheless, that many prisoners were subsequently assigned to them.

The existing buildings were later renovated and floor was added to fourteen barracks. The construction of eight new blocks began. At some point after August 1941, the blocks were numbered one to 28; not all 28 buildings, however, were used to accommodate prisoners. Several served other purposes: warehouse space for prisoners' clothing and "deposits", showers, a delousing station, a canteen, and administrative offices. While the residential blocks were being renovated, the prisoners who were living there were transferred to other

---

[2] APMO, Collection of Testimonies, vol. 22, card 149.

blocks. This, of course, worsened living conditions throughout the entire camp. The process of adding new floors to the buildings continued until the spring of 1943.

The number of prisoners housed in each block varied and depended on the total number of prisoners at the camp. The need to accommodate Soviet prisoners-of-war, who were assigned to nine blocks in the fall of 1941, and the arrival of women prisoners in 1942, who were subsequently assigned to ten blocks, exacerbated the already difficult living situation.

During the first months of the camp's existence, prisoners at KL Auschwitz slept in large halls on straw mattresses laid in rows. After the wakeup call in the early morning, the prisoners had to gather up the straw mattresses and arrange them in one corner of the room. As a result, the straw inside the mattresses rapidly decayed, and the distribution and collection of mattresses was accompanied by clouds of dust inside the room. In the five-meter wide halls called "*Stube*", prisoners had to lie side-by-side on three rows of straw mattresses, as closely together as humanly possible. Prisoners could only sleep on their side. Given the lack of space, the prisoner-functionaries had to use force to coerce the prisoners to sleep. Whenever someone left the chamber to relieve himself at night, he would return to find that there was no place left to sleep.

The camp authorities were fully informed about the catastrophic living conditions at the camp. The special presentation that accompanied Himmler's first visit to KL Auschwitz on March 1, 1941, bears witness to this fact. Before his announced visit, the necessary preparations were made at the camp. As part of the program for the visit, a "tour" of one of the housing blocks was planned. Block Nr 6 was selected for the tour (later Block Nr 14). To start off, all prisoners in visibly poor condition were removed from the block, the remaining prisoners had to leave, and wooden, tri-level bunk beds were installed. A corresponding number of blankets were distributed. Of course, the beds had to be made up to military standards, with a pronounced edge on the mattresses and blankets. Also taking part in the preparations were the prisoners, whose external appearance was to bear witness to the alleged orderliness that prevailed at the camp. Of course, only as many prisoners were accommodated in the renovated block as there were mattresses, in order to give the appearance that everyone slept alone. [3]

Everything went according to plan. Himmler and his entourage "toured" the prepared block. Scarcely had the SS "dignitaries" left the camp before everything was returned to its original state: the beds were dismantled and the mattresses were spread out again on the floor.

The first tri-level wooden bunks were delivered to KL Auschwitz at the end of February 1941 and successively installed in the residential blocks during the following months. [4] The bunks, which held three mattresses and measured 80 cm × 200 cm with a height of 225 cm, were theoretically intended for only three prisoners. In practice, however, at least two prisoners slept on each

---

[3] Ibid., vol. 72, card 130, account of former prisoner Erwin Olszówka.

[4] APMO, D-Aua-31/1, inventory number 29720, report of the head of the camp's employment division, *SS-Hauptsturmführer* Heinrich Schwarz.

mattress, for a total of six in each of three-level bank. After the additional floors were added to the buildings, several hundred wooden tri-level bunks were installed in each block. According to an inventory dated January 25, 1943, [5] twenty-one blocks were designated as living quarters at KL Auschwitz (including Blocks Nr 24 and 25, which were only partly used for housing). At this time, for example, Block Nr 2 contained 234 beds with 702 mattresses, but the total number of prisoners residing there number 1193 — thus, 982 prisoners had to sleep two-to-a-mattress. Only the prisoner-functionaries, who had their own, small living space in the block, slept in separate iron beds. A similar overcrowding existed in all of the residential blocks.

Due to the overcrowding at Auschwitz I, stable-type wooden barracks were installed on a temporary basis. Cellars and garrets were used for temporary accommodation. The designated sleeping area in each block measured around 2900 cubic meters. Given that more than 1200 people slept in each building, each prisoner had only around 2.5 cubic meters of space.

Besides the tri-level wooden bunks, each block had the following furnishings, which had been successively installed in all the blocks: coal-burning furnaces, around 20 wooden tables, several wooden chairs, and several dozen simple stools. Each two-story residential block at the main camp was divided administratively into two parts: the ground floor (e.g., Block Nr 1) and the second floor (e.g., Block Nr 1a). Each floor represented a self-contained administrative unit, except that the second floor of each block normally contained only two halls, while the ground floor was divided into several smaller units. There were common sanitary facilities, normally located on the ground floor (a lavatory with 22 toilet seats and urinals, as well as a washroom with 42 taps, installed above stone drainage spouts). It should be stressed that all these facilities were installed only after the camp had been established. In the summer and fall of 1940, several thousand prisoners had only two wells where they could wash; and they had to meet their physiological needs by using a provisional field latrine. After toilets were installed inside the blocks, their use was limited in accordance with various prohibitions announced by the prisoner-functionaries.

On the grounds of KL Auschwitz II-Birkenau, there were two types of barracks — brick and wood — that were assigned as living space. They were built with great speed; in section BI (later the women's camp), brick barracks were constructed on swampy terrain without the necessary insulation. These barracks measured 36.25 × 11.40 m and were 5.80 m high (a surface area of 413.25 sq. m with a total of 1235 cubic meters living space) and had seventeen windows barred shut, two vents and one entrance. On either side of the entrance to the barracks, there stood two small rooms — one allocated to the *Blockältester* as his *Stube*, and the other used for storing bread. Each barrack was divided by brick walls into 60 sleeping areas, each of which held three makeshift beds; altogether, each barrack contained 180 provisional beds with a surface area of 4 m². According to the regulations of the SS

---

[5] APMO, D-AuI-4/34, inventory number 161197.

administration, at least four prisoners were to sleep on each pallet. Under such crowded conditions (more than 700 people per barrack), each individual only had 1.7 m³ of space. Such barracks had practically no heating, although there were two iron stoves, installed mainly for appearances. At first, there was only a dirt floor, which was eventually replaced with a flat layer of bricks or a thin layer of concrete. There were no sanitary facilities. It was 1944 before small areas were divided off for toilets and a washroom. This work could not be finished, however, before the camp was liberated. At first, these barracks did not even have electric lights.

The second type of accommodation assigned to prisoners at Birkenau were wooden stable-type barracks (*Pferdestallbaracken OKH — Type 260/9*), built from wooden planks delivered to the camp. The barracks each measured 40.76 × 9.56 m with a height of 2.65 m (surface area of 389 m² with 1248 m³ of space). Instead of windows, skylights were installed on either side of the barracks. The walls were made of poorly-fitting planks. The roofs — which also served as ceilings — were a layer of boards covered with tar paper. The roof was supported by the outside walls and two rows of posts that divided the barracks lengthwise into three. The only entrances were double doors (actually gates) at either end of the barracks. The interior, which normally provided space for 52 horses, was divided into eighteen cells.

In each barracks of this type, the two cells closest to the main entrance were allocated to the prisoner serving as *Blockältester*, while the last two stalls on the opposite end, next to the secondary entrance, were used as a substitute latrine. The remaining fourteen cells, contained either tri-level bunks measuring 280 cm × 185 cm and 200 cm high, or wooden shelves. Fifteen prisoners were expected to sleep in each cell — altogether, more than 400 people per barrack. A chimney, flue which ran almost the length of the barracks, completed its facilities. There were, of course, no sanitary facilities in the barracks. According to the assumed, "theoretical" density of prisoners, each had about three cubic meters of space.

All the figures given above for prisoner quarters — e.g., the measurements for brick and wooden barracks — should be considered mere approximations. In reality, the number of prisoners housed in each barrack was sometimes much larger; the situation constantly changed, depending on the number and size of transports arriving at the camp. Each transport could carry up to several thousand people. Sometimes more than fifteen prisoners would have to sleep in the tri-level bunks, and as a result, boards would often break, and prisoners would fall to the ground.

In the brick barracks, the improvised beds on which the prisoners slept were covered with a thin layer of straw (sometimes, though, prisoners had to sleep on bare boards). In the wooden barracks, on the other hand, there were paper mattresses stuffed with wood shavings. Blankets were distributed for covering up.

The humidity in the barracks, the leaking roofs, the straw mattresses soiled by prisoners suffering from starvation diarrhea — all worsened the already difficult living conditions, especially since it was forbidden to open the doors at night, even to air out the buildings. The barracks swarmed with various types of vermin; the rats running through the camp attacked both the living and the dead. The constant lack of wash water and the lack of necessary sanitary facilities contributed to this problem.

At construction site BI at KL Birkenau, the only water during the first year was in the kitchen barracks, and prisoners were not allowed to use it. Given the lack of showers and washrooms, the prisoners went around dirty for months and had to relieve themselves in primitive, open-air field latrines. Given such conditions and the overcrowding, it is not surprising that epidemics of contagious diseases returned time after time to literally decimate the prisoners. Rather than radically improving the living conditions and sanitation at the camp, the central German authorities, who understood the situation quite well, worried instead about their inability to increase the number of prisoners at the concentration camps. [6] A regulation of August 19, 1942, which ordered concentration-camp commandants to make certain that Jewish prisoners washed their legs each day because it would decrease the rate of disease and increase their productivity, smacks of irony. [7] It is not known why this regulation only applied to Jews, who represented, at the time, around 50% of the prisoners at KL Auschwitz.

The sanitary conditions improved slightly with the construction of buildings that housed showers and facilities for disinfecting clothing and underwear. Such buildings were put up one at a time in sections BIa, BIb and at construction site BII. In 1943, barracks with latrines and washrooms were put into use at camp BI. These brick buildings, measuring 4.50 m × 36.25 m with a height of 2.50 m, housed either washrooms with more than 90 faucets and drainage gutters or latrines with 58 toilet holes and solid concrete drains. For the 62 residential barracks that housed women prisoners at camp BI in 1943, there were only ten sanitation barracks: four washroom-barracks, four latrines, and two barracks with latrines on one end and washrooms on the other. The female prisoners were allowed to use the latrines and washrooms, however, for only a couple minutes before leaving for work eaxch morning and after their return in the evening. Given the crowding and pushing, the female auxiliary prisoners "regulated movement" in the latrines and washrooms by hitting, yelling and cursing.

On the grounds of section BII at Birkenau, stable-type barracks housed the sanitary facilities. At camp BIIa, three barracks with washrooms and toilets were supposed to serve a total of sixteen residential barracks. In all the other camps (BIIb, BIIc, BIId, BIIe), six sanitation barracks (three washrooms and three latrines) served a total of thirty-two residential barracks. As was the case in camp BI, the time allotted for using these facilites was very short. Given the number of persons living in each camp (from several to twenty thousand), using the facilities confronted the prisoners with many difficulties. Although showers had been installed, the prisoners were rarely allowed to use them. When they were, they had to take off their clothes in their block or barracks, and then they were driven naked — no matter what the weather — to the showers. More than a few prisoners lost their lives as a result of this routine.

---

[6] APMO, D-RF-9/WVHA/8/1, Collection *Sammlung von Erlässen*, card 10.
[7] APMO, D-RF-8/WVHA/9, Collection *Sammlung von Erlässen*, card 40.

The residential and sanitary conditions at KL Auschwitz III (Monowitz), as well as the several dozen affiliated camps, were similar to those described above.

3. Clothing

When they arrived at Auschwitz, prisoners received a special denim uniform at registration. It had blue and gray stripes, which allowed prisoners to be distinguished from a distance and thus made difficult their escape. Male prisoners received a shirt, long pants, a blouse and trousers. Depending on the time of year, they received either summer clothes (*Sommeranzug*) made of denim, or winter clothes (*Winteranzug*), which differed only in the thickness of the material. In the winter, prisoners received striped "overcoats" made of thicker material, but without any additional layers for warmth. In terms of shoes, prisoners received either wooden, Dutch-type clogs, made of one piece of wood, or wooden clogs with a leather exterior. Dirty and ridden with lice, the camp uniform and clogs — which did not fit the prisoners, shrank in the rain, and made movement difficult — represented an additional torment for the prisoners.

Difficulties that existed from the very beginning in supplying KL Auschwitz with the requisite number of uniforms and clogs explain why prisoners, although they received winter uniforms, did not receive any clogs in the very cold and snowy autumn of 1940. The prisoners had to walk to work barefoot, and stand for hours on end during roll-calls. The fact that prisoners were always cold and shivering accelerated their bodies' decline and contributed to an increase in deaths. "Winter" clothing did not protect the prisoners from the winter, especially against the uncommonly bitter cold of that time. In order to protect themselves from losing heat and becoming frostbitten, many prisoners wore pieces of paper from cement sacks beneath their blouses, although they were threatened with severe punishment for doing so. Only on September 24, 1941, did a new regulation allow the prisoners to inform their families about the possibility of sending them warm underwear and sweaters at the camp. [8]

The increasing difficulties from year to year in securing denim and the other materials necessary for producing camp uniforms forced the SS authorities to permit prisoners to wear civilian clothes at the concentration camps. An administrative circular of February 9, 1943 [9], allowed Poles and Russians to wear civilian clothes taken from the so-called depository, and a second circular, dated February 26 of the same year, ordered the general distribution of civilian clothes, marked in a special way, for prisoners employed inside the camp. [10] From then on, the special camp uniforms were only distributed to prisoners working outside the camp, where civilian clothes would make it difficult to recognize prisoners if they escaped.

---

[8] Ibid., card 18.
[9] Ibid., card 20.
[10] Ibid., card 23-24.

A subsequent circular from May 26, 1943 [11], ordered that the prisoners' caps were to be collected for the summer; they would be redistributed on a suitable date. The most drastic regulation came on November 7, 1944. It ordered the SS staff to distribute only the summer uniform and forbade the distribution of overcoats and warmer clothes to prisoners who worked inside the camp. It stipulated that civilian clothes should be worn in a larger number of cases. [12] The regulation went so far as to mention that prisoners could wear waistbands (*Leibbinde*) and sweaters — in reality, however, such articles remained unavailable to prisoners in Nazi concentration camps.

At KL Auschwitz, actual practice had long preceded the regulations mentioned above; since the spring of 1942, the camp authorities had been distributing uniforms from exterminated Soviet POW's to newly-arrived female prisoners. The camp administration made similar use of the underwear, clothes, and shoes of Jews murdered in the gas chambers. Civilian clothing, as mentioned above, was specially marked by applying stripes with oil paint and by sewing portions of the camp uniform to the shoulders of the civilian clothes. From then on, only prisoners who were employed outside the camp or worked together with civilians (e. g., prisoners employed at the sub-camps or at the branch of IG Farbenindustrie in Monowice) had to wear the camp uniform. In accordance with existing regulations, prisoners being sent to other concentration camps also wore camp uniforms.

The prevailing conditions at KL Auschwitz — overcrowding and excessive congestion in the barracks, the lack of sanitary facilities, the complaints that afflicted the prisoners (such as starvation diarrhea), and — worst of all — the impossibility of maintaining personal hygiene — meant that prisoners' clothes became torn, dirty, louse-infested, often stained with excrement and urine, smelly, and repugnant. Only those prisoners who came into direct contact with SS men during their work could keep their uniforms clean, since the SS men feared lice as potential carriers of typhus.

In the beginning, since KL Auschwitz had no washing machines and the laundry facilities that were later installed proved insufficient, camp uniforms and underwear were sent to a laundry in Bielsko. The insufficient number of washing machines and their lack of productivity, as well as the lack of necessary facilities for disinfecting louse-ridden underwear and other clothing, explains why the prisoners did not change their underwear for weeks on end, or even months. The half-measures taken by the camp administration were directed as much, in fact, against the prisoners — e.g., during de-lousing actions (*Entlausung*), men and women prisoners had to stand naked outside their barracks for the entire day. The barracks were disinfected with the gas Zyklon-B, and the prisoners' underwear and other clothes were dipped in vats filled with a solution of cyklon. It is not difficult to imagine what impact such actions had on the exhausted and ill, especially when the delousing occurred during rainy weather. When prisoners become wet during work or at roll-call, they had to go bed in their wet clothes in order to dry them with the heat of

---

[11] Ibid., card 43.
[12] APMO. D-RF-3/RSHA/117/1 cords 79-80.

their bodies while they slept. The lack of water — even for drinking — made it impossible to wash underwear on one's own.

A separate problem was the issue of shoes, which particularly affected prisoners who had to walk long distances during the day. During marches, the poorly-fitting clogs caused painful sores on the feet and legs. Given the lack of vitamins in the prisoners' diet and their general exhaustion, these sores developed into festering wounds that were difficult to heal and became an indirect cause of many deaths. During the "selections" carried out by the SS doctors, wounds on the lower extremities often served as a pretext for declaring a prisoner unfit for work and thus superfluous. As a result, the prisoner was either killed with an injection of phenol to the heart or liquidated in the gas chambers.

4. Rations

Prisoners at the camp received three meals a day: in the morning, in the afternoon, and in the evening. The nutritional value of such meals depended on many factors, including the binding nutritional norms for Nazi concentration camps, which changed several times during KL Auschwitz's existence. On the basis of these norms, daily and weekly menus were developed that specified the items to be served, their ingredients, and caloric value. Such were the principles, but the reality of the situation looked quite different.

The SS personnel administered the food warehouses and kitchens. According to the accounts and testimony of former prisoners, the SS men removed the most valuable produce and foods from the warehouses — e.g., meat, margarine, sugar, buckwheat, flour and sausage. Thus, the available ingredients were insufficient for preparing meals in accordance with the established norms.

Based on surviving documents from the SS Hygienical Institute in Rajsko, which received samples of the food distributed to prisoners, it has been established that the soup served at the camp lacked 60-90 procent of the margarine forseen in the official recipe, the bread was stale and hard, and the sausage that prisoners received contained about half the fat of the sausage eaten by the SS staff, despite the fact that it was produced in the same slaughterhouse. [13]

The distribution of food and meals was a separate problem. In accordance with the established system at Nazi concentration camps, the auxiliary prisoners took responsibility for serving the meals. They carried pots of soup, "coffee", "tea", and other food products from the kitchen and its warehouses and distributed it to the prisoners. The corrupt prisoner-functionaries, recruited from among convicted German criminals (especially at the beginning of the camp's existence) worried above all else about themselves and their

---

[13] The German doctor, Dr. Hans Münch, employed during the war at the SS Hygienical Institute in Rajsko, near Auschwitz, prepared in 1947 a series of reports based on documents from the institute, including works on the subject of the quality of meals served to prisoners at KL Auschwitz. APMO, Collection of Studies (Münch), 103, vol. 25.

companions. They reduced — with impunity — the amount of food distributed, especially such high-calorie foods as bread, sugar, sausage, and margarine, which they then kept as "leftovers" for their own consumption. Thus, instead of the caloric intake foreseen in the regulations — around 1700 calories for prisoners engaged in light work and 2150 calories for those engaged in hard labor — the actual caloric intake was, in fact, around 1300 and 1700 calories, respectively.

In the morning, prisoners received around a half liter of black coffee (hot water with coffee substitute) or a mixture of hot water and herbs, called "tea". These concoctions were rarely sweetened. According to menus that have been saved and interviews with survivors [14], the prisoners' dinner consisted of soup "with meat" four times a week, and "vegetable" soup without meat three times a week. It should be stressed that the "fresh vegetables" mentioned in the camp nutritional norms were merely turnips and potatoes. The basic ingredients in the soup were turnips, potatoes, and a small quantity of other ingredients, such as barley, millet, rye, and "Awo", a nutritional extract.

Beginning in 1942, whatever produce could be found in the baggage of Jews murdered in the gas chambers was also put into the soup. A ca. 3/4 liter portion of soup contained 350-400 calories. The soup was unappetizing and watery; new arrivals, not yet starving, often ate it with disgust. The soup tasted worse and did little to satiate the prisoners' hunger when eaten cold, as was often the case, for example, when prisoners returned to the camp from work in the evening or at night (e.g., prisoners employed at the IG Farbenindustrie plant).

For the evening meal, prisoners received about 300 g of bread with ca. 25 g of sausage, 25 g of margarine, a teaspoon of jam, or some cheese. Often, these foods were old and spoiled. The evening meal contained 900-1000 calories. The bread distributed in the evening was supposed to suffice for the next morning as well, but given the hunger prevailing at the camp, only a few prisoners could bring themselves to split the bread and save part of it for breakfast. In order to calm their hunger temporarily, most of them ate the bread right away. Prisoners engaged in hard labor also received a special supplement (*Schwerarbeiterzulage*): bread, margarine, or sausage, according to the established norms at the time. The hard-labor supplement also diminished in the course of being distributed.

After several weeks of such hunger rations at the camp, most prisoners began to show signs of emaciation, leading up to so-called "Muselmannism". Thousands of emaciated prisoners, starved within inches of their lives, tried on every possible occasion to get something to eat and could not be held back from even digging through the dumpsters next to the kitchen for garbage. [15] The consumption of vegetable peels, rotten turnips and potatoes, did not placate their hunger, however, and merely contributed to its ill effects, especially diarrhea.

---

[14] One such menu can be found in the documents on the sub-camp at Trzebinia — a branch of KL Auschwitz III, APMO, Collection Trzebinia, vol. 3/2, card 12).

[15] APMO, D-Aul-1/132, Collection of *Standortbefehle* (orders issued by commander of the camp garrison), vol. 2.

In each section of KL Auschwitz, there were also "canteens", as was the case at the other Nazi concentration camps. Prisoners could make purchases in the canteens on rare, pre-established days, if they had deposited marks in an account during registration or had received a postal money-order from their families. In terms of the articles of food offered for sale, the canteens hardly played a positive role. From time to time , one could buy pickled beets, salted snails and mineral water, along with cigarettes, shaving articles, articles for brushing one's teeth, camp letterhead, postage stamps, or other articles of little value to prisoners. Thus, the section of the camp's regulations — stamped on prisoners' letters to the outside world — that forbade shipments of food, "because the prisoners can buy everything at the camp", represented a cynical attempt to mislead public opinion and conceal the prisoners' starvation. Only the difficult situation at the front and the need to utilize the prisoners' labor led the SS central authorities to lift the ban on sending food packages in a circular dated October 29, 1942[16]. This only improved the situation for prisoners whose families could afford to send packages of food. The change in regulations did not apply to Soviet prisoners-of war, Jewish prisoners, and prisoners whose families lived in liberated areas.

Packages of food began to arrive at KL Auschwitz in autumn 1942. Because there were no restrictions, they could be sent as often as one wanted. This food allowed some of the prisoners to save themselves from death through starvation, although the situation did not improve for everyone, especially not for Jewish prisoners.

In 1943, in addition to the packages mailed by families, packages also began to arrive at KL Auschwitz from the International Committee of the Red Cross. The packages were addressed to individual prisoners, who had to verify their receipt by filling out a special form to be mailed back to the donor. Because the International Red Cross (IRC) did not have a large number of addresses for prisoners held in Nazi concentration camps, these shipments, despite their psychological importance, did not play a significant role. The existing regulations required that the prisoner's name, camp number, and the name of the camp be specified in the package's address. Nonetheless, the arrival of the first packages from the IRC demonstrated that the prisoners at KL Auschwitz could not be isolated from the outside world, as the SS authorities had wanted. The camp administration, angered by the incoming packages, began an inquiry into how prisoners' addresses had reached outside the country. (The camp resistance movement had provided some of the addresses). The central administration of the SS, apparently also concerned about the matter issue, authorized the commandants of the concentration camps in a circular from August 1, 1944, to requisition all packages delivered from abroad or by the Red Cross.[17] The contents of the packages were to be given to the camp's kitchens. The likely grounds for the new regulation was to prevent prisoners from signing the receipts attached to the packages, which would prove that they were being held at a concentration camp. This did not stop the

---

[16] APMO, D-RF-9/WVHA/8, Collection *Sammlung von Erlässen*, card 52.
[17] APMO, Höss Trial, vol. 12, card 141.

KL Auschwitz II-Birkenau. The interior of a barrack for prisoners, where often more than several hundred people were crowded together.

KL Auschwitz II-Birkenau. Camp latrine.

KL Auschwitz II-Birkenau. Roll-call for newly-arrived women prisoners in the summer of 1944.

A report from October 4 1944, on the population of the women's camp at Birkenau.

Frauen-Lager,KL.Au.II
Abteilung III/a
BIa-b/B-II b.g.c/B.III   Birkenau,den 4.lo.44

                S t ä r k e m e l d u n g .

St rke am 3.lo. 1944   43.462 Hftl.

Zu in e an 3.lo.1944
Einlieferungen   16
Durchgangs-Juden   488   504   "

Abgänge am 3.lo.1944
gestorben nat.Todes   4
S.B.   989   993   "

                    SA.:   42.973 Hftl.
                    ===========================

        SS- Obersturmführer.:

KL Auschwitz I. Camp orchestra.

Auschwitz. Column of prisoners on their way to work to build factories for the Krupp concern.

KL Auschwitz II-Birkenau. Prisoners at work digging ditches to drain water from the swampy terrain of the camp.

KL Auschwitz. Male and female prisoners at work excavating gravel.

KL Auschwitz I. Prisoners constructing central heating lines.

KL Auschwitz II-Birkenau. Prisoner labor always took place under the supervision of the SS.

Dwory near Oświęcım. Panorama of the Buna-Werke facilities belonging to IG Farbenindustrie, which exploited the labor of prisoners from KL Auschwitz.

Aerial photograph taken by the Allies in 1944 of the camp at Monowice (Monowitz), also known as KL Auschwitz III, situated near the Buna-Werke.

Betr.: G.U.v.21.8.43.

120

1. Fogielman,	Pola	27319	51. Bahar,	Consola	39237
2. Szafranska,	Sima	30218	52. Kovo,	Gracia	39253
3. Zucker,	Sara	33863	53. Kanchi,	Luna	39256
4. Rakowics,	Michla	33874	54. Cohen,	Elvira	33268
5. Heytkop,	Tina	33891	55. Koen,	Mary	39274
6. Batyr,	Sara	34015	56. Franko,	Sara	39282
7. Fuchter,	Hana	34896	57. Chason,	Sara	39287
8. Putersmit,	Lotte	37969	58. Haskieli,	Bella	39294
9. Neumann,	Genia	38399	59. Isak,	Regine	39308
10. Katz,	Allalouf	38723	60. Levy,	Sarina	39313
11. Daisy,	Sarina	38827	61. Menehm,	Donna	39320
12. Ischak,	Rikete	38857	62. Mayer,	Rachel	39334
13. Markisado,	Ruena	38859	63. Majl,	Klara	39342
14. Malia,	Diamanta	38870	64. Menane,	Mary	39346
15. Moche,	Lora	38890	65. Missin,	Rosa	39351
16. Pitchon,	Matyka	38891	66. Pizon,	Beveneda	39373
17. Parenta,	Alegre	38892	67. Peres,	Katerine	39374
18. Parente,	Desi	38896	68. Fardo,	Reketa	39375
19. Pitschon,	Silda	38971	69. Rosales,	Alegra	39387
20. Angel,	Sol	38973	70. Sides,	Marie	39390
21. Amsic,	Marta	38974	71. Sedaca,	Duca	39397
22. Arama,	Marica	38990	72. Samuel,	Regine	39398
23. Awlas,	Regina	38997	73. Samuel,	Signore	39400
24. Amarijo,	Paloma	39004	74. Sadyka,	Luna	39410
25. Arueste,	Sara	39008	75. Algousti,	Luna	39632
26. Baruch,	Matyka	39010	76. Algava,	Oro	39647
27. Angel,	Stella	39019	77. Alchech,	Martha	39648
28. Kune,	Rikieta	39034	78. Sarsion,	Regine	39667
29. Coen,	Klara	39047	79. Cohen,	Ester	39671
30. Reformes,	Buena	39048	80. Cohen,	Esterina	39673
31. Elisseras,	Stella	39050	81. Calof,	Marie	39682
32. Franko,	Ruena	39069	82. Errere,	Mathilde	39723
33. Chason,	Diamante	39079	83. Nachman,	Lies	39726
34. Levi,	Rose	39100	84. Nachman,	Flore	39733
35. Mano,	Buena	39101	85. Pinchas,	Marie	39733
36. Mano,	Dora	39113	86. Parfeta,	Gilde	39751
37. Menachem,	Rachel	39119	87. Sulena,	Reketa	39756
38. Mallach,	Vida	39120	88. Sulena,	Sol	39799
39. Marcos,	Jemina	39124	89. Fajaylar,	Chana	39975
40. Nachmann,	Ida	39131	90. Attias,	Mathilde	39990
41. Pesach,	Lidia	39155	91. Azar,	Mathilde	39994
42. Sedicario,	Dudu	39163	92. Angel,	Perl	39995
43. Sevi,	Rachel	39173	93. Albachanowitz,	Bella	39996
44. Situvi,	Sol	39183	94. Alias,	Rachel	40003
45. Taboch,	Estera	39187	95. Benjamin,	Julie	40017
46. Testa,	Matica	39193	96. Benosilio,	Sylvia	40054
47. Allaluf,	Mercada	39208	97. Cohen,	Rosa	40056
48. Asevi,	Alegra	39212	98. Calderon,	Anna	40052
49. Amir,	Lisa	39215	99. Cemmi,	Sarah	40059
50. Allaluf,			100. Esrati,	Luzzie	

1. Benamtchi,	Bella	43845	451. Aelion,	Nini	44935
2. Beraha,	Paloma	43853	452. Alkabes,	Esther	44933
3. Cohen,	Allegre	43883	453. Benveniste,	Mathilde	44972
4. Dassa,	Corina	43887	454. Kliacjim,	Ida	44999
5. Barztty,	Etty	43894	455. Jahiel,	Djeny	45007
6. Estru,	Lina	43898	456. Kazez,	Rosa	45010
7. Franco,	Lilly	43905	457. Levy,	Berthe	45016
8. Gattegn,	Olga	43911	458. Ousiel,	Djina	45042
9. Gattegno,	Grazia	43913	459. Paranto,	Sofia	45051
10. Gourbis,	Rachel	43914	460. Chasan,	Anna	45099
11. Hassid,	Vida	43916	461. Gottschalk,	Luzie	45208
12. Juda,	Astrea,	43936	462. Lewy,	Margarethe	45235
13. Madcar,	Mathilde	43951	463. Plajewer,	Gertrud	45253
14. Mansano,	Doudoun	43958	464. Klasen,	Helene	45419
15. Moche,	Lea	43965	465. Klinger,	Johanna	45501
16. Kamias,	Denny	43983	466. Rassing,	Martha	45610
17. Nahmias,	Ida	43991	467. Klein,	Kate	45612
18. Nachmias,	Regina	43993	468. Gross,	Bella	45616
19. Namen,	Sara	43995	469. Kariach,	Betty	45628
20. Nahmias,	Irene	43997	470. Müller,	Ilse	45974
21. Nahmias,	Lily	43998	471. Errera,	Sarika	46027
22. Saoumias,	Luna	44001	472. Sion,	Nina	46067
23. Nasias,	Daisy	44003	473. Sciaky,	Riquetta	46068
24. Usiel,	Bella	44007	474. Klinger,	Nisle	46146
25. Perahia,	Allegra	44009	475. Hofmann,	Jetchen	46175
26. Pessach,	Martha	44016	476. Bleckmann,	Simone	46987
27. Sibi,	Laura	44054	477. Citrinowitz,	Francoise	46972
28. Sarfati,	Elvira	44035	478. Levy,	Rebecca	46665
29. Sarfati,	Gilda	44037	479. Koch,	Edith	47521
30. Samuel,	Djilda	44060	480. Kamarek,	Rachela	47887
31. Simha,	Esther	44081	481. Lewin,	Sara	47918
32. Sevi,	Djulia	44083	482. Sarniewicz,	Faja	48071
33. Veisal,	Rachel	44089	483. Birman,	Helene	48381
34. Jehaskiel,	Daisy	44092	484. Ickowics,	Sabina	48541
35. Sier,	Gita	44261	485. Ogólnik,	Alina	48551
36. Molnar,	Leopoldina	44290	486. Rochman,	Estera	48561
37. Myer,	Julie	44295	487. Szpajzman,	Ernestine	48575
38. Pinto,	Marta	44300	488. Wolrauch,	Sara	48591
39. Angel,	Oro	44383	489. Goldberg,	Nechama	48655
40. Angel,	Lisa	44404	490. Korn,	Bajla	48767
41. Sereshi,	Jeanne	44425	491. Ryszan,	Renée	48940
42. Coen,	Etty	44445	492. Badmarów,	Belle	49531
43. Hassid,	Beatrice	44486	493. Fruchtgarten,	Alice	49978
44. Michel,	Daisy	44511	494. Krawiec,	Chasa	49488
45. Matalon,	Allegra	44513	495. Lonza-Lonczynska,	Romana	49949
46. Matarasso,	Angela	44523	496. Zajdfuden,	Ryfka	49730
47. Rahman,	Dora	44553	497. Ginoberg,	Szprynca	49552
48. Chiesel,	Kade	44603	498. Jäger,	Elsa	50062
49. Venezia,	Elza	44618			
50. Bek,	Sidonie	44838			

Die Lagerführerin:

Oberaufseherin.

List of the names and numbers of the Jewish women "selected" at the Birkenau camp on August 21, 1943, and sent to the gas chambers, signed by the director of the women's camp, Maria Mandel. Polish prisoners from the camp resistance movement smuggled the list out of the camp. (Shown are the first and last pages of the list).

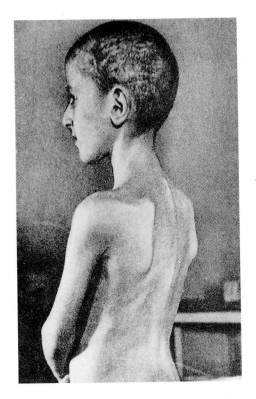

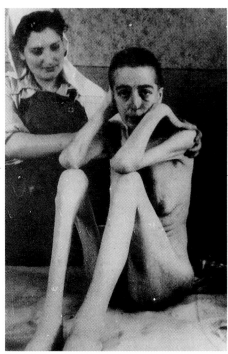

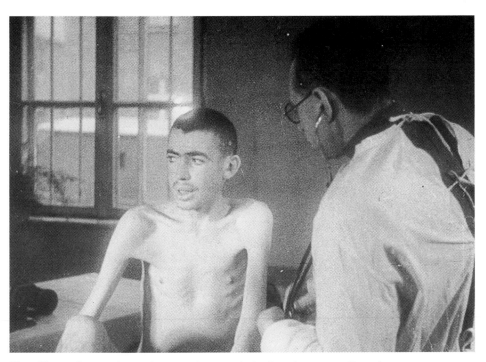

The effects of starvation: prisoners photographed after the camp's liberation.

VIKTOR BRACK
SS-OBERFÜHRER

Geheime Reichssache

BERLIN, den 23. Juni 1942
S B, Voßstr. 4

An den
Reichsführer-SS. und Chef der
Deutschen Polizei
Heinrich H i m m l e r

Berlin SW 11
Prinz Albrecht Str. 8

Sehr geehrter Reichsführer!

Ich habe dem Brigadeführer G l o b o c n i k auf Anweisung von Reichsleiter Bouhler für die Durchführung seiner Sonderaufgabe schon vor längerer Zeit einen Teil seiner Männer zur Verfügung gestellt. Aufgrund einer erneuten Bitte von ihm habe ich nunmehr weiteres Personal abgestellt. Bei dieser Gelegenheit vertrat Brigadeführer Globocnik die Auffassung, die ganze Judenaktion so schnell wie nur irgend möglich durchzuführen, damit man nicht eines Tages mitten drin steckenbliebe, wenn irgendwelche Schwierigkeiten ein Abstoppen der Aktion notwendig machen. Sie selbst, Reichsführer, haben mir gegenüber seinerzeit schon die Meinung geäußert, daß man schon aus Gründen der Tarnung so schnell wie möglich arbeiten müsse. Beide Auffassungen, die ja im Prinzip das gleiche Ergebnis zeitigen, sind nach meinen eigenen Erfahrungen mehr als berechtigt; trotzdem möchte ich Sie bitten, in diesem Zusammenhang folgende Überlegung von mir vortragen zu dürfen:

Bei ca. 10 Millionen europäischen Juden sind nach meinem Gefühl mindestens 2 - 3 Millionen sehr gut arbeitsfähiger Männer und Frauen enthalten. Ich stehe in Anbetracht der außerordentlichen Schwierigkeiten, die uns die Arbeiterfrage bereitet, auf dem Standpunkt, diese 2 - 3 Millionen auf jeden Fall herauszuziehen und zu erhalten. Allerdings geht das nur, wenn man sie gleichzeitig fortpflanzungsunfähig macht. Ich habe Ihnen vor ca. 1 Jahr bereits berichtet, daß Beauftragte von mir die notwendigen Versuche

- b.w. -

für diesen Zweck abschließend bearbeitet haben. Ich möchte diese Tatsachen nochmals in Erinnerung bringen. Eine Sterilisation, wie sie normalerweise bei Erbkranken durchgeführt wird, kommt in diesem Fall nicht in Frage, da sie zu zeitraubend und kostspielig ist. Eine Röntgenkastration jedoch ist nicht nur relativ billig, sondern läßt sich bei vielen Tausenden in kürzester Zeit durchführen. Ich glaube, daß es auch im Augenblick schon unerheblich geworden ist, ob die Betroffenen dann nach einigen Wochen bzw. Monaten an den Auswirkungen merken, daß sie kastriert sind.

Sollten Sie, Reichsführer, sich im Interesse der Erhaltung von Arbeitermaterial dazu entschließen, diesen Weg zu wählen, so ist Reichsleiter Bouhler bereit, die für die Durchführung dieser Arbeit notwendigen Ärzte und sonstiges Personal Ihnen zur Verfügung zu stellen. Ebenso hat er mich beauftragt, Ihnen zu sagen, daß ich dann auf schnellstem Wege diese so notwendigen Apparaturen in Auftrag geben soll.

Heil Hitler!

Ihr

Viktor Brack

Letter of *SS-Oberführer* Viktor Brack, director of Hitler's chancellery and initiator of the experiments on mass-sterilization, to *Reichsführer-SS* Heinrich Himmler on the issue of sterilizing two to three million European Jews and exploiting them for forced labor.

Luftwaffe Lieutenant and *SS-Sturmbannführer* Horst Schumann, M.D.

Letter regarding Horst Schumann's work on the influence of x-rays on the human reproductive organs. Schumann declared himself in favor of operative castration as a quicker and more effective method of sterilization.

Geheime Reichssache! ODPIS 7

Berlin W 8,den 29 April 1944
Vosstrasse 4
Fernruf:Ortsverkehr 120054
Fernverkehr 126621

Kanzlei des Führers
der NSDAP

An den

Aktenzeichen:IIa/Kt

Reichsführer-SS und Chef der
Deutschen Polizei
Heinrich Himmler
B e r l i n   SW 11

Prinz Albrecht Str. 9

Sehr verehrter Reichsführer!

Im Auftrage von Reichsleiter Bouhler überreiche ich Ihnen anliegend eine Arbeit des Dr. Horst S c h u m a n n über die Einwirkung der Röntgenstrahlen auf die menschlichen Keimdrüsen.

Sie baten seinerzeit Oberführer Brack um Durchführung dieser Arbeit und unterstützten dieselbe durch Zurverfügungstellung des entsprechenden Materials im KL. Auschwitz. Ich verweise speziell auf den 2. Teil der vorliegenden Arbeit, der den Nachweis führt, dass eine Kastration des Mannes auf diesem Wege ziemlich ausgeschlossen ist oder einen Aufwand erfordert, der sich nicht lohnt. Die operative Kastration, die, wie ich mich selbst überzeugt habe, nur 6 - 7 Minuten dauert, ist demnach zuverlässiger und schneller zu bewerkstelligen als die Kastration mit Röntgenstrahlen.

Eine Fortsetzung der Arbeit werde ich Ihnen demnächst überreichen können.

Anlage.

Heil Hitler!

Ihr sehr ergebener

/-/podpis nieczytelny.

Prof. Carl Clauberg, a specialist who conducted sterilization experiments on female Jewish prisoners.

Letter from Clauberg to Himmler, in which he suggests the possibility of sterilizing several hundred to a thousand women in a single day.

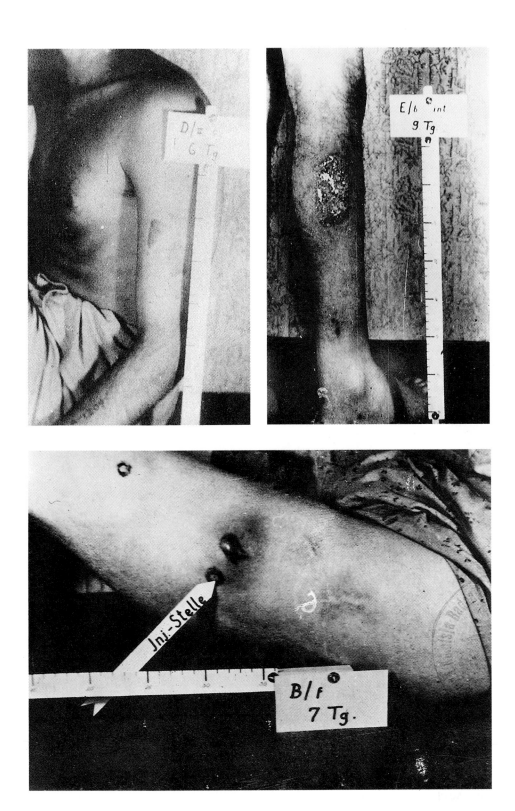

Inflammation, infections, and ulcerations caused by Emil Kaschub's experiments.

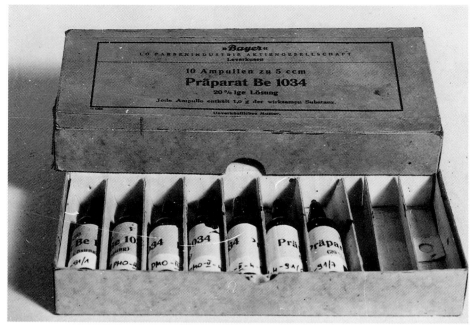

Preparation Be 1034, a product of the firm Bayer (part of the IG Farben trust), which SS doctors experimentally administered to prisoners suffering from contagious diseases.

SS-Hauptsturmführer Prof. August Hirt, who initiated the idea of creating a skeleton collection for anthropological studies at the Institute for Anatomy in Strassburg.

Letter from *SS-Standartenführer* Wolfram Sievers, General Secretary on the *Ahnenerbe* foundation, to *SS-Obersturmbannführer* Dr. Brandt on the issue of supplying Hirt with 150 skeletons of Jewish prisoners from the Auschwitz concentration camp.

Doc. NO-086

Das Ahnenerbe
Der Reichsgeschäftsführer

Berlin an 2.11.42
Persönlicher Stab RF-SS
Schriftgutverwaltung
Akt.Nr. Geh./51/16

An

G e h e i m !

SS-Obersturmbannführer
Dr. B r a n d t

B e r l i n

Lieber Kamerad Brandt !

Wie Sie wissen, hat der Reichsführer-SS seinerzeit angeordnet, dass SS-Hauptsturmführer Prof.Dr. H i r t für seine Forschungen alles bekommen soll, was er braucht. Für bestimmte anthropologische Untersuchungen - ich berichtete dem Reichsführer-SS auch bereits darüber - sind nun 150 Skelette von Häftlinge, bezw. Juden notwendig, die vom KL Auschwitz zur Verfügung gestellt werden sollen. Es ist dazu nur noch erforderlich, dass das Reichssicherheitshauptamt eine offizielle Anweisung des Reichsführers-SS erhält, die aber auch Sie in Auftrag des Reichsführers-SS erteilen können.

Mit kameradschaftlichem Gruss

Heil Hitler !

Ihr Sievers

Z oryginałem zgodny

Jan Sehn

/Tom L.d.n. 9 k.8 akt procesu
lekarskiego/

SS-Sturmbannführer Dr Eduard Wirths, *SS-Standortarzt* (SS garrison doctor) from September 1942 at the Auschwitz concentration camp.

Professor of Anatomy at the University of Münster, *SS-Obersturmbannführer* Johann Paul Kremer, M.D. and Ph.D.

SS-Hauptsturmführer Josef Mengele, M.D. and Ph.D., the camp doctor responsible for criminal experiments on children, youths, and the disabled.

Hyg.-bakt. Unters.-Stelle
der Waffen-SS, Südost

29. JUN. 1944

Auschwitz OS., am **29. Juni 1944.**

46774/VIII/50

Anliegend wird übersandt:

(12-jähriges Kind)

Material: **Kopf einer Leiche** entnommen am

zu untersuchen auf **Histologische Schnitte**

Name, Vorname:

siehe Anlage

69/41

Dienstgrad, Einheit:

Klinische Diagnose:

Anschrift der einsendenden Dienststelle: **H.-Krankenbau**
Zigeunerlager Auschwitz II, B II e

Bemerkungen: **Der 1.Lagerarzt**
K.L. Auschwitz II

SS-Hauptsturmführer.
(Stempel, Unterschrift)

Letter bearing Mengele's signature regarding research to be carried out on the head of a 12-year-old child.

Child prisoners from KL Auschwitz, victims of the criminal experiments conducted by SS doctor Josef Mengele.

 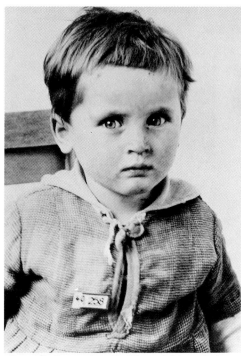

Gypsy children from the Schmidt family: Johanna (age 6) and Erdmann (age 7). These children died at the camp in June 1943.

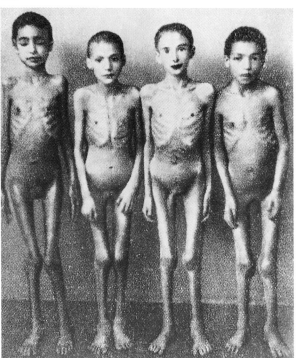

Girls (most likely Gypsies). The photograph was taken at the photo service of the camp Gestapo *(Erkennungsdienst)* on Mengele's orders.

The card of a eleven-year-old boy originating in the card file for Soviet POW's.

The personal chart of a child-prisoner at KL Auschwitz.

Birth certificate for a child born at KL Auschwitz.

Death certificate for Auschwitz prisoner Vladimir Kamlov, born May 5, 1943.

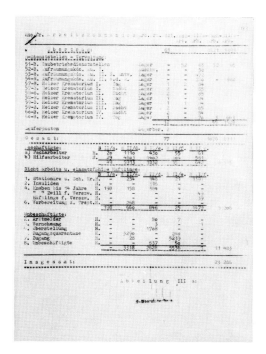

Messages smuggled out of the camp by the camp resistance movement to the Cracow committee for Assistance to Concentration-Camp Prisoners *(Pomoc Więźniom Obozów Koncentracyjnych, PWOK)*, containing a copy of a Nazi list of 22 Polish women and 10 Polish children delivered to KL Auschwitz from Bydgoszcz on September 7, 1943, who were given camp numbers and then exterminated in a gas chamber. Later, the camp authorities received an order to release the prisoners from the given transport.

The third page of a list from October 3, 1944, containing employment statistics for the prisoners at KL Auschwitz-Birkenau. Among those listed as unemployed are boys and twins age 14 and under.

**Photographs of Jewish children, who were sent to their deaths
in the gas chambers immediately upon arrival at KL Auschwitz.**

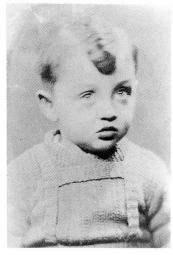

Eva Meisel (born November 1, 1936). Arrived at KL Auschwitz on October 30, 1944, with her parents and younger brother (born 1942) in a transport of Jews from the Theresienstadt ghetto.

Frania Pilcer (born September 28, 1935 in Katowice). Sent to KL Auschwitz with her parents in June 1942 in a transport of Polish Jews from Chrzanów. They were gassed along with the other people in the transport (a total of 4,000) immediately upon arrival.

A Jewish boy named Peter (family unknown, born 1938 in Opawa). He was most likely sent to KL Auschwitz with his family in a transport of Czech Jews from the Theresienstadt ghetto. The photograph is from a collection of family photographs of people sent to KL Auschwitz.

The family of former prisoners Lili Jacob, a Hungarian Jew. From left to right: her aunt Tauba with her four children, all of whom were sent to the gas chamber after selection on the railway platform at Birkenau. The transport carrying them arrived at KL Auschwitz from the Beregszasz ghetto in Hungary in June 1944.

Byelorussian children liberated from KL Auschwitz, a majority of whom were adopted by Polish families. Photograph taken at the Children's Home in Harbutowice in May-June 1945.

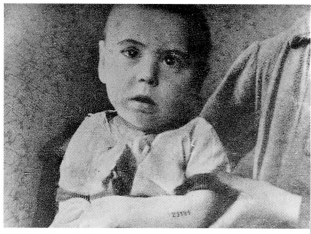

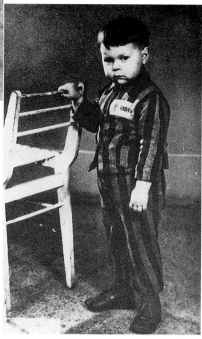

Jewish baby of unknown gender, age one to two, who was liberated from KL Auschwitz. The camp number on the child's forearm was corrected by mistake (likely while the number was being outlined before the picture was taken). The child could be a baby girl with camp number A-25141 or A-5141 or a boy with camp number A-5141 or B-5141.

A Jewish child, Józef Gomez-Fefferling (Nr. 155910), born at KL Auschwitz in April 1943, who was hidden by his mother and her co-prisoners from the camp authorities until the camp's liberation.

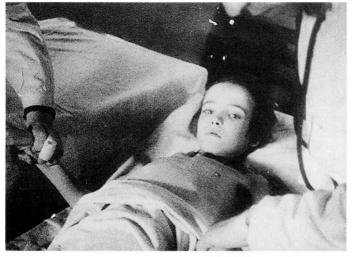

A Jewish girl, Jana Ecksteinova, age 9, at the Polish Red Cross (PCK) Hospital after the camp's liberation. The PCK hospital was located on the grounds of the former main camp.

A group of children exiting Barrack 2 at construction site BIIe at Birkenau after the camp's liberation on January 27, 1945.

Liberated children at KL Auschwitz. The photo was taken in the spring of 1945 on the grounds of the former main camp.

KL Auschwitz I. Execution Wall (reconstructed) between Blocks 10 and 11, where thousands of prisoners — mainly Poles — were executed.

Syringe used for killing prisoners with phenol injections and a requisition for 5 kg of phenol, signed by the SS sanitarian Klehr.

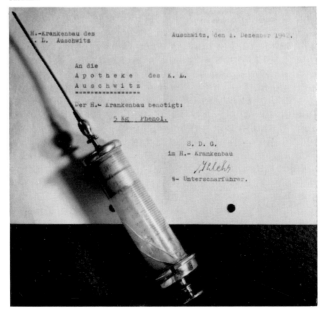

KL Auschwitz I. Portable gallows on which prisoners were hung.

KL Auschwitz I. Collective gallows (reconstructed) in front of the camp kitchen. On July 19, 1943, twelve prisoners were executed there for making contact with civilians and for the escape of three prisoners from their work-detail.

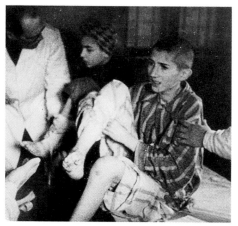

Prisoners suffering from frostbitten feet after being forced to stand for long periods of time in the frost as a punishment.

KL Auschwitz II-Birkenau. Stand used for flogging in the courtyard of the former punishment company at the men's camp.

KL Auschwitz I. Entrance to the standing cell (reconstructed), where prisoners had to stand for the night as punishment.

commandant at Auschwitz from assuring a representative of the International Red Cross that packages were still being distributed individually and that "trusted individuals", including the *Judenältester*, were dividing up collective parcels among the prisoners. [18] This was a bald lie, since there were no "trusted individuals" at KL Auschwitz and the IRC's collective parcels had gone to the SS warehouses, rather, than to the kitchens serving the prisoners.

The starving prisoners tried in various ways to appease their hunger and acquire additional food. The most common method was "organizing", or acquiring food at work — for example, while cultivating vegetables or carrying food to the SS warehouses. Most highly-desired and sought-after were fresh fruits and vegetables, since they were not part of the camp's menus. Although prisoners caught at "organizing" were subject to the severest punishments, the practice was widespread at KL Auschwitz and all other concentration camps. The prisoners traded food acquired in this illegal way — even articles "organized" from the warehouses containing the personal effects of individuals murdered in the gas chambers — on the camp's "black market".

5. The Daily Routine

The prisoner gained knowledge about the camp's discipline, punishments, and work schedule based on his own, often tragic, experiences. The advice given to new arrivals by friends, colleagues, or simply kind individuals helped them quickly acquaint themselves with living conditions at the camp and avoid unpleasant experiences.

At the camp, all activities took place on the basis of an order or a particular signal. Prisoners who did not understand the orders (given in German) or who failed to carry them out immediately were subject to chicanery and beatings by the SS men or auxiliary prisoners.

In the morning, around four o'clock, a gong sounded the wake-up call. Amid curses and beatings, the prisoners arose from their mattresses as quickly as possible. Prisoners sleeping in three-tier bunks with pallets had to make their beds up to army standards. The smallest error could cost the "guilty" party dearly. After the wakeup call, there was little time for relieving oneself, "washing", standing in line for food, and eating "breakfast". In certain blocks and barracks that held more than several hundred prisoners, all these activities took place at a feverish pace; many prisoners were unable to get to the water, and the last ones in line often went without coffee.

At roll-call, the prisoners stood in rows of ten, which made it easier for the SS men to count. The amount of time spent at the morning roll-call (and other roll-calls) depended on how quickly all the prisoners were accounted for. After the roll-call, orders came to fall into work details (*Arbeitskommandoformieren*), and the prisoners went to specified locations on the grounds of the camp,

---

[18] For an account of the visit: Comité International de la Croix-Rouge, *Documents sur l'activité du Comité International de la Croix-Rouge en faveur des civils détenus dans les camps de concentration en Allemagne (1938-1945), I — Visite au Commandant du camp d'Auschwitz d'un délégué du CICR (Septembre 1944)* (Geneva, April 1947), pp. 91-2.

where their detail left for work. As they marched off to work, the camp orchestra (there was one at each of the camp's three divisions) would play. Beyond the gates, SS guards would join the work-details to supervise the day's work.

The effective work-day, established by the internal orders of the commandant's office [19], lasted eleven hours (6 a.m. to 5 p.m.) with a half-hour break for dinner. Some prisoners — e.g., those employed in the camp kitchens and in the horse stalls — worked much longer. Depending on the distance to their workplace, some prisoners had to walk 10-20 km on foot each day (e.g., prisoners employed at the IG Farbenindustrie plant, before they were moved to what became KL Auschwitz III in Monowice).

At the beginning of the camp's existence, work was often done on the run. The SS guards and prisoner-functionaries were constantly rushing the prisoners with curses and beatings. A terror, particularly for the women prisoners, were the SS men's dogs, which were specially trained to knock down their victims and inflict painful injuries. Certain SS guards, wanting a few days extra leave, would order prisoners to leave their established work area and then shoot them. When the work-detail returned to camp, the guard would report to his superiors that a prisoner had been shot while "trying to escape". If the guard successfully proved his "alertness", he would receive a commendation or a couple extra days of vacation. Therefore, it is not surprising that many prisoners died at work and that their comrades had to carry their bodies back to camp.

When they returned to the camp in the evening, the prisoners, exhausted from work and the day's chicaneries, had to bring themselves to make yet another exertion: they had to march in rows through the camp gates at the pace of the march being played by the camp orchestra. This made it easier for the SS men to count the prisoners. At the gate, the returning prisoners would also be searched. Anyone caught stealing anything — even if it were only a piece of a turnip — could expect severe punishement for "sabotage" and violating camp regulations.

After all the prisoners had returned, the evening roll-call was held and the evening meal was distributed. Then, around 9 p.m., curfew was imposed, after which no one was to leave the residential blocks. The SS sentries holding watch in the guard towers would shoot at anyone who violated this rule. The imposed quiet of the curfew was occasionally broken by the sound of rifle fire — a sign that one of the prisoners, psychologically broken, had tried to "run into the fence". In camp jargon, "running into the fence" meant committing suicide by running into the electrical fence surrounding the camp. The guards, responsible for preventing anyone from approaching the fence, usually fired without warning.

Beyond the hard work, punishments, and other chicaneries that they suffered, the most difficult and hated aspect of camp life for the prisoners were roll-calls, which could last up to ten hours a prisoner seemed to have escaped.

---

[19] APMO, D-AuI/40, 43. Collection of *Standortbefehle* (orders issued by command of the camp garrison vol. 2.

After prisoner Tadeusz Wiejowski fled the camp on July 6, 1940, a nineteen-
-hour roll-call was held as punishment. Former prisoner Henryk Król
described what happened in his memoirs:

> The night was macabre .... At daybreak, everyone was shivering from the cold ....
> Only for a brief period did the rays of the rising sun provide relief. Soon the heat
> from the sky compounded our suffering. We fainted one after the other. Those who
> fainted had water poured on them. At night, an unpleasant event took place....
> A translator, a prisoner named Baworowski, stepped out of rank at a certain moment
> and asked the SS man guarding us for permission to relieve himself. In vain. After
> a certain time, we smelled a stench. This Baworowski had not been able to hold it and
> had gone in his pants. The SS man, as soon as he noticed who had committed this
> "offense", ordered Baworowski to take off his pants, roll them up, and hold them in
> his teeth. In addition, he ordered him to crouch and bark. This act of the SS man
> infuriated all the prisoners and gave us a preview of what awaited us at the camp. [20]

After the next escape, in October 1940, the prisoners had to stand at the
assembly square from noon until nightfall. After this long period of standing at
attention, around 120 dead and unconscious prisoners had to be carried from
the square. Snow had fallen during the roll-call, and the prisoners had only
been clothed in the thin, denim camp uniform, without any shoes, caps or
overcoats. During 1941, ten or more prisoners would be selected at various
roll-calls (mainly in the evening) and, in revenge for escapes, condemned to
death by starvation. The SS "selected" these prisoners from among those who
lived in the same block as the escapee.

For female prisoners at Auschwitz, particularly arduous were so-called
"general" roll-calls. During such roll-calls, beyond having their camp numbers
verified, a selection was also conducted. Ill women considered unfit for work
were selected for liquidation in the gas chambers. Women prisoners had to
stand outside their barracks during these roll-calls, which could last 10-20
hours. Two such assemblies took place, for example, on February 7 and 28,
1943, on the grounds of the women's camp at Birkenau.

The prisoners, worn down by hard labor, could not even rest on Sundays
and holidays. Some had to work, and the rest were subjected by the SS men to
a so-called "lice hunt" (*Läuseappelle*).

Among the measures of terror adopted by the SS authorities, the highly-
developed system of punishments method out to the prisoners played a central
role. The most common punishments included bans on sending and receiving
letters, punitive drills, punitive labor during hours off, starvation
(e.g., denying prisoners "dinner" during a full day's work); flogging, often
carried out in public, during which the victim had to count the number of
lashes in German; "posting" (hanging a prisoner by his hands, which were tied
behind his back); assignment to a punishment company; and imprisonment in
the cells of the camp jail. Each of these punishments, in addition to the
physical pain and psychological humiliation they caused, could also hasten or
directly contribute to a prisoner's death (see p. 145).

---

[20] APMO, Collection of Testimonies, vol. 76, card 199.

When discussing punishments, one should distinguish between those carried out — in terms of documentation [21] — with a certain degree of formality, and those meted out at will by individual SS men, for which no evidence remains, except the scars on the bodies of their victims.

6. Contacts with the Outside World

Given the total isolation of prisoners at KL Auschwitz, the only official possibility for contacting relatives was through the mail. According to regulations, each prisoner could send and receive only two letters each month. Of course, all incoming and outgoing letters were submitted to the strict censorship of the SS men employed at the *Postzensurstelle*, which, in organizational terms, was directly subordinated to the commandant's office (*Abteilung I*).

The prisoners were required to write their correspondence in German. In order to be mailed, letters had to be written in fifteen lines or less on a special form, stamped with the name of the camp and listing the general guidelines for correspondence with prisoners. On the days when prisoners were allowed to write, the prisoner-functionaries in each block would remind them that in accordance with the orders of the SS administration, all letters had to contain the phrase, "I am healthy and feel well" (*Ich bin gesund und fühle mich gut*) — no matter what the prisoner's actual physical state was. When the letters were censored, suspicious sentences were struck out and entire passages deleted. It was not permitted to attach or enclose anything in letters to the camp — e.g., photographs. Prisoners with the designation "*Nacht und Nebel*" (NN), Soviet prisoners-of-war, the majority of Jewish prisoners at the camp, and prisoners whose families lived in areas liberated from the Nazis — were not allowed to correspond.

A regulation from March 30, 1942, limited the amount of correspondence that could be carried out by Jews and people from the East (*Ostvölker*). Up to then, they had been allowed to send and receive only one letter every two months. Moreover, people from the East had had to use a special, returnable card for correspondence (*Karten mit Rückantwort*). [22]

In 1943, Jews were forbidden to use camp stationery and cards for correspondence; they received special cards without the KL Auschwitz stamp. The Jews had to give as their address the work camp at Birkenau (*Birkenau, Arbeitslager*) for the sake of camouflage. They were also not allowed to give out their camp numbers. A special stamp on the cards informed recipients that correspondence could be carried out henceforth only through the *Reich's Union for Jews in Germany* (*Reichsvereinigung der Juden*), located in Berlin. [23] Using these methods, the SS authorities sought to calm the fears of Jews

---

[21] For certain punishments, the camp administration would draw up a formal *Strafmeldung*, announcing the punishment to be administered, followed by a *Strafverfügung*, which confirmed that the punishment had been carried out.

[22] APMO, D-RF-9/WVHA/8, Collection *Sammlung von Erlässen*, card 31.

[23] APMO, D-Au-I/4167. Collection of letters and camp correspondence cards, vol. 20 (photocopies), card 15.

residing in ghettoes. The so-called "letter campaign" (*Briefaktion*) ordered at the beginning of March 1944, which applied to Jews who had arrived at the camp from the Theresienstadt (Terezin) ghetto in Czechoslovakia provides direct evidence of this goal. On March 5, the prisoners received the special cards, which they were ordered to post-date to March 25-27 and send to their family and friends with their greetings. Follwing the *Briefaktion*, the prisoners were liquidated in the gas chambers on March 9. Their families and friends, however, remained convinced that they were still alive and residing at the "work camp" Birkenau bei Neu Berun.

As was the case at other concentration camps, the prisoners at KL Auschwitz tried to evade the existing restrictions and send home uncensored letters through civilian laborers who they met at work. After the central SS authorities became aware of this problem through SS intelligence reports, they ordered on December 11, 1942, that prisoners be more closely watched, particularly those with communist leanings. [24]

The camp authorities were advised to monitor the prisoners closely during sporadic visits by outside individuals and institutions to KL Auschwitz. The visitors could only tour special residential blocks and infirmary barracks set up for that very purpose. On such occasions, the prisoners (e.g., at the sub-camp Fürstengrube) would receive better dinners. [25] It was forbidden, however, to show the crematoria or even discuss the subject. [26] Prisoners, of course, did not have any opportunities to discuss or point out the conditions prevailing at the camp. It is therefore not surprising that the representative of the International Red Cross who visited Auschwitz in the fall of 1944 could only speak with several prisoners in the presence of SS men. The fact that he only heard of the existence of mass-extermination facilities at KL Auschwitz from British POW's being held at a camp in Cieszyn [27] testifies to the likely character and quality of the discussion that he had held at Auschwitz.

7. The Camp Hospital

In the evening, after they returned from work, long lines of prisoners seeking medical attention would form outside the doors to the camp's outpatient hospital. Some of the prisoners in line could barely stand on their feet; others, having lost consciousness, were simply lying on the ground. The prisoner--doctors employed at the outpatient infirmary would either give first aid after a preliminary examination and dress wounds with paper bandages, or apply to have the prisoner admitted to the camp hospital. The final decision in such matters lay with the SS doctor responsible for prisoners' health at the given section of the camp. In the branch camps, SS sanitarians (*Sanitatsdienstgrade* — SDG) made such decisions.

---

[24] APMO, D-RF-9/WVHA/8/1, Collection *Sammlung von Erlässen*, card 7.

[25] APMO, Collection of Testimonies, vol 60, card 100; vol. 50, card 94, accounts of former prisoners Jan Ławnicki and Józef Łabudek.

[25] APMO, D-RP-9/WVHA/8/1, Collection *Sammlung von Erlässen*, card 23.

[27] *Comité International la Croix-Rouge...*, p. 93.

In the first months of its existence, the hospital for prisoners (*Häftlingskran-kenbau* or HKB) at KL Auschwitz did not have any equipment, so the work of the handful of prisoner-doctors was reduced to nursing and cleaning duties. The prisoner holding the title *Lagerältester des HKB* (lit., "Senior of the Prisoners' Hospital") was responsible for routine matters at the hospital. At the beginning, this title was held almost exclusively by German prisoners. Despite their lack of qualifications, they often decided whether to admit ill prisoners to the hospital and even meddled with their treatment. As early as 1941, selections were conducted at the camp hospital. "Selected" individuals were either murdered with injections of phenol or sent to the gas chambers. Thus, the camp hospital gained the dismal reputation among prisoners of being the "vestibule to the crematorium" and "waiting room to the gas chamber".

The furnishings of the hospital buildings and barracks did not differ in the least from that of the residential blocks. The sick had to lie on paper mattresses filled with wood shavings. The three-floor wooden beds made access to patients difficult, and it was not easy for them to climb out of bed. Most of the ill, beyond their other complaints, suffered from starvation-diarrhea. Hence, the mattresses were soiled with excrement and secretions from the prisoners' wounds. Prisoners admitted to the hospital had their clothes and underwear taken away. This meant that the sick had to lie naked, often two-to-a-mattress, covered with dirty, lice-infested blankets. In the halls and barracks of the hospital, a smell that is hard to describe prevailed; the groans of those who were dying and raging with fever mingled with cries for water and for help.

The official allocation of medicines was insufficient, both in terms of assortment and of quality. Most of the time, there were tablets for pain (*Schmerztabletten*), aspirin, pyramidone and cough drops, along with coal and tannalbin for the prisoners' diarrhea. There were also very small quantities of bandages and gauze. The lack of preparations for fighting scabies was a most serious deficiency. In this situation, the most generous efforts on the part of the hospital personnel were ineffective, particularly when epidemics of such contagious diseases as typhus and spotted fever broke out at the camp. The unsanitary conditions at the hospitals in all the sections of KL Auschwitz and at its branch camps, the lack of medicine, and the frequent selections that were conducted — all discouraged ill prisoners from going to the outpatient infirmaries, except at the very last moment.

SS doctors also used the hospitals for conducting pseudo-scientific experiments (see p. 88), which affected thousands of prisoners at KL Auschwitz. Most of the victims of such experiments perished before the research was finished, and those who survived were crippled for life.

The secretariat of the camp hospital kept files on all patients and filed reports on deceased prisoners, which, in keeping with forms and methods established by the SS, cited false causes of death. Before cremation, all dental work made from precious materials was removed from the mouths of the prisoners' corpses. The surviving reports from the supervisor of the camp's dental station (*Leiter der Häftl. Zahnstation des KL Auschwitz*) show that a total of 16,325 gold and platinum teeth were taken from 2,904 corpses in

1942. These reports only counted, of course, prisoners who had been officially registered at the camp. [28]

*

Of the many Nazi concentration camps, KL Auschwitz was one of those that maintained extremely difficult living conditions — practically impossible to survive — from the moment of its establishment to its liquidation. The excessive overcrowding in the residential barracks and blocks; the lack or insufficient number of sanitary facilities; the lack of water and means to maintain personal cleanliness; clothing and underwear that was most often dirty and did not fit; insignificant rations and the inhuman exploitation of forced labor — all contributed to an extremely high mortality rate among the prisoners. Those who perished from malnutrition, cold, or contagious diseases, or who were liquidated as a depleted source of labor were constantly being replaced by prisoners from new transports.

Defenseless prisoners, denied effective medical treatment, often became the victims of criminal medical experiments, whose results were used to advance the Nazi's genocidal goals.

Under these inhuman conditions, which hastened the prisoners' biological destruction, the SS also strived to break their psychological resistance. The procedure for receiving prisoners at the camp and the highly-evolved system of punishments and prohibitions contributed to this process, beginning with registration, when the prisoners became numbers without names. The ultimate goal of all this was to transform the prisoners into passive creatures, denied all human rights, whose only destination, in the end, was extermination.

---

[28] The originals of these reports have been preserved in the archives of the Auschwitz- -Birkenau State Museum at Oświęcim.

IRENA STRZELECKA

EXPERIMENTS

In the realization of Hitler's plans for exterminating entire nationalities, Nazi doctors played an important role. Some who assisted the Nazis worked at higher or lower levels of the central medical organizations of the SS and *Wehrmacht*, while others worked at research institutes and medical schools at German universities and bore high titles. Openly violating basic medical ethics, often on their own initiative, they offered their skills in the service of National Socialist ideology, fully aware of its criminal aims.

SS doctors who held offices at the concentration camps, including KL Auschwitz, played a special role in this regard. In violation of the Hippocratic Oath, they assisted in the mass murder of Jews. They conducted selections among the Jews who arrived in mass transports and oversaw the procedures used in their annihilation. They sentenced the most severely ill and physically--exhausted prisoners to death in the gas chambers or murdered them in the camp hospital with phenol injections to the heart; later, they falsified the cause of death. They carried out criminal medical experiments on the prisoners and fulfilled other duties incompatible with the medical profession. On the basis of their contributions, the camp's program of extermination became reality; they went down in history as criminal doctors.

A particularly drastic departure from medical ethics on the part of many German doctors was their participation in criminal medical experiments conducted on concentration-camp prisoners. The initiators and organizers of these experiments were *Reichsführer SS* Heinrich Himmler; *SS-Obergruppenführer* Ernst Grawitz, head doctor for the SS and police; and *SS-Standartenführer* Wolfram Sievers, General Secretary of the *Ahnenerbe* ("Ancestral Heritage") society and director of the Research Institute for the Military-Scientific Goals of the *Waffen-SS*. The Main Economic-Administrative Office of the SS (to whom the concentration camps were subordinated in March 1942) saw to administrative and financial matters. The Hygienical Institute of the *Waffen-SS*, directed by *SS-Oberführer* Joachim Mrugowsky, MD, professor of bacteriology at the Medical Faculty of the University of Berlin, provided assistance with all special analytical research.

Experiments that were planned at the central level were meant to serve the needs of the army (some had the goal of improving the state of health of the soldiers), help achieve postwar plans (e.g., in the area of population policy) or provide scientific underpinnings for racial theories (e.g., the superiority of the Nordic race).

Independent of the experiments planned at the central level, a number of Nazi doctors conducted experiments on prisoners at request of German pharmaceutical firms and medical institutes or for their own motives, interests and scientific careers.

During World War II, many German doctors cooperated with the Third Reich's ruling elite and supported Nazi demographic policies by experimenting with potential methods for mass sterilization, to be applied to nationalities that the Nazis considered inferior. Based on surviving correspondence and the postwar testimony of several high Nazi officials, [1] we can conclude that the Nazis were planning the sterilization of both the Jews and the Slavs. [2] Once the mass murder of Jews in the gas chambers began, the sterilization of the Slavs and German-Jewish citizens (so-called *Mischlingen*) was contemplated. [3]

At a series of secret conferences at Himmler's headquarters in 1941, the main issue was the question of mass sterilization. Among those taking part were leading SS functionaries; representatives of Nazi medicine, including the head physician of the SS, Dr. Ernst Grawitz; and Himmler himself. The assembled individuals debated what might be the simplest and most effective method for sterilizing an unlimited number of persons in the shortest period of time possible.

As a result of a conference on July 7-8, 1942, attended by Himmler, Prof. Karl Gebhardt, and Richard Glücks (Inspector of Concentration Camps), the task of finding a method of sterilization answering all these criteria was entrusted to

---

[1] For example, Viktor Brack, director of Hitler's chancellory; Karl Brandt, professor of medicine, Hitler's personal physician, and *Reichskommissar* for Health and Sanitation; Adolf Pokorny, MD; Rudolf Brandt, J. D., personal advisor to Himmler; and Rudolf Höss, the commandant of the camp at Auschwitz.

[2] In October 1941, Pokorny wrote to Himmler (in his office as *Reich* Plenipotentiary for Strengthening Germandom):

If we are able to discover as quickly as possible the means that could imperceptibly cause sterilization in a relatively short period of time, then we will have acquired a new, very effective weapon. The broad possibilities are alone suggested by the thought that three million Bolsheviks currently held as German prisoners could be sterilized, and as a result, they would stand at our disposal as workers, but without the ability to multiply.

Document NO 035, as cited in Alexander Mitscherlich and Fred Mielke, *Medizin ohne Menschlichkeit. Dokumente des Nürnberger Ärzteprozesses.* (Frankfurt am Main und Hamburg, 1949), p. 237.

Several months later, on June 23, 1942, Brack wrote to Himmler:

Among the 10 million European Jews there are, in my estimation, at least two to three million men and women fully capable of work. Taking into account the exceptional difficulties that a deficit of laborers has created for us, I am of the opinion that these two to three million should be selected out, in any case, and preserved. This can only take place, however, if they are at the same time impotent.

Document NO 205, as cited in ibid., p. 242. Also see the documentation from the trial against the Nazi doctors before the American Military Tribunal in Nuremberg.

Also see Yves Ternon and Socrate Helman, *Historia medycyny SS czyli mit rasizmu biologicznego* (Warszawa, 1973), pp. 169-218; Jan Mikulski, *Medycyna hitlerowska w służbie III Rzeszy* (Warszawa, 1981), pp. 56-78; Stanisław Sterkowicz, *Zbrodnicze eksperymenty medyczne w obozach koncentracyjnych Trzeciej Rzeszy* (Warszawa, 1981), pp. 82-96.

[3] Raul Hilberg, *Die Vernichtung der europäischen Juden* (Berlin, 1982) p. 636; Ternon and Helman, pp. 171-77.

Prof. Carl Clauberg, an authority in the field of female infertility, a participant in international gynecological conferences, and, during the war, head of the ward for womens' diseases at the hospital in Chorzów (Königshütte).

In response to Clauberg's persistent requests, Himmler gave him permission to conduct sterilization experiments at the Auschwitz concentration camp. Clauberg began his work at the end of 1942 in Barrack 30 on the grounds of the hospital at the women's camp (BIa) at Birkenau. In April 1943, Rudolf Höss, in accordance with orders he received, placed at Clauberg's disposal part of Block 10 at the main camp. The two upstairs chambers of that block held 150-400 female Jewish prisoners from various countries. The records of the camp's employment office listed them as "prisoners for experimental use" (*Häftlinge für Versuchszwecke*). [4] Most of the women subjected to Clauberg's experiments had already had at least one child and had not stopped menstruating at the camp.

The method of mass sterilization without surgery that Clauberg developed was based on introducing into the women's sex organs — under the pretext of gyneco-logical examination — a specially-prepared chemical irritant that caused an extreme inflammatory state. As a result, the oviducts would over-expand after several weeks and occlude. The results of the experiments were verified each time by x-ray.

Clauberg's co-workers included: Dr. Johannes Goebel (Göbel), a representa-tive of the firm Schering Werke and inventor of the chemical agent used by Clauberg in his sterilization experiments, and an SS sanitarian named Binning. His medical and nursing staff consisted mainly of female Jewish prisoners. Beginning in September 1943, the head doctor at Block 10 — with the same rights as a *Blockältester* — was surgeon and gynecologist Alina Białostocka (registered at the camp under the name Brewda), a Polish Jew. [5]

The procedure described above was executed in a brutal fashion and often caused complications in the form of peritonitis and hemorrhaging in the oviducts, accompanied by a high fever and heavy bleeding. In many cases, such complications were the cause of collapse, leading to death. Some of the Jewish women died from Clauberg's experiments, and others were put to death so that their corpses could be dissected. [6]

---

[4] APMO, D-AuI-3a. Monthly figures for the employment of male and female prisoners at KL Auschwitz.

[5] Jan Sehn, "Carl Claubergs verbrecherische Unfruchtbarmachungs-versuche an Häftlings--Frauen in den Nazi-Konzentrationslagern" *Hefte von Auschwitz* 2 (1959) pp. 3-32, 53-87; Reimund Schnabel, *Macht ohne moral. Eine dokumentation über die SS* (Frankfurt am Main, 1957), pp. 263-82; Dorota Lorska, "Block 10 in Auschwitz" in *Hamburger Dokumente. Die Auschwitz-Hefte. Texte der polnischen Zeitschrift "Przegląd Lekarski".* (Weinheim und Basel 1987), pp. 209-212.

Czesław Głowacki, "Z dokumentacji zbrodniczych doświadczeń Carla Clauberga". *"Przegląd Lekarski — Oświęcim* 1976, pp. 85-90; *Criminal Experiments on Human Beings in Auschwitz and at War Research Laboratories*, ed. Lore Shelley (San Francisco, 1992).

APMO, Collection of Testimonies, vol. 54, cards 169-75, account of former prisoner Kazimiera Topór; APMO, Höss Trial, vol. 7, cards 74-83; vol. 17, cards 59-67; vol. 59, cards 44-46, testimony of former prisoners Felicja Pleszowska, Alina Brewda and Ilona Vohryskova. In the archives of the State Museum at Auschwitz, one can find several accounts by female Polish prisoners who were victims of Clauberg's experiments.

[6] *Amidst a Nightmare of Crime. Notes of Prisoners of Sonderkommando found at Auschwitz*, (Oświęcim, 1973), pp. 31-68, account of former prisoner Alter Feinsilber; APMO, Höss Trial, vol. 17 card 80, testimony of former prisoner Stefan Markowski.

Himmler was constantly informed of progress and results from the experiments. On June 7, 1943, Clauberg wrote:

> The method that I have conceived for sterilizing women without an operation is already nearing completion .... In response to the question posed to me by the *Herr Reichsführer*, regarding how long it would take to sterilize 1,000 women with this method, I can give, as requested, the following reply: If the experiments that I am conducting continue to have the same results as up to now — and there is no reason to believe that this will not be the case — I will be able to declare in a short period of time that one trained physician located in a reasonably-equipped outpost, assisted by ten staff members, will most likely be able to sterilize in the course of a single day several hundred or even a thousand women. [7]

In May 1944, Clauberg's research station was moved to Block 1 of the women's camp, on the grounds of the so-called camp extension (*Schutzhaftlagererweiterung*). In addition to his sterilization experiments, Clauberg was using new caustic substance and conducting experiments in the field of artificial fertilization. Along with Dr. Goebel, he experimented with new developments in the field of radiology as well, with the goal of applying them to his sterilization experiments. In January 1945, Clauberg moved his operations to KL Ravensbrück, where he continued his experiments on female Jewish prisoners — transferred from Auschwitz — and on Gypsy women.

At Victor Brack's initiative, *SS-Sturmbannführer* Horst Schumann, MD, also began sterilization experiments in November 1942 (about the same time as Clauberg). Schumann was a lieutenant in the *Luftwaffe*, former director of the division for terminal patients at Castle Grafeneck in Wurttemburg and then at a clinic in Sonnenstein. He was also a member of the special "doctor's commission" that visited the concentration camps to select ill and emaciated prisoners to be sent to the gas chambers. Schumann, just like Clauberg, was striving to discover the most effective method for mass sterilization, which would allow the leadership of the Third Reich to destroy lower races using "scientific methods", by denying them the ability to reproduce. According to Höss, before Schumann arrived at Auschwitz, he had received an order from Himmler to give Schumann as many male and female prisoners as he requested and all other necessary assistance.

In Barrack 30 at the women's camp (BIa) at Birkenau, a previously-installed station for "x-ray sterilization" was placed at his.disposal. Schumann made the station — composed of two x-ray devices. ("*Röntgenbombe*") from the firm Siemens — operational by linking it with cables to a control chamber, protected from x-rays with sheets of lead. Every now and then, groups of several dozen male and female Jewish prisoners were taken to the station from the grounds of the camp at Birkenau (sometimes from Block 10 of the main camp) and subjected to sterilization experiments based on irradiating the

---

[7] Documents from the trial of doctors at Nuremberg, NO 212 and NO 213. The question had been contained in a letter from Brandt to Clauberg dated July 11, 1942: "Once you initiate your work, the *Reichsführer SS* requests that you inform him of the amount of time it will take to sterilize a thousand female Jews." Citation according to Y. Ternon and S. Helman, p. 203.

testicles in men and the ovaries in women. In seeking the optimal dose of radiation for achieving complete infertility, Schumann applied varying doses at different intervals. Customarily, the prisoners subjected to these experiments were sent back to work, although they suffered from serious burn wounds from the radiation, particularly beneath their stomachs, in the groin area, and on their buttocks. They had radiation burns on their skin and hard-to-heal, festering wounds. Complications from the experiments resulted in many deaths. Other victims of Schumann's experiments were sent to the gas chambers as a result of the "selections" conducted at the camp. [8]

The Jews subjected to sterilization experiments worked at a number of jobs, including on the work detail for road construction. The following is an excerpt from the written testimony of former prisoner Franciszek Gulba:

> I returned to building roads at camp BIb. Right away, on my second day there, a group of seven or eight prisoners were assigned to the work detail who crouched as they walked, holding their underbellies, groaning, rolling on the ground and writhing in pain. I could not understand them either in Polish or in German. I took the trouble to go to their block and found out that they were 15-17-year-old Greek Jews, who had been subjected to some experiments. Over the next two days, similar groups were sent out to us. [9]

Former prisoner Jan Szpalerski also came into contact with a victim of Schumann's experiments:

> During my stay at the hospital (BIIf), I met a formerly well-known Jew from Warsaw, a shoemaker from Wiśniowa Street. His entire family had been murdered at the camp, and he himself had become a victim of some criminal experiment based on irradiating the testicles with x-rays. He was severely crippled and suffering terribly. He explained to me that such experiments were being carried out on an entire group of Jews, 50 men and the same number of women. After a short interval, they were all gassed. [10]

Several weeks later, in the second stage of the experiment, sperm samples were taken from several prisoners at the infirmary of the main camp and examined beneath a microscope to determine the presence and vitality of spermatozoon. Other male and female prisoners subjected to Schumann's sterilization experiments were surgically castrated (on one or both sides), in order to examine the irradiated genitals in the laboratory and to gain samples for a comparative histology. The operations were carried out — often in the presence of Dr. Schumann — in Block 21 (the surgery), or sometimes in Blocks 10 and 28 in the main camp. Most often, prisoner-doctors carried out the

---

[8] Stanisław Kłodziński, "Sterylizacja i kastracja promieniami Roentgena w obozie oświęcimskim: Dr. Horst Schumann", *Przegląd Lekarski — Oświęcim* (1964), pp. 105-11; accounts and testimony of former prisoners — e.g., APMO, Collection of Testimonies, vol. 63, cards 153-190 (copies), vol. 49, cards 84-86, account of former prisoner Kazimierz Szwemberg; APMO, Höss Trial, vol. 2, cards 82-83, testimony of former prisoner Michał Kula.

[9] APMO, Collection of Testimonies, vol. 70, see the attachment to the account.

[10] Ibid., vol. 94, card 248.

surgical castration, including both Dr. Władysław Dering, a Pole released from the camp in 1944 and employed by Clauberg at his private clinic, and a Jew, Dr. Maximilian Samuel, who was later exterminated at the camp. Some of the individuals subjected to the operation died from infections or internal bleeding. [11]

A number of former male and female prisoners have given depositions on the subject of sterilization experiments and surgical castration, including a Jewish woman from Greece:

Around the middle of March 1943, I was deported along with other Jews from Thessaloniki to Birkenau .... In summer 1943, during the morning roll-call, the female *Blockältester* summoned a number of girls, including me .... Under guard, we were taken to Auschwitz, to Block 10. Other Greek women and girls were already there. One day Dr. Schumann appeared — I learned his name during my stay at Block 10 — and ordered all the girls to step forward. He pointed to several girls, including me, and took down our numbers. The next day, we were taken .... back to Birkenau and irradiated. We entered a room where we undressed, and from there we were summoned one after the other, to a dark room. Two people were there, Dr. Schumann and a male assistant. The assistant attached two plates to my body, one to my stomach, and the other to my back. Dr. Schumann entered a protected cabin, observed me through a window, and turned on the device, of which the plates were a part. The device that I stood inside of was turned on for several minutes — how long I do not exactly know. On yet the same day, we were taken back to Auschwitz. On the way, all of us vomited. We did not know what had happened to us. After several days, festering wounds appeared in the areas where they had been attached .... After around two months, we were sent back to work at Birkenau, although our wounds had not yet healed .... One day, during the morning roll-call, my number was called, along with the numbers of the other girls who had been irradiated. Once again, we were taken to Auschwitz, to Block 10 .... There, we were examined by Dr. Samuel .... He chose Gilda and Bella from among us for an operation. Dr. Samuel operated on Gilda and Bella, as far as I can remember, on the same day as he had examined us .... The operation took place in the same Block 10, where we were being held .... Sometime in November 1943, I was taken, along with nine other girls, to the neighboring Block 21, and we were operated on there .... In the vestibule to the operating room, we had to undress and receive an injection .... After I received the injection, I lost all feeling in the lower part of my body. A little bit later, I was taken to the operating room and laid on the table. In the room, there were Dr. Schumann, Dr. Dering, another prisoner-doctor and a woman, Dr. Brewda. She kept my spirits up. Between my upper and lower body, there was a screen. I know that Dr. Dering operated on me, and the second prisoner-doctor assisted. After the operation, I was taken back to Block 10. We all lay in the same room and screamed in pain .... Bella died the very same night. Beuna had a terrible, open wound. Her wounds, as well as ours, were festering .... After one or two months .... Dr. Schumann appeared at the

---

[11] One can find around 180 entries testifying to the castrations carried out in Blocks Nr. 21 and 28 in a surviving book from the surgical division of the hospital at Auschwitz's main camp. APMO, D-AuI-5/1-3, Surgical Book.

Also see APMO, D-AuI-52, which contains various documents related to the hospital; APMO, Collection of Reminiscences, vol. 172, card 135, memoirs of former prisoner Rudolf Diem; APMO, Collection of Testimonies, vol. 53, cards 205-208, account of former prisoner Tadeusz Paczuła.

block, observed our wounds, and ordered us back to work at Birkenau, no matter how difficult it still was for us to move. This meant certain death for Beuna, whose injury was still in a particularly bad state.... She died at Birkenau. [12]

The results of the experiments on sterilization through irradiation turned out unsatisfactory. In his paper, "On the Impact of X-Rays upon the Human Genitals", which Schumann wrote on the basis of his experiments, at KL Auschwitz and sent to Himmler in April 1944, Schumann declared himself in favor of surgical castration as a more effective and quicker method of sterilization. He nevertheless continued his experiments at KL Ravensbruck beginning in April 1944.

Only a small number of victims from Clauberg's and Schumann's experiments, fully aware of their permanent mutilation, survived the concentration camp at Auschwitz. [13] The remainder perished at the camp either from phenol injections or in the gas chambers, where they were sent after selection.

Schumann's x-ray device was removed from the Auschwitz camp in December 1944, and Czech prisoner Stanisław Ślezak, who had maintained and serviced the device and was thus considered a "carrier of secrets" (*Geheimnisträger*), was transferred to KL Mauthausen in January 1945, where he was shot.

While the goal of Clauberg's and Schumann's experiments was the development of a method for the biological extinction of nationalities considered undesirable by the Nazis, another criminal doctor, *SS-Hauptsturm-führer* Josef Mengele, MD and PhD, conducted research on the subject of twins, [14] as well as on the physiology and pathology of dwarfism. He worked in close cooperation with the Kaiser Wilhelm Institute for Anthropological Questions and the Sciences of Heredity and Eugenics, directed by Prof. Ottmar Freiherr von Verschauer at Berlin-Dahlem. Mengele's other research interests included people with different-colored irises (heterochromia iridii) and causes and methods of treatment for *noma facie* or "water cancer" — up to that point, a little-known disease that afflicted some of the Gypsy prisoners at Auschwitz.

---

[12] APMO, Collection of Testimonies, vol. 63, cards 160-62, copy of an account by the former prisoner and Greek Jew, Dora Akunis. Her name, as well as the names of nine other Greek-Jewish women subjected to hysterectomies, appear in the surgery book mentioned above under the date November 10, 1943. Also see the testimony of other former women prisoners who were victims of Schumann's experiments in *Criminal Experiments on Human Beings in Auschwitz...*

[13] The numerical data on the number of prisoners subjected to experiments by Clauberg and Schumann are varied and fluctuate between several hundred to over one thousand.

[14] According to Y. Ternon and S. Helman, Josef Mengele wanted to use his experiments on identical twins to establish scientifically the racist theory of the superiority of the Nordic race and also to prove the absolute superiority of heredity over environment. Y. Ternor and S. Helman, p. 231.

According to Dr. Miklos Nyiszli, a Hungarian pathologist employed in the dissection room of crematorium II in the sections for the corpses of twins, the goal of Dr. Mengele's experiments was to uncover the secret of the birth of twins, which would assist the increase of the German population. Miklos Nyiszli, *Auschwitz Doctor's Eyewitness Account* (New York, 1960) p. 60; Gerald L. Posner and John Ware, *Mengele: The Complete Story* (New York, 1986); Helena Kubica, "Dr. Mengele i ślady jego działalności", *Przegląd Lekarski — Oświęcim* (1989), pp. 96-106.

One of Dr. Mengele's workrooms was located on the grounds of the family camp for Gypsies (in the showers near Barrack 32), where he assumed his duties as a camp doctor upon his arrival at the end of May 1943. After the camp's reorganization in November 1943, Mengele was appointed head doctor at KL Auschwitz II-Birkenau. He began his research on Gypsy children, supplied to him from the so-called "Kindergarten" in Barracks 29 and 31. For his experiments, he sought out twins and individuals with unusual physical characteristics (i.e., manifesting dwarfism or gigantism) during the selections conducted on transports of Jews sent to Auschwitz for extermination; at the family camp for Jews from the Theresienstadt ghetto (BIIb); and at camp BIII ("Mexico"). (Jewish women from Hungary were being sent directly to camp BIII, since the large number of transports made it impossible to conduct a selection immediately upon their arrival at the unloading ramp.) After the family camp for Gypsies was liquidated, the human subjects of Dr. Mengele's experiments were transferred to Barrack 15 at the men's infirmary camp (BIIf) and to certain hospital barracks at the women's camp.

In the first stage of his experiments, Dr. Mengele, assisted by medical personnel from different fields — chosen from among the prisoners — conducted specialized medical examinations on twins and individuals with congenital anomalies. Along with radiological, dental, laryngological, and surgical exams, the subjects were submitted to anthropometrical exams, in which the length and width of their heads, noses, hands and shoulders were measured with precision instruments; and morphological exams, in which their blood was tested, among other things, for its transfusability.[15] The examinations, which lasted for hours and were at times painful and exhausting, were a terrible ordeal for the terrified and starving children who predominated among the twins placed at Mengele's disposal.

Former prisoner Elżbieta Piekut-Warszawska, assigned to take care of the twins housed in one of the barracks at the women's camp in Birkenau in July 1944, had to present the children for these examinations. She later described what occurred:

The anthropometrical examinations took place as follows: the children were stripped naked and measurements were made for hours (two to five hours) with the assistance of precision instruments (protractors, compasses, and sliderules). The pairs of twins were examined and checked to see if their measurements were identical. A good deal was written down. This was a difficult ordeal for the children. Terrified, worn-out, hungry and shivering, they had to get up at six in the morning and walk the one-and-a-half kilometer road from the block to the outpatient hospital. The x-ray examinations took place under similar conditions. It was already very cold, it was the end of September or beginning of October, and the room in which the tests were

[15] See the copy of a list containing personal data and the results of anthropometrical examinations on several hundreds Jewish prisoners, including Jewish twins from Hungary. APMO, Files of the Camp Resistance, vol. 16, cards 22-36; APMO, D-AuII-5, inventory number 154381, Prisoners's Documents — Camp Hospital at Birkenau, divs. BIa, BIIa BIIe, BIIf, cards 9, 10, 23; APMO, D-AuI-5, inventory number 154368, Documents from the Dental Station for Prisoners; APMO, Documents from the SS Hygienical Institute — for example, the documents in file 43.

conducted was unheated. The children being tested stood before the x-ray screen from five to fifteen minutes, since the exposure on display was being talked over and discussed. The results of these tests were not long in coming. After they returned [to the block], the children had fevers, caught colds, terrible coughs, sinus infections, and even pneumonia .... Particularly traumatic were the morphological tests. Blood was collected from the children's fingers, then from their veins, sometimes two or three times from the same victims. The children screamed, shielded themselves, would not let themselves be touched. They were very afraid of being pricked .... Drops were also put in their eyes. I did not witness the actual procedure, since the children were taken into the adjacent room. Some pairs of children received drops in both eyes, others in only one .... The results of this action were very painful for the victims. A large swelling of the eyelids resulted; their eyes burned and ran .... (and) the children suffered very much. [16]

Both the twins and handicapped individuals designated for experiments were photographed; their jaws and teeth were cast in plaster; fingerprints and toe-prints were made. On Mengele's orders, prisoner Dina Gottliebova (from the camp for Jews from Theresienstadt, BIIb) produced comparative sketches of the twins: of their heads, auricles, noses, mouths, hands and feet. All the original documentation from these experiments were kept in the individual files maintained on each person designated for experimental purposes. Jewish prisoners had to assist Mengele in his scientific research on twins (and on the disease *noma faciei*) — e.g., the world-renowned pediatrician, Dr. Bertold Epstein from the University of Prague and Rudolf Vitek (under the name Weiskopf at the camp).

After these tests had been completed upon the midgets and pairs of twins, they were murdered upon Dr. Mengele's orders with a phenol injection, so that the next stage of experimentation could begin: the comparative analysis of their internal organs on the basis of autopsies. In cases indicated by Mengele, Dr. Jancu Vexler or — beginning in June 1944 — the Hungarian Jew and doctor of pathology, Miklos Nyiszli, would carry out autopsies and give their scientific appraisal of the results. [17] In his memoirs, Dr. Nyiszli wrote:

These experiments, carried out *in vivo* — that is, upon a living organism — under the pretense of medical research, were far from exhaustive on the subject of twins from a scientific point of view. They were mediocre. They did not tell much. Thus, the next and most important stage of research followed: analysis on the basis of an autopsy. The comparison of normal and pathologically-developed, relatively-diseased organs. But to be able to do this, a corpse is required. Because the autopsy and analysis of the organs had to be carried out simultaneously, the twins had to die simultaneously. Thus, they perished at the same time in the barracks for experiments at the Auschwitz concentration camp .... Thus, a medically-unique coincidence occurred — two twins died at the very same moment. [18]

Skeletons that were interesting from a scientific point of view were conserved and shipped to the Institute in Berlin-Dahlem for closer study. In order to

---

[16] APMO, Collection of Reminiscences, vol. 129, cards 78, 79.

[17] Dr. Vexler worked in a dissecting-room on the grounds of the Gypsy camp and later at the camp hospital in section BIIf. Dr. Nyiszli performed his autopsies in a modernly-equipped dissecting room in Crematorium II.

[18] Nyiszli, pp. 58-59

insure that they were not disturbed and arrived promptly, the shipments were sealed with the stamp: "Urgent, shipments important for war aims". [19]

A division for several dozen Gypsies afflicted with *noma faciei* was established in part of Block 22 on the grounds of the family camp for Gypsies. As the disease progressed, the soft tissue of the cheeks would diminish to the point that the individual's teeth, gums and bones would be left exposed. Those who were ill with noma, a portion of whom were children, were treated for a period with pharmaceuticals and received a special, nutritious diet. Dr. Mengele often visited the division to test and photograph Gypsies at various stages of the disease's development that interested him. He also directed a Czech prisoner, Vladimir Zlamal, to paint their faces. Mengele ordered that certain Gypsy children afflicted with noma be murdered and that their bodies be shipped to the Hygienical Institute in Rajsko for histo-pathological research. The Institute preserved individual organs, and even conserved the entire heads of children in jars. [20] Former prisoner Mieczysław Kieta, employed at the SS Hygienical Institute in Rajsko, as a witness for the prosecution at the trial against the Commandant at KL Auschwitz, Rudolf Höss, testified:

In spring 1944, so-called noma (water cancer) began to spread at the Gypsy camp. In conjunction with this, the institute in Rajsko began to receive corpses of Gypsy children to be subjected to histo-pathological research. Entire heads from children were preserved in jars as specimens for demonstrations. [21]

Dr. Mengele maintained the experimental facilities in which he had conducted his heredity research until January 17, 1945 — that is, until the camp's final evacuation. On the very same day, he left KL Auschwitz, taking with him the documentation from his experiments.

Also connected with the extermination of prisoners were experiments on changes in the human organism caused by hunger, particularly at the point of "brown deterioration" (*braune Atrophie*) of the liver. On the basis of an understanding with *SS-Standortarzt* Eduard Wirths (director of medical services at the Auschwitz camp), *SS-Obersturmführer* Johann Paul Kremer, MD and PhD, professor of anatomy at the University of Münster and lecturer on anatomy and the science of human heredity, conducted such experiments at Auschwitz. Kremer had been recruited from the SS hospital in Prague to replace Bruno Kitt. He held the office of camp doctor from August 30 to November 18, 1942. It would have been difficult for Kremer to find a more suitable place for his research.

Each morning, he examined the prisoners seeking admission to the camp hospital in Block 28. Among them were many extremely-emaciated prisoners ("Muselmänner"), at the point of complete starvation, who were normally

---

[19] Ibid., p. 47

[20] A letter signed by Dr. Mengele from June 29, 1944, has been preserved, ordering that the head of a 12-year-old Gypsy child be sent to the SS Hygienical Institute in Rajsko for histological examination. APMO, SS Hygienical Institute, file 41, card 64.

[21] APMO, Höss Trial, vol. 7, card 14.

killed by a phenol injection to the heart. From among these prisoners, or sometimes the prisoners at the camp hospital, Kremer would select individuals whom he considered suitable subjects for research. Immediately before their liquidation, as they lay on the dissecting table, he asked them about their vital statistics (e.g., about their body weight before arrest or medications that they had last used). In certain cases, he had them photographed. Prisoners appointed by Kremer would remove livers, spleens, and pancreases from the still-warm bodies of the victims for his use. When he left Auschwitz in November 1942 to return to his duties at the University of Münster, Kremer brought with him both the photographs of his victims and the specimens that he had collected. [22]

During the years 1941-44, the camp SS doctors [23] tested new preparations and medicines on prisoners at KL Auschwitz for their tolerance and effectiveness — medicines known by such cryptonyms as B-1012, B-1034, B-1036, 3582, P-111, as well as rutenol and periston, medicines not yet approved for use. [24] They were acting at request of the German chemical concern, IG Farbenindustrie, and specifically for the firm Bayer, one of its holdings. These preparations were given in varying doses to prisoners suffering from contagious diseases (including trachoma, typhus, tuberculosis, diphtheria, and erysipelas) and in various forms (tablets, powders, liquids, intravenous and intramuscular injections, and even rectal enemas). In many cases, the prisoners were artificially exposed to these diseases for the purpose of research. The pharmacological experiments were conducted in the hospital blocks of the main camp (usually in the block for contagious diseases), in the infirmary (HKB) at the women's camp at Birkenau, and the camp hospital at Monowice. Prisoners subjected to these experiments underwent laboratory testing and x-rays at given intervals of time. If they died, an autopsy was conducted in order to identify potential changes in their internal organs that might demonstrate the effects of the medications that they had received. According to the testimony of former prisoner-doctors employed at the camp hospital, who directly witnessed the pharmacological experiments — Władysław Tondos, Władysław Fejkiel and Stanisław Kłodziński — all the medications mentioned proved to be ineffective. The ill individuals forced to take them would begin to have troubles with their digestive tracts, as witnessed by persistent vomiting of blood, painful and bloody stools with strands of mucous membrane, and circulatory difficulties. According to Stanisław Kłodziński,

---

[22] Jan Sehn, "Sprawa oświęcimskiego lekarza SS J. P. Kremera", *Przegląd Lekarski — Oświęcim* (1962), pp. 49-61; "Pamiętnik Johanna Paula Kremera", in *Oświęcim w oczach SS* (Oświęcim, 1980,) pp. 191-270.

[23] Friedrich Entress, Helmuth Vetter, Eduard Wirths; and on a less scale, Fritz Klein, Werner Rhode, Hans Wilhelm König, Victor Capesius (director of the camp pharmacy) and Bruno Weber, Director of the SS Hygienical Institute in Rajsko.

[24] Stanisław Kłodziński, "Zbrodnicze doświadczenia farmakologiczne na więźniach obozu koncentracyjnego w Oświęcimiu (Preparat 3582, rutenol, Be 1034, periston)", *Przegląd Lekarski — Oświęcim* (1965), pp. 40-46; Jan Mikulski, "Pharmakologische Experimente im Konzentrationslager Auschwitz-Birkenau". *Hefte von Auschwitz* 10 (1967), pp 3-18; Władysław Fejkiel, "Eksperymenty dokonywane przez personel sanitarny SS w głównym obozie koncentracyjnym w Oświęcimiu", *Przegląd Lekarski — Oświęcim* (1964), pp. 101-105.

of the 50 individuals afflicted with typhus who were treated with preparation "3582", fifteen died, and of the 75 individuals treated for tuberculosis with rutenol, 40 died. [25]

Dr. Władysław Tondos (before his arrest, director of the sanatorium for tuberculosis patients in Zakopane) testified after the war:

In 1942, Dr. Helmuth Vetter appeared on the grounds of the concentration camp at Auschwitz as an SS doctor. Medical colleagues, now prisoners, knew Vetter from the period between the wars, when he traveled through Poland as a representative for Bayer, promoting the firm's various medications. After his arrival [at the camp — IS], unknown preparations began to be used. To test these medications, healthy prisoners were infected with typhoid-contaminated blood, 5 cc injected intravenously. The individuals who were artificially infected with the virus in this way were then treated with the new preparations. These preparations were produced by the firm Bayer. On the basis of our observations, we concluded that the preparations did not work on typhus, and the majority of the sick patients died. [26]

In the field of pharmacological experiments, the camp pharmacist, Victor Capesius, along with camp doctors Bruno Weber and Werner Rhode, tested the effects of an unknown narcotic substance with the smell and color of coffee on prisoners. As a result of its use, several prisoners died. The substance was planned for use in interrogating prisoners of war in order to make them reveal military secrets.

The firm Bayer, dissatisfied with the pharmacological experiments being conducted in the camp hospitals at KL Auschwitz, bought 150 female prisoners from the camp for 170 RM apiece in order to test newly-developed stupefacients. (The commandant's office had initially demanded 200 RM per prisoner, but the firm considered this price too high.) In one of the surviving letters submitted to the camp administration, the firm Bayer reported:

The transport of 150 women arrived in good condition. Because they died during the experiments, however, we could not reach any binding conclusions. Thus, we are turning to you to request that you send the next group of women — the same number at the same price. [27]

SS doctors Helmuth Vetter and Friedrich Entress also carried out experiments on several dozen of prisoners at KL Auschwitz in order to measure more precisely the incubation period for typhoid and to determine at what point blood infected with typhoid is most contagious and when it ceases to be so. In this case, the SS doctors also infected healthy prisoners with the virus through injections of contaminated blood and then tested a hardly-known anti-typhus vaccine on prisoners suffering from the illness. These experiments led to numerous health complications for the already severely-ill and emaciated prisoners.

---

[25] APMO, SS Staff Trial, vol. 59, cards 53-67; APMO, D-AuI-5, inventory number 29713, 29714, various documents related to the hospital.

[26] APMO, SS Staff Trial, vol. 59, card 55.

[27] Jan Sehn, *Obóz koncentracyjny Oświęcim-Brzezinka (Auschwitz-Birkenau)*, (Warszawa, 1964), pp. 80-84.

Dr. Eduard Wirths, independent of the pharmacological experiments, began research in spring 1943, along with his younger brother, a gynecologist from Hamburg, on uterine cancer. (He hoped to advance his brother's scientific career.) He chose female subjects for his experiments from among the Jewish women being held upstairs in Block 10 at the main camp. The women were examined in order to detect the early stages of the cancer in the vagina. Whenever the disease was detected or suspected, a conical amputation of the uterus was carried out, and the tissue removed was sent to a histological laboratory in Hamburg. In certain cases indicated by Wirths, prisoners working in the darkroom of the political division would come and photograph the operation in progress. The female prisoners subjected to these experiments were then sent to the camp at Birkenau.

On the subject of these experiments for the early detection of uterine cancer, former prisoner Felicja Pleszowska, employed as an attendant in Block 10, later testified:

> The operations at Wirths's station went as follows: The women designated for this goal were first gynecologically examined, both externally and internally. Then, they were subjected to a "colcoscoping", examined with the assistance of a device called a colcoscope, to determine whether and at what place the female sex organs might be susceptible to the development of cancer. The results from this procedure were examined in detail, and on the basis of the resulting diagnosis, the women were divided into two groups. The first group was composed of those who were completely healthy and thus not subject to additional procedures. Women in the second group were operated on under anaesthesia, during which small strips of tissue were gathered from the spots discovered earlier with the colcoscope at the opening of the uterus. These samples were then shipped to Hamburg for further study .... Dr. Wirths was initially interested in the station to a larger degree. The station was equipped with first-rate medical equipment. Wirths carried out the operations and examinations himself.
> After several weeks, Dr. Max Samuel, a gynecological surgeon, a Jewish prisoner with German citizenship, was sent to Wirths' station. He was supposed to be famous I heard, in his profession .... Dr. Wirths delegated all of his work to Dr. Samuel; personally, he only attended to supervising Samuel and checking his work. [28]

In late 1944, in order to unmask various methods of dereliction of duty spreading among German soldiers especially on the Eastern front, in the form of simulated illnesses, self-induced injuries, ulcers, fevers and hepatitis, Emil Kaschub (doctor at the ensign level) was dispatched to Auschwitz on the *Wehrmacht's* behalf. He tested various toxic substances on Jewish prisoners, which he applied to their skin, injected in their arms or legs, or administered orally (atabrine). He wanted to learn how to duplicate the symptoms that German soldiers had been reporting. Kaschub's experiments were carried out in one of the upstairs wards at Block 28 in the main camp, which was strictly isolated and guarded. Tomasz Bardyj, a Hungarian Jew and former prisoner who was subjected to these experiments, testified later:

---

[28]   According to the former prisoner Felicja Pleszowska, around 120-150 Jewish women were subjected to amputation of the uterus. APMO, Höss Trial, vol. 7, cards 78, 79.

I was sent to the Auschwitz camp in July 1944. At the beginning of August, because my knees had swollen up from hunger, I was being held as an ill prisoner in Block 19 at Auschwitz. Around August 22, 1944, a commision arrived at Block 19, of which *SS-Oberfeldwebel* Emil Kaschub was a member. During an inspection, they chose twenty people, men, all my height, and directed us to Block 28, where we were quartered in isolation ward nr. 13. Emil Kaschub forbade the SS men to let us go out anywhere or have contact with other prisoners. We were taken out only once during the day in order to carry out our physiological functions. At other times, we were given a bucket in the room. On the second day after our relocation to ward 13, Emil Kaschub, assisted by a prisoner-attorney, Dr. Schtern [Samuel — IS], and a Hungarian surgeon, Schwarz [Laszlo — IS], began to carry out various experiments on us. Emil Kaschub, using a special saw, personally removed the outer layer of skin on our shins, and then he smeared oil on the resulting wound on some of us, and others, he smeared with a liquid. He proceeded in this fashion with all twenty of us. After that, he began observing how our wounds festered and healed. Every day, he photographed our wounds, and at the moment when they had competely festered, he removed that portion of skin, along with the flesh, from all of us, and collected it [...] Whenever Kaschub photographed the wounded portions of our bodies, we stood on a stool. They covered up the windows in the ward and took photographs by the light of the reflectors. During this time he asked, "Does it hurt?" and then, having received a positive reply, he said, "But the German soldier is suffering every type of hardship because of you rotten Jews." Later, Emil Kaschub went to Brussels. While he was away, Dr. Schwarz helped save many of us by performing emergency treatment and by sending those of us who recovered to other blocks. Those whom he could not heal .... were sent to the crematorium to be burned. [29]

The samples of pus and skin were sent, along with the flesh, to the VIII Sanitary District in Wrocław (Breslau) for analysis. Several dozen young Jewish prisoners had to suffer and be crippled in order to help unmask Germans evading or attempting to leave military service. Kaschub had basically induced an inflammatory state on the young men's skin, along with abscesses and hard-to-heal ulcerations that ultimately led to necrosis of the tissue. As a result, some of the young men were sent to the gas chambers during the selections conducted at the HKB.

In 1942, *SS-Hauptsturmführer* Prof. August Hirt, chairman of the department of anatomy at the *Reichsuniversität* in Strasbourg, wanting to create a collection of Jewish skeletons under the auspices of the *Ahnenerbe* foundation. He received Himmler's permission to select the necessary number of prisoners at Auschwitz for his goals. The selection of 115 prisoners (79 Jewish men, 30 Jewish women, two Poles, and four "Asiatics" — probably Soviet prisoners of war) and their subsequent "study" was carried out by *SS-Hauptsturmführer* Dr. Bruno Beger, a co-worker at the Military-Scientific Research Institute of the *Ahnenerbe* foundation. Arriving at Auschwitz in the first half of 1943, he made anthropometrical measurements and collected the prisoners' personal data. He finished his work on June 15, 1943. A portion of

---

[29] APMO, IZ-1/1. Other collections [*Inne Zespoły*], Documents of the Soviet Commission for the Research of Hitlerite Crimes, vol. 2, cards 75-77. Also includes the testimony of Zak Frejdin, a victim of the experiment (vol. 3, cards 154-156), and of Samuel Schtern, a nurse in Block Nr. 28 (vol. 2, cards 68-74).

the prisoners selected by Beger were then sent at the end of July or beginning of August to the concentration camp Natzweiler-Struthof, [30] where they were liquidated in the gas chambers. Their corpses were then placed at Hirt's disposal for his skeleton collection, to be used for anthropological studies demonstrating the superiority of the Nordic race. [31]

In December 1944, twenty Jewish children were taken from Auschwitz to KL Neuengamme and placed at Dr. Kurt Heismeyer's disposal for his research on tuberculosis. In April 1945, these children were hanged on heating pipes at the school on Bullenhuserdamm in Hamburg. The prisoner-doctors who knew about these experiments were hanged along with the children. [32]

Undoubtedly, one should also count as experiments the operations carried out on prisoners by SS doctors (including Friedrich Entress, Horst Fischer, and Heinz Thilo) without the necessary surgical qualifications. (Although the operations were unnecessary from a medical point of view, they were carried out for the sake of self-education.) One should also count in this category the practice they gained in collapsing lungs by practicing on prisoners afflicted with tuberculosis (i.e., pneumothorax), as well as spinal taps carried out on prisoners ill with meningitis. Although survivors' accounts and memoirs contain references to other types of experiments, it is objectively impossible to establish their goals.

All the medical experiments, conducted on individuals who — by any standard — had to live under extreme conditions, represented the equivalent of a death sentence for many of them. The fate of prisoners subjected to such experiments was of no concern to the SS doctors. Often, in order to conceal their criminal activities, they sentenced their victims to death, either in the gas chambers or by phenol injection.

---

[30] According to Josef Kramer, then Commandant at KL Natzweiler, there were a total of 36, sent between May and November 1944.

[31] Mitscherlich and Mielke, pp. 174-83; S. Kłodziński, „Zbiór szkieletów żydowskich dla uniwersytetu III Rzeszy w Strassburgu", *Przegląd Lekarski* (1984),pp. 96-101.

[32] Fritz Bringmann, *Kindermord am Bullenhuserdamm, SS Verbrechen in Hamburg 1945: Menschenversuche an Kindern* (Frankfurt a. M., 1978); Günter Schwarberg, *Der SS Arzt und die Kinder. Bericht über den Mord vom Bullenhuser Damm* (Hamburg, 1979).

FRANCISZEK PIPER

PRISONER LABOR

One of the decisive factors in determining the living conditions and chances for survival of prisoners in Nazi concentration camps was the type of work to which they were assigned. On the one hand their forced labor allowed the camp itself to function (prisoners had to carry out most of the tasks related to the maintenance and administration of the camp) and provided a source of profit for the German state. On the other hand, their labor was also exploited by the Nazis as a means of extermination (*Vernichtung durch Arbeit* or "destruction through work").

The general political and economic situation of the Third Reich influenced the type of work to which prisoners at Auschwitz were assigned. Conditions peculiar to the camp also influenced how prisoners were employed, based upon its two basic functions: as a camp for gradual annihilation of actual, suspected, or potential enemies of the Third Reich, mainly Poles; and as a center of immediate extermination for Jews, shipped from practically every European country.

1. Construction of the Camp

At the beginning of the camp's existence, there was no specific plan or even a general conception for the employment of prisoners. Until 1941, the camp authorities solved the problem extemporaneously by employing prisoners as they were needed. Given its location, KL Auschwitz, unlike other camps founded after 1938, did not have any possibilities for employing prisoners on a mass scale. Its location was chosen on the basis of its links to transportation and the possibilities it offered for housing prisoners. Initially, it was planned as a transit camp, where prisoners from Silesia and the General Government would spend quarantine before being transferred to camps in Germany. Given the urgency at the time, the construction of a camp from the bottom up was never considered; instead, existing buildings were adapted to new purposes. A group of 22 barracks in Zasole, a suburb of Oświęcim (German: Auschwitz) were requisitioned for this purpose.

The original plans for building the camp also served as the first guidelines for employing prisoners. Little information survives on this subject. We only know from Höss' memoirs that the camp was originally designated for around 10,000 prisoners. The buildings to be adapted had neither drainage nor sanitary facilities and several had been partially destroyed during military operations in September 1939. Himmler gave new orders to expand the main camp during his first inspection of it on March 1, 1941. The main camp at Auschwitz (Oświęcim) was to be enlarged to accommodate 30,000 people, and a new camp was to be built nearby at Birkenau (Brzezinka) to accommodate 100,000 prisoners of war (later this capacity was increased to 200,000). [1]

During its four-and-a-half years of existence, on the basis of these and subsequent orders, the camp at Auschwitz expanded to become an enormous complex of several dozen camps, including — in addition to the main camp, Auschwitz I — the camps at Birkenau (Auschwitz II) and at Monowitz (Monowice) with affiliates in Silesia (Auschwitz III).

A majority of the prisoners employed in 1940 worked on the maintenance and expansion of the camp. In the following years, the percentage of prisoners employed in this type of work remained high. The initial tasks included fencing off the territory of the future camp, erecting guard towers, renovating the barracks into living quarters for the prisoners, and levelling the grounds of the camp. Sixty prisoners would be harnessed to an enormous roller to flatten the ground at the roll-call square and to help build roads. Driven from morning to evening by the German criminal, kapo Krankenmann, the prisoners quickly lost their strength. He killed on the spot anyone who could not take this kind of work.

To acquire building materials for adding new floors to the one-story buildings at camp, and at the same time to eliminate unnecessary buildings near the grounds of the camp, prisoners were employed at demolishing the houses of Poles that had been expulsed in 1940-41 from the villages of Birkenau (Brzezinka), Babice, Harmęże, Pławy, Rajsko, Budy and Brosz-kowice, as well as on the left-bank of the town of Auschwitz (Oświęcim). Work in the special *Abbruchkommando*, assigned to this task, represented one of the most difficult and dangerous work possibilities at the time. In the winter and spring of 1941, in the cold, foul weather, hundreds of prisoners — armed with shovels, pickaxes, and crowbars — worked each day at dismantling houses. The walls, which were demolished with logs and sometimes even battering rams, would fall and crush prisoners to death who did not move in time. The resulting corpses were carried to the crematorium, and anyone who was injured was killed. The demolition work was considered finished only after the last scrap of a building's foundation had been removed from the ground and the entire terrain had been leveled and seeded. As if that had not sufficed for a day's exertion, the staggering prisoners had to lug bricks obtained from the demolition back to the camp on their shoulders.

Other work details returned to the camp around the same time. The most tragic sight was the *Strafkompanie* or "penal company". Prisoners, attached to it for the most insignificant disciplinary violations or for general "laziness", were often killed at work. They were employed, among other places, in the

---

[1] *Wspomnienia Rudolfa Hössa komendanta obozu oświęcimskiego* (Warszawa, 1965,) pp. 110, 119; Report, Glücks to Himmler, February 21, 1940, in *Trials of War Criminals before the Nürnberg Military Tribunals,* vol. V (Washington, 1950), pp. 356-358.

gravel pits. To this day, one can see enormous pits around the camp, where thousands of tons of gravel and sand had been obtained to build roads and buildings at the camp, including the residential blocks, crematoria, and gas chambers.

The prisoners named one of the gravel pits *"Palitzschkiesgrube"* after one of the camp's infamous butchers, *Rapportführer* Palitzsch. The prisoners who worked at this pit, driven without pause, had to dig up and sift gravel and then haul it up shaking boards in wheelbarrows to the edge of the pit. When a prisoner could no longer hold a shovel or wheelbarrow in his worn-out, bleeding hands — and if he did not want to be beaten to death with a staff — he would "go to the post" — cross an established security line and duck a shot from the guard. This was the work detail distinguished by its daily "contingent" of deaths.

A warehouse for building materials or *Bauhof* occupied around a dozen hectares on the west side of the camp. While the camp was being expanded, more than a dozen wagons would arrive each day at the train platform located there. They were carrying bricks, cement, reinforced steel, roofing tiles, limestone, building fixtures, etc. Given the general shortage of rolling-stock, camp officials strived to limit the stay of each wagon to a minimum. Thus, the unloading work had to be carried out at a maximum speed. Although new arrivals, not yet exhausted from staying at the camp, were assigned, as a rule, to this work, few could last longer than a couple of weeks. In the space of two hours, ten prisoners had do unload 480 bags of cement, weighing 50 kg apiece, and carry them to a warehouse located 150 m away. Altogether, each prisoner had to cover a distance of more than 15 km during these two hours, and half the time with a burden of 50 kg. SS-men and kapos, lined up in two rows, would beat the prisoners incessantly with their staffs in order to drive them forward. When Professor Sedlaczek from Warsaw tripped and fell while running with his load, one of the supervising SS-men ran up, raised up a bag of cement, and threw it with his entire strength upon the prone professor's back. He died immediately from a crushed spine. Similar bestial murders were a daily occurence during the unloading.

Labor in other work details was no different. Of the 10,000 Soviet prisoners of war shipped to KL Auschwitz in October 1941, more than 9,000 perished within five months, mainly during construction of the camp at Birkenau, begun in October 1941. The construction of that camp continued up to the last months of KL Auschwitz's existence. In the end, only around 300 of the 600 buildings, intended for housing prisoners and other uses, were actually erected. As a result of Himmler's decision to concentrate the machinery for the mass extermination of all European Jews at KL Auschwitz, the construction of four buildings housing gas chambers and crematorium ovens began in 1942. The facilities were put into operation in 1943. [2]

---

[2] Until that time, two provisional gas chambers, so-called bunkers, were used, and before that, the gas chamber at Crematorium I in the main camp.

2. Maintenance of Administrative and Economic Divisions at the Camp

A significant number of prisoners were also employed at various economic and administrative units of the camp, including every type of warehouse — for clothes, food and equipment; at workshops engaged in ironmaking, carpentry, painting, tailoring, shoemaking, and repairing automobiles; at the camp offices and kitchens; in the hospitals and sick wards. Some prisoners also had to help maintain the facilities for mass extermination, by carrying corpses from the gas chambers, burning them in the crematoria ovens or in piles; and then collecting, sorting and shipping the stolen possessions of the victims. [3]

In terms of its effect upon the prisoners, the work in the different areas named above varied greatly. There was relatively less-strenuous work, such as that in the kitchens, offices, and workshops. In other types of work, the possibility for survival was slim. Storing the potatoes and turnips that arrived at the camp in large quantities each year — which, along with bread, formed the basis of the prisoners' diet — was one of the more dangerous assignments. To carry these products, the prisoners used so-called "carriers" — large wooden boxes with handles. Two prisoners would lift each box. This work, which would have strained even a healthy and well-fed person, was murderous for the prisoners. Horrible scenes played out. Despite their greatest exertions — since everyone recognized that the price was one's life — people would fall beneath the crushing burden that they carried. Whoever failed to stand up immediately would perish beneath the blows of a wooden staff.

It was terrible to watch how those who instinctively remained on their feet were murdered because they were no longer able to keep hold of the "carrier" with their bleeding hands. Sometimes, SS men or kapos would yell and instruct them to bend down. When the prisoner did, one of them would take a stuffed stool specially prepared for that very purpose and deal him a blow to the neck with his entire strength. This resulted in immediate death. The corpse was thrown into the nearest pit. Frightened prisoners ran to escape the blows of their torturers across the chains of the guard post in order to be killed by a guard's bullet instead. Each day, this work detail would return with around twenty corpses.

The prisoners steadfastly believed that the pace of their work had nothing at all to do with the completion of their work by a given deadline — often, they finished earlier than expected. The actual goal, they believed, was to torment and kill them. No one ever doubted that the use of basic means of transport, such as a wagon or wheelbarrows, would have made the work still strenuous, but not deadly.

3. Agriculture

Agriculture was one of the main fields of economic endeavor at the camp. Prisoners began to work at farming immediately after the camp authorities drove out the local population and occupied farmland in the so-called

---

[3] For more on the subject of prisoner labor in economic and administrative areas, see Franciszek Piper, *Arbeitseinsatz der Häftlinge aus dem KL Auschwitz*, (Oświęcim, 1995), pp. 152-187.

"security sphere" around the camp. This area included, along with residential buildings, farms with harvested and unharvested crops, which the expellees had been forced to leave behind. In order to cultivate the evacuated land, the camp authorities created a special agricultural brigade (*Landwirtschaftskommando*) in the summer of 1940. At first, it only continued the work that the resettled Polish population had begun.

In 1941, on Himmler's orders, the camp's administrative area was expanded, and additional residents from the Oświęcim (Auschwitz) area were resettled. As a result, the camp's "sphere of interest" (*Interessengebiet*) expanded by around 4,000 ha. In keeping with Himmler's order, a special SS agricultural holding was established there, which would exploit the prisoners' labor. In the years 1940-44, a total of six farms were established next to the camp.[4] At Harmęże (Harmense) a large chicken farm was established; at Pławy, facilities for fish; and at Rajsko, horticultural facilities, where flowers and vegetables were cultivated on a large scale. The flowers, tomatoes and cucumbers sent to Berlin in the early spring with the KL Auschwitz stamp were a source of pride for Himmler, proof of his "all-round contribution to the cause of bulding Hitler's *Reich*". At the horticultural facilities, they experimented with the cultivation of kok-saghyz, a rubber-producing plant from the southern regions of the Soviet Union. The mass cultivation of kok-saghyz, it was hoped, would allow Germany to overcome its shortage of rubber in the near future.

Farm work, mainly performed by women prisoners, was no easy task, given the conditions prevailing at the camp. Once the sowing and harvesting were over, the women had to work in fall and winter at removing stones from the fields, digging ditches, draining fields and meadows, deepening and cleaning ponds, and building dikes.

4. Sub-camps

From 1941, several industrial operations became interested in the prisoners of the Auschwitz concentration camp as a potential source of labor, including the SS firm, *Deutsche Ausrüstungswerke* (DAW), and the chemical combine, IG Farbenindustrie. DAW employed prisoners at wood and iron works that had been established at the camp, while IG Farbenindustrie rented them out to help build a chemical plant that would provide the German economy with deficit rubber and synthetic gasoline. The number of prisoners employed at these enterprises was, however, small. Only the collapse of Germany's *Blitzkrieg* strategy and the entry of the United States — with its enormous economic and military potential — into the war in December 1941 presented Germany with the need to increase its armaments production and thus

---

[4] The following works, all by Anna Zięba, are the only ones published to date specifically on the subject of the sub-camps engaged in agriculture at Auschwitz: at Babitz (Babice) — "Wirtschaftshof Babitz. Nebenlager beim Gut Babice", *Hefte von Auchwitz* 11 (1970), pp. 73-87, at Harmense (Harmęże) — "Die Geflügelfarm Harmense. Die Errichtung der Farm", *Hefte von Auschwitz*, 11 (1970), pp. 39-72; at Rajsko — idem. "Das Nebenlager Rajsko" *Hefte von Auschwitz* 9 (1966), pp. 75-108; at Budy — "Wirtschaftshof Budy", *Hefte von Auschwitz* 10 (1967), pp. 67-85.

mobilize all its reserves, including the concentration-camp prisoners as a potential source of labor. Germany's war economy not only faced difficulties at the time in increasing employment, but also suffered from a lack of manpower due to the conscription of additional age cohorts of men for the planned offensive in the East.

In order to mobilize all reserves, including foreign labor, Hitler established the Office of Plenipotentiary for Labor Questions under Firtz Sauckel on March 21, 1942. Another measure taken at the time was the subordination of the Inspectorate of Concentration Camps to the Main Economic-Administrative Office of the SS on the basic of a March 3, 1942 order. The order reflected the SS's desire to achieve better economic results with prisoner labor and to exploit it for armaments production. The SS hoped to achieve the latter goal by retooling existing factories at the camp for armaments production and by converting several factories in the nearby area.

In the case of KL Auschwitz, the German concern Krupp, interested in leasing prisoners, began negotiations with the camp in July 1942. It was June 1943, however, before they could employ prisoners at their factory built near the camp. Krupp was unable, however, to even begin production at its Auschwitz facilities. Because the detonator factory of the firm Weichsel--Metall-Union had to be evacuated from Zaporozhiye in the USSR, the Supreme Command of the *Wehrmacht* ordered that Krupp's facilities be liquidated to make room for Union's factory. Union took over the facilities and machines left behind on October 1, 1943. Union's facilities and a plant for salvaging airplanes, established on October 29, 1943, were the two armament plants in the strict sense of the word that were established near the camp.

The second idea, to build affiliated camps on or near the grounds of already-existing industrial facilities, proved more economical. In 1942, KL Auschwitz's first four affiliated camps or sub-camps were established in Goleszów (Golleschau); Jawiszowice (Jawischowitz); Monowice, near Oświęcim (Monowitz), and Chełmek. In 1943, an additional five were founded: in Świętochłowice (Eintrachthütte); Jaworzno (Neu-Dachs); Libiąż (Janinagrube); Wesoła, near Mysłowice (Fürstengrube), and Łagisza (Lagischa). In 1944, seventeen sub-camps were founded: at Bobrek near Oświęcim (Bobrek), Lędziny (Günthergrube), Gliwice (Gleiwitz, three sub-camps), Blachownia Śląska-Sławięcice (Blechhammer), Siemianowice (Laurahütte), Sosnowiec (Sosnowitz), Zabrze (Hindenburg), Trzebinia, Stara Kuźnia (Althammer), Chorzów (Bismarckhütte), Rydułtowy (Charlottegrube) Prudnik (Neustadt), Czechowice-Dziedzice (Tschechowitz, two subcamps), and Łagiewniki (Hubertushütte). [5] In the years 1942-44, a total of 26 camps affiliated with the Auschwitz

---

[5] *Hefte von Auschwitz* has published monographs to date on the following sub-camps, founded alongside industrial concerns: In issue Nr. 9 — Golleschau (Goleszów), Lagischa (Łagisza); Nr. 10 — Blechhammer (Blachownia-Sławięcice), Janinagrube (Libiąż), Laurahütte (Siemianowice); Nr. 11 — Sosnowitz II (Sosnowiec), Hindenburg (Zabrze); Nr. 12 — Chełmek, Neu-Dachs (Jaworzno), Günthergrube (Lędziny), Bismarckhütte (Chorzów), Hubertushütte (Łagiewniki); Nr. 13 — Althammer (Stara Kuźnia), Neustadt (Prudnik); Nr. 14 — Gleiwitz I-III (Gliwice); Nr. 15 — Jawischowitz (Jawiszowice); Nr 16 — Fürstengrube (Wesoła), Trzebinia; Nr. 17 — Charlottegrube (Rydułtowy), Eintrachthütte (Świętochłowice); Nr. 18 — Tschechowitz (Czechowice-Dziedzice).

concentration camp were established in Upper Silesia, next to metalworks, mines and other industrial facilities. Two additional sub-camps were established alongside industrial facilities located outside Silesia in Czech territory; at Freudenthal (Bruntal) and Lichtewerden (Světla). In terms of the different types of labor, prisoners performed construction and renovation work at five camps: at Sośnica near Gliwice, SS Hütte Porombka (Międzybrodzie), Brünn (Brno, in occupied Czech territory), Sosnowitz I (Sosnowiec), Gleiwitz IV (Gliwice). At seven, prisoners worked in agriculture: Babitz (Babice), Budy (two sub-camps), Harmense (Harmęże), Rajsko (two sub-camps), and Pławy. At three, they worked in forestry: Kobior, Altdorf (Stara Wieś), and Radostowitz (Radostowice). There was a penal sub-camp at Budy, and one sub-camp without any established location, which employed prisoners at clearing rubble and repairing damage caused by bombing. Altogether, more than 40 sub-camps had been established by 1945.

The sub-camps located next to industrial facilities answered to the commandant of the concentration camp at Auschwitz until November 21, 1943, when Auschwitz was divided into three camps. Thereafter, all the affiliated camps answered to the commandant of KL Auschwitz III at Monowice (Monowitz; sub-camp Buna), except for those engaged in agriculture and forestry. *SS-Hauptsturmführer* Heinrich Schwarz, assisted by *Lagerführer* and *SS--Obersturmführer* Vinzenz Schöttl, served as commandant of Auschwitz III until the end of the camp's existence. The commandant at Auschwitz III, just like the commandant at Auschwitz II (Birkenau), was obligated to work in close cooperation with the commandant of Auschwitz I (the main camp in Oświęcim), who was senior in rank as head of the Auschwitz SS garrison.[6]

Each sub-camp had a supervisor (*Lagerführer*) appointed by the commandant, who was assisted by a *Rapportführer* (lit., "assembly leader"). The *Rapportführer* was responsible for holding roll-calls, keeping count of the prisoners, and overseeing his subordinates: the *Blockführers*, who were assigned to oversee the prisoners in each residential block, and the SS sanitarians (*Sanitätsdienstgrade* — SDG), who administered the prisoner's infirmaries (*Häftlingskrankenbau* — HKB) at each camp. The *Rapportführer's* oversight over the sick ward was purely administrative, and the SS sanitarians did not possess the qualifications needed to treat the prisoners. This was left to the prisoner-doctors. The HKB had little in the way of furnishings, and the assortment and number of medications sent from the pharmacy at KL Auschwitz I were completely inadequate. SS doctors, who occasionally visited the sub-camps, were not interested in the treatment or state of health of prisoners. They limited themselves to finding chronically-ill prisoners who were unable to work. They would carry out selections, based on the prisoners' outer appearance. They would either send crippled and emaciated prisoners to a camp infirmary (at the sub-camp Buna/Monowitz or occasionally, Birkenau) or to immediate death in the gas chambers. Depending

---

[6] APMO, D-AuI-1, Collection of Standortbefehle (orders issued by the commander of the camp garrison) Nr. 53/43 from November 22, 1943.

on the number of prisoners at the sub-camp, the doctors would select out anywhere from a handful to several hundred prisoners during one visit.

The bodies of dead prisoners were sent to KL Auschwitz for burning. Sometimes, at distant sub-camps, corpses would be buried in local cemeteries (eg., in Rydułtowy, in the case of the Charlottegrube camp, or in Prudnik, in the case of Neustadt). In 1944, crematoria with one oil-burning furnace apiece were installed at the Blechhammer (Blachownia-Sławięcice) and Trzebinia sub-camps, where the death rates were extremely high. In fall 1944, construction was begun on a crematorium at the Charlottegrube sub-camp (Rydułtowy), but was never finished. [7]

At the sub-camps, besides the SS men, sometimes soldiers from normal military formations were assigned to a given production facility and would guard the prisoners. For example, soldiers from German air units supervised prisoners employed in producing antiaircraft guns at the Eintrachthütte facilities in Świętochłowice (today, the "Zgoda" works). Soldiers from the *Wehrmacht* oversaw the work of women prisoners producing ammunition at the "Donnersmarck" plant (currently the "Zabrze" works) in Zabrze. This was also the case at the following sub-camps: Charlottegrube (Rydułtowy), Bismarckhütte (Chorzów), Sosnowitz (Sosnowiec), Golleschau (Goleszów), and Laurahütte (Siemianowice). At Laurahütte, SS men held only top offices; normal soldiers from antiaircraft units composed the remainder of the staff. Some factories had their own security teams (*Werkschutz*), which also held watch over the prisoners.

Given the small number of SS guards available, their supervision was usually reduced to watching fences, gates, and other entryways to prevent prisoners from escaping. At the various coal mines, SS men would only go below ground in exceptional cases. They conducted spot checks to make sure that prisoners were at their workplaces. The kapos and *Vorarbeiter* constantly supervised the prisoners, while the civilian personnel provided technical oversight.

The prisoners usually worked in brigades of several people, along with civilian workers. It normally went as follows: either there were several trained prisoners under the supervision of a civilian expert, or a couple prisoners assigned to several civilian workers. In the latter case, the prisoners would bring the civilian workers raw materials, carry the finished product, clean and maintain machines or clean up the work area. The system of piece-work that prevailed undoubtedly created an interest among the civilian personnel in maintaining a suitable level of discipline and productivity among the prisoners.

At most sub-camps, the main contractor would rent prisoners out to his subcontractors — smaller or larger specialized firms. At the largest sub-camps, Monowitz (Monowice) and Blechhammer (Blachownia Śląska-Sławięcice), there were several dozen such firms.

[7] Andrzej Strzelecki, "Das Nebenlager 'Charlottegrube", *Hefte von Auchwitz* 17, (1985), pp. 41-90.

5. The Working Conditions for Prisoners Employed in Industry

Prisoners employed in industry faced, as a rule, very difficult working conditions. Although they worked at very different industrial facilites — in mining, metallurgy, chemical and textile industries — more than half of the prisoners were engaged in very strenuous construction work: excavating, leveling, carrying. This applied in particular to prisoners at the sub-camps Lagischa (Łagisza), Althammer (Stara Kuźnia), Monowitz (Monowice), Blechhammer (Blachownia Śląska-Sławięcice), Trzebinia, Günthergrube (Lędziny) and Neu-Dachs (Jaworzno). At Althammer, they built a power plant; at Trzebinia, a chemical works; at Güthergrube, a mine; and at Neu-Dachs, a mine and power plant. The prisoners worked in haste and under poor conditions, with little machinery and no protective gear.

Prisoners employed in actual production experienced slightly better conditions. If nothing else, they were not exposed to the weather. The SS men and kapos were also more lax in their supervision. Often, however, the prisoners received dangerous or particularly arduous tasks. In the mines at Neu-Dachs, prisoners had to work in the depths of the shaft, flooded with water, at such jobs as loading. Most worked without helmets or rubber safety boots.

Women prisoners at the Gleiwitz II (Gliwice) sub-camp, employed in the production of lamp-black at the facilities of the Deutsche Gasrusswerke, labored under particularly difficult conditions. In the production rooms, where the fine, black soot was produced from anthracite coal, sulphur and oil, the temperature would reach 60-70°C (140-158°F). The situation worsened at night, because the windows could not be opened due to the compulsory blackout. The women had to work in hermetically-sealed overalls because the soot, dust, and toxic fumes in the air were difficult to wash out. Similar conditions prevailed in the packing room for the lamp-black. A very dangerous job, particularly for the weakened and emaciated prisoners, was to carry out buckets of dirty oil, whose temperature could reach 300°C (572°F). This resulted in cases of severe burns. [8]

At several sub-camps — Monowitz (Monowice), Trzebinia, Blechhammer (Blachownia-Sławięcice), and Tschechowitz (Czechowice) I — *Bombensucher-kommando*, prisoners were utilized for removing unexploded bombs and shells. At Tschechowitz I, this was their main employment. The around 100 prisoners assigned to this task worked under the supervision of two German pyrotechnicists. The work went as follows:

At a radius of about two meters from where a bomb had landed, the prisoners would dig a large crater, at the bottom of which, at a depth of several meters, lay the unexploded shell. One of the prisoners would clean the dirt from it, then a pyrotechnicist or one of the trained prisoners would enter the crater to disarm the bomb by unscrewing the detonator .... The disarmed bombs were carried on a wagon to a shop located on the grounds of the sub-camp, where they were stored and subsequently shipped to an unknown destination. [9]

---

[8] Irena Strzelecka, "Arbeitslager Gleiwitz II", *Hefte von Auschwitz* 14 (1973), pp. 119-20.
[9] Irena Strzelecka and Tadeusz Szymański, "Die Nebenlager Tschechowitz I Bombensucher-kommando und Tschechowitz-Vacuum", *Hefte von Auschwitz* 18 (1990), pp. 189-224.

Although the sub-camps were established, in principle, near their respective workplaces, prisoners at several sub-camps had to work at different locations. Each day, they had to walk several kilometers on foot, to their workplace and back. Prisoners who had to help build IG Farbenindustrie's chemical plant in Dwory near Oświęcim had to walk around 12 km each day, to the plant site and back, until a sub-samp was established in the vicinity of the plant. Around 3 a.m., while everyone else at the camp was still sleeping, prisoners from this detail were awakened and led off to work. When they returned to the camp, it was already dark. Given the constant rushing — at the beginning, prisoners had to work on the run, or at a *Laufschritt* — the harsh working conditions outside (torrid heat during summer, bitter cold in the winter) and numerous beatings, the prisoners in this work detail suffered a high death rate. The very prospect of employment in this detail would fill prisoners with horror. It detail maintained this gloomy reputation as long as the camp existed. [10]

The hours that prisoner-employees could be forced to work was, in principle, unlimited. The firms decided themselves on the length and schedule of the prisoners' workday. This led to a wide variation in methods and hours of employment. The factories that employed prisoners had anywhere from one to three shifts, and the prisoner's workday could last anywhere from eight to twelve hours.

The contract of March 27, 1941 between IG Farbenindustrie and the SS (the first of its kind in the history of KL Auschwitz), established a workday for prisoners of 10-11 hours during the summer and 9 hours in winter. [11] At the Hindenburg sub-camp in Zabrze, the women prisoners had to work eleven-hour shifts. Prisoners employed by the concern *Reichsbahnausbesserungswerk* at their *Wagenwerk* factory at the Gleiwitz I sub-camp in Gliwice worked twelve-hour shifts.

Usually, prisoners working in the mines were assigned to three eight-hour shifts. At foundries, prisoners usually worked 12 hours, in one or two shifts. At the remaining industrial facilities, particularly where prisoners were employed in construction, the workday lasted anywhere from 10 to 12 hours.

Often, such norms were exceeded. Prisoners repairing train tracks at the *Wagenwerk* plant in Gliwice, for example, might not be allowed to leave their workplace for an entire week; they would sleep several hours each days in railway cars at the factory. At the mine "Brzeszcze-Jawiszowice", if the day's quota was not met, the prisoners would be held at work until the designated work was finished. Sometimes, prisoners would be kept at work through the entire next shift. As a result, shortly after they returned to camp, the prisoner-workers would have to get ready to return to work. [12] Such practices became so widespread that the commandant of KL Auschwitz III had to address the problem with a circular. In an order from July 14, 1944, he

---

[10] *Schuldig im Sinne des Rechts und des Völkerrechts* (Berlin, 1966). This publication contains documents and materials related to the employment of prisoners at the Buna Werke that were submitted to a court in the trial of former SS doctor Horst Fischer.

[11] Danuta Czech, *Kalendarz wydarzeń w KL Auschwitz* (Oświęcim 1992), p. 56.

[12] Andrzej Strzelecki, "Das Nebenlager Jawischowitz". *Hefte von Auschwitz* 15 (1975), p. 224.

declared that the prisoners needed a suitable rest period in order to maintain an adequate level of productivity. "It is unacceptable — he announced — for foremen to keep skilled prisoners at work during the night, after they have completed their shift for the day". [13]

Prisoners only had one or two Sundays free from work each month. During this time off, as was the case during the week, they had to perform various tasks at the camp, such as cleaning, washing and repairing clothes. On Sundays, prisoners at the sub-camp Gleiwitz I (Gliwice) were punished by flogging at Sunday roll-calls. In general, if one adds up the time spent coming and going to work, attending roll-calls (drawn-out, despite orders from higher SS authorities), waiting in line for food and similar tasks, the time available for rest was limited to several hours of sleep each night.

How prisoners were treated at the different sub-camps varied. The type of work undoubtedly influenced it. Work outdoors, constantly supervised by the SS men and kapos, presented more opportunities for hitting and mistreating the prisoners than work carried out with machines, whose rhythm and tempo was regulated to a greater extent by technical processes. The attitude of civilian supervisors was also of central importance to the prisoners' situation. In general, workers and lower-level civil servants behaved decently towards the prisoners, while mid-level and higher supervisors competed with the SS and kapos in mistreating them.

The prisoners employed at the mines attached to the following sub-camps were treated particularly badly: Neu-Dachs (Jaworzno), Jawischowitz (Jawiszowice), Blechhammer (Blachownia Śląska-Sławięcice), Janinagrube (Libiąż), and Charlottegrube (Rydułtowy). In a number of cases, supervisors, directors and foremen brutally beat prisoners and even killed them.

The particularly difficult sub-camps included Buna at Monowitz (Monowice), Blechhammer (Blachownia-Sławięcice), Trzebinia, Tschechowitz II (Czechowice), and Gleiwitz I (Gliwice). At the Trzebinia sub-camp, prisoners returned from work almost every day with the corpses of comrades who had been murdered by the kapos and SS men. The refinery directors repeatedly stressed in their reports to KL Auschwitz that the SS men should drive the prisoners at work without mercy, because this was the only way to improve productivity. [14] Inspector Bergman from the management of the Jaworzno mines apparently expected the same. On June 28, 1944, he wrote to *Lagerführer* Pfütze at the Neu-Dachs sub-camp that the Jewish kapos needed to be replaced by non-Jews in order to improve productivity. [15] In justifying his request, Bergman referred to his own experience. This was in fact unnecessary; assigning supervising functions to prisoners of a different nationality (most often German) had been a standard practice at the camp since its establishment. One report from the refinery at Trzebinia, which employed Jewish prisoners, reported that "thanks to the employment of German kapos, the prisoners' productivity has improved". [16]

---

[13] APMO, D-AuIII-1, Kommandanturbefehl KL Auschwitz III Nr. 8/44.
[14] APMO, Collection Trzebinia, vol. 3/2, card 3.
[15] Franciszek Piper, "Das Nebenlager Neu-Dachs", *Hefte von Auschwitz* 12 (1971), p. 103.
[16] APMO, Collection Trzebinia vol. 3/2 card 29.

Another method for maintaining productivity, besides beating the prisoners, was to constantly exchange new and healthy prisoners for worn-out ones. The leasing contracts between the firms and the SS even stipulated that such exchanges should take place.[17]

Several firms fed the prisoners themselves, or occasionally gave out food bonuses to prisoners who distinguished themselves at work. Most often, however, the prisoners received a cash bonus as an incentive. Such incentives were of little value to the unfed, constantly starving prisoners, who could only use such money for buying toiletries, writing paper, and other small items at the camp commissary, which were essentially worthless.

6. The Employment Structure of Prisoners in Industry

The chemical industry held first place from the very beginning in terms of the number of prisoners it employed. It was also the first industry to employ prisoners from KL Auschwitz. Already in 1941, as noted above, they had been exploited for the construction of a chemical plant for IG Farbenindustrie in Dwory. The concern IG Farbenindustrie held a privileged position in terms of leasing prisoners from KL Auschwitz. In 1941, the Buna-Werke complex employed nearly 100% of the prisoners employed in industry; in 1942, 60%; in 1943, 40%; and in 1944, 25%. One of the first Auschwitz sub-camps, was built in 1942 next to the IG Farbenindustrie plant.

In 1944, five new sub-camps were established next to chemical plants: Blechhammer (in Blachownia Śląska-Sławięcice), Trzebinia, Gleiwitz (Gliwice), and Tschechowitz (Czechowice-Dziedzice). Thanks to the new camps, the number of prisoners employed in the chemical industry as a percentage of all the prisoners employed in industry remained near 40%.

The mining industry commanded second place in terms of prisoner employment. The "Brzeszcze-Jawiszowice" mines, part of the state--run Herman Göring Werke, were the first coal mines to employ Auschwitz prisoners, in mid-August 1942. This was the first case in the history of the concentration camps in which prisoners were utilized underground for mining. In 1943, three new sub-camps arose next to mines: the Neu-Dachs sub-camp on June 15 in Jaworzno, next to the mines "Neu-Dachs", "Friedrich August", and "Rudolf"; on September 2, the sub-camp Fürstengrube (Wesoła near Mysłowice); and on September 4, the sub-camp Janinagrube (Libiąż). In 1944, two additional sub-camps were founded next to mines: on February 1, the sub-camp Günthergrube (in Lędziny; today, the "Ziemowit" mines), and on September 1, the sub-camp Charlottegrube (next to the present-day "Rydułtowy" mines in Rydułtowy). The number of prisoners employed in coal mines grew rapidly. At the end of 1944, 8,200 prisoners were working at coal mines attached to sub-camps.

---

[17] Franciszek Piper, "Das Nebenlager Eintrachthütte", *Hefte von Auschwitz* 17 (1985), pp. 92-94. Contract between SS-WVHA and the firm OSMAG.

In 1943, in third place, in terms of prisoners employed, was the electrical industry. Prisoners helped build the following power plants: Jaworzno II (originally "Wilhelm"), Łagisza ("Walter"), and "Halemba" in Stara Kuźnia (Althammer). At the Neu-Dachs sub-camp (Jaworzno), some of the prisoners helped construct a power plant; two other sub-camps were established at the sites of power plants — the Lagischa sub-camp (Łagisza) in September 1943 and the Althammer sub-camp (Stara Kuźnia) in mid-September 1944. When construction was suspended on the power plant in Łagisza on September 6, 1944, the prisoners at the sub-camp were transferred to the Neu-Dachs sub-camp in Jaworzno.

In 1944, the number of prisoners employed in steel and metalworking more than tripled. In 1943, the steel and metal industries only employed around 2,000 prisoners (at Eintrachthütte in Świętochłowice, Union in Oświęcim [18], and Siemens-Schuckert in Bobrek) and there was only one sub-camp for metal-working. By 1944, there were already nine sub-camps and around 7,300 prisoners working in the industry.

All prisoners (with the exception of the prisoners at the sub-camp Gleiwitz I, employed in repairing train tracks) worked at armaments plants producing weapons, ammunition, or military parts. They worked at machines, carried parts, assisted, cleaned, etc. At *Donnersmarckhütte* (today, the foundry "Zabrze"), women prisoners worked at machines, carried sand and molding materials and welded and assembled bomb carriers for German aircraft. Prisoners also worked at other types of firms in Silesia: e.g., at a cement factory in Goleszów (1942-45), the Bata shoe factory in Chełmek (1942), and a textile factory in Prudnik (1944-45).

Several large German concerns and 150-200 other firms exploited the labor of prisoners from KL Auschwitz, from the great joint-stock companies down to small subcontractors renting prisoners from the main contractors. The concern IG Farbenindustrie, which, thanks to Göring's support, already won the right in 1941 to employ prisoners from KL Auschwitz, also held 51% of the shares in the corporation Fürstengrube GmbH, which employed prisoners at the coal mines "Fürstengrube" and "Janinagrube". These mines, in turn, supplied the complex in Dwory with coal for producing synthetic rubber and gasoline. [19] The concern also had trade contacts with the Günthergrube mine, belonging to Fürstlich Plessische Bergwerks AG, which cooperated with IG Farbenindustrie in matters related to the employment of prisoners from KL Auschwitz. Because of its importance to the German economy and the influence that it wielded in Third Reich political circles, this chemical combine was able to claim priority in employing concentration-camp prisoners.

The state-run enterprises Energieversorgung Oberschlesien AG, Hermann Göring Werke, and Berg- und Hüttenwerkgesellschaft-Berghütte also employed a significant number of prisoners. Albert Speer, General Inspector for

---

[18] The factory in Oświęcim belonged to the Krupp concern until September 30, 1943, when Union took it over.

[19] Tadeusz Iwaszko, "Das Nebenlager Fürstengrube", *Hefte von Auschwitz* 16 (1978), pp. 6-11.

Water and Energy Questions and, simultaneously, Minister for Armaments and Ammunition, established the first of these firms in 1942. Energieversorgung exploited the labor of prisoners from the Neu-Dachs sub-camp (Jaworzno) to construct the power plant "Wilhelm" (Jaworzno II) and to mine coal. It also used prisoners from the Lagischa sub-camp (Łagisza) in the construction of the power-plant "Walter". In 1943, around 3,200 prisoners worked for the electrical concern; in summer 1944, around 4,700; and at the beginning of 1945, 4,150.

Already in 1942, the Hermann Göring Werke employed prisoners at the "Brzeszcze-Jawiszowice" coal mine and, beginning in 1944, at the "Charlottegrube" mine (Rydułtowy). The number of Auschwitz prisoners employed at the Hermann Göring Werke reached its peak in the spring of 1944 with a total of 3,400.

The employment of prisoners at the armaments factories of the Berghütte concern also experienced a rapid increase. While, in 1943, only one of the concern's factories (Eintrachthütte in Świętochłowice) was employing a total of 700 prisoners, by the following year, five of its factories employed a total of around 3,600 prisoners. In addition to the Eintrachthütte facilities in Świętochłowice, prisoners also worked at plants in Siemianowice (Laurahütte), Chorzów (Bismarckhütte), Sosnowiec (Sosnowitz), and Łagiewniki (Hubertushütte).

Other concerns that made use of Auschwitz prisoners included: Oberschlesische Hydrierwerke AG (ca. 4,100 prisoners at the sub-camp Blechhammer in Blachownia-Sławięcice in 1944); the Fürstengrube corporation, mentioned above (around 1,150 prisoners in 1943 and 2,200 in 1944, at the sub-camps Fürstengrube and Janinagrube); Reichsbahnausbesserungswerk (1,300 prisoners at the sub-camp Gleiwitz I in 1944); Deutsche Gasrusswerke with headquarters in Dortmund (around 1,100 prisoners from sub-camp Gleiwitz II); Weichsel-Metall-Union in Auschwitz/Oświęcim, mentioned above (1,223 prisoners in 1943 and 1,088 women in 1944; there is no data on men for that year); Erdöl Raffinerie Trzebinia GmbH (around 800 prisoners from the Trzebinia sub-camp in 1944).

Among the industrial concerns of the SS, Deutsche Ausrüstungswerke (DAW) represented the largest employer of prisoners, used in the production of ammunition boxes, furniture, and wooden building supplies. Its branches included metalworks, textile workshops (DAW Weberei und Flechterei, established on March 22, 1943), factories for salvaging aircraft (Luftwaffen Zerlege-Betriebe, from October 29, 1943). In 1944; DAW employed a total of around 3,300 prisoners, 1,300 of whom worked in the factories for salvaging airplanes. A large number of prisoners also worked at a cement plant in Goleszów, Ostdeutsche Baustoffwerke GmbH (ca. 350 prisoners in 1942, ca. 450 in 1943; ca. 1,100 in 1944).

7. The Economic Impact of the Prisoners' Labor

The prisoners' labor benefited the SS, private capital and the German state. Their work in the SS's factories represented one source of profit for organization. Until mid-1943, the SS held a virtual monopoly over the prisoners' employment. In the years 1941-42, the SS paid the state treasury the symbolic figure of 0,30 marks for each day's work by each prisoner, regardless of his or her qualifications. [20] The low labor costs and resulting possibility of reducing prices on goods made by the prisoners gave SS enterprises a significant market advantage over enterprises making use of free labor. Thus, under pressure from business circles, [21] beginning January 1, 1943, the SS raised the rate that its firms paid for each day's labor and made a differentiation in rates between skilled and unskilled workers. They subsequently paid 1.5 marks for each day's work by a skilled laborer and 0.5 marks for each unskilled laborer. Since most prisoners were considered unskilled, the actual rate was only raised slightly, by 0.2 marks — the situation, in fact, had not changed. Only after subsequent interventions in mid-1943 did the SS raise the rates that it paid once more, and in several cases, to the prevailing rate at other factories. For example, the SS cement factory at Goleschau (Goleszów) began to pay, as of July 1943, four marks per day for each skilled laborer and 1.5 marks for each unskilled assistant. Between July 1 and September 30, 1943, the factories of the Deutsche Ausrüstungswerke paid three marks per day for each skilled laborer and one mark per day for each unskilled worker or female prisoner (regardless of her qualifications). [22]

The rate paid for prisoners at other private and state enterprises (most often private firms) was significantly higher. On the basis of the March 27, 1941 contract between the SS authorities and IG Farbenindustrie — the first firm to rent prisoners from KL Auschwitz — the chemical combine agreed to pay four marks per day for the work of each skilled laborer and three marks per day for each unskilled assistant. The same rate was paid for prisoners employed at the sub-camps: Jawischowitz (coal mine) Neu-Dachs (coal mines and power-plant construction), Lagischa (construction of a power plant) and at the Krupp works in Auschwitz/Oświęcim and — following its liquidation — by the firm Union. A higher rate was introduced in May 1943 for several enterprises that sought to employ prisoners, beginning with the Eintrachthütte steelworks: six marks per day for each skilled laborer and four marks per day for each unskilled worker. This rate applied to the work of prisoners at the sub-camps: Janinagrube (coal mines), Sosnowitz (armaments factory of Ost-Maschinenbau GmbH) and Trzebinia (refinery of Erdöl Raffinerie GmbH). This rate was also used in 1943 for prisoners working at the coal mine Fürstengrube in Wesoła, but was later reduced to four and three marks, respectively.

The money offered for prisoners' labor was significantly lower than the amount paid for free labor. For private firms, the difference amounted to 50%,

---

[20] APMO, Documents from the Trial of G. Maurer, vol. 12, cards 88-90, Doc. NO-576, "Häftlingssätze", wage table from February 24, 1944 signed by the chief administrator at SS-WVHA, Gerhard Maurer.

[21] Enno Georg, *Die wirtschaftlichen Unternehmungen der SS* (Stuttgart 1963), pp. 116-17.

[22] APMO, D-AuI-3a. Monthly statistics on the employment of prisoners from KL Auschwitz and bills prepared for the prisoners' work.

and for SS enterprises, it was even greater. This explains why private firms requested that prisoners also be made available to them as a work force. The private enterprises were also happy to exchange prisoners of war, mainly English, for a labor force unbound by restrictions, both in terms of organizational questions and in terms of treatment. Such an exchange took place, for example, at the sub-camps Janinagrube and Trzebinia. The employment of prisoners from Auschwitz remained profitable, despite their lower productivity, which the firms estimated at 40-60% of that of free labor. Longer work hours, savings on work uniforms, lower standards of safety, and similar savings on other costs normally associated with employment more than compensated for the lower level of productivity. In calculations regarding the prisoners' work, daily rates, rather than hourly rates, were binding, and the length of the work day was set by the firm in question.

The prisoners' labor also represented an important source of income for the state. The concentration camps were, after all, state institutions run by the SS, and all payments collected by the SS for the prisoners' work went to the state treasury through the camp's account. [23] According to the surviving invoices (*Forderungsnachweisen*) prepared by the administration of KL Auschwitz for firms and institutions employing prisoners, more than 12,000,000 marks flowed into the state treasury in 1943 for seven months of work by male prisoners (January-May, November and December) and nine months of work by female prisoners (January-June, October-December). State revenues from leasing the prisoners grew rapidly because both the rates demanded for their employment and the number of prisoners being rented out had increased. While the state treasury received 362,356.50 marks in Januray 1943 for 288,452 days of work by the prisoners [24], in December, it received 2,041,381.45 marks for 674,147 days of work. [25] Of the latter sum, the directorate for camp construction owed 779,505.50 marks; IG Farbenindustrie, 459,844.50 marks; Energieversorgung Oberschlesien AG, 179,474 marks; Hermann Göring Werke, 100,554.40 marks; and the remainder was owed by other firms and institutions. State revenues from renting prisoners at KL Auschwitz in 1943 likely amounted to 15-20 million marks, and in 1944, 30-40 million marks.

As a labor force, the prisoners at KL Auschwitz and other concentration camps represented the cheapest labor force at the German economy's disposal. Prisoners were denied any sort of personal property; the living quarters, clothing, and food that they received did not even meet their minimal needs in these areas. The same applied with regard to their personal hygiene and health. According to the SS's figures, the total daily cost for maintaining the prisoners — in terms of nutrition, clothing and quarters — amounted to 1.34 marks for

---

[23] "[A]ll private and other firms to whom prisoner-workers were made available had to pay a certain fee to the state treasury through the administration of the given concentration camp." E. Georg, pp. 115-16.

[24] APMO, D-AuI-3a. The monthly figures for the employment of male and female prisoners are based upon 41 surviving invoices from January 1943.

[25] Ibid., according to 33 surviving invoices for December 1943.

each male prisoner and 1.22 marks for each woman. [26] If one accepts these figures (although we know that prisoners normally did not even receive the official quota of food and services allocated to them), then more than half of the revenues collected for their labor represented pure profit for the German state.

These profits were realized at the cost of the prisoners' lives and health. Despite Germany's economic difficulties and labor shortages, the predatory exploitation of prisoners at KL Auschwitz continued in its most drastic form until the end of the camp's existence. Given the concentration at the camp of machinery for mass extermination and the related possibility of replacing depleted factors of labor with new ones, the life of a prisoner at Auschwitz never achieved — even according to Nazi standards — too high a price.

---

[26] APMO, DR-F-9, WVHA, Korespondencja dotycząca formularzy [Correspondence Related to Forms] 2, p. 6. "Übersicht über die Unterhaltskosten für Häftlinge des KL,"17 March 1944.

SUB-CAMPS OF KL AUSCHWITZ

Altdorf in Stara Wieś near Pszczyna, 1942-43, forestry work for Oberforstamt Pless, ca. 20 prisoners.

Althammer at Stara Kuźnia near Halemba, Sept. 1944 — Jan. 1945, construction of a thermal power plant, 486 prisoners (Jan. 17, 1945).

Babitz at Babice near Oświęcim, March 1943 to January 1945, work on an SS farm, 159 male prisoners (Jan. 17, 1945) and around 180 female prisoners (summer 1944).

Birkenau at Brzezinka, 1943 to Jan. 1945, work on an SS farm, 204 prisoners (January 17, 1945).

Bismarckhütte in Chorzów, Sept. 1944 — Jan. 1945, work at the steelworks (today, Batory steelworks) in the production of guns and armored cars. Firm: Berghütte, Königs- und Bismarckhütte AG, 192 prisoners (Jan. 17, 1945).

Blechhammer at Sławięcice near Blachownia Śląska, Apr. 1944 — Jan. 1945, construction of a chemical plant (today, Zakłady Koksochemiczne). Firm: O/S Hydrierwerke AG, 3,958 male prisoners (Jan. 17, 1945) and 157 women prisoners (Dec. 30, 1945).

Bobrek in Bobrek near Oświęcim, Apr./May 1944 — Jan. 1945 (prisoners employed from Dec. 1943), work in a factory producing electrical parts for airplanes and submarines. Firm: Siemens-Schuckertwerke AG, 213 male prisoners (Jan. 17, 1945) and 38 female prisoners (Dec. 30, 1944).

Brünn in Brno (Czech territory), Oct. 1943 — Jan. 1945, work on completing the construction of the main building of the Technical Academy for the SS and Police. Employer: Administration C of SS-WVHA, *Bauleitung* Brünn, 250 prisoners (Oct. 1943), 36 prisoners (Jan. 17, 1945).

Budy at Budy near Oświęcim, Apr. 1943 — Autumn 1944, work on an SS agricultural holding, several hundred female prisoners.

Budy at Budy near Oświęcim, Apr. 1942 — Jan. 1945 (with a break in the autumn and winter of 1942/43), work on an SS agricultural holding, 313 prisoners (Jan. 17, 1945).

Budy at Budy near Oświęcim, June 1942 — Spring 1943, work on SS farms at leveling (ditch-digging), as well as cleaning and deepening fish ponds, around 400 female prisoners from a punishment company (summer 1942).

Charlottegrube in Rydułtowy, Sept. 1944 — Jan. 1945, work in the Charlottegrube coal mine (today, Rydułtowy Mine) at mining coal and expanding the mine. Firm: Hermann Göring Werke, 833 prisoners (Jan. 17, 1945).

Chełmek in Chełmek, Oct. — Dec. 1942, work for a shoe factory (deepening and cleaning a water-collection pond). Firm: Ota Schlesische Schuhwerke, formerly "Bata", ca. 150 prisoners.

Eintrachthütte in Świętochłowice, May 1943 — Jan. 1945, work at the Eintrachthütte steelworks (today, ZUT Zgoda) in the production of antiaircraft guns. Firm: Berghütte — OSMAG and OST-Maschinenbau, 1,297 prisoners (Jan. 17, 1945).

Freudenthal in Bruntal (Czech territory) 1944 — Jan. 1945, firm Emmerich Machold, 301 female prisoners (Dec. 30, 1944).

Fürstengrube in Wesoła near Mysłowice, Sept. 1943 — Jan. 1945, work in the Fürstengrube mine at mining coal and building a new mine. Firm: Fürstengrube GmbH, 1,283 prisoners (Jan. 17, 1945).

Gleiwitz I in Gliwice, March 1944 — Jan. 1945, repair of railroad tracks. Firm: Reichsbahnausbesserungswerk, 1,336 prisoners (Jan. 17, 1945).

Gleiwitz II in Gliwice, May 1944 — Jan. 1945, production of lamp-black (women); repair and maintenance of machines, expansion of the factory (men). Firm: Deutsche Gasrusswerke GmbH (currently Gliwickie Zakłady Chemiczne Carbochem), 740 male prisoners (Jan. 17, 1945) and 371 female prisoners (Dec. 30, 1944).

Gleiwitz III in Gliwice, July 1944 — Jan. 1945, work at Gleiwitzer Hütte (today, Gliwickie Zakłady Urządzeń Technicznych) at renovating the plant and then at producing arms, ammunition and wheels for railway cars. Firm: Zieleniewski-Maschinen und Waggonbau GmbH, Cracow, 609 prisoners (Jan. 17, 1945).

Gleiwitz IV in Gliwice, June 1944 — Jan. 1945, work at expanding the barracks as well as repair and renovation of military vehicles, 444 prisoners (Jan. 17, 1945).

Golleschau in Goleszów, July 1942 — Jan. 1945, work at an SS cement factory. Firm: Ostdeutsche Baustoffwerke GmbH — Golleschauer Portland Zement AG, 1,008 prisoners Jan. (17, 1945).

Günthergrube in Lędziny, Feb. 1944 — Jan. 1945, coal mining at the "Piast" mine and construction of the Günthergrube coal mine (today, "Ziemowit" mine). Firm: Fürstlich Plessische Bergwerke AG, 586 prisoners (Jan. 17, 1945).

Harmense in Harmęże near Oświęcim, Dec. 1941 — summer 1943, work on an SS farm (raising chickens, rabbits and fish), around 70 prisoners.

Harmense in Harmęże near Oświęcim, June. 1942 — Jan. 1945, work at an SS farm (raising chickens and rabbits), ca. 50 female prisoners.

Hindenburg in Zabrze, Aug. 1944 — Jan. 1945, work at the foundry Donnersmarkhütte (today, Zabrze steelworks) in the production of armaments and munition. Firm: Vereinigte Oberschlesische Hüttenwerke AG, 50 male prisoners (Jan. 17, 1945) and 470 female prisoners (Dec. 30, 1944).

Hubertushütte in Lagiewniki, Dec. 1944 — Jan. 1945, work at the Hubertushütte foundry (today, Zygmunt). Firm: Berghütte König und Bismarkhütte AGs-, 202 prisoners (Jan. 17, 1945).

Janinagrube in Libiąż, Sept. 1943 — Jan. 1945, work at the coal mine Janinagrube, mining coal. Firm: Fürstengrube GmbH, 853 prisoners (Jan. 17, 1945).

Jawischowitz in Jawiszowice, Aug. 1942 — Jan. 1945, mining coal in the "Brzeszcze-Jawischowitz" mine and construction work above ground. Firm: Reichswerke Hermann Göring, 1,988 prisoners (Jan. 17, 1945).

Kobior in Kobiór, 1942-43, forestry work, employer: Oberforstamt Pless, 158 prisoners (Apr. 25, 1943).

Lagischa in Łagisza, Sept. 1943 — Sept. 1944, construction of the thermal power plant "Walter". Firm: Energie-Versorgung Oberschlesien AG, ca. 1,000 prisoners.

Laurahütte in Siemianowice, Apr. 1944 — Jan. 1945, work at the Laurahütte foundry (today, "Jedność") in the production of antiaircraft guns. Firm: Berghütte — Königs- und Bismarckhütte, 937 prisoners (Jan. 17, 1945).

Lichtewerden in Světlá, (Czech territory), Nov. 1944 — Jan. 1945, work in a thread factory. Firm: G. A. Buhl und Sohn, 300 female prisoners (Dec. 30, 1944).

Monowitz (Buna) in Monowice near Oświęcim, Oct. 1942 — Jan. 1945 (employment from Mar./Apr. 1941), construction of a chemical plant (today, Zakłady Chemiczne Oświęcim). Firm: IG Farbenindustrie AG, 10,223 prisoners (Jan. 17, 1945).

Neu-Dachs in Jaworzno, June 1943 — Jan. 1945, work in the coal mines (today, the mines "Komuna Paryska" and "Jaworzno") and construction of the power plant "Wilhelm" (today, "Jaworzno"). Firm: Energieversorgung Oberschlesien AG, 3,664 prisoners (Jan. 17, 1945).

Neustadt in Prudnik (Sept. 1944 — Jan. 1945), weaving at a textile factory (today, Prudnickie Zakłady Przemysłu Bawełnianego). Firm: Schlesische Feinweberei AG, 399 female prisoners (Dec. 30, 1944).

Plawy in Pławy near Oświęcim, 1944? — Jan. 1945, work on an SS agricultural holding, 138 male prisoners (Jan. 17, 1945) and ca. 200 female prisoners (Jan. 17, 1945).

Radostowitz in Radostowice near Pszczyna, 1942-43, with a break during the winter of 1942-43, forestry work. Employer: Oberforstamt Pless, ca. 20 prisoners.

Raisko in Rajsko, June 1943 — Jan. 1945, work on an SS agricultural holding (horticulture, experimental cultivation of kok-saghyz, around 300 female prisoners (1944).

Sonderkommando Kattowitz in Katowice, Jan. 1944 — Jan. 1945, construction of a shelter and barracks for the Gestapo, ten prisoners.

Sosnowitz I in Sosnowiec, Aug. 1943 — Feb. 1944, renovation of offices, 100 prisoners.

Sosnowitz II in Sosnowiec, May 1944 — Jan. 1945, work at a foundry (today, Cedler) producing shells and barrels for anti-aircraft guns. Firm: Berghütte-Ost-Maschinenbau GmbH, 863 prisoners (Jan. 17, 1945).

Sośnica, near Gliwice, July — Aug. 1940, dismantling of a prisoner-of-war camp, ca. 30 prisoners.

SS Hütte Porombka in Międzybrodzie, Oct./Nov. 1940 — Jan. 1945, construction and maintenance of an SS rest home; several dozen prisoners for its construction and several female prisoners for its maintenance.

2 SS Bauzug in Karlsruhe, Sept. — Oct. 1944, removing rubble from the city and repairing train tracks. Employer: Administration C of SS-WVHA, ca 500 prisoners. [27]

---

[27] The prisoners were housed in freight trains. Around the middle of October 1944, the sub-camp was subordinated to the concentration camp Buchenwald; several days later, it was renamed "7-*SS Eisenbahnbaubrigade*" and transferred to Stuttgart.

Trzebinia in Trzebinia, Aug. 1944 — Jan. 1945, expansion of a refinery. Firm: Erdöl Raffinerie GmbH, 641 prisoners (Jan. 17, 1945).

Tschechowitz I — Bombensucherkommando at Czechowice Dziedzice, Aug. — Sep. 1944, removal of unexploded bombs from the grounds of an oil refinery and the neighbouring area. Firm: Vacuum Oil Company, ca. 100 prisoners.

Tscheschowitz II — Vacuum at Czechowice-Dziedzice, Sept. 1944 — Jan. 1945, removal of rubble and protection of the refinery. Firm: Vacuum Oil Company, 561 prisoners (Jan. 17, 1945).

HELENA KUBICA

CHILDREN AND YOUTHS AT KL AUSCHWITZ

Of the crimes that the Nazis committed during the war, particularly egregious were those committed against children and young people. Children and youths perished not only as a direct result of military activity, but also from executions, pacification, forced resettlement, and captivity in prison and various types of Nazi camps — youth, penal, and concentration camps. The youngest children, if they displayed "Nordic" racial characteristics, were taken from their families and sent to Germanization centers. The greatest number of children, however, perished in ghettoes and at centers for mass extermination. Among the latter, the Auschwitz camp played a central role, serving simultaneously as a concentration camp and as a center for mass extermination.

On the basis of surviving documents, it is difficult to establish how many children and youths were deported to the camp, how many were registered there, and how many died or were killed. On the basis of the surviving documents from KL Auschwitz related to deportations to the camp — mainly name lists from individual transports and various estimates — one can state that of the at least 1.3 million people deported to the camp, around 234,000 were children and young people. [1] This figure includes around 220,000 Jews, more than 11,000 Gypsies, and the remainder are children of other nationalities: Poles, Byelorussians, Ukrainians, Russians and others. [2]

The fate of the children deported to the camp was tragic. Jewish children were normally murdered immediately upon arrival, along with old people, the handicapped, and everyone who was otherwise unable to work. A group of several hundred Jewish children, mainly twins, represented one exception; they were used for criminal medical experiments. Another exception were the children from the ghetto at Theresienstadt (Terezin). Only certain Jewish youths considered fit for labor were allowed to live and registered as prisoners at the camp. Under the difficult living conditions there, however, they perished

---

[1] For the sake of this study, prisoners under the age of 15 are considered to be "children", and prisoners aged 15-18, "youths" or "young people". The camp authorities used similar age rankings in correspondence and reports on prisoner employment. Where a lack of access to original camp documents has made it necessary to use other authors' figures, their age rankings are specified.

[2] Specific data for each nationality will only be available after a computer analysis of the comprehensive card-files for prisoners is completed.

quickly. Although almost all non-Jewish children and youths went through registration and became prisoners at the camp for a certain period of time, they came to share the same fate as most of the deportees in relatively short order.

The surviving camp documents contain the names and numbers of more than 21,000 children and youths who were registered at the camp. Children and youths perished rapidly under the living conditions that prevailed at the camp, so, at any point in time, they represented only an insignificant percentage of the total prisoners. Their number was lowest in the first years of the camp's existence, increased slightly thereafter, and then peaked in the second half of 1944. According to the daily employment records for prisoners at KL Auschwitz II-Birkenau, on April 23, 1944, there were 2,846 male children and youths living at the camp (not including Gypsies); on August 21, 1944, 779 boys (14 and below); on October 2-3, 1944, 2,510 boys and girls.[3] From other documents (delivery receipts for foodstuffs from the warehouse),[4] we know that several days before the camp was evacuated — on January 10, 1945 — there were 611 children of both genders at the women's camp at Birkenau.

In evaluating the data cited above, we have to keep in mind that these figures are incomplete because the Nazis destroyed most of the documents that contained such statistics. That the surviving documents rarely give separate figures for children represents yet another difficulty for research. When they were registered at the camp, children received numbers from the same series as the adult prisoners. Documents in which children appear as a separate statistical category (see examples above) are relatively few.

A special category of child prisoners at KL Auschwitz were those born at the camp, who numbered at the very least — based on the surviving documents — 680.

1. Jewish Children and Youths

The largest group of children and youths shipped to the camp were of Jewish origin. They began arriving, along with adults, in the first months of 1942 as part of the Nazi campaign for the "final solution of the Jewish question", or the complete extermination of Europe's Jewish population.

According to the fragmentary data that have been preserved, of the at least 1.1 million Jews deported to KL Auschwitz, around 220,000 were children and young people, or around 20% of all the Jews deported to the camp.

Among the first Jews brought to the camp as part of the "final solution" were Jews from Slovakia. The transports from Slovakia brought not only adults, but also a large number of Jewish youths and even children under 14. Based on the surviving transport lists from April 17 — July 17, 1942, containing the names of 8,749 males, we find among them 656 children and

---

[3] APMO, D-AuII-3a, vol. 8/1, 8/2, 8/3. Daily figures for the employment of male and female prisoners at KL Birkenau.

[4] APMO, D-AuII-4/20, segr. 25. "Różne" [Various]; receipts for food that had been taken from the camp warehouses for children, pregnant and nursing women on the grounds of the women's camp at Birkenau from January 8 and January 10, 1945.

youths. The youngest were only 11-12 years old. They remained at the camp for only a brief period; most of them perished shortly thereafter. [5]

Among the Jewish women deported from Slovakia, there were also a large number of young girls. The register of names from the first transport to Auschwitz, from Poprad, on March 25, 1942 (it arrived at the camp on March 26), bears witness to this fact. In this transport of 999 women, there were 116 girls 16-17, as well as one girl who was only 14. [6]

Unfortunately, other documents related to the transports of Jews from Slovakia do not list the ages of the deportees, so we cannot establish the total number of Jewish youths and children deported to the camp from Slovakia. We only know — based on second-hand accounts — that the proportion of children and young people in the transports was significant.

The name lists for the transports of French Jews, on the other hand, mainly sent to Auschwitz via the transit camp in Drancy, have survived in their entirety. From March 27, 1942, to August 11, 1944, more than 69,000 French Jews were delivered to the camp in 69 larger and two smaller transports. Of these Jews, more than 9,800 were youths and children (17 and under) of whom 7,400 were children (14 and under). The largest number of Jewish children deported from France arrived in 1942. In the transport from August 19, 1942, for example, more than half of the 1000 Jewish deportees — 538 — were children; in the transport from August 26 of the same year, there were 553 children out of a total of 1057 people. [7]

The name lists of Jews deported from Belgium in 1942-44 have also survived practically in their entirety. Of the 24,906 Belgian citizens of Jewish origin deported in 27 transports to Auschwitz, there were more than 4,600 children and youths, 16 and under. A transport of 1,000 Jews from September 1, 1942, for example, carried a total of 344 children; the transport from September 26, 1942, carried 523 children and youths out a total of 1,742 prisoners. [8]

Name lists have also survived for the transports of Jews from Germany (mainly from Berlin) and Austria. Of the more than 20,000 German Jews deported to the camp in the years 1942-44, there were more than 2,500 children and young people (to age 17). [9]

Transport Nr. 32 from March 2, 1943, carried along with Jews from Germany, 158 Norwegian Jews, of whom 22 were children (14 and under). A total of 84 children and youths (17 and younger) were deported from Norway and exterminated at KL Auschwitz. [10]

Jews from Austria were routed to the camp mainly through the ghetto in Terezin (Theresienstadt). Only 200 Jews were sent directly from Vienna,

[5] APMO, D-AuII-2, vol. 1-2, transport lists of Jews for the period April 17 — July 17, 1942.

[6] APMO, RSHA-3/128, inventory number 155590, "Transporty RSHA ze Słowacji w 1942 r. [RSHA Transports from Slovakia in 1942]".

[7] APMO, D-RF-3/1-74, vol. 1-26, transport lists from Drancy.
See also Serge Klarsfeld, *Le Memorial de la deportation des Juifs de France* (Paris, 1979).

[8] Serge Klarsfeld and Maxime Steinberg, *Memorial de la deportation des Juifs de Belgique* (Bruxelles, 1982), pp. 22-23.

[9] APMO, D-RF-3/121/1-16. Gestapo Berlin — Auschwitz Transporte.

[10] Ibid.; *Dokumentensammlung über "Die Deportierung der Juden aus Norwegen nach Auschwitz" zusammengestellt von Towiah Friedmann* (Ramat Gan, 1963).

between March and September 1944. Among them were fifteen children (14 and under). [11]

In July 1942, transports of Jews from Holland began to arrive at the camp on a mass scale, mainly from the transit camp at Westerbork. In the years 1942-44, more than 60,000 Jews were shipped to the camp from Holland in a total of 68 transports. If we examine the Dutch Red Cross's statistical analyses for only 38 of these transports, which list the number of children up to 15 years of age (in some cases, to 16 years of age) and youth (to 17 years of age), we find that of the 31,661 Jews brought to the camp in these transports, there were 3,832 youths and children. [12] The largest number of Jewish children arrived from Holland in 1942, especially during July and August. A transport from August 14, for example, which held a total of 505 male and female prisoners, contained as many as 129 children (to age 15) and eight youths (15-17). As was the case with other transports, these children were dispatched immediately after the selection to be exterminated. The only exception was a transport from June 3 (it arrived at the camp on June 6, 1944), which held 17 children. Everyone who arrived in this transport, from adults down to children of only two years of age, were sent directly to the camp without a selection being conducted. Most likely, an exception was made because these prisoners — skilled workers from the firm Philips AG and their families — represented to the Nazi authorities a particularly valuable labor force, indispensible for specialized work at armaments plants. [13]

Of the ca. 300,000 Polish Jews sent to the camp, we can only estimate the number of children and youths. We can base such an estimate on the existing data on the demographic structure of the Jewish population that had to reside in the Łódź ghetto. These data show that in January 1944, of the ca. 70,000 Jews, more than 17,000 were aged 19 or below, or 24% of the total population. [14] This proportion barely changed at all up to the end of the ghetto's existence in August 1944, when its residents were deported to KL Auschwitz. If we assume a similar age structure for the other transports of Polish Jews to the camp, we arrive at the figure of 72,000 Jewish youths and children.

We also lack specific data on the age structure of the around 10,000 Jews deported from Yugoslavia between August 1942 and August 1944. [15] We only know that of the 1,800 Jews deported to KL Auschwitz in August 1942 from the transit camp in Tenje, there were around 700 children; [16] of the 323 Jews deported from the Prekmurja area in Slovenia on May 2, 1944, there were 48

---

[11] APMO, D-RF-3/119/1. Gestapo-Transportlisten, Auschwitz-Transporte.

[12] APMO, Collection Studies, vol. 26, „Transports of Jews from Holland to Auschwitz, Analyzed by the Dutch Red Cross".

[13] APMO, Collection of Materials, vol. 191; syg. Mat./1416; Günther Schwarberg, *Dziecióbójca. Eksperymenty lekarza SS w Neuengamme* (Warszawa, 1987), p. 20.

[14] Abraham Melezin, *Przyczynek do znajomości stosunków demograficznych wśród ludności żydowskiej w Łodzi, Krakowie i Lublinie podczas okupacji niemieckiej* (Łódź , 1946), pp. 44, 51. See also the report from the inspection of the Łódź ghetto, submitted on January 24, 1944 by Horn, head of the company *Ostindustrie* to the chief of SS-WVHA Pohl, entitled *Przedsiębiorstwa getta łódzkiego i Ostindustrie* ("Industries in the Łódź Ghetto and *Ostindustrie*) in Artur Eisenbach, *Hitlerowska polityka zagłady Żydów* (Warszawa, 1961). p. 562.

[15] Franciszek Piper, *Auschwitz: How many perished; Jews, Poles, Gypsies* ... (Cracow, 1992), p. 53.

[16] Ibid., pp. 35, 36.

children and youths.[17] (Yugoslavian Jews, it should be pointed out, also arrived at Auschwitz in transports from Hungary and Italy).

At the end of 1942, numerous transports began arriving at KL Auschwitz from Terezin (Theresienstadt) in Czech territory. Initially, these transports were subjected to the same treatment as other Jewish transports — the Jewish prisoners went through a selection, after which the majority, including children, were sent to the gas chambers. Beginning in September 1943, however, transports of Jews from Theresienstadt (Terezin) were no longer subjected to selections; instead, the Jews from these transports were held in a special family camp on the grounds of Birkenau, created for propaganda purposes: the "Theresienstadt Family Camp" (*Familienlager Theresienstadt*).

In September 1943, this special camp held around 5,000 people, including more than 470 children and youths, 17 and under (including more than 280 children from two months to 14 years of age). In December 1943, an additional 4,984 Jews from the Theresienstadt (Terezin) ghetto were brought to the camp, including 568 children and youths (of whom 467 were children, 14 and under). On May 16, 17, and 19, 1944, new transports arrived, carrying a total of 7,949 people, of whom more than 700 were 17 or under (including 500 children, 14 and below).

The Jewish prisoners housed in the "family camp" received better treatment and were granted certain privileges: they could correspond, were not subjected to selections, and could live together as families, although they were divided by gender. Smaller children were allowed to remain with their mothers. Something quite extraordinary, given the general conditions at the camp, was the creation of a "kindergarten" for younger children in two of the camp's barracks, along with a school for older children. At the kindergarten, the younger children learned songs and poems and played games. The older children, aged 6-10, were divided into three classes for schooling. The older boys were even allowed to write a "newspaper" on packing paper that they had received. The camp administrators even allowed the children to organize a puppet theater. On a simple stage erected inside one of the barracks, the children held performances twice a week. Children at the kindergarten also received better rations: specially-prepared soup, at times a larger portion of beet jam or margarine, or even pats of butter.

Six months after the first transports had arrived, on the night of March 8-9, 1944, the family camp for Jews from Theresienstadt was partially liquidated. The 3,791 surviving men, women, and children from the transports of September 1943 were taken by truck to the gas chambers and exterminated. The final "liquidation" of the family camp took place on July 10-11 and 11-12, 1944; the remaining 7,000 Jews, including almost all the children, were killed.[18]

---

[17] *Auschwitz-Birkenau, KL Koncentracijsko taborišče* (Maribor, 1982), pp. 512-75.

[18] Before the final "liquidation" of the Jewish family camp, a selection was conducted. As a result, several thousand young and healthy men and women were kept as laborers, as well as the twins upon whom SS doctor J. Mengele was conducting experiments, and a group of around 90 boys, age 14-16, who were supposed to be sent to the *Reich*, but ended up, fact, in the penal company at the men's camp (BIId) at Birkenau.

Miroslav Kárný, "Terezinski obóz familijny w Brzezince", *Zeszyty Oświęcimskie* 20 (1993); John Freund, *After those Fifty Years. Memoirs of the Birkenau Boys*. 1992.

On the basis of the surviving, nearly complete transport lists, we can calculate that during the years 1942-44, more than 46,000 Jews were sent to KL Auschwitz from Theresienstadt (Terezín), including at least 6,460 children and youths, to age 17 (including more than 5,000 who were 14 or younger). Only very few survived the camp. [19]

In March 1943, Jews began to be deported from Greece to Auschwitz. Between March 15 and August 7, 1943, 48,633 Jews were deported from Thessaloniki, of whom only 11,747 survived the initial selection. The remaining deportees — almost 80% of the Jews who had arrived on the transports, including ca. 12,000 children — were immediately killed in the gas chambers. [20] In 1944, another ca. 6,000 people were deported from Athens and the islands of Corfu and Rhodes. These transports also contained a significant, but unspecified, number of children.

Children also arrived at Auschwitz in the transports of Jews from Italy, whose deportations began in the second half of 1943. The first transport, numbering 1,030 people, arrived in October 23, 1943, from Rome. The transport included 296 children and youths (aged 17 or younger). Up to 193 had yet to reach their tenth birthday, and 20 of them were babies, only several months old. [21] Altogether, more than 7,500 Jews were deported from Italy between October 23, 1943, and October 28, 1944. With the exception of the first transport of Jews from Rome mentioned above, we lack the necessary documentation to establish how many of the deportees were children or youths. Only nine Jewish children from Italy survived to witness the camp's liberation.

In mid-May 1944, the mass deportation of Jews from Hungary to Auschwitz began. Although the deportations basically took place over a span of only two months, around 438,000 Jews were deported to the camp. The transports of Jews from Hungary distinguished themselves by the exceptionally large number of children that they carried, as confirmed by numerous accounts and testimonies from former prisoners and other witnesses, as well as secret reports that the camp resistance movement smuggled out of the camp.

Not all the children faced immediate death in the gas chambers. Beginning in June 1944, some of them were shipped along with adults to transit camps (*Durchgangslager*) for a short period of time. Entire transports would be sent to such camps without an initial selection taking place. The children only remained in the transit camps, however, for a short period; they either died from the severe conditions or were sent to their deaths after a selection was conducted. A few teenage youths considered fit to work were sent with adult prisoners to other camps inside the Third Reich or to the Auschwitz

---

[19] APMO, D-RF-3/84-87, vol. 1-27, photocopies of the transport lists of Jews shipped from the Theresienstadt ghetto to Auschwitz in 1942-44. The list of children and young people is incomplete because several photocopies of transport lists are illegible.

[20] Danuta Czech, "Deportation und Vernichtung der griechischen Juden im KL Auschwitz", *Hefte von Auschwitz*, 11 (1970), pp. 17-24; Miriam Nowitch, "Los dzieci żydowskich w Grecji", in *Dzieci i młodociani w latach II wojny światowej* (Warszawa, 1982), p. 81.

[21] Liliana Picciotto Fargion, *L'occupazione tedesca e gli ebrei di Roma* (Milano, 1979), pp. 43-73; *Il libro della memoria. Gli Ebrei deportati dall' Italia (1943-1945)*.

sub-camps — for example, Trzebinia (a group of more than 100 boys aged 14-17) or Jawischowitz (a group of several dozen boys). [22] Unfortunately, the number of Jewish children brought to the camp in transports from Hungary remains unknown, since no documents on the subject have survived. On the basis of the data we do have, however, regarding the age structure of the Hungarian Jews, we know that in 1941, youths and children, 20 and below, made up 22.2% of the total Jewish population. If we round the percentage down to 20% and assume that no significant change in the age structure took place before the deportations — that is, until 1944 — we can estimate that of the 438,000 Jews deported from Hungary, around 90,000 were children and youths. [23]

A certain number of children and youths also arrived at KL Auschwitz from other concentration camps. There are few surviving documents regarding such transfers, however. We know, for example, that on July 26, 1944, 524 women and 899 children were brought to Auschwitz from the Stutthof concentration camp. [24] On August 1, 1944, 129 Jewish boys aged 8-14, originally from Kowno in Lithuania, were brought to Auschwitz from the concentration camp in Dachau. On September 12, 300 Jewish children arrived at the camp from the Kowno region and were killed the same day in a gas chamber. [25]

2. Gypsy Children and Youths

After the Jews, the largest group of children and youths to be sent to KL Auschwitz were Gypsies. An examination of the data contained in the registration books shows that of the close to 21,000 Gypsies registered at the Gypsy camp in Birkenau, there were more than 11,000 children and youths, including 9,432 children (up to age 14). Among the latter children, 378 were born at the camp. [26]

Given the camouflaged, propagadistic character of the Gypsy camp, the Gypsy children were guaranteed better living conditions for a limited period of time. Because it was a family camp, the children could stay together with their relatives. They also received better rations, according to the norms for

---

[22] APMO, Collection Trzebinia, nr. mikr. 1340/7, 8, 9; APMO, Collection Brzeszcze, segr. I, p. 218.

[23] Sari Reuveni, "Antisemitism in Hungary 1945-1946. After the Holocaust: National Attitudes to Jews", *Holocaust and Genocide Studies* vol. 4, Nr. 1, pp. 41-62. Contains the age structure of Jews in Hungary in percentages for the years 1930, 1941, and 1946. I rounded down the percentage in which I was interested, for the ages 0-20 in 1941, because it went two years beyond the age-range for youths used in this study.

[24] Archives Museum Stutthof (henceforth AMSt). Collection of orders from the commander of the camp, I-I-1, nr. 49.

[25] APMO, Files of the Camp Resistance, vol. VII, card 460; APMO, Collection of Testimonies, vol. 117, card 2-9, statement of former prisoner Łazar Grejs. See also AMSt, Syg. mikr. 264 for a photocopy of a telegram from the Commandant of KL Stutthof, P.W. Hoppe, to SS-WVHA, as well as syg. 1-II-14, registration book for prisoners.

[26] APMO, D-AuII-3/1/1, D-AuII-3/2/1, ledgers for men and women held at the Gypsy camp; APMO, D-AuI-3a, vol. 6, "Stärkemeldungen" AuII-FKL dated July 17, 1944, and July 28, 1944, daily reports on the number of female prisoners at Birkenau referring to section BIIe (the Gypsy camp).

so-called "Eastern workers". [27] A "Kindergarten" for children at the age of six and under was established at the Gypsy camp in the summer of 1943 on the orders of Dr. Josef Mengele. A playground was installed in the enclosed area between Barrack 31 and the washroom, including a sandbox, carousel and seesaws. High-ranking SS officers and civilian visitors often photographed the children playing there for propaganda purposes. [28] The children in the "Kindergarten", especially twins, were the true source of Dr. Mengele's interest, to be used for his criminal medical experiments.

After a short time, however, the effects of overcrowding in the barracks, along with the catastrophic hygienic and sanitary conditions, caused by a lack of water, began to take their toll. An epidemic of typhus broke out and greatly accelerated the death rate among the Gypsies, particularly among the children. After a certain time, the children and pregnant women stopped receiving higher-quality rations. At the same time, Himmler gave SS doctors a secret order to "liquidate" Gypsies who fell ill, particularly children, in a discreet way inside the provisional hospital on the grounds of the Gypsy camp. [29] This shows quite clearly that the "Kindergarten", as well as the higher quality rations and special treatment that the Gypsy prisoners had received, were simply a camouflage to conceal the actual goal behind their imprisonment — namely, their extermination.

At the end of May 1944, the step-by-step liquidation of the Gypsy camp began. Some of the men, women, and children — mainly German Gypsies — were gathered together and housed temporarily at the main camp, before being sent on August 2, 1944, to camps in the *Reich* proper. The remaining men, women and children at the Gypsy camp — around 3,000 — were exterminated on the same day in Crematorium V's gas chamber. This completed the liquidation of the Gypsy camp. [30] On September 26 and October 5, Gypsy children arrived at Birkenau once more. They were brought from KL Buchenwald. These children most certainly included those who had been transferred, along with their parents, to KL Buchenwald in August 1944, at the time of the Gypsy camp's liquidation. [31] They were also killed in the gas chambers.

---

[27] Letter, Persönlicher Stab Reichsführer SS [Personal staff of the *Reichsführer* SS — i.e., Himmler's staff] to *SS-Obergruppenführer* Oswald Pohl, head of SS-WVHA, 15 April 1943. Archiwum Głównej Komisji Badania Zbrodni przeciwko Narodowi Polskiemu — Instytut Pamięci Narodowej. Microfilm documents, sygn. M-315.

[28] Ota Kraus and Erich Kulka, *Die Todesfabrik* (Berlin, 1958), p. 169.

[29] Autobiography of Rudolf Höss, in *KL Auschwitz Seen by the SS: Höss, Broad, Kremer* (Oświęcim, 1978), p. 68.

[30] See the testimony of former prisoners Kazimierz Smoleń, Bertold Epstein, and Otto Wolken for the trial of former camp commandant Höss in: APMO, Höss Trial, vol. 1, card 26; vol. 5, card 31; vol. 6, card 43.

[31] "The Manuscript of Salmen Lewental" in *Amidst a Nightmare of Crime — Manuscripts of Members of Sonderkommando* (Oświęcim, 1973), p. 129.

See also the report of the *SS-Standortarzt* at KL Buchenwald from August 5, 1944, regarding the number and ages of the Gypsies who arrived on August 3, 1944 from KL Auschwitz in: Reimund Schnabel, *Macht ohne Moral. Eine Dokumentation über die SS* (Frankfurt a. M., 1957), p. 152.

3. Polish Children and Youths

Polish children made their first appearance at the camp in June-August 1940, when the first transports of Poles began to arrive at the camp. They were schoolchildren or Scouts who had been brought along with adults from other prisons or who had simply been caught in the streets during round-ups.

Based on the incomplete name lists for the first prisoners arriving from Tarnów, Wiśnicz, Silesia, Cracow and Warsaw between June and mid-August, we can establish that at least 100 of the 3,000 prisoners were teenage boys. [32] Later transports of men also brought boys, aged 15-17, and in isolated cases, even 13- and 14-year-old boys to the camp. The partially-preserved lists of newly-arrived prisoners registered at the camp, the *"Zuganslisten"*, confirm this fact. These lists, which include each prisoner's date of birth, show, for example, that the transport from Warsaw that arrived at the camp on February 1, 1941, carried 39 youths among its 596 prisoners. The transports that arrived on April 5 and 7, 1941, also contained a large number of younger prisoners, including 14-year-olds. [33]

The situation was similar for the first transports of Polish women to the camp, beginning in April 1942. In addition to the adults, there were schoolgirls and teenage Girl Scouts who had been arrested for cooperating with the resistance movement, as well as other girls being held as part of the German occupier's campaign of repression against Polish youth.

In December 1942 and February 1943, entire families were expelled from the Zamość region and deported to the camp. Three transports (December 13 and 16, 1942, and February 5, 1943) brought a total of 1,301 Poles to the camp, including at least 119 children and youths of both sexes. [34] The fate of these children at the camp, particularly that of the boys, was tragic. After several weeks at the men's camp (BIb) at Birkenau, they were murdered on the orders of the camp authorities with phenol injections in Block 20 (HKB) at the main camp. To destroy all evidence of their crimes, the SS camp doctors fabricated death certificates giving various illnesses as the cause of death. In doing so, they were complying with the regulations of the Main Security Office for the Reich (*Reichsicherheitshauptamt*) which required that Poles, unlike Jews, should die a natural death (or, at least, be documented as having died such a death). [35]

The first Polish children to be killed by injection were two boys: nine-year-old Tadeusz Rycyk and 12-year-old Mieczysław Rycaj. They were murdered

---

[32] Irena Strzelecka, "Die ersten Polen im KL Auschwitz I", Hefte von Auschwitz 18 (1990), pp. 68-145; APMO, Numerical Register of the the Polish Red Cross [*Książka numerowa PCK*]; Helena Kubica, "Pierwszy transport z Warszawy", *Biuletyn Informacyjny MKO*, Nr. 10/211 (October 1978), pp. 1-4.

[33] APMO, Collection *Zugangsliste*, vol. 1-5, lists of newly-arrived prisoners for the period January 7 — December 22, 1941.

[34] Calculations based on documents and materials in the archives of APMO.

[35] Report of *SS-Untersturmführer* Heinrich Kinna from December 1942 regarding a transport of Poles to KL Auschwitz from the Zamość region, contained in: *Zamojszczyzna. Sonderlaboratorium SS. Zbiór dokumentów polskich i niemieckich z okresu okupacji hitlerowskiej*, vol. I (Lublin, 1977), p. 220.

on January 21, 1943. On February 23, another 39 boys were murdered, and on March 1, a new group of 80 boys. The last group included not only boys from Zamość, but other also Polish, Jewish and Russian boys from earlier transports. [36] The girls deported from Zamość were not subjected to such a "spearing" campaign, but the majority of them nevertheless perished from typhus and the horrible sanitary and hygienical conditions that prevailed at the women's camp at Birkenau.

The next largest group of Polish children and youths arrived at the camp in August-September 1944, deported from Warsaw after the uprising had broken out. At least 13,095 Polish men and women were dispatched from the transit camp at Pruszków to Auschwitz on August 12 and September 4, 13, and 17, 1944. Among these prisoners were 1,400 children to age 18, including 684 who were 14 or under. [37]

When we speak about Polish youths and children at the camp, we should not forget those who never formally became prisoners at the camp, but were held along with adults in Block 11 at the main camp, the so-called "Death Block", beginning in February 1943. These Poles, prisoners of the Katowice Gestapo, were called "police prisoners" at the camp. They were tried by the police court-martial (*Standgericht*) from Katowice, which held special sessions in one of the rooms on the ground floor of Block 11. For alleged political and criminal acts against the *Reich* — including such minor offenses as stealing or smuggling food or running away from forced labor — the "police prisoners" were sentenced, as a rule, to death. After the court completed its session, the condemned were executed in front of the Execution Wall, situated in the courtyard to Block 11 (or, beginning in 1944, inside the crematoria at Birkenau).

From the fragmentary lists of names of men and women condemned to death by the police court-martial, compiled illegally by the camp resistance movement, one discovers that on September 2, 1943, the court-martial condemned 94 prisoners to death, including eight children under 17. One child, Leokadia Samarzyk, was only nine. The court-martial also condemned children to death, along with adults, at its sessions on October 22, November 29 and December 29, 1944. [38]

A rare exception was the case of four girls held temporarily at the women's camp in Birkenau while awaiting trial. The court-martial failed to pass sentence on the four girls: Augustyna Borowiec (14), Maria Bar, Maria Orlicka, and Rozalia Kowalczyk (each under 15). The court-martial ordered

[36] APMO, Files of the Camp Resistance, vol. V, cards. 49-50; APMO, Książka kostnicy [Mortuary Register], entries for January 21, 1943 (p. 46), February 23, 1943 (pp. 77-8), March 1, 1943 (pp. 83-5); Death certificates prepared by the camp doctor for Mieczysław Ryca (actually Rycaj), born May 3, 1930; and for Tadeusz Rycyk, born October 9, 1933, Microfilm Nr. 227/43.

[37] APMO, Files of the Camp Resistance, vol. VIIIa, numerical list of men sent from Warsaw to KL Auschwitz after the armed uprising, illegally assembled by prisoners at the camp; APMO, Files of the Camp Resistance, vol. VIIIb, incomplete list of names of the women sent to the camp from Warsaw after the outbreak of the uprising. The list contains the names of about half the women and girls deported to the camp.

[38] APMO, Files of the Camp Resistance, vol. IV, cards 254-9.

that they be sent to the security police's camp for Polish children in Łódź (*Polen-Jugendverwahrlager der Sicherheitspolizei*). This decision even caught the German police off guard, who — on the basis of previous sentences — had already informed the parents of one girl that she had been executed at Auschwitz. [39]

Particularly disturbing is the following account of SS man Pery Broad, a former official from KL Auschwitz's Political Division (*Politische Abteilung*), an eyewitness to one of the court-martial's proceedings:

> They led in a 16-year-old boy. Because he was hungry, he had stolen something from a store, and is thus considered one of the few "criminal" cases. After reading the death sentence, Mildner [head of the Katowice Gestapo, who conducted the trial — HK], slowly picks up the paper on the table and gives a sharp glance at the small, feeble figure standing next to the wall in his thin clothes. Slowly accentuating each word, he says: "Do you have a mother?" The boy avoids his glance and replies, barely audibly, in a voice choked by tears: Yes. "Are you afraid of death?" The butcher, at the neck of his prey, surveys the onlookers and sadistically basks in the horror of his victim. The boy does not speak up; he simply trembles. "We will shoot you today", Mildner says, striving to give his voice a judgmental tone. "You would have been hung someday anyway. In one hour you will be dead." [40]

Given the fragmentary evidence that exists, we cannot even venture a guess regarding the number of children and youths condemned to death by the court martial or sent to concentration camps as a result of its proceedings.

4. Youths and Children from Byelorussia and Ukraine

In the years 1943-44, not only Jewish, Gypsy, and Polish children were sent to the camp, but also children from the occupied territories of the former Soviet Union. This took place in accordance with a January 6, 1943, order from Himmler, who decreed that:

> ... whenever campaigns are being conducted against bandits [partisans —HK], you should round up men, women and children suspected of contacts with the bandits and send them in organized transports to the camp in Lublin or to Auschwitz. [41]

The German *Einsatzkommandos*, which operated in the occupied territories of the East, and particularly *Einsatzkommando 9*, sent entire families to Auschwitz and Majdanek (in Lublin) in the course of the "pacification" campaigns conducted in Byelorussia, particularly in the area of Minsk and Vitebsk, and in

---

[39] WAP Katowice, Collection Provinzialverwaltung, syg. 5309, 5320, 5454, 5402, 5431. See also Józef Witkowski, *Hitlerowski obóz dla małoletnich w Łodzi* (Wrocław, 1975), pp. 87-8; Alfred Konieczny, *Pod rządami wojennego prawa karnego Trzeciej Rzeszy. Górny Śląsk, 1939-1945* (Warszawa and Wrocław 1972), p. 369.

[40] "Reminiscences of Pery Broad" in *KL Auschwitz Seen by the SS.* (Oświęcim, 1978), p. 156.

[41] Nuremberg Document, sygn. NO-2031. Polish version published in Roman Hrabar, *Na rozkaz i bez rozkazu* (Katowice, 1968), pp. 117-118. See also Andrzej Kamiński, *Hitlerowskie obozy koncentracyjne i ośrodki masowej zagłady w polityce imperializmu niemieckiego* (Poznań, 1964), p. 172.

the Ukraine, particularly in Lwów (Lviv). At least 15 transports of civilians arrived at KL Auschwitz from the occupied areas of the Soviet Union. The largest number of children were brought to the camp in transports from Vitebsk on September 9, October 22 and November 23, 1943, and in a transport from Minsk on December 4 of the same year. Russian children were also brought to the camp in evacuation transports from the Majdanek and Stutthof concentration camps.

Among the Soviet prisoners of war shipped to the camp, one could also find children 11-17 years of age. A certain number of Russian children also arrived with adults in collective transports from different areas of the *Reich*. Most had been caught running away from forced labor and were being sent to the concentration camp as punishment.

A lack of documentation prevents us from establishing the exact number of children held at KL Auschwitz from the former Soviet Union. If we take into account only the four transports mentioned above from Minsk and Vitebsk, for which we have established partial figures, we can cite as an initial estimate that at least 907 children and young people arrived at the camp in these transports. [42]

5. Children Born at the Camp

After the women's camp was established at KL Auschwitz in March 1942, there were cases in which women prisoners who had been pregnant upon their arrival would give birth to children. [43] At first, such women, considered unfit for work, were put to death by phenol injection as part of the euthanasia campaign being conducted at the concentration camps. Such killings normally took place after the evening roll-call, during which the pregnant women were asked to report to the sick ward. Even if some women prisoners successfully bore their children, they would be murdered along with the child. Several Polish women from the Zamość region suffered such a fate.

In the first half of 1943, the practice of exterminating women who were pregnant or bore children was discontinued, likely as a result of Himmler's new directives for the euthanasia campaign. [44] Instead, the women were forced to have an abortion, sometimes by surgery, irregardless of the stage of their pregnancy. If the child was nevertheless born alive, then the new-born would be killed by phenol injection or drowned. Such babies were never entered into the camp's records.

Beginning in the second half of 1943, children born to non-Jewish prisoners at the camp were allowed to live. After their birth at the camp hospital, they

---

[42] APMO, Mat/1345, vol. 108 c, cards 131-50, list of Byelorussian children arriving at KL Auschwitz from Vitebsk and Minsk in 1943.

[43] APMO, D-RF-3/RSHA. Collection Allgemeine Erlässe. Correspondence of the RSHA, vol. 80a, card 135, order of the head of RSHA from May 6, 1943, regarding a renewed ban on the Gestapo's sending pregnant women to the camps at Ravensbrück, Auschwitz, and Lublin. The regulation applied only to women sent to the camp individually by police units.

[44] See the order of Richard Glücks, Inspector of Concentration Camps, from April 27, 1943, informing the concentration-camp commandants that Himmler's decision regarding killings under the euthanasia campaign applied only to the mentally-ill. (Nuremberg Doc. PS 1933 in A. Kamiński, p. 172).

were given to their mothers. Because the mother lacked the necessary milk and the baby had to live under the extremely primitive hygienical and sanitary conditions at the HKB, the child would most often die. Only a few cases have been documented in which a mother who gave birth at the camp was released along with her child.

Children born at the women's camp were registered after several days as "new arrivals" (the first documented case took place on July 22, 1943). [45] They would receive their respective camp numbers (girls, from the women's series; boys, from the men's series). As a rule, it was tattooed on the child's thigh or buttocks, or, in a few cases, on the hand. The camp's Civil Registration Office (*Standesamt II*) documented the child's birth. When filling out birth certificates, instead of giving the camp as the place of birth in the space indicated on the form, they would write down the name of the town and the particular street (e.g., "Auschwitz, Kasernenstrasse"). [46]

Children born to German women, as well as the Polish women brought to the camp from Warsaw during the 1944 uprising, were not tattooed with camp numbers. Quite likely, this was also the case with non-Jewish children whom the SS doctors qualified for Germanization during their inspections of the infirmary-blocks (HKB). Children who met the physical criteria of the Nordic race were taken from their mothers and sent to so-called "exit quarantines", where initial anthropological tests were run. They then were sent to a Resettlement Center in Łódź, Nakło or Potulice, or to the special facilities of the *Lebensborn* foundation — an organization that, women took part in the Germanization of children. [47]

Children born to Jewish women were usually exterminated immediately upon birth (without any sort of registration) until the end of October 1944, when the mass extermination of Jews was discontinued. For unknown reasons, in violation of established norms, the births of eight Jewish children were recorded in the camp's records during 1944, and the babies were registered (i.e., received camp numbers). The first such registration took place on February 21, 1944. [48] One of the new-borns survived at the camp for several months, but perished shortly before the camp's liberation.

As part of the privileged treatment that its residents received, children born at the so-called family camp for Jews from Theresienstadt (Teresín) were not exterminated during that camp's existence at Birkenau. No documents have survived, however, recording how many children were born at this camp. It is only known that all of them perished during the camp's liquidation in July 1944.

A similar situation prevailed at the family camp for Gypsies. Gypsy women were allowed to give birth, and a special maternity ward was even established. Newborns were entered into the main register for the Gypsy camp

---

[45] APMO, D-AuI-2/1, 2, 3, Collection Geburtsurkunde [Birth Certificates].

[46] Ibid. See also APMP, Höss Trial, vol. 3a, cards 136-137, testimony of former prisoner Stanisława Rachwałowa.

[47] The tasks of the *Lebensborn* "Foundation", established on December 12, 1935, on Himmler's initiative, included the Germanization of children born in Eastern Europe.

[48] APMO, Files of the Camp Resistance, vol. 20 b, c, list of transports for men and women, illegally compiled by prisoners on the basis of official transport lists.

A total of 378 Gypsy children were born there. The death rate for newborns, however, was even higher than at the women's camp, although the Gypsy children received better rations for a brief period. The deaths resulted from the sanitary and hygienical conditions at the Gypsy camp, which were worse than anywhere else, (at first, there was no water or sewage) and the terrible overcrowding, both of which increased the spread of contagious diseases.

If we add up all the figures cited above, we find that on the basis of the surviving camp documents from 1943-45 and documents prepared in the course of campaigns of assistance for liberated prisoners, a total of 680 children were born in capitivity at the women's camp and the Gypsy family camp. Of these children, eight were released from the camp with their mothers, and 46 survived until the camp's liberation. Of the latter, several died immediately after their liberation at the Polish Red Cross (PCK) hospital on the grounds of the former Auschwitz camp and at the PCK hospital in Brzeszcze. [49]

6. The Living Conditions for Children and Youths

During the initial years of its existence (1940-43), except for isolated cases, there were no children under 14 years at the camp. There were, however, youths aged 15-17, as mentioned above. They lived together with the adults and were treated the same. In the second half of 1940, one block at the men's camp was set aside for boys under 18 (Block 5), subsequently called the "young prisoners' block". During its several months of existence, it held around 300 boys. The young men who resided there did not have to work at the beginning; they first had to learn a profession at the so-called bricklayer's school (*Maurerschule*). [50] The block existed in various forms at the main camp and at Birkenau, with occasional interruptions, until 1944. Not only Polish boys, but also Jews and Russians, were sent to the school. Their professional training lasted several weeks, after which they were transferred to the work detail for construction. [51]

---

[49] According to memoirs and accounts of former women prisoners employed in the HKB, a significantly larger number of children were born at the camp than one can find documented in the surviving records. The largest number of births took place among the Jewish women. A former prisoner and professional midwife, Stanisława Leszczyńska, who assisted in births at the women's camp beginning in May 1943, asserts in her camp memoir/report published in 1957 that from May 1943 to the camp's liberation, she alone had assisted in ca. 3,000 births. In the opinion of other women prisoners who worked on the staff at the camp hospital at the time, this figure is highly-inflated.

Stanisława Leszczyńska, "Raport położnej z Oświęcimia", *Przegląd Lekarski — Oświęcim* (1965), pp. 104-6.

[50] APMO, Collection of Testimonies, vol. 72, cards 18-19; vol 73, card 1; vol. 74, cards 3-4; vol. 96, cards 34-7; accounts of former youth-prisoners: Nikodem Pieszczoch, Stanisław Miarkowski, Czesław Sułkowski, Stanisław Hantz.

[51] APMO, Collection of Testimonies, vol. 16, card 52, account of former prisoner Abraham Dawid Feffer; APMO, Höss Trial, vol. 2, card 3, testimony of former prisoner Mojżesz Kleinstein. See also F. Piper, *Zatrudnienie więźniów KL Auschwitz* (Oświęcim, 1981), pp. 329-30.

At the women's camp, a so-called children's work detail (*Kinderkommando*) was created for several months in 1942. The teenage girls attached to it would work at gardening. One of these girls later wrote:

Exactly two days after I arrived at the camp [she arrived at the end of May 1942 — HK] I was sent to the *Kinderkommando*. It was a group of very young girls, 12-16 years old. The *Kommando* worked at gardening in Rajsko. [52]

In addition to the hard labor, which sometimes exceeded the physical capabilities of the poorly-nourished teenage boys and girls, they were subjected to every possible form of chicanery and severe punishment for what were often minor offenses. For example, the 16-year-old prisoner, Czesław Kempisty, was punished with several hours of "posting" after he threw several rutabagas to starving Soviet prisoners-of-war on their way to work. (He was unloading them from a wagon). Halina Grynstein, a Jewish girl, thirteen years of age, was shot in the shoulder by a German guard simply because she approached the camp fence to speak with another female prisoner. Youths at the camp were also victims of the depravity of certain male and female prisoners, mainly criminals.

Due to changes in conduct on the part of camp authorities with regard to non-Jewish children in the second half of 1943, children began to appear at the women's camp, particularly in September 1943, after transports of civilians — mainly mothers with children — arrived at the camp from Byelorussia. Separate barracks were established for children over two years of age, away from their mothers. Most of these children were sent shortly thereafter in several large transports to special camps for children from the East in Konstantynów near Łódź and in Potulice, most likely for Germanization. At the beginning of November 1943, one single transport carried 542 Byelorussian children from Auschwitz to Potulice. [53]

The conditions that the children housed in the separate barracks faced — in terms of both food and shelter — did not differ from those faced by the adults. Only the children in the camp infirmary fared slightly better, but only thanks to the extraordinary efforts of the prisoners on the infirmary staff. They strived to get a hold of extra blankets, warmer clothing, and extra portions of food for children, especially white bread and milk. The staff used illegal contacts with prisoners working in the men's infirmary and the "Canada" warehouses to obtain such items.

Adult prisoners also assisted children outside of the infirmary. Prisoners who held administrative functions related to the other prisoners, as well as those who labored in work details with access to clothing, food or medicine had the greatest possibilities in this regard. Not only individual prisoners, but also the camp resistance movement organized such assistance.

---

[52] APMO, Collection of Testimonies, vol. 47, card 32, testimony of former prisoners Ruth Milarowa (under the name Hermansztadt at the camp).

[53] APMO, IZ-2/1-8, Other Collections, Akta Centrali Przesiedleńczej — Obóz w Potulicach [Documents of the Resettlement Center/Camp in Potulice] (UWZ Lager-Potulic), vol. 1, 1a.
See also Władimir Litwinow, *Pojezd iz noczi* (Kiev, 1989).

Particularly strong efforts were made to obtain additional food and adequate clothing. Women employed in the kitchen at the camp would "organize" additional rations for the children. Women prisoners who worked in the gardens would "organize" vegetables. Prisoners who worked at the "Canada" warehouses would smuggle children's clothing and underwear into the camp. Women who worked at the camp's tailoring workshops would sew clothes for smaller children and babies from used sheets. In work details at the camp, the adult prisoners strived to protect children and youths from particularly strenuous work, and in some cases, even defended them from brutal prisoner-functionaries. [54] Adult prisoners decorated the children's barracks with color drawings of games and scenes from fairy tales. Such pictures have survived until today on the walls of Barrack 16 in the women's camp at Birkenau, on the grounds of construction site BIa, reserved for Polish children.

Another special form of protection was making certain that the daily struggle for survival would not deform the weak, developing psyches of the children at the camp. Adult prisoners took pains to see that the children, especially the older ones, would not succumb to demoralization. They sought to arouse feelings of patriotism. In the evenings, the adults would tell stories and recite poems to the children and teach geography, history, and literature to the older ones.

Organizing assistance for Jewish children and youths, constantly under the threat of selection to the gas chambers, represented a most difficult task. Thanks, however, to the courage and quick thinking of certain prisoners, some Jewish children were saved. The effort to save Jewish children began at the camp's train platforms. Prisoners assigned to unload transports of Jews would use Dr. Mengele's order to gather together twins for "experimental purposes" as a way to smuggle children who were more or less similar into the camp, where they at least had a chance of survival.

In a few cases, prisoners — mainly those who held an office — were able to conceal Jewish children in the barracks for non-Jewish children with the goal of protecting them from selections. In one case, Polish prisoners, led by the *Blockältester* of Barrack 7 at Birkenau, Czesław Gaszyński, were able to save more than 120 Jewish children at the quarantine camp for men at Birkenau. After bribing several SS men, they hid them at first among the Polish children and then organized their transfer to the camp KL Flossenbürg, where they no longer faced the threat of selection to the gas chambers. [55] They also rescued Jewish newborns by exchanging them for non-Jewish children who had died in the infirmary at the women's camp.

---

[54] APMO, Collection of Reminiscences, vol. 71, card 128, memoirs of former prisoner Eulalia Kurdej; Lech Szawłowski, "Z przeżyć warszawskich dzieci w obozach hitlerowskich "*Przegląd Lekarski — Oświęcim* (1972), p. 160; Bogdan Bartnikowski, *Dzieciństwo w pasiakach* (Warszawa, 1977), pp. 71-5.

[55] APMO, Collection of Reminiscences, vol. 108, cards 20-28, memoirs of former prisoner Czesław Gaszyński. See also APMO, Höss Trial, vol. 6, card 31 and vol. 1, card 68, and the additional testimony of former prisoners Otto Wolken and Luigi Ferri.

See also Alfred Fiderkiewicz, *Brzezinki — wspomnienia z obozu* (Warszawa, 1956), pp. 119.

The extermination of child prisoners, as well as their transfer to other camps (especially during the camp's evacuation), meant that only a few children survived to witness Auschwitz's liberation. The children left behind by the camp authorities, along with ill prisoners who were unable to march, were housed at the women's camp on the grounds of BIIe. According to the latest research in the available documents, more than 600 children and youths aged 17 or younger were liberated from the camp, including more than 400 children, 14 or below. [56]

The liberated children were extremely emaciated; some had frozen limbs. The majority of them found themselves immediately after liberation either at the Soviet field hospitals organized on the grounds of the former main camp or at the PCK's Camp Hospital, directed by Dr. Józef Bellert.

After examining a group of 180 children aged six months to 14 years, the judicial committee of doctors established that the majority of them suffered from diseases contracted at the camp: 60% suffered from vitamin deficiency and emaciation and 40% were stricken with tuberculosis. Each child was 5-17 kilograms underweight, although most of them had arrived at the camp in the second half of 1944 — i.e., they had been at the camp for only three to six months. [57]

Among the liberated children, Jewish children, predominated, particularly those who had been used for medical experiments, along with Polish children from Warsaw. Having gained their freedom, their tragedy and suffering were not over yet. Not all of them could return to their homes and lead normal lives. Many of them had nothing to return to. Their parents had either died or were still alive at camps inside the Third Reich, having been brought there in evacuation transports. Quite often, the younger children did not know their family name or where they came from. Those children who still had families would often return home in a state of extreme physical and psychological exhaustion. Before they could begin studying like their contemporaries, they first had to recover. Some would spend years and years in hospitals and sanatoria, or would be invalids for the rest of their lives. Neuroses, tuberculosis, anemia, diseases of the circulatory and respiratory systems and kidneys — these were the enduring results of their imprisonment at the camp. That these former child-prisoners were five times as likely to suffer from disabilities than their peers who had not lived through the hell of the camp bears the most telling witness to the living conditions at the camp.

---

[56] On this subject, see the notes of former prisoner Stanisława Jankowska for the period January 17-27, 1945. She gives the figure of 435 for children being held on January 26 among the women prisoners at camp BIIe at Birkenau. She does not give, however, an upper age-limit for her definition of "children".

APMO, Collection of Reminiscences, vol. 61a, card 19.

[57] APMO, Collection IZ, syg. IZ-1/3 pp. 39-42, medical report of the Extraordinary Commision for Research into Nazi Crimes (*Nadzwyczajna Komisja d/s Badania Zbrodni Hitlerowskich*).

EXTERMINATION
AT KL AUSCHWITZ

FRANCISZEK PIPER

LIVING CONDITIONS AND WORK AS METHODS OF EXTERMINATING PRISONERS

1. Hunger and Disease

Because of the political situation at the time, the Nazis had not decided before 1941, to undertake mass extermination to solve the so-called "Jewish Question". Only after the Nazi attack on the Soviet Union did this change. At first, prisoners were killed slowly by denying them the basic needs of life; the main tool for was hunger. The prisoners received mass murder an amount of food that would only allow them to survive three to six months. Denied the necessary number of calories, the prisoner's body would meet the deficit by consuming the energy stored in its own fatty tissue. After this energy was depleted, the prisoner's muscles began to deteriorate. This reduced the body's resistance and led to internal-organ damage. A high rate of illness prevailed with regard to every type of infectious disease.

Among the numerous diseases that afflicted the prisoners, starvation diarrhea claimed the largest death toll. Under normal conditions this disease did not exist, but was widespread at all the concentration camps. The symptoms of this disease included a deterioration in the body's ability to digest food, extreme emaciation, and a rapid decrease in body weight. Resembling skeletons, prisoners afflicted by it would die on the streets of the camp and in the residential blocks and were killed in large numbers at work. Only a few were admitted to the camp infirmary, which resembled only in name an institution dedicated to saving human lives. The only privilege of those who made it into the hospital was being freed from work duties and the strenuous roll-calls; they could die in relative peace.

Another common and fatal disease, a result of the terrible sanitary conditions at the camp, was spotted fever. This disease returned time and again in the form of a rapidly-spreading epidemic, and plagued the camp practically without a break from April 1941 to spring 1944. At its peak, hundreds — or even thousands — of prisoners would die each month. The 1942 epidemic of spotted fever took the gravest course. The first cases were noticed in March at the men's camp in Birkenau (Brzezinka), and by July, the epidemic had spread through the entire camp. The number of deaths grew every day. A total of 2,192 prisoners men and prisoners of war died in April of that year; in May, 2,982; in June, 3,688; in July, 4,124; and in the first three weeks of August, 4,113.

The rapidly-spreading epidemic of spotted fever presented a major obstruction to exploiting the prisoners as a work force. The resulting break in work of the several thousand prisoners employed by the IG Farbenindustrie concern in the construction of their Buna-Werke facilities from August to October 1942 led to heavy losses and a long delay in completing this priority investment for the German war economy.

This fact, along with the fear of the SS staff that the epidemic could spread to themselves and their families, given the growing number of cases of SS men falling ill and even dying (at the beginning of the epidemic, the garrison's doctor, *SS-Hauptsturmführer* Siegfried Schwela died from the disease on May 10, 1942), finally led the SS authorities to take steps to limit the effects of the epidemic and partially eliminate it.

2. Work

A proven and effective method of extermination at the camp was work. Every prisoner had to work; if there was no sensible task to be done, the prisoners received senseless tasks. Indeed, although this formula of annihilation through work (*Vernichtung durch Arbeit*) was first articulated in a 1942 letter to Himmler from the *Reich's* Minister of Justice, Thierack, it had been practiced since the very beginning of the concentration camps' existence. Such camps as Mauthausen, Flossenbürg, Natzweiler and Gross-Rosen were not founded by accident next to stone quarries, which for centuries had stood as a symbol for murderous, unfree labor. The entire system for organizing work — its intensity, conditions and facilities in terms of tools and installations — was based on the principle that work was to serve as a punishment for the prisoners in and of itself; it was to serve as a means to their physical destruction. The binding rule was the maximal exploitation of physical labor with the minimal — unjustified even under wartime conditions — use of machines and tools. The necessary technical means were only employed in those areas in which optimal economic results, quality or the timely completion of a given task were required. Most often, however, prisoners had to use the most basic tools and means of transport, such as shovels, pickaxes, and wheelbarrows.

Although there were vehicles and horse carts at the camp, the universal method for transport at the camp was forcing the prisoners to carry loads by hand, often over long distances. Prisoners were harnessed to so-called roller-wagons (*Rollwagen*) — large freight wagons, used for carrying building materials, food, clothes, excrement from the latrine, or corpses. Universally employed was the system of pendular transport, in which prisoners would carry a load from one place to the other, while running through a gauntlet of kapos and SS men, who would rush them by constantly hitting them with wooden staffs. Even in 1943, when Germany faced an enormous labor deficit, the following method was used for transporting building materials for road construction at Birkenau: the prisoners were ordered to hold their blouses or overcoats up part-way to form an improvised basket, which they then used to carry earth or gravel to a location several hundred meters away.

At the camp, no work existed that was not deterimental from a logical or economical — not to mention humanitarian — point of view. It is sufficient to recall that in spring 1944, after the horses had been requisitioned for military needs, women prisoners were harnessed to the plough at the SS farm in Babice, next to the camp. The vision of these women of a "lower race" pulling a plough can be considered a symbol of the essence of Nazism, with slave labor at the Auschwitz camp on the one hand and its gas chambers on the other forming a traverse of bitter experience.[1]

3. Punishments

Essential for the proper functioning of the camps's extermination apparatus was the absolute obedience of the prisoners. Every reflex of open resistance, no matter how insignificant, met with the harshest possible reprisals. In the October 1, 1933, regulations for the concentration camp at Dachau, written by the future inspector of concentration camps, Theodor Eicke, it states:

> Anyone who attacks a guard or SS man, refuses to obey or refuses to finish the work at their workplace, calls on others to do so or calls on them to revolt, leaves the march column or place of work or urges others to do so, screams during the march or at work, yealls, agitates or gives speeches — will be shot on the sport or alternatively hanged.[2]

In fact, every SS man could kill prisoners without any consequences. Not only camp officials, but also the highest state authorities condoned and encouraged this type of behavior. It was Hitler himself who on November 29, 1935, pardoned some guards from KL Hohenstein sent to prison "who — as the Ministry of Justice acknowledged — had taken part in tormenting [the prisones — FP] in a very harsh and cruel way".[3]

Hitler, after all, had never concealed his belief that physical force and terror were effective methods for governing:

> I do not want — he said — the concentration camps to be transformed into sanatoria. Terror is the most effective political weapon. Everybody supports undertaking something against us, until he learns about what awaits him at a concentration camp ...I need people who act severely and do not even begin to think when they have to kill someone ... A conscience is a Jewish creation ... Every deed makes sense, even criminal ones.[4]

Thedor Eicke, the first inspector and — as Höss call him — the founder of the concentration camps, schooled and trained cadrés for the camps in this spirit a Dachau — at the time, a celebrated school for the butchers beneath the death's head.

---

[1] Franciszek Piper, *Arbeitseinsatz der Häftlinge aus dem KL Auschwitz*, (Oświęcim, 1995).

[2] *Der Prozess gegen die Hauptkriegsverbrecher dem Internationalen Militärgerichtshof*, vol. XXVI, (Nürnberg, 1949), pp. 291-93.

[3] Nuremberd Document PS 785-788; *Der Prozess...*, Vol. XXVI, pp. 300-27.

[4] Hermann Rauschining, *Gespräche mit Hitler* (Zürich-Vienna-New York 1940), pp. 79, 81, 82, 95, 210, 211.

The prisoners, to him, were eternal enemies of the state, who had to be closely watched and dealt with severely, and who, if they resisted, were to be annihilated. [5]

The cadré for the camp staff at Auschwitz also came from Eicke's school: camp commandant Rudolf Höss — a pedantic criminal, steering the entire mechanism for extermination from his office; the first camp supervisor (*Lagerführer*), Karl Fritzsch, founder of the system of individualized terror that remained in place until the end of the camp's existence; his deputy, former director for special schooling at KL Dachau, Hans Aumeier; and the executioner, *Rapportführer* Gerhard Palitzsch, among others.

The prisoners at KL Auschwitz did not know what regulations, if any, applied to their behavior, as had been the case at the Dachau camp. There was no standard list of prohibitions, orders, or punishments. What was allowed and not allowed at the camp was taught with a wooden staff. That is how former prisoner Czesław Jaworski, a doctor before the war, arrested by the Gestapo and sent to the camp on suspicion of membership in an underground resistance organization, described the situation:

Walking up the stairs, I noticed a bulletin board in the corridor with various announcements in German hanging on it. I looked for the regulations that applied to us at the camp in the belief that they could be found in certain paragraphs and communicated for general information. Unfortunately, I did not find them. I suddenly saw Schreiber, the *Blockführer*, so I turned to him: "Excuse me, sir, are there certain regulations that apply to prisoners at the camp? I would like to know them, in order to avoid any unpleasantries." He looked at me like an idiot, hit me in the face and replied, "There you have your regulations, mister lawyer!" This explanation cost me two teeth. [6]

The most common punishment, not mentioned in any regulation, was the summary beating of a prisoner at the scene of his "crime". Every SS man and every prisoner holding an office, from the camp senior (*Lagerältester*) down to the block barber, had the right to strike — and even kill — the prisoners. Such beatings and maltreatment were also part of the so-called regulation punishments, such as: punitive labor during free time from work, assignment to the penal company, and punitive exercises. The commandant — or in his absence, the *Lagerführer* — allotted such punishments on the basis of a report from an SS man with a special punitive order. On the basis of the 275 surviving reports and 110 punitive orders, one can establish the relationship between the violations committed by prisoners and the punishments meted out to them.

The most frequent causes for punishing prisoners included: failing to report to work with one's work detail, evading work, leaving one's workplace without permission, committing sabotage during work (including, for example, dropping and breaking concrete pipes during unloading), preparing meals during work, stealing food or clothing, trading with civilian workers, illegally mailing letters and smoking cigarettes at forbidden times.

---

[5] *Wspomnienia Rudolfa Hössa, komendanta obozu oświęcimskiego* (Warszawa, 1965), p. 269.
[6] Czesław W. Jaworski, *Wspomnienia z Oświęcimia* (Warszawa, 1962), p. 46.

The punishment reports shed an interesting light on the conditions at the camp. On June 13, 1944, the leader of the sub-camp in Jawischowitz (Jawiszowice), Wilhelm Kowol, announced the punishment of prisoner Lazar Anticoli (born January 3, 1910, in Rome) who tried with another prisoner to break into a pigsty at 11 o'clock at night to steal the bread crumbs left for the pigs. The *Schutzhaftlagerführer* (camp supervisor) of KL Auschwitz III, Vinzenz Schöttl, sentenced Anticoli to ten weeks of punitive labor under supervision. [7]

Flogging was frequently the official punishment. It was usually administered publicly, during roll-call, on a special table that was constructed in such a way that the legs of the prisoner lying on it were immobilized. The SS men used a cudgel, or less often a whip, as the regulations specified. According to the regulations, the strokes were to be administered quickly, one after the other, and were not to exceed 25 at one time. The actual practice, however depended on the mood of the SS man supervising the punishment. The flogging of five prisoners following the camp's first escape (Tadeusz Wiejowski) demonstrates the latitude that the SS men had for reinterpreting the regulations related to this type of punishment. The five prisoners selected were to receive 25 strokes on there separate occasions. After they received the first 25 strokes, they were sent to the cellar of the "Death Block", were they stayed for 21 days without medical treatment, although the wounds that they had received were festering and infected. After the 21 days, prisoner-sanitarians led them back to the assembly square, where they received the remaining 50 strokes all at once. Once the flogging was finished, they had to be carried to the camp infirmary, where one of them, Stanisław Mrzygłód, died from his wounds and another, Bolesław Bicz, lay unconscious for two weeks.

According to the annoucement of punishment, dated February 1, 1944, prisoner Josef Engel, working in the pits of the "Brzeszcze-Jawiszowice" coal mine, having decided that he could no loger bear the hard work and poor treatment, slashed his throat with a knife. As punishment, it was proposed to administer 25 strokes. On January 25, 1944, Juda Calvo was ordered flogged for having purchased bread smuggled into the camp with two of his gold teeth, wchich he had torn from his mouth.

Women were also punished by flogging. In her memoirs, Seweryna Szmaglewska remembers one occasion in which female prisoners were punished in this fashion:

Two hundred women were to be flogged, 25 strokes apiece ... In the beams of light, one could see a line of women slowly approaching in an orderly fashion the place where they all were to lie down beneath the whip. Against the doors of the blosk, there was the figure of Schultz bending down and cracking the whip with his hand.

Suddenly, confusion broke out. In the darkness, women who had not been flogged were trying to slip though to join those who had already received their punishment. Schultz noticed, threw down his whip, and seized an emaciated figure who was fighting with difficulty through the mud. He grasped her by the hips, raised her up,

---

[7] APMO. D-AuI, II, III-2/284, Meldungen und Strafverfügungen [Announcements and Notifications of Punishment].

and bashed her head on the ground. After he saw to his swollen hands, he returned to the flogging .... The screams, moans, and yells resounded through the darkness of that fall evening. [8]

Another, equally painful punishment was so-called "posting", in which the prisoner was hung from his hands, tied behind his back, so that his feet could not touch the ground. During this unbelievably painful punishment, the prisoner would lose consciousness from pain. It was also very dangerous in terms of its possible effects. If a prisoner hung on the post for a longer period, the tendons in his shoulders would rip. As a result, he or she would lose control of his hands and, unable to work, would fall victim to a "selection".

Incarceration in the "standing cell" (*Stehzelle*) represented one of the most severe punishments. The cells in question were located in the basement of Block 11 at the main camp. Each of the four cells had a surface area of less than one square meter. A deep manhole, closed off by a grate and tight doors, led beneath the ground to the cell. In the cell, total darkness prevailed, since even the single entrance for air, measuring 5 × 5 cm, was covered by a metal screen. Up to four prisoners were locked up in each cell; this made any movement or change of position impossible. After standing the entire night, the victims would be driven along with the other prisoners to work. Prisoners were sentenced to this punishment for several nights or even longer than ten nights.

In 1943, the commandant of KL Auschwitz ordered all affiliated camps to build their own standing cells. Such cells are known to have existed at Birkenau, Eintrachthütte (Świętochłowice), Fürstengrube (Wesoła) and other camps. Prisoners were sentenced to these cells, as well as other punishments, for the most trivial violations.

Prisoner L. Lens (60970) had to spend ten nights in a standing cell because he had tried to go to another block to get a second helping of food. L. Katz (64495) received three nights for having relieved himself behind one of the buildings. Prisoner H. Cahn (104909) was condemned to ten nights for picking some fruit in a nearby garden after relieving himself at work. For the same violation, a female prisoner, M. Tajfelbaum (Teitelbaum, 47332) had to spend five nights locked in a standing cell.

Prisoners could also be sentenced to a dungeon, to a normal cell with standard camp rations, or to a normal cell, where they would receive only bread and water, except for every fourth day, when they would receive the normal camp rations.

Among the severest punishments was a sentence in the penal company (*Strafkompanie*), established in August 1940. The office of supervisor for the punishment company was held consecutively by *SS-Unterscharführer* Gerlach, *SS-Rottenführer* Stermberg, *SS-Hauptscharführer* Otto Moll, *SS-Hauptscharführer* Rüf and *SS-Unterscharführer* Umlauf. A total of around 6,000 prisoners passed through it; its normal size was 150-600 prisoners. Prisoners in the *Strafkompanie* were housed separately and not allowed to contact other prisoners or to correspond by mail. They slept either on beds composed of bare

---

[8] Seweryna Szmaglewska, *Dymy nad Birkenau* (Warszawa 1945), pp. 195-96.

boards or on the concrete floor in their underwear. In the years 1940-42, when the penal company was housed in Block 11 of the main camp, prisoners belonging to it were not even admitted to the camp infirmary when they suffered from a serious disease.

When he received prisoners into the penal company, Otto Moll, future head of the crematoria and one of the greatest war criminals ever to wear the SS insignia, would ask them why they had been sent to his command. Regardless of their answer, he would hit them with a heavy staff and then, after they fell to the floor, kick and trample them and then set the dog on them that he normally walked around the camp.

Although they worked at the most strenous jobs — for example, at the gravel pit — prisoners in the punishment company received worse rations than the other prisoners. They always had to work at an accelerated pace. Loaded down with wheelbarrows of gravel, the prisoners had to run up sloped boards to the edge of the pit. Whenever they paused, the kapos and SS men would beat them without mercy. If someone fell, they would stand on his throat and suffocate him. The bodies of murdered prisoners, carried back to camp on the shoulders of prisoners returning from work, bore witness to the ardour and zeal of the kapos and *Vorarbeiter* of the punishment company. If the higher SS authorities in the camp administration considered the number of returning corpses too small, the next day would exact a bloodier toll.

In the penal company, one of the greatest thugs was the kapo Ernst Krankemann. He arrived at KL Auschwitz on August 29, 1940, in the second transport of German criminals, who assumed the offices of *Blockältester* and kapos at the camp. By profession, he was a barber. Stout, short, but powerfully-built, Krankemann could kill a prisoner by crushing his head on the edge of a wall with a single blow to the shoulders. He was the one straddling the shaft of the enormous roller, driving the Jews and priests harnessed to it from morning to evening. Anyone who fell would perish beneath the weight of the roller. No prisoner could escape with his life if Krankemann glimpsed gold teeth. After all, he paid with his life, in the end, for speculating in "gold" with the SS men. In order to dispose of their partner, who knew too much, they sent him along with the first transport of invalids on July 28, 1941, to be "cured" at the euthanasia facility in Sonnenstein. Most likely, the prisoners hanged him in the wagon in order to avenge the deaths of his victims.

In May 1942, the penal company was transferred to Birkenau and housed in Block 1 on the grounds of the men's camp. As one of the former prisoners, Józef Kret wrote, "... the block reminded one of a stinking hovel. Clouds of thick straw-dust intensified the normal darkness there. In this cloud of dust, similar to a thick fog, a throng of people ran around like a swarm of insects." [9]

At Birkenau, the penal company helped dig the central drainage ditch, the Königsgraben. This was a site known for bestial murders. It was at this site that it came to an open rebellion and escape by prisoners on June 10, 1942.

---

[9] Józef Kret, "Ein Tag in der Strafkompanie", *Hefte von Auschwitz* 1 (1959), p. 124.

Making use of the confusion caused by a violent downpour, some prisoners, disregarding the danger from the SS men and kapos, rushed to escape. After the initial shock, the SS men opened fire and together with the kapos, regained control of the situation. Although thirteen prisoners were killed, nine were able to escape. The remaining prisoners were driven back to the camp by *Kommandoführer* Otto Moll. The next day, in the courtyard to the block of the punishment company, an improvised inquiry took place. During it, the camp supervisor, *SS-Hauptsturmführer* Hans Aumeier shot seventeen prisoners for refusing to talk, and *SS-Hauptscharführer* Franz Hössler shot three more. The remaining 320 prisoners, their hands restrained by barbed wire, were driven into the gas-chamber bunker and killed. New prisoners were sent to the penal company to take their place.

The excavation work on the Königsgraben continued. Every day, when they returned to the camp, the column of prisoners from the penal company would pull a cart behind them, loaded with the bodies of murdered prisoners. The prisoners of the penal company had to work even after the evening roll-call, when other prisoners had free time. Without any tools, they were ordered, for example, to crush pieces of brick stacked outside the buildings. During this work, the kapo Alfons Göttinger, called Sepp by the prisoners — "tall, thin, with an oblong face like Mephisto" — entertained himself by catching the prisoners with a lasso. He would throw the noose around a prisoner's neck, twist it around several times, and then throw the prisoner into a chest of corpses standing in one corner of the courtyard.

Shortly after the women's camp was established, a penal company for women prisoners was founded. At first, it was located in the village of Budy, and then transferred to the camp at Birkenau. It consisted of around 400 women, who were employed in cleaning fish ponds, building dikes and other earthwork. Regardless of the time of year, these women often had to work in cold water up to above their waists. The work lasted, depending upon the time of year, up to fourteen hours. It is thus not surprising that they suffered a high mortality rate. On one night in October 1942, the SS men and female kapos (German criminal prisoners) murdered 90 French Jews for allegedly planning a revolt. Camp commandant Rudolf Höss commented after visiting the area that "the French women had been killed with poles and axes, some had been completely decapitated, others perished after being thrown through an uspstairs window". [10]

Another punishment were drills, or, in camp jargon, "sports". Routinely applied to new arrivals passing through quarantine, it was also used as a punishment. During "sports", the prisoners would perform various exercises upon command, such as marching and singing, running, crawling on one's elbows and on the tips of one's toes, rolling on ground covered with gravel and crushed-up bricks; and spinning around in circles with one's hands raised. These exercises were carried out at a rapid pace, irregardless of the age and health of a given prisoner.

---

[10] *Wspomnienia Rudolfa Hössa*, p. 140.

A specialist at thinking up new types of exercises was *SS-Oberscharführer* Ludwig Plagge. He could drill prisoners for hours on end while holding a pipe in his mouth (thus, the prisoners nicknamed him "little pipe"). Anyone who fell was beaten by Plagge's assistants and had to do additional exercises. Prisoners resisting were killed. This was the way in which the commander of the Warsaw fire department, Stanisław Gieysztor, died. Given his weight (around 100 kg), he was unable to run and fell down. Then, *Lagerältester* Leo Wietschorek began to beat him with a stick five centimeters thick. Lying on his back to protect himself from the blows, Gieysztor caught hold of the stick for a moment. This only outraged his attacker even more, who then started to beat him in a brutal fashion. After Gieysztor lost consciousness, Wietschorek suffocated him by forcing the pole down his throat. [11]

A punishment often applied at the women's camp was to force a prisoner to kneel with her hands up, in which she was forced to hold stones. Other punishments included a ban on sending and receiving letters, not receiving dinner during a full-day's work, additional work during free-time, etc.

---

[11] APMO, Höss Trial, vol. 25, card 5, testimony of former prisoner Michał Kula.

For more on the subject of punishments, see Henryk Kuszaj, "Strafen die von der SS an Häftlingen des Konzentrationslagers Auschwitz vollzogen wurden," *Hefte von Auschwitz* 3 (1960), pp. 3-45.

FRANCISZEK PIPER

DIRECT METHODS FOR KILLING PRISONERS

1. Executions

One direct method of extermination at the camp was execution. While it was officially maintained that only *Reichsführer-SS* Himmler — or, actually, the *Reichsicherheitshauptamt* (RSHA) — could order a prisoner's execution, in fact, most executions were carried out on the orders of the camp authorities without any formalities. The regulations regarding executions only served to camouflage the crimes being committed at the camp.

The execution orders that the RSHA occasionally promulgated were drawn up at the request of camp authorities in response to violations of discipline by prisoners that were considered particularly dangerous — for example, in the case of group escapes. In most cases, however, the head of the camp's Gestapo or *Politische Abteilung*, Maximilian Grabner, ordered the executions that were carried out. He usually decided whom to execute during his routine inspections of the camp prison, the so-called bunker, to which prisoners were sentenced for disciplinary violations or on suspicion of illegal activity at the camp. SS man Pery Broad, one of Grabner's subordinates, described one such inspection:

Grabner normally used the weekend — as he cynically said — to "clean out" the bunker. After he gave a briefing, the entire division had to follow him to the camp, to Block 11. Although only three or four officials were actually needed, Grabner brought everyone with him because he felt better together with a numerous staff. In the duty room of Block 11, he waited for the arrival of the *Lagerführer, SS-Hauptsturmführer* Aumeier. After a period of waiting, which he used to underline his importance, the little Bavarian walked into the room with a powerful stride. His harsh, screeching voice betrayed his drunkenness .... The supervisor of the bunker and several *Blockführer* complete the commission, which now proceeded to the cellar to begin "cleaning" .... The air in the cellar was so stale that you could hardly breathe .... The warden on duty opened the first cell doors with a key from his key-ring .... Holding the list of prisoners up to the door, Aumeier, together with Grabner, began to hold court. The first prisoner gave his name and told how long he had been sitting in the bunker. The *Lagerführer* questioned the *Rapportführer* briefly regarding why the prisoner had been thrown into the bunker. In those cases in which Division II had sentenced the prisoner, Grabner held the deciding voice. Then the two camp dignitaries decided: punishment report one or punishment report two .... With his blue pen, Aumeier would draw next to the name of the prisoner, so that all could see, a large cross .... since it was no longer a secret to anyone what "punishment report two" meant. [1]

The individuals sentenced to execution were led from the cellar of Block 11 to the first floor, to the washroom, where they disrobed and waited to be shot. In the neighboring room, women also waited naked to be shot. In the first years of the camp's existence, when the prisoners did not have camp numbers tattooed to their hands, it was written on their breasts with an indelible pencil. Until the end of 1942, the hands of the condemned were bound with wire, but this practice was discontinued, because cases of resistance had proven rare. In the face of their untimely death, the condemned men and women usually remained peaceful and dignified. They were killed individually or in twos with a bullet to the back of the head. The wall at which the executions took place, made of wood, sand and insulating board, was enclosed by the two walls to the courtyard between Blocks 10 and 11. Beneath the wall, where the victims's blood fell, sand had been strewn. Regardless of the time of year, the prisoners were shot naked and barefoot — first women, then men. The still bleeding corpses were transported to the crematorium. A path of blood marked the route that the vehicles had taken through the camp.

Many members and organizers of the camp underground perished in such a fashion after being jailed by the *Politische Abteilung*. On January 25, 1943, after a selection at the bunker, 53 prisoners were shot. They included high-ranking Polish officers: Colonel Jan Karcz, former head of the Cavalry Department in the Ministry for Military Affairs; Colonel Karol Kumuniecki, and major Edward Gött-Getyński. After a selection on October 11, 1943, 54 prisoners accused of a military conspiracy at the camp were executed, including famous Poles from the social, political, and military spheres. The following individuals were lost: Wacław Szumański from Warsaw and Józef Woźniakowski from Cracow, renowned attorneys; the prewar conservative politician and publicist, Jan Mosdorf; the former assistant commander of the first air regiment in Warsaw, Wing-Commander Teofil Dziama; Colonel Juliusz Gilewicz; and Captain Tadeusz Paolone-Lisowski.

The first to go before the screen [The Execution Wall-FP] — wrote former prisoner Ludwik Rajewski — were Colonel Dziama and Captain Lisowski-Paolone. They went in a fashion befitting a soldier. As they came before the screen, Dziama turned to the executioners carrying out the death sentence, Stiewitz and Clausen, with the request not to be shot in the back of the head, but like a soldier — right in the face .... Lisowski shouted one last time, "Long live Free and Indep..." These were his last words. [2]

Sometimes during the roll-call, anywhere from a few to several dozen names would be called out with the order to report to the camp chancellory in Block 24. The individuals summoned included prisoners whose files had been stamped "return undesirable" by the local Gestapo unit that had sent them to

[1] *Oświęcim w oczach SS: Höss, Broad, Kremer* (Oświęcim 1972), pp. 138-9.
[2] Ludwik Rajewski, *Oświęcim w systemie RSHA* (Warszawa and Kraków, 1946), p. 112.

the camp. After the details regarding each prisoner were reviewed in the chancellory, they were led to the Execution Wall in Block 11 and shot. In the official documents related to their death, as was the case with the prisoners executed after tours of the bunker, some common disease was given as the cause of death. The documents of some prisoners were doctored to show a previous admission to the camp hospital.

Upon the orders of higher police officials in the *Reich* or the General Government, hostages were also executed at the camp. At times, individuals were specially shipped to the camp with this goal in mind, as was the case with the 40 Poles shot on November 22, 1940. At other times, prisoners already residing at the camp were executed as hostages. The executions took place in revenge for activities of the resistance movement in the area where the hostages were from.

For example, 168 Polish actors, performers and officers arrested in a Cracow café were killed on May 27, 1942, in revenge for an attack against a high officer of the Luftwaffe. In revenge for acts of sabotage in Silesia, 56 prisoners from the area were executed on August 18, 1942. Around 280 prisoners from Lublin and Radom were murdered on October 28, 1942, in revenge for the activities of the resistance movement in their home areas.

The police court-martial (*Polizei-Standgericht*) from the Gestapo post in Katowice assembled every few weeks at Auschwitz to pass judgment on Poles from Silesia who were accused of illegal, conspiratorial activity against the occupiers, usually of a political nature. Among these individuals, however, one could find people who had been arrested for merely possessing a radio or discussing current political events. Such people — men, women, and even children — never became formal prisoners at the camp, but stood at the disposal of the Gestapo post in Katowice.

The court proceedings to decide each person's fate represented the final chapter of a long investigation during which — in order to obtain clarifications and a confession from the accused — the most refined torture had been applied. At the beginning of this process, the prisoner was normally whipped and kicked all over. If the resulting clarifications did not satisfy the "investigators", or if the suspect refused to give testimony that might have sometimes implicated his nearest friends or family, the suspect was beaten on the so-called "seesaw". After his torturers bound the prisoner's hand with chains, they ordered him to encircle his bent knees with them, beneath which an iron bar was inserted. The bar was secured, in turn, to a suitable pole, so that the prisoner was left hanging with his head towards the ground. This allowed his torturers to strike him at will on the buttocks and sex organs. The interrogators would strike the prisoners with such force that their bodies would move in rhythm like a pendulum and, at times, would even complete an entire revolution around the axis of the metal bar. If the victim cried out, they would cover his face with a gas mask.

Another method for forcing a confession was to pour hot water into the mouth or nose with a special funnel, which would make the tormented individual choke. The tormenters would occasionally tear off the fingernails of a suspect, or stick needles into particularly sensitive areas of his body. Even more gruesome tortures were applied. It thus comes as no surprise that the suspects confessed to all the deeds of which they were accused, whether they had committed them or not; the sessions of the court-martial represented a pure formality. Typically, the judgement would state:

> As a result of an investigation by the state police, the Pole... violated the laws of the German state... so the police court-martial of the Gestapo post in Katowice hearby condemns him to death. [3]

In a handful of cases, the accused only received a sentence in the concentration camp. Only a small portion of the documents from the proceedings of the court-martial have survived. On the basis of documents from the camp's resistance organization, which tried to document the crimes of the camp authorities as closely as possible, one finds that during the court-martial's sixth session, [4] of the 580 individuals judged, 556 people, including 76 women, were condemned to death. The remaining 24 persons, including one woman, received a sentence at the concentration camp. Altogether, an estimated 3,000-4,500 people were executed on the orders of the court-martial.

Functionaries from the *Politische Abteilung* applied the same methods of torture when questioning prisoners at the camp.

KL Auschwitz also served as a site for executing civilians who were partisans or members of underground organizations. The police would ship such individuals — men, women and children — to the camp to carry out their death sentence. These individuals, shot immediately upon their arrival, were never entered into the camp records. A former prisoner at the camp, Dr. Bolesław Zbozień, described one such execution:

> Sometime, I cannot remember the exact date, we encountered Palitzsch on the streets of the camp at Auschwitz. Before him, he was driving a man and a woman. The woman was carrying a small child in her arms, and two larger children, around four and seven years old, walked next to her. The entire group was walking in the direction of Block 11. I made it with some colleagues to Block 21 in time. From a window in a room on the ground floor, we gazed out at the courtyard to Block 11, standing on a table inside the room. As long as I live, the scene that played out before our eyes will remain engraved in my memory. The man and woman did not resist when Palitzsch stood them before the Wall of Death. It all took place in the greatest calm. The man held the hand of the child who stood on his left side. The second child stood between them; they both held his hand. The mother clasped the youngest to her breast. Palitzsch first shot the baby in the head. The shot to the back of the head exploded its skull .... and induced massive bleeding. The baby struggled like a fish, but the mother only held him more firmly to herself. Palitzsch next shot the child standing in the middle. The man and woman .... continued to stand without moving, like statues. Later, Palitzsch struggled with the oldest child, who would not allow himself to be shot. He threw him to the ground and shot him at the base of the head while standing on his shoulders. He then shot the woman, and at very last, the man.

---

[3] *Oświęcim w oczach SS*, p. 149.

[4] The court-martial met during its sixth session on the following dates: on Sept. 2, 1943; Oct. 22, 1943; Nov. 29, 1943; Sept. 29, 1944; Oct. 30, 1944, as well as in Mar. 1944.

This was the greatest monstrosity .... After that, although many executions were carried out, I did not watch them. [5]

Former prisoner Franciszek Gulba, sent to Block 11 as a punishment, also witnessed such an execution:

One evening, a dozen or so people were led to Block 11 .... In this group, there were men, women, and children... they were held in the basement of Block 11 .... Around noon the next day, the men of the group were the first to come out. They were led to the courtyard of Block 11 in twos. Their hands were bound with wire behind their backs. After he had driven them out, the *Blockälteste* brought the condemned before the "Wall of Death". *Rapportführer* Palitzsch carried out the executions. During breaks, while the next group was being brought out, he would throw his carbine over his shoulders and smoke a cigarette, maintaining complete calm while pacing around the courtyard. At the end, a woman was brought out with a child — a mother and daughter, we assumed. The mother .... held the daughter's hand. Both had been stripped to their underwear. Palitzsch shot the mother first. When she fell to the ground, the weeping child flung herself upon the body and screamed, "Mama! Mama!" Palitzsch shot at the girl, but he apparently missed, because the child continued to grasp her mother's body and shake her. The *Blockführer* ran out and held the girl still so that Palitzsch could aim freely. Shortly thereafter, the child was dead. We saw such executions almost every day. [6]

Such executions were carried out under a veil of secrecy. The prisoners were not allowed to leave their blocks while the executions took place or while the corpses were being loaded up and taken from Block 11 to the crematorium. Windows in Block 10 overlooking the Death Block were boarded shut with special screens, while the windows to Block 11 were partially walled shut. Before the firing began, prisoners were evacuated from rooms adjacent to the courtyard to the other side of the building.

Whenever particularly loud and bold escapes from the camp transpired, the escapees, if they were captured, were hanged. Unlike the executions by firing squad, such hangings had a public character. The goal was to terrorize the prisoners and convince them of the futility of resistance. The hangings took place during roll-calls so that everyone could see. Two special, portable gallows, located in the courtyard of Block 11, were used for this purpose. When necessary, temporary gallows were also constructed. Twelve prisoners from the surveyor's detail, accused of assisting there colleagues in escaping, were hanged on July 19, 1943, on such an improvised gallows — railroad tracks bolted down to three pillars. On December 6, 1943, at the sub-camp Neu-Dachs in Jaworzno, nineteen prisoners were hung, who were suspected of a plan to escape through a tunnel. In July or the first half of September 1944, a Pole, Edward Galiński, was hanged after being captured in a joint escape with a Jewish woman, Mala Zimetbaum, who also perished.

The prospect of execution by starvation particularly horrified the prisoners. Whenever a prisoner escaped, the commandant or *Lagerführer* would choose

---

[5] APMO, Collection of Testimonies, vol. 70 card 159-160.

[6] Ibid. cards 46-7.

ten or more prisoners at roll-call from the block where the escapee had resided and lock them up in a cell in the basement of Block 11. Once there, they received neither food nor water. Within a week or two, the tormented prisoners would perish. On the basis of the register from Block 11 one can establish several dates on which such "selections" took place. On April 23 and June 17, 1941, for each escapee from the camp, ten prisoners were selected for death by starvation. During one such "selection" at the end of July or beginning of August 1941, Maximilian Rajmund Kolbe, a Franciscan missionary-priest well-known to Polish Catholics before the war, voluntarily stepped forward from the ranks of prisoners and requested that *Lagerführer* Karl Fritzsch let him take the place of one of the individuals condemned to death by starvation, Franciszek Gajowniczek. After surviving for almost two weeks in the bunker of Block 11 and the deaths of most of his comrades, the priest was put to death with a phenol injection to the heart. [7]

From 1942 on, death by starvation was only applied to individual prisoners for disciplinary violations.

In addition to the 12,000 Soviet prisoners-of-war housed and registered at KL Auschwitz, in accordance with an order from the head of the Sipo and SD, Heydrich, political officers and other Soviet prisoners in POW camps were simply sent to Auschwitz for execution by special units, the so-called *Einsatzgruppen*. Such POWs were neither identified nor registered, but simply liquidated upon their arrival at the camp. The first such group of around 300 prisoners, mainly political officers from the Red Army, arrived in July 1941. Within several days, they were all murdered during work at the gravel pit next to the camp kitchen. The SS men standing at the top of the pit shot down at the POWs at the bottom. If any of the POWs failed to perish from an SS man's bullet, then the kapos would kill him with staffs, shovels or axes.

Given the falsification and destruction of most camp documents, one cannot establish how many prisoners lost their lives at the camp as a result of executions. [8]

In addition to the Jews sent to the camp in mass transports, smaller or larger groups of Poles — members of underground organizations, partisans, and hostages — and Soviet prisoners of war, were also shot in the gas chambers and crematoria. Sometimes the camp authorities attached them to transports of Jews to be killed by gassing. A member of the *Sonderkommando*, Alter Feinsilber, alias Stanisław Jankowski, wrote as follows:

In addition, two or three times each week a "demolition" would take place in the mortuary — i.e., a smaller or larger group of up to 250 people (various genders and ages) would undress and be shot. Since these people had walked in from outside the

---

[7] APMO, Mat. 605/47a, Materials about Father Kolbe. Accounts of former prisoners: Brunon Borgowiec, Maksymilian Chlebik, Franciszek Gajowniczek and others.

[8] An estimate for the number of executions only carried out before the Execution Wall would number several thousand. According to the account of former prisoner Ciechanowiecki, SS man Palitzsch declared that he alone had shot 25,000 prisoners. APMO, Höss Trial, vol. 1 card 156; Alfred Konieczny, *Pod rządami wojennego prawa karnego Trzeciej Rzeszy: Górny Śląsk, 1939-45*, Part VII. Warszawa-Wrocław 1972.

camp, they were not prisoners from Auschwitz. They had been arrested by
the Gestapo in various localities and sent to the crematorium for execution
without being entered into the camp records. In only a few cases did the
"demolition" also include prisoners from Auschwitz itself. Quakernack, I would
point out, carried out these executions with his own hands. At the time of
the executions, he would assemble all the Jews [from the *Sonderkommando* — FP]
at the cokery and carry out the executions in the presence of the Poles and Germans
employed at the crematorium. Since the cokery plant was only a dozen or so
meters away, we Jews heard the shots, the sound of people falling, and screams.
With my own ears I heard how the victims screamed that they were innocent;
I heard the screams of children. Quakernack would reply to them: "More of
ours are dying at the front." Then we were summoned inside the chamber where
the executions had taken place, and we Jews carried the still warm and bleeding
bodies out of the chamber to the ovens of the crematorium. Each hour, we
carried out 30 human bodies. Quakernack stood there with his gun in his hand,
stained and dripping blood. Besides Quakernack, the *Lagerführer* at Auschwitz,
Schwarz, and the commandant of the entire camp, along with his SS retinue, would
take part in such executions .... Every week, ten to fifteen Russian prisoners-of-war,
who had been held for several days in the bunker of Block 11, would be shot next to
the crematorium's oven. They were not entered into the camp's records, they were
not registered in general, so their deaths could not be verified even in the camp
documents. I observed such executions over the span of one year at Auschwitz, and
then more of the same at Birkenau, except that more Soviet POWs were shot each
week at Birkenau. [9]

Another member of the *Sonderkommando* wrote in his memoirs — which were
found after the war — about how Poles from the resistance movement,
brought in from outside the camp, were executed:

Sometime at the end of 1943, the following event came to pass. One hundred
sixty-four Poles were brought in from the area, including twelve young women — all
members of a secret organization. A number of personages from the SS came. At the
same time, several hundred Dutch Jews were brought in, prisoners of the camp, to be
gassed. One young Polish woman, already stripped naked, gave a brief, but
passionate speech to everyone, stigmatizing the Nazis' crimes and oppression. She
concluded: "We will not perish; our nation's history will immortalize us, our deeds
and spirit will live and flourish; the German nation will pay a price for our blood that
we can only imagine. Down with the barbarity of Hitler's Germany! Long live
Poland!" Then she turned to us, the Jews in the *Sonderkommando:* "Remember that
you bear the sacred burden to avenge us, the innocent. Tell our brothers, our nation,
that we went to death conscientiously, full of pride." Then the Poles kneeled to the
ground and solemnly repeated a prayer in a way that made a deep impression.
Then they all rose and sang the Polish national anthem together, and the Jews sang
the *Hatikwa* .... With a sincerity that was deeply moving, they expressed their last
feelings in this way, with a hope and belief in the future of their nation. After that,
they all sang the *Internationale* together. During the song, a Red Cross vehicle
arrived, gas was thrown into the chamber, and all of them breathed their last
breath. [10]

---

[9] *Wśród koszmarnej zbrodni*, pp. 41-3.
[10] Manuscript of "Unknown Author" in *Wśród koszmarnej zbrodni*, pp. 110-11.

2. The Killing of Prisoners in the Gas Chambers

The SS also used the gas chambers and crematoria for exterminting registered prisoners of different nationalities (Jews until October 1944, non-Jews until April 1943) who were considered terminally ill under the "euthanasia" campaign begun in Auschwitz in July 1941. The frequent selections at the camp's infirmaries (HKB) meant prisoners would go there only as a last resort. A contagious illness or longer stay at the HKB sufficed for ending up on the list of prisoners to be gassed.

Selections were conducted not only among sick prisoners at the HKB, but also among the nominally healthy prisoners as well. At Auschwitz I, selections took place in the showers between Blocks 1 and 2 and at other locations. One functionary who carried out such selections, *Rapportführer* Oswald Kaduk, was sentenced to life imprisonment in the Federal Republic of Germany in 1965. Often drunk, not able to stand on his own two feet, he would sit on a stool with a bottle of vodka in his hands and review the naked prisoners filing past him. One eyewitness testified as follows:

Selections were a daily thing at the sick wards. An indescribable panic fell upon the prisoners, however, when a *Lagersperre* was called after the evening roll-call, and a group of SS with *Lagerführer* Baer, *Arbeitsdienst*[11], *SS-Untersturmführer* Sell and Kaduk arrived at the showers .... When the *Blockführer* gave the signal, we set off at a brisk pace in single file, so that the SS men could get a look at all of us. We had to be very careful, since the landings beneath the inoperative showers had been unevenly laid. It was thus easy to twist one's leg and fall down. To stumble or fall led to one's immediate dispatch to the group selected for death. The SS men eyed us with a greedy look. They were seeking victims. The more, the better. After the inspection, during which we had transversed the entire shower barrack, we all lined up on Birch Alley, not far from the barbed-wire fence. The *Blockführer* re-counted the prisoners again. From our block, six colleagues had remained in the showers, destined either to the gas or to a phenol injection. We had survived these terrible few minutes. Some had lost their entire energy, others felt exhilirated. After we returned to the block, Adolf could not believe that he had survived this trial by fire. He tried to cross the room at the same tempo as he had in the showers only minutes before — he stumbled on the even floor. He touched his swollen legs, lovingly carressed them and repeated over and over: *Mein Gott, mein lieber Gott. Wie habe ich das fortgebracht.*[12] Then he walked around the room naked, as if he wanted to make certain that he was still among the living. He was as elated as a child who had unexpectedly received a gift and made everyone marvel at how he looked like a young god. In October of that year, we went through this test of strength and nerves again. This time, Adolf did not return with us.[13]

At the women's camp, selections normally took place when the work details returned in the evening or during so-called general roll-calls. During such roll-calls, the prisoners were ordered to run a dozen meters or so in their heavy

---

[11] Translator's note: The officer responsible for prisoner employment at the concentration camp.

[12] Translator's note: "Oh, God, my dear God. How did I make it?"

[13] Franciszek Stryj, *W cieniu krematoriów* (Katowice, 1960), pp. 225-6.

wooden clogs. The SS men would pull anybody who ran too slowly out of line with their wooden staffs and group them together nearby. If the gas chambers were full, the women would be held in Block 25, fully isolated from the rest of the camp. The block had barred windows, and the gate that led to its courtyard was always guarded. The screams and cries of the women awaiting their deaths issued forth from the block; they lifted their hands through the bars to beg for water. No one was permitted, however, to approach the block. The loading of the victims — pleading for their lives — into the trucks took a particularly brutal course. Women who struggled hopelessly to defend themselves were taken by their arms and legs and thrown violently onto the platforms. The dead were loaded along with the living.

Block 7 of the men's camp at Birkenau served the same function. The severely ill were assembled there both from Birkenau and the main camp. On average the block held 1,200 prisoners. Every three to five prisoners received one liter of soup. Bread was almost never distributed. For days on end, the prisoners would stand in front of the block, or would have to stand in rows at night. Drunken SS men would strike and kill them. When the trucks came to take them to the gas chambers, Dantesque scenes unfolded. Prisoners would try to hide, if only to stay until after the vehicles had left. They were found buried in garbage, under the straw in the sleeping area, in every recess of the block. When they were finally herded onto the vehicles, some resigned themselves apathetically, while others still tried to escape and save themselves by jumping out of the truck on the way. The condemned would sing patriotic and religious songs. One day, the prisoners were particularly moved by a transport of French women being sent to the gas chambers, who loudly sang the *Marseillaise*. Such scenes remained deeply engraved in the prisoners' memories. They would watch as the trucks reached the crematorium gates, where the last act of the tragedy would play out for its unfortunate victims. What occurred was supposed to remain a secret of the butchers forever. This would have certainly occured, except that by some miracle, a handful of workers from the *Sonderkommando* survived. Dr. Mikloś Nyiszli, a former prisoner who dissected corpses on the orders of Dr. Mengele in a specially--equipped laboratory in Crematorium II, wrote the following about the final moments of the selection victims' lives:

Two large, barred windows, covered with mosquito wire, looked out from my chamber to the courtyard. Every day, at about seven in the evening, a truck came up to the gate of the crematorium. It carried around 70-80 men or woman to be liquidated. The daily allotment of prisoners selected at the concentration camp. They came here from the barracks and the hospitals. Most had been residents at the concentration camp for many years or at least a number of months and did not have any illusions regarding their fate. When the truck drove through the gate, the entire courtyard was filled with a monstrous pre-death scream. Those who had been chosen for death knew that there was no escape beneth the chimney of the crematorium. They did not have enough strength left to jump from the high platform of the truck. The SS guards yelled and pressured them. The non-commissioned officer driving the truck lost his patience. He sat down behind the wheel and started the engine. The front of the gigantic platform rised up slowly and dumped the people out. The sick prisoners, already half-dead, fell on their heads, their faces, one on top of the other — onto the concrete. A horrible cry rose to the heavens. A terrible scene .... The *Sonderkommando* had already torn the rags of the victims and thrown them into a pile in the courtyard. They carried the prisoners into the boiler room, where *Oberscharführer* Muhsfeld waited for them in front of the furnace grates. Today, it was his turn. He had rubber gloves on his hands and was carrying a gun. The people standing in front of him fell to the floor, one after the other, making room for the next ones. In the course of several minutes, Muhsfeld had 'knocked off' all eighty — that was what he usually said, '*umgelegt*'. A half hour later, all that remained of them was a handful of ashes. [14]

During the typhoid epidemic that spread through the camp, not tens, but hundreds of prisoners were killed at a time in the gas chambers. On August 29, 1942, the newly-appointed doctor for the SS garrison, Kurt Uhlenbroock, ordered that everyone afflicted with typhus be executed, including prisoners recuperating at the HKB. 746 prisoners were taken from the HKB and exterminated in the gas chambers.

On the days and nights of July 10-11 and 11-12, 1944, around 7,000 people were gassed during the liquidation of the family camp for Jews from Theresienstadt, located at Birkenau. On August 2, during the liquidation of the Gypsy family camp at Birkenau, 2,897 Gypsies were gassed to death — men, women and children. This was the last remaining group of the more than 20,000 Gypsies sent to the camp since February 1943. Except for a small number who were freed or sent to other camps (ca. 2,000), all of them perished from starvation, disease or manslaughter.

Prisoners from the affiliated camps also perished in the gas chambers after SS doctors visiting the HKB designated them as unable to return to work quickly. Between November 1943 and January 1945, Dr. Horst Fischer, a camp doctor at KL Auschwitz III, selected ca. 1,300-1,600 prisoners from the sub-camps Neu-Dachs (Jaworzno), Eintrachthütte (Świętochłowice), Janina-grube (Libiąż) and Jawischowitz (Jawiszowice) for death. SS sanitarians appointed by him also carried out selections at the sub-camps. Anywhere from a dozen to several dozen prisoners could be selected during one visit. In the largest sub-camps, Buna in Monowitz (Monowice) or Neu-Dachs (Jaworzno), the number of prisoners selected could run into hundreds. On January 18, 1944, for example, 254 prisoners were selected at the Neu-Dachs sub-camp. By February 3, of these prisoners, four had died, three had been stricken from the selection list, and the remaining 247 had been murdered in the gas chambers of KL Auschwitz II.

During 1942-43, selections took place every two weeks at the largest Auschwitz-affiliated camp, KL Monowitz, situated next to the facilities of IG Farbenindustrie. Thereafter, they took place less often. As a result, between November 1942 and December 1944, more than 8,000 prisoners were shipped to KL Auschwitz II-Birkenau or — less often — to KL Auschwitz I for extermination.

---

[14] Mikloś Nyiszli, *Auschwitz, A Doctor's Eyewitness Account* (New York, 1960), p. 126-27.

New prisoners, healthy and strong, would replace those who had been murdered. The enterprises that leased the prisoners considered this constant rotation of the labor force necessary for maintaining a suitable level of productivity. It was even specified as a condition in the contracts between the firms and the SS. The contract between the Main Economic-Administrative Office of the SS (*Wirtschafts- und Verwaltungshauptamt der SS*) and the firm Ost-Machinenbau GmbH in Sosnowitz (Sosnowiec), clearly stated in Point 4: "Ill prisoners will be returned to the concentration camp at Auschwitz to the extent that their illness is not of a temporary character and their return to work cannot be expected." [15]

Another guarantee that this system for rotating the labor force would function effectively were the principles that governed the settlement of accounts. The firms paid the camp administration exclusively on the basis of the days worked by each prisoner. So, the state treasury, in whose name the camp received payments, would lose money whenever a prisoner fell ill. Thus, removing sick prisoners from the sub-camps lay in the interest of both parties to the agreement.

It also occurred that representatives from the various enterprises would themselves take part in the selections and designate prisoners to be removed from the sub-camps. Some even allowed the camp staff to use the firm's vehicles to this end. Stanisław Pluta, employed as a driver at the Trzebinia refinery, testified about one such incident:

On the orders of my dispatcher, I drove with my truck to the camp at Trzebionka, where around fifteen ill, clearly emaciated Jewish prisoners were loaded onto the truck. Under the escort of some SS men, I brought the prisoners to the concentration camp in Birkenau [Brzezinka]. After they got out of the truck at the camp, several dozen new, healthy prisoners from Birkenau got onto the truck, and we took them to the camp at Trzebionka. [16]

Prisoners who were selected out were usually murdered immediately in the gas chambers or held for a period of time in a ward of the men's HKB at Birkenau. Former prisoner Juliusz Ganszer wrote about the subject in his memoirs:

One day, a whole group of emaciated prisoners were brought to us [the HKB at Birkenau — FP] from the coal-mining camps nearby. They were locked up in the *Waschraum* [17] for three nights and two days. The *Blockälteste* at the *Waschraum* was Staszek Paduch. Without any thought as to what might await us, we decided to give them a barrel of soup. In my block there were many Poles who had received packages, so the soup had been left over. When we lugged the barrel into the *Waschraum* which Paduch unlocked, the mustiness and stench overpowered our noses. The condemned men, completely naked, kept the cold, concrete shower room

---

[15] Wojewódzkie Archiwum Państwowe w Katowicach, Collection Berghütte, sygn. 25-11, s. 6-6a.

[16] Akta Okręgowej Komisji Badania Zbrodni Hitlerowskich w Krakowie, sygn. 18/67.

[17] Translator's note: washroom.

warm with the heat of their own bodies. Some of them prayed aloud, others were talking. All of them rushed to the soup. The following evening, they were all taken and gassed. [18]

The gas chambers and crematoria were the most enduring buildings constructed at KL Auschwitz. They — along with the planned crematorium number six, which was to surpass all previous ones in its size and capabilities — outlined the camp's future evolution. In order to destroy all traces of the crimes that they had committed, the Nazis blew up the crematoria. Today, however, the concrete ruins of these buildings remain a grim, eternal "memorial" to the victims of Nazi genocide.

3. Extermination by Injection

The political situation in Europe, Germany's military successes, and above all else, the predicted collapse of the Soviet state in the near future — all contributed to a sense of impunity within the Nazi administration and presented the necessary conditions for accelerating the genocide being conducted at the concentration camps. Since the methods of extermination applied up to that time had proved insufficient, the Nazis began to kill prisoners with lethal injections and through asphyxiation in the gas chambers. Up to that point such methods had only been applied in Germany at so-called "euthanasia" facilities, used for murdering the mentally ill. The facilities had specially-equipped shower rooms where, under the pretense of bathing, carbon monoxide had been pumped in through the water pipes to kill off the mental patients.

Special commissions of doctors would designate prisoners to be sent to the euthanasia facilities for extermination based on their ability to work. The transports often included terminally-ill and invalid prisoners, who were told that they were being sent off to lighter work or to recover. The transports also included prisoners whom the SS simply wanted to get rid of.

At KL Auschwitz, the first selection of this type took place on July 28, 1941. The 575 prisoners who were selected, rather than being killed on the spot, were shipped to the euthanasia center at Sonnenstein in Saxony to be gassed.

The practice of liquidating ailing prisoners with an injection of phenol to the heart first began in August 1941. It represented a continuation of the euthanasia campaign referred to in administrative correspondence with the cryptonym "14 f 13". The SS doctors who selected the ill prisoners to receive such injections during various periods of the camp's history included: Friedrich Entress, Erwin von Helmersen, Heinz Thilo, Edmund König, Josef Mengele, and Bruno Kitt. Most often, the SS sanitarians Josef Klehr (serving a life sentence since 1965 in the Federal Republic of Germany) and Herbert Scherpe would administer the injections, or prisoners who had been trained to do so, such as Alfred Stesel and Mieczysław Pańszczyk. Prisoners selected for "skewering" had to report to Block 20. There, they were called into the out

---

[18] APMO, Collection of Reminiscences vol. 2, card. 379.

patient hospital one at a time and sat down in a chair. Then two prisoners assigned to do so would restrain the victim's hands, and a third would cover his eyes with a towel. Klehr would then stick the needle into the victim's heart and inject the phenol. The corpse would be thrown onto a pile in the adjoining washroom, and the next prisoner would be immediately called in. During certain periods, several dozen prisoners would be killed each day using this method. For example, during four months in 1942 (August, September, November, and December), 2,467 people were killed by phenol injection.

FRANCISZEK PIPER

THE MASS EXTERMINATION OF JEWS IN THE GAS CHAMBERS

At about the same time as the first ailing prisoners were being sent to the euthanasia facilities at Sonnenstein and executions by phenol injections had commenced, large numbers of Soviet prisoners of war began to arrive at the camp, who were to be immediately exterminated upon the orders of R. Heydrich, chief of the Third Reich's Security Police and Security Services (Sipo and SD). It was *Lagerführer* Fritzsch, however, who decided to test the gas Zyklon B on the POWs as a potential means for the mass extermination of Jews. Up to that point, Zyklon B was only used at the camp for delousing.

After several small-scale attempts in August, on September 3, 1941, a transport of around 600 Soviet POWs were driven into the cellar of Block Nr 11, along with 250 prisoners selected from the camp hospital. After the windows were sealed with dirt, the gas was thrown inside. Because a few victims were still alive the next day, the amount of gas was doubled and the room was sealed once more. On the night of September 4, the prisoners from the punishment company and male nurses from the camp hospital were summoned to the courtyard of Block 11. They were to carry out a special task, they were told, about which they were to tell no one, upon penalty of death. They were ordered to put on gas masks and directed inside the cellar, where the bodies of the gas victims lay. The prisoners had to carry the corpses to the courtyard, remove the victims' clothes and underwear, and carry the bodies to the crematorium. The work lasted for two days. Because the camp staff had had to remove all the prisoners from the block [1] during the gassing — an inconvenience — and the rooms had to be aired out for a long time, the next gassing of Soviet POWs took place at the mortuary located next to the crematorium, a former ammunition bunker with a surface area of 78 m². The former commandant, Höss, later described how the extermination of the transport of 900 POWs proceeded:

While the transport was being unloaded, several holes were made in the ceiling of the mortuary. The Russians had to take off their clothes in the vestibule, and then they entered the mortuary quite peacefully, having been told that they were to be deloused. The transport filled up the entire mortuary exactly. Next, the door was

---

[1] The block housed the camp jail and the penal company.

closed, and gas was dropped through the holes. I do not know how long it took to kill them, but one could hear some of them murmuring for a long time. After the gas was thrown in, several POWs yelled, 'Gas!', then a loud bellowing began, they began to press against the door, but the door withstood the pressure. It was several hours later before it was opened up and the rooms aired out. [2]

The SS exterminated subsequent transports of Soviet POWs in a similar fashion.

The Commandant of KL Auschwitz, Rudolf Höss, responsible for preparing the camp for the mass extermination of Jews, verified the effectiveness of Zyklon B. He recognized that it was a more effective tool for poisoning people on a mass scale than the carbon monoxide used at the euthanasia facilities. He informed Adolf Eichmann of the Main Security Office of the Reich (*Reichssicherheitshauptamt*, RSHA) about Zyklon B during one of his routine visits to Auschwitz, associated with the ongoing preparations for the "final solution of the Jewish question". They both decided that Zyklon B should be employed for killing the Jews.

We do not know the exact date when the mass extermination of Jews at KL Auschwitz began. Most likely, small, individual transports of Jews were exterminated in the gas chamber next to Crematorium I already in the fall of 1941. Transports of Jews from Silesia began to arrive on a larger scale after the Wannsee Conference in January 1942.

At first the Jews were exterminated, just like the Soviet prisoners of war, in the mortuary next to the camp's crematorium. Transports would arrive by train at the unloading ramp next to the camp. SS guards would escort the new arrivals to the courtyard of the crematorium. Then all roads and passages to the courtyard were sealed off; nobody was allowed to leave. After the victims removed their clothes, they were driven into the mortuary, the improvised gas chamber. The SS men told them that they were going to have a shower, and after that, they would receive food and be sent to work. At the moment when they dropped the Zyklon B into the gas chamber, a truck purposely placed nearby was turned on in order to drown out the yells and screams of the dying.

After the chamber was aired out, prisoners assigned to the crematorium would arrive to burn the corpses. All of this took place with the greatest secrecy; only the smallest circle of SS men from the camp administration and political division initially took part. These individuals included Maximilian Grabner, Franz Hössler, and Adolf Theuer (responsible for disinfection).

The small capacity of the crematorium, which could burn only about 340 corpses per day, and the difficulty in keeping the entire action secret, resulted in its transfer to the camp at Birkenau, as the SS had originally planned. Already during Eichmann's first visit to Auschwitz, they had taken one of the vacated residential buildings in Birkenau, walled up the windows, bolted down

---

[2] *Wspomnienia Rudolfa Hössa komendanta obozu oświęcimskiego* (Warszawa, 1965), p. 150. Crematorium I at the main camp, Auschwitz I, had been opened in August 1940. At first, it was used for burning the bodies of prisoners who died from natural causes or from executions. At that time only one oven was in operation, which had two grates. In 1941-1942, two other ovens were built.

the doors to make it airtight, and made special holes in the walls for dropping in gas. The entrance doors bore the inscription: "To the Showers." The new gas chamber was called Bunker 1.

Jews to be killed in the gas chambers were brought by train to the unloading ramp of the freight station at Auschwitz and driven on foot to the bunker. At the beginning, selections were carried out among the arriving transports only on an irregular basis. In July 1942, they began to take place regularly. After they had cordoned off the area, the SS men would open the doors to the train's cars. Yelling instructions as the people disembarked, they would begin dividing them up. The men had to stand in one line along the ramp; women and children, in another. People, uncertain about their fate, began to cry and scream at the prospect of being split up. Once in line, they had to file in front of an SS doctor, who would decide a prisoner's ability to work on the basis of his or her external appearance. With a movement of his hand, he would send some to the left, others to the right.

Depending on the actual labor needs at the time and the age and gender structure of the transport that arrived, a larger or smaller percentage of its passengers (20% on average) — strong and healthy young people — were sent to the camp. The remainder — the old, the lame, mothers with children, pregnant women, and individuals who looked physically weak — were sent to their deaths. The latter were led up portable steps into a truck, which delivered them to the bunker. At times, when not enough trucks were available, some of the victims would be led on foot to the area that later became the third construction site (BIII) at Birkenau.

The SS men escorting prisoners sought not to provoke them. They tried in fact to dismiss their victims' fears about the future with false information. The view of the village house that stood nearby, surrounded in spring by trees blooming in the orchard, must have had a calming effect upon the prisoners. After their arrival at the site, the SS men told them that disinfection and showers awaited them; they ordered the people to undress in two barracks designated for this purpose. They then drove the people inside the house. People who sensed a ruse, whose behavior might have unleashed a panic, were discretely led behind the building and killed with a gunshot to the base of the head.

Around 800 people could fit at a time into the gas chamber, which was divided into two rooms. Once the space was filled, the SS men would immediately shoot the remaining victims. After they bolted the doors shut and tightened the screws, specially-trained SS "disinfectors" would drop Zyklon B into the interior in the form of lumps of diatomite soaked in hydrocyanic acid. The people inside died within several minutes from internal suffocation, caused by a breakdown in the process of oxygen exchange between their blood and tissues, an impact of the cyanide. The people standing closest to the openings in the ceiling died almost immediately; people who screamed, old people, the sick and children would also perish quickly. To make certain that no one was left alive, the chamber was only opened after half an hour. At times when a larger number of transports arrived, the time for gassing was shortened to ten minutes. Most of the corpses were found next to the doors because people would try to flee from the gas as it rapidly spread throughout the chamber. The bodies, found half-sitting or curled up, would cover the entire floor of the gas chamber. The bodies were covered with excrement, vomit, and blood. The skin had taken on a pink color.

After the gas chamber was aired out, the corpses were removed, loaded onto iron carts and carried several hundred meters away on the tracks of a narrow-gauge railway to the deep pits where they were buried.

After the mass extermination of the Jews had already begun, Eichmann arrived at the camp with an order from Himmler. It directed the camp administration to cut and save the hair from the women's corpses and to extract the gold teeth from all the victims. The hair was subsequently sold to German textile firms for the production of haircloth at the price of 50 pfennig per kilogram. The firm Alex Zink in Roth, near Nuremburg, was one recipient of the hair. The gold teeth, on the other hand, were melted at the SS hospital building in the main camp and delivered to the Main Sanitation Office of the SS (*SS-Sanitätshauptamt*) in Berlin in the form of gold bars. Rings and other jewelry were also removed from the corpses.

The Jews had to leave the earthly possessions that they had brought with them at the unloading ramp. Their possessions, they were told, would be delivered separately to the camp. Prisoners belonging to a special work detail (*Aufräumungskommando*), or "Canada" in camp jargon, would load the goods into waiting trucks, which then carried them to special warehouses (see p. 170). A small portion of these goods ended up on display at a camp "museum" in Block 24 of the main camp, toured by SS dignitaries whenever they visited.

Due to the rising number of transports, a new gas chamber was installed in an adapted house in the summer of 1942, as had been the case with the first gas chamber. Called Bunker Nr. 2, it had four rooms, where 1,200 people could be liquidated at a time. The camp staff made use of the gas chamber during Himmler's two-day visit to the camp in July 1942 to demonstrate the entire process for gassing Jews, from the arrival of the transport and the selection at the unloading ramp to the emptying of the gas chamber at the end. Also present for the demonstration were the Supreme President and *Gauleiter* of Upper Silesia, *SS-Brigadeführer* Fritz Bracht, and the Commander of the SS and Police for the Southeastern Region, headquartered in Wrocław (Breslau), *SS-Obergruppenführer* Ernst Schmauser.

Shortly after Himmler's visit, *SS-Standartenführer* Paul Blobel from Eichmann's office arrived at the camp with an order that the mass graves be excavated and the corpses burned. Since June 1942, Eichmann's Office had been directing the effort to obliterate all traces of the mass executions carried out on Polish and Soviet territory. In order to acquaint themselves with the latest technology for cremating corpses, a delegation from KL Auschwitz, composed of Commandant Rudolf Höss, *SS-Untersturmführer* Franz Hössler (from the prisoner employment office), and *SS-Untersturmführer* Walter Dejaco, visited the camp at Kulmhof (Chełmno on Ner). After they observed the experimental methods being used there (e.g., attempting to destroy a large number of corpses by making use of explosives), they decided that the most effective and quickest way for liquidating corpses was simply to burn them in the open air.

From the end of September 1942, corpses from the gas chambers at Auschwitz were burned in piles of more than 2,000 bodies interspersed with wood. The SS also began to burn corpses exhumed from the pits. To keep the excavated corpses burning, they poured on oil or methanol mixed with fat from the burning corpses.

Prisoners from a special work detail, the so-called *Sonderkommando*, had to perform all the auxiliary work: removing the bodies from the gas chambers, cutting the hair, tearing out gold teeth, and burning corpses. The *Sonderkommando* consisted mainly of Jewish prisoners originating from the countries from which the latest transports were arriving. This work detail varied in size depending on the intensity of the killing in the gas chambers at a given time. Prisoners from this group lived apart and isolated from the other prisoners — at the main camp, in the basement of Block 11. At Birkenau, they resided in a special block assigned to them until mid-1944, and thereafter, in various rooms of the crematoria themselves.

According to Eichmann's orders, these prisoners were to be liquidated after every large operation. In practice, however, the *Sonderkommando* was liquidated only once every several months, and so-called skilled workers were spared: stokers, mechanics and prisoners functionaries of so-called self-government.

One of the first *Sonderkommandos*, numbering 80 prisoners, worked at digging up the victims who had been gassed in Bunkers 1 and 2 during August 1942. The next group of 150-300 prisoners worked at the bunkers from September to the end of November 1942 and burned the 107,000 corpses that had been exhumed from the mass graves. This second *Sonderkommando* was liquidated on December 3, 1942, in the gas chamber of Crematorium I. [3]

The original gas chambers installed in the bunkers, as well as the pits for burning corpses, were considered temporary facilities. They continued to be used until the four gas chambers and crematoria, built especially for exterminating the Jews, were finished.

The construction of the new facilities began in summer 1942 and rapidly progressed until mid-1943. Several hundred prisoners worked day and night to finish their construction. The first new facility put into operation was Crematorium IV, on March 22, 1943; then Crematorium II, on March 31; Crematorium V, on April 4; and Crematorium III, on June 25. Crematorium II, almost identical in construction to Crematorium III, contained five three-chamber ovens with two furnaces apiece. Crematoria IV and V, on the other hand, each contained one eight-chamber oven with four furnaces.

Before the new crematoria were officially put into operation, representatives of the camp administration and employees of the firm Topf und Söhne conducted a trial run of Crematorium II in the presence of a special delegation of higher SS officers from Berlin. Having been acquainted with the new crematoria's operation by August Brück, the kapo responsible for the

---

[3] Salmen Lewental, *Amidst a Nightmare of Crime. Notes of Prisoners of Sonderkommando Found at Auschwitz* (Oświęcim, 1973). Member of one of the *Sonderkommando*, has described in his notes the psychological difficulties of prisoners assigned to this special work detail.

crematoria at KL Buchenwald, the prisoners from the *Sonderkommando* lit the pilot lights to the furnaces on the morning of March 5, 1943, and kept them burning until 4 p. m. Then, in the presence of the special delegation, who timed the start-up procedure with watches in hand, the prisoners put three bodies into each chamber (a total of 45). Because they took 40 minutes to burn up, contrary to expectations, it was ordered that the ovens be heated for ten to twenty days. In the end, according to a letter from the *Zentralbauletung der Waffen SS und Polizei Auschwitz* to Administrative Groups C of SS-WVHA of June 28, 1943, [4] it was found that each crematorium had the following capacities in 24 hours:

Crematorium I   —   340 corpses
Crematorium II   —   1440 corpses
Crematorium III —   1440 corpses
Crematorium IV   —   768 corpses
Crematorium V   —   768 corpses

Altogether, the crematoria could burn a total of 4,756 corpses a day. This represented only their theoretical capabilities, based on the assumption that they would function regularly, without need for repair, as long as they were serviced on a regular basis — e.g., the slag would be cleaned out of furnaces. According to former prisoners in the *Sonderkommando*, however, the productivity of the crematoria was in fact twice as high; during periods when numerous transports arrived, up to 5,000 corpses would be consumed each day in Crematoria II and II alone, and as many as 3,000 in Crematoria IV and V. [5]

From then on, corpses were only burned in pits outside when larger transports arrived and it was impossible to burn all the bodies in the crematoria. Given the unlimited capabilities for burning corpses outside, the number of corpses burned in the open depended on the number of transports arriving and the capabilities of the gas chambers. The death-factory Auschwitz-Birkenau reached its highest "productivity" in spring and summer of 1944 during the deportation of Jews from Hungary, the so-called "Hungarian Action." Because the capabilities of Crematoria II-V and their gas chambers proved insufficient, Bunker 2 was returned to operation, the old burning pits were reexcavated, five additional large pits were established next to Crematorium V, and the railroad tracks that carried the trains full of victims were extended right up to the crematoria.

A barbed-wire fence surrounded the crematoria. They had separate entrances from the rest of the camp and were hidden from it by willow trees. Perfectly-maintained flowerbeds gave the whole area an innocent look.

The gas chambers and the undressing rooms to Crematoria II and III were situated underground. The large halls for undressing not only had misleading inscriptions on the wall, but also contained numbered hooks with benches beneath them. The gas chambers themselves contained water pipes and fake

---

[4] *SS im Einsatz. Eine Dokumentation über die Verbrechen der SS* (Berlin, 1960), p. 169; APMO, BW 30/42/2.

[5] APMO, Höss Trial, vol. 11, card 139, testimony of Henryk Tauber, former member of the *Sonderkommando*.

showers. People were driven to the wall as they entered the gas chamber, behind a cordon of SS men. As the chamber filled up, the SS guards would move closer to the door. Using this method, around 2,000 people could be packed into a gas chamber measuring $30 \times 7 \times 7 \times 2.4$ m with a surface area of 210 m^2 (later divided into two rooms).

The gas chambers to Crematoria IV and V, on the other hand, had been built above ground, for financial reasons. Each gas chamber was divided at first into three, and later four rooms, with a total capacity of around 2,000 people. The holes for dropping gas into the gas chambers of Crematorium IV and V, as had been the case with the bunkers, were built into the walls. In Crematoria II and III's gas chambers, on the other hand, Zyklon B was dropped through holes in the ceiling, down special chutes made of several layers of thick wire mesh with a moving core that ran down to the tiled floor. An SS "disinfector" would throw the contents of a can of Zyklon B into a special distribution cone, which — by speading the lumps of diatomite evenly within the core of the chute — accelerated the gassing process. According to the testimony of the former commandant, Höss, five to seven kilograms of Zyklon B sufficed to murder 1,500 people. In the years 1942-43, the firm Tesch und Stabenow delivered a total of 19,652.69 kg of Zyklon B (which was also used for disinfection) to the camp.

Peepholes in the doors to the gas chamber allowed the SS doctor supervising the gassing to observe the interior. Among the few people to watch the victims suffocating inside, besides the SS doctors and crematoria staff, was Höss himself. He later wrote:

> Through the peephole in the doors one could see how the people standing nearest to the entry pipe immediately fell dead. Close to one-third of the victims died immediately. The others began to press forward, scream, and gasp for air. Rather quickly, however, the screams faded into murmurs, and after a couple of minutes, everyone was lying on the floor. After 20 minutes at the most, no one was moving. [6]

Once the ventilators were turned on and the gas was dispersed from inside, the doors to the gas chamber were opened. The *Sonderkommando* carried out the corpses, cut the hair from the heads of the dead women, and transported the bodies in electric freight elevators below ground to the crematorium.

Once all jewelry and gold teeth had been removed, the victim's bodies were placed in special stretchers (at the beginning, in wagons) and dispatched into the ovens. It took 20-30 minutes to burn three to five bodies. The ashes, along with the remains from any bones that had not been consumed, were ground up in special pestles; they were then either dumped in rivers (mainly the Vistula) or transported by truck to the village of Harmense (Harmęże), where they were thrown into the fish ponds, used to fill in swamps, or used to fertilize fields at the camp's farms. The gold teeth taken from the corpses were melted in a special crucible installed in one of the rooms inside Crematorium III. The garrets of the crematoria, warmed by the ovens below, were used to dry the hair shorn from the corpses of the female victims.

---

[6] *Wspomnienia Rudolfa Hössa*, p. 209.

The prisoners of the *Sonderkommando* carried out all these tasks under the supervision of SS men. From 1942-45, the following were the supervisors of the crematoria: *SS-Haumptscharführer* Otto Moll (sentenced to death in a trial at Dachau and executed on May 28, 1946); *SS-Hauptscharführer* Hirsch, *SS-Unterscharführer* Steinberg, *SS-Scharführer* Buch and *SS-Oberscharführer* Erich Muhsfeld (on December 22, 1947, sentenced by Poland's Supreme National Tribunal and executed). The *Sonderkommando* grew to its largest proportions in the summer of 1944 — around 900 prisoners — at the height of the campaign to exterminate Hungarian Jews. According to data from August 30, 1944, 874 prisoners alternated work in two shifts, day and night, at Birkenau's four crematoria.

When the number of Jews sent to the camp for extermination began to dwindle at the end of 1944, it was decided to gradually liquidate the prisoners working in the *Sonderkommando*. In September 1944, 200 of its members were sent from Birkenau to the camp at Auschwitz, where they were deceitfully gassed in rooms that had never been used for that purpose before. When the SS tried to liquidate the next group, a revolt broke out on October 7, 1944, which resulted in the death of several hundred prisoners, killed during the fighting or subsequently murdered. Figures from October 9, 1944, show that the *Sonderkommando* numbered only 212 prisoners. Fourteen were arrested the next day and jailed in the bunker of Block 11 at the main camp. The arrested included one of the rebellion's organizers, Jankiel Handelsman from Radom. The 198 remaining prisoners contained to work at Crematoria II, III and V. Crematorium IV, destroyed during the revolt, was not operating anymore.

In the final period of the camp's existence, the prisoners of the *Sonderkommando* were employed in destroying all traces of the crimes committed at the camp. In October 1944, under the supervision of SS men, they demolished the burnt-out walls of Crematorium IV. In November, after the transports ceased, they removed the equipment from the gas chambers and demolished the ovens in Crematorium II and III. In January 1945, Crematorium II, III and V were blown up. On November 26, 100 of the around 200 prisoners in the *Sonderkommando* at the time were assembled, allegedly to be shipped to KL Gross-Rosen; they were, in fact, murdered near the camp. On January 5, 1945, six members of the *Sonderkommando* were shipped to KL Mauthausen and shot, 30 were assigned to maintain the last active crematorium, and 70 were employed at cleaning out and leveling the pits where corpses had been burned. [7]

The last two groups of prisoners from the *Sonderkommando,* about 100 in number, left the camp on January 18, 1945, under SS escort, along with the other prisoners being evacuated on foot in the direction of Wodzisław Ślaski. Of these prisoners from the *Sonderkommando*, several dozen survived the war, including:

Alter Feinsilber alias Stanisław Jankowski, who had arrived at the camp in March 30, 1942, from Drancy and had received camp number 27675. In

---

[7] Handwritten accounts from "Unknown Author" and Chaim Herman in *Amidst a Nightmare of Crime.*

November 1942, he was attached to the *Sonderkommando*. During the evacuation from the camp in January 1945, he escaped in Jastrzębie;

Szlama Dragon, who had arrived at the camp on December 6, 1942, from the ghetto in Mława and received camp number 80359. He became a member of the *Sonderkommando* on December 10, 1942. During the camp's evacuation, he fled in the vicinity of Pszczyna;

Henryk Tauber, who had arrived at the camp on January 19, 1943, from the ghetto in Cracow. He was a member of the *Sonderkommando* beginning in February 1943 and ran away while prisoners were being evacuated in January 1945.

These former prisoners presented Polish judicial officials with detailed testimony regarding the procedures and facilities used for mass extermination in the gas chambers.[8] After the war, written testimonies from six other members of the *Sonderkommando* were also found, buried next to the crematoria, including accounts by Salmen Gradowski, Salmen Lewental, Chaim Herman, a prisoners with the first name of Lejb, and a Greek Jew, likely named Nadsari (vel Marcel Nadjary, Nadsari, Nadjar). Their accounts, along with the testimony of the prisoners mentioned above, have born invaluable — if horrifying — witness to the crimes that were committed at Auschwitz.[9]

---

[8] APMO, Höss Trial, vol. 1, cards 3-28; vol. 11, cards 103-121 and 122-170. Testimony of Jankowski, Dragon, and Tauber; Jankowski's testimony was also published in *Amidst a Nightmare of Crime*, pp. 31-68.

[9] Handwritten accounts by Gradowski, Lewental, Herman and an unknown author can be found in *Amidst a Nightmare of Crime*, pp. 75-190. Lejb's handwritten account was published in *Hefte von Auschwitz* 14 (1973), pp. 17-71.

ANDRZEJ STRZELECKI

THE PLUNDERING OF PERSONAL EFFECTS FROM THE JEWISH VICTIMS OF MASS EXTERMINATION

When expelling Jews from the various ghettoes and transit camps for deportation to death camps, including KL Auschwitz, the Nazi authorities presented the Jews with the perspective of resettlement to new territories. In keeping with this prospect, the Jews would gather together their most valuable possessions so that they could begin their lives anew under unknown conditions and survive for an unspecified length of time in an unknown place. Following the Nazis' instructions, they usually arrived at Auschwitz with bags weighing no more than 10-50 kilograms, containing food, clothing, toiletries, various housekeeping items (pots, bedding, quilts, rugs, etc.) and specialized instruments and materials. Doctors, for example, brought along drugs and medical equipment.

It was generally forbidden to bring along valuables and large sums of money. Many people violated these restrictions, however, and hid valuables that they had saved from previous theft in their luggage, clothes and shoes — even in their food. The Jews were often required to bring with them a two to three days' supply of food. Sometimes, a fourteen days' supply of food was conveyed in separate freight cars for all the people in a given transport.

Items brought to KL Auschwitz by the Jews destined for extermination were subject to arbitrary plundering by the SS central administration, in co-operation with the Ministries of Economics and Finance of the *Reich* and other Nazi organs, under the codename "Operation Reinhard" (*Aktion Reinhard*). [1] The stolen goods became the property of the Nazi state.

The thefts committed against the Jewish victims were considered top secret. Thus, the SS authorities responsible for administration of the concentration camps and other centers of mass extermination would refer to the stolen property in administrative documents and instructions with various euphemisms: the property of the resettled Jews (*Besitz der umgesiedelten Juden*), the left-over Jewish effects (*die anfallenden jüdischen Effekten*), the goods from the Jewish thieves and fences (*das Jüdische Hehler- u. Diebesgut*). Old cloth that could still be used in textile production became "left-over textile

---

[1] This cryptonym was also used for the extermination of Jews and the theft of their property in the General Government. The SS conceived the name in honor of the late director of the *Reichsicherheitshauptamt* (Main Security Office of the *Reich, RSHA*), *SS-Obergruppenführer* Reinhard Heydrich, assassinated in May 1942 by members of the Czech resistance movement.

materials from the Jewish deportation" (*Textil-Altmaterial aus der Judenaus-siedlung*), or "rags from among the unusable civilian items left behind during individual operations at Auschwitz and other camps" (*Lumpen von den nicht brauchbaren Zivilsachen aus den einzelnen Aktionen von Auschwitz und anderen Lagern*).

The theft of extermination victims' possessions at KL Auschwitz, as was the case at other concentration camps, lay within the jurisdiction of the Economic-Administrative Division of the SS, Division IV. In July 1943, it began to operate under a new name — the "Administration for the SS Garrison at Auschwitz" (*SS-Standortverwaltung Auschwitz*), directed in succession by *SS-Untersturmführer* Max Meyer, *SS-Hauptsturmführer* Rudolf Wagner (until July 1942), *SS-Sturmbannführer* Wilhelm Max Josef Johann Burger (until April 1943) and *SS-Obersturmbannführer* Karl Ernst Möckel (until the camp's liquidation). The office called the "Administration for Prisoners' Property" (*Gefangeneneigentumsverwaltung* or *Häftlingseigentumsverwaltung*), directed by *SS-Obersturmführer* Theodor Krätzer, was the unit most directly involved in stealing Jewish property.

1. The Procedure for Pillaging and Preparing Stolen Property for Use

The pillaging began immediately after the Jewish deportees arrived at the camp's railway platforms. The prisoners, following the orders of the SS men, who purposely created a rushed atmosphere, would place their larger and heavier bags inside the railway cars or leave them at specified locations on the train platforms. They were only permitted to keep their hand luggage. Resistance, they learned, would only lead to their being beaten or shot. On the way to the gas chambers, they were forced to leave their remaining clothes and baggage either inside the special undressing rooms or outside under the open sky. Once they entered the gas chamber, the items that they had left behind underwent an initial sorting. After they were killed, the bodies of the Jewish deportees were also closely examined before they were burned. All jewelry was removed, and any teeth made of precious metals were torn out. Even the genitals and rectums of the victims were searched.

The property that had been appropriated on the train platforms and at the crematoria were then stored in the camp's many warehouses. At the warehouses, everything was sorted out and prepared either for shipping or for use at the camp. [2] In official camp parlance, these storage areas, along with the warehouses that held clothing and utensils deposited by prisoners at the camp, were called "property storage" (*Effektenkammern, Effektenlager*), and the prisoners who worked at them, "cleaning details" (*Aufräumungskommandos*).

The enormous quantity and high value of the goods plundered from the Jewish victims became associated in the prisoners' minds with what, for them, was a symbol of enormous wealth: Canada. They began referring to this stolen

---

[2] The following publication contains photographs of the stolen goods being transported to the camp warehouses and the prisoners working to sort it: *L'Album d'Auschwitz. D'apres un album découvert par Lili Meier survivante du camp de concentration* (Paris, 1983), pp. 144-46, 150-61.

property, the warehouses that it filled and the work detail attached to these warehouses as "Canada". After a period of time, some administrators and camp staff adopted this term as well.

Whenever the extermination campaign against the Jews was accelerated, such a large quantity of stolen goods would arrive at the "Canada" warehouses that it would have to be stacked up outside the barracks. Vast piles of clothing, luggage and assorted bundles, stacked several meters high, would stand in front of the warehouses for weeks on end. The goods were hastily unpacked. Any valuables that were found were thrown down special openings that led to padlocked chests. Money, foodstuffs, medicines, and various utensils were put in separate piles. When items of clothing were sorted, they were closely examined to find any valuables that might have been hidden in them. At the same time, the "Jewish" star was removed. Once it was sorted, the clothing, underwear, bedding, quilts, blankets, and numerous other items were assembled into packages and made ready for shipping. Other stolen goods, such as luggage and quilts, were also thoroughly searched for any hidden money or valuables. At the leather workshop (*Lederfabrik*) situated near the main camp, hundreds of shoes were taken apart each day to discover any hidden valuables.

The men and women prisoners employed in the *Aufräumungskommandos* ("Canada" work-detachments), in comparison to prisoners in other work details, had significantly larger possibilities for illegally "organizing" food products, clothing, and other items that were highly-valued at the camp. In order to improve their chances for survival, they often made use of this opportunity, or at least tried to make use of it. Given this fact, the SS men would closely watch the "Canada" work details, especially the prisoners who were sorting stolen goods or searching them for money and other valuables. Prisoners caught "organizing" goods were usually punished quite severely or simply shot on the spot. After they finished work, or sometimes in the middle of it, they were often subjected to arbitrary and brutal body searches. They were particularly painful and humiliating for the women prisoners.[3]

2. Distribution and Use of the Plunder

A large number of surviving orders and reports show that the Nazis distributed the plunder from the victims of mass extermination at KL Auschwitz in a way that benefited numerous industrial facilities and state institutions that were central to the Third Reich's economy. One of the most crucial documents is a September 26, 1942, directive from SS-WVHA to the directors of the administrative divisions at the Auschwitz and Majdanek concentration camps, which regulated the distribution and use of objects plundered from the Jews at the two camps.[4] According to the order, the two camps were to deposit all

---

[3] The best-known account of the working conditions in the camp's Canada warehouses can be found in the memoirs of Kitty Hart: *Return to Auschwitz. The Remarkable Story of a Girl Who Survived the Holocaust* (London, 1981).

[4] Nuremberg Document NO-724; Raul Hilberg, *Die Vernichtung der europäischen Juden. Die Gesamtgeschichte des Holocausts* (Berlin, 1982), p. 645.

Fernspruch · Fernschreiben · Funkspruch · Blinkspruch

Nachr.-Stelle | Nr. 4645 | Befördert: an | Tag | Zeit | durch

20 Feb 1943

Vermerke:

Angenommen oder aufgenommen: von | Tag | Zeit | durch

Abgang: Tag: | Zeit: | Dringlichkeitsvermerk

An: W.V.-Hauptamt
Amt D II
Oranienburg

Absendende Stelle

Fernsprech-Anschluß:

513

Inhalt

20.2.43

Betreff: Überstellung von 5022 Juden aus Theresienstadt

Bezug : Dort. FS v. 17.2.43 Nr. 1023

Gesamtstärke der Zugänge vom 21.1.43 2.000 Juden, davon ausgesucht zum Arbeitseinsatz 418 = 254 Männer u. 164 Frauen = 20,9 %. vom 24.1.43 2029 Juden davon zum Arbeitseinsatz 228 = 148 Männer u. 80 Frauen = 11,2 % vom 27.1.43 993 Juden, davon zum Arbeitseinsatz 284 = 212 Männer u. 72 Frauen = 22,5 %. Gesondert untergebracht wurden am 21.1.43 1582 = 602 Männer u. 980 Frauen u. Kinder, am 24.1.43 1801 = 623 Männer u. 1178 Frauen und Kinder, am 27.1.43 709 = 197 Männer u. 512 Frauen und Kinder. Die Sonderunterbringung der Männer erfolgte wegen zu grosser Gebrechlichkeit, die der Frauen, weil der grösste Teil Kinder war.

– 66 –

gez. Schwarz

Wenden !

Telegram from the director of the employment division at KL Auschwitz, H. Schwarz, to Administration DII at SS-WVHA, reporting the results of the selection conducted on 5,022 Jews brought to KL Auschwitz from the Theresienstadt ghetto. Of the 5,022, 4,092 were exterminated in the gas chambers, and only 930 were kept alive for forced labor.

Inl. II 1408 g

Telegramm
(G-Schreiber)

Budapest, den 11. Juli 1944 15.15 Uhr
Ankunft, den 11. Juli 1944 19.30 Uhr

Nr. 1927 vom 11.7.44.

Geheim!

+) Inl II a (V.S.)

Im Anschluß an Fernschreiben Nr. 1838 +) vom 30. Juni.

I. Konzentrierung und Abtransport Juden in Zone V einschließlich Aktion Vorstädte Budapest am 9. Juli planmäßig mit 55.741 abgeschlossen. Gesamtziffer aus Zonen I bis V einschließlich Vorstadtaktion nunmehr 437.402.

II. Über Fortgang Aktion gegen Budapest ist gesondert nach Fuschl berichtet worden.

Veesenmayer

St.S. [illegible]
U.St.S. Pol
Botschafter Ritter
[illegible]
L[illegible]
" " [illegible] Pol
" " [illegible]
" " [illegible] Pol
" " [illegible]
" " [illegible]funk
Chef [illegible]
Dg. Pol
Gr. Leiter Inl. I
[illegible]

Inl II

Telegram of the German ambassador to Hungary, Veesenmayer, to the German Foreign Office, in which he reports that 437,402 Jews were deported from Hungary as of July 9, 1944.

KL Auschwitz II-Birkenau. The unloading of a transport of Jews at the railway platform in 1944. On the left is a barracks for SS men, and in the distance, the barracks of the women's camp (BIb) and Crematoria II and III. An SS man photographed the process by which the Jews from these transports were deported, selected, and sent to their deaths. Prisoner Lili Jacob found an album containing 200 such photographs after the war; it is one of the most important pieces of evidence on the extermination of Jews.

KL Auschwitz II-Birkenau. Jews deported to the camp leaving the freight cars.

KL Auschwitz II-Birkenau. Jews standing on the unloading ramp after leaving the freight cars, before being divided up into two groups — men, on the one hand, and women and children, on the other. In the distance are the barracks of the women's camp and Crematorium II.

KL Auschwitz II-Birkenau. Women and children on the unloading ramp, awaiting selection.

KL Auschwitz II-Birkenau. Men awaiting selection after being separated from the women and children.

KL Auschwitz II-Birkenau. Men and women on the unloading ramp before selection.

KL Auschwitz II-Birkenau. Two Jewish boys from Hungary on the unloading ramp, awaiting selection.

KL Auschwitz II-Birkenau. Jews standing in two lines — men to the right, women and children to the left — before the selection began. In the distance is the main gate to the camp, and to the right, the barracks of the women's camp.

KL Auschwitz II-Birkenau. Jewish women and children awaiting selection after being separated from the men.

KL Auschwitz II-Birkenau. Selection at the unloading ramp. SS men — most often doctors —designated people as fit or unfit for work based upon their appearance (sometimes their profession was also taken into account). Based on statistics, around 80% of the new arrivals were sent to the gas chambers, and the remainder were driven to the showers ("Sauna" — BIIg), given camp clothes, registered in the camp records, tattooed with camp numbers, and subsequently employed at Auschwitz or its sub-camps, or transferred to other concentration camps.

KL Auschwitz II-Birkenau. Selection at the unloading ramp. In the distance is the camp gate.

KL Auschwitz II-Birkenau. Selection at the unloading ramp. In the distance, a column of Jews condemned to death is walking in the direction of Crematoria II and III. In the far distance are the barracks of the women's camp, BIb.

KL Auschwitz II-Birkenau. A group of men designated unfit for work, on the way to the gas chambers at Crematoria IV and V.

KL Auschwitz II-Birkenau. Columns of people condemned to death during the selection being led in the direction of Crematoria II and III. On the left is the gate to the women's camp, and to the right is a barracks for SS men, and behind it are the showers and kitchen (with numerous chimneys) at the women's camp, BIb.

KL Auschwitz II-Birkenau. A group of women and children designated unfit for work on the way to the gas chambers at Crematoria IV and V. In the distance: barracks at the men's camp.

KL Auschwitz II-Birkenau. People waiting before being exterminated in the gas chambers.

KL Auschwitz II-Birkenau. Unloading ramp. Possessions brought to the camp by the Jews were transferred to warehouses, where they were searched through and sorted.

Uscha. Fischer Alfred

Verpflichtungsschein.

1.) Mir ist bekannt und ich bin heute darüber belehrt worden, daß ich mit dem Tode bestraft werde, wenn ich mich an Judeneigentum jeglicher Art vergreife.

2.) Über alle während der Judenevakuierung durchzuführenden Maßnahmen habe ich unbedingte Verschwiegenheit zu bewahren, auch gegenüber meinen Kameraden.

3.) Ich verpflichte mich, mich mit meiner ganzen Person und Arbeitskraft für die schnelle und reibungslose Durchführung dieser Maßnahmen einzusetzen.

Auschwitz 22 5. 44

Alfred Fischer
44- mila

Members of the KL Auschwitz staff had to sign an oath not to steal any items that had been plundered from the Jewish victims of mass extermination and to keep the camp's operations secret. A large number of such oaths have been preserved in the archives of the State Museum at Auschwitz (PMO) in the files of individual SS men.

B e t r e f f :

Über die übertägige Verwertung von Textil-Altmaterial aus
der Judenumsiedlung.

Aus der anliegenden Aufstellung ist die bisher aus den Lagern
Auschwitz und Lublin abgeführte Menge an Altmaterial aus der
Judenumsiedlung zu ersehen. Es muss hierbei besonders berück-
sichtigt werden, dass der Anfall an Lumpen ein sehr hoher ist.
Hierdurch vermindert sich natürlich die verwertbare Altbekleidung, insbesondere an Männer-Garnituren. Eine Befriedigung der
gestellten Anforderungen an Männer-Garnituren konnte daher nicht
in vollem Umfange erfolgen.

Ganz besondere Schwierigkeiten machte die Abtransport mit der
Bahn. Durch die dauernd einsetzenden Transportsperren stockte
die Abfuhr, sodass es zeitweilig zu Anhäufungen in den einzelnen Lagern kam.

Besonders bemerkbar machte sich die seit Dezember 1942 beste-
hende Transportsperre nach der Ukraine, welche verhinderte, dass
die für die dortigen Volksdeutschen bestimmte Altbekleidung ge-
liefert werden konnte. Die Gesamtmenge für die Volksdeutschen in der Ukraine wurde daher von der Volksdeutschen Mittelstelle nach Litzmannstadt geleitet und dort in einem großen
Lager untergebracht. Sofort bei Lockerung der Transportlage
wird die Vomi die Verteilung durchführen.

Die Gestellung der in grosser Anzahl benötigten Waggons konnte
bisher in engster Zusammenarbeit mit dem Reichswirtschaftsministerium durch dieses erfolgen. Auch in Zukunft wird das RWM bemüht
bleiben, beim Reichsverkehrsministerium unter Hinweis auf die
schlechte textile Rohstofflage Waggons für die Abfuhr von Altmaterial aus dem Generalgouvernement beschaffen.

gez.: Pohl

SS-Obergruppenführer und
General der Waffen-SS

Report of the head of the Main Economic-Administrative Office of the SS,
Oswald Pohl, from February 6, 1943
(Nuremberg Document NO-1257). Already during the initial phase of the
so-called "final solution of the Jewish
question", 825 freight cars left the Auschwitz and Majdanek camps carrying
clothing and shoes plundered from the
Jewish victims of mass extermination, as
well as one freight car carrying women's
hair.

A b s c h r i f t   Geheim

A u f s t e l l u n g

Über die von den Lagern Lublin und Auschwitz auf Anordnung des SS-Wirt-
schafts-Verwaltungshauptamt abgelieferten Mengen an Textil-Altmaterial:

1. Reichswirtschaftsministerium

Männer-Altbekleidung ohne Wäsche	97 000 Garnituren	
Frauen-Altbekleidung ohne Wäsche	76 000 Garnituren	
Frauen-Seidenwäsche	89 000 Garnituren	
	insgesamt:	34 Waggons

Lumpen	400 Waggons	2 700 000 kg
Bettfedern	130 Waggons	270 000 kg
Frauenhaare	1 Waggon	3 000 kg
Altmaterial	5 Waggons	19 000 kg
insgesamt:		2 992 000 kg

insgesamt: 536 Waggons
570 Waggons

2. Volksdeutsche Mittelstelle

Männerbekleidung:			Kinderbekleidung:		
Mäntel	99 000	Stck.	Mäntel	15 000	Stck.
Röcke	57 000	"	Knabenröcke	11 000	"
Westen	27 000	"	Knabenhosen	3 000	"
Hosen	62 000	"	Hemden	3 000	"
Unterhosen	38 000	"	Schals	4 000	"
Hemden	132 000	"	Pullover	1 000	"
Pullover	9 000	"	Unterhosen	1 000	"
Schals	2 000	"	Mädchenkleider	9 000	"
Pyjamas	6 000	"	Mädchenhemden	5 000	"
Kragen	10 000	"	Schürzen	2 000	"
Handschuhe	2 000	Paar	Schlüpfer	5 000	"
Strümpfe	10 000	"	Strümpfe	10 000	Paar
Schuhe	31 000	"	Schuhe	22 000	"

Frauenbekleidung:			Wäsche usw.:		
Mäntel	155 000	Stck.	Bettbezüge	37 000	Stck.
Kleider	119 000	"	Bettlaken	46 000	"
Jacken	26 000	"	Kopfkissen-		
Röcke	30 000	"	bezüge	75 000	"
Hemden	125 000	"	Geschirrtücher	27 000	"
Blusen	30 000	"	Taschentücher	135 000	"
Pullover	60 000	"	Handtücher	100 000	"
Unterhosen	49 000	"	Tischdecken	11 000	"
Schlüpfer	60 000	"	Servietten	8 000	"
Pyjamas	27 000	"	Zolltücher	6 000	"
Schürzen	36 000	"	Krawatten	25 000	"
Büstenhalter	25 000	"	Gummischuhe		
Unterkleider	22 000	"	und Stiefel	24 000	Paar
Kopftücher	85 000	"	Mützen	9 000	Stck.
Schuhe	111 000	Paar	insgesamt:	211 Waggons	

-2-

- 2 -

3. Reichsjugendführung - Landdienst

Männer-Altbekleidung	4 000	Garnituren
Männer-Mäntel	4 000	Stück
Männer-Schuhe	3 000	Paar
Frauen-Altbekleidung	4 000	Garnituren
Frauen-Mäntel	4 000	Stück
Frauen-Unterwäsche	3 000	Garnituren
Frauen-Pullover	20 000	Stück
Frauen-Schürzen	5 000	Stück
Schals versch. Art	6 000	Stück
Frauen-Schuhe	3 000	Paar

4. Unternehmen "HEINRICH"

Männer-Altbekleidung	2 700	Garnituren

5. I.G.Farbenindustrie Auschwitz

Männer-Altbekleidung	4 000	Garnituren

6. Organisation "TODT" - Riga

Männer-Altbekleidung	1 500	Garnituren

7. Generalinspektor des Führers für das Kraftfahrwesen

Männer-Altbekleidung	1 000	Garnituren
Männer-Unterwäsche	1 000	"
Männer-Schuhe	1 000	"
Männer-Mantel	1 000	Stück

8. Konzentrationslager

Männer-Jacken	28 000	Stück
Männer-Hosen	25 000	"
Männer-Westen	7 000	"
Männer-Hemden	44 000	"
Männer-Unterhosen	34 000	"
Männer-Pullover	1 000	"
Männer-Mantel	6 000	"
Frauen-Mäntel	25 000	"
Männer-Schuhe	100 000	Paar

insgesamt: 44 Waggons

zusammen: 825 Waggons

F.d.R.d.R.:

SS-Hauptsturmführer

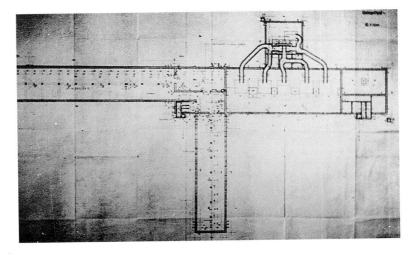

KL Auschwitz II-
-Birkenau. Plan for
Crematorium II or
III from January
23, 1942. On the left
is the undressing
room, at the bottom
is the gas chamber,
and to the right are
the oven chamber,
sanitation and admi-
nistrative rooms,
and the coke store.

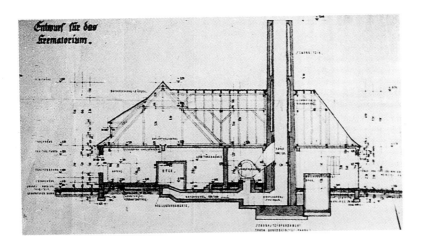

KL Auschwitz II-
-Birkenau. Plan for
Crematorium II or
III — cross-section
of the oven chamber
and the chimney.

KL Auschwitz II-
-Birkenau. Crema-
torium II. Constru-
ction of the ovens
in 1943.

KL Auschwitz II-Birkenau. Crematorium II during its construction in 1943.

KL Auschwitz II-Birkenau. Crematorium IV. The gas chambers were located at the lower left. Beneath the room, three small windows are visible — holes for dropping in Zyklon B. The undressing chambers and administrative rooms were located in the middle section. The oven chamber was located on the right, along with the two chimneys, the sanitary and administrative facilities, and the coke store.

Letter of the Main Construction Office at Auschwitz to Kammler at SS-WVHA, in which he cites the daily capabilities of the individual crematoria. Altogether, the five crematoria were capable of burning 4,756 corpses a day.

KL Auschwitz I. The interior of the gas chamber at Crematorium I. The gas chamber, used from the autumn of 1941 to the autumn of 1942, could hold 700-800 people at a time. After the bunkers for gassing were established at Birkenau, it was used only as a backup facility.

Can of Zyklon B with the Degesch trademark and lumps of kieselguhr soaked in prussic acid (i.e., cyanide). According to Commandant Rudolf Höss, five to seven kilograms of Zyklon B sufficed to kill 1,500 people.

Permit to drive a truck to Dessau to pick up material for *Sonderbehandlung* or "special treatment"   i.e., Zyklon B.

German banknotes directly into the account of SS-WVHA at the *Reichsbank* in Berlin. They were to send all other hard currency, jewelry, and precious metals to the *Reichsbank* via SS-WVHA. Other administrative organs also had authorization to take possession of pillaged goods: economic units subordinated to SS-WVHA; the *Volksdeutsche Mittelstelle* (Ethnic German Mediation Agency, VoMi), an organization established by SS men for the resettlement of Germans; and the Economics Ministry of the *Reich*. The Economics Ministry served as a receiver for used or perished goods, which were nonetheless shipped to industrial facilities for use as raw materials.

On October 14, 1942, the *Reichsführer* SS, Heinrich Himmler, on the basis of the same regulation, ordered the head of SS-WVHA, Oswald Pohl, and the head of VoMi, Werner Lorenz, to provide more than 230,000 *Volksdeutsche* and German settlers with clothing, shoes and utensils from the warehouses at Auschwitz and Majdanek for the Christmas holiday. (This group included 45,000 settlers and *Volksdeutsche* in the Żytomierz region of Ukraine.) Himmler stressed in his order that each settler should receive an overcoat, headwear, other clothing and necessities. Particularly needy families were to receive blankets, bed linens and down quilts as well. [5]

By February 1943, despite the existing difficulties with rail transportation, 824 railway cars had already departed from KL Auschwitz and KL Majdanek, filled with textile and leather goods from "Jewish resettlement" (aus der *Judenumsiedlung*) — i.e., stolen from the Jewish victims of mass extermination. A majority of the railway cars (569), containing worn-out clothing and other cloth items (particularly *"Lumpen"*, rags and pieces of cloth), went to the *Reich's* Ministry of Economics for industrial use. VoMi received 211 wagons filled with hundreds of thousands of articles of men's, women's and children's clothing, comforters, tablecloths, towels, and other items for distribution to German colonists. The remaining 44 railway cars of clothing and shoes went to other concentration camps, several paramilitary units and the chemical plant of IG-Farbenindustrie in Auschwitz-Monowitz (Dwory). IG-Farben received, for example, 4,000 men's suits. (Pohl cited all these figures in a special report to Himmler, dated February 6, 1943.) [6] According to Rudolf Höss, the camp's former commandant, up to twenty freight cars were loaded each day at the camp's railway platforms with the personal effects of the victims. [7]

A letter of January 24, 1944, from Administration DII of SS-WVHA to the SS authorities at KL Auschwitz confirmed the receipt (not in any particular order) of successive shipments of watches, watch cases and parts, watchbands, fountain-pens, mechanical pencils and other small, unspecified devices. The letter also contained instructions to the camp staff regarding future shipments of such items. [8] Karl Sommer, a former official at Administration DII, asserted in January 1947 that their division, in keeping with a special order from the head of SS-WVHA, Oswald Pohl, was constantly receiving shipments of

[5] Nuremberg Doc. NO-606 (NO-5395); compare to R. Hilberg, p. 646.
[6] Nuremberg Doc. NO-1257.
[7] *Wspomnienia Rudolfa Hössa, komendanta obozu oświęcimskiego* (Warszawa, 1965), p. 205.
[8] Nuremberg Doc. NO-4468.

confiscated watches from Auschwitz and Majdanek. They would send the watches for appraisal and repair to a watchmaker's workshop established on the grounds of KL Sachsenhausen. [9]

In addition to the 1942 regulation of SS-WVHA mentioned above, other surviving reports, regulations and correspondence from the SS for five months of 1943 (May, August, September, November and December) and two months of 1944 (July and August) [10] demonstrate that even the smallest items stolen from the Jewish victims of KL Auschwitz and other extermination centers were submitted for appraisal, cleaning and repair at special workshops belonging to SS-WVHA. These items included watches, fountain pens, mechanical pencils, shaving equipment, razor blades, scissors and flashlights. Stolen wrist watches (only occasionally made of precious metals) and fountain pens were distributed to SS divisions at the front, pilots in the *Luftwaffe*, and submarine crews. The razors and razor blades went to SS field hospitals and canteens (for resale), while SS barber facilities received scissors, depending on the type. In July 1944, 2,500 watches were given to Berlin residents who had been victims of the Allied bombing.

According to the memoirs and accounts of a number of former SS staff members at KL Auschwitz, such a large amount of plundered valuables and money (mainly jewelry and watches made of precious metals) flowed into the camp's *Häftlingseigentumsverwaltung* division that the SS functionaries employed there had to work constantly in order to appraise, sort and count them. Every few weeks, trucks guarded by armed SS men would carry the sorted valuables in sealed containers to the SS central administration. [11]

Based on an understanding of mid-1942 between Himmler and the *Reich's* Minister of Economics, Walter Funk, the SS central administration turned over these shipments from KL Auschwitz and other extermination centers of money and valuables to the *Reichsbank* in Berlin. *SS-Hauptsturmführer* Melmer of Administrative Group A at SS-WVHA organized these shipments. The *Reichsbank* immediately added to its assets some of the valuables that it received, such as hard currency and bars of precious metals, and sent other items, such as jewelry and gemstones, on to other institutions that were subordinate or cooperating with it. The *Berliner Pfandleiheanstalt* sold the plundered gemstones and securities and transferred the profits to the state treasury (*Reichshauptkasse*) by depositing them in a special account established by the Ministry of Finance under the assumed name, "Max Heiliger". Some valuables ended up being sold outside the Third Reich, in Switzerland and elsewhere. The financial needs of the SS also did not go neglected. In an arrangement similar to the "Max Heiliger" account, the *Reichsbank* and

---

[9] APMO, Pohl Trial, vol. Pd 1, card 79-80, clarification of K. Sommer. Compare to *Wspomnienia Rudolfa Hössa*, p. 206.

[10] Nuremberg Documents NO-2003, NO-2749, NO-2751, NO-2753-55 and others. Compare to R. Hilberg, p. 647.

[11] APMO, Höss Trial, vol. 17, card 148, statement of Włodzimierz Bilan; APMO, SS Staff Trial, vol. 52, cards 153, 194, 197-8, 213, 220-1, 227-33, 241-2; vol. 55, card 241, statements of former SS functionaries Georg Höcker, Karl Heinrich Hykes, Karl Ernst Möckel, Karl Morli and Heinrich Neumann, as well as the account of former prisoner Marian Prząda.

Golddiskontbank, using profits made from the stolen property, established a special loan fund for the SS, the so-called "Reinhardtfonds". They remained a constant source of financing for SS economic enterprises.

A few years after the war, the former head officer of the *Reichsbank*, Albert Thoms, released a statement on that institution's role in handling property that had been stolen from Nazi extermination victims. According to his report, he had witnessed the bank receiving deliveries from KL Auschwitz. Former SS officials Rudolf Höss and Karl Möckel also mentioned the *Reichsbank's* role in receiving stolen valuables from the camp. Möckel even implicated Melmer (the SS official mentioned above) as the intermediary between SS-WVHA and the *Reichsbank.* [12]

A large number of German organizations and firms received various textiles, leather goods and utensils that had been stolen from the victims of KL Auschwitz. Not only Nazi documents, but also the testimony and memoirs of various witnesses demonstrate this fact. In her 1976 memoirs, the former slave-laborer Barbara Adamkiewicz asserts that the factory she worked at in Kiel, "Berthold Steinkopf", had received mass shipments of clothing from Auschwitz and other camps for processing in the winter of 1942-43. The clothing was cut into 40 x 40 cm strips, which were later used in German factories for cleaning machines. Józef Kubiścik, a resident of Chełmek (near Auschwitz), stated in 1960 that the "Bata" factory in Chełmek, run by Germans during the war, received a large quantity of shoes from KL Auschwitz and the General Government. [13]

Stolen clothes were also delivered *en masse* from Auschwitz to other concentration camps. After the clothes were inspected and repaired at camp workshops they were distributed to newly-arrived prisoners as a substitute for the standard camp uniform. Leather-goods were taken apart and used with wood for making clogs.

Medicine and medical equipment were taken from the camp's warehouses and shipped to first-aid stations and medical units providing care to SS men and their families. Fine foods were either distributed to SS dignitaries visiting the camp (they would receive, along with other gifts, vintage wine) or handed over to the mess-halls and clubs that served the camp SS staff. Low-quality food items were given to the kitchens that prepared rations for the prisoners.

Among the stolen items were also baby carriages, which were gathered together in front of the "Canada" warehouses. Former prisoner Wanda Szaynok witnessed one day a large number of baby carriages being removed from the grounds of the camp in the direction of the Auschwitz (Oświęcim) train station. Brought out in rows of five, the procession of carriages lasted an hour. [14]

---

[12] Statement of Albert Thoms from May 8, 1946, Nuremberg Doc. PS-3951; APMO, SS Staff Trial, vol. 52, cards 198, 220, statement of Karl Ernst Möckel; *Wspomnienia Rudolfa Hössa,* p. 206, Cf. Hilberg, pp. 647-50.

[13] APMO, Collection of Testimonies, vol. 12, cards 40-3, account of J. Kubiścik; Barbara Adamkiewicz, "Nie chciałam zasilić niemieckiej rasy", in *Z literą P. Polacy na robotach przymusowych w hitlerowskiej Rzeszy 1939-1945. Wspomnienia* (Poznań, 1976), pp. 53-4.

[14] APMO, Höss Trial, vol. 5, card 133.

The staff at KL Auschwitz and other citizens of the Third Reich ran to the camp administration to take part in the allocation or re-sale of the plunder taken from the victims of mass extermination, including clothes, baby carriages and home products.

The Jews brought to the camp for extermination, in keeping with the instructions of the Nazi authorities, would often write their names, addresses and (sometimes) their dates of birth on their suitcases. According to the Nazis, this would help them later identify their luggage. Today, the numerous suitcases marked with the personal data of their long-dead owners, on display at the State Museum in Oświęcim (Auschwitz), are one of the most basic pieces of material evidence that extermination victims' possessions were systematically plundered.

3. Plundering by Individual SS Men

According to the orders of *Reichsführer* SS Himmler, all staff members at KL Auschwitz were obliged to observe the "principle of the holiness of property" (*Grundsatz über die Heiligkeit des Eigentums*); they were not to appropriate for themselves any goods considered to be the property of the German state, the SS, other Nazi bodies, or full citizens of the Third Reich. Nevertheless, orders from the camp's commandants, Rudolf Höss and Arthur Liebehenschel, demonstrate that the SS men stole, again and again, various objects stored at the camp — e.i., pluner from the victims of mass extermination. The camp commandants tried to combat this type of activity through various orders. [15]

On May 22, 1944, undoubtedly in conjunction with the "Hungarian Action" (the extermination of the Hungarian Jews already in progress), a special initiative was undertaken among the camp staff. They were to sign an oath obligating them not to disturb any property of the Jews and to keep the annihilation of Jews at the camp a secret. One point of the oath regarding Jewish property reads as follows: "I know and have been informed today that I will be punished by death if I take any Jewish possessions." [16]

A surviving judgment from an SS court in the case of *SS-Unterscharführer* Franz Wunsch from July 18, 1944, demonstrates what severe punishments the SS authorities meted out to staff members found to have stolen property from the victims of extermination. [17] Wunsch, a supervisor of prisoners working at the "Canada" warehouses, was sentenced to five weeks' arrest for stealing small items worth a total of 30 Marks (including leather gloves and cigarettes). One factor that spoke in his favor was that he had not stolen any valuables for himself.

One Auschwitz staff member who regularly appropriated plundered objects at the camp was *SS-Obersturmführer* Johann Paul Kremer, MD and PhD.

---

[15] APMO, D-AuI, Sturmbannbefehl Nr. 85/43 from May 25, 1943; APMO, D-AuI-1, Standortbefehl Nr. 31/43 from August 6, 1943, and Nr. 51/43 from November 16, 1943, point 4.

[16] APMO, Personal Files of SS Men — e.g., Ludwig Damm, Alfred Fischer, and Otto Klauss.

[17] APMO, Personal Documents of F. Wunsch; APMO, SS Staff Trial, vol. 37, cards 199-203.

Entries in his memoirs show that time after time he would send packages from Auschwitz containing valuable war-time items, stolen from the "Canada" warehouses. [18]

Several leading staff members at the camp played no small role in illegally appropriating confiscated goods, including Camp Commandant Höss and the Head of the Political Division (the camp Gestapo), *SS-Untersturmführer* Maximilian Grabner. With the silent acquiescence of Höss, his wife, Hedwig, would supplement their household budget with fine foods and other goods taken from the warehouses and other economic units at the camp. She paid nothing or only a symbolic price for the goods. Some SS men gave the Höss family food, including wine, preserved fish and cigarettes — e.g., *SS-Unterscharführer* Franz Schebeck, from the food warehouse that he oversaw, and *SS-Oberscharführer* Engelbrecht, from the camp canteens that lay under his supervision. Erich Grönke, the director of the workshops and warehouses on the grounds of the former tannery in Oświęcim — thankful to Höss for his release from the camp and subsequent employment as a civilian in its administration — spared no effort in providing the Höss family with leather goods, including shoes, women's pocketbooks and leather chairs.

In the second half of 1943, a special commission headed by *SS-Sturmbann-führer* Dr. Konrad Morgen, J.D., began a special investigation at Auschwitz into graft and fraud by SS men. Grabner was among those who stood accused. A search of their quarters yielded a large quantity of valuables and other goods that had been stolen from the victims of mass extermination. These objects, material evidence of the theft of state property, were stored in the chambers of the Political Division, in the barracks next to Crematorium I. On the night of December 7-8, 1943, this material evidence was destroyed in a fire, under circumstances that were never clarified. Most likely, the SS men decided to set the barracks on fire in order to destroy the evidence gathered against them.

The surviving documents from the Nazi administration do not contain the necessary data that would allow us to establish the total or even partial profits that the Nazis realized by plundering the belongings of KL Auschwitz's victims. It is not baseless, however, to suggest that their value must have exceeded several hundred million *Reichsmark*. [19]

---

[18] "Diary of Johann Paul Kremer", in *KL Auschwitz seen by the SS. Höss, Broad, Kremer* (Oświęcim, 1972), pp. 222, 224, 227.

[19] APMO, Höss Trial, vol. 22, card 74; "Obóz koncentracyjny Oświęcim w świetle akt Delegatury Rządu RP na Kraj", *Zeszyty Oświęcimskie* (Special Edition Nr. I, 1968), p. 52.

FRANCISZEK PIPER

THE NUMBER OF VICTIMS AT KL AUSCHWITZ

The immense number of victims and the industrial form of annihilation at the camp made KL Auschwitz a symbol of Nazi genocide for the entire world. The truth about the camp has been spread through thousands of publications — memoirs, articles, and relations of former prisoners. Events at the camp and the survivors' individual tragedies have left an indelible mark upon their consciousness for life. Many have considered it their life's mission — in fulfillment of the last wishes of those who perished at the camp — to spread the truth about the suffering and death of these innocent victims of hate, contempt and selfishness. Due to the survivors' efforts, KL Auschwitz has become a subject of scholarship, literature and art and has entered into the consciousness of millions of people around the world.

Auschwitz has become an universal symbol of genocide despite the fact that since research began on the camp's history, there has been no unanimity among historians regarding how many people were murdered at the camp. In various publications on the camp, the figure has ranged anywhere from one to four million. These differences have arisen because the Nazis, wanting to avoid any legal or moral responsibility for the crimes that they committed, destroyed the camp's records, which might have provided the necessary evidence for establishing the number of victims.

The question arises: To what extent can we today, after almost fifty years of research on Nazi crimes, establish the actual number? [1]

1. The Number of Victims in the Accounts of Prisoners and Nazi Officials

It was prisoners, members of the camp resistance movement, who first tried to estimate the number of people deported and murdered at KL Auschwitz. Based on information from various sources, they compiled reports and estimates, which they subsequently handed over to the Polish resistance movement outside the camp. These data were made public in the underground press, submitted to the Polish Government-in-Exile in London, and kept in the Polish underground archives, "Pro Memoria".

---

[1] For more on this subject, see Franciszek Piper, *Die Zahl der Opfer von Auschwitz. Aufgrund der Quellen und der Erträge der Forschung 1945 bis 1990* (Oświęcim, 1993).

One such note from the resistance movement, dated February 24, 1943, [2] reads as follows:

> Oświęcim. From the Auschwitz camp, the following horrifying statistics regarding victims have arrived in the capital [i.e., Warsaw-FP]. They verify that from the beginning of the camp's existence to December 15, 1942, 640,000 people have perished.

Jerzy Tabeau (Wesołowski, referred to in reports as "a Polish major"), who escaped from the camp on November 19, 1943, estimated in his report to the Polish underground that the number of Jews alone killed at the camp numbered 1.5 million by the time he escaped. [3]

Several months later, on April 7, 1944, two Jewish prisoners, Alfred Wetzler and Walter Rosenberg (Rudolf Vrba), escaped from the camp, before the enormous wave of transports carrying Hungarian Jews began to arrive. In their account, they estimated the number of Jews murdered at the camp from April 1942 — April 1944 to be 1,765,000. [4]

If one adds up all the figures from notes and documents from the resistance movement, we obtain the figure of around 2,000,000 victims, the majority of whom were Jews, followed by Poles and prisoners of other nationalities. Although it will later be shown that the figures cited above are inflated, they nonetheless indicate the scale of the crimes that were committed at the camp.

The workers of the *Sonderkommando,* assigned to burn corpses, also wrote about millions of people being liquidated in handwritten notes that were found after the war, buried near the ruins of the crematoria. The authors, as they foresaw themselves, would not survive the war. One of them, Salmen Gradowski, wrote:

"I have buried this under the ashes, deeming it the safest place, where they will certainly dig to find the traces of millions of exterminated people." [5] Another member of the *Sonderkommando,* Salmen Lewantal wrote in his note: "The history of Auschwitz-Birkenau as a labour camp in general and in particular as the camp of extermination of millions of men will remain — I am sure of it — not sufficiently imparted to the world." He later states: "Such was daily life at the camp. Every day, thousands were murdered — this is no exaggeration, literally thousands." [6]

Other prisoners from the *Sonderkommando* who survived, thanks to their escape during the camp's evacuation in January 1945, gave similar testimony. On April 16, 1945, Alter Feinsilber (alias Stanisław Jankowski) offered the following testimony to Edward Pęchalski, a member of the Commission to Investigate German-Hitlerian Crimes at Auschwitz (*Komisja Badania Zbrodni Niemiecko-Hitlerowskich w Oświęcimiu*) in Cracow:

---

[2] "Obóz koncentracyjny w Oświęcimiu w świetle akt Delegatury RP na kraj, *Zeszyty Oświęcimskie* 1 (special edition, 1968), p. 89; Henceforth, "Oświęcim w świetle akt Delegatury...".

[3] APMO, Höss Trial, vol. 44, card 24; APMO, Files of the Camp Resistance, vol. 1, card 50.

[4] Tadeusz Cyprian and Jerzy Sawicki, *Sprawy polskie w procesie norymberskim* (Poznań, 1956), pp. 132-3.

[5] *Amidst a Nigthmare of Crime. Notes of Prisoners of Sonderkommando found at Auschwitz* (Oświęcim, 1973), p. 75.

[6] Ibid., pp. 146-47.

In accordance with my own observations and discussions with other prisoners from the *Sonderkommando*, I came to the conclusion that during the existence of that *Sonderkommando*, which was two years, more or less, no fewer than 2 million people were cremated in the crematoria and bunkers of Birkenau. This number does not include persons cremated at Birkenau by other previous *Sonderkommando* which had been liquidated by the SS men and could not give us information regarding the number of people cremated while these Sonderkommandos were active. .... The number of unregistered individuals who were burned exceeded several million. [7]

Szlama Dragon, another member of the *Sonderkommando* — from December 9, 1942, to January 1945 — testified, "I estimate the number of people gassed to death in the two bunkers and four crematoria to have been more than four million. [8]

Henryk Tauber, a member of the *Sonderkommando* from February 1943 to January 1945, stated that during his tenure on the work detail, two million people were gassed, in addition to two million before. [9]

Former prisoners who had been employed in various offices and administrative units of the camp associated with mass extermination or its documentation offered similar figures in their testimony. For example, the head scribe in the *Lagerführer* or camp supervisor's office, Erwin Olszówka, estimated the number of victims to have been 4.5 million, or at least four million, based on reports submitted by the camp's infirmaries and crematoria. [10] The *Sonderkommando's* doctor, Dr. Mikloś Nyiszli, whose memoirs are known around the world, writes: "The flames consumed millions of bodies." [11] Bernard Czardybon, who held the office of kapo in the work detail "Canada I" after 1942 and was responsible for sorting the personal effects of the annihilation victims, arrived at the figure of 5-5.5 million people based on the quantity of the possessions that they had left behind. [12]

The SS men also estimated the number of victims to be in the millions. Former prisoner Stanisława Rachwałowa, who had worked in the office of the Political Division (*Politische Abteilung*) at Birkenau, testified: "Based on the conversations that the SS men held in the political office, I concluded that this number [of the victims — FP] lay somewhere between four and five million." [13] Włodzimierz Bilan, an SS man from the Political Division at Birkenau, verified this figure. He testified at Höss's trial that the SS men estimated the number of victims to have been five million. [14] Another SS man from the Political Division wrote in his memoirs:

Auschwitz was an extermination camp! The biggest to exist in the history of the world. Two or three million Jews were murdered there in the course of its existence! Not to mention thousands of Poles, Russians, Czechs, Yugoslavs, etc. [15]

---

[7] Ibid., p. 63.
[8] APMO, Höss Trial, vol. 11, card 113.
[9] Ibid., vol. 11, card 149.
[10] Ibid., vol. 7, card 221.
[11] Mikloś Nyiszli, *Auschwitz. A Doctor's Eyewitness Account* (New York, 1960), p. 5.
[12] APMO, Höss Trial, vol. 24, cards 254-55.
[13] Ibid., vol. 3, card 117.
[14] Ibid., vol. 17, card 148.
[15] *KL Auschwitz Seen by the SS. Reminiscences of Pery Broad* (Oświęcim, 1972), p. 143.

The SS doctor Friedrich Entress, who had held the post of camp doctor from 1942-43, testified that according to his estimates, 2-2.5 million people had been murdered at KL Auschwitz. [16]

Statements by former camp commandant Rudolf Höss, among the most-frequently cited authorities in scholarship on the camp, have attracted considerable attention. Central to Höss's credibility is the fact that he still had insight into the camp's functioning even after his transfer in December 1943 from Auschwitz to the head position at the Main Economic-Administrative Office of the SS (*SS-Wirtschaftsverwaltungshauptamt*). He also returned to KL Auschwitz in 1944 for a period of time to direct personally the largest annihilation campaign in the camp's history — the mass murder of around 400,000 Hungarian Jews. After the war, Höss went into hiding in Germany and was arrested on March 11, 1946, by the British Field Security Section in the area of Flensburg. Before he was extradited to Poland, he testified before several Allied investigative bodies, including the International Military Tribunal in Nuremberg. On April 15, 1946, he testified at Nuremberg:

According to my calculations, at least 2,500,000 people were gassed there [at KL Auschwitz — FP] and subsequently burned; another 500,000 perished from emaciation and disease, for a total of 3,000,000 victims. This number represents 70-80% of all the prisoners at Auschwitz; the remainder were sent to industries exploiting concentration-camp prisoners as a source of forced labor. Around 20,000 Russian prisoners of war, gathered together by the Gestapo at prisoner-of-war camps and shipped to Auschwitz in *Wehrmacht* transports, manned by officers and enlisted men of the *Wehrmacht*, are included in this figure. The remainder consisted of 100,000 German Jews and a large number of people — mainly Jews — from Holland, France, Belgium, Poland, Hungary, Czechoslovakia, Greece, and other countries. We liquidated around 400,000 Hungarian Jews in the course of one summer, in 1944. [17]

After Höss's extradition to Poland, he changed his testimony in places. He asserted:

At previous hearings I have asserted that the number of Jews brought to Auschwitz for extermination numbered 2,500,000. This figure came from Eichmann. Shortly before Berlin was surrounded, he told this to my superior, *Gruppenführer* Glücks, before he (Glücks) was summoned to the *Reichsführer SS* for a report. Only Eichmann and his permanent assistant, Günther, kept data on the total number of people who had been liquidated. On the orders of the *Reichsführer SS* all documents that might become a source of information regarding the number of people who had been murdered were to be burned at Auschwitz after every major campaign. As the head of Office DI, I personally destroyed all the documents kept in my office. The same was done in other offices. Based on Eichmann's comments, all documents were also being destroyed at RSHA and the office of the *Reichsführer SS*. Only the documents that he kept for reference might still contain some indicators. Even if through negligence some letters or telegrams might have been retained in certain offices, they would not contain information regarding the total number of victims. I never knew the total number; I also did not maintain any data that might have

---

[16] APMO, SS Staff Trial, vol. 45, card 230.
[17] T. Cyprian and J. Sawicki, pp. 438-39.

allowed me to arrive at one. The numbers from the larger campaigns still remain in my memory; Eichmann or his deputy recited these figures to me a number of times: Upper Silesia and the General Government — 250,000; Germany and Theresienstadt [Terezín] — 100,000; Holland — 95,000; Belgium — 20,000; France — 110,000; Greece — 65,000; Hungary — 400,000; Slovakia — 90,000. Already, I cannot remember the numbers from the smaller campaigns, but they were insignificant, anyway, in comparison to the numbers above. I consider the figure of two-and-a-half million much too high. The possibilities for extermination had their limits, even at Auschwitz.

These later figures cited by Höss totalled 1,130,000. Nevertheless, his closing statement on January 11, 1947, however, Höss declared once more: "During my tenure at Auschwitz, millions of people died, whose exact number I cannot determine." [18]

2. Estimates by Investigative and Judicial Organs

The first estimates regarding the number of victims at KL Auschwitz came from the Special Soviet State Commission for the Investigation of Crimes by the German-Fascist Aggressors. Representatives from the Commission arrived at Auschwitz on February 4, 1945, a week after the camp's liberation. At the site, there remained several thousand prisoners — eyewitnesses to the events — and the ruins of the gas chambers and crematoria that the SS had blown up. There were also documents left scattered about. On the basis of the witnesses' testimony, an analysis of the documents left behind and an inspection of the ruins of the machinery for mass destruction, the Commission declared:

At Auschwitz, millions of people were annihilated, poisoned, and burned. In the five crematoria by themselves (52 retors), during the entire period of their existence, the Germans had the capability to destroy:

Nr. Crematorium	Period of Existence in Months	Monthly Burning Capabilities	Burning Capabilities, Entire Period
I	24	9,000	216,000
II	19	90,000	1,710,000
III	18	90,000	1,620,000
IV	17	45,000	765,000
V	18	45,000	810,000
		279,000	5,121,000

Taking into account the Germans' wide-scale application of pyres for burning corpses, the total capability of the facilities for murdering people at Auschwitz should have been even greater than cited above. Yet, if we take into account other factors, such as their partial use during certain periods, the technical commission of experts has come to the conclusion that for the period of the Auschwitz camp's existence, the

---

[18] *Wspomnienia Rudolfa Hössa komendanta obozu oświęcimskiego* (Warszawa, 1965), pp. 22-23, 204-5.

German butchers annihilated no fewer people there than four million citizens of the USSR, Poland, France, Jugoslavia, Czechoslovakia, Rumania, Hungary, Bulgaria, Holland, Belgium and other countries. [19]

The Polish Commission for the Investigation of German Crimes (*Komisja Badania Zbrodni Niemieckich*), which later investigated at the camp, arrived at similar conclusions. On the basis of the Polish commission's figures, Höss stood accused of taking the lives of "around 300,000 people held at the camp as prisoners and entered into the camp's records; around 4,000,000 people, mainly Jews, who were brought to the camp in transports from other European countries for immediate extermination, and were thus not listed in the camp's records; and around 12,000 Soviet prisoners of war held at the concentration camp, in violation of the regulations of international law regarding the treatment of POWs. [20]

Poland's Supreme National Tribunal, which heard the charges against Höss, only partially concurred with the numbers presented in the indictment. It declared Höss guilty of:

> participating in the perpetration of murders against around 300,000 people held at the camp as prisoners, who had been entered into the camp records; other people, mainly Jews, whose numbers cannot be precisely established, but who numbered at the very least more than 2,500,000, who were brought by transports to the camp from various European countries for immediate extermination and were thus not listed in the camp's records; and at least 12,000 Soviet POWs. [21]

The question regarding the number of victims was touched upon several times at Nuremberg before the International Military Tribunal and before American tribunals in the cases against IG Farben, RuSHA and Pohl.

With regard to Auschwitz, the Tribunal has heard as a witness the commandant of that camp for the period May 1940 to December 1943. He has stated that at the Auschwitz camp alone, 2.5 million people were exterminated during that period and that an additional half million perished from starvation and emaciation. [22]

In the cases tried by the American military tribunals, the figure of three to four million victims was stated in the indictments. [23]

3. Scholarly Works

The decided majority of scholarly works, not to mention popular-scientific and press articles, have repeated either the figures of the Soviet commission or Höss's figures in increments between 1-2.5 million. Works published in Poland

---

[19] APMO, Höss Trial, vol. 8, cards 28-9.
[20] Ibid., vol. 32, card 3. Judgement of the Supreme National Tribunal in the Höss case.
[21] Ibid., card 6.
[22] *Materiały Norymberskie* (Warszawa, 1948), p. 232.
[23] Andrzej Pankowicz, "Das KL Auschwitz in den Nürnberger Prozessen", *Hefte von Auschwitz* 18, (1990) pp. 309-312.

(including those of the Central Commission for the Investigation of Hitlerite Crimes and the State Museum at Auschwitz),[24] in the former Czecho-slovakia,[25] and in the former East Germany,[26] have most often cited either the figures of the Soviet commission or those of the Supreme National Tribunal in Poland. In the West, on the other hand, the scholarship has usually only cited the number of Jews killed — ca. 1-2.5 million, based on Höss's figures.[27]

The Polish researcher Jan Sehn, who personally interrogated Höss during the investigation against him, has taken part from the very beginning in projects aimed at probing deeper into the crimes committed at KL Auschwitz. In his book, one of the first scholarly works on the history of the camp, he states:

All the assembled evidence has proved that — taking into account the time during which all the crematoria were in operation, as well as the supplemental facilities at Birkenau — the number of people gassed and burned in these facilities was no fewer than four million.[28]

In his reflections on the number of victims at the Auschwitz camp, Czesław Madajczyk, a renowned Polish historian, uses the figures of Poland's Supreme National Tribunal, which decided that 2.5 million people, mainly Jews, had been exterminated without any documentation in the camp records. With regard to the Soviet commission's figure of four million, he comments as follows:

Among the four million victims, 2.7 million were supposed to have been Jews, and 1.3 million were of Polish and other nationalities. Many researchers question this figure as being too high, both in the aggregate and in terms of its individual components.[29]

Professor Michael Foot, in his foreword to *Fighting Auschwitz* by Polish--emigré historian Józef Garliński, asserts:

---

[24] Krzysztof Dunin-Wąsowicz, *Resistance in the Concentration Camps 1938-1945* (Warsaw, 1982), p. 44; Anna Pawełczyńska, *Values and Violence in Auschwitz. A Sociological Analysis* (London, 1979), p. 25; Czesław Pilichowski, *Es gibt keine Verjährung* (Warschau, 1980), pp. 120, 144; Kazimierz Smoleń, *Auschwitz 1940-1945. Guidebook through the Museum* (Oświęcim, 1978), p. 21; *Bestrafung der Verbrecher von Auschwitz,* in *Auschwitz. Geschichte und Wirklichkeit des Vernichtungslagers* (Reinbek bei Hamburg, 1980), p. 211; Danuta Czech, "Konzentrationslager Auschwitz. Abriss der Geschichte", in *Auschwitz. Geschichte und Wirklichkeit...*, p. 42; Franciszek Piper, "Ausrottung" in *Auschwitz. Geschichte und Wirklichkeit...*, p. 135.

[25] Ota Kraus and Erich Kulka, *Noc a mlha* (Prague, 1958), p. 112; and by the same authors, *Tovarna na smrt. Dokument o Osvetimi* (Prague, 1956).

[26] Klaus Drobisch, "Die letzte Phase des Faschistischen Massenmordes 1943-1945", in *Juden unterm Hakenkreuz* (Berlin, 1973), p. 360; Bruno Baum, *Widerstand im Auschwitz* (Berlin, 1957), p. 5.

[27] According to Raul Hilberg, three million Jews perished in all the Nazi camps, and more than one million at Auschwitz. He gives the following figures for the remaining camps: Treblinka, more than 750,000; Bełżec, up to 600,000; Sobibor, up to 200,000; Chełmno, 150,000; and Lublin-Majdanek, 50,000; Raul Hilberg, *Die Vernichtung der europäischen Juden* (Berlin, 1982), p. 821.

[28] Jan Sehn, *Konzentrationslager Oświęcim-Brzezinka (Auschwitz-Birkenau)* (Warschau, 1957), p. 173.

[29] Czesław Madajczyk, *Polityka III Rzeszy w okupowanej Polsce*, vol. II (Warszawa, 1970), pp. 293-4.

... there is no other place where so many people have been put to death so fast: over three million souls, in an area of fifteen square miles, in less than five years. [30]

As mentioned above, the works of Western historians, as a rule, only cite figures for the number of Jews murdered at Auschwitz. Raul Hilberg and Edward Crankshaw put the number at 1,000,000; [31] Leon Poliakow, Lucy Dawidowicz, and Martin Gilbert, 2,000,000; [32] and Yehuda Bauer, 2,500,000. [33] These authors, as a rule, give neither the source from which they have derived their figures nor the method they have used for calculating them.

Gerhard Reitlinger and George Wellers, on the other hand, have each made an attempt to analyze both the figures for individuals deported to Auschwitz and the figures for victims murdered there. [34] Reitlinger rejects the figure of four million based on the method used in arriving at it. He asserts that fewer than one million people perished at the camp: 790,000-840,000 of the 851,000 Jews shipped to the camp and a portion of the 100,000 non-Jewish prisoners held at the camp. In calculating the number of Jews deported to Auschwitz, Reitlinger adds up the figures for Jews deported from individual countries as they were known to him at the time. Reitlinger's numbers have turned out to be deflated in a number of cases. [35]

Using a similar method — i.e., adding up the number of people deported from individual countries — Wellers comes to the conclusion [36] that a total of 1,613,455 people were deported to the camp (1,433,405 Jews; 146,605 mainly Poles; 21,665 Gypsies and 11,780 Russians), of whom 1,471,595 perished (1,352,980 Jews; 86,675 mainly Poles; 20,255 Gypsies; and 11,685 Russians). [37] These figures, we shall demonstrate below, need to be closely examined.

4. The Number of Victims and Deportees in Light of the Most Recent Research

From a methodological point of view, the deportees and victims at KL Auschwitz can be divided into two groups: the first consisting of the registered prisoners, designated with successive camp numbers from several series; and a second group composed of individuals who were never formally prisoners and who were killed in the gas chambers or executed without having been registered and

---

[30] Józef Garliński, *Fighting Auschwitz. The Resistance Movement in the Concentration Camp* (London, 1975), p. 13.

[31] Hilberg, p. 821; Edward Crankshaw, *Die Gestapo* (Berlin, 1959), pp. 191.

[32] Leon Poliakow, *Breviere de la Haine* (Paris, 1951); Lucy Dawidowicz, *The War Against the Jews 1933-1945* (Aylesburg, 1979), p. 191; Martin Gilbert, *Atlas of the Holocaust* (London, 1982), p. 100; idem., *Final Journey. The Fate of the Jews in Nazi Europe* (London-Boston-Sydney, 1979), p. 70.

[33] Yehuda Bauer, "Auschwitz", in *Der Mord an den Juden im zweiten Weltkrieg* (Stuttgart, 1985), p. 173. (The author has borrowed the citation from a Polish publication).

[34] Gerald Reitlinger, *The Final Solution* (London, 1971), pp. 500-501; Georges Wellers, "Essai de determination du nombre de morts au camp d'Auschwitz", *Le Monde Juif* (1983: 112).

[35] For example, Reitlinger uses the figure of 380,000 for Jews deported from Hungary. This is 58,000 less than the actual figure.

[36] Wellers's work concentrates exclusively on the issue of the number of victims at KL Auschwitz.

[37] Wellers, pp. 153, 155.

given a camp number. (Only a relatively small number of deportees to Auschwitz were not registered and then transferred to other camps.)

Although most documents at the camp were destroyed, the number of registered prisoners can be established with a large degree of precision, thanks to our knowledge of the last — or, more accurately, near-last — numbers that were given out in each series. This figure totals more than 400,000 and is somewhere in the neighborhood of 400,207.[38] It includes ca. 205,000 Jews; 130,000-140,000 Poles; 21,000 Gypsies; 12,000 Soviet prisoners of war; and around 25,000 prisoners of other nationalities (Byelorussians, Russians, Ukrainians, Czechs, Yugoslavs, French, Germans, Austrians and others).[39]

The second group, significantly larger than the first, consists almost exclusively of Jews brought to the camp in mass transports as part of the Nazi campaign for the complete and final annihilation of the Jews. As a result of the selections that were normally conducted on such transports, a portion of those who were considered able to work were registered as prisoners, while the remainder — the majority — were taken directly to the gas chambers and exterminated. On a smaller scale, besides the Jews, groups of Soviet POWs, Poles sent to the camp for execution, and prisoners delivered from other concentration camps and found unfit for labor were also murdered without being registered at the camp.

Registered prisoners at KL Auschwitz

Series	Men	Women	Total
General	202,499	89,325	291,824
Jews, Series A	20,000	29,354	49,354
Jews, Series B	14,897	—	14,897
EH, *Erziehungshaftlinge*	9,193	1,993	11,186
RKG (Soviet POWs)	11,964	—	11,964
Z (Gypsies)	10,094	10,888	20,982
Total	268,647	131,560	400,207

Source: Author's determinations based on camp records.

---

[38] In some publications, 405,222 is the number given for registered prisoners. See, for example, Kazimirz Smoleń "Auschwitz Concentration Camp", in *Selected Problems from the History of KL Auschwitz*, (Oświęcim, 1979), pp. 16. This number comes from adding in so-called "police prisoners", who were not formally prisoners at KL Auschwitz (although they spent time at the camp) and from rounding up several figures.

[39] Wellers gives 201,405 as the figure for registered Jews. He arrives at this figure by adding up the number of Jews who were selected along with those brought to the camp in RSHA transports. A number of other, so-called "collective" transports — which carried different categories of prisoners — also brought Jews to the camp. (According to the calculations of Tadeusz Iwaszko, based on lists of new arrivals, between May 21 and December 22, 1941, 1,079 Jews arrivals at the camp in such transports.) A certain number of Jews were also registered in the general series after Series A and B were introduced for Jewish prisoners. Taking these factors into account, we must increase the figure for registered Jews to around 205,000. The figure given for Poles is an estimate, arrived at by adding up the size of transports from prewar Polish territories, increased proportionally on the basis of deportees from other, unspecified localities.

Because Jews represented the decided majority of the camp's unregistered victims, the establishment of their numbers is of decisive importance for determining the total number of people deported and killed at KL Auschwitz.

This number could have been established on the basis of the reports sent by the camp authorities to their SS superiors, which gave the results from the selections conducted on each transport. Unfortunately, only reports for three such transports have been preserved. Given this state of affairs, the surviving documents related to the organization and dispatch of transports from individual countries to Auschwitz represent the only possible source for establishing a complete figure. The correspondence associated with the preparation and departure of the transports, the name lists for individuals deported to the camp, and other statistical materials related to the functioning of the ghettoes and transit camps are thus of the most crucial importance. Such lists and other documents have survived for Germany and Austria; for the occupied countries of Western Europe; and for the former allies of the Third Reich — France, Belgium, Holland, Norway, Bohemia and Moravia, Slovakia, and Italy. We also have exact figures for the number of Jews deported from Hungary, thanks to the surviving telegrams to the German Foreign Ministry from the German representative-plenipotentiary for Hungary, Edmund Veesenmayer, who reported on the progress being made in deporting Hungarian Jews.

As such archival materials have become available, they have been systematically published. On the basis of these materials, we can now establish the number of Jews who were deported from each of these countries to Auschwitz. Unfortunately, such materials are lacking with regard to transports of Jews from Poland. Most likely, such transport lists were never compiled for Polish Jews; at any rate, they have not survived. Reitlinger estimates that around 200,000 Jews from Poland and the Baltic States perished at KL Auschwitz. [40] Wellers, on the other hand, estimates the number of Polish Jews deported to the camp to be ca. 600,000. [41] He arrives at this figure by multiplying the figure of 119 transports by the average of 5,000 individuals per transport, which yields a total of 595,000. He then adds another 20,000 for Jews who were brought to the camp in other smaller transports. An analysis of all known transports, however, shows that the figure of 5,000 people per transport is an inflated estimate; the actual number was closer to 2,000. [42] On the basis of the various source materials related to the extermination of Polish Jews, we can assert that around 300,000 Jews deported from the territories of prewar Poland perished at Auschwitz. This figure does not include these Polish Jews who were shipped to the camp from other countries and concentration camps.

---

[40] Reitlinger, p. 500.

[41] Wellers.

[42] Danuta Czech cites the figures for the transports of Polish Jews in the expanded and corrected German edition of her *Kalendarz wydarzeń w obozie koncentracyjnym Oświęcim-Brzezinka*: Danuta Czech, *Kalendarium der Ereignisse im Konzentrationslager Auschwitz-Birkenau 1939-1945* (Reinbek bei Hamburg, 1989).

See also Raul Hilberg, *Sonderzüge nach Auschwitz* (Frankfurt a.M., 1987), pp. 211-12, 215.

Altogether, at least 1,100,000 Jews were brought to KL Auschwitz: 438,000 from Hungary; [43] 300,000 from Poland; [44] 69,000 from France; [45] 60,000 from Holland; [46] 55,000 from Greece; [47] 46,000 from Bohemia and Moravia (Theresienstadt); [48] 23,000 from Germany and Austria; [49] 27,000 from Slovakia; [50] 25,000 from Belgium; [51] 10,000 from Jugoslavia; [52] 7,500 from Italy; [53] 690 from Norway; [54] and 34,000 from other concentration camps and undesignated areas. Of these 1,100,000 Jews deported to the camp, around 200,000 were registered as prisoners, and the remaining ca. 900,000 were murdered, almost without exception, shortly after their arrival, without being registered at the camp.

In addition to the 130,000-140,000 Poles mentioned above, who were entered into the camp's records, a certain number of Poles were shipped to the camp and killed without being registered. This would include the Poles who were sentenced to death by the German Police Court-Martial in Katowice. On the basis of the preserved documents from that court, the number of Poles who lost their lives at KL Auschwitz as a result of its verdicts numbered between 3,000-4,500. [55]

Poles were also executed at the Auschwitz camp in the course of so-called "special treatment" (*Sonderbehandlung*) — that is, without any sort of trial, on the basis of a decision by the police, and confirmed by the Main Security Office of the *Reich* (*Reichsicherheitshauptamt*, RSHA). On July 2, 1942, for example, seventeen members of a Polish underground organization, the Polish Secret Insurgent Organization (*Polska Tajna Organizacja Powstańców*), were executed under the auspices of "special treatment". [56]

---

[43] Randolph L. Braham, *The Destruction of Hungarian Jewry* (New York, 1963), p. 443.

[44] D. Czech, *Kalendarium...*, passim. This figure can also be derived from the balance of Polish Jews lost during the Nazi extermination campaign. According to Czesław Madajczyk, a total of 2.7 million Polish Jews perished during the war: ca. 500,000 in ghettoes; 200,000 from various forms of execution; and around 2,000,000 in Nazi camps. The decided majority of Polish Jews died at Treblinka, Sobibór, Bełżec, and Chełmno. Altogether, around 1.6-1.95 million Polish Jews perished at these camps.

[45] Serge Klarsfeld, *Memorial to the Jews Deported from France, 1942-1944* (New York, 1983).

[46] *Documenten van de Jodenvervolging in Nederland 1940-1945* (Amsterdam, 1965), pp. 115-120.

[47] Danuta Czech, "Deportation und Vernichtung der griechischen Juden", *Hefte von Auschwitz* 11 (1970).

[48] H.G. Adler, *Theresienstadt 1941-1945* (Tübingen 1955).

[49] APMO, D-RF-3/121/1-16, "Gestapo Berlin Auschwitz Transportlisten"; APMO, D-RF/3/120/1-3, "Auschwitz Transporte".

[50] Based on figures for the transports from March 26 to October 20, 1942, from the Moreshet Archives in Givat, Chaviva, Israel.

[51] Serge Klarsfeld and Maxime Steinberg, *Memorial de la deportation des Juifs de Belgique* (Brüssel, 1982).

[52] Jasa Romano and Ladoslav Kadelburg, *The Third Reich: Initiator, Organizer and Executant of Anti-Jewish Measures and Genocide in Yugoslavia, 1933-1945* (Belgrade, 1977); D. Czech, *Kalendarium*, pp. 488-93.

[53] Table by Giuliana Donati in *Ebrei in Italia: Deportatione, Resistenza* (Giuntina-Firenze 1975).

[54] *Dokumentensammlung über die Deportierung der Juden aus Norwegen nach Auschwitz* (Ramat Gan, 1963).

[55] Alfred Konieczny, *Pod rządami wojennego prawa karnego Trzeciej Rzeszy, Górny Śląsk* (Warszawa-Wrocław, 1972).

[56] Konieczny, pp. 354-6.

The executions that prisoners so often refer to in their post-Auschwitz accounts most likely took place under this rubric of *Sonderbehandlung*. Alter Feinsilber, who worked at the crematoria from November 1942 to January 1945, testified that groups of up to 250 people, brought into the camp from outside and never entered into the camp's records, would be executed two or three times each week. [57] One document from the resistance movement dated March 1943 reads: "In the first week of this reporting period, around 300 officers, along with their wives, but not their children, were taken to Auschwitz; they originally came from the General Government, their fate is unknown." [58] Former prisoner Stefan Wolny asserts that at the end of 1943, elderly people from the Polish territories annexed directly to the *Reich* were gassed. [59] Former prisoners Joachimowski and Drozd testified that Polish and Czech partisans were secretly gassed at the camp. [60] On June 23, 1942, 566 patients were taken from the psychiatric hospital in Kobierzyn, near Cracow, and gassed at the camp. [61] Another document from the resistance movement reported that based on observations and calculations, one could assume that "50,000 or more Poles — men, women, and children" had been gassed at KL Auschwitz without being registered at the camp. [62]

These represent only a few examples of the large number of testimonials given by former prisoners and the resistance movement. As a cautious estimate, we can assert that in addition to the 130,000-140,000 registered Poles who were shipped to KL Auschwitz, around 10,000 were executed without being registered.

Soviet prisoners of war were also killed without being entered into the camp's records. They were mainly officers selected at POW camps by special commissions of police and security officials. In his work on the fate of Soviet POWs at KL Auschwitz, Jerzy Adam Brandhuber mentions four such groups of POWs who were murdered without being registered: 300 soldiers in July 1941; 600 gassed in September 1941; 900 gassed in the mortuary of Crematorium I at the main camp; and eighteen killed in February 1944. [63] These four groups undoubtedly represent only a small portion of the unregistered POWs murdered at the camp. According to Alter Feinsilber's testimony: "Every week, 10-15 Russian prisoners of war were shot near the cremating oven .... [T]he same was happening at Birkenau, where even more Russian POWs were shot every week." [64]

A report from the resistance movement, dated October 10, 1942, states: "Since July 1941, Bolshevik POWs have been arriving at the camp, and almost all of them, numbering in the tens of thousands, have been poisoned in the gas

---

[57] See Feinsilber-Jankowski's account in *Amidst a Nightmare of Crime*, p. 42-3.

[58] *Oświęcim w świetle akt Delegatury*, p. 92.

[59] APMO, Höss Trial, vol. 4, card. 91.

[60] APMO, SS Staff Trial, vol 44, card 108.

[61] Czech, *Kalendarium...*, p. 234.

[62] APMO, Files of the Camp Resistance, vol. 7, card 485.

[63] Jerzy Adam Brandhuber, "Die Sowjetischen Kriegsgefangenen im Konzentrationslager Auschwitz" *Hefte von Auschwitz* 4 (1961), p. 45, 46.

[64] *Amidst a Nightmare of Crime*, p. 44.

chambers." [65] Former camp commandant Höss cited the largest figure. In his initial testimony to the English, he asserted: "I personally remember that during my tenure as commandant at Auschwitz, on the orders of the top leaders of the Gestapo, 70,000 Soviet prisoners of war were gassed." [66]

Since the necessary evidence is not available, it is impossible to verify these numbers. We can merely ascertain, based on the examples cited, that in addition to the ca. 12,000 registered Soviet POWs murdered at KL Auschwitz, at least 3,000 unregistered ones were also killed — although we cannot preclude the possibility that this figure, in fact, was significantly higher.

A number of people of other nationalities were also murdered at the camp without being listed in any records. These unregistered individuals included completely used-up and worn-out prisoners from other concentration camps, judged unfit for to work. It also included around 2,000 Gypsies, murdered for similar reasons. [67]

When we add up all the figures reached above, we can conclude that from 1940-45, at least 1,300,000 (1,305,000) people were deported to KL Auschwitz: around 1,100,000 (1,095,000) Jews from all parts of Europe; ca. 140-150,000 (147,000) Poles; ca. 23,000 Gypsies (mainly from Germany, Austria, Bohemia and Moravia); ca. 15,000 Soviet POWs and around 25,000 prisoners of other nationalities (Czechs, French, Yugoslavs, Byelorussians, Ukrainians, Germans, Austrians, and others).

5. How Many of the 1.3. Million Deportees Perished at the Camp?

On the basis of the partially-preserved camp documents we can establish only a small portion of the camp's total victims. Among the death certificates that can be found in the archives of the State Museum at Oświęcim (Auschwitz) in the form of originals or duplicates, [68] a certificate from December 31, 1942, has the highest number for 1942 — 45,616; for 1943, the highest number is 36,991, for a prisoner who died on December 18, 1943. Thus, for the years 1942-43, around 83,000 death certificates were issued for registered prisoners. An analysis of these and other documents leads one to conclude that at the end of February or beginning of March 1943, death certificates stopped being issued in most cases for registered Jews, brought to the camp in the RSHA's mass transports. If one takes into account these death certificates and the other fragmentary evidence that has survived, [69] one can establish only around 100,000 cases of registered prisoners dying.

---

[65] Oświęcim w świetle akt Delegatury, pp. 45-6.
[66] From Höss's testimony. APMO. Höss Trial, vol. 21, card 13.
[67] Czech, Kalendarium..., p. 448.
[68] The Russians took around 69,000 death certificates from KL Auschwitz in 1945. The International Read Cross was first granted access to them in 1989.
[69] These documents include: the register from the mortuary at the main camp, which contains the camp numbers of 22,902 deceased prisoners for the period October 1941-August 1943; the daily register for male prisoners at the camp for the period January 19 to August 19, 1942, which contains the names of 20,000 prisoners who died, as well as the numbers for 1,500 dead POWs and a death register for Soviet prisoners of war, which documents the deaths of more than 8,000 Soviet POWs.

Since not all the camp documents directly related to the deaths of prisoners have survived, the only method for establishing the number of victims is to balance the number of arrivals with the number of prisoners who departed, based on surviving documents from the camp, material from the camp resistance movement and other sources of information. According to these data, most of which have been published in Danuta Czech's *Kalendarz wydarzeń w obozie koncentracyjnym Oświęcim-Brzezinka,* [70] around 25,000 prisoners were transferred to other camps in the years 1940-43. According to Andrzej Strzelecki's estimates, another 187,820 were transferred out of Auschwitz during 1944-45, of whom ca. 163,000 had been registered and ca. 25,000 had not. [71] Thus, for the years 1940-45, a total of around 188,000 registered prisoners and 25,000 unregistered ones were transferred to other camps, around 1,500 were released, around 500 escaped and around 8,000 survived to be liberated at KL Auschwitz and its sub-camps, [72] — all tolled, around 233,000 of the 1,300,000 people who passed through the camp survived. Thus, according to these figures, the remaining 1,100,000 people perished at the camp. Among those who perished were 960,000 Jews, [73] 70,000-75,000 Poles, [74] 21,000 Gypsies, 15,000 Soviet prisoners of war, and 10,000-15,000 prisoners of other nationalities.

Both the figure of 1.3 million for individuals deported to the camp, as well as the figure of 1.1 million for those who perished should be considered minimum figures, based on the sources available to date. The actual number of victims might turn out to be higher, given the following factors: the death sites of a number of victims to the Nazis have not yet been identified; in the scholarship on the subject, there are always differences regarding not only the figure for the total number of victims, but also with regard to the figures for individual camps and other places of execution; and the numbers arrived at for the transports of Polish Jews are estimates, based in part on the numbers used in planning such transports. The actual number may, in fact, have been higher. [75] The latest research does not indicate, however, that the total could have been any higher than 1.5 million. [76]

---

[70] Translator's note: "Calendar of Events at the Concentration Camp Auschwitz-Birkenau".

[71] See the table of figures in Andrzej Strzelecki, *Ewakuacja, likwidacja i wyzwolenie KL Auschwitz* (Oświęcim, 1982).

[72] Lidia Krysta, "Opracowanie statystyczne — Przeniesienia, ucieczki, zwolnienia z KL Auschwitz". APMO, Zespół Opracowania.

[73] The figure of 960,000 includes 865,000 who were killed without any documentation, as well as the ca. 95,000 registered Jews who perished.

[74] The figure of 70,000-75,000 includes the ca. 60,000-65,000 registered Poles who perished and ca. 10,000 unregistered individuals. As was the case with the 95,000 registered Jews, it is a preliminary figure arrived at on the basis of the proportion of Poles among the various nationalities at the camp. The figure of 60,000-65,000 includes the ca. 7,700 deceased Polish men whose names can be found in the daily register for the period January 19 to August 19, 1942, as well as ca. 6,600 deceased Polish women whose names were recorded in an underground list.

[75] As a rule, former prisoners have given larger figures for the number of people who arrived in each transport.

[76] According to Wellers, the number of people who died or who were murdered at KL Auschwitz totalled 1,471,595.

THE RESISTANCE
MOVEMENT

HENRYK ŚWIEBOCKI

PRISONER RESISTANCE

The history of KL Auschwitz, replete with death and martyrdom, also had another aspect. At the camp, resistance arose; the prisoners, as the Austrian author Hermann Langbein rightly notes in the title to his book, did not simply go *wie die Schafe zur Schlachtbank* ("like sheep to the slaughter"). [1] Many prisoners refused to give in to feelings of resignation or to fall into apathy. They sought instead to oppose the Nazis' criminal activities in a wide variety of ways. Their activities — often characterized by spontaneity, sometimes by anonymity — also took on, in many cases, an organized form deserving of the term "underground struggle" or "resistance movement" in the full sense of the word.

Naturally, the realities of life at the camp limited the possibilities for resistance in the universally understood meaning of the term. As the Polish publicist Jerzy Zaborowski rightly points out, under the conditions at KL Auschwitz, "underground struggle" consisted of:

> any deed, even carried out in secret as an act of individual heroism, that had as its goal to assist other prisoners, the damage — if only a single gear — of the camp's machinery of death, or to establish contact with the world outside the fence in order to send news about the camp or to request help. [2]

The Italian psychologist and psychiatrist, Andrea Devoto, an expert on the subject of concentration camps, defines the phenomenon as follows:

> Anything could be resistance, because everything was forbidden. Every activity represented resistance that created the impression that the prisoner retained something of his former personality and individuality. [3]

Prisoners' resistance expressed itself mainly in the attempt to save the individual. It was a struggle for biological survival, to keep human beings alive

---

[1] Hermann Langbein, *...nicht wie die Schafe zur Schlachtbank. Widerstand in den national-sozialistischen Konzentrationslagern 1938-1945* (Frankfurt a.M., 1980).

[2] Jan Zaborowski in the introduction to Tomasz Sobański, *Fluchtwege aus Auschwitz* (Warszawa, 1980), p. 23, 24.

[3] Andrea Devoto, "Aspekty socjopsychologiczne i socjopsychiatryczne obozów koncentracyjnych", *Biuletyn Głównej Komisji Badania Zbrodni Hitlerowskich w Polsce* XVIII (1968), p. 120.

to the greatest extent possible. This struggle for survival was accompanied by efforts to oppose corruption, demoralization, and "de-humanization" — the fight to maintain human dignity under extreme conditions, the non-acceptance of the behavior imposed by the camp authorities. The Italian Jew and former prisoner Primo Levi (Nr. 174517), a well-known author after the war, clarified the significance of such activities by quoting an opinion of one of the prisoners:

> .... that precisely because the *Lager* was a great machine to reduce us to beasts we must not become beasts; that even in this place one can survive, and therefore one must want to survive, to tell the story, to bear witness; and that to survive we must force ourselves to save at least the skeleton, the scaffolding, the form of civilization. We are slaves, deprived of every right, exposed to every insult, condemned to certain death, but we still possess one power and we must defend it with all our strength — the power to refuse our consent. [4]

The prisoners who participated in the struggle to defend man and his dignity also constantly strived to make sure that the world learned the truth about what was happening at KL Auschwitz and that it would become part of its history. At the risk of their lives, they assembled documents and other evidence of the Nazis' criminal deeds — specifically, about the Holocaust against the Jews; the extermination of Poles and Gypsies, and other nationalities and groups; the martyrdom of these groups; and the methods of physical and psychological torture. They hid some of these documents on the grounds of the camp with the hope that they would someday be found. Most often, however, they succeeded in smuggling them outside the camp still during KL Auschwitz's existence.

The struggle for biological survival and the preservation of human dignity, on the one hand, and documenting and revealing Nazi crimes, on the other, represented the most essential forms of resistance at KL Auschwitz. A large number of prisoners took part in this struggle, whether as individuals, groups, or part of the camp-wide conspiracy. Military, political and cultural activity, as well as the secret practice of religion, also represented forms of resistance. They shared the goal of redeeming man, in both a physical and moral sense, while also disclosing and censuring the crimes against humanity taking place at the camp. Not directly linked to these basic principles were yet other resistance activities that damaged the Nazi system in some way. This included sabotage, which prisoners mainly carried out at their work sites, and spying for the Allies. Although such activities did not directly benefit the camp community, they gave one the satisfaction of having fulfilled one's duty and inspired one to continue the struggle.

One outside factor had a considerable influence upon the prisoners' struggle to resist — namely, the attitude of Poles in the local population and in conspiracies outside the camp. The assistance that the Poles gave to prisoners at the camp — repeatedly subjecting themselves to danger and risking their lives — was of no small importance. They facilitated and made possible the

---

[4] Primo Levi, *If this is a Man* (Abacus, 1987), p. 47.

prisoners' efforts to save individuals and to send information outside the fences of the camp. It was also of great moral significance. The prisoners realized that they were not alone; they could count on outside assistance. This knowledge helped them maintain their spirits and stiffened them psychologically; it helped them to face the enduring terror that raged at the camp.

HENRYK ŚWIEBOCKI

ATTITUDES, BEHAVIOR AND SPONTANEOUS ACTIVITY
BY THE PRISONERS

The attitudes and behavior of the prisoners had a significant impact upon the morale of the camp community and its willingness to fight. Their attitudes and actions varied, however. Each prisoner brought to KL Auschwitz his or her own experiences from "the entire life that they had lived up to then". Each had a different past; some had led a peaceful life before their arrest, while others, including former military personnel, political activists, and participants in various conspiracies had been hardened in the struggle with the occupier. Their behavior at the camp varied, however. Some wanted to survive at all costs, even at the cost of others. Others, having the same goal, would act in such a way as to not harm anyone else, but also would not help them, and expected no help themselves. Another group of prisoners were those who failed to develop any defense mechanisms and, having lost all hope of living, stopped offering resistance and fighting for survival. There were also a large number, however, who considered helping others and resisting the SS to be their main goals. [1]

Mainly those who were imprisoned at the camp had the possibility to offer resistance. Most deportees perished, however, immediately upon their arrival in the gas chambers. They had neither the time nor the opportunity to organize resistance. Nevertheless, spontaneous acts containing elements of struggle and rebellion did occur. They could take the form of passive defiance or active resistance. Such acts were characterized by a heroic, patriotic attitude before the SS — deportees would condemn the Nazis to death for their crimes or express contempt for the death that awaited them.

On October 23 or 24, 1943, a rebellion broke out among Jews brought to the camp from Bergen-Belsen who were awaiting their deaths. After the selection was concluded, the Jews were led to the extermination facilites — women to Crematorium II and men to Crematorium III. In the changing-room to Crematorium II, one woman, realizing that death awaited her, tore the pistol away from SS man Josef Schillinger before she entered the gas chamber. She shot him several times and severely wounded him. Then she shot a second SS-man, Wilhelm Emmerich. The other women took this as a signal to throw themselves upon the SS men. The rebellion was put down in the end and the

---

[1] See Kazimierz Godorowski, *Psychologia i psychopatologia hitlerowskich obozów koncentracyjnych. Próba analizy postaw i zachowań w warunkach ekstremalnych obciążeń* (Warszawa, 1985), pp. 90-91.

women perished. Schillinger died on the way to the hospital from the wounds he had received. Emmerich recovered, but was permanently crippled; from then on, he walked with a limp. [2]

There were also cases of Jews escaping while being driven to their deaths in the gas chambers. On the night of May 25-26, 1944, several hundred Jews who had arrived in a transport from Hungary tried to flee. The SS men tracked them down with spotlights and murdered them. Two days later, a similar occurence took place among other Jews brought to the camp from Hungary. [3] Apparently, such escapes were not an isolated incident. [4] Of the relevant SS documents that have survived, one finds Garrison Order Nr. 17/44, citing a letter of June 3, 1944, instructing that the electricity to the barbed-wire fence surrounding KL Birkenau should not be shut off. [5] This order undoubtedly resulted from the repeated escape attempts of deportees being led to the extermination facilities.

A number of eyewitness reports describe the attitudes of the deportees as they neared their deaths. In 1952, a Yiddish manuscript was unearthed near the ruins of Crematorium III, written by a member of the *Sonderkommando* during the camp's existence. It included the following passage:

It was Passover 1944. A transport arrived from Vittel in France. It contained many honored Jewish personalities, including the rabbi from Bayonne, Rabbi Mosze Friedman, blessed be his memory, one of the greatest scholarly authorities for Polish Jewry .... He undressed along with everyone else. Then, a certain *Obersturmführer* came in. The Rabbi went up to him and, holding him by the collar of his uniform, told him in German: 'You vulgar, barbaric murderers of humanity, don't think that you will succeed in exterminating our people; the Jewish nation will live forever and never disappear from the arena of world history. But you, you base murderers, will pay quite dearly; for every innocent Jew, you will pay with ten Germans, and you will not only vanish as a power, but as a nation itself. The day of reckoning approaches, the blood that has been shed will cry out for retribution. Our blood will not know peace until the fiery wrath of destruction vents itself upon your nation and destroys your bestial race.' He spoke these words with great force in a strong lion's voice. He then put on his hat and shouted with great zeal 'Szema Israel!' Everyone present cried with him, 'Szema Israel!', and the extraordinary enthusiasm of a deep faith penetrated all of them .... [6]

---

[2] APMO, Files of the camp Resistance, vol. Va, cards 324a, 324b, Report of Jerzy Tabeau (so-called "Report by a Polish Major", *Raport polskiego majora*), compiled in Cracow at the end of 1943/beginning of 1944 after his escape from the camp; APMO, Files of the Camp Resistance, vol. I, card 37, Smuggled letter from prisoner Stanisław Kłodziński from August 27 (?), 1943, to Teresa Lasocka-Estreicher from the conspirative Committee to Assist Concentration-Camp Prisoners (*Pomoc Więźniom Obozów Koncentracyjnych*, PWOK) in Cracow; APMO, Höss Trial. vol. 6, cards 27-28, testimony of former prisoner Otto Wolken; Hermann Langbein, *Menschen in Auschwitz* (Frankfurt a.M., Berlin, and Vienna, 1980), pp. 142-3.

[3] Sprawozdanie okresowe PWOK od 25.V.1944 do 15.VI.1944 (Report of PWOK for the period May 25 — June 15, 1944). APMO, Files of the Camp Resistance, vol. VIII, cards 445-446.

[4] APMO, Files of the Camp Resistance, vol. Va, cards 323c, 324a.

[5] Standortbefehl Nr. 17/44 from June 9, 1944, in APMO, Standortbefehle 1944, vol. 3, card 331.

[6] "Rękopis Nieznanego Autora" in *Wśród koszmarnej zbrodni. Notatki więźniów Sonderkommando* (Oświęcim, 1975), 170. For an earlier translation of the document, see "Manuscript of an Unknown Author", in *Amidst a Nightmare of Crime* (Oświęcim, 1973), pp. 116, 118.

On another page of the same manuscript, the author relates the following:

Sometime at the end of 1943, the following event came to pass. One hundred sixty-four Poles were brought in from the area, including twelve young women — all members of a secret organization. A number of personages from the SS came. At the same time, several hundred Dutch Jews were brought in, prisoners of the camp, to be gassed. One young Polish woman, already stripped naked, gave a brief, but passionate speech to everyone, stigmatizing the Nazis' crimes and oppression. She concluded: 'We will not perish; our nation's history will immortalize us, our deeds and spirit will live and flourish; the German nation will pay a price for our blood that we can only imagine. Down with the barbarity of Hitler's Germany! Long live Poland!' Then she turned to us, the Jews in the *Sonderkommando*: 'Remember that you bear the sacred burden to avenge us, the innocent. Tell our brothers, our nation, that we went to death conscientiously, full of pride.' Then the Poles kneeled to the ground and solemnly repeated a prayer in a way that made a deep impression. Subsequently, they all arose and sang one verse of the Polish national anthem together, and the Jews sang the *Hatikwa* .... [7]

Often, prisoners from the camp would behave in a similar fashion as their death approached. They did not plead for mercy, but awaited their fate proudly, with their heads held high. They would often shout out patriotic slogans during their execution. Pery Broad, a former SS man and functionary in the Political Division (*Politische Abteilung*), the camp Gestapo, described how prisoners behaved before being executed in front of the Death Wall in KL Auschwitz I:

Next to the black wall stood a prisoner with a shovel. Another prisoner, chosen for his strength, brought out the first victims at a run .... Although they were faltering skeletons — some had vegetated for months in a putrid basement-cell, where one would not even keep an animal — barely able to stand on their feet, many of them would still cry at the last second: 'Long live Poland!' or 'Long live freedom!' In such cases, the executioner-flunky would hurry up with his shot to the back of the head or try to silence them with violent blows .... Thus died the Poles and the Jews, whom Nazi propaganda had always proclaimed to be slavish creatures, whimpering for mercy, not entitled to any rights in life, or a least not to the same rights to which Germans were entitled. It made no difference whether they were men or women, young or old; almost without exception, one would see the same picture: people mobilizing the remainder of their strength to die with dignity. [8]

On December 30, 1944, the last execution took place at the main camp. Five members of the camp resistance movement were hung there: Ernst Burger (Nr. 23850), Rudolf Friemel (Nr. 25173), and Ludwig Vesely (Nr. 38169) — all Austrians; and two Poles, Piotr Piąty (Nr. 130380) and Bernard Świerczyna (Nr. 1393). The condemned did not allow their eyes to be covered. Before they were hung on the gallows, they managed to let out one last cry, "Down with

---

[7] Ibid.

[8] "Wspomnienia Pery Broada", in *Oświęcim w oczach SS* (Katowice, 1980), pp. 140-41. For an earlier, complete translation, see "Reminiscences of Pery Broad", in *KL Auschwitz seen by the SS* (Oświęcim, 1972), pp. 148-49.

Hitler!", "Down with fascism!", "Today, us; tomorrow, you!", and "Long live Poland!". [9]

Cases of active resistance also occurred among those who were taken to be executed. Such was the case, for example, on October 28, 1942, when 280 Poles were killed. Two of them, Captain Dr. Henryk Suchnicki (Nr. 19456) of the Polish Army and Leon Kukiełka (Nr. 16465), rose up to fight. They defended themselves in Block 11 (the Death Block) with wooden stools. They were eventually shot by the SS men. [10]

The noble sentiments and behavior of individual prisoners, particularly the example of those who were endowed with exceptional personalities and charisma — famous people from political, social and cultural life — greatly influenced the morale of the camp community. An act committed by Father Maksymilian Rajmund Kolbe (Nr. 16670), the Polish Franciscan from Niepokalanów, became an enduring symbol of sacrifice, heroism and resistance. In the summer of 1941, he volunteered to take the place of a prisoner who was selected for death by starvation — a man with a family — and thus saved his life. Kolbe perished from an injection of phenol on August 14 in the basement of the infamous Death Block. The Polish prisoner whose life he had saved, Franciszek Gajowniczek (Nr. 5659), survived the war. Father Maksymilian's heroic attitude deeply moved his fellow prisoners and was often commented upon at the camp. [11]

Less well-known at he camp, but also requiring a great deal of courage, was the act of Dr. Adelajda Hautval (Nr. 31802), a French prisoner. She refused to work together with an SS doctor, Dr. Eduard Wirths, in conducting criminal experiments on female prisoners in Block 10 of the main camp. She gave as her reason that such activities were not in keeping with her oath and conscience as a doctor. [12]

Among the well-known figures from Polish political life held at KL Auschwitz was Jan Mosdorf (Nr. 8230), leader of the pre-war Radical--National Camp (*Obóz Narodowo-Radykalny*) — a right-wing organization of

---

[9] Leon Mackiewicz, "Ostatnia egzekucja w Oświęcimiu", APMO, Collection of Reminiscences, vol. 3, card, 454; APMO, Höss Trial, vol. 8, card 107, Testimony of former prisoner Jan Dziopek; Tomasz Sobański, *Fluchtwege aus Auschwitz* (Warszawa, 1980), p. 217.

[10] Tadeusz Iwaszko and Stanisław Kłodziński, "Bunt skazańców 28.X.1942 r. w oświęcimskich bloku nr 11", *Przegląd Lekarski — Oświęcim* (1977), pp. 119-21.

See also Danuta Czech, *Kalendarz wydarzeń w KL Auschwitz* (Oświęcim, 1992), p. 272.

[11] APMO, Materials about Father Kolbe, vol. 47, 47a, 47b, 47c, 47d, 47e (most importantly, the accounts of former prisoners: Brunon Borgowiec, Tadeusz Chróścicki, Franciszek Gajowniczek, Tadeusz Paczuła, Tadeusz Pietrzykowski, and Henryk Sienkiewicz, held in t. 47a); APMO, D-AuI-2/1, *Sterbebuch* [Death Register], t. I/1941, p. 508, Death Certificate nr. 510/1941 for Rajmund Kolbe, prepared by the camp's *Standesamt* (*Myocardinsuffizienz*, or cardiac insufficiency, was given as the cause of death); compare with APMO, Files of the Camp Resistance, vol. XII, card 39, smuggled letter of prisoner Konrad Szweda from the end of 1941; compare with Jan Ptakowski, *Oświęcim bez cenzury i bez legend* (New York, 1985), p. 55.

[12] Dorota Lorska, "Blok X w Oświęcimiu," *Przegląd Lekarski — Oświęcim*, (1965), pp. 102-3; Ella Lingens, Dr Adelajda Hautval, *Przegląd Lekarski — Oświęcim*, (1964), pp. 119-21; compare with Hermann Langbein, *...nicht wie die Schafe zur Schlachtbank. Widerstand in den national-sozialistischen Konzentrationslagern 1938-1945* (Frankfurt a. M., 1980), p. 178.

a nationalistic and antisemitic character. Mosdorf, who participated in the camp resistance movement, became an advocate for cooperation among the prisoners, regardless of their nationality or worldview. He gave considerable assistance to the Jews. [13] Postwar accounts, including some by Jews who survived the Holocaust, have emphasized his behavior and assistance in saving fellow prisoners. Mieczysław Maślanko, a former Jewish prisoner (registered at the camp as Mojżesz Maślanko, Nr 128153), gave the following testimonial after the war:

At Auschwitz, I met Jan Mosdorf. He also had a big heart and helped Jews. I personally received a large amount of help from him, which perhaps decided my survival. I was lying in the hospital in Block Nr. XIX. Mosdorf held some low-level office position in this block. And then suddenly, at the beginning of September 1943, Kuryłowicz ran into the hospital block with information that I was personally threatened with liquidation and that I should promptly and immediately leave. Mosdorf, not pausing for a single moment, at the risk of his own life, literally in the course of several minutes arranged all the complicated formalities at the camp, and I was transferred after a few minutes to another hospital block, Nr. IX. And I lived anew. [14]

Another former prisoner, also a Jew, the writer Wolf Glicksman, writes in an article contained in *Yiwo. Annual of Jewish Social Science* VII (New York, 1953):

Another well-known individual, the pre-war leader of the antisemitic youth movement in Poland, Jan Mosdorf, repeatedly risked his life to bring my letters to relatives held at the women's camp at Birkenau. Mosdorf worked at Birkenau and often brought me vegetables, and sometimes a slice of bread or some clothes. [15]

A historian from the United States, Philip Friedman, a Jew born in Poland, writes the following in his book:

At the camp, Mosdorf changed his relationship to Jews. Some of the food-packages that he received from friends .... he would share with Jews. In his work at a camp office, he sometimes saved Jews threatened with being selected and gassed. [16]

Such attitudes, behavior and activity on the part of individual prisoners inspired others. They strengthened feelings of solidarity, induced activity, called forth new strength, and demonstrated that hope still existed to those who had lost all hope. The camp constantly provided new examples and proof of solidarity, friendship, assistance, sacrifice, and self-denial.

---

[13] APMO, Höss Trial, vol. 27b, card 176, testimony of former prisoner Józef Cyrankiewicz; APMO, Collection of Testimonies, vol, 78, card 31, account of former prisoner Edward Halek; Tadeusz Hołuj, "Rozejm Jana Mosdorfa", *Odrodzenie 35* (1946); Ptakowski, ibid., p. 40; also see footnotes 14-16.

[14] *Ten jest z ojczyzny mojej. Polacy z pomocą Żydom 1939-1945*, ed. Władysław Bartoszewski and Zofia Lewinówna (Kraków, 1969), p. 670.

[15] Ibid., p. 91.

[16] Philip Friedman, *Their Brother's Keepers* (New York, 1978), p. 114.

HENRYK ŚWIEBOCKI

PRISONER SELF-HELP

Among the many activities directed against terrorization and destruction, prisoner self-help played a central role. It was characterized by a wide range of activities and had a broad scope. It consisted of everyday acts of comradery, friendship, mutual assistance, and solidarity. Self-help was a form of self-defense against physical destruction. It also served to raise the prisoner's morale and prevent psychological collapse.

Self-help arose in different forms. It could be individual and spontaneous or organized and directed. Its borders are difficult to draw with any precision. Organized activity resulted from the work of self-help groups and underground organizations established by the prisoners. Since mainly Poles were initially held at KL Auschwitz, self-help and conspiratorial groups first arose among Polish political prisoners. The Polish underground was composed of military organizations, along with socialist and nationalist political parties, all of whom were linked to the Home Army (*Armia Krajowa*, AK). Conspirational groups, mainly of a leftist nature, were later formed by prisoners of other nationalities at the camp. There were Austro-German, French, Jewish, Yugoslavian and Russian groups. In 1943, they united with some of the Polish socialists and other leftists to form a common, international underground organization at the camp: *Kampfgruppe Auschwitz*, or Auschwitz Fighting Group (for information on these organizations, see p. 216).

Different factors influenced how self-help organizations formed. Often, prisoners from the same transport or prison, having experienced similar ordeals, would support one another. In many cases, self-help arose on the basis of comradery and solidarity among prisoners from the same locality. Groups also arose on the basis of similar careers. Particularly strong were the bonds among teachers, doctors and clergy. Members of Scouting organizations maintained close contacts. Not without significance for the creation of self-help groups were also ties of kinship, friendships from before arrest, acquaintance through schooling or the military and previous connections through conspiratorial groups, political parties and clubs. A common language or common membership in an ethnic or nationality group could also bring prisoners together.[1]

---

[1] Krzysztof Dunin-Wąsowicz, *Resistance in the Nazi Concentration Camps 1933-1945* (Warszawa, 1982), p. 56; Stanisław Hüpsch, Artur Krzetuski, Władysław Plaskura, "Wpływ więźniów z 'grupy mościskiej' na warunki bytowe i sanitarne w obozie oświęcimskim", „*Przegląd Lekarski — Oświęcim* (1973), pp 137-147; Zenon Jagoda, Stanisław Kłodziński and Jan Masłowski, „Przyjaźnie Oświęcimskie", *Przegląd Lekarski — Oświęcim* (1978), pp. 35-7, 50-51, 53, 55, 57.

The postwar memoirs, testimony and accounts of Auschwitz survivors contain a great deal of information about the different forms that self-help could take. Sociologist Anna Pawełczyńska (Nr. 44764), a Pole, lists the following forms of self-help, among others:

.... the concealment of the weakest in the middle of a row of prisoners (the ends of every row were very exposed to beatings), taking the place of the weakest prisoner at work, giving him the warmest clothes, sharing food. To this category of activity also belong all the techniques of shoring up those prisoners who had lost their reserves of mental endurance. This meant releasing tension in dangerous situations through humor, the telling of stories, a song, a laugh, recollections, plans for the future; it meant finding the most varied subjects or games to distract attention from the present. Every proof of loyalty and sympathy, every hour of a shared life of the imagination (personal as well as historical), every moment of laughter, every joke was part of the arsenal of collective defense and thus an element of the resistance movement. [2]

Of particular importance to new arrivals at the camp were warnings about potential dangers, protection, advice, friendly words and kind gestures from other prisoners who had found themselves behind the fence earlier. Wiktoria Klimaszewska (Nr. 48517), a Pole, relates in her account how, when she was brought to KL Birkenau in November 1942, a female prisoner working in the reception office purposely lowered her age when filling in her personal data. "I was surprised", she explains in her account, "but I came to understand that it would certainly be better that there were women prisoners who would watch over us. I later found out that in the opinion of the camp authorities, older people had no right to live."[3]

Two Jews — Viktor E. Frankl (Nr. 119104), a psychologist from Austria, and Elie Wiesel (Nr. A-7713), a recipient of the Nobel Peace Prize after the war — described how prisoners already at the camp would try to assist new arrivals in various ways and help keep their spirits up.

Although it was strictly forbidden to leave the barracks — Victor Frankl asserts — ... one of our well-known colleagues, who had been taken to Auschwitz several weeks before us, stole into our barrack. He tried to calm us down, teach us, console us. .... Affecting good humor and nonchalance, he hastily gave us several tips .... I only ask and request one thing of you, shave every day, even with a piece of glass, or give your last piece of bread to anyone who is willing to shave you. That way, you will look younger, and your scraped cheeks will take on color. Just do not get sick and try to look young. Furthermore, in order to live, there is only one way: create the impression that you are fit for work. Here it is enough to hobble because of some unnoticed scratch or corn. If an SS sees its, he will wag his finger and two days later, dead certain, it will be the gas. [4]

---

[2] Anna Pawełczyńska, *Values and Violence, A. Sociological Analysis* (London, 1979), p. 119.
[3] APMO, Collection of Testimonies, vol. 15, card 4, account of former prisoner Wiktoria Klimaszewska.
[4] Viktor E. Frankl, *Ein Psycholog erlebt das Konzentrationslager* (Wien, 1947), pp. 22, 29.

Elie Wiesel relates the following occurrence:

> After a few minutes of this mad race we arrived in front of another block. The prisoner in charge was waiting for us. He was a young Pole, who smiled at us. He began to talk to us, and, despite our weariness, we listened patiently.
>
> 'Comrades, you're in the concentration camp of Auschwitz. There's a long road of suffering ahead of you. But don't lose courage. You've already escaped the gravest danger: selection. So now, muster your strength and don't lose heart. We shall all see the day of liberation. Have faith in life. Above all else, have faith. Drive out despair, and you will keep death away from yourselves. Hell is not for eternity. And now, a prayer — or rather, a piece of advice: let there be comradeship among you. We are all brothers, and we are all suffering the same fate. The same smoke floats over all our heads. Help one another. It is the only way to survive. [5]

Weakened, emaciated and ill prisoners required special care. For many of them, assistance from friends at the camp helped them overcome the crisis and regain their strength. Often, they would strive to arrange lighter work for such prisoners, and if possible, indoors — for example, in the kitchen, in the room where potatoes were pealed, in warehouses or in camp offices. The camp employment office was responsible for distributing jobs. The German prisoner Otto Küsel (Nr. 2), held the top office in the so-called *Arbeitsdienst* during the years 1940-42. This was one of the most important offices that a prisoner could hold. Küsel answered to an SS man from the employment office, but, in most cases, made decisions regarding employment himself. Although he was a criminal prisoner, chosen by the camp authorities for the realization of their criminal goals, Küsel turned out to be a decent individual. Whenever he had the time and opportunity, he would help other prisoners. [6] Those who survived the camp remember him with great sympathy. The Pole Ryszard Dacko (Nr. 4044) characterized Küsel as follows:

> I can only speak of him using superlatives. He was very obliging and helped other prisoners whenever he could. Prisoners of various nationalities would come to him, including those who were extremely emaciated, so-called 'Muslims'. If he was not able to solve a problem, he would swear helplessly like a sailor. [7]

Prisoners would sometimes work to save their fellow prisoners who were ill and in a critical state but who were afraid to report to the HKB. In the opinion of many prisoners, the HKB was the "vestibule to the crematorium". This reputation arose from the fact that prisoners were exterminated at the HKB by phenol injection and that selections were conduced among the ill for the gas chambers, especially during epidemics. The Pole Kazi-

---

[5] Elie Wiesel, *Night* (Fontana Books, 1972), pp. 52-53.

[6] Józef Garliński, *Fighting Auschwitz* (London, 1975), pp. 56, 57; H. Langbein, *Menschen in Auschwitz* (Frankfurt a.M., Berlin and Vienna, 1980), pp. 180-81; J. Ptakowski, *Oświęcim bez cenzury i bez legend* (New York, 1985), pp. 96-7; APMO, Collection of Testimonies, vol. 39, card 67; vol. 50, cards 135, 138, 143; vol. 67, card 67; vol. 71, card 188 — Accounts of former prisoners Franciszek Balzar, Stanisław Witek, Kazimierz Szczerbowski and Ryszard Dacko.

[7] Account of R. Dacko, ibid., card 188.

mierz Hałoń (who went under the assumed name Kazimierz Wrona, Nr. 20687, at the camp), relates how, during an illness, he was able to overcome the crisis with the assistance of colleagues, without having to enter the hospital:

> When I began to feel bad, I went to Antek Rychter for an 'anti-typhoid' pill .... I walked around with a fever for a couple days, but did not go to a doctor, because at that time, several ill people had been taken to Birkenau [i.e., to the gas chambers — HS]. I worked in a work-detachment led by Zepel, an Austrian — a socialist with a red triangle. My colleagues 'hid' me so that I would not have to go to the hospital. In the morning, on the way to work, as we went through the gates to the camp, where the SS men always counted the groups of five, my colleagues would brace me behind the shoulders, as was the case when we returned. I had such a high fever that I did not have the strength to walk alone. At work, I was immediately led down into the pit, where a machine for carrying earth was being repaired by our work detail. One had a certain degree of protection there from the SS men who directed our work. The kapo even delegated one colleague to look after me. Carrots and beets were brought down to me, and I was given boiled water to drink. When work was over, I was brought out, put in the column, and led back to the camp for roll-call. [8]

Despite everything, the HKB was also a place where self-help activity was highly-developed. The prisoners employed there — doctors and nurses, as well as administrative personnel — made superhuman efforts to decrease the death rate among the ill. They strived to surround the patients with security and to create an atmosphere of comradeship and warmth. The lack of medicine presented an enormous problem. The amount of medicine that was officially distributed was negligible in comparison to the enormous need. Thus, they attained it by stealing from the SS pharmacy and warehouses. A great deal of medicine also flowed into the camp through secret channels from the outside, from the Polish population and the underground (see p. 217).

The prisoners on the HKB staff sought to protect their ill counterparts from selections to the gas chambers. The Polish doctor Władysław Fejkiel (Nr. 5647) wrote the following on the subject:

> At that time, the greatest extermination ever conducted by the commandant's office came down upon us. It consisted of frequent selections to the gas and injections of phenol. If it had not been for the responsible attitude of the majority of the personnel working as nurses, doctors, and administrators, significantly more people would have perished than was the case. Before every expected selection to the gas, the strongest among the ill would sign up for work. The doctor at the outpatient hospital would receive the list and admit them to the infirmary only after the risk had subsided. Very weak patients learned how they had to behave while selections were being conducted. They were taught how they had to respond to the questions that they were asked by the SS doctor and how to create the impression that they were strong. The prisoner-doctor who had to introduce such an ill individual to the SS

---

[8] Account of former prisoner Kazimierz Hałoń, as cited in: Stanisław Kłodziński, „Dur wysypkowy w obozie Oświęcim I", *Przegląd Lekarski — Oświęcim* (1965), p. 63.

doctor had the duty not to give the actual data regarding the illness, to conceal from him any diagnoses that were of disuse to the ill patient, shorten the disease's length and present the best prognosis possible. The ill, who were particularly threatened, were hidden in the garrets and other recesses during the selection itself or taken from the rooms that the SS doctor had not yet inspected to rooms that had already been looked over. [9]

Thanks to this activity, some prisoners were saved from death. One of them was the Pole Józef Kret (Nr. 20020). He remembers the following:

When my fever peaked, unbeknownst to me, I eluded the greatest possible danger: that was when the trucks pulled in and carried away those in our block who were ill with typhus to the gas chamber. I was hidden under a mattress, making use of the fact that I was not visible in the top bunk from the ground. My body was emaciated and the flatness of the mattress, filled with shavings, was propitious for camouflaging a person unconscious from fever. I was informed about the danger that had passed once I returned to consciousness. On my new chart, the name of another illness was now displayed. I do not know the name of the courageous doctor who saved me from being gassed. I presume that not only I, but many others as well, have him to thank for their lives. [10]

In terms of self-help, there were also cases in which prisoners employed in camp offices falsified data at the risk of their own lives to protect comrades from the misery of death. One example of this was the rescue of the Jew Benedykt Kautsky (Nr. 68510). In January 1943, while he was in the hospital at KL Auschwitz III-Monowitz, his documents were switched with those of a German political prisoner. As a result, Kautsky avoided selection to the gas chamber and death. Gustav Herzog (Nr. 68485), a Jew from Austria, who held the office of *Rapportschreiber* ("report writer") at the camp, played a leading role in this dangerous switch of data. [11] In his book after the war, Kautsky wrote that he was quite shocked when he suddenly discovered that he was an "Aryan" political prisoner, a German, which permitted him to stay longer in the HKB without worrying about selection to the gas chamber. [12]

Maria Kozakiewicz (Nr. 7551), a Polish Jew, was saved in a similar way. The personal questionnaire that she had received, for Jews, was switched for an "Aryan" one, and she was subsequently transferred to another camp. Two Polish women were behind this risky undertaking: Walentyna Konopska (Nr. 13156), employed in the identification office, and Wanda Marossanyi (Nr. 7524), working in the camp employment office. [13] Maria Kozakiewicz survived

---

[9] Władysław Fejkiel, "O służbie zdrowia w obozie koncentracyjnym w Oświęcimiu I (Obóz główny)", *Przegląd Lekarski — Oświęcim* (1961), p. 48.

[10] Józef Kret, "Lekarze znaleźli wyjście", *Przegląd Lekarski — Oświęcim* (1966), p. 186.

[11] Benedikt Kautsky, *Teufel und Verdammte* (Wien, 1961), p. 56; APMO, "Zugangslisten: Juden — nicht fotografiert [Entry Register — Jews, not photographed]", vol. 2, pp. 272, 274 (Kautsky is listed as a Jew), and "KL Buchenwald-Zugangslisten vom KL Auschwitz, Männer", vol. 7, k. 77 and 78 (Kautsky is listed as a political prisoner).

[12] Kautsky, p. 56.

[13] APMO, Collection of Testimonies, vol. 30, cards 3-4, account of former prisoner Hanna Schyller-Palarczykowa. Compare to ibid., vol. 4, card 417, account of former prisoner Maria Żumańska.

the concentration camps and the war. Józef Mikusz (Nr. 7794), a Pole, asserts in his account from after the war that at the men's camp at KL Birkenau, as part of the campaign of self-help, there were cases in which Jewish prisoners were registered as non-Jews. He cites the example of a lawyer from Lwów (Lviv) name Margulicz, who was registered at the camp as a Pole under an assumed named, Onyszkiewicz, and was employed at the packaging office. He survived the war. [14]

Among the forms of material help, assistance in the form of food played an important role. Situations are known in which a prisoner would give up part of his daily starvation-ration for the sake of a colleague. To this group belonged the communist Georges Varennes, one of the organizers of a self-help group among the French prisoners. Former prisoner Roger Abada (Nr. 45157) from France writes in his memoirs:

> We shall never forget our dear comrade, Georges Varennes, a teacher from Yonne .... Varennes created solidarity among the internees under such terrible conditions .... He refused his own scant ration of food in order to sustain his young comrades. [15]

There are a number of accounts in which former prisoners relate how Father Maksymilian Kolbe, already mentioned, would share his ration of camp food with others, often with comrades-in-suffering whom he did not even know. [16] It also demanded a great deal of sacrifice to divide up the packages that some prisoners (so-called "Aryans") were allowed to receive from their families from the end of 1942. Jews and Soviet prisoners of war, who were not allowed to receive packages, could sometimes make use of such assistance. The Pole Józef Majchrzak (Nr. 33204) stated:

> I received my first package of food, in my *Stube* [17] (numbering around 200 prisoners). It was a holiday for us. It was good that my family, though poor and resettled, had sent me dried-up, sliced bread with fat. The onions and fat, in a separate package, had disappeared along the way, although there had only been a small quantity of them. This bread from freedom, as we all called it, was the most delicious and most valuable thing under the sun. I consumed the contents of the package in the evening in the *Stube* with my colleagues. It was not a meal, but more a food-tasting. [18]

Packages from families represented a small drop of water in a sea of need. Most often, additional food was obtained by deceiving the camp authorities. Food was stolen from the SS warehouses or the camp's production facilities, such as the slaughter house, dairy and bakery. A certain number of food items were smuggled out of "Canada" — that is, from the warehouses where the property of Jews who had been murdered in the gas chambers was storted and

---

[14] Ibid., vol. 68, card 34, account of former prisoner Józef Mikusz.

[15] Ibid., vol., 31, card 122, account of former prisoner Roger Abada.

[16] APMO, Materials about Father Kolbe, vol, 47a, cards 16, 48, 52, accounts of former prisoners Henryk S. Cyankiewicz, Tadeusz Pietrzykowski and Zygmunt Ruszczak.

[17] Translator's note: A room in the barracks.

[18] Account of former prisoner Józef Majchrzak, as cited in Z. Jagoda, S. Kłodziński, and J. Masłowski, *Przyjaźnie Oświęcimskie*, p. 48.

stored immediately after their arrival at the camp. Food was procured from these warehouses, along with other necessities for the prisoners, such as medicine, warm clothing, underwear and shoes. This type of activity was known in camp jargon as "organization" or "organizing".

The camp's reserves were not the only resource available for the prisoners' campaign of self-help. A significant amount of food and medicine also reached the prisoners from outside the camp. Poles — the local population, charities, and the underground — supplied them through secret channels.

Solidarity campaigns also played a central role in the self-help effort. Such campaigns could take various forms. One campaign, for example, was based on the principle of providing food for those prisoners who had no possibility of receiving food beyond the rations at the camp. Another example was the cigarette collection conducted by French prisoners for Christmas 1944. The collected cigarettes — a total of 4,000 — were distributed to ill prisoners and women. [19] Nina Gusiewa (Nr. 65781), a member of the conspiracy among Russian prisoners at KL Birkenau, wrote about her experiences during her employment at the children's barracks in spring 1944. Around 200 Russian, Byelorussian, Ukrainian, Polish and Jewish children lived there under horrible conditions. The women prisoners who worked there, after explaining the conditions, turned to the prisoner community with an appeal for assistance to the children. Gushieva later described what happened:

> The men quickly responded to our appeal. The prisoners brought food, clothing, and shoes to our camp and sent bread, sugar, medicine and underwear to the children. The doctors Olga Nikiticzna Klimienko, Lubov Alpatova, a Polish woman named Marysia, and Zoya Taralina, a student in her second year at the Rostov medical institute, visited the children every day, observed them, gave instructions about how we should care for them, and prescribed medicine. .... We also turned to our female comrades for assistance, who, ignoring the fact that they were hungry and emaciated themselves, would share their last crumb of bread with the children. Female prisoners who worked in the agricultural brigade brought us carrots, beets, potatoes and other vegetables, which we secretly prepared in our barracks .... The women who received packages from their families helped us greatly. They were women, no-longer young, from Barrack 7: Maria Juryńska from Warsaw, Jadwiga, Wanda, Zosia, and others. They sacrificed a significant portion of their packages for the children. I will always remember the good eyes of the loving Mrs. Maria from Warsaw, who knew nothing about the fate of her three children, because they had all been arrested before her. The Czechs, Yugoslavs and French also helped the children. Women of all nationalities shared their scant rations with them. [20]

Solidarity campaigns extended not only to the material, but also to the moral, sphere. They included such political activities as the fight against nationalism and chauvinism and the struggle against antisemitism. The goal was the creation of a united front of prisoner cooperation against the SS staff. This represented the chief concern and main focus of the camp conspiracy's activities.

---

[19] See K. Dunin-Wąsowicz, p. 67.
[20] Nina Gusiewa, "O tym zapomnieć nie wolno," *Zeszyty Oświęcimskie* 5 (1961), pp. 136-7.

The effectiveness of such activities depended in many cases on the attitudes of the prisoner-functionaries — kapos, block seniors and their assistants. Their possibilities for lightening the burdens of their fellow prisoners were enormous. It was with this fact in mind that efforts were made — especially on the part of the conspiratorial movement among the prisoners — to assure that offices in the camp hierarchy ended up in the hands of prisoners of a high moral stature, who would preserve their human dignity and not become a tool in the hands of the SS for oppressing their comrades. Political prisoners, imprisoned at the camp for their ideals, represented the best guarantee in this regard. At the same time, efforts were made to force the removal of criminals from the majority of positions that they had received — with the blessing of the SS, of course. This applied in particular to certain criminals who had distinguished themselves as kapos or block seniors with their exceptional brutality and had cooperated with the camp authorities in the annihilation of other prisoners. In such cases, the prisoners took the so-called path of lesser evil. This was the case, for example, with Leo Wietschorek (Nr. 30), the *Lagerälteste* (camp senior) from division BIb at KL Birkenau, a German criminal who brutalized prisoners. The prisoners made a special effort to infect him with typhus. He subsequently died at the beginning of July 1942. [21] In most cases, however, political prisoners took over such offices as a result of the camp's constant expansion. It forced the SS men to seek skilled individuals to fill such positions. In most cases, they found such qualified individuals among the political prisoners.

The self-help campaign was the most extensive and one of the most effective forms of prisoner self-defense against extermination. It presented many with an opportunity for survival. It also had a great moral significance; it restored the prisoners' belief in humanity. It helped them avoid psychological break-down and gave them the strength to survive the nightmare of the camp.

---

[21] APMO, Collection of Testimonies, vol. 67, card 151, account of former prisoner Stanisław Grudziński; Stanisław Kłodziński, "Rola kryminalistów niemieckich w początkach obozu oświęcimskiego", *Przegląd Lekarski — Oświęcim* (1974), p. 125; compare to J. Ptakowski, p. 97.

BARBARA JAROSZ

ORGANIZATIONS OF THE CAMP RESISTANCE MOVEMENT AND THEIR ACTIVITIES

1. Organizations of the Camp Resistance Movement

The first organizations of a camp resistance movement appeared at KL Auschwitz in the second half of 1940. It was mainly Poles, the majority of prisoners at the time, who established them. In the fall of 1940, a group affiliated with the Polish Socialist Party (*Polska Partia Socjalistyczna*, PPS) was founded. Its leaders and organizers were PPS leftists from the interwar period: Stanisław Dubois (under the assumed name Dębski at the camp, executed on August 21, 1942) and Norbert Barlicki (d. September 21, 1941). [1] Its members included Adam Kuryłowicz, a PPS activist from the interwar period, and Konstanty Jagiełło, a member of the Red Scouting organization (*Czerwone Harcerstwo*). In a later period, peasant activists and communists also joined its ranks, including Julian Wieczorek (d. January 9, 1943), Juliusz Rydygier, Stefan Bratkowski and others. This very close-knit group engaged in intensive political activity and developed a campaign of assistance for fellow prisoners. They made contact with the PPS organization in Cracow and Warsaw — where they sent news about the camp — through civilian workers and organizations that were active near the camp.

Professional soldiers were particularly active in camp resistance organizations. In October 1940, Witold Pilecki (under the name Tomasz Serafiński at the camp) founded a group that adopted the name Union of Military Organizations (*Związek Organizacji Wojskowej*, ZOW). The organization was composed of five-member cells or "fives". Its membership included Edward Ciesielski, Lieutenant Kacperski, Captain Henryk Bartosiewicz, and cavalry Captain Włodzimierz Makaliński. The group's work centered on "organizing" food and warm clothing, keeping the prisoners' spirits up, and spreading news from outside the camp. They delivered reports to Warsaw about the situation at the camp through escapees, such as Lieutenants Wincenty Gawron and Stefan Bielecki, who escaped on May 16, 1942, on the orders and with the assistance of the organization. It was the same case with Lieutenant Stanisław Jaster, who succeeded in escaping with three other prisoners in an automobile on June 20, 1942.

---

[1] Translator's note: Unless otherwise noted, individuals designated as deceased ("d.") or "executed" perished at KL Auschwitz.

Witold Pilecki, who arrived at the camp on September 22, 1940, after voluntarily joining a group of people captured during one of the Gestapo's round-ups in Warsaw, also escaped from the camp. He escaped not in order to save his own life, but to bring out evidence of the Nazis' crimes, to serve as an eyewitness to the world about the camp, and to make plans with other underground organizations for breaking into the camp and freeing the prisoners. When he left the camp, he handed over leadership of the group to Major Zygmunt Bończy-Bohdanowski (shot before the Execution Wall on October 11, 1943) and Captain Henryk Bartosiewicz.

In February 1941, Colonel Kazimierz Rawicz (held under the name Jan Hilkner at the camp and subsequently transferred in August 1942 to KL Mauthausen), established the Union for Armed Struggle (*Związek Walki Zbrojnej*, ZWZ) at the camp. Its leadership consisted of Air Force Colonel Teofil Dziama (executed on October 11, 1943), Captain Tadeusz Paolone (under the assumed name Lisowski at the camp, executed on October 11, 1943), and Bernard Świerczyna (who was hanged after a failed escape on December 30, 1944).

Soon thereafter, other military organizations arose to take their place, including one under the leadership of Colonel Aleksander Stawarz (executed on June 15, 1942) and cavalry Captain Włodzimierz Koliński. In the spring of 1942, Colonel Jan Karcz organized a group at Birkenau on the grounds of camp BIb, whose members included Czesław Ostańkowicz, Władysław Ostrowski, Janusz Krzywicki, and Stanisław Grudziński. The group's main goal was to save prisoners at the HKB from selections, to protect prisoners in the penal company and to "organize" additional food. After Karcz was executed on Jauary 25, 1943, Ostrowski assumed the organization's leadership. In March of the same year, some of the group's members were sent off in a transport to KL Buchenwald; consequently, the group ceased to exist. [2]

In the fall of 1941, right-wing Polish organizations began to form, composed of former sympathizers of the National Democracy and the National-Radical Camp (*Obóz Narodowo-Radykalny*). These groups were established on the initiative of Professor Roman Rybarski (d. March 6, 1942) and the publicist Jan Mosdorf (executed on October 11, 1943).

At the end of 1941, the Union for Armed Struggle initiated a campaign for unity. Colonel Rawicz assumed leadership of the new organization. A committee of representatives from each political and military group sat atop the new organization. The leadership committee consisted of Rybarski (chairman), Dubois (vice-chairman), Mosdorf (from the youth wing), Rawicz and Pilecki. The committee functioned until August 1942, when Rawicz was transferred to KL Mauthausen. Colonel Juliusz Gilewicz (executed on October 11, 1943) succeeded Rawicz as chairman. Until October 1942, all resistance groups, except Karcz's and Koliński's, subordinated themselves to a common command.

The command structure of the united forces underwent changes. The system of "fives" was eliminated, and the organization was divided into batallions,

---

[2] APMO, Collection of Testimonies, vol. 49, card 65, account of former prisoner Czesław Ostańkowicz.

companies and platoons with designated areas of activity. Major Bończa-
-Bohdanowski was appointed commander of the united military forces, with
Captain Stanisław Kazuba in charge of its First Battalion; Captain Edward
Gött-Getyński, in charge of the Second Battalion; Captain Tadeusz Paolone,
in charge of the Third Battalion; and Captain Julian "Trzęsimiech", at the
head of the Fourth Battalion. [3]

In 1943, the military leadership of the camp resistance movement was
thrown into disarray by a series of actions undertaken by the German camp
administration against the resistance movement. Several dozen military and
political activists perished during the campaign. (On January 25, 1943,
fifty-one prisoners suspected of illegal activities against the SS were shot; on
October 11, 1943, fifty-four prisoners.) Despite their bloody campaign of
repression, the SS failed to achieve their goals.

Two new centers of resistance arose. One, at the main camp, had a leftist
character. Its membership embraced former PPS members, communists,
prisoners without a political affiliation, and new arrivals at the camp. Among
the latter were Józef Cyrankiewicz, Tadeusz Hołuj, Ludwik Rajewski, Stanisław Kłodziński, Adam Kuryłowicz, and Lucjan Motyka. A second center
arose at Birkenau. In 1943, several left-wing groups were established with
contacts to the organization at KL Auschwitz. One organization was founded
by Alfred Fiderkiewicz in the infirmary at site BIIf. Its members included
Henryk Korotyński, Tadeusz Borowski and Andrzej Kobyłecki. The central
goal of the group was to save ill prisoners, particularly well-known scholars
and political activists. They worked to gather additional food together and
medicine for them and conducted propaganda work. To raise the prisoners'
spirits, they spread political news and news about the front. They also made
preparations for self-defense in case of an uprising or a decision by the SS to
liquidate all the prisoners.

At camp BIId, a leftist group also arose, consisting of Konstanty Jagiełło,
Zygmunt Balicki, Wincenty Rutkiewicz, and Dawid Szmulewski. There was
also a military group at the camp, led by Commander Aleksander Żytkiewicz.
Its leadership included Jan Dmochowski, Zygmunt Idziak, Stanisław Racz-
kowski, and Zygmunt Majewski. [4] The organization's members worked in
different work details and thus had contact with the entire camp. They thus
ended up serving as intermediaries between the conspiracies at the men's and
women's camps. They distributed food and medicine and smuggled letters and
other documents.

The womens's camp also witnessed the establishment of an underground
organization during the summer of 1943. Stanisława Rachwałowa, Antonina
Piątkowska, Helena Hofman, Wiktoria Klimaszewska and Zofia Bratro
formed its first five-member cell. [5] Other prisoners at the women's camp joined

[3] APMO, Collection of Reminiscences, vol. 130, card 111, memoir of Witold Pilecki.

[4] APMO, Collection of Testimonies, vol. 67, card 7, and vol. 52, card 23, accounts of former
prisoners Aleksander Żytkiewicz and Zygmunt Idziak.

[5] Ibid., vol. 15, cards 39-43 and vol. 15 card 9, accounts of former prisoners Zofia Bratro and
Wiktoria Klimaszewska.

the organization: Anna Pawełczyńska, Maria Mazurkiewicz, Wanda Marossanyi, Maria Maniak, and Wanda Jakubowska. The women prisoners
maintained contact with the organization at the men's camp. They delivered
news and documents that they had assembled to the male conspirators. In the
spring of 1944, the women's organization fell under Żytkiewicz's leadership.
After Żytkiewicz was transferred to the Gross-Rosen concentration camp in
the middle of the year, Colonel Władysław Smereczyński, transferred to the
camp from Majdanek, assumed his former office.

Independent of the Polish conspiracy, prisoners of other nationalities began
to establish resistance groups at the camp at the end of 1942 and beginning of
1943. One of the first to begin operations was an Austrian group formed in
1942. Despite its small size, the group was close-knit and active. Its members
were mainly communists, social democrats and former volunteers from the
International Brigades during the Spanish Civil War. They arrived at KL
Auschwitz with political skills and experience acquired at other camps and in
battle during the Spanish Civil War. The organization's nucleus consisted of
Ernst Burger, Hermann Langbein, Alfred Klahr (under the assumed name
Ludwig Lokmanis at the camp), Rudolf Friemel, Ludwig Vesely, Heinrich
Dürmayer, and Ludwig Soswinski. Their activities concentrated on the
prisoner infirmary (HKB), where many of them worked.

In 1942, a French group was established. Its founder — George Varennes,
a schoolteacher and communist organizer — had initiated self-help activities
among the French prisoners. After his death on November 1, 1942, Roger
Abada, Eugéne Garnier and Roger Pelissou took over the organization's
leadership. [6] On January 27, 1943, the first French women — political
prisoners — arrived at the camp: Danielle Casanova, Maie Politzer, Raymon-
de Salez, Ivonne Blech and others. They initiated conspiratorial activities and
made contact with the men's group. Danielle Casanova (who died on May 10,
1943, from typhus) and Marie Claude Vailland-Couturier headed the women's
organization. A Belgian group under the leadership of a communist named
Berliner cooperated with the French group.

The Russians also had a large resistance organization, active at both the
Auschwitz and Birkenau camps. Captain Viktor Ivanov, Valentin Sitnov
(a pilot) and Colonel Kuźma Karcew formed the organization's nucleus at the
main camp. Alexander Lebiediev and Fyodor Skiba directed the group. Active
at Birkenau were Professor Ivan Mironov, Piotr Miszyn, Michaił Wino-
gradow, Władimir Soroko and — beginning in 1944 — General Djmitr
Karbyshew [7] and Władimir Diegtiariew. Women also participated in the
organization: Nina Gusiewa, Anna Trynda, Żenia Saryclewa, Nina Char-
wamova and the doctor Lubov Alpatova, among others.

In 1943, a German grouping arose, composed of communists, social
democrats, and members of other antifascist parties who had been imprisoned
in concentration camps for a number of years. Organized by Bruno Baum, it

---

[6] Ibid., vol. 31, cards 120-36, accounts of former prisoners Roger Abada and Eugéne Garnier.
[7] General Karbyshew, transferred to KL Auschwitz from Majdanek in 1944, was subsequently evacuated to KL Mauthausen in the fall, where he perished in February 1945.

worked closely together with the Austrian group. Its participants included Karl Lill, Alfred Ponthius, and Rudolf Göbel at Auschwitz; Horst Jonas at Birkenau; Kurt Posener, Stefan Heymann, and Ludwig Wörl at Monowice (Monowitz); and Orli Reichert, Judith Dürmayer, and Gerda Schneider at the women's camp.

A Czech group was also active at the Auschwitz and Birkenau camps. Its ranks included Emil Panevic, Dr. Jan Čespiva, Dr. Miloš Nedvěd, Igor Bistric, Karel Beran, Erich Kulka and Ota Kraus. The following women also deserve mention: Herta Soswinski (under the assumed name Mehl at the camp), Vera Foltynowa, Vlasta Kladivova, Zdenka Nedvedova and Dr. Slava Klein. A small Yugoslavian group also formed under the leadership of Norka Vuksanovic,[8] composed mainly of female partisans. Its members included Stefka Štibler, Jelena Vasiljevic, Zora Rakovič, Nada Čalic and other women.

The Jewish prisoners at KL Auschwitz carried out conspiratorial activities both within the nationality groups mentioned above and in their own resistance organizations. Among the most active and determined Jewish groups was formed by the prisoners of the *Sonderkommando*. Composed of prisoners who worked at the crematoria and the pits where corpses were burned, it was led by Salmen Gradowski, Jankiel Handelsmann and a third man, named Kamiński. They were one of the most-endangered groups at the camp; the camp SS administration regularly liquidated the workers attached to the *Sonderkommando* in order to rid themselves of witnesses to their crimes.

Each national grouping strived to assure that prisoners would survive by arranging material assistance for them in the form of food, medicine and clothes. Each also tried to save prisoners from being murdered, organized escapes and gathered information about the situation at the camp.

It was in the interest of the entire camp resistance movement that the different nationality groups coordinate their activities. At the beginning of 1943, the Austrian group began negotiations to establish a united, international resistance organization at the camp. During one such negotiating session in May 1943, a united organization, *Kampfgruppe Auschwitz* ("Auschwitz Fighting Group"), was established. At the head of the organization sat a Steering Committee, composed of Józef Cyrankiewicz, Tadeusz Hołuj, Ernst Burger, and Hermann Langbein. After Langbein was evacuated to the camp at Neuengamme on August 25, 1944, Heinrich Dürmayer and Ludwig Soswinski assumed his duties. After Burger made an unsuccessful escape attempt on October 27, 1944, Bruno Baum joined the committee.

Cells in each work detail represented the basic organizational unit of the new organization. Together, the cells formed a united group. The group's leadership would either meet in the cellar to Block 4, where Burger worked as a clerk, or at the HKB, where many of its members worked, along with prisoners cooperating with them.

The Polish military groups did not join the international organization. It was only in 1944, that an agreement was reached to establish a joint military council (*Rada Wojskowa Oświęcim*, RWO). The steering committee

---

[8] APMO. Collection of Testimonies, vol. 37, card 33, account of former prisoner Tadeusz Hołuj.

for RWO was composed of Lucjan Motyka and Heinrich Dürmayer from *Kampfgruppe Auschwitz* and Bernard Świerczyna and Mieczysław Wagner from the military group. RWO concerned itself with military matters — training cadres, establishing fighting groups and assigning them various tasks.

Kampfgruppe Auchwitz's sphere of activity extended only to the main camp and Birkenau. At Monowice (Monowitz), a separate organization arose, with its own leadership: Leon Stasiak (alias Leiser Sylmann), Stefan Heymann, Kurt Posener, and Piotr Machura. Contacts did exist, however, between the two organizations.

2. The Resistance Movement Outside the Camp

It was possible for a resistance movement to exist and engage in activities at the camp thanks to assistance from outside. The resistance movement that operated immediately outside the camp worked under difficult conditions. The Oświęcim area (German — Auschwitz) had been annexed directly to the Third Reich under Hitler's decree of October 8, 1939, and had become part of the Katowice (Kattowitz) administrative district. The Polish population residing in these areas faced greater oppression and exploitation than Poles inside the General Government. Furthermore, geographical conditions — the flat terrain and the lack of a large wooded area — made it impossible to organize larger partisan units and engage in armed struggle. Nevertheless, illegal organizations already formed in the early months of the occupation. The organizations outside the camp mainly concentrated in their activities on establishing contact with the prisoners inside the camp and giving them assistance.

The first organization to form — in the winter of 1939 — was the Union for Armed Struggle (*Związek Walki Zbrojnej*, ZWZ), established on the initiative of Polish reserve officers: Mieczysław Jonkisz (codename "Mietek"), Stanisław Matuszczyk, Stanisław Krępa-Trojacki („Trojacki") and career military officer Jan Wawrzyczek (codenames "Marusza" and "Danuta"). In the spring of 1940, an "Oświęcim Section" (*Obwód Oświęcimski*) of the organization was established under the leadership of Alojzy Banaś ("Zorza"). His staff included two couriers, Stanisław Dembowicz ("Radom") and Antoni Szlachcic ("Laura"); Marian Feliks, quartermaster; Maksymilian Niezgoda, head of intelligence; Father Władysław Grohs de Rosenburg, chaplain; Stanisław Krępa- -Trojacki; Jan Wawrzyczek; and two female liaison officers, Bronisława Kubisty and Jadwiga Dylik. The Oświęcim Section, which answered to the Bielsko Inspectorate of ZWZ, was divided into four subunits: Oświęcim (under the leadership of Jan Jakuczek), Kęty (Jan Barcik), Brzeszcze (Rudolf Wittek) and Zator (Roman Żabczyński).

In 1942, ZWZ adopted the name *Armia Krajowa* (AK) or Home Army. In October of that year, due to a betrayal, the Germans arrested practically the entire staff of the Oświęcim Section. The arrested conspirators were sent to the prison at Mysłowice, tried by a German court-martial, and executed at the Auschwitz camp on Jauary 25, 1943. Jan Wawrzyczek subsequently took over as commander and assembled a new staff: Józef Górkiewicz ("Górnik"), assistant commander; Antoni Chowaniec ("Antoni"), quartermaster, and Franciszek Hoszek ("Beethoven"), intelligence officer. Antoni Szlachcic remained as a courier, and Zofia Gabryś ("Wera"), Bronisław Dłuciak ("Dzidka") and Waleria Kubajak became liaison officers.

ZWZ/AK was active in two main areas: military activity, or armed struggle with the occupier, and civil activity, or assisting prisoners. The AK was able to establish contacts with prisoners at the camp — Stanisław Furdyna, Bernard Świerczyna and Antoni Wykręt — through Polish civilian workers employed inside the camp. Through this channel, they were able to obtain information about the situation at the camp, incoming and outgoing transports, etc. The information was then passed on to Home Army headquarters for the Silesian District in Katowice.

The executive organ responsible for civil activity was called the Committee to Assist Prisoners at the Camp in Oświęcim (Auschwitz). Helena Stupka ("Jadzia") directed the Committee's work. Her assistants included Wincencja Stolarska, Janina Kostecka, Maria Zębata, Michalina Gretka, Janina Kajtoch, Zofia Cicha, and Julia Ilisińska. The Committee worked to supply the camp with medicine, food and clothing and was a channel for uncensored correspondence by the prisoners.

Partisan units from the Oświęcim Section took part in the armed struggle with the occupier. In 1941, under Wawrzyczek's leadership, a first partisan unit, "Marusza", was founded in the area of Łęki and Jawiszowice. In 1942, two additional units were founded — around Kańczuga and Bielany — under the leadership of Captain Jan Barcik ("Soła") and Sergeant Jan Jamroz ("Maczuga"). In 1943, the three units merged and adopted the name "Sosienki". Wawrzyczek assumed leadership of the united organization. The "Sosienki" unit offered active resistance. It organized escapes from the camp, took part in sabotage and diversionary activities, and fought skirmishes with SS patrols. Several dozen escapees from the camp found refuge in its ranks, including Stanisław Furdyna, Antoni Wykręt, Stanisław Zyguła, Jan Prejzner, Marian Szayer, Wincenty Ciesielczuk, and Edward Padkowski. Because the partisans sometimes dressed in SS uniforms, the commander of the SS garrison had to introduce a special system of controls, including a daily password, to make sure that members of the SS staff and auxiliary services would be able to identify each other. [9]

In addition to the Home Army organization, the Polish Socialist Party (PPS) was also active near the camp. In 1940, experienced PPS organizers from the interwar period established their first underground branches, which evolved over time into strong conspiratorial centers. In the Brzeszcze area, Piotr Hałoń, Jan Nosal, and Władysław Malik, helped organize for the socialists; in Oświęcim, Jan Krzemień; in Jaworzno, Franciszek Mazur and Franciszek Kobielski.

Initially, the PPS's activities included political work, sabotage, and hiding people who were fleeing from the Gestapo. The PPS's main goal when it first made contact with the Auschwitz camp was to offer the prisoners assistance. In

---

[9] APMO, SS Staff Trial, vol. 39, card 236, Standort-Sonderbefehl from November 7, 1944.

this regard, the PPS group in Brzeszcze played the most important part. It mobilized entire families to cooperate: the Hałońs, the Golczyks, the Pytliks, Nikiels, Gachs and others.

In 1942, the arrival of young people, who had been arrested in April 1940 and held for over a year at the Dachau and Gusen camps, expanded the activists' ranks. They assumed leadership of the organization. At its head stood Edward Hałoń ("Boruta"), who directed a nucleus composed of Władysław Pytlik ("Birkut"), Emil Golczyk ("Jantar"), Bogusław Chmielewski ("Bodgan"), Marian Skubis ("Brom"), Marian Gach ("Alfons") and the Nikiel brothers — Julian, Franciszek, Tadeusz and Wiktor. In 1944, escapees from the camp joined the organization: Konstanty Jagiełło ("Kostek" or "Bezzębny"), Tomasz Sobański and Jerzy Tabeau. It kept in contact with the camp through its two liaison officers, Danuta Bystroń and Natalia Szpak. The establishment of a standing link to the camp organization through Edward Hałoń's brother, Kazimierz (alias Wrona at the camp) enlivened the PPS's contacts with the camp. Kazimierz Hałoń smuggled information and documents out of the camp through civilian workers. After he escaped on February 10, 1943, another prisoner, Józef Róg, assumed his former role.

In addition to food and medicine, the PPS group supplied the camp with underground publications, explosives, civilian clothing and wigs for prisoners planning an escape. Fugitives from the camp were hidden in Brzeszcze, given fake papers and cared for there until they could be smuggled across the border to the General Goverment or transferred to partisan units. The PPS in Brzeszcze represented the main link between the camp organization and the District Workers' Committee of the PPS in Cracow. At the end of 1944, the PPS group outside the camp dissolved. Edward Hałoń had already left the area in 1943 to avoid arrest. Emil Golczyk, Marian Gach and Władysław Pytlik had then taken over leadership of the group. In September 1944, they also left for Cracow, and other members of the organization joined partisan units.

Peasant activists were also engaged in operations in villages near the camp. The Peasant Party (*Stronnictwo Ludowe*), whose activities had been interrupted by the outbreak of war, began to revive in 1940 under new forms of organization. Military units, or a "Peasant Guard" (Chłostra) formed, which later adopted the name "Peasant Battalions" (*Bataliony Chłopskie*, BCh), in 1941. The First District Commander of the Peasant Battalions was Wojciech Jekiełek (codenames "Żmija" and "Łysy"). Beyond their basic goals of undermining the occupation and conducting information activities within Polish society, the BCh — as was the case with the other organizations — made assisting prisoners at the camp a first priority. Many individuals who had been feeding prisoners on their own up to that point started cooperating with veteran peasant activists, including Helena Płotnicka, Władysława Kożusznik, Irena Kahanek, Anna Szalbut, Zofia Zdrowak, Kazimierz Jędrzejowski, Piotr Jarzyna, and Antoni Mitoraj. The BCh established their first contacts with the camp through prisoners employed on the surveying and gardening details in Rajsko: Kazimierz Jarzębowski, Edward Biernacki, Jan Winogroński, and Janusz Pogonowski (alias Skrzetuski at the camp). Women and even children would hide parcels of food and medicine at prearranged locations.

The Peasant Battalions suffered grave losses in 1943. Already in December 1942, Wojciech Jekiełek had been arrested in Osiek, and Anna Szalbut, who had accompanied him, was killed. (Jekiełek was able, however, to escape to Cracow.) Kazimierz Jędrzejowski ("Kazek") assumed the organization's leadership, but was then arrested in October 1943. Imprisoned in Mysłowice after a hearing, he was sentenced to death by a court-martial and executed at KL Auschwitz on May 26, 1944. Helena Płotnicka, an activist with distinguished service, met with a similar fate. After being arrested in May 1943 and imprisoned at Birkenau, she died from typhus on March 17, 1944. Because many activists had to flee the area to avoid arrest, the Peasant Battalions ceased operations in the area of the camp.

Despite the Nazis' doggedness in fighting communists and the exceptionally difficult conditions under which they operated, cells of the Polish Workers' Party (*Polska Partia Robotnicza*, PPR) began a campaign of assistance for prisoners at the camp. Members joined the PPR's ranks from such organizations as the Society of Friends of the USSR, Sickle and Hammer, and others. The PPR formed its own fighting units in 1942, the Peoples' Guard (*Gwardia Ludowa*, GL), which later became the People's Army (*Armia Ludowa*, AL). The PPR established partisan units near the camp and assisted prisoners planning to escape.

GL units also conducted diversionary activities, sabotaged transportation facilities and high-voltage lines, disorganized German transport, and interrupted work at industrial facilities employing Auschwitz prisoners. Beyond the material damage inflicted upon the occupier, all these activities contributed to a sense of danger among the Germans; the SS staff was in a constant state of alarm.

Before the May 1 holiday in 1944, the PPR Central Committee called on party members to increase their sabotage activity. Thus, the commandant's office ordered the SS guard units at KL Auschwitz to be in a state of readiness. The camp authorities increased patrols inside and immediately outside the camp, postponed staff members' vacations, and intensified surveillance of Polish civilian workers. [10]

Despite their political differences, all the underground organization operating near the camp cooperated when it came to assisting the prisoners. They often used the same people and channels for contacting prisoners. They often received money, food and medicine from the same sources.

In addition to the political organizations, charities also participated in the campaign to assist prisoners at Auschwitz. In 1940, the local and regional administration of the Polish Red Cross (PCK) in Cracow established a special section for "Assistance to Prisoners of War, Expellees and Political Prisoners". The Prisoner Care division, or "*Patronat*", tried to assist prisoners and their families. Another charity, the Main Assistance Council (*Rada Główna Opiekuńcza*) was established in 1941 to conduct similar activities. In March 1943, a committee for Assistance to Concentration Camp Prisoners (*Pomoc Więźniom Obozów Koncentracyjnych*) was established on the initiative of Teresa

---

[10] APMO, D-AuI-1/99, Standort-Sonderbefehl from April 29, 1944.

Lasocka-Estreicher, Helena Szlapak, Wojciech Jekiełek and Adam Rysiewicz. In constant contact with the camp underground, the organization received smuggled letters and documents and cared for escapees from the camp. Scouting organizations from Silesia, Cracow and Oświęcim also played a significant role in charitable activities.

The resistance movement outside the camp suffered serious losses; many activists ended up in camps and prisons or were killed. The Gestapo used every means at their disposal to uncover Polish conspiracies. They achieved certain successes, as an extensive report from the security police command in Katowice from December 18, 1944, demonstrates. During their campaign against the Home Army in the Silesia District, the Gestapo had uncovered the group's organizational structure, including the codenames of its leaders inside and outside the camp. Only the approaching front and the need to evacuate the German administration ended the investigation and saved the underground activists from exposure and arrest. [11]

3. Types of Activity Undertaken by the Camp Resistance Movement

The activities of the camp resistance movement spanned a broad spectrum. To present all of them would require a separate study.

The border between organized and spontaneous resistance is often difficult to define. The most significant and common forms of resistance included:
— providing material assistance for prisoners in the form of food and medicine;
— documenting Nazi crimes at the camp;
— arranging escapes from the camp;
— committing acts of sabotage;
— political organizing;
— struggling to fill camp offices with political prisoners;
— making preparations for the eventual outbreak of an uprising at the camp.

At the beginning of KL Auschwitz's existence, the most important task was to gather additional food and medicine. The rations that the prisoners received did not meet the body's daily requirements. At the end of November 1942, the SS central administration finally allowed packages of food to be mailed to the camp. This regulation did not apply, however, to all prisoners. Thus, prisoners had to collect food by "organizing" it from SS warehouses, other warehouses holding the property of murdered prisoners, the camp slaughterhouse and the camp dairy. Significant amounts of food also arrived from outside the camp. The local population hid packages of food and medicine in areas where the prisoners worked. Among those who distinguished themselves through such assistance were Helena Płotnicka and Władysław Kożusznik from Przecieszyn, Maria Górecka and her daughter Wanda from Brzeszcze, Janina Kajtoch and Janina Cicha from Babice, Helena Stupka from Oświęcim and many others.

---

[11] Zygmunt Walter-Janke, "Armia Krajowa na Śląsku w świetle dokumentów niemieckich", *Najnowsze Dzieje Polski* 3 (1959), p. 199.

Der Höhere SS- und Polizeiführer
beim Oberpräsidenten in Schlesien
und beim Reichsstatthalter im Sudetengau
im Wehrkreis VIII

Breslau 18, den 22. Juli 1940.
Ebertschenallee 14

I.Nr. 394/40.(g)

Geheim!

2 4. JULI 1940

An den

1. Inspekteur der Sicherheitspolizei

   in B r e s l a u

2. Inspekteur der Ordnungspolizei

   in B r e s l a u

nachrichtlich:

An den
Kommandanten des Konzentrationslagers Auschwitz
SS-Hauptsturmführer H ö ß

in A u s c h w i t z.

Der Kommandant des Konzentrationslagers Auschwitz meldet mir,
daß er die Sicherheit seines Lagers, in dem z.Zt. etwa 1 300
Schutzhäftlinge verwahrt werden, nur mit größter Anstrengung mit
der ihm zur Verfügung stehenden verhältnismäßig kleinen Wach-
truppe von 2 Kompanien aufrecht erhalten kann.
Da das Lager laufend aufgefüllt wird, erschweren sich somit die
Sicherungsverhältnisse des Lagers mehr und mehr.
Durch Beihilfe von 5 im Konzentrationslager beschäftigten Zivil-
arbeitern ist es am 6.7.1940 bereits einem Häftling gelungen,
die Freiheit zu gewinnen.
In der Nacht vom 11. zum 12.7.1940 ist von Außenstehenden ein
gewaltsamer Befreiungsversuch unternommen worden, wobei es den
Tätern gelang, bereits den 1. Zaun zu überwinden. Nur durch die
Wachsamkeit eines Postens konnte Schlimmeres verhindert werden.
Wie weiterhin festgestellt wurde, werden immer wieder, besonders
in den in der Nähe des Lagers befindlichen bereits geräumten An-
wesen, verdächtige Personen beobachtet und angetroffen. Die Bevölkerung des Ortes ist fanatisch polnisch und wie durch V-Männer
in Erfahrung gebracht wurde, zu jedem Vorgehen gegen die verhaßte
Bewachungsmannschaft bereit. Auch hat jeder Häftling, dem die Flucht
gelingt, alle Hilfe zu erwarten, sobald er das nächste polnische

polnische Gehöft erreicht hat.
Das Lager befindet sich erst im Aufbau und zwar jetzt im Kriege
unter erschwerten Verhältnissen. Ich muß daher von jeder der
mir unterstellten Einheiten erwarten, daß sie den Kommandanten
und seine Mannschaft in jeder Weise unterstützen.
Soweit dies bisher nicht geschehen ist, behalte ich mir besondere Maßnahmen vor.
Um die Sicherheit des Lagers zu gewährleisten und der Bevölkerung vor Augen zu führen, daß sie schärfste Maßnahmen
zu erwarten hat, wenn sie das besonders mit Draht abgezäunte
und mit Verbotstafeln versehene, geräumte Anliegergebiet des
Konzentrationslagers verbotswidrig betritt, ordne ich folgendes
an:

1. Der Inspekteur der Sicherheitspolizei führt im Einvernehmen
   mit dem Kommandanten des Konzentrationslagers und mit Unter-
   stützung von Kräften des Inspekteurs der Ordnungspolizei
   schlagartig eine Räumungsaktion durch.

2. Bei dieser Räumungsaktion wird jeder männliche Pole, der
   in dem besonders mit Draht umsäunten und mit Verbotstafeln
   versehenen Räumungsgebiet angetroffen wird, auf der Stelle
   erschossen.
   Frauen und Kinder soweit sie angetroffen werden, sind der
   Staatspolizeistelle Kattowitz zwecks Überprüfung zu über-
   stellen.

3. Der Zeitpunkt der Aktion ist mir rechtzeitig zu melden.
   Der Inspekteur der Sicherheitspolizei legt mir einen aus-
   führlichen Bericht über das Ergebnis der Razzia vor.

SS - Gruppenführer.

Letter from the Superior Commander of the SS and Police in Wrocław (Breslau), Erich von dem Bach-Zelewski from July 22, 1940, on the campaign of expulsions from the area surrounding the camp. It contains information about the patriotism of the Polish population living near Auschwitz.

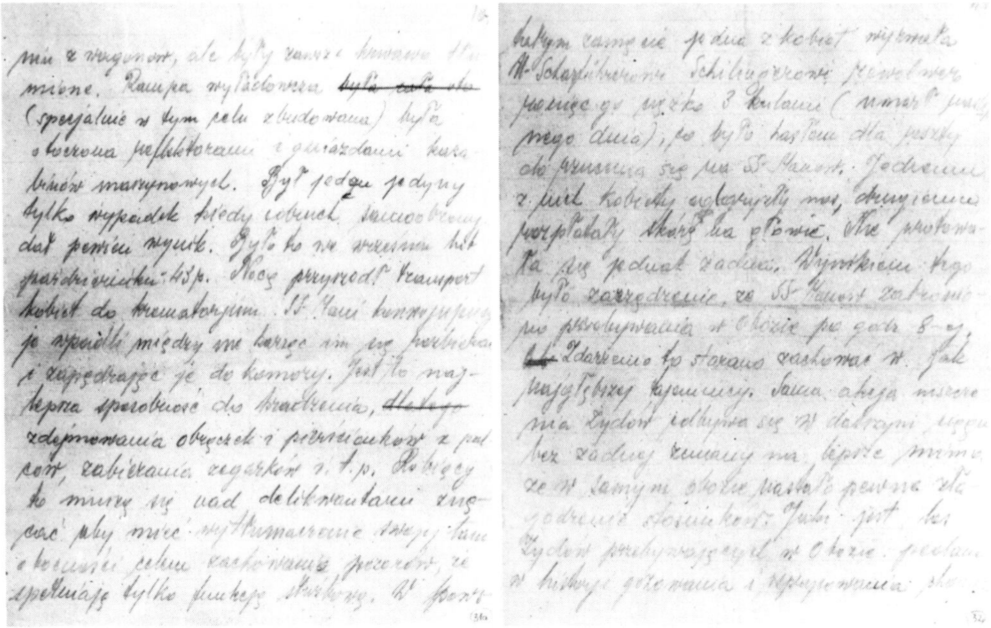

nie z wagonów, ale były zawsze [illegible] [illegible]
mione. Rampa wyładowcza ~~była cała~~ [illegible]
(specjalnie w tym celu zbudowana) była
otoczona reflektorami i gwiazdami karabinów maszynowych. Był jednak jedyny
tylko wypadek kiedy [illegible] samoobrony
dał pewien wynik. Było to we wrześniu lub
październiku 43 r. Nocą przyszedł transport
kobiet do krematorjum. SS-mani konwojujący
je wpadli między nie każąc im się rozbierać
i zapędzając je do komory. Jest to naj-
lepsza sposobność do kradzieży, ~~dlatego~~
zdejmowania obrączek i pierścionków z pal-
ców, zabierania zegarków i t. p. Będący
tu mnożą się nad delikwentami znę-
cać aby mieć wytłumaczenie swojej tam
obecności celem zachowania pozorów, że
spełniają tylko funkcję straży. W pewnym

takim czasie jedna z kobiet wyrwała
SS-Scharführerowi Schillingerowi rewolwer
raniąc go ciężko 3 kulami (umarł jeszcze tego dnia), co było hasłem dla reszty
do rzucenia się na SS-manów. Jednemu
z nich kobiety wydrapały oczy, drugiemu
rozpłatały skórę na głowie. Nie [illegible]-
ła się jednak żadna. Wynikiem tego
było zarządzenie, że SS-manom zabronio-
no przebywania w obozie po godz. 8-ej.
~~[illegible]~~ Zdarzenie to starano zachować w. jak
największej tajemnicy. Sama akcja niszcze-
nia Żydów odbywa się w dalszym ciągu
bez żadnej zmiany na lepsze mimo,
że w samym obozie nastąpiło pewne zła-
godzenie stosunków. Żydów jest bez
Żydów przebywających w Obozie. przesta-
[illegible] [illegible] golenia i [illegible] [illegible].

Pages from the report written by the Pole Jerzy Tabeau in 1943/44 after his escape from KL Auschwitz. The pages shown describe the rebellion of the Jewish women at Crematorium II.

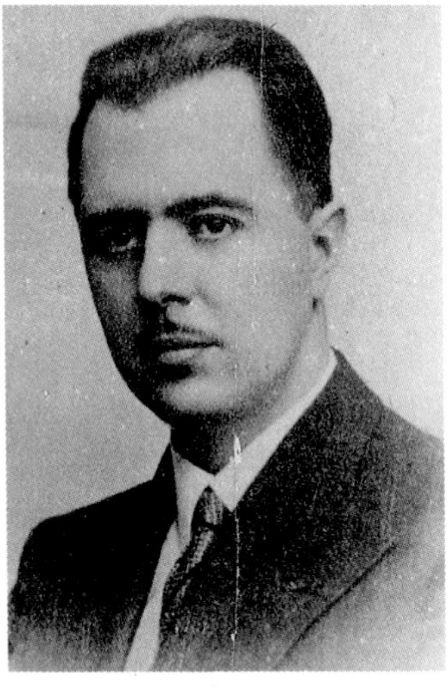

Jan Mosdorf, prisoner at KL Auschwitz (Nr. 8230), a participant and co-organizer of the self-help campaign among the prisoners and activist in the Polish conspiracy at the camp. He was shot in a collective execution on October 11, 1943, before the Execution Wall.

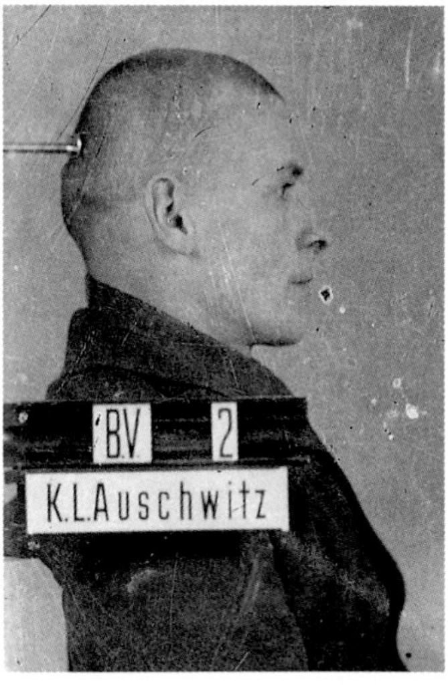

Otto Küsel, a German prisoner at KL Auschwitz (Nr. 2), participant and co-organizer of the prisoner self-help campaign, who cooperated with the camp underground. In 1942, he escaped from the camp.

Maksymilian Maria Kolbe (Rajmund Kolbe),
a Polish Franciscan, who voluntarily took the
place of another prisoner condemned to death
by starvation. He died in the cellar of the Death
Block.

The death certificate for Rajmund Kolbe
prepared by the camp Registration Office.
It gives a false cause of death.

KL Auschwitz II. Block Nr. 11, called the "Death Block" by prisoners. It served many functions,
including as the infamous camp prison, where escapees and members of the resistance movement from
both inside and outside the camp were held.

Witold Pilecki, prisoner at KL Auschwitz (under the name Tomasz Serafiński), one of the founders and leaders of the Polish conspiracy at the camp. He authored a number of secret reports smuggled out of the camp to the Home Army (Armia Krajowa AK).

Tadeusz Paolone, prisoner at KL Auschwitz (Nr. 329 under the last name Lisowski at the camp), captain in the Polish Army and one of the leaders of the Home Army organization among the prisoners at KL Auschwitz. He was shot during a collective execution on October 11, 1943.

Juliusz Gilewicz, prisoner at KL Auschwitz and colonel in the Polish Army, commander of the Home Army organization at KL Auschwitz. Shot during a collective execution on October 11, 1943.

Teofil Dziama, prisoner at KL Auschwitz and colonel in the Polish Army, one of the leaders of the Home Army organization among the prisoners at KL Auschwitz. Shot during a collective execution on October 11, 1943.

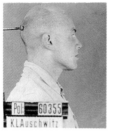

Józef Cyrankiewicz, prisoner at KL Auschwitz (Nr. 62933), one of the leaders of the international organization *Kampfgruppe Auschwitz* and the author of a number of messages smuggled out of the camp.

Hermann Langbein, prisoner at KL Auschwitz and organizer of the Austrian resistance movement at KL Auschwitz; one of the leading figures in the international underground organization at the camp, *Kampfgruppe Auschwitz.*

Roza Robota, prisoner at KL Auschwitz (Nr. 24961), member of a Jewish conspiratorial group. She was hung by the SS men on January 6, 1945, for supplying explosives to the Jews in the *Sonderkommando.*

Jankiel Handelsman, prisoner at KL Auschwitz, a leader of the Jewish conspiracy in the *Sonderkommando* and one of the organizers of the rebellion on October 7, 1944. He was murdered during interrogation.

Stanisław Kłodziński, prisoner at KL Auschwitz (Nr. 20019), an active member of the camp resistance movement and an author of numerous messages smuggled out of the camp.

Antonina Piątkowska, prisoner at KL Auschwitz, member of the Polish conspiracy, who sent documents about the crimes being committed by the SS outside the camp.

Aleksander Lebiediew, prisoner at KL Auschwitz (Nr. 88349), one of the organizers and leaders of a Russian conspiracy at the camp.

Vera Foltynowa, prisoner at KL Auschwitz (Nr. 42808), member of an underground Czech group.

Maria Stromberger, an Austrian nurse employed in the hospital for SS men at KL Auschwitz, secretly gave help to the prisoners and served as a contact between the underground outside the camp and the camp resistance movement.

Maria Bobrzecka, a member of the underground PPS organization outside the camp, actively participated in the campaign to assist prisoners.

Władysław Pytlik, an active member of the PPS group in Brzeszcze.

Wojciech Jekiełek, leader of the local Peasant Battalions unit outside the camp.

Stefan Jasieński, parachutist sent by the Main Command of the Home Army to the Auschwitz area with the goal of establishing contact with the camp conspiracy. Captured by the SS, he likely perished in the cellar of the Death Block.

Jan Wawrzyczek, commander of the Oświęcim section of the Home Army (AK) and leader of the "Sosienki" partisan unit.

Teresa Lasocka-Estreicher, member of the Main Assistance Council (*Rada Głównej Opiekuńczej*) in Cracow, co-founder of the organization Assistance for Concentration Camp Prisoners (*Pomoc Więźniom Obozów Koncentracyjnych*), who received messages and documents smuggled outside the camp by the resistance movement.

Edward Hałoń, leader of the PPS in Brzeszcze.

Helena Jedlińska, member of the Oświęcim section ZWZ/AK, an active participant in the campaign of assistance for the prisoners.

Helena Datoń, who served as a contact between the prisoners and the underground PPS.

Helena Stupka, member of ZWZ/AK and organizer of assistance for prisoners at Auschwitz.

Zofia Zdrowak-Dętkoś, contact for the Home Army in the area outside the camp. She gave prisoners assistance and helped them escape from the camp. After being sent to KL Auschwitz for her activities, she escaped from an evacuation transport in January 1945.

Władysława Kożusznik (left) and Helena Płotnicka, contact persons for the Peasant Battalions group outside the camp. For assisting the prisoners, Płotnicka herself was sent to Auschwitz and perished there on March 7, 1944.

Łęki-Zasole. House of the Jedliński family, local quarters of the Home Army and one of the transit points for escapees from KL Auschwitz.

Łęki-Zasole. The restaurant belonging to Julian Dusik (first from the left), where escapees from the camp hid and were given assistance.

Franciszek Walisko, a civilian worker and contact between the prisoners at KL Auschwitz and the underground PPS group.

Ludwik Kandzia, a civilian worker and contact between the prisoners at KL Auschwitz and the PPS.

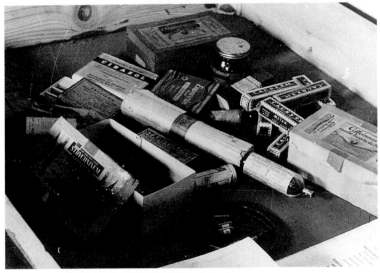

Packages used for smuggling medicine into the camp.

Specially-made objects used to smuggle messages out of the camp.

Jewish women being driven into the gas chambers and corpses of extermination victims being burned under the open sky. The photographs were taken in hiding by Jewish prisoners attached to the *Sonderkommando* in 1944 and smuggled out of the camp to the Polish underground in Cracow.

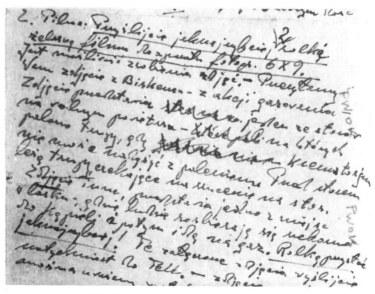

Fragment of a secret message written by Józef Cyrankiewicz and Stanisław Kłodziński on September 4, 1944, regarding photographs that had been submitted of the "gassing campaign" and the possibility of taking additional pictures.

The Pole Eugeniusz Bendera (in 1980) with the former SS warehouse (*Hauptwirtschaftslager*, HWL) in the background. He and his colleagues carried out a daring escape from the warehouse on June 20, 1942.

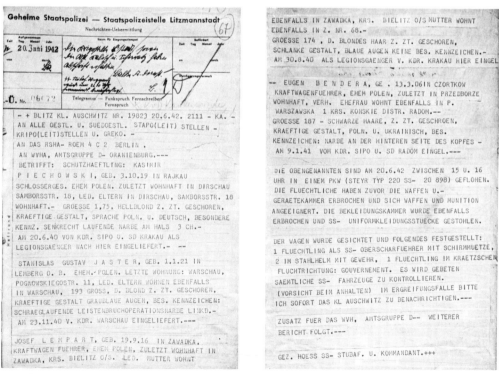

Geheime Staatspolizei — Staatspolizeistelle Litzmannstadt
Nachrichten-Uebermittlung

20. Juni 1942

Telegramm — Funkspruch Fernschreiber
Fernspruch

- + BLITZ KL. AUSCHWITZ NR. 19823 20.6.42. 2111 - KA. -
AN ALLE OESTL. U. SUEDOESTL. STAPO(LEIT) STELLEN -
KRIPO(LEIT)STELLEN U. GREKO. -
AN DAS RSHA- ROEM 4 C 2 BERLIN .
AN WVHA, AMTSGRUPPE D- ORANIENBURG.---
BETRIFFT: SCHUTZHAEFTLING: KASIMIR
P I E C H O W S K I, GEB. 3.10.19 IN RAJKAU
SCHLOSSERGES. EHEM POLEN. ZULETZT WOHNHAFT IN DIRSCHAU
SAMBORSSTR. 18, LED. ELTERN IN DIRSCHAU, SAMBORSSTR. 18
WOHNHAFT.- GROESSE 1,75, HELLBLOND Z. ZT. GESCHOREN,
KRAEFTIGE GESTALT, SPRACHE POLN. U. DEUTSCH, BESONDERE
KENNZ. SENKRECHT LAUFENDE NARBE AM HALS 3 CM.-
AM 20.6.40 VON KDR. SIPO U. SD KRAKAU ALS
LEGIONSGAENGER NACH HIER EINGELIEFERT.- --

STANISLAS GUSTAV J A S T E R, GEB. 1.1.21 IN
LEMBERG O. B. EHEM. POLEN. LETZTE WOHNUNG: WARSCHAU,
POGNOWSKIEGOSTR. 11, LED. ELTERN WOHNEN EBENFALLS
IN WARSCHAU, 193 GROSS, D. BLOND Z. ZT. GESCHOREN,
KRAEFTIGE GESTALT GRAUBLAUE AUGEN, BES. KENNZEICHEN:
SCHRAEGLAUFENDE LEISTENBRUCHOPERATIONSNARBE LINKD.-
AM 23.11.40 V. KDR. WARSCHAU EINGELIEFERT.---

JOSEF L E M P A R T, GEB. 19.9.16 IN ZAWADKA,
KRAFTWAGEN FUEHRER, EHEM POLEN, ZULETZT WOHNHAFT IN
ZAWADKA, KRS. BIELITZ O/S. LED. MUTTER WOHNT

EBENFALLS IN ZAWADKA, KRS. BIELITZ O/S MUTTER WOHNT
EBENFALLS IN Z. NR. 68.-
GROESSE 174 , D. BLONDES HAAR Z. ZT. GESCHOREN,
SCHLANKE GESTALT, BLAUE AUGEN KEINE BES. KENNZEICHEN.-
AM 30.8.40 ALS LEGIONSGAENGER V. KDR. KRAKAU HIER EINGEL

-- EUGEN B E N D E R A, GE . 13.3.06 IN CZORTKOW
KRAFTWAGENFUEHRER, EHEM POLEN, ZULETZT IN PRZEDBORZE
WOHNHAFT, VERH. EHEFRAU WOHNT EBENFALLS IN P.
WARSZAWSKA 1 KRS. KONSKIE DISTR. RADOM.--
GROESSE 187 - SCHWARZE HAARE, Z. ZT. GESCHROEN,
KRAEFTIGE GESTALT, POLN. U. UKRAINISCH, BES.
KENNZEICHEN: NARBE AN DER HINTEREN SEITE DES KOPFES -
AM 9.1.41 VOM KDR. SIPO U. SD RADOM EINGEL.----

DIE OBENGENANNTEN SIND AM 20.6.42 ZWISCHEN 15 U. 16
UHR IN EINEM PKW (STEYR TYP 220 SS- 20 898) GEFLOHEN.
DIE FLUECHTLICHE HABEN ZUVOR DIE WAFFEN U.-
GERAETEKAMMER ERBROCHEN UND SICH WAFFEN UND MUNITION
ANGEEIGNERT. DIE BEKLEIDUNGSKAMMER WURDE EBENFALLS
ERBROCHEN UND SS- UNIFORMKLEIDUNGSSTUECKE GESTOHLEN.

DER WAGEN WURDE GESICHTET UND FOLGENDES FESTGESTELLT:
1 FLUECHTLING ALS SS- OBERSCHARFUEHRER MIT SCHIRMMUETZE,
2 IM STAHLHELM MIT GEWEHR, 1 FLUECHTLING IM KRAETZSCHEN
FLUCHTRICHTUNG: GOUVERNEMENT. ES WIRD GEBETEN
SAEMTLICHE SS- FAHRZEUGE ZU KONTROLLIEREN.
(VORSICHT BEIM ANHALTEN) IM ERGREIFUNGSFALLE BITTE
ICH SOFORT DAS KL AUSCHWITZ ZU BENACHRICHTIGEN.----

ZUSATZ FUER DAS WVH, AMTSGRUPPE D-- WEITERER
BERICHT FOLGT.----

GEZ. HOESS SS- STUBAF. U. KOMMANDANT.+++

Telegram from June 20, 1942, reporting the escape of four Polish prisoners in a car: Kazimierz Piechowski, Stanisław Gustaw Jaster, Józef Lempart, and Eugeniusz Bendera.

Edward Galiński, a Pole who escaped from the camp, but was later caught. He perished at the camp.

Mala Zimetbaum, a Jewish prisoner who escaped but was captured. She perished at the camp.

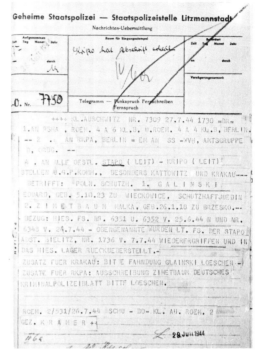

Telegram from July 28, 1944, reporting the capture and return to the camp of escapees Edward Galiński and Mala Zimetbaum.

The names of Mala Zimetbaum and Edward Galiński with the date July 6, 1944, scratched on the wall of Cell Nr. 19 in the cellar to Block Nr. 11 at the main camp. The inscription was most likely made by Galiński, who was jailed there after his failed escape.

Telegram from April 27, 1943, about the escape of two Poles from the camp: Tomasz Serafiński (Witold Pilecki) and Jan Retko (Jan Redzej).

Wiśnicz, 1943. Polish escapees from the camp (l-r): Jan Redzej, Witold Pilecki, and Edward Ciesielski.

Telegram from February 7, 1944, about the escape of the Gypsy Weronika Woloncewicz.

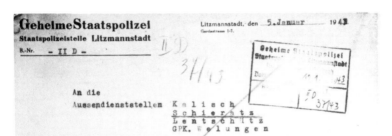

GeheimeStaatspolizei
Staatspolizeistelle Litzmannstadt

Litzmannstadt, den 5.Januar 1943
Gardestrasse 1-7.

B.-Nr. - II D -

An die
Aussendienststellen K a l i s c h
S c h i e r a t z
L e n t s c h i t z
GPK. W e l u n g e n

- - - -

Betrifft: Schutzhäftlinge Russin Paraska S a w e n k o, geb.
1915 in Jekatrynoslaw, Russin Wassa L o c z w i n e n-
k o, geb.16.8.19 in Sulober-Kosowka, Russin Pydosyja
C i n h a n k o w a, geb.6.8.00 in Timoszewka, Russin
Dora G a w r e l u k, geb.Lomaczuk, geb.5.7.14 in
Sosniewiec, Russin Wera G u n s k a j, geb.27.12.19
in Konela, Krs.Kiew, Russin Taissa P a n o w a, geb.
23.9.15 in Kiew, Russin Nadja N e t r e b k o, geb.
17.8.24 in Pryluky, Russin Wira B o w s c h a, geb.
30.10.24 in Kiew, Russin Lena A w t o m i e n k o,
geb.18.2.23 in Krasnodary.

Vorgang: Ohne.-

Die Obengenannten sind in der Nacht vom 29. - 30.12.4
aus dem KL.-Auschwitz - Zweiglager Budy - geflohen. Ich bitte,
die erforderlichen Fahndungsmassnahmen einzuleiten und im
Erfolgsfalle umgehend zu berichten.

Im Auftrage:

gez.: N e u m a n n
Kriminalkommissar

Beglaubigt:
Kanzleiangestellte.

/Lu.

A letter from the Gestapo in Litzmannstadt (Łódź) from January 5, 1943, reporting the escape of nine Russians from the Budy sub-camp.

Bernard Świerczyna, a Polish activist in the resistance movement at KL Auschwitz and staff member of the Home Army organization at the camp, which cooperated with the international organization, *Kampfgruppe Auschwitz*. He was hung at the camp on December 30, 1944, for trying to escape.

Rudolf Friemel, an Austrian prisoner at KL Auschwitz, one of the organizers and leaders of the Austrian conspiracy and the international organization *Kampfgruppe Auschwitz*. He was hung at the camp on December 30, 1944, for helping organize the escape of Bernard Świerczyna and four other prisoners active in the camp underground.

Siegfried Lederer, a Jewish escapee from KL Auschwitz.

Pawel Stienkin, a participant in the rebellion and collective escape of Soviet POW'S on November 6, 1942.

Oświęcim, 1983. A meeting between the escapees Cyla Zacharowicz-Cybulska (Stawiska), a Jew, and the Pole Jerzy Bielecki many years later.

In the Miechów area The independent AK partisan battalion "Skała". The following escapees from KL Auschwitz fought in the battalion: Ryszard Kordek (first from the right), Henryk Dzięgelewski (second from the right), Kazimierz Andrysik, Zdzisław Michalak, and Józef Papuga.

San Francisco, 1989. The Jews (1-r) Herman Shine (Hermann Scheingesicht) and Max Drimmer, escapees from KL Auschwitz III-Monowitz holding a small portrait of Józef Wrona.

Honorary Diploma from the Yad Vashem Institute in Israel, bestowed upon the Pole Józef Wrona for assisting Jews during the war, including Hermann Scheingesicht and Max Drimmer (above), whom he helped escape from the camp and hid until the area around Auschwitz was liberated.

The Pole Jerzy Tabeau (Jerzy Wesołowski), who wrote a report about the camp after his escape.

The Jew Rudolf Vrba (Walter Rosenberg), who wrote a report about KL Auschwitz after his escape.

The Jew Alfred Wetzler, author of a report about KL Auschwitz after his escape from the camp.

Telegram about the escape from KL Auschwitz of Walter Rosenberg (Rudolf Vrba) and Alfred Wetzler.

Title page to the brochure "German Extermination Camps — Auschwitz and Birkenau", published in Washington in November 1944. The brochure contained reports written by escapees from the camp: the Pole, Jerzy Tabeau, and four Jews — Alfred Wetzler, Rudolf Vrba, Czesław Mordowicz, and Arnošt Rosin.

Page from the French-language brochure "Les camps d'extermination", published in Geneva in mid-1944. It contained information about the transports of prisoners arriving at KL Auschwitz and the gassing of Jews.

Note from the German radio monitoring service regarding the broadcast of Radio London from June 15, 1944, reporting the murder at KL Auschwitz II--Birkenau of Jews from the Theresienstadt ghetto. The broadcast included a threat that the individuals responsible for the killings would be brought to justice.

SPRAWOZDANIE ZA OKRES OD 1/II do 1/III 1944.

Oświęcim.
W obozie czynione są gorączkowe przygotowania do wywozu więzionych Polaków do innych obozów w Rzeszy. Więźniowie liczą się z możliwością gazowania: przy tej okazji wysyła się systematycznie w na gaz więźniów chorych i niedołężnych. 12 lutego przywieziono z Radomia 60 Polaków, których rozstrzelano na bloku 11-tym nie wciągając na listę internowanych. Rozstrzelanym wystawiono karty śmierci z zapodaniem powodu "egzekucja" co dowodzi, że rozkaz rozstrzelania przyszedł z poza obozu.
W wszystkich bowiem wypadkach,w których egzekucję przeprowadza się na podstawie decyzją władz obozowych rozstrzelanym na kartach śmierci wpisuje się notatkę "śmierć na skutek choroby w Krankenbau". Wciągu dwóch pierwszych tygodni lutego przywieziono do obozu 7.000 Żydów z Włoch, Francji i Danji. Transporty te znikneły poszły na gaz.
W obozie kobiecym w Birkenau znajduje się 15.000 kobiet. Ostatni zarejestrowany numer wynosi 75.520.
Eksperymenty. Przybyła do obozu specjalna komisja lekarsko sądowa SS z Berlina, przeprowadziła badania na kilkudziesięciu chorych Żydach z sanitarju szach. Nieszczęśliwym ofiarom zastrzykiwano domięśniowo jakiś tajemniczy preparat, skrupulatnie badając reakcję. Ofiary po 15-tu minutach wyprowadzono na podwórze, gdzie przez pół godziny przeprowadzano z nimi ćwiczenia gimnastyczne /biegi, osłędzania, skoki/ poczem poszczególni ośrodkowie z komisji wypytywali tych nieszczęśliwych; czy nie występuje obiaw całkowitego zobojętnienia do życia - czy chcą żyć, czy umierać, czy czują strachacy obojętność - a przedewszystkim kilkakrotnie zadawano pytanie; kto jest twoim osobistym wrogiem. Należy więc przypuszczać, że gestapo pracuje nad odkryciem jakiegoś środka chemicznego, któryby w działaniu swoim wprowadzał ofiary w stan kompletnego zobojętnienia psychicznego, co w konsekwencji ułatwiłoby im otrzymywanie od nieszczęśliwych ofiar szczerych zeznań. Jak narazie jednak ten ohydny eksperyment nie udał się. Zaobserwowano tylko obiawy lekkiego znarocznenia, senność, brak orientacji i brak stolca. Więźniowie na których przeprowadzano to ohydne doświadczenie zostali po kilku dniach poszła-i do komory gazowej.
Śmierć 160 robotników cywilnych.
Trudno nam ze względów zrozumiałych podawać przyczynę aresztowania 160-ciu robotników pracujących na terenie obozu. Tak,czy inaczej jednak wszyscy oni po 2-dniowym śledztwie zostali skazani na śmierć przez sąd wojenny. Egzekucja została wykonana natychmiast. Wszystkich ich przewieziono na blok 11-ty do gazowni i krematorjum. Po wyładowaniu z aut przed szereg wystąpiła kobieta i w sposób zdecydowany wygłosiła do skonsternowanych SS-manów krótkie przemówienie. "Wszyscy tu obecni znaz zdajemy sobie dobrze sprawę ze za chwilę zginiemy w sławnej oświęcimskiej gazowni, a spaleni zostanie my w sławnym oświęcimskim krematorjum. Minął jednak czas kiedy waszych zbrodni dopuszczaliście się w tajemnicy. Dziś cały świat wie, co się tutaj dzieje i za każde zamordowanego w Oświęcimiu ciężko w przyszłości zapłacą hitlerowskie Niemcy. Żegnamy świat z przekonaniem, że niedaleki jest kres waszych ohydnych zbrodni. W tym momencie jeden z rozjuszonych SS-manów podskoczył do dzielnej Polki i uderzeniem kolby rewolweru w twarz powalił ją na ziemię. Reszta eskorty rzuciła się na nieszczęśliwych i kolbami karabinów wepchnęła ich do krematorjum nr.4 Robotnicy jeszcze parę minut w środku śpiewali"Jeszcze Polska nie zginęła " i "Na barykady".
Tak zginęło 160-ciu, których jedyną zbrodnią było to, że podczas rewizji znaleziono przy nich trochę więcej chleba, niż zwykł zabierać do pracy hitlerowski robotnik.
Listy z zaświata.
W Czechach istnieje specjalne miasto, Theresienstadt, w którym skupieni są Żydzi czescy. Mają tam oni swój samorząd, swoje pieniądze i t d. a opiekuje się nimi międzynarodowy Czerwony Krzyż. Gestapo ubiegłego roku sugerując mieszkańcom Theresienstadt pracę na terenie GG na dobrych warunkach - potrafiło wywieźć znakomak stamtąd blisko 6.000 osób. Jakim cudem ludzi ci uwierzyli obłudnym zapewnieniom gestapowców, tego naprawdę nie możemy zrozumieć. W każdym razie jednak przywieziono ich do Oświęcimia i umieszczono w specjalnym lagrze. Początkowo obchodzono się z nimi w sposób podejrzanie grzeczny. Pozwolono im mieszkać w obozie razem z rodzinami, zachowali własny personel lekarski i sanitarny. Sielanka ta trwała kilka miesięcy, niemalże do dni dzisiejszych. Obecnie ponieważ przybyły mają w Theresienstadt nowe transporty z Berlina, przyszedł rozkaz zlikwidowania pierwszego transportu. Cały więc pierwszy transport - 1.800 kobiet i ponad 2.000 mężczyzn został zagazowany. Dnia 19 marca blisko 4.000 przewanino zdrowych ludzi /mężczyzni, kobiety, dzieci/ stłoczono w komory gazowe, a po kilku godzinach przewieziono do krematorjów. Dobrana specjalna ekipa SS-manów i Capów w sposób nieludzki przez kilka godzin obchodziła się z skazanymi na śmierć. Około 60 osób zatłuczono kijami i uderzeniami kolb karabinów. Cała operacja przeprowadzona była mocą przy zachowaniu jaknajdalej posuniętych ostrożności, aby pozostali w obozie Żydzi z Theresienstadt niczego nie domyślili się. Aby wprowadzić w błąd resztę Żydów w Theresienstadt i międzynarodowy Czerwony Krzyż kazano wszystkim tym nieszczęśliwym na 4 dni przed zagazowaniem napisać listy do swoich bliskich w Czechach. Listy te kazano wszystkim zaopatrzeć datą 25 marca 1944. Listy te przechowuje Politische Abteilung a wyśle je dopiero po 25-tym marca. W ten oto sposób chce gestapo udowodnić że w Oświęcimiu nikogo nie gazuje się, a zarazem usiłuje zwabić nowe ofiary z Theresienstadt. Listy te przyjdą do adresatów wtedy, gdy ich autorzy tych listów od kilkunastu dni byd przestali. Ogrom hitlerowskiego zwierzęcego okrucieństwa da się tylko porównać z ogromem tchórzostwa z jakim te bydlęta starają się zacierać ślady swych zbrodni.
100.000 zamordowanych.
Oświęcim stał się synonimem hitlerowskiej kultury i hitlerowskiej cywilizacji. W potwornych warunkach, których umysł ludzki nie jest wstanie sobie wyobrazić więzi się tysiące ludzi tylko poto, aby po dłuższym, czy krótszym okresie potwornych męczarni posłać ich na śmierć. Śmierć staje się tu wyzwoleniem, jest jedną z najprzyjemniejszych chwil spędzonych przez więźnia w obozie. Masowe mordy opracowywane są naukowo i nikt na świecie nie będzie wstan iż w przyszłości znaleźć śladów hitlerowskiego barbarzyństwa. Każda bowiem ofiara palona jest w olbrzymich krematorjach, które pracują bez przerwy. Inxxxxxxprzedstawixxxabiszxxz Tak,czy inaczej jednak żaden gestapowiec nie jest wstanie zapodać, czy bieżący numer w lagrze przekroczył 174.000.xxxxxxiiixxxnxxx Jeżeli równocześnie ponad 49.000 więźniów przebywa w obozie tylko ponad 49.000 Co się więc stało z resztą. Naturalnie, że część zwolniono, a część wysłano do innych obozów w Rzeszy. Dla orientacji podajemy ilość zwolnionych i wysłanych do innych obozów koncentracyjnych z Rzeszy. W roku 1940 wysłano i zwolniono razem 100 osób, - w 1941 - 3.300, w 1942 - 2.100, w 1943 -fxxxxx muixx 15.600, w 1944 do 22/II - 2.300, a więc opuściło lager około 25.000 więźniów. Brakuje zatem 100.000 ludzi, którzy lagru nie opuścili, a których w nim nie ma. Tych sto tysięcy zostało zamordowanych w obozie różnymi sposobami. Biciem,wykańczaniem, choroby, epidemje, zapikowanie, gazowanie i rozstrzeliwanie. W żadnym więc razie zamordowano z normalną numeracją 100.000 tysięcy ludzi. Do ogólnej liczby ofiar w Oświęcimiu dodać należały zmarłych t.zw. Erziehungshäftlingów, a więc robotników zbiegłych z robót z Rzeszy /ogólna suma 9.549/. Dalej 19.000 jeńców sowieckich, dalej kobiety i wreszcie przeszło miljon zagazowanych,ztransportów Żydowskich i tysiące - rozstrzeliwanych cywilów. Oto pokłosie jednego, jedynego lagru.

Prosimy o opublikowanie tych danych, a przedewszystkim zawiadomienie nieszczęśliwych mieszkańców Theresienstadt o losie jaki spotkał ich braci i o niecnym podstępie gestapa.

Smok,26/III 1944   POMOC WIĘŹNIOM
                                    OBOZÓW KONCENTRACYJNYCH.

Periodical report of the organization Assistance for Concentration Camp Prisoners in Cracow, containing information about the crimes being committed at KL Auschwitz received from the camp underground.

A March 1943 dispatch sent by the Polish resistance movement from a secret radio station to the Polish Government-in-Exile in London. The report contained figures on the number of people murdered at KL Auschwitz. It reads:

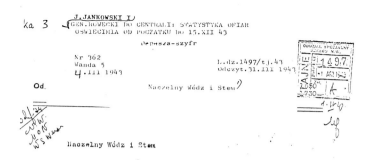

"The statistics for Oświęcim from the establishment of the camp until December 15, [1942] show that more than 640 thousand people have perished there, with 30 thousand still alive. 65 thousand Poles have been executed, hung, tortured, gassed, or have died from starvation and disease, with 17 thousand still alive. More than 26 thousand Soviet POW's have been liquidated; 100 are still alive. More than 520 thousand Jews have been gassed, including 20 thousand from Poland and the rest from France, Belgium, Holland, Yugoslavia, etc. 6,800 women are alive — mainly Poles — and 19,000 have died. Only a portion are registered in the camp records. Thousands are dying without being identified — e.g. almost all the Jews. Now packages are allowed [but] rarely arrive — fat, sugar, etc. usually disappear."

1) Stanisław Mikołajczyk

Sobol Kalina
1/Stanisław Mikołajczyk N.W.

Sobol Kalina

Polish **Underground** Movement
(1939 - 1945) **Study Trust**
11, **Leopold** Road, London W5 3PB

Szyfr-depesza.

L.dz.K.3175/44   Lena, dn.5 kwietnia 1944
Nr.26.   Otrzym. i odczyt. dn. 5 czerwca.

Orkan.

Przekazuję dep. dla dr.Szerera i dr.Szwarcbardt

Sobol.

Z Teresienstadtu w protektoracie, skupisku
Żydów czeskich wywieźli Niemcy pod pretekstem pracy w GG
siedem tys. Żyd. do obozu w Oświęcimiu. Przed dwu tygodn.
ich zagazowali. Przed straceniem wyjobyli od nich
napisane listy do krewnych i znajomych z opisem dobrych
warunk. pracy.

To zasadzka na dalsze grupy. Trzeba natychm.
ostrzedz przez radio i ulotkami przed takową zbrodnią
Żydów Teresienstadtu i Miedzynar. Cz. Krzyż, pod kt.
opieką mają się znajdować.

Na Węgrzech przebywać ma obecnie osiemset
tys. Żyd. Niemcy zaczęli już akcję ich likwid.

Zróbcie coś realnego dla urat. straceńców.
U nas akcja tropienia i likwid. resztek trwa nadal.
Ruiny ghetta warsz. są wysadzane. Ma ono być zrówn. z
ziemią.
            Za C.K.T.Z.M. Pr. p. Berezowski.
                 ZKN Borowski.

czyt. i przep.H.Z.

Dispatch sent by a secret radio station to the Polish government in London by the Polish resistance movement in 1944. It contains information regarding the fate of the Theresienstadt Jews at KL Auschwitz. The last two paragraphs read:

"There are supposed to be currently 800 thousand Jews in Hungary. The Germans have already begun the campaign to exter[minate] them.

Do something effective to rescue the doomed. Here, the campaign to pursue and liquidate the remainder is still continuing. The ruins of the Wars[aw] ghetto have been blown up. It is to be leveled to the ground..."

Berczowski
ZKN Borkowski

List of women prisoners brought to KL Auschwitz, secretly assembled on the basis of transport lists and smuggled out of the camp.

Fragment of a report from August 1944, to Stefan Jasieński ("Urban") and the Home Army command for the Silesian District, regarding a plan for beginning an uprising at the camp.

A smuggled message from Edward Biernacki, written in 1942, acknowledging the receipt of medicines smuggled into the camp.

A smuggled message from August 21, 1944, listing the number of prisoners at the various camps that made up KL Auschwitz.

Title page to the brochure about KL Auschwitz entitled, *Obóz śmierci* ("Death Camp").

Title page to a publication that contained excerpts from the Polish government's note of May 3, 1941, to Allied and neutral states.

being devoured by vermin ; we awaited the time to get up, shivering with cold.

Reveille was marked by the curses of our guards, and by blows with sticks ; we queued up at the entrance of the latrine, after which we received a bit of dry bread, our only breakfast ; then to work : some were engaged in digging up the stumps of trees, others had to saw wood, still others were employed on navvying. Tormented and emaciated faces, eyes with circles round them, badly healed wounds, ragged clothes : that was how my fellow prisoners appeared to me. Our German guards boxed our ears and beat us, right and left, with truncheons or the butt end of rifles or kicked us, in order to goad us to work.

At evening roll call we were lined up, then there came a bawled "Attention !" A whipping bench was brought along ; one after the other the prisoners had to lie on this ; their trousers were pulled down and they were beaten with a stick or a truncheon ; the number of blows varied from case to case. I heard terrible cries ; usually the victim fainted ; the executioners then threw cold water on them ; they came to—and the torment was resumed.

Smoking was forbidden, writing was forbidden, it was forbidden to receive parcels, forbidden to take a rest during work.

On the . . . ten prisoners were executed and I had to be present.

APPENDIX 168

TESTIMONY OF M . . . N. Y., DELIVERED AT V . . .

on April 15, 1940

(Extract from Statement)

Since the end of March, 1940, Fort No. VII of Poznan had ceased to serve as a prison. It became a sort of school for Gestapo agents, who perfected themselves there in the art of treating prisoners with a refined sadism. The course in question lasted three to four weeks, and experiments were then carried out on people who were subjected to the most frightful tortures. One experiment consisted in beating the victim into insensibility, reviving him with cold water—then resuming. Another consisted in pumping air from a special valve into the victim's duodenum, until—in some cases—his intestines burst.

Note.—The witness also quoted four other methods of torture employed by the Gestapo authorities.

APPENDIX 168a

SUMMARY OF TESTIMONIES AND REPORTS CONCERNING THE GERMAN CONCENTRATION CAMP AT OŚWIĘCIM

Poles are being deported to Oświęcim, Oranienburg, Sachsenhausen, Mauthausen, Dachau and other concentration camps of lesser importance. It is chiefly people of educated appearance who are being arrested, their service testimonials from private employers or public institutions being ignored.

174

They are sometimes taken away incompletely dressed, even during the winter, marched to the railway station and herded into goods trucks (70 to a truck). The trucks are sealed, then moved to a siding and left there until a sufficient number of prisoners are gathered in to make up a train. In some cases these trucks have been kept on a siding for three or four days, or even a week, regardless of whether the prisoners had any warm clothes, in 48 degrees of frost.

At first there was the sound of voices and stamping feet from the trucks, the prisoners were trying to keep warm in this way. The guards reacted by banging on the walls of the trucks with rifle butts to warn the unfortunate people to keep quiet. After two days' waiting the trucks would be very silent indeed.

The journey to Oświęcim took from three to five days. Once a day during the journey rations consisting of bread and lumps of frozen boiled paste were thrown into trucks through the air holes.

Sometimes anything from 6 to 10 dead bodies were dragged out of the trucks after a few days' wait at the station, and some 40 per cent. of the prisoners had frozen hands and feet. The survivors pulled the clothes off the corpses and used them for themselves. On arrival at the station of destination, the train was shunted to a specially prepared detraining platform, which was very steep and covered with ice and snow. There the transport was kept until late at night. Then the doors were suddenly opened, powerful searchlights were turned on, and the prisoners were ordered to leave the trucks. Dazzled by the strong light, stiff from cold, starving, and stunned by the fresh air, the unfortunate prisoners were unable to alight at once, so the German police " helped " them, beating them with rifle butts and kicking them. The older people slipped and fell on the ice-covered sloping platform. Those too weak to rise from the floor of the trucks were dragged out by their hands or feet and thrown down the slope of the platform. The dead bodies were probably burnt in the local crematorium. Amidst incessant beating the prisoners were loaded into lorries.

On arrival of a transport at the concentration camp the prisoners were divided according to height ; those unable to stand on their feet were laid on the ground. It took from two to four hours to check the list of prisoners, who were then marched to some barracks. These were cold, unheated and full of holes. At the entrance of one of them hung the dead body of a man. He was one of a number of hunger strikers who thus protested against the horrible, inhuman treatment after being compelled to work in wet overalls in freezing weather. The sleeping space in the barracks is so restricted that if a prisoner turns round he disturbs his neighbours. Towels have to be piled up in one heap, so that the individual prisoner has no towel of his own, and there is danger of infection. Many prisoners suffering from venereal disease were purposely sent to the Oświęcim camp.

The prisoners have to get up at 5 o'clock in the morning and are allowed only three minutes to wash under a cold shower, clean their clothes and dress. Sick prisoners have to do the same work as well. Only prisoners with a temperature of 38 deg. C. may apply to the infirmary. Anyone calling there with a lower temperature is sent to the penal section. The prisoners are afraid of illness, as there is practically no medical aid.

The guards at the concentration camps are ex-convicts with commuted life sentences, including a few German Communists who had also been sentenced to life imprisonment. All are degenerates, yet they are arbiters of life and death over the unfortunate Poles.

The prisoners are forced to perform exhausting but purposeless tasks.

175

Appendix Nr. 168a — regarding KL Auschwitz — to the Polish government's note of May 3, 1941.

Oſtſchweizeriſches Tagblatt
und
Rorſchacher Tagblatt

(bei Oſtſchweizeriſchen Wochenblattes 102. Jahrgang)

The Swiss press — in this case, the *Ostschweizerisches Tagblatt* — published information in mid-1944 about the deportation and extermination of Jews from Hungary and the extermination facilities at KL Auschwitz based on reports from the Polish Government-in-Exile in London.

62 EISENBAHNEN VOLL JÜDISCHE KINDER...
WOHIN?

London, 8. Juli. (Reuter.) Das polnische Innenministerium hat vom Delegierten der polnischen Regierung in Polen Einzelheiten über das Schicksal der aus Ungarn deportierten 400.000 Juden erfahren. Der grösste Teil der Deportierten wurde nach dem Vernichtungslager von Auschwitz in Oberschlesien übergeführt. Am 15. Mai wurden von den Deutschen in Ungarn 62 Eisenbahnwagen mit jüdischen Kinder im Alter von 2 bis 8 Jahren abtransportiert und seither verliessen täglich Eisenbahnzüge mit Erwachsenen den Bahnhof von Plaszow bei Krakau.

Nach den beim polnischen Hilfskomitee für die Juden in Polen vorliegenden Informationen sind seit dem Jahre 1939 2 Millionen polnische Juden in drei Konzentrationslagern Polens ums Leben gekommen.

Diese Reutermeldung wird auch von der Exchange-Agentur verbreitet mit folgenden Zusätzen:

„Es konnte festgestellt werden, dass die meisten der durchfahrenden Erwachsenen nach Oswiecim geschafft und in den Gaskammern des Lagers hingerichtet wurden." Die polnische Regierung warnt, Briefen, aus denen hervorgeht, dass der Schreiber anscheinend guten Mutes ist, und die aus Oswiecim datiert sind, Glauben zu schenken. Es sei festgestellt worden, dass diese Briefe erzwungen wurden. Das polnische Innenministerium stellte ferner die tägliche Vergasungskapazität in den Kammern von Oswiecim mit 6000 fest. Das Innenministerium erklärt schliesslich, dass in der zweiten Hälfte des Jahres 1942 zwei weitere Todeslager von den Deutschen in Polen errichtet wurden, das Lager Tremblinka und das Lager Rawaruska. Ob auch dort Gaskammern eingerichtet wurden, sei unbekannt.

Die Massenmorde an den Juden wurden übrigens bis heute von deutscher Seite gar nicht bestritten; sie liegen ganz in der Linie der von Hitler ausgegebenen Parole, das Judentum müsse „ausgerottet" werden.

The Brickyard

WEDNESDAY MORNING, MARCH 22, 1944

Poles Report
Mass Murder

LONDON, March 21. (*AP*)—The Polish Ministry of Information said today that more than 500,000 persons, mostly Jews, had been put to death at a concentration camp at Osweicim, southwest of Krakow.

In a lengthy report on Nazi atrocities the ministry declared three crematoriums had been erected inside the camp to dispose of 10,000 bodies a day. Gas chambers were said to have been attached to the crematoriums.

The report asserted that men, women and children arrive by truckloads and are removed to the gas chambers where 10 to 15 minutes are required for execution, but since the supply of poison gas is limited some persons are not dead when they are thrown into the crematorium.

Information about KL Auschwitz in the *Los Angeles Times* from March 22, 1944, based on a report from the Polish Government-in-Exile in London.

The manuscript of Jewish prisoner Salmen Gradowski from the *Sonderkommando*, found in 1945 near the ruins of Crematorium Nr. II. In the report, the author describes, among other things, the mass extermination of Jews at KL Auschwitz.

Szyfr depesza.

L.dz.K.3918/44   Lena dn.

Nr.66.   Otrzym. i odczyt. 13 lipca 44r.

Orkan.

Zaczęło się od 15.V. w Oświęcimiu masowe mordowanie ludzi, pierwsi idą Żydzi, potem jeńcy sow. i t.zw. chorzy. Masowo przywozi się Żydów węg. Na dobę przybywa 13 pociągów po 40 - 50 wagonów. Ofiary przekonane, że idą na wymianę za jeńców niem. lub na osiedlenie. Komory gazowe czynne bez przerwy. Trupy palą w krematorjach i na wolnym powietrzu. Zagazowanych już ponad 100 tys. Ostra propaganda może osłabić tempo likwidacji 5 a a l w t i w g o ł

Telegram of July 13, 1944, from the Polish resistance movement to the Polish government in London, containing information about the extermination of Hungarian Jews at KL Auschwitz.

Fragments of a secret message written by Polish prisoners Stanisław Kłodziński and Józef Cyrankiewicz on September 6, 1944, and sent outside the camp to the Polish resistance movement. It contained information about the plans of the SS ("Moll-Plan") to liquidate KL Auschwitz and murder the prisoners.

DEPESZA SZYFR   TAJNE

Nr 213/1/XXX

118   Mowa to 59 es 09 ie 40

Śnicz Nr.213 dnia 23.9. Garda.-

Otrzymaliśmy wiadomość, że Niemcy planują zlikwidowanie Oświęcimia i Buchenwaldu.

Komendant Oświęcimia Höss, mąż zaufania Himmlera, zwracał się do różnych SS-Führerów o projekty takiej likwidacji obozu wraz z ludźmi.

Obecnie w Birkenau znajduje się 16727 mężczyzn i 39125 kobiet.

Zgłosił się z projektem komendant Birkenau Moll, żądając zmotoryzowanych oddziałów SS, artylerii do ostrzeliwania bloków, 16 samolotów bombardujących, wreszcie odpowiednią ilość ludzi do splantowania terenu.

DEPESZA SZYFR   TAJNE

Nr 213/2/XXX

118   Mowa to 59 es 9 de 40

D.c. Nr.213.

Projekt byłby przyjęty, lecz Moll chce polecenia pisemnego zn Berlina, a to jest właśnie jedna z robót, która przeprowadza się nieoficjalnie.

Potworną tę zbrodnię należy uniemożliwić - na co tu w Kraju, a tym mniej na Śląsku nie mamy sił ani żadnych możliwości.

Skazańcy czekają na ratunek - każdy dzień może już być za późno.

W obozie w Płaszowie ostatnio większe egzekucje Polaków.

L. dz. 8932/7/4/8/44   21

Dispatch from September 23, 1944, sent by the Polish resistance movement via underground radio station to the Polish government in London, regarding the plans of the SS to liquidate the camp and murder the prisoners ("Moll-Plan").

LONDON
55 New Cavendish St. W 1

GENEVA
17 Quai Wilson

BUENOS AIRES
Corrientes 1879

JERUSALEM
Vaad Leumi P. O. D. 471

MONTREAL
1121 St. Catherine St. W

MEXICO CITY
Ramos 1744

CABLES: CONGRESS, NEW YORK
TELEPHONES: Circle 6-1900

August 9, 1944

Hon. John J. McCloy
Under Secretary of War
War Department
Washington D. C.

My dear Mr. Secretary:

Doc. 54

164

I beg to submit to your consideration the following excerpt from a message which we received under date of July 29 from Mr. Ernest Frischer of the Czechoslovak State Council through the War Refugee Board:

"I believe that destruction of gas chambers and crematoria in Oswiecim by bombing would have a certain effect now. Germans are now exhuming and burning corpses in an effort to conceal their crimes. This could be prevented by destruction of crematoria and then Germans might possibly stop further mass exterminations especially since so little time is left to them. Bombing of railway communications in this same area would also be of importance and of military interest."

Sincerely yours

A. Leon Kubowitzki
Head, Rescue Department

ALK:dl

Letter from Leon Kubowitzski of the World Jewish Congress to the U.S. Department of War from August 9, 1944, requesting that they consider the possibility of bombing the extermination facilities at KL Auschwitz along with the railway lines leading to the camp.

WDOAS:JJMcC:NZW

ASW 400.38 Czechoslovakia

14 August 1944

Dear Mr. Kubowitzki:

I refer to your letter of August 9 in which you request consideration of a proposal made by Mr. Ernest Frischer that certain installations and railroad centers be bombed.

The War Department has been approached by the War Refugee Board, which raised the question of the practicability of this suggestion. After a study it became apparent that such an operation could be executed only by the diversion of considerable air support essential to the success of our forces now engaged in decisive operations elsewhere and would in any case be of such doubtful efficacy that it would not warrant the use of our resources. There has been considerable opinion to the effect that such an effort, even if practicable, might provoke even more vindictive action by the Germans.

The War Department fully appreciates the humanitarian motives which prompted the suggested operation, but for the reasons stated above it has not been felt that it can or should be undertaken, at least at this time.

Sincerely,

(SIGNED) JOHN J. McCLOY

JOHN J. McCLOY
Assistant Secretary of War

Doc. 55

165

384.2
Bombardments
Czechoslovakia

Mr. A. Leon Kubowitzki
Head, Rescue Department
World Jewish Congress
1834 Broadway
New York 23, N. Y.

14 Aug 44

Letter of Assistant Secretary of War John J. McCloy from August 14, 1944, rejecting the possibility of bombing the extermination facilities at KL Auschwitz.

The amount of food that local residents supplied ran into tens of kilograms. Julian Dusik's store in Łęki, for example, contributed 14.5 kg of butter, 100 kg of bread, 10.5 kg of sugar and 4 kg of margarine on one October day in 1941.

Because the system introduced for rationing food by the occupier made it difficult to feed the prisoners, the underground organizations near the camp and charities in Cracow began the cooperate. In December 1940, the Section for Assistance to Prisoners-of-War, Expellees, and Political Prisoners of the PCK sent 1,000 holiday packages to the camp. In January 1942, they sent 2,500 packages. The Main Assistance Council, the Committee to Assist Concentration Camp Prisoners and Scouting organizations also offered significant help.

The camp resistance organization, cognizant of the difficulties related to food collection in the area, decided to seek other sources of assistance. In mid-1943, they compiled lists of prisoners at the camp — including their names, camp numbers, and block numbers — and smuggled them out through their contacts to Cracow. From there, the lists were sent to the International Committee of the Red Cross in Geneva. In a smuggled message dated June 20, 1943, Stanisław Kłodziński wrote:

We should see that the outside world receives our addresses in order to prove to the Germans that the entire world knows about Auschwitz. We should conduct this operation on a mass scale and give various countries more than 200-300 of our addresses. It has to be a mass campaign so that we cannot be called to account for it. At the same time it would also be good to give out addresses of Germans at the camp, Czechs and others, such as Sov. [iet] communists. In a word, so that the camp will be flooded with international packages. [12]

The campaign had positive results; packages began to flow into the camp from the International Red Cross. Although the SS requisitioned most of them, the fact that prisoners' names and numbers at Auschwitz were known abroad proved that the secrecy that the camp authorities had sought so urgently to protect had been breached.

Medicine was also smuggled into the camp in significant quantities. The official supplies that the camp received for treating the ill were only a drop in the ocean compared to the conditions prevailing at the camp. Seventy percent of the medications that prisoners used were supplied illegally. Some were brought to the camp by prisoners assigned to outside work details. A number of secret messages have survived that list needed medicines or verify their receipt. For example, a smuggled message, dated July 31, 1942, from Janusz Pogonowski (alias Skrzetuski at the camp) asserts: "I received around 1,000 ampules of various medications (coramina, digipuratum, calc., gluc., etc.), all given to sick ward at KL Au." [13] Another prisoner, Edward Biernacki, reported: "In the months: June, July and August, I brought to the grounds of

---

[12] APMO, Files of the Camp Resistance, vol. I, card 33.
[13] Ibid., vol. I, card 5.

the camp hospital around 7,500 cc of injections .... and 70 series of anti-typhus vaccinations." [14]

Some medicine was delivered to the camp through the mail. In 1944, five to ten kilogram packages of medications arrived at the camp packaging office, addressed to deceased prisoners. They reached prisoner-doctors through underground channels. Stanisław Kłodziński asserted in a clandestine message from January 20, 1944:

> You in Ośw. or Zator send a well-packed package with medications to a fictitious person: Pris. Nr. 71825, Śliwiński Stephan, b. 12.I.1912, Bl. 25, St. 6 KL Auschwitz Post 2 O/S, and we will collect it at our post office without inspection. At the time, small risk of uncovering. Send such packages twice a week. [15]

An important source of supplies to the camp was the drugstore in Brzeszcze, run by Maria Bobrzecka. Pharmacists in Oświęcim, Kęty, Zator, and Chrzanów, along with the Main Assistance Council, also supplied medications. The need for food and medicine was enormous. It was impossible, however, to deliver by illegal means packages to all the thousands of prisoners imprisoned at the camp. Even small amounts were of vital importance, given the conditions at hand, and helped save the lives of numerous prisoners.

Another significant activity of the resistance movement was collecting evidence of the crimes that the SS was committing and delivering it outside the camp. Among the most important documents to leave the camp were:

1. Registration books or "Bunker Registers" from the jail in the basement of Block 11. They listed the names of the prisoners who had been incarcerated there, along with information about their subsequent fate. A scribe from Block 11, Jan Pilecki, had given the books to members of the resistance organization.

2. Copies of registers from the camp morgue (*Leichenhalle*) assembled by prisoner Stefan Markowski, and then the registers themselves, which listed the camp numbers of prisoners who had been killed by phenol injections or shot.

3. Lists of more than 6,000 Polish women who had perished or been murdered at the camp. The list was compiled by prisoner Monika Galica on the basis of the original death registers in the chancellory of the HKB, where she worked.

4. Plans for the crematoria and gas chambers stolen in 1944 from the SS construction office at Birkenau (*SS-Bauleitung-Birkenau*) by Krystyna Horczak, a Polish prisoner, and two Czech prisoners, Vera Foltynova and Valeria Valova.

5. Copies of documents related to Dr. Josef Mengele's anthropological experiments on twins and Jewish women, made by prisoner Martyna Puzyna.

6. Three photographs that had been taken illegally during the summer of 1944 by prisoners employed in the *Sonderkommando* at Crematorium V. Among the participants in this action were Alex from Greece (his last name is unknown); Szlojme Dragon and his brother, Josel; and Alter Szmul Fajnzylberg (at the camp, Stanisław Jankowski) and Dawid Szmulewski.

---

[14] Ibid., vol. I, card 10.
[15] Ibid., vol. II, card 58.

7. Transport lists of the men and women brought to the camp, including Jews with camp numbers from the A and B series. The lists were assembled in September 1944 by prisoners employed in the receptions office (*Aufnahme*) of the political division: Kazimierz Smoleń, Ludwik Rajewski, Tadeusz Szymański, Tadeusz Wąsowicz, and Jan Trembaczewski. The lists contained data about the arrival of transports at the camp, the numbers distributed to the prisoners, and the origin of each transport.

Not only original documents, but also reports were smuggled out of the camp in the form of *grypsy* (illegal letters). They recorded the exact number of prisoners at the camp, the number of transports arriving and leaving, the names of prisoners condemned to death by the police court-martial of the Katowice Gestapo, the names of SS men on the camp staff, descriptions of living conditions at the camp, and proposed routes and schedules for prisoner escapes. For example, a *gryps* from September 16, 1944, entitled "The Butchers of Auschwitz", gave the names and discriptions of the several dozen SS men who were the most vicious criminals at the camp. Commandant Rudolf Höss headed the list. The message, addressed to Teresa Lasocka--Estreicher ("Tell") began as follows:

Tell
We are sending rough sketches of the butchers of Auschwitz. All the data are authentic beyond any doubt. It would be quite desirable that London declare death sentences against them as quickly as possible. [16]

The information contained in the smuggled reports was compiled by prisoners employed in various administrative units at the camp — in the main writing office, the HKB, the offices of the Political Division (*Politische Abteilung*) and the prisoner employment office. At the risk of their lives, they copied documents, plans and reports. Spot inspections conducted by the SS forced the prisoners to find a suitable way to hide secret messages and smuggle them out of the camp. They were put inside specially-made candles, attached to cigarettes, indelible pens, keys, the wrapping paper around sweets, etc. The prisoners, wanting to shrink the format of the smuggled messages to a minimum, sometimes used cigarette paper to this end. Along with such smaller messages, one also found reports 10-20 pages long. Messages that contained more important information were written in code. The signatures included such codenames as "J", "Tor", "Cyr" (Józef Cyrankiewicz), "St", "Stakło" (Stanisław Kłodziński), "Max", and "Benek" (Bernard Świerczyna).

Established channels were used for smuggling both documents and smaller messages out of the camp. Civilian workers employed by German firms served as go-betweens between the camp organization and the underground outside the camp: Stanisław Mordarski, Józef Cholewa, Franciszek Walisko, and Helena Datoń, the cashier at the mess for SS men in "*Haus 7*". They would smuggle messages from the prisoners outside the camp and send them on to

---

[16] Ibid., vol. VII, card 462.

Brzeszcze. From there, the Kornaś family from Spytkowice or Aniela Kieres from Chrzanów would deliver the secret materials to Cracow.

In 1944, the organization gained yet another contact — the Austrian nurse Maria Stromberger, known as "Sister Maria". Employed at the hospital for SS men, she joined the camp conspiracy. She was used as a conduit for delivering larger manuscripts, books, and documents. She would either contact Helena Datoń or carry the materials to Brzeszcze or Chrzanów herself. She also delivered newspapers, medicine, explosives and arms to the camp. Stanisław Kłodziński wrote to Cracow in a smuggled message dated September 26, 1944: "Make contact with the Sister as often as possible — it is a safe and quick way — we can always pick up." [17]

In the summer of 1944, an SS man, Frank, the *Blockführer* from Block 5, was drawn into cooperating with the resistance. At first, he gave the prisoners information about the strength of the guard staff, their weaponry, and new orders that had been given at the camp. Later, they entrusted him with the role of intermediary. In smuggled messages, Frank was called the "ambassador":

> On Friday around 7:30 at the same meeting place, where he once met with Jantar, our ambassador will arrive and bring the plans — which we did not want to send the normal way given their size. [18]

Some information that reached Cracow was published in the underground press. Other information, marked "give to London", was delivered to England to be announced on the radio. Certain materials could not be published immediately, given safety considerations for the prisoners who had delivered them.

Yet another activity of the camp resistance movement was organizing and preparing escapes (see p. 225).

The camp resistance movement, besides assisting prisoners, also carried out various diversionary activities. Prisoners employed at German industrial facilities and mines conducted sabotage. For example, prisoners who salvaged wrecked airplanes would deliberately destroy important parts, let gas out of the tanks, etc. Similarly, women prisoners cultivating kok-saghyz in Rajsko — a plant with high-quality rubber in its roots — would dilute it with chemicals and falsify key data to delay the pace of experimentation on rubber production.

The camp resistance organization also conducted political education work among the prisoners. The goal was to achieve international solidarity in the struggle against Nazism. It sought to counteract the German propaganda claiming that only criminals were being held at the concentration camps. To this end, a resolution was prepared that demonstrated the number of criminals being held, mainly Germans, were less than five percent of all the prisoners. The majority, the resolution asserted, was composed of political prisoners of all nationalities. One part of the resolution read:

---

[17] Ibid., vol. II, card 164.

[18] Ibid., vol. II, card 142. Smuggled message from September 7, 1944, written by Stanisław Kłodziński.

Although we are slaves at the camps, we are people of freedom, sending the free world news of our existence, of our unprecedented struggle for the rights of political prisoners. [19]

In response to the threat of mass murder, the Auschwitz Military Council (RWO) began reviewing possibilities for sparking an uprising at the camp to free the prisoners. Colonel Kazimierz Rawicz had already developed a plan in 1942 for a rapid, mass effort both inside and outside the camp and had sent it to the commander of the Home Army (AK), General Stefan Rowecki ("Grot"), with the goal of establishing a timetable for initiating the action. The plan, considered too bold at the time, was not implemented. The question arose again in 1944 as a result of developments on the Eastern front. The front was rapidly moving to the west as a result of the Red Army's offensive. In July, the second-largest concentration camp, Majdanek, was liberated; the officials at the camp were taken by surprise and did not have time to destroy the facilities for mass extermination and murder the prisoners. At Auschwitz, it was feared that the SS men, having learned from experience, would strive at all costs to destroy every trace of the crimes that they had committed.

In response to the mounting risk of the camp's liquidation, the leadership of the camp resistance made contact with the Home Army command for the Silesian District. They requested not only explosives and weapons, but also assistance in the form of organized diversions outside the camp to tie down some SS forces while the prisoners tried to escape. They stressed that the camp's complete or even partial liberation would have an enormous moral impact given KL Auschwitz's international significance as one of the most dismal symbols of Nazi Germany. The liberation of the camp, they argued, should not be viewed exclusively in terms of assistance for the prisoners; the prisoners also represented an enormous potential in terms of manpower, fit to take part in an armed uprising. [20] At the camp, reports were prepared evaluating the situation and presenting details about the number of prisoners at Auschwitz and its sub-camps, the strength of the SS garrison, their weaponry and technical capabilities, the state of organizational preparations, etc. [21]

Stefan Jasieński ("Urban"), dispatched to the area by the Home Army's Supreme Command, received all this information. He was supposed to make contact with the camp organization and evaluate possibilities for conducting warfare in the area. He was arrested in September 1944 by a German patrol and imprisoned at the camp, where he most likely perished.

The plans for an uprising at the camp were never realized. Thousands of prisoners, mainly Poles and Russians, began to be evacuated from the camp on a mass scale in the second half of 1944, which threw the resistance movement into disarray. Furthermore, the Home Army leadership considered the escape

---

[19] Ibid., vol. II, card 87.
[20] Ibid., vol. II, card 114.
[21] Ibid., vol. II, card 98. Report from August 22, 1944 signed by Józef Cyrankiewicz.

plan unrealistic for a number of reasons, including the lack of necessary weaponry. More importantly, the number of prisoners at the camp was enormous, and many of them, ill and unable to fight, could not be guaranteed the necessary security and assistance.

4. Rebellions

Although a general uprising never broke out at the camp, rebellions by individuals or entire groups did take place. There exist numerous examples of prisoners who displayed an unshaken attitude in the face of death (see p. 195).

In a number of publications, the massacre of woman prisoners in the penal company at the Budy sub-camp has been designated a rebellion. In June 1942, in revenge for the escape of a Polish woman, a penal company was established for women at Budy, a village seven kilometers away from Auschwitz. The company was composed of 400 women of various nationalities, including Jews from France and Czechoslovakia and 200 Polish women. These women lived under inhuman conditions and worked at strenuous jobs. The German women assigned to auxiliary functions — criminals and prostitutes — tormented the female prisoners in the penal company.

In the first days of October 1942, the prisoner-functionaries and SS guards massacred the French-Jewish women assigned to the company. Around 90 women perished, killed with clubs and axes or thrown from the attic windows of their residential block. During an investigation, functionaries from the Political Division were unable to clarify what had provoked the incident. Commandant Rudolf Höss explained it away as a revolt by the women prisoners, who had tried to threaten a kapo with clubs and rocks to escape from the camp. [22]

Pery Broad, who took part in the inquiry as an official from the Political Division, later offered a different version of events:

> When one of the Jewish women returned the evening before from the toilet to the sleeping area on the top floor of the school, one of the German women thought that she saw a rock in her hand. Of course, this was only an hysterical illusion .... She called out the window for help, claiming that the Jewish woman was beating her. All the guards standing around at the camp then ran up the stairs and, along with the women functionaries, devoid of any humanity, attacked the Jewish women. They threw some women down the winding stairs into a heap, one on top of the other. Some were thrown out of the window and lay there dead. [23]

Because the contradictory testimony of the women prisoners and the SS guards prevented the establishment of guilt, the commandant did not decree any punishments in the case. After the hearings were finished, the injured Jewish

---

[22] APMO, Höss Trial, vol. 21, card 42-3.
[23] "Wspomnienia Pery Broada", in *Oświęcim w oczach SS* (Oświęcim, 1972), p. 157. Cf. "Reminiscences of Pery Broad", in *KL Auschwitz seen by the SS* (Oświęcim, 1972), p. 166.

women, along with six German prisoners-functionaries who had taken part in the massacre, were put to death with injections of phenol. [24]

On June 10, 1942, an organized rebellion and escape broke out inside the men's penal company at the Birkenau camp. The prisoners' desire to save their own lives had caused the rebellion. Prisoners were sent to the punishment company for violations committed at the camp, along with political prisoners who were considered particularly dangerous, with the goal of isolating them from the remaining prisoners. On May 27, 1942, around 400 Polish prisoners brought to the camp in 1940-41 from the districts of Warsaw and Cracow were assigned to it. At the time, the punishment company was digging a drainage ditch at Birkenau, the so-called "Königsgraben". Every other day, around a dozen prisoners from the latter group were sent to the main camp at Auschwitz to be shot. The surviving prisoners realized that all of them would eventually be killed in a similar fashion. Several of them took up the idea of organizing a mass escape during work. One of the organizers later recounted:

All of us were burdened and condemned to death anyway, so we considered it better to risk it so that somebody could be saved. It was only a question of making the escape as massive as possible. [25]

Only trusted prisoners were informed of the plan to prevent its betrayal. The plan foresaw the escape taking place when *SS-Hauptscharführer* Otto Moll, *Kommandoführer* of the punishment company, gave the signal to end work and return to camp. Everyone was supposed to run away on their own. On the day of the escape, it was raining heavily and most likely as a result, the signal to quit work came earlier than usual. This disoriented the prisoners and aroused fears and uncertainties; they thought their plan had been betrayed. Some prisoners ran to escape. The sentries began to shoot at the fleeing prisoners, and the kapos succeeded in turning around a dozen back. During the pursuit, thirteen prisoners were shot, and two others were imprisoned in the bunker of Block 11 and later sent to the gallows.

On June 14, two other prisoners who had taken part in the attempted escape met with the same fate. Only seven prisoners succeeded in escaping. The remaining prisoners in the punishment company were brought back to the camp. The next morning, after the roll-call, around 100 prisoners were sent to work, while around 320 remained at the camp in the courtyard outside the barracks of the penal company. Then *Lagerführer* Hans Aumeier arrived with a group of SS men and demanded that the prisoners reveal the organizers of the rebellion. When they refused to talk, he selected a group of 20 prisoners and, to frighten the others, ordered that they be shot. Around a dozen prisoners originally assigned to the penal company were taken from the camp infirmary and added to the group. The hands of the assembled prisoners were

---

[24] SS man Josef Klehr carried out the executions of the women prisoner-functionaries on October 24, 1942.

[25] APMO, Collection of Testimonies, vol. 11, card 4, account of former prisoner Tadeusz Chróścicki.

bound with barbed wire, and they were led to Bunker 1, where they were murdered.

A German prisoner assigned to the penal company, who had to help bind the prisoners' hands, later recounted:

> The blood gushed like a fountain from their bound hands, but not a single complaint crossed the lips of the tormented Poles, one could not even discern any suffering in the faces of many of them; only their hate and contempt for the Nazi butchers glistened in their eyes. .... Young people went to their deaths without complaining and cursing, without whimpering and pleading — they died like heroes. Probably only Poles are able to die like that. [26]

To camouflage what had happened, the names of the murdered prisoners were recorded over several days in the camp's daily strength register (*Stärkebuch*).

The largest pre-planned rebellion, by the Jews employed in the *Sonderkommando*, took place on October 7, 1944. The prisoners in the *Sonderkommando* labored under a greater threat than other work details, given the nature of their work. They understood that the SS officials wanted to annihilate them more than anyone else, since they were inconvenient witnesses to mass murder. They thus decided to fight and defend themselves, even at the cost of their lives. For many months, they had been preparing for a rebellion. Soviet POWs brought to the camp from KL Lublin in April 1944 and attached to the *Sonderkommando* also took active part in the preparations.

The prisoners planned to blow up the crematoria, burn down the barracks, cut the wire fence surrounding the camp and flee. Thanks to the cooperation of women prisoners at the Union-Werke armaments factory and male prisoners on the *Zerlegebetriebe* work detail (which salvaged wrecked airplanes), they were able to assemble enough explosive materials to produce primitive grenades. [27] The majority of the workers in the *Sonderkommando* knew about the plan and had been assigned a role. The uprising was planned for June 1944. They were awaiting the Red Army's offensive because they thought that it would provide their plan with a better chance of success. [28]

Due to the large number of people involved in the plan and a failure to maintain the necessary secrecy, SS officials caught scent of the rebellion. Repressive measures were taken that led to a significant loss of people. The prisoners in the *Sonderkommando* were transferred out of Camp BIId and housed in the garrets of Crematoria II and III and in the undressing room to Crematorium IV, in order to isolate then from the other prisoners and to prevent any contacts with them.

At the end of the summer of 1944, the number of transports arriving at the camp for extermination decreased, as did the number of people needed for servicing the crematoria. The SS slowly began to liquidate the prisoners in the *Sonderkommando*. In September, the SS assembled 200 of its members and

---

[26] APMO, Files of the Camp Resistance, vol. VII, card 450.

[27] Manuscript of Salmen Lewental in *Amidst a Nightmare of Crime*, (Oświęcim, 1973), pp. 167-168.

[28] APMO, Höss Trial, vol. 11a. cards 115, 145, accounts of former prisoners Szlama Dragon and Henryk Tauber.

under the pretext of transferring them to the Gleiwitz sub-camp, sent them to Auschwitz I. They were gassed there in a building that had been previously used for delousing and disinfecting clothes (*Entwesungskammer*).

The prisoners foresaw further reductions in the *Kommando*. When news arrived on the morning of October 7 that 300 prisoners from Crematoria IV and V were going to be sent off in a transport, the prisoners realized that they would meet the same fate as their predecessors. So, they decided to carry out their plan and not let themselves be taken without a fight.

When Crematorium IV was set ablaze, it was supposed to be a signal to start activity at all the other crematoria. At noon, SS men arrived at Crematorium IV to assemble the prisoners. The prisoners attacked[29] them with hammers and axes and set the crematorium on fire. Some sought refuge in the nearby woods. The prisoners at Crematorium II also took action. They cut the wire fence surrounding the crematorium and ran to escape in the direction of Rajsko. They barricaded themselves inside a barn there.[30] The prisoners from Crematoria III and V were not able to join the fighting because SS reinforcements quickly arrived and took control of the situation. To hunt down the escapees, the SS staff from sub-camps near Brzezinka (Birkenau) joined in. The SS men threw grenades inside the barn where the prisoners were hiding and set in ablaze. Many were killed by machine-gun fire. The Allied aircraft that were flying by for air-raids in Silesia made pursuit difficult. In the evening, the corpses of the prisoners killed during the escape were returned to the camp. Around 200 survivors from the rebellion were shot. After the revolt, the *Sonderkommando* shrank in size from 663 to 212 prisoners; 451 perished. The remaining prisoners from the *Sonderkommando* were housed in Crematorium III.

The rebellion's organizers were Polish Jews: Jankiel Handelsman, Josef Deresiński, Salmen Gradowski, and Josef Dorębus (alias Josef Warszawski). All of them, with the exception of Handelsman, perished during the rebellion. He was imprisoned along with around a dozen other prisoners in the bunker of Block 11 at the main camp on October 10, where he was tortured to death during interrogation. The SS staff suffered insubstantial losses. Three *Unterscharführer* were killed, and a dozen or so were injured.[31] On October 9, the camp resistance organization sent a report to Cracow describing the *Sonderkommando*'s revolt.[32]

After the revolt was put down, the Political Division investigated how the prisoners got ahold of explosives. Their investigation showed that the Jewish women employed at the Union Werke had smuggled out the explosives and given them to Róża Robota, a Jewish women from Ciechanów working in the *Bekleidungskammer* at Birkenau. She had given them, in turn, to the resistance group from the *Sonderkommando*. The following prisoners were subsequently

---

[29] Ibid., vol. 26, cards 161-2, testimony of former prisoner Henryk Mandelbaum; Z. Lewental, p. 232.

[30] Filip Müller, *Sonderbehandlung* (Munich, 1979), p. 257.

[31] APMO. D-Au-I-1/102, Standortsonderbefehl Nr. 26/44 from October 12, 1944.

[32] APMO, Files of the Camp Resistance, vol. III, card 175.

arrested and condemned to death: Róża Robota, Ala Gartner, Regina Safirsztain and Ester Wajcblum. [33] They were hung at Auschwitz on January 6, 1945, on the grounds of the camp "extension" (*Erweiterung*). The executions took place in two parts. Two women were hung during a roll-call at which women prisoners from the night shift at the Union-Werke were present. The others were hung after the daytime work detail returned.

The camp resistance movement operated under exceptionally dangerous conditions, significantly more difficult than in freedom. Many of its members perished, but their heroic struggle was not in vain. Thanks to them, other prisoners were saved, and the "free world" learned still during the war about the tragedy taking place at KL Auschwitz.

---

[33] Michał Grynberg, *Żydzi w rejencji ciechanowskiej 1939-42* (Warszawa, 1984), pp. 126-27.

HENRYK ŚWIEBOCKI

ESCAPES FROM THE CAMP

1. Motives For Escaping

In a state of constant danger and uncertainty about their fate, prisoners sought salvation through escape. The desire to save one's life was accompanied by yearnings for freedom, family, friends and one's homeland. Sometimes escapes were an act of despair in the face of the threat of immediate death. In many cases, other factors played a role. Prisoners also escaped to tell the outside world the truth about Auschwitz as a place of death, to document the crimes being committed by the SS, to make contact with Polish underground groups and to supply them with important political or military information. Such escapes were often the result of an order given by the camp resistance organization. The desire to join the partisans and take part in the armed struggle against the enemy represented one of the most basic motivations for attempting an escape. Many escapees from KL Auschwitz were active in underground organizations, including those operating near the camp.

2. Factors Influencing Escapes (Difficulties, Acts of Repression, Possibilities)

To escape, however, presented enormous difficulties. The camp was well-guarded by the SS staff and protected by a special security system, which was constantly being improved. Beyond the fence, there was a strip of land that isolated the camp from the outside world and was constantly being patrolled. This so-called "interest area" of the Auschwitz concentration camp (*Interessengebiet des KL Auschwitz*) encompassed an area of around 40 km². This vast area was devoid of any local Polish population due to resettlements, which had left behind only a few skilled workers essential to the German economy, such as miners and railway workers. A "closed-off area" or *Sperrgebiet* had been established next to the camp, which could only be entered and left with a permit from the commandant of KL Auschwitz. Signs in this area bearing the inscription — "Forbidden area! Fire without warning!" — showed how dangerous it was to cross this terrain without permission. An SS "settlement" (*SS-Siedlung*) had also arisen near the camp, which housed the families of the SS staff at KL Auschwitz — who, of course, were hostile to the prisoners. The German settlers (*Volksdeutsche*) who had taken over Polish expellees' farms near the camp (but outside the camp's *Interessengebiet*) bore a similar attitude. [1]

Whenever an escape was reported, the SS men would immediately sound an alarm and organize a search. Motorized SS columns would join the pursuit, and hounds would be used for tracking the escapees. Telegrams were sent to the Gestapo outpost, the criminal police (*Kripo*), and the border police (*Greko*). The telegrams listed the personal data and camp numbers of the escapees, their date of escape, and sometimes even details about their method of escape. This heightened the vigilance of the German police, who would inspect the area more thoroughly than usual.

Other measures served to isolate the camp and the surrounding area from the outside world. SS sentries were posted at guard towers along the so-called *Grosse Postenkette* or "great *cordon*", running at a distance of between several hundred meters to several kilometers away from the fence to the camp. SS men would hold guard day and night on a rotating basis for three days, unless the escapee was caught earlier. Only then would the guards be called back from their posts along the *Postenkette*.

It was quite likely that an escapee would be caught, particularly since his appearance — with a shaved head and clothing from the camp — immediately gave him away. Jews and Gypsies were at the greatest risk because their swarthy complexion and features often stood out. The camp numbers tattooed on prisoners' left hands made it easier for the German police to identify escapees from Auschwitz. A lack of knowledge of the local terrain and an inability to understand Polish — the language of the only local population that might provide assistance — presented escapees with other, significant problems. Polish escapees had a better chance.

The prisoner who decided to attempt an escape realized that if he were caught, his fate was sealed. Most often, those who tried to escape received the death penalty. Before the prisoner perished (shot, hung or starved to death), he or she would also have to undergo a brutal interrogation by the camp Gestapo, which wanted to find out how the escape was conducted, who had assisted the prisoner, etc. Captured escapees were not the only ones to suffer repressive measures. Often, other prisoners also had to face the consequences. The camp authorities, in order to prevent escapes, frequently applied the principle of collective responsibility. This took different forms. It could take the form of an extended roll-call (the longest lasted 19 hours on July 6-7, 1940), accompanied by numerous chicaneries. Another repressive measure was to imprison selected prisoners from the escapee's work detail in the camp jail, submit them to interrogation, and then send them to the penal company, where their chances of survival were practically nil.

The most drastic form of collective punishment were cases in which ten to twenty prisoners were condemned to death. They were either executed or hung on the gallows. In 1941, the brutal principle of starving to death a group of ten

---

[1] Tadeusz Iwaszko, "Häftlingsfluchten aus dem Konzentrationslager Auschwitz", *Hefte von Auschwitz* 7 (1964), pp. 8-10; cf. Henryk Świebocki, "Przyobozowy ruch oporu w akcji niesienia pomocy więźniom KL Auschwitz", *Zeszyty Oświęcimskie* 19 (1988), pp. 8-10.

or more prisoners from the same work detail or living quarters (block or barrack) was applied. The victims would be imprisoned inside the dark cell located in the basement of the Death Block, where, denied any food or water, they would perish within one to two weeks.

Prisoners were not the only ones to suffer such repressions. The Polish population near the camp was also punished for offering assistance — or being suspected of offering assistance — to escapees. Such individuals were imprisoned at the camp, sometimes with their families. There were cases in which an escapee's parents would be arrested and held at the camp. They would be held, it was announced, until their son or daughter was found. Punishment on the basis of collective responsibility was consistently applied only until the second half of 1943. Thereafter, it was used only sporadically. [2] At times, for prisoners who wanted to escape, it represented an impassable barrier.

Certain conditions were also conducive, however, to risking an escape. One significant factor in this regard was the fact that prisoners were employed outside the fence in the vast area adjoining the camp. Prisoners could more easily escape from their workplaces than from inside the camp itself. The SS guards overseeing the prisoners at work could not watch everybody at once. The prisoners thus had opportunities to use the area's topography to throw the SS men off guard and flee. As a result, most escapes occurred at work, outside the fence.

The attitude of the local population was also of great importance for the success of an escape. It should be stressed that area residents — at the risk of their freedom or very lives — often played a role in planning escapes. As early as July 1940, the Commandant at KL Auschwitz informed the Supreme Commander of the SS and Police in Wrocław (Breslau):

The local population is fanatically Polish and — as verified by our intelligence — is prepared to do anything against the hated SS camp staff. Every prisoner who manages to escape can count on every possible assistance, if he simply reaches the nearest Polish farm. [3]

Thanks to the attitude of the local population and the stance of the Polish underground near the camp, which concentrated most of its efforts on assisting prisoners (see p. 211), escapees from the camp were not left to their own devices and luck. Often, they received assistance on the way to freedom. Such assistance proved most effective when the escape had been pre-arranged and coordinated through secret channels with the resistance outside the camp. In terms of preparations, the underground would secretly deliver to the camp civilian clothes, wigs, identity papers and maps of the area with suggested escape routes. Representatives from one of the underground organizations would meet the escapees at a pre-designated location near the camp, provide

---

[2] Tadeusz Iwaszko, "Häftlingsfluchten", pp. 21-22, 53-56.
[3] APMO, D-AuI-1/13, documents related to the escape of Tadeusz Wiejowski, p. 25 (citation from a letter of Rudolf Höss from July 19, 1940, to Erich von dem Bach-Zelewski).

them with protection and hide them in a safe place until they could direct them to a partisan unit or help smuggle them into the General Government.

Changes and transformations in how the camp functioned were also not without significance in preparing escapes. In 1942, KL Auschwitz also became a center for the mass extermination of Jews, who were murdered in gas chambers. All possessions that they had brought with them were stored in warehouses inside the camp before being shipped to various agencies of the Third Reich. Prisoners who decided to escape were sometimes able to gain clandestine access to these effects and equip themselves with civilian clothes, shoes and other necessities. The money, gold and jewels that had been the property of the murdered Jews often "leaked" into the hands of the prisoners, who were sometimes able to buy off several SS men and gain their assistance in escaping. This was accompanied, however, with a grave risk — the threat of betrayal or a setup, simply aimed at tricking the prisoner out of the payment agreed-upon.

3. Routes and Methods of Escape. The Fate of Escapees

Prisoners used different methods for reaching freedom. On July 6, 1940, Tadeusz Wiejowski (Nr. 220), a Pole, fled the camp. Five Poles, civilian workers (*Zivilarbeiter*) for a German construction firm operating on the grounds of the recently-established camp, helped him. Wiejowski, attired in one of the Pole's workclothes, walked outside the camp with them. The workers gave him food and money and shipped him away from the area of the camp on a freight train. This was the first escape in the history of KL Auschwitz. Two days later, the Polish workers were arrested and condemned to death after a brutal interrogation. Their sentence was later reduced to flogging and imprisonment at the camp. Only one of them, Bolesław Bicz, survived the camp, but he died shortly after the war. [4]

Other prisoners followed Wiejowski's example. They displayed a great deal of flair and ingenuity. They fled alone or in groups. Many escapes were spontaneous, carried out on the spot; others were scrupulously planned in advance. Planned escapes had the greater chance of success.

Prisoners repeatedly used SS uniforms in their quest for freedom. Such was the case with the daring escape of four Poles working at the *Hauptwirtschafts-lager* (HWL), the food warehouses for SS men located near the main camp. Two prisoners employed at the HWL — Kazimierz Piechowski (Nr. 918) and Stanisław Gustaw Jaster (Nr. 6438) — escaped, along with Józef Lempart (Nr. 4319) and Eugeniusz Bendera (Nr. 8502), who worked in the garage of the warehouses. On the afternoon of Saturday, June 20, 1942, they slipped through a passageway to the cellars of the locked *Hauptwirschaftslager*, where an SS man was standing guard. From there, they went through a boiler room to a warehouse, using keys that they had duplicated in advance. They broke into

---

[4] Ibid., pp. 5-8, 22-23; APMO, Höss Trial, vol. 3, cards 32-35, account of former prisoner Bolesław Bicz; Danuta Czech, *Kalendarz wydarzeń w KL Auschwitz* (Oświęcim, 1992), pp. 19-20, 24, 32, 34.

a warehouse containing clothing and uniforms for the SS, as well as sidearms and ammunition. They put on SS uniforms and armed themselves. They left the HWL in a car (Steyer Model 220) that they had stolen from the nearby garages. After they made it through the SS checkpoint, they happily left the area of the camp and drove to the General Government. One of the escapees, Jaster, brought with him a report that Witold Pilecki had compiled at the camp, which he was to give to the commanders of the Home Army (AK). We can assume that he completed his assignment. Jaster, who subsequently served in the ranks of the Home Army, perished under tragic circumstances in Warsaw a year later. The remaining escapees survived the war. [5]

The Pole Jerzy Bielecki (Nr. 243) was also able to escape from the camp disguised as an SS man, along with a Jewish woman, Cyla Cybulska (known at the camp as Cyla Stawiska, Nr. 29588). Bielecki got ahold of a uniform through Tadeusz Srogi, prisoner Nr. 178, employed in the SS clothing warehouse (*SS-Bekleidungskammer*). Srogi also helped him obtain an SS identity card. On July 21, 1944, Bielecki — disguised as an SS man — appeared at the staff building (*Stabsgebäude*) where Cybulska was employed. In a conversation with a female SS overseer, he acted like an official of the camp Gestapo. He demanded that she present prisoner Nr. 29588 for interrogation. Without a second thought, the overseer followed his orders. Then Bielecki escorted Cybulska through the *Sperrgebiet* surrounding the camp. At the SS checkpoint, he used his fake identity card. After ten days of marching, coming out only at night, the pair reached and successfully crossed the border to the General Government. Both escapees remained there. The Czerniakows, a Polish family in the village of Przemęczany (near Racławice), hid Cybulska. Bielecki joined a partisan unit of the Home Army. Both survived the war. After the war, the Yad Vashem Institute in Israel honored Jerzy Bielecki with the Medal for the Righteous Among Nations, given to those who assisted Jews during the Holocaust. [6]

The escape attempt of Edward Galiński (Nr. 531), a Pole, and Mala Zimetbaum (Nr. 19880), a Jewish woman shipped to KL Auschwitz from the Malines camp in Belgium, followed a similar pattern. Unfortunately, their attempt did not succeed. They had carefully planned the escape. Galiński had taken care of the uniform, which he had bought from an SS man. Zimetbaum, employed by a female SS overseer as a messenger — which allowed her access to the SS guardhouse (*SS-Blockführerstube*) — had secured identification forms.

---

[5] APMO, IZ-8/3, Documents from the Gestapo, pp. 67, 67a (telegrams regarding the escape of K. Piechowski, S.G. Jaster, J. Lempart, and E. Bendera); APMO, Collection of Testimonies, vol. 4, cards 572-77; vol. 27, cards 66-70; vol. 67, cards 169-73, accounts of former prisoners: Józef Lempart, Eugeniusz Bendera, Kazimierz Piechowski; Józef Garliński *Fighting Auschwitz* (London, 1975), pp. 102-103, 272-273; cf Jerzy Ambroziewicz, "Zdrajca czy bohater", *Za wolność i Lud* 22 (1971), p. 10.

[6] APMO, IZ-8/4a, Documents of the Łódź Gestapo, pp. 67-8 (telegrams regarding the escape of C. Stawiska and J. Bielecki); APMO, Collection of Testimonies, vol. 16, cards 57, 61; vol. 104, cards 104-8; vol. 52, cards 126-28; accounts of former prisoners Jerzy Bielecki, Cyla Zacharowicz--Cybulska, and Tadeusz Srogi; Jerzy Bielecki, *Kto ratuje jedno życie... Pamiętnik z Oświęcimia* (Warszawa, 1990), pp. 203-9, 211-14, 216-18, 220-2, 231-2, 235-8, 240-318.

On June 24, 1944, Galiński, wearing the SS uniform, escorted Zimetbaum through the *Sperrgebiet* surrounding the camp. The fake identification sufficed to get them through the SS guardpost at the fence. Within two weeks, however, a German border patrol caught the escapees in the Beskid Żywiecki Mountains. They were returned to the camp, interrogated and condemned to death. They most likely perished in September 1944. [7]

The Polish prisoners Antoni Wykręt (Nr. 613) and Henryk Kwiatkowski (Nr. 3002) also used SS uniforms in their escape on September 9, 1944. They drove out of the camp with three other colleagues, also Poles: Stanisław Furdyna (Nr. 193), Stanisław Maliński (Nr. 69) and Stanisław Zakrzewski (Nr. 118410). A similar escape took place on September 28, 1944. Leonard Zawadzki (Nr. 13390) and Alfons Szumański (Nr. 23483), who spoke excellent German, dressed up like SS men and fled. They brought with them four other Poles: Jan Prejzner (Nr. 14046), Tadeusz Donimirski (Nr. 2009), Wacław Maliszewski (Nr. 59195) and Tadeusz Żaboklicki (Nr. 21668).

In both cases, the prisoners had made thorough preparations before fleeing. Thanks to prisoner-colleagues employed in the SS warehouses and the camp printing office, they had been able to obtain SS uniforms and identification forms. They had managed to arrange all the details related to their escapes through messages smuggled out of the camp by Zofia Zdrowak, a secret contact between the Home Army and the prisoners. They had coordinated their escape with the commander of the local AK partisan unit ("Sosienki"), Jan Wawrzyczek, including how to meet up with representatives of his organization. After their successful escape, all the Poles listed above joined the partisans; they strengthened the ranks of the "Sosienki" unit, operating next to the camp, and the AK unit "Garbnik" in Beskid Żywiecki. In 1944, more than 20 fugitives from KL Auschwitz were fighting in the two units. [8]

Escapees who joined underground units outside the camp often distinguished themselves with their bravura. Dressed in their SS uniforms, two of the fugitives mentioned above, Stanisław Furdyna and Antoni Wykręt, stopped a horse-drawn cart carrying two prisoners and a three-man escort near the camp. Acting like officials of the camp Gestapo, they thoroughly searched the cart and checked the papers of one SS man. At the end, they announced that they were taking over the prisoners in the name of the Gestapo. This was how the Polish prisoners Stanisław Zyguła (Nr. 682) and Marian Szayer (Nr. 17036) were liberated from the camp. They, in turn, joined the "Sosienki" unit. [9]

---

[7] APMO, IZ-8/4a, Documents from the Łódź Gestapo, pp. 20-23; IZ-8/2, p. 172 (telegrams regarding the escape and capture of M. Zimetbaum and E. Galiński); Wiesław Kielar, "Edek i Mala", *Zeszyty Oświęcimskie* 5 (1961), pp. 109-19; Tomasz Sobański, *Fluchtwege aus Auschwitz* (Warszawa, 1980), pp. 65-76; D. Czech, pp. 694, 760.

[8] APMO, Collection of Testimonies, vol. 4, cards 504-6; vol. 65, cards 58-60; vol. 12, cards 175-8; vol. 16, cards 70-71; vol. 52, card 125; vol. 11, cards 12-13, accounts of former prisoners: Stanisław Maliński and Stanisław Zakrzewski, Henryk Kwiatkowski, Jan Prejzner, Wacław Maliszewski, Tadeusz Srogi and Zofia Zdrowak; H. Świebocki, "Przyobozowy ruch oporu", pp. 99-100, 113.

[9] APMO, Collection of Testimonies, vol. 4, cards 442-4, account of former prisoner Stanisław Zyguła; H. Świebocki, "Przyobozowy ruch oporu", pp. 100-102.

Sometimes escapes took place with the assistance of SS men. Siegfried (Vitezslav) Lederer, a Jew deported to the camp from the Theresienstadt ghetto, took this path to freedom. SS man Viktor Pestek, a *Volksdeutscher* from Romania — and, in the prisoners' opinion, a decent man — helped him escape. On April 5, 1944, Lederer, disguised as an SS man and accompanied by Pestek, made it out of KL Auschwitz II-Birkenau. The two then traveled to Prague by train, successfully passing through the border control. Lederer went to the Theresienstadt ghetto to inform its Council of Elders about the fate of the Jews at KL Auschwitz. He subsequently joined the Czech resistance and survived the war. Pestek, however, met with a tragic end. The SS captured him when he returned to KL Auschwitz to organize yet another escape. After a brutal interrogation, he was executed on October 8, 1944. [10]

Escapes organized with the assistance of SS men, however, brought with them enormous risks. They could end in betrayal or turn out to be set-ups. For example, two Jewish prisoners — Daniel Obstbaum, active in the *Sonderkommando* conspiracy at KL Birkenau, and Fero Langer — were among those who fell victim to the provocation of an SS man named Dobrovolny, a *Volksdeutscher* from Slovakia. In 1944 — the exact date cannot be established — they were led several kilometers away from the camp and shot. [11]

An attempted escape by five members of the camp resistance movement also ended in tragedy: an Austrian, Ernst Burger (Nr. 23850) and four Poles — Czesław Duzel (Nr. 3702), Piotr Piąty (Nr. 130380), Władysław Raynoch (Nr. 60746) and Bernard Świerczyna (Nr. 1393). They wanted to coordinate and enhance the cooperation between the camp conspiracy and the Polish resistance movement. The escape was scheduled for October 27, 1944. According to the plan, the two SS men whom they had bribed — one named Frank, who had been cooperating with the underground inside and outside the camp for a period of time, and a second, named Johann Roth — were to bring the prisoners out of the camp in a truck carrying dirty clothes to the laundry in Bielsko. On the way to Bielsko, the truck was supposed to stop in the forest outside the village of Łęki, where members of the Polish underground were to meet the escapees. The SS man Roth, however, had informed the camp Gestapo about the plan, and they had made the necessary preparations. On October 27, the truck did bring the prisoners outside the camp gate, but it stopped near the checkpoint and a group of armed SS men jumped in. The truck returned to the main camp and stopped outside Block 11. The prisoners hiding in the truck were led out. All of them succeeded, however, in taking poison. Raynoch and Duzel died, but the other three were saved and

[10] APMO, IZ-8/4, Documents form the Łódź Gestapo, pp. 61-3, telegram regarding the escape of S. Lederer; Hermann Langbein, *Menschen in Auschwitz* (Frankfurt a. M., Berlin, Vienna, 1980), pp. 497-500; Erich Kulka, "Escapes of Jewish Prisoners from Auschwitz-Birkenau and Their Attempts to Stop the Mass Extermination", in *The Nazi Concentration Camps. Proceedings of the Fourth Yad Vashem International Historical Conference (Jerusalem, January 1980)* (Jerusalem, 1984), pp. 406-7; H. G. Adler, *Theresienstadt 1941-1945. Das Antlitz einer Zwangsgemeinschaft — Geschichte, Soziologie, Psychologie* (Tübingen, 1955), p. 152.

[11] Filip Müller, *Sonderbehandlung. Drei Jahre in den Krematorien und Gaskammern von Auschwitz* (Munich, 1979), pp. 88-9; E. Kulka, pp. 405-6; APMO, Collection of Testimonies, vol. 114, cards 23, account of former prisoner Alter Fajnzylberg.

imprisoned in the bunkers of Block 11. Two other prisoners, who had helped organize the escape, were also imprisoned there. Both were Austrians, members of the international resistance group, *Kampfgruppe Auschwitz*: Rudolf Friemel (Nr. 25173) and Ludwig Vesely (Nr. 38169). After being interrogated, all five of them (Burger, Piąty, Świerczyna, Friemel, Vesely) were hung on December 30, 1944. [12]

Quite often, prisoners planning an escape would use hiding places or "bunkers" that they had prepared in advance near their worksites outside the camp fence. Fellow prisoners would often assist such escapees by concealing their hiding places and by spreading shag tabacco or pouring turpentine nearby to prevent them from being scented by the SS men's dogs during the pursuit. The escapees would hide in their place of concealment for three days, until the SS guards were withdrawn from the *Große Postenkette*. At that point, they would leave their hiding place and continue fleeing. Two Jewish members of the underground organization *Kampfgruppe Auschwitz* escaped in mid-June 1944 by using such a ploy: Alfred Klahr (registered at the camp as Ludwig Lokmanis, Nr. 58933) from Austria and Stefan Bratkowski (Nr. 64783) from Poland. At the beginning of their escape, the goal of which was to establish contacts with Polish communists (*Polska Partia Robotnicza*, PPR) and the Red Army, they hid on the grounds of the Deutsche Ausrüstungswerke (DAW), an SS armaments plant near the main camp. With the assistance of the Polish underground outside the camp, the fugitives made it to Warsaw. Klahr and Bratkowski would not survive the war, however. Both perished in Warsaw; Bratkowski fell while fighting in the Warsaw Uprising. [13]

Prisoners escaped from KL Auschwitz II-Birkenau using the same method. In mid-July 1944, four Poles escaped from Birkenau after hiding in a bunker dug in Section BIII of the camp ("Mexico" in camp jargon). Once the escapees — Kazimierz Andrysik (Nr. 89), Zdzisław Michalak (Nr. 180), Ryszard Kordek (Nr. 10291) and Józef Papuga (Nr. 12049) — made it outside the camp, they met up with their contact person (Sylwester Pawela from Chełmek), who led them to the tugboat "Piast", moored on the Vistula in Gromiec, near Oświęcim. Captain Stanisław Szydłowski and his Polish crew hid the fugitives on board and brought them through a checkpoint on the border between the Third Reich and the General Government to the port of Dąbie, near Cracow. The fugitives changed boats to a small passenger ship, which took them to Nowy Korczyn. From there, they reached a Home Army unit, which they joined, in order to fight the occupier in the Kielce, Miechów and Jędrzejów regions. [14]

---

[12] T. Sobański, pp. 208-213; D. Czech, pp. 795, 828; H. Świebocki, "Przyobozowy ruch oporu", pp. 110-11.

[13] APMO IZ-8/4a, Documents of the Łódź Gestapo, pp. 5-6 (telegram regarding the escape of L. Lokmanis and S. Bratkowski); T. Iwaszko, "Häftlingsfluchten", p. 33.

[14] APMO IZ-8/4a, Documents from the Łódź Gestapo, pp. 58-9 (Telegram regarding the escape of R. Kordek and Z. Michalak); APMO, Collection of Testimonies, vol. 67, cards 73-4; vol. 85, cards 120-21; vol. 86, cards 28-9, 31-4; vol. 89, cards 11-12, accounts of former prisoners Józef Papuga, Sylwester Pawela, Józef Nosek, Stanisław Sosin; Ryszard Kordek, "Powrotna droga", in *Ucieczki ku wolności. Wspomnienia Polaków z lat wojny i okupacji* (Poznań, 1980), pp. 376-419; T. Sobański, pp. 102-112.

In the night of July 28, 1942, three women prisoners escaped from the so-called "Penal Camp" at Budy through its barbed-wire fence: Alicja Zarytkiewicz (Nr. 7585), a Pole, and two women listed in camp documents as Germans — Pauline Górski and Erika Krause (Nr. 858). The women used the absence of an SS sentry to throw a blanket over the fence and climb over it to freedom. At the very moment when they climbed over, the sky darkened and the moon clouded over. This greatly facilitated their escape. The women made it to the outskirts of the forest and then split up. Alicja Zarytkiewicz successfully made it to Cracow, where she made contact with an underground organization. She later fought in a partisan unit. Erika Krause was caught and re-imprisoned at KL Auschwitz. In August 1944, she was transferred to KL Ravensbruck. [15] There is no information available regarding the third woman.

Other escapes from the penal camp at Budy took place. The largest was on the night of December 29-30, 1942, when nine Russian women fled: Paraska Sawenko, Wassa Loczwinenko, Fydosyja Cinhankowa, Dora Gawreluk, Wera Gunskaj, Taissa Panowa, Nadja Netrebko, Wira Bowscha and Lena Awtamienko. We do not have any further information regarding the method of escape or the fate of these women. This is also the case for Weronika Woloncewicz, a Polish Gypsy, who fled the Gypsy camp at Birkenau on February 6, 1944. [16]

Prisoners also tried in some cases to tunnel their way outside the camp to freedom. Such an attempt took place during the summer of 1944 at the Eintrachthütte sub-camp in Świętochłowice. A group of prisoners dug a tunnel between one of the barracks still under costruction and a ditch outside the camp, near the guard tower. The ditch was used by the SS men for anti-aircraft cover. It took two months to burrow through. On the night of July 3, the tunnel finally reached the ditch and the prisoners begen to flee in groups of three to the outside. When the third group left the tunnel, an SS man in the guard tower sounded an alarm. The dark of the night aided the prisoners' escape. The following prisoners succeeded in escaping: Władisław Rutecki (Nr. 175641), a Pole; Leib Zizmemski (Nr. 98143), a Polish Jew; and seven Russians — Luka Didenko (Nr. 175682), Fedor Ryschynowytsch (Nr. 175681), Jakub Wischniewskyj (Nr. 125038), Ivan Wasiukow (Nr. 175728), Sergiej Michalewskij (Nr. 175769), Nikola Titow (Nr. 175696) and Nikolaj Iwanenko (Nr. 129985). After the escape, Rutecki and Ryshinovitch joined the Peasent Battalions near Ryczów, while Didenko joined the Home Army in the Pilica region. Ziziemski was captured on July 13, 1944, near Bielsko and returned to KL Auschwitz. He survived both the camp and the war. [17]

---

[15] APMO IZ-8/3, Documents from the Łódź Gestapo, pp. 84-84a (Telegram regarding the escape of A. Zarytkiewicz, P. Górski and E. Krause); APMO, Collection of Testimonies, vol. 11, cards 26-28, account of former prisoner Alicja Zarytkiewicz; Tadeusz Iwaszko, "Fluchten weiblicher Häftlinge aus dem KL Auschwitz", *Hefte von Auschwitz* 18 (1990), pp. 159-160.

[16] APMO, IZ/10, nr. inw. 155988, Documents from the Gestapo Sieradz, p. 4 (letter from the Gestapo Łódź from January 5, 1943, informing about the escape of the Russian women mentioned in the text); APMO, IZ-8/4, Documents from the Łódź Gestapo, p. 19 (telegram regarding the escape of W. Woloncewicz).

[17] APMO, D-AU-1, Meldeblatt, D-AuI-13, pp. 334-6 (circular from the Gestapo Breslau [Wrocław] from July 15, 1944, containing the names of the escapees mentioned in the text); Franciszek Piper, "Das Nebenlager 'Eintrachthütte', *Hefte von Auschwitz* 17 (1985), pp. 133-137; Ber Mark *The Scrolls of Auschwitz* (Tel Aviv, 1985), p. 110.

A similar attempt by around 30 prisoners at the Neu-Dachs sub-camp in Jaworzno during the second half of 1943 had a quite different outcome. A kapo noticed that someone had been tunneling from one of the barracks to the neighboring woods. He immediately alerted the SS. As a result, the authorities at the sub-camp arrested several dozen prisoners, some of whom were transferred to the punishment company at Birkenau. The rest were imprisoned in the bunkers of Block 11 at the main camp, KL Auschwitz I. Nineteen prisoners — eleven Poles and eight Czechs — were selected from among those imprisoned in the bunkers and condemned to death. On December 6, 1943, they were hung on the grounds of the Neu-Dachs sub-camp.[18]

Prisoners also tried to escape from the grounds of the German industrial facilities where they worked. Numerous attempts were made from the grounds of Auschwitz III-Monowitz (Monowice) in Dwory, where prisoners worked in the chemical plants of IG Farbenindustrie. In September 1944, two Jews fled from the plant: Max Drimmer (Nr. 69932) and Hermann Scheingesicht. A Polish civilian employed at the plant, Józef Wrona from Nowa Wieś near Oświęcim, helped them. On September 20, 1944, during the dinner break, he concealed them in one of the warehouses at the chemical plant in a hiding place that he had prepared beneath some fiberglass. The following evening, Wrona returned to the warehouse, led them out from under the fiberglass, gave them civilian clothes, and escorted them out of the plant. He then hid them at his home in Nowa Wieś. They remained there until November 15, 1944. By that time, Wrona, sought by the Gestapo himself, had to go into hiding, but he was able to find the two Jews a new hiding place at a friend's house near Rybnik. Drimmer and Scheingesicht stayed there until liberation. For his assistance to Jews, including the escapes mentioned above, Wrona was honored in 1990 with Yad Vashem's Medal for the Righteous Among Nations.[19]

Attempts at group escapes were also made during rebellions, which occurred several times in the history of KL Auschwitz. The mutiny of the Poles in the penal company on June 10, 1942, and the rebellion of the Jews in the *Sonderkommando* on October 7, 1944 — both at KL Birkenau — have been discussed above (see p. 222). Another rebellion and group-escape attempt took place on November 6, 1942. Several dozen Soviet POWs at Birkenau organized the action. The camp authorities had assigned them to find a prisoner whose absence had been noticed during the roll-call. They searched the grounds of Section BII, still under construction. Taking advantage of the approaching dusk and rising fog, the Soviets rushed in the direction of the SS sentries and — after making it past them — fled into the underbrush nearby. They continued to run. During the pursuit organized by the SS, many of them were captured or shot. Several were able, however, to elude their pursuers, including

---

[18] Franciszek Piper, "Das Nebenlager 'Neu-Dachs'", *Hefte von Auschwitz* 12 (1970), pp. 100-101; APMO, D-AuI-3. Bunker Register, Part II, pp. 54-56 (entries for the deaths of the nineteen prisoners).

[19] APMO, Collection of Testimonies, vol. 125, cards 37-49; account by Józef Wrona and other attached documents, including a photocopy of his Diploma of Honor from Yad Vashem, letters written by Max Drimmer and Hermann Shine (Scheingesicht). HPK, vol 7, card 572.

Andrei Aleksandrovich Pogorzhev, Wiktor Kuźniecow, and Paweł Stienkin. Two weeks later, Pogorzhev and Kuzhnietsov were captured by regular German police near Rybnik, but were not identified as escapees from KL Auschwitz. They were subsequently imprisoned at the Lamsdorf prisoner of war camp in Łambinowice. Sitenkin encountered a similar fate; he was imprisoned at a second POW camp in Heydebreck (Kędzierzyn). He escaped from this camp as well, however, and returned to the Red Army after crossing the Soviet lines in the East. He later took part in the conquest of Berlin. [20]

4. Escapes Resulting in the Disclosure of Information About the SS's Crimes

Of particular importance were escapes that resulted in former prisoners disclosing information about the camp and the extent of Nazi crimes. Witold Pilecki's report, handed over to the Home Army command by Stanisław Gustaw Jaster in 1942, has already been mentioned, as have Siegfried Lederer's efforts to inform the Council of Elders at Theresienstadt about the fate of Jews at KL Auschwitz. On June 28, 1944, after a day of hiding in a concrete cellar at the plant, two Polish prisoners — Konstanty Jagiełło (Nr. 4507) and Tomasz Sobański (Nr. 13609) — escaped from the premises of the Deutsche Ausrüstungswerke (DAW). They met up with representatives of the local PPS organization, who dispatched them to Cracow. The escapees gave the Cracow organization of the PPS various materials that they had brought with them from the camp, including maps, sketches, situation reports on the location of SS forces and other materials. In keeping with their arrangements before the escape, they then joined the underground PPS unit operating near the camp to help assist prisoners. On October 27, 1944, during one such action — a rendezvous with escaped prisoners from KL Auschwitz — Konstanty Jagiełło fell in battle with the SS. [21]

In several cases, escapees wrote reports or personal accounts about the camp. Several were even published during the war. In November 1944, a brochure, "German Extermination Camps — Auschwitz and Birkenau", was published in Washington, D.C. It contained reports written by escapees from KL Auschwitz: Jerzy Tabeau (aka Jerzy Wesołowski, Nr. 27273), a Pole; Alfred Wetzler (Nr. 29162), Rudolf Vrba (in the camp Walter Rosenberg, Nr. 44070), and Arnošt Rosin (Nr. 29858) — Slovakian Jews; and Czesław Mordowicz (Nr. 84216), a Polish Jew.

Tabeau escaped in an extraordinary manner from Section BIIe (the Gypsy camp) at KL Birkenau, along with a second Pole, Roman Cieliczko (Nr. 27089). On the evening of November 19, 1943, Tabeau and Cieliczko caused a short-circuit in the camp fence, which extinguished the floodlights. Protected by rubber gloves, they used pliers to cut the barbed-wire fence and made it

---

[20] APMO, Collection of Testimonies, vol. 29, cards 11-14, letter dated May 17, 1962, from former prisoner Andrei Alexandrowich Pogorzhev; Michail Stiepanowicz Zaboczen, "Antifashistkoe podpol'e Osvyenchima", *Novaya i novejshaya istorija* 3 (1965), p. 112 "Reminiscences of Pery Broad" in *KL Auschwitz seen by the SS* (Oświęcim, 1972), p. 169; cf. T. Sobański, pp. 148-151.

[21] APMO IZ-8/4a, Documents from the Łódź Gestapo, pp. 25-6 (Telegram about the escape of K. Jagiełło and T. Sobański); T. Sobański, pp. 79-86, 211-214; D. Czech, p. 795.

outside. The shocked and disoriented SS men in the guard towers began shooting. Under the cover of darkness, the escapees were able to make it outside the area of the camp. After their escape, they took part in the struggle against the occupier. Cieliczko joined the partisans and later fell during one of their operations. Tabeau linked up with the underground PPS. Until the occupation was over, he fought in socialist partisan units, especially in the area of KL Auschwitz. At the end of 1943 or beginning of 1944, he assembled in Cracow a report about the camp, which the Polish resistance movement delivered through secret channels to the West. It eventually ended up in the brochure published in Washington, mentioned above. [22]

Rudolf Vrba (Walter Rosenberg) and Alfred Wetzler escaped from KL Birkenau. On April 7, 1944, they hid inside a bunker that they had prepared on the grounds of "Mexico". Three days later, they left. Moving south, they were able to make it to Slovakia with the assistance of the Polish population along the way. In the town of Żylina, they secretly met with representatives of the Slovakian Jewish Council (*Judenrat*). They spent two days reporting to the *Judenrat* about the camp. From their accounts, a larger report was assembled and smuggled to the West.

Vrba and Wetzler remained in Slovakia after their escape, where they joined the resistance movement. Vrba, who joined the partisans and fought in the mountains of Western Slovakia, was decorated for bravery. Wetzler joined the partisans as well. [23]

Arnošt Rosin and Czesław Mordowicz fled from KL Birkenau at the end of May 1944. They used the same method as Vrba and Wetzler, but hid in a different location — in a bunker that they had dug on the grounds of the gravel pit outside the camp's fence. After they reached Slovakia, the two escapees gave the Slovakian *Judenrat* an account about KL Auschwitz at a secret meeting in the town of Liptowsky Svaty Mikulaš. The information was subsequently sent to the West in a form of a written report. Although both escapees survived the war, Czesław Mordowicz would suffer a great deal more before liberation. He was arrested in the fall of 1944 in Bratislava and imprisoned anew at KL Auschwitz. Fortunately, the SS men failed to recognize him, and this saved his life. He was later transferred to another camp, from which he was liberated. [24]

A pamphlet was published in the second half of 1944 in England under the title, *The Camp at Drancy and the Extermination Camps in Poland*. Its author

[22] APMO IZ-8/3a, Documents from the Łódź Gestapo, pp. 113 (telegram regarding the escape of J. Wesołowski and R. Cieliczko); APMO, Collection of Testimonies, vol. 98, cards 12-31; account of former prisoner Jerzy Tabeau; Henryk Świebocki, "Auschwitz — czy w czasie wojny świat znał prawdę o obozie?" *Zeszyty Oświęcimskie* 4 (Special edition, 1992), pp. 12-17, 42; Martin Gilbert, *Auschwitz und die Allierten* (Munich, 1982), pp. 384-86.

[23] APMO IZ-8/4, Documents from the Łódź Gestapo, pp. 65-7 (telegram regarding the escape of W. Rosenberg and A. Wetzler); APMO, Collection of Testimonies, vol. 40, cards 35-42; account of former prisoner Alfred Wetzler; Rudolf Vrba, Alan Bestic, *Ich kann nicht vergeben* (Munich, 1964), pp. 225-7, 261-85, 290, 298-9; H. Świebocki, "Auschwitz", pp. 21-31 39-42.

[24] APMO IZ-8/4, Documents from the Łódź Gestapo, pp. 118-19 (telegram regarding the escape of Cz. Mordowicz and A. Rosin); APMO, Collection of Testimonies, vol. 50, cards 103, 107-11; account of former prisoner Czesław Mordowicz; H. Świebocki, "Auschwitz", pp. 33-9, 42; M. Gilbert, pp. 253, 272, 384-6.

was an anonymous Jew, who had escaped from the Neu-Dachs sub-camp in Jaworzno. Most likely, the escape had taken place on September 7, 1943, from the grounds of a coal mine employing prisoners from Auschwitz.[25]

Although they were not published during the war, the reports of two Polish escapees — Witold Pilecki, mentioned above, and Stanisław Chybiński (Nr. 6810) — also deserve to be mentioned. Pilecki escaped on April 27, 1943, with two other Poles, Jan Redzej (registered at the camp as Jan Retko, Nr. 5430) and Edward Ciesielski (Nr. 12969). They escaped at around two in the morning while working in the building that housed the camp's bakery, situated about two kilometers away from KL Auschwitz I. The prisoners cut the wire to the alarm system, unlocked the bolted doors with a forged key, unscrewed the iron bar that reinforced the door and made it outside the bakery. They then barricaded the doors from the outside to prevent the SS guards from leaving the bakery, whose windows were reinforced by grates. They successfully fled the area of the camp and reached the General Government. They contacted the Polish underground (AK) and joined its ranks to fight against the occupier. Pilecki assembled reports about KL Auschwitz, which he sent to the Home Army's leadership. The three escapees later took part in the Warsaw Uprising in 1944. Redzej fell during the battle. Ciesielski and Pilecki survived the war. The Polish communist authorities, however, would later condemn Pilecki to death. He was executed in 1948.[26]

The second author mentioned above, Stanisław Chybiński, fled on May 20, 1943, with two other Poles assigned to do surveying work around the camp. Following his escape, in the summer of 1943, he composed a report about the camp entitled "Scenes from Auschwitz" (*Obrazki Auschwitzu*) for the Polish underground. Chybiński then joined the AK unit operating immediately outside the camp and fought. He survived the war.[27]

5. Escapes During the Camp's Evacuation

A separate topic are the escapes that occurred during the camp's liquidation and evacuation in January 1945. Tens of thousands of prisoners were evacuated from Auschwitz and its sub-camps. Escorted by SS men, the prisoners walked in columns to the west, in the direction of Wodzisław and Gliwice. While marching through villages, settlements, and towns, prisoners tried to escape. They would decide to make an attempt when they approached some underbrush, the woods, or uneven terrain. They fled from where the columns halted, having been revived from a longer or shorter rest. They were often downed by bullets from the SS escort. Frequently, they fell into the

---

[25] Polish Institute and General Sikorski Museum in London, Archives, A. 12 73/5, copy of the pamphlet, *The Camp at Drancy and the Extermination Camps in Poland*.

[26] APMO, D-AuI-1, Telegrams Regarding the Escapes of Prisoners, vol. 1, cards 116-18 (regarding the escapes of T. Serafiński, J. Retko, and E. Ciesielski); APMO, Collection of Reminiscences, vol. 130, cards 3-14 and vol. 183, cards 4-71 (report by W. Pilecki prepared after his escape); J. Garliński, pp. 166-174, 267-268.

[27] T. Iwaszko, "Häftlingsfluchten", pp. 20-21; H. Świebocki "Przyobozowy ruch oporu", pp. 53-4.

hands of the German police and were executed. Many, however, succeeded in escaping and were taken in by the Polish population, who hid them in their houses, shops, barns and piles of straw, where they remained until liberation.

6. Statistics on Escapes

Escapes represented a type of prisoner resistance. Despite the extreme isolation of the camp and the close oversight of the SS, some were able to make it out. According to the author's calculations, from the establishment of KL Auschwitz until its liquidation and evacuation on January 18-19, 1945, 757 male and 45 female prisoners escaped — a total of 802 people. The largest group of escapees were Poles (396), followed by residents of the former USRR (179), Jews (115), Gypsies (38), Germans, Czechs, Austrians and Yugoslavs. The largest number of escapes occurred in the years 1943 (295) and 1944 (312).

The 802 escapees met with various fates. 144 successfully escaped and survived the war. 327 were caught during the attempt or after it had succeeded — sometimes months or even years after — and returned to the camp. This figure includes prisoners shot while attempting to flee. For 331 prisoners, there is no evidence that they were ever captured, but this does not prove that they had succeeded. Undoubtedly, many of them had failed.

The number cited above is a minimum and reflects only a portion of the prisoners who risked escapes. It does not include prisoners who tried to flee during rebellions (the Poles in the punishment company in 1942, Soviet POWs in 1942, and especially the Jews of the *Sonderkommando* in 1944), whose names have not been established. It also does not include the several hundred male and female prisoners who sought to escape or run away while being evacuated from the camp on foot in January 1945.

HENRYK ŚWIEBOCKI

DISCLOSURE AND DENUNCIATION OF SS CRIMES

1. Activities by the Polish Resistance Movement and the Polish Government in London to Disclose SS Crimes

The SS authorities did not succeed in keeping secret the crimes being committed at KL Auschwitz. The truth about the camp was disclosed still during the war. The Polish resistance movement — both in the area of the Auschwitz camp and at its headquarters in occupied Poland — provided an important service in this regard. Thanks to its organized network of secret contacts, it was able to receive information and documents from prisoners at the camp, including smuggled messages and reports from the camp underground. These materials disclosed the conditions prevailing at the camp, the death rate and exterminations. They represented a crucial, although not exclusive, source of knowledge about KL Auschwitz. The oral and written accounts of escaped prisoners (including Witold Pilecki, Stanisław Chybiński and Jerzy Tabeau — see p. 235) also provided an enormous amount of important information. The rare individuals who were released from the camp would sometimes reveal the truth in a way that preserved their complete anonymity. The Polish resistance movement also received intelligence reports about the camp — for example, from *Zivilarbeiter* (civilian laborers) who worked for private German companies near (or even inside) the camp and thus came into direct contact with prisoners.

The Polish underground publicized the information, documents and reports obtained by such methods throughout Polish society. They used such materials in publishing underground fliers, brochures and books. Three brochures, clandestinely printed in Warsaw in 1942, based on the accounts of prisoners released from the camp, are examplary of such publications: *Oświęcim. Pamiętnik więźnia* ("Auschwitz. A Prisoner's Memoir"), by the publicist and novelist Halina Krahelska; *W piekle* ("In Hell"), by the well-known Catholic writer Zofia Kossak, who described prisoners' daily life at Auschwitz and other camps; and *Obóz śmierci* ("Death Camp"), by the journalist Natalia Zarembina. The third publication became known outside Poland's borders. In 1943, it was reprinted in London in Polish; in 1944, it appeared in English translation in London and Washington, and was also published in Spanish in Mexico. In 1944, the brochure *W piekle* ("In Hell") was translated into English and published in London.[1] In 1944, the Polish resistance printed up a flier for the German population entitled *Die Zähne von Auschwitz* ("The Teeth of Auschwitz"). It explained how European Jews were being murdered in the gas chambers and how their gold teeth were being used to pay for the current needs of the Third Reich.[2]

The underground press in Poland published a large amount of news about the camp. *Biuletyn Informacyjny* ("Information Bulletin"), the press organ of ZWZ/AK published two long reports in 1940, four in 1941, four in 1942, three in 1943, and three in 1944. The newsletter of PPS-WRN, entitled *WRN*, contained four reports about the Auschwitz camp in 1940, two in 1942, seven in 1943, and one in 1944. *Wolność* ("Freedom"), WRN's local newsletter in Cracow, published nine extensive reports about the camp in 1943. The left-wing socialist *Barykada Wolności* ("Freedom's Barricade") reported on the camp, as did the peasant publications *Przez Walkę do Zwycięstwa* ("Through Struggle To Victory") and *Agencja Informacyjna — Wieś* ("Information Agency — Countryside"), which contained four reports on the camp in 1944. The press organ of the PPR, *Trybuna Wolności* ("Freedom Tribune") also reported on the camp. The first short story about KL Auschwitz, *"Biała Noc* ("White Night") by Juliusz Kydryński, appeared in January 1943 in the underground publication *Miesięcznik Literacki* ("Literary Monthly") in Cracow.[3]

The Polish resistance movement also sent information about the camp outside the borders of occupied Poland. The main recipient of this information was the Polish Government-in-Exile in London. By radio and by courier, the exile government received messages, communiqués and reports about the situation in Poland, including the terror and crimes of the occupier, and the situation at KL Auschwitz. The following sources of information from occupied Poland deserve to be mentioned: the monthly *Pro memoria o sytuacji w kraju* ("Pro Memoria About the Situation at Home"), the biweekly *Aneksy do raportów dotyczących terroru niemieckiego* ("Annexes to the Reports About the German Terror"), and the weekly *Przeglądy najważniejszych wydarzeń w kraju* ("Overview of the Most Important Events at Home"). All were sent to London by the exile government's underground representative in Poland, or "Delegatura" (*Delegatura RP na Kraj*). By sending such information to London, the Polish resistance sought not only to document the crimes being committed, but also to prompt the Allies and the entire civilized world to intervene on behalf of those who were being terrorized, enslaved, and killed.

---

[1] Natalia Zarembina, *Obóz śmierci* (n.d.); idem., *Obóz śmierci. Zbiór relacji z obozu w Oświęcimiu opublikowanych w kraju przez ruch oporu mas pracujących* (London, 1943); *The Camp of Death* (London, 1944); *Oświęcim — The Camp of Death. Underground Report.* (New York, 1944); *Oświęcim. Campo de la Muerte. Documentos Publicados par el Movimento Clandestino de Polonia* (Mexico, 1944); Władysław Bartoszewski, "Publikacje konspiracyjne o Oświęcimiu", *Więź* Nr. 1-3, 1985.

[2] Stanisław Kłodziński, "Z zagadnień gospodarczej eksploatacji zwłok ludzkich w Niemczech hitlerowskich", *Przegląd Lekarski — Oświęcim* (1964), p. 95.

[3] Krzysztof Dunin-Wąsowicz, *Resistance in the Nazi Concentration Camps 1933-1945* (Warszawa, 1982), p. 167.

The Government-in-Exile in London was motivated by similar considerations in its actions. Through press and information activity, as well as through diplomacy, they earnestly sought to reveal the truth — about Auschwitz and other camps and prisons, about the terror being unleashed by the occupier in Poland, and about the mass murder being committed aqainst Poles and Jews. On May 3, 1941, the Government-in-Exile addressed a note to the Allies and neutral states regarding the arrests being made in Poland, the mass executions, the deportations to Auschwitz and other camps and the conditions prevailing at these facilities. It described the violence that had been committed against the Jews during the first year-and-a-half of occupation. The note was accompanied by a series of attachments, including Attachment No. 168a, a three-page summary of testimonies and reports about the situation at Auschwitz until November 1940. In 1941, excerpts of the note and its attachments were published in London under the title, *The German Occupation of Poland. Extract of a Note Addressed to the Governments of the Allied and Neutral Powers on May 3, 1941.* [4] Attachment No. 168a, entitled "Oświęcim Concentration Camp", was published on November 15, 1941, in the *Polish Fortnightly Review*, the biweekly, English-language bulletin of the Polish Government-in--Exile's Information Ministry. One sentence was added to the original document: "During the winter months, the crematoria ovens have not sufficed for burning all the corpses." [5]

In January 1942, the Polish government published a "black book" of several hundred pages in London, entitled *The German New Order in Poland*. The book, which detailed Nazi policies in Poland between September 1939 and the end of June 1941, contained numerous documents and photographs. The publication not only dealt with the fate of the Poles under German occupation, but also devoted a large space to the fate of the Jews under the heading, "Persecution of the Jews and the Ghettoes". The black book also disclosed information about KL Auschwitz. [6] We should point out that as early as 1940, the Information Ministry of the Polish Government-in-Exile had overseen the publication of a brochure, *The Persecution of Jews in German-Occupied Poland*. The Poles had also been the initiators of the joint declaration of April 28, 1940, by the governments of Poland, Great Britain and France, denouncing Nazi atrocities in Poland. The declaration had also made reference to the brutal treatment of the Jewish population. [7]

On a number of occasions, the *Polish Fortnightly Review* devoted space to the subject of Auschwitz. On July 1, 1942, it reported on the mass murder of

---

[4] See Władysław Bartoszewski's introduction to "Raport komórki Więziennej Delegatury Rządu z 1944 r. o Pawiaku, Oświęcimiu, Majdanku i Ravensbrück", *Najnowsze Dzieje Polski. Materiały i studia z okresu II wojny światowej*, t. XII (Warszawa, 1968), p. 156; idem., "Po obu stronach muru", in *Ten jest z ojczyzny mojej. Polacy z pomocą Żydom 1939-1945* (Kraków, 1969), p. 26; Martin Gilbert, *Auschwitz und die Alliierten* (Munich, 1982), pp. 15-16.

[5] M. Gilbert, p. 403, fn. 5.

[6] *The German New Order in Poland*, published for the Polish Ministry of Information (London, n.d.), pp. 86-9 (information about the Auschwitz camp); W. Bartoszewski, "Po obu stronach...," p. 29.

[7] W. Bartoszewski, "Po obu stronach...," p. 28, 1003-4 (joint declaration of the governments of Poland, Great Britain and France).

Jews in Poland and the German occupier's repression of the Polish population. It provided general information about the camp — the conditions prevailing there, pharmacological experiments on prisoners, the establishment of the women's camp and the worsening conditions, suicides, the experimental use of Zyklon B on Soviet and Polish prisoners in September 1941, the gas chambers at Birkenau, and other methods for killing prisoners, as well at the high death rate. Two weeks later, on July 15, 1942, it provided detailed information about the crimes being committed against the Poles. The July 15 issue contained a map with the locations of 22 camps where Poles were being held. A section devoted to Auschwitz reported on the arrival of new transports at the camp, the high mortality rate among the prisoners and the exploitation of their labor for building a synthetic-gasoline factory. [8]

The *Polish Fortnightly Review* was not the only publication used by the exile government to inform the world about KL Auschwitz. The daily bulletin of the Polish Information Ministry, *Dziennik Polski*, also reported on the camp. After its merger in 1944 with *Dziennik Żołnierza*, formerly published in Scotland, *Dziennik Polski i Dziennik Żołnierza* continued to print articles on the subject. On June 9, 1944, based on reports from the Polish Telegraph Agency (*Polska Agencja Telegraficzna*), information appeared in the merged newspaper about the murder in the Auschwitz gas chambers of several thousand Czech Jews from the ghetto-camp at Theresienstadt. It reported that before they were exterminated, the Jews had been forced to write letters to relatives in Czechoslovakia about the "good working conditions in Poland". [9] The exile press's source of information was likely a telegram received by the Polish authorities in London on June 5, 1944. The message, transmitted by the *Delegatura's* radio station in occupied Poland, contained along with the information about the Jews from Theresienstadt the following appeal: "You should immediately warn the Jews in Theresienstadt by radio and with leaflets about these crimes, as well as the Int. R. Cross, under whose protection they should fall." [10]

A report dated March 25, 1944, compiled by the Polish prisoner, Józef Cyrankiewicz, and smuggled out of the camp by the Polish underground, was undoubtedly the basis for the June 5 telegram. Cyrankiewicz's report, entitled "Letters from the Beyond", contained extensive information about the fate of the Jews from Theresienstadt. The following is an excerpt:

In Czech territory, there is a special city for Jews, Theresienstadt, where Czech Jews are concentrated. .... The Germans, promising work under good conditions, tricked two transports of Czech families into leaving there; numbering 6,000, they resided last year in a special *Lager* near Oświęcim. They were dealt with in a suspiciously polite fashion. They were allowed to live at the camp with their families and were not

---

[8] M. Gilbert, pp. 51, 57, 58.

[9] Miroslav Kárný, "Ein Auschwitz-Bericht und das Schicksal des Theresienstädter Familienlagers", *Judaica Bohemiae* XXI/1 (1985), p. 12.

[10] Studium Polski Podziemnej w Londynie [Studies Center for the Polish Undergound in London], Akta MSW [Documents from the Ministry of Internal Affairs], file 26, p. 52, citation from Telegram Nr. 26 L. dz. K.3175/44.

ordered to work. .... This went on for a couple of months. Currently, more large transports are supposed to be arriving from Theresienstadt. In order to make room for the new guests, on orders from Berlin, all of the 3,800 people (1,800 women, 2,000 men) from the first transport, who had been at the camp for a couple months, were assembled. .... and packed into a gas chamber. Those who are still alive, the second transport (around 2,500), are not supposed to suspect what has happened with the first transport .... To mislead the remaining Jews in Theresienstadt and the International Red Cross, the favorite German trick of mailing letters was used. Only four days before they were gassed everyone was ordered to write letters to their loved ones — in Czech territory — with the news that they are doing well here. Everyone was ordered to date the letters March 25, while their authors were gassed already on March 15. These letters will remain in the *Politische Abteilung* until March 25, when they are supposed to be sent out to attract new victims and proof the fact that anyone who claims the people were gassed is a liar. [11]

On July 21, 1942, the Polish Government-in-Exile published a report on Nazi crimes in Poland. It told about the mass murder of "Polish citizens of the Jewish confession" in Lublin, Lwów, Stanisławów and at the camp in Chełmno, where "tens of thousands have been killed in gas chambers". It also contained information about KL Auschwitz — about the trial use of gas on Soviet POWs and Poles in September 1941 and the transports of women being brought from the Ravensbrück camp to Auschwitz. [12]

The Polish government in London was constantly providing the Allies with new evidence of Nazi crimes against the Polish and Jewish nations. At a press conference in London on July 9, 1942, the Polish government presented the English public with documents on the extermination of Jews that had been received from occupied Poland. On December 10, 1942, the Government-in-Exile's foreign minister, Edward Raczyński, presented a detailed note to the governments of the United Nations that described the enormity of the tragedy confronting the Jewish nation. He appealed to the governments of the United Nations to condemn and punish the guilty individuals and to find "effective means by which one can hope to prevent the Germans from continuing to apply methods of mass extermination". [13]

Raczyński's note resulted in a joint declaration by twelve governments, announced simultaneously in London, Moscow and Washington on December

---

[11] APMO, Files of the Camp Resistance, vol. II, card 68a, smuggled report from Józef Cyrankiewicz to Adam Rysiewicz, Secretary of OKR-PPS in Cracow.

To clarify the information contained in the report, the ghetto-camp at Theresienstadt was initially intended for Jews from the so-called German "protectorate" of Bohemia and Moravia; later, Jews from other European countries were sent there as well. On September 8, 1943, 5,006 Jews were transferred from Theresienstadt to KL Auschwitz II-Birkenau and housed in a separate camp — the so-called "family camp" — on the grounds of BIIb; on December 16 and 20, 1943, an additional 4,964 Jews arrived from Theresienstadt. On the night of March 8-9, 1944, the 3,791 Jews (men, women and children) brought from Theresienstadt in the transport on September 8, 1943 were murdered in the gas chambers of KL Auschwitz II-Birkenau. The letter-writing action most likely took place on March 5, 1943.

[12] M. Gilbert, p. 58. The information contained in the report about the transports of women from KL Ravensbrück was incorrect and unclear in parts.

[13] W. Bartoszewski, *Po obu stronach ...*, p. 29, 1007-11 (note from Minister E. Raczyński).

17, 1942. The twelve governments condemned the policy of exterminating Jews and declared that "those responsible for these crimes will not go unpunished" and demanded "the most rapid adoption of the necessary steps leading to the practical realization of this goal". [14]

The Polish National Council in London, the exile equivalent of the Polish parliament, adopted a similar stance regarding the repression and extermination of Jews. In four resolutions — passed on June 10 and November 27, 1942, and on January 7 and December 20, 1943 — they appealed to the Allied governments and their publics to adopt measures to oppose the Nazis' crimes. [15]

In addition to its information activities, aimed at disclosing Nazi crimes, and its diplomatic notes and appeals, seeking the adoption of concrete steps to assist the oppressed and prevent further exterminations, the Polish Government-in-Exile also turned to the Vatican for assistance. Polish officials informed the Holy See about the growing atrocities in Poland, including the mass destruction at the camps, and requested that the Pope intervene. In a January 2, 1943 letter to the Pope, the President of the Polish Republic, Władysław Raczkiewicz, described the massacre of civilians, the kidnappings of children for the goal of Germanization, and the deportations to KL Auschwitz. He appealed to Pius XII to speak out publicly and condemn the crimes. [16]

On March 22, 1944 the *Los Angeles Times* published a summary of an extensive report on the extermination campaign against prisoners at Auschwitz, made public the day before by the Polish Information Ministry in London. The *Washington Post* (20 lines) and the *New York Herald Tribune* (23 lines) published summaries the same day. [17]

In Switzerland, the St. Gallen newspaper, *Die Ostschweiz*, carried an article on the extermination of Hungarian Jews at KL Auschwitz on July 10, 1944, entitled "People are Disappearing" (*Menschen verschwinden*). The article was based on information from their London correspondent; the source, once again, were the materials that the Polish Government-in-Exile was receiving from home. [18] Another Swiss newspaper, the *Ostschweizerisches Tagblatt und Rorschacher Tagblatt*, ran information about the camp from the Reuters and Exchange agencies in July 1944 (most likely on July 10). Quoting a Reuters story from July 8, 1944, the Swiss newspaper reported that the Polish Ministry of Internal Affairs had received information from its *Delegatura* in occupied Poland about the fate of the 400,000 Jews deported from Hungary. The majority of them, the newspaper reported, had been sent to the Auschwitz extermination camp in Upper Silesia. According to data from the Polish Committee to Assist Jews, two million Polish Jews had been murdered since 1939 in three camps inside Polish territory. The Exchange agency repeated the

---

[14] Ibid., pp. 1013-14 (joint declaration of the governments of twelve states).

[15] Ibid, pp. 1006-7, 1015-6 (Declarations and Resolutions of the National Council in London).

[16] Vittorio E. Giuntella, *Il nazismo e i Lager* (Rome, 1979), pp. 158-9.

[17] Mel Mermelstein, *By Bread Alone. The Story of A-4685* (Los Angeles, 1981), p. 61; Deborah E. Lipstadt, *Beyond Belief. The American Press and the Coming of the Holocaust 1933-1945* (New York, 1986), p. 223.

[18] APMO, Documents from the *Bundesarchiv* in Koblenz, mikr. 1624/101.

Polish government's assertion that the Auschwitz gas chambers were capabl. of killing up to 6,000 people on a daily basis. [19]

In Istanbul, the office of the Polish Consul-General, A.N. Kurcyusz, published news about camp. On a duplicating machine, his office ran off a newsletter based on reports from the Polish resistance movement entitled, *Poland under German Occupation*. An article from March 15, 1944, reported that between the summer of 1942 and the fall of 1943, 850,000 Jews had been liquidated in the gas chambers at KL Auschwitz, including 60,000 from Greece; 60,000 from France, Belgium and Holland; and 50,000 from Slovakia, Bohemia and Moravia. It also mentioned the fate of 15,000 Polish Jews from Będzin and Sosnowiec, exterminated in the gas chambers during the summer of 1943. [20]

In 1944, demands and appeals began to appear in the West, along with speculation, about the bombing of several death camps, including Auschwitz. On August 18, 1944, the British Foreign Office informed Joseph Linton, the political secretary of the Jewish Agency in London, that the lack of topographical maps for the camps at Auschwitz (Oświęcim) and Treblinka presented serious difficulties for realizing any plans to bomb the two camps from the air. After receiving this news, Linton immediately obtained detailed maps of Auschwitz and Treblinka from the Polish Government-in-Exile and immediately passed them on to the Foreign Office. [21]

Based on the information sent to London by the Polish resistance movement, Allied broadcasters informed the entire world about KL Auschwitz. They spread this information to the farthest corners of the globe via radio. The BBC in particular reported in its news programs about conditions at the camp, the mass murder of prisoners and the plans of the SS officials.

2. KL Auschwitz in the Western Mass Media

The Polish resistance movement, the Government-in-Exile in London and the circles affiliated with them were not the only ones to disclose the truth about the camp at Auschwitz. Other groups, institutions and individuals worked to reveal the Nazis' crimes. News about the camp only occasionally appeared in Allied and neutral countries until mid-1944, when the mass media in these countries began carrying a great deal of information on the subject. The information came from various sources. Poles often provided the information.

In 1941, Jon Evans published a book in London on Nazi crimes in Poland, based on materials obtained from the Government-in-Exile and Poles residing in England. The book also contained information about KL Auschwitz, based

---

[19] Jenö Lévai, *Zsidósors Európában* (Budapest, 1948), p. 90.

[20] M. Gilbert, pp. 212, 419 (fn 27). The numbers given in the text regarding the number of murders should be approached with some degree of caution. They were published hastily and without any possibility for verification. One should also be cautious in making use of the information cited below regarding the number of victims at the camp, taken from the mass media during the war.

[21] Ibid., p. 358. For the sake of accuracy, we should point out that by that time, Treblinka no longer existed as a death camp.

on the account of an escapee, a former Polish artillery officer. The author gave a brief overview of conditions at the camp: rations, work, the system of punishments and torture and the disposal of bodies through cremation. [22]

From 1942-44, articles about the camp appeared in the *Neue Volkszeitung* in New York and in the *Bulletin der Jüdischen Telegrafen Agentur* in London (1943-44). On June 1, 1943, the London *Times* published an article entitled "Nazi Brutality to Jews", in which the newspaper's diplomatic correspondent named Oświęcim near Cracow (using the Polish name) as a destination to which Jews were being brought. The Jews, he added, were being deported to the camp from the ghetto in Cracow. [23] Despite the strict censorship applied in Switzerland, references to the camp began appearing in the Swiss press, especially about the annihilation of Jews in 1942-44 — e.g., in the *Schaffhauser Intelligenzblatt* and the social-democtratic *Schaffhauser Arbeiter--Zeitung*.

A publication of the French resistance movement, *Les Cahiers du Témoignage chrétien*, contained a detailed report about conditions at the camp under the title, "*Défi* [A Challenge]", in its January and February 1943 issues (Nr. 13-14). It reported that 40,000 prisoners, mainly Poles, were being held at the camp; that there were three crematorium ovens; and that the number of deaths exceeded 150 people per day. Another periodical of the French resistance movement, *Défense de la France*, carried an extensive article on the subject in its September 30, 1943 issue (Nr. 39). Not only Poles, it reminded its readers, but also 100 French women were in mortal danger at the camp. The biweekly *Reports from France*, published by the French Ministry of Information in London, ran a six-page article "The Camp at Drancy and the Extermination Camps in Poland" in its September 15 issue. The article was based on the testimony of a Jewish escapee from the Neu-Dachs sub-camp of KL Auschwitz in Jaworzno. It described conditions not only at the sub-camp, but also at KL Auschwitz II-Birkenau and the Drancy transit camp. [24]

3. Escapees' Accounts and the West's Reaction

The publication in mid-1944 of three accounts by escapees from KL Auschwitz also influenced public opinion in the West. The authors of the three reports were Jerzy Tabeau, a Pole; three Jews from Slovakia — Rudolf Vrba (Walter Rosenberg), Alfred Wetzler and Arnošt Rosin, and Czesław Mordowicz, a Jew from Poland (see. p. 235).

The first of them, Jerzy Tabeau, wrote an account of the camp on the orders of the Polish resistance movement at the end of 1942 or beginning of 1943 in Cracow. He recounted events that had taken place at KL Auschwitz

---

[22] Jon Evans, *The Nazi New Order in Poland* (London, 1941), pp. 13, 65-6.

[23] K. Dunin-Wąsowicz, p. 168; "Eine Stätte des Grauens. Ein Bericht aus dem Konzentrationslager Oświęcim (Auschwitz)", in *Auschwitz. Zeugnisse und Berichte*, ed. H.G. Adler, Hermann. Langbein, Ellas Lingens-Reiner (Cologne — Frankfurt a.M., 1979), pp. 191-3, M. Gilbert, p. 170.

[24] K. Dunin-Wąsowicz, p. 165; Archives of the Polish Institute and Gen. Sikorski Museum in London (henceforth, Polish Institute and Sikorski Museum), A12 73/5 (copy of the article "The Camp at Drancy and the Extermination Camps in Poland").

between the spring of 1942 and the fall of 1943. He described his stay, conditions at the camp, the methods used to annihilate and destroy Poles and other prisoners, and the extermination of Jews in the gas chambers. Based on his own calculations, he estimated the number of Jews who had already been killed at more than 1,500,000. Tabeau's report was delivered in mid-1944 through clandestine channels in Slovakia to Switzerland. (Likely, it was also sent from occupied Poland to London via Stockholm.) On conspiratorial grounds, the author's name was not given. The account thus became known as "the report of a Polish Major". Long after the war, Tabeau's report continued to appear in historical works under the same name. [25]

The second report evolved from the accounts given to the Slovakian *Judenrat* by Rudolf Vrba and Alfred Wetzler at a secret meeting on April 25-26, 1944, in Żylina, Slovakia. Their 60-page manuscript was prepared in both Slovak and German versions. Numerous copies were printed in both languages. The account, which dealt with events at KL Auschwitz between April 1942 and April 1944, was often reproduced. Vrba and Wetzler recounted their stay at the camp and its living conditions, told about the arrival of transports of prisoners from all over Europe and illustrated the different methods used for liquidating prisoners, including the mass murder of Jews in the gas chambers. They described the extermination facilities and estimated that between April 1942 and April 1944 around 1,765,000 Jews from different parts of Europe had been murdered in the gas chambers. Part of the report also dealt with the camp at Majdanek (KL Lublin), where Vrba had been imprisoned before his transfer to KL Auschwitz. [26]

When they gave their accounts to the Slovakian *Judenrat*, Vrba and Wetzler also told about the preparations being made for the reception and extermination of Jews from Hungary, who were supposed to begin arriving at the camp in the near future. They urgently requested that the Jews of Hungary be warned about the danger that awaited them at Auschwitz. Thus, one copy of Vrba's and Wetzler's report was secretly delivered at the end of June 1944 to Dr. Rudolf Kastner, one of the leading Zionists in Hungary and director of the Jewish Assistance Committee in Budapest. [27]

The third report was also based on depositions given to the Slovakian *Judenrat* — this time, by Czesław Mordowicz and Arnošt Rosin, who secretly met with its representatives in Liptovsky Svaty Mikulaš in mid-June 1944. Their account of events at KL Auschwitz, covering the period April-May 1944, placed particular emphasis on the tragedy that had befallen the Jews deported

[25] APMO, Files of the Camp Resistance, vol. Va, cards 307-32 (report of J. Tabeau); APMO, Collection of Testimonies, vol. 98, card 24, account of former prisoner Jerzy Tabeau; M. Gilbert, p. 276; Henryk Świebocki, "Auschwitz — czy w czasie wojny świat znał prawdę o obozie?" *Zeszyty Oświęcimskie* (Special Volume Nr. IV, 1992), pp. 15-16.

[26] APMO, Files of the Camp Resistance, vol. XXIIa, cards 1-39 (report of A. Wetzler and R. Vrba); APMO, Collection of Testimonies, vol. 40, cards 41-42, account of former prisoner Alfred Wetzler; Rudolf Vrba and Alan Bestic, *Ich kann nicht vergeben* (Munich, 1964), pp. 284-5; John S. Conway, "Frühe Augenzeugenberichte aus Auschwitz. Glaubwürdigkeit und Wirkungsgeschichte", *Vierteljahrshefte für Zeitgeschichte* 2 (1979), pp. 268-9; H. Świebocki, pp. 27-8.

[27] Vrba and Bestic, pp. 225-7, 285-6; M. Gilbert, p. 241; account of A. Wetzler, pp, 37, 42.

from Hungary in May, victims of mass extermination in the camp's gas chambers. [28]

These three reports, in terms of the intentions of their authors and the circles standing behind them — viz., the Polish resistance movement and the Slovakian *Judenrat* — were not meant to be just a documentation of Nazi crimes. Above all else, it was hoped that their rapid publication would provoke a worldwide reaction. A campaign was initiated with this goal in mind.

We have already recounted how a copy of Vrba's and Wetzler's report was delivered to Dr. Kastner for the sake of Hungary's Jews. It was also decided to send a copy of Tabeau's report to Switzerland. Dr. Jaromir Kopecký, Czechoslovakia's standing delegate to the League of Nations, obtained a copy in Geneva in June 1944. On May 22, 1944, the chargé d'affaires for the Holy See in Bratislava, Monsignore Giuseppe Burzio, received a copy of the report and dispatched it to the Vatican. In the second half of June 1944, Vrba and Mordowicz secretly met with the papal nuncio to Switzerland, Monsignore Mario Martilotti, in the village of Svaty Jur, ca. 15 km outside Bratislava. The papal representative, transferred on a temporary basis to Bratislava, listened to their accounts of the camp at Auschwitz. In June 1944, Dr. Kopecký acquired a copy of Vrba's and Wetzler's report in Geneva, as well as that of Mordowicz and Rosin, through underground channels. He worked to bring the new reports, along with Tabeau's, to the attention of Allied governments, international organizations (e.g., the World Jewish Congress and the International Red Cross) and the general public, through the mass media. [29]

On June 14, 1944, Dr. Kopecký and Dr. Gerhart Riegner, the Geneva representative of the World Jewish Congress, sent a telegram to London from the British Consulate in Bern. The telegram, which cited Vrba's and Wetzler's reports without disclosing their names, told the fate of the Jews deported from Theresienstadt to KL Auschwitz II-Birkenau: around 4,000 had been murdered in the gas chambers on March 7, 1944, and the camp authorities were planning to exterminate another 3,000 by June 20, 1944. Kopecký and Riegner requested that this information be aired by Allied broadcasters and that the German authorities be warned about the potential consequences. [30] In response, BBC radio broadcast a communiqué the very next day, June 15, which repeated the contents of the telegram regarding the fate of the Theresienstadt Jews. The communiqué also contained the following warning:

.... In London there is a most accurate report about the mass murders at Birkenau. Everyone responsible for these mass murders, from the highest authorities through mid-level officials down to the organs carrying out the orders will be called to account for it. [31]

---

[28] M. Gilbert, p. 272; H. Świebocki, p. 38.
[29] J. Conway, pp. 276-8; M. Gilbert, pp. 273, 276; M. Kárný, pp. 13-15, 24.
[30] M. Gilbert, pp. 273-4.
[31] APMO, Documents from the *Bundesarchiv* in Koblenz, mikr. 1624/72, report of German radio monitoring from June 16, 1944.

Over the following days, Radio London repeated the warning. The issue also found a certain resonance in the press. American newspapers published short articles about the fate of the Theresienstadt Jews: the *New York World Telegram* (June 16, 1944), the *Los Angeles Times* (June 17), the *New York Times* (June 20), and the *Washington Times Herald* (June 20). [32] We should remember at this point that the Polish emigrant newspaper, *Dziennik Polski i Dziennik Żołnierza*, had already reported on this subject on June 9, 1944.

The mass media's activities regarding the fate of the Theresienstadt Jews developed into a press campaign, resulting in the publication of additional information about KL Auschwitz. The access of the press to the escapees' reports played a significant role in the publicity. While Dr. Kopecký played an important role in all of this, the person mainly responsible was correspondent for the British Exchange Telegraph press agency, Walter Garrett. On June 24, 1944, Garrett sent to London four detailed dispatches, on the fate of Hungary's Jews and their mass deportation to Auschwitz, conditions at the camp, and the murder of a total of 1,765,000 Jews at the camp. Garrett based his telegrams on information he had obtained from the First Secretary of the Salvadoran consulate in Geneva, Georges Mandel-Mantello. The director of the Palestinian Office in Budapest, Miklos Krausz, had sent Matello's information about the deportation of Hungary's Jews, as well as a condensed version of Wetzler's and Vrba's report in English, through secret channels. [33]

Garrett's telegrams met with an appropriate level of response in the British media — for example, in the *Manchester Guardian* on June 27 and 28, 1944. [34] Garrett then began an energetic campaign in Switzerland to reveal the truth about Auschwitz and to interest the Swiss media in it. His activity brought results. At least 383 references and columns on Auschwitz, including excerpts from Vrba's and Wetzler's report, appeared in the Swiss press by mid-1944, within 18 days after Garrett had disclosed the information. This was the first time during the war that the Swiss censors allowed the publication of such complete information about the Nazi genocide. [35] Then, a 66-page brochure on the Nazi camps was published in Geneva in French: *Les camps d'extermination* („The Extermination Camps"). The brochure made use of Vrba's and Wetzler's report, as well as that of a "Polish Major" (i.e., Tableau). A condensed, German-language version of Vrba's and Wetzler's report was also published in Geneva under the title, *Die Vernichtungslager* (the Extermination Camps). [36]

A number of U.S. newspapers carried information about the camp during the first two weeks of July 1944, following the publication of Vrba's and Wetzler's report — e.g., the *New York Times*, the *Christian Science Monitor*, the *Los Angeles Times*, the *Washington Times Herald*, the *Seattle Times*, the *Washington Star* and the *Kansas City Star*. Although the articles differed on

[32] D. Lipstadt, pp. 233-4.

[33] J. Conway, p. 278; Karný, pp. 25-6; Lévai, pp. 68-72 (W. Garrett's telegrams in English).

[34] Cf. David S. Wyman, *Das unerwünschte Volk. Amerika und die Vernichtung der europäischen Juden* (Ismaning bei München, 1986), pp. 401, 544 (fn 4).

[35] J. Conway, p. 278.

[36] *Les camps d'extermination. Dépositions de témoins oculaires*, Troisième serie (Geneva, 1944); Dunin-Wąsowicz, p. 168.

certain details and varied in their thoroughness, almost all of them contained the message that from April 1942 to April 1944, between 1,500,000 and 1,700,000 Jews had been murdered at Auschwitz. With the exception of Jews from Lithuania which the newspapers failed to mention, the newspapers' lists conformed in their entirety with the Vrba's and Wetzler's estimates of the Jews murdered at KL Auschwitz-Birkenau. [37]

American radio stations also reported on the number of Jews murdered at the camp, including stations in New York (July 3), Cincinnati (July 8), and American broadcasters in Europe (July 9, 1944), German radio monitors recorded this information and reported it to authorities of the Third Reich. [38]

On July 4, 1944, the Czechoslovakian Government-in-Exile in London delivered to the eight Allied governments a documentary report, entitled "Report on the Conditions in the Concentration Camps of Oświęcim and Birkenau". The report was attached to an appeal that a strong warning be addressed to the Nazi regime, stressing that it would be held fully responsible for the crimes it had committed. The report was based on excerpts from Wetzler's and Vrba's report, distributed by Dr. Kopecký, and supplemented with information from the account of the "Polish Major" (Tableau) and recent news about the deportation of Hungarian Jews to Auschwitz. [39]

The escapees' reports on KL Auschwitz, now in the hands of the Allies, still awaited individual publication. This took place in November 1944, when the American War Refugee Board published in Washington a 59-page brochure entitled, *German Extermination Camps — Auschwitz and Birkenau*. The text was divided into two parts. The first part contained the account by Alfred Wetzler and Rudolf Vrba, supplemented with information from Czesław Mordowicz's and Arnošt Rosin's report. The second half carried the report of the "Polish Major", Jerzy Tableau. [40]

On November 25, 1944, the War Refugee Board distributed texts of the reports to the American press. On the following day, November 26, a number of newspapers — e.g., the *New York Herald Tribune*, the *Louisville Courier Journal*, the *Philadelphia Inquirer*, the *New York Times*, and the *Washington Post* — carried articles on the subject, informing their readers about the Nazis' crimes at KL Auschwitz. [41]

4. Activities Undertaken to Stop the Crimes (The Question of Bombing KL Auschwitz and Allied Activities to Assist Prisoners)

The publication of material from the escapees' reports from KL Auschwitz in mid-1944 generated a press campaign in the West, which was accompanied by activities to prevent the Nazis from committing further crimes. This campaign

[37] D. Lipstadt, pp. 234-5.
[38] APMO, Documents from the *Bundesarchiv* in Koblenz, mikr. 1624/128, 116, 114, report of the German radio monitors from September 4 and July 10, 1944.
[39] M. Kárný, p. 24.
[40] Executive Office of the President, War Refugee Board, *German Extermination Camps — Auschwitz and Birkenau* (Washington, D.C., 1944).
[41] M. Gilbert, p. 385; D. Lipstadt, p. 264.

gained strength when dispatches began arriving in mid-May 1944 from various sources about the deportation of Jews from German-occupied Hungary to KL Auschwitz and their annihilation in the gas chambers. Reports on the tragic fate of the Hungarian Jews aroused public indignation and protests, which led to measures being taken to prevent further exterminations and to rescue those who were still alive.

On June 25, 1944, Pope Pius XII sent a telegram to the Regent of Hungary, Admiral Miklos Horthy, calling on him to save the Jews, demanding that he "spare these many unfortunate people from any further suffering". Others delivered similar appeals to the Hungarian government to stop deporting Jews: Gustavus Adolphus V, King of Sweden; the International Committee of the Red Cross; and the governments of Turkey, Switzerland and Spain. The Allies published a list of 70 individuals — Germans and Hungarians — who bore the greatest responsibility for the deportations. The President of the United States, Franklin Delano Roosevelt, delivered an ultimatum, threatening that "Hungary's fate will be different from that of all other civilized nations" if it did not stop the deportations. Heavy Allied bombing of Budapest on July 2, 1944, backed up the President's threat. Under pressure from all sides, Admiral Horthy ordered on July 6, 1944, that the deportation of Jews from Hungary be discontinued. [42]

The activities aimed at stopping the crimes were quite often accompanied by appeals and demands that the extermination facilities at Auschwitz, along with the railway lines to the camp from Hungary, be bombed. Numerous individuals, groups and organizations, particularly Jewish organizations, put forth these demands, which were mainly addressed to the government of the United States. Among those who called for bombing the crematoria and gas chambers, as well as the railway lines from Hungary, was Dr. Gerhart Riegner. With Dr. Kopecký's approval, on June 24, 1944, he delivered a six-point proposal on the question to Washington through the American consulate in Bern. [43]

Beginning in mid-1944, appeals and demands for bombing the camp intensified. Many were addressed to the War Refugee Board, established by President Roosevelt in January 1944. The board intervened on the issue of bombing the camp several times at the War Department. President Roosevelt and the War Department also received direct appeals to bomb the extermination facilities and rail lines to the camp. Unfortunately, the appeals were ineffective. The War Department opposed bombing. They were of the opinion that military forces and equipment should not be used for non-military goals. The Department formulated this stance in a confidential memorandum released at the beginning of 1944. The War Department also based its rejection on the fact that the proposed operations could "not be carried out". Bombing the camp, they argued, would require the disengagement and use of significant air capabilities that were urgently needed to win decisive battles in other areas.

---

[42] J. Conway, p. 279; M. Gilbert, pp. 312-13; Hannah Arendt, *Eichman in Jerusalem. Ein Bericht von der Banalität des Bösen* (Reinbeck bei Hamburg, 1978), p. 243.

[43] M. Gilbert, p. 289; D. Wyman, pp. 402-6, 409-15.

They pointed out the possible technical difficulties in carrying out the bombing, and even raised the objection that it might lead to acts of vengeance on the part of the Germans. The most effective assistance for victims of persecution, they believed, would be a rapid victory of the Allies over the Third Reich and the other Axis powers, a victory to be won by applying every possible means at their disposal. [44]

The British Air Ministry had similar views regarding the impossibility of bombing the camp. On July 6, 1944, two representatives of the Jewish Agency, Chaim Weizmann and Mosche Shertok, discussed with British Foreign Minister Anthony Eden their proposal to bomb the railway tracks from Budapest to KL Auschwitz, as well as the extermination facilities at the camp itself. Their request met with the understanding on the part of the Foreign Minister and of Prime Minister Winston Churchill. On July 7, 1944, Eden sent a letter on the subject to the Minister for Air, Archibald Sinclair. He requested that Sinclair reply regarding the possibility of conducting the proposed action. In his reply of July 15, 1944, Sinclair asserted that the English would not be able to bomb the railway lines and extermination facilities at KL Auschwitz and that the prisoners would not benefit much as a result. He suggested at the same time, however, to interest the Americans in the subject. [45]

Such a stance on the part of the Allies prevented the initiation of any military activities to stop the Nazi extermination campaign. KL Auschwitz did not become a target for bombing. Nevertheless, Allied planes often flew over the area of the camp. In April 1944, reconnaissance planes began appearing in the area to photograph industrial facilities, particularly the factories for synthetic rubber and gasoline at the Buna-Werke in Monowice (Monowitz). The pilots' photographs also included the grounds of the camp. The first aerial photographs in which KL Auschwitz was visible were taken on April 4. The best-known photographs of the camp were taken by pilots during a surveillance flight on August 25. In the photographs, one can clearly see, among other things, the crematoria and gas chambers, the unloading ramp and even a group of people on their way to the crematoria. [46]

In July 1944, the Allies began systematic bombing runs against industrial targets in outlying areas of Upper Silesia. The main targets were fuel refineries. Between July 7 and November 20, 1944, the Allies bombed the synthetic fuel plant at Blechhammer (Blachownia Śląska) at least ten times. This plant was located several dozen kilometers to the northwest of KL Auschwitz. The squadrons that made the bombing runs undoubtedly flew through the area, perhaps even over the grounds of the camp. On August 7, the Americans bombed the oil refinery at Trzebinia, only 20 km away from KL Auschwitz. On August 20, 127 Flying Fortresses of the U.S. Air Force, escorted by 100 Mustang fighters, dropped 1,336 five-hundred pound bombs on the Buna-

[44] D. Wyman, pp. 404, 406, 409-15, 421.

[45] Bernard Wasserstein, *Britain and the Jews of Europe 1939-1945* (London, 1979), pp. 309-12.

[46] M. Gilbert, pp. 225, 363; Dino A. Brugioni and Robert G. Poirer, *The Holocaust Revisited: A Retrospective Analysis of the Auschwitz-Birkenau Extermination Camps* (Washington, D.C., 1979).

-Werke in Monowice, only several kilometers away from the extermination facilities at KL Auschwitz II-Birkenau. [47] On September 13, 96 American B-24 Liberator bombers renewed the attack on the Buna-Werke. From an altitude of 7,500 meters, they dropped more than 1000 five-hundred pound bombs on their target. Some fell on KL Auschwitz — probably by mistake — and damaged, among other things, the side-tracks leading up to the crematoria at Birkenau. The bombs also mortally wounded some SS men and prisoners at the "camp extension" (Lagererweiterung) next to the main camp.

A September 20, 1944 report from the underground group, Assistance for Concentration Camp Prisoners (Pomoc Więźniom Obozów Koncentracyjnych, PWOK) in Cracow, contains the following information on the bombing, based on reports from the resistance movement at the camp:

> During the general attack of the American planes against the I.G. Farben industrial facilities on 13.IX.1944 .... the aviators also dropped bombs on certain camp facilities. At Auschwitz I, two SS barracks along the Große Postenkette were destroyed, killing 15 SS men and severely wounding 28 others. One part that lies beneath the rubble has yet to be searched through. .... A barrack of the Bekleidungswerkstätte [49] was also destroyed and 40 prisoners, including 23 Jews, died there, unfortunately, and 65 were severely wounded. Thirteen persons still remain beneath the rubble, presumably alive. At Auschwitz II, only two bombs fell, as if the air force had more deserving targets for destruction than the gas chambers. One of the bombs damaged the railway and side-track leading up to the crematorium, and the second destroyed a shelter located between the tracks, killing around 30 civilian workers. [50]

Before the end of 1944, the Americans would bomb the Buna-Werke facilities twice more — on December 18 and 26. [51]

It should be pointed out at this juncture that proposals for bombing KL Auschwitz did not appear for the first time in 1944 in connection with the deportation and extermination of Jews from Hungary. The Polish government had put forth a proposal on this issue much earlier. On January 4, 1941, cavalry Captain Stefan Zamoyski, an associate of General Władysław Sikorski, Supreme Commander and Prime Minister of the Polish Government-in--Exile, had sent a letter to Marshal Richard Peirse of the Royal Air Force. In the letter, the Polish authorities had proposed that KL Auschwitz be targeted in bombing raids. Peirse replied directly to General Sikorski in a letter dated January 15, 1941:

> Dear General,
> I very carefully weighed your proposal, put forth by Captain Zamoyski in his letter Nr. 46/41 from January 4, regarding an aerial attack against the concentration camp in Oświęcim. I also discussed the matter with Sir Charles Portal. We both decided,

---

[47] M. Gilbert, p. 354, 360; D. Wyman, pp. 417-18.

[48] M. Gilbert, pp. 369-70; D. Wyman, p. 418.

[49] Translator's note: garment works.

[50] PWOK, "Sprawozdanie okresowe (od 1 IX 1944 do 20 IX 1944). Komunikat specjalny", APMO, Files of the Camp Resistance vol. VII, card 459.

[51] M. Gilbert, pp. 389-90; D. Wyman, p. 418.

I regret to inform you, that a successful attack against Auschwitz cannot be carried out in practice. Two major factors contribute to this. First, our bombing forces have as their main assignment attacking certain industrial centers — and we can assume that if we are able to achieve the necessary concentration of attacks, we will likely accelerate the crisis in the German armaments industry during this year. It is imperative that we take advantage of every occasion to attack selected targets with all of the forces that we have at our disposal. .... Second, we know from our experience that sporadic attacks against such targets as Auschwitz would most likely not achieve the desired result — i.e., destruction of the barbed-wire fences and ammunition dumps in such a way that would allow the prisoners to escape. Aerial bombardment of this type would require an enormous amount of precision if it were not to lead to significant casualties among the prisoners themselves.

I greatly regret giving you such a response, General, but I know that you will understand the reasons, and the fact that only a close concentration of our bombing forces against major targets will prove effective in the fight against our common enemy. [52]

Among the documents at the State Museum in Oświęcim is a smuggled message from June 14, 1943, in which the Polish prisoner Stanisław Kłodziński reported as follows to Teresa Lasocka-Estreicher of the PWOK committee in Cracow:

Here, around our blocks on the grounds of the camp, a gigantic *Werkhalle* is being built for the firm Krupp. Currently, machinery is being installed. I assume that within a month it will already be time for the birds to come flying. As far as we are concerned, do not hold back, we are willing and able to prove once again with our blood that we are intent on destroying the enemy. So do not hesitate because we are living here. The Krupp firm should be destroyed and leveled to the ground. [53]

Another document that touches on the subject of bombing is a telegram from the Polish government in London to the Home Army command in occupied Poland from August 24, 1943. It reads as follows:

The British general staff has expressed their readiness to bomb Auschwitz, particularly the factories for synthetic rubber and gas, and other such factories in Silesia. For our part, we want to link this with a mass liberation of the prisoners. Our closest cooperation is imperative to free them immediately after the attack and to give them assistance. In addition, you must help us identify targets based on their importance and guide the airplanes to targets in such a way that will avoid casualties among the Poles. Report what you think about this and what you expect from us in this regard, including whether you can prepare the prisoners for it in advance. This operation is planned for the period when the nights are longest. [54]

---

[52] Polish Institute and Sikorski Museum, Archives, KOL. 1 Dz. Cz. NW, Copy of January 15, 1941 letter from Marshal Peirse to Gen. Sikorski.

[53] APMO, Files of the Camp Resistance, vol. I, card 32, citation from Kłodziński's smuggled message.

[54] Citation from B. Wasserstein, p. 308.

Activities aimed at publicizing the truth about KL Auschwitz and hindering Nazi crimes did not let up in 1944. Allied broadcasters addressed warnings to those responsible for the extermination, annihilation, and suffering of people at the camp. The BBC communiqué of June 15, 1944, regarding the Jews from Theresienstadt has already been mentioned. On July 28, 1944, in its 8:20 a.m. broadcast, Radio London cited several figures regarding Nazi crimes in Poland, along with the reminder that the "Allied Commission is preparing a precise list of German criminals". The figures used in the broadcast were undoubtedly taken from a report prepared by the Prisoner Section of the Polish Government's *Delegatura* in occupied Poland. The report, requested by the Government-in-Exile, was delivered to London by courier at the end of July 1944. The 74-page manuscript contained four sections — the first dealt with the prison at Pawiak; the second, more-detailed report, with KL Auschwitz; the third, with the camp at Majdanek, and the last, with KL Ravensbrück. [55]

During the first half of 1944, the BBC broadcast a list of SS men on the Auschwitz camp staff who were the most responsible for the crimes being committed there. All the individuals listed, the broadcaster added, had been given death sentences. This aroused a great deal of commotion among the camp's SS personnel. [56] In a clandestine message from May 9, 1944, the prisoners informed the Polish underground:

They are afraid of all this clamour .... The death sentence announced by London a while back against 15 *SS-Führer* at Auschwitz has made a deep impression upon the accused, and has caused some of them to even break down. It is thus a very effective method, and you must strive to do everything possible so that eventual news will go out as quickly as possible — this would be short things, suitable for radio-telegram. [57]

The Allies' initiatives in the fall of 1944 to hinder the Nazis' plans for destroying all traces of their crimes had a great impact upon the prisoners' fate. On September 6, 1944, the resistance movement at KL Auschwitz dispatched a secret report to the Polish underground. It contained information about the SS's plans for liquidating the camp — namely, destroying its structures, including first and foremost the extermination facilities, leveling everything to the ground, and murdering the prisoners as witnesses to the crimes. The message also named the director of the crematoria and gas chambers at Birkenau, Otto Moll, as the person responsible for carrying out the plan. [58] So plans for liquidating the camp were often referred to as the "Moll-Plan".

---

[55] See W. Bartoszewski's introduction to *Raport komórki więziennej*, pp. 158-59.

[56] APMO, Files of the Camp Resistance, vol. II. card 75; smuggled message from J. Cyrankiewicz dated May 9, 1944; Hermann Langbein, *Menschen in Auschwitz* (Frankfurt a. M. -Berlin-Vienna, 1980), p. 293; Józef Garliński, *Fighting Auschwitz* (London, 1971), pp. 230-231; cf. "Reminiscences of Pery Broad" in *KL Auschwitz seen by the SS* (Oświęcim, 1972), p. 197.

[57] APMO, Files of the Camp Resistance, vol. II, card 75, citation from a smuggled message of J. Cyrankiewicz.

[58] Ibid., cards 140, 141, smuggled messages from S. Kłodziński and J. Cyrankiewicz.

The Polish resistance movement informed The Government-in-Exile about the Nazis' plans for the camp in a coded message transmitted from a secret radio-telegraph station on September 23, 1944. The dispatch included besides the information, the following appeal:

This hideous crime must be prevented — here at Home, or at least in Silesia, we have neither the forces nor the possibility. The condemned are waiting on salvation — any day might be too late. [59]

The Polish Government-in-Exile shared its information about the SS's desire to murder the prisoners at Auschwitz with the British Ministry of Foreign Affairs and the U.S. State Department. The information was accompanied with request that the planned crimes be prevented. The American and British governments, after agreeing upon their stance, issued a joint declaration that made public the SS's plans and warned that those who committed such crimes would receive the punishment that they deserved. This warning was broadcast by Radio Washington on October 10, 1944, at 12 a.m. and by the BBC at 6 p.m. and 9 p.m. [60] Radio Moscow also broadcast information about the plan to murder the prisoners. [61] Officials of the Third Reich responded immediately to the declaration and warnings of the Western Allies. On October 11, 1944, the German telegraph service reported that it was not true that any plan existed for murdering the prisoners and that the information publicized by the Allies was false. [62]

That the Germans denied these reports does not prove that a plan for murdering the prisoners at KL Auschwitz did not exist. The Third Reich authorities, we can assume, abandoned their original plans because the Allies had publicized the planned crime. Undoubtedly, the military situation at the front, which pointed to a rapid collapse of the Nazi state, also influenced the situation. The plan to liquidate the prisoners at KL Auschwitz was never realized. As a result, thousands of lives were saved, mainly those of Jews, who represented the largest group of prisoners at the camp at that time.

The SS authorities did not succeed in concealing their crimes. During the war, the world already knew that KL Auschwitz was a place where Jews were being exterminated and Poles — along with other nationalities — were being liquidated. The fact that the world already knew was, to a great extent, a contribution of the Polish resistance movement, which kept the West constantly informed about the camp with documents and other materials.

---

[59] Ibid., vol. XXX, cards 63, 64, Dispatch Nr. 213/XXX from 23 September 1944 — photocopy of the original held at Studium Polski Podziemnej in London.

[60] M. Gilbert, p. 381; cf. Halina Wróbel, "Die Liquidation des Konzentrationslagers Auschwitz-Birkenau", *Hefte von Auschwitz* 6 (1962), p. 7-8.

[61] Cf. Philip Friedman and Tadeusz Hołuj, *Oświęcim 1940-1945* (Warszawa, 1946), p. 139; APMO, Höss Trail, vol. 25b, card 146, account of Teresa Lasocka.

[62] M. Gilbert, pp. 381-2.

LIBERATION

ANDRZEJ STRZELECKI

EVACUATION, LIQUIDATION AND LIBERATION OF THE CAMP [1]

The growing pressure of the Allied forces on the Third Reich in the last years of the war forced the German authorities successively to liquidate the concentration camps and other centers of confinement and mass extermination. In 1944, the facilities that were liquidated included *Konzentrationslager* (KL) Lublin, also known as Majdanek, and KL Natzweiler; and in January 1945, KL Stutthof and KL Auschwitz. Upon entering the camps — either liquidated or in the process of being liquidated — the Allies were able to save throngs of prisoners from certain death and disclose the magnitude of the crimes being committed there.

While the camps were being disbanded, a total of at least 500,000 prisoners were evacuated from them to areas quite distant from the front lines. During this unprecedented transfer of prisoners from camp to camp, tens of thousands lost their lives. (It is impossible to establish the exact number of victims in this chain of evacuations.) Not without reason were the evacuation transports and evacuation marches called "death transports" and "death marches".

By evacuating prisoners, the Nazi authorities sought to keep them at their disposal as a source of slave labor. They also wanted to prevent the Allies from using them militarily. A significant number of prisoners were ready to support the Allies with weapons in hand. The concentration camp prisoners, however, were few in number and not well-trained militarily, unlike the prisoners of war held inside the Third Reich; most of them were also physically debilitated. They did, however, represent a force ready to take part — with a significant degree of commitment — in the struggle against Nazism; if not in the military ranks of the Allies, then at least spontaneously, within the resistance movement. The so-called "self-liberation" of the prisoners at KL Buchenwald on April 11, 1945, bears witness to this fact.

The Third Reich's efforts to keep the masses of prisoners at the disposal of the German war economy by evacuating them did not save the Third Reich from defeat; it merely showed the illogic of the Nazi regime's efforts in its final stages of activity.

---

[1] This chapter is a summary of the author's research from the following publications: *Wyzwolenie KL Auschwitz* (Oświęcim, 1974); *Ewakuacja, likwidacja i wyzwolenie KL Auschwitz* (Oświęcim, 1982); *Marsz śmierci. Przewodnik po trasie Oświęcim — Wodzisław Śląski* (Katowice, 1989). It also contains more recent findings.

1. The Camp During the Initial Stage of Evacuation and Liquidation (August 1944 — mid-January 1945)

In July-August 1944, Red Army units reached the Wisła (Vistula) Wisłoka line. The Red Army only had around 200 km left to go from their bridgehead in the Sandomierz region to the camp at Auschwitz. Given the situation, Nazi officials began considering two possibilities: liquidating the camp in response to further Soviet military successes, or keeping the camp at their further disposal. Given the possible need to retreat, they began taking steps in August 1944 to retain the prisoners held at the camp as a potential labor force and to save the property stored at the camp. During the first stage of the camp's liquidation, which lasted until mid-January 1945, the SS took the following steps:

1) To the greatest extent possible, they continued to exterminate in the gas chambers most of the Jews deported to the camp immediately upon their arrival; at the same time, they used the camp as a center for assembling and dispatching the prisoner labor force to the Third Reich proper. The mass extermination of Jews was discontinued in November 1944.

2) In November 1944, the practice of selecting "unproductive" individuals from among the Jewish prisoners held at the camp for liquidation in the gas chambers was also discontinued. Before this change took place, however, between August 29 and October 29, 1944, 3,824 prisoners were exterminated from the men's quarantine camp (BIIa) at Birkenau alone.

3) During September-November 1944, most of the prisoners employed at servicing the crematoria and gas chambers were liquidated as direct witnesses to the exterminations.

4) From August 1944 to mid-January 1945, around 65,000 male and female prisoners were evacuated from the camp, including almost all the Poles, Russians and Czechs (around 15,000 people). The Poles and Russians were transferred not only to enable their continued exploitation as a labor force, but also because the SS considered them to be the most dangerous element, more inclined to escapes and rebellions, particularly as the front neared Oświęcim.

The evacuated prisoners were employed inside the Reich at different industrial facilities; they had to work, for example, at expanding underground armaments factories in the Harz Mountains and in Austria. This initial evacuation was of a limited nature, since around 67,000 prisoners remained at the camp until the final stages of the camp's liquidation. The majority of the prisoners, unaffected by this initial transfer, remained employed to the very last minute at industrial facilities on the grounds of the camp and in the surrounding area, mainly in the industrial region of Upper Silesia.

5) By the fourth quarter of 1944, the Nazis had developed a contingency plan for evacuating prisoners on foot if a Soviet advance into Upper Silesia proved unavoidable.

6) At the end of 1944, while the expansion of the central portion of KL Auschwitz (the main camp and the camp at Birkenau) was halted, the sub-camps established next to industrial facilities continued to expand. (The agricultural facilities next to the camp were also not neglected in this regard.) Until the beginning of January 1945, around two weeks before Soviet forces

entered Upper Silesia, the Hubertushütte sub-camp, recently established next to a steelworks in Bytom-Łagiewniki, continued to function. [2]

7) In the final months of 1944, several dozen wooden barracks were dismantled at Birkenau (in sections BI and BIII) and shipped in pieces to the Third Reich. Prisoners from the different sections of the largely-depopulated camp at Birkenau were all transferred to Section BII and housed at camps BIIb-f. On October 6, all the women who had been held up to that point in Section BIII were transferred to Section BIIc, while a few were also sent to the main camp and held on the grounds of the "camp extension" (*Lagererweiterung*). During the first days of November, the quarantine camp (BIIa) was evacuated, and the men inside were transferred to camps BIId and BIIf. Finally, on November 24, the women prisoners at camps BIa and BIb were ordered to go to camps BIIb (healthy prisoners) and BIIe (the ill), with a portion also going to the *Lagererweiterung*.

8) On November 25, 1944, on the orders of Oswald Pohl, the head of SS-WVHA, concentration-camp Auschwitz II-Birkenau was incorporated into the main camp, Auschwitz I, undoubtedly in conjunction with the significant decrease in prisoners and the liquidation of camps BIa, BIb, BIIa and BIII. The two camps were administratively united once more under the common name of *Konzentrationslager Auschwitz*. [3] In accordance with the same order, Auschwitz III, composed of the sub-camps situated next to industrial facilities, was renamed *Konzentrationslager Monowitz*. The constant striving of the SS authorities to camouflage what was occurring at Auschwitz undoubtedly had no small influence upon the latter name change.

9) The property at Auschwitz — consisting of, for example, an extremely large quantity of building materials and possessions stolen from the Jewish victims of mass extermination — was also not forgotten in the final months of the camp's existence. These items had been stored in numerous barracks and other buildings inside the camp, particularly in the warehouse barracks known as "Canada" I and II. A significant portion of these goods were rapidly shipped inside the *Reich*.

According to a report by *SS-Oberscharführer* Karl Reichenbacher, director of the clothing warehouses at the main camp, [4] they were planning to ship out a total of 514,843 articles of men's, women's and children's clothing for the period December 1, 1944 — January 15, 1945 alone. At least 96,310 pieces of this clothing ended up at KL Dachau, KL Gross-Rosen, KL Ravensbrück and other camps.

10) The SS officials devoted a greate deal of attention to obliterating all traces of their crimes in the second half of 1944. Shortly after the liberation of Majdanek on July 24, 1944, where several SS men were caught and numerous

---

[2] On December 11, 1944, representatives from a number of chemical firms were still discussing at a conference in Katowice various methods for increasing the productivity of Auschwitz prisoners employed at their facilities, as if the issue would remain relevant throughout all of 1945. APMO, Gerhard Maurer Trial, vol. 12, cards 33-36, Protocol from a conference of representatives from chemical plants in Katowice on December 11, 1944.

[3] APMO, D-AuI-1, Standortbefehl Nr. 29/44.

[4] A copy of the report has been preserved in the archives of the State Museum at Oświęcim.

pieces of evidence revealing SS crimes were seized, the camp Gestapo at Auschwitz, along with the camp's other administrative units, intensified their long-standing effort to destroy old and unnecessary documents, including prisoner lists and card files. The name lists of the Jews deported to the camp for extermination began to be burned.

The process of liquidating the pits containing human remains at Birkenau — formerly used for burning corpses and burying ashes from the crematoria ovens — most likely began in September 1944. A special work detail composed of male and female prisoners was given the assignment of cleaning out the pits, filling them in and covering them with sod. As much as possible, the prisoners tried to sabotage this work while their supervisors were not looking. They tried, for example, to fill in the pits without first removing the burnt human remains.

11) From mid-October to the end of 1944, Crematorium IV, damaged by the prisoners of the *Sonderkommando* during their rebellion, [5] was leveled to the ground. During November-December 1944, in accordance with an order from *Reichsführer — SS* Himmler, three crematorium buildings were made ready for demolition. Holes were drilled in the walls for charges of dynamite; the technical facilities inside the gas chambers were dismantled, along with the ovens in Crematoria II and III, and shipped inside the Third Reich. Crematorium V and its gas chambers remained untouched, however, until the second half of January 1945. [6]

On January 17, 1945, the last general roll-call took place at KL Auschwitz. According to a surviving report from the camp resistance movement, a total of 67,012 male and female prisoners reported — 31,894 from the main camp and Birkenau and 35,118 from the sub-camps of KL Monowitz. [7]

2. The Final Evacuation and Liquidation of the Camp

If the Nazi authorities did not at first seem in a rush to take steps to evacuate and liquidate KL Auschwitz, their stance dramatically changed in mid-January 1945 with the Red Army's Wisła-Odra (Vistula-Oder) offensive, which commenced eight days ahead of schedule. The camp's final evacuation and liquidation now took place.

2.1. Death Marches and Death Transports

A unique document has survived in the files of the Military-Historical Archives in Prague: the December 21, 1944 order of Fritz Bracht, *Gauleiter* and Commissar for Defense of the *Reich* in Upper Silesia, regarding the evacuation of civilians, POWs, slave laborers and other prisoners from the so-called Province of Upper Silesia. [8] Bracht instructed that in the face of an immediate

---

[5] See p. 223.

[6] The small Crematorium I at the main camp was demobilized in 1943, and its internal facilities were removed in the first half of 1944.

[7] APMO, Files of the Camp Resistance, vol. III, card 208.

[8] A copy of the full text can be found in A. Strzelecki, *Ewakuacja*, pp. 265-75.

The evacuation routes from the camp at Auschwitz were littered with the bodies of dead prisoners. One of the victims of the evacuation.

The corpses of Auschwitz prisoners murdered during the evacuation in January 1945, found in the village of Přelouč in what is . now the Czech Republic (Pardubice district). A resident of Přelouč named Dostál illegally took the photo.

One of the evacuation transports for prisoners, photographed during its departure from train station in Kolin in the Czech Republic on January 24, 1945. The photograph was taken from a short film that was illegally made by a resident of Kolin, engineer Jindřich Kremer, with his amateur film camera.

Der Reichsverteidigungskommissar
für den Reichsverteidigungsbezirk
Oberschlesien
Oberpräsidium   Kattowitz, den 21.Dezember 1944

O.P.I 3 a / Az. 870/2/OP.Fl.I 554/44 g   **Geheim**

An
s. Verteiler

Betr.: Räumung; hier: U-Plan (Treckplan).
Bezug: Die verschiedenen Besprechungen der beteiligten Dienststellen
beim Landesplaner.

Anlagen: pp.

Die arbeitsgebundene Bevölkerung, die Häftlinge, Kriegsgefangenen,
ausländische Arbeiter, Justizgefangenen und ggf. Flüchtlinge aus
den Oberschlesien benachbarten Räumen werden im Falle unmittelbarer
Feindbedrohung mit Trecks umquartiert.
Falls die Reichsbahn nicht in der Lage ist, zur Umquartierung
der Nichtarbeitsgebundenen (s.meinen Erlass vom 19.12.44 O.P.I 3 a
Az. 870/1/L OP.Fl.) genügend Wagenraum zur Verfügung zu stellen,
müssen auch diese mit Trecks zurückgeführt werden. Den Trecks
kommt deshalb die grösste Bedeutung zu. Oberster Grundsatz:
Den Vorrang hat vor der Bergung von Gütern die Umquartierung
der deutschen Menschen.

A
Beteiligte Treckführungsstellen.
Die Verantwortung für die Vorbereitung und Durchführung der
Treckmassnahmen tragen folgende Stellen:
1.) Für die Trecks der Zivilbevölkerung (landwirtschaftliche
und nichtlandwirtschaftliche) die Kreisleiter (NSV).
2.) Für die Trecks der Polizeigefangenen einschl. der
KL-Häftlinge der Höhere SS und Polizeiführer. Diesen
angeschlossen sind die durch die Vomi betreuten Ausländer.
3.) Für die Trecks der Kriegsgefangenen der Höhere
Kommandeur der Kriegsgefangenen.
4.) Für die Rückführung der ausländischen Arbeiter das
Gauarbeitsamt zusammen mit der DAF.
5.) Für die Rückführung der Justizgefangenen der General-
staatsanwalt.

Die verkehrspolizeiliche Steuerung auf den Strassen und Brücken
übernehmen die Kommandeure der Ordnungspolizei bei den
Regierungspräsidenten mit Hilfe ihrer Strassenkommandanten.

B.
Auslösung der Treckmassnahmen.

Stichworte: a) Umquartierung der nichtarbeitsgebundenen
Bevölkerung mit Bahn oder Trecks: "Nikolaus".

b) Umquartierung der arbeitsgebundenen Bevölkerung ,
soweit nicht für Notwirtschaft und -verwaltung
oder für unmittelbare Zwecke der Landesverteidigung
benötigt: "Goldfisch".

c) Umquartierung der Polizeigefangenen (einschl.
KL Auschwitz) und Justizgefangenen: "Karla".

d) Umquartierung der Kriegsgefangenen: "Krebs".

e) Umquartierung der ausländischen Arbeiter: "Amerika".

Gegebenenfalls werden die Stichworte zu gleicher Zeit oder in
verschiedener Reihenfolge ausgelöst. Siewerden von mir über
Konferenzschaltung der Gauleitung an die Kreisleiter und unteren
Verwaltungsbehörden bekanntgegeben, soweit möglich auch unmittel-
bar an die Treckführungsstellen. Aufnahme und Weitergabe der
Stichworte nur mit eindeutiger Bezeichnung des Gebietes, für die
sie gelten.

A fragment of the instruction given by the Commissar for the Defense of the Reich in Upper Silesia — the *Gauleiter* and High President of the province of Upper Silesia, Fritz Bracht — on December 21, 1944, regarding the evacuation on foot from Upper Silesia of the civilian population, slave laborers, prisoners-of-war and other prisoners, including the ones being held at KL Auschwitz.

Trecke der Kriegsgefangenen.
Die ausser Lamsdorf noch vorgesehenen Rastlager (für 3tägige
Zwischenrast) werden vom Kommandeur der Kriegsgefangenen im
Benehmen mit den zuständigen Landräten und zunächst und dem
Reichsverteidigungskommissar mitgeteilt. Die Kriegsgefangenen
werden nach der Zwischenrast möglichst schnell nach Oberschlesien
abtransportiert.

Trecke der KL-Häftlinge.
Besondere Berücksichtigung erfordert wegen ihrer Länge und
Bedeutung für die allgemeine Sicherheit die Marschstrasse der
KL-Auschwitz. Um ihre Marschleistung nicht zu beeinträchtigen,
wurde ihr die Benutzung eines "Kunsttreckweges" für die zivile
Bevölkerung und das Vormarschrecht bei Kreuzungen zugestanden,
die im linken Odergebiet nicht ganz zu vermeiden waren. Dieser
Treckweg ist also von Rastplatz zu Rastplatz fortschreitend auf
rd. 20 km für alle anderen Trecks gesperrt. Das gleiche gilt für
die nördliche Ausweichstrasse, über Alt-Berun, Nichau usw.,
falls diese gewählt werden muss.

wenden!

Miedzna, den 19.Januar 1945.

Betr.: Häftlinge aus dem K.L.Auschwitz.

An den

Herrn Ortspolizeiverwalter

in P Y S K I L E S .

Im Bereich des Gendarmerie Postens P i e d ż n a sind auf
dem Transport von Auschwitz 39 Häftlinge verstorben. Darunter
waren 10 männliche und 29 weibl.Personen. Nur 15 davon hatten eine
Nummer, bei den übrigen konnte kein Kennzeichen festgestellt werden
Folgende Kennnummern wurden festgestellt:
-300, 4292, 36143, A6737, 9699, 10369, 18927, 17243, 15244,
-1993, 17770, 13221,27645, 76596, 30816, 32716,33910, 19974,
30631, 31204, 156775, 135285, 2 1917.0, 195333, 175252.

Löw,

Hptw.d.Gend.d.Res.

Memorandum from the commander of the civilian police in Miedźna (near Pszczyna) from January 19,
1945, reporting the discovery of the corpses of 39 prisoners who had been murdered during their
evacuation (death march) from KL Auschwitz.

Lfd.-lfd.-Nr.	Jahr, Monat, Tag und Stunde	Namen und Vorname	Beruf	Stand	Alter	Religions-Bekenntnis	Ort des Todesfalls (genaue Adresse)	Todesursache	Serierung Wann und wo?	Mehrkkosmi	Amt, Datum und Nummer der Bewilligung zur Einäscherung	Amt, Datum u. Nummer der Bewilligung	Wann u. wo? Amt, Datum und Nummer der Bewilligung	Jahr, Monat, Tag und Stunde	Obergehen (Name, Adresse des Übernehmers) Amt, Datum und Nummer der Bewilligung	Ort der Hinterlegung der Asche	Bemerkung
30 87	1945	163238	Geheime Staatspolizei Olmütz					Bordwaffen erschossen						1945 7-2 Mittwoch			K
30 88	1945	129276	Geheime Staatspolizei Olmütz					Bordwaffen erschossen						1945 7-2 Mittwoch			K
30 89	1945	A8812	Geheime Staatspolizei Olmütz					Bordwaffen erschossen						1945 7-2 Mittwoch			K
30 90	1945	B6356	Geheime Staatspolizei Olmütz					Bordwaffen erschossen						1345 7-2 Mittwoch			K
30 91	1945	187301	Geheime Staatspolizei Olmütz					Erfroren						1945 7-2 Mittwoch			K
30 92	1945	175510	Geheime Staatspolizei Olmütz					Erfroren						1945 8-2 Donnerstag			K
30 93	1945	18734	Geheime Staatspolizei Olmütz					Erfroren						1945 8-2 Donnerstag			K
30 94	1945	B 8635	Geheime Staatspolizei Olmütz					Erfroren						1945 8-2 Donnerstag			K
30 95	1945	B 1344	Geheime Staatspolizei Olmütz					Erfroren						1945 8-2 Donnerstag			K
30 96	1945	B 13461	Geheime Staatspolizei Olmütz					Erfroren						1945 8-2 Donnerstag			K

Fragment of the daily log book from the crematorium of the cemetery at Olomouc reporting the
cremation of the corpses of 14 prisoners from KL Auschwitz, who had either perished from exposure or
been shot by SS guards during their evacuation from KL Auschwitz through Moravia to the Third Reich
proper.

The warehouse barracks at Birkenau that had held the property of Jewish extermination victims burned for five days after being set on fire by the retreating SS men.

The SS men blew up the crematoria and gas chambers before leaving the camp.

On January 27, 1945, the camp at Auschwitz was liberated. The health service of the Soviet army and the Polish Red Cross gave immediate assistance to the surviving prisoners.

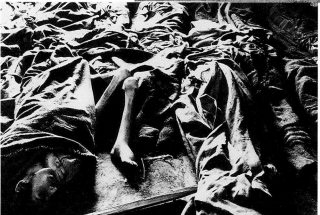

Not all the prisoners at KL Auschwitz survived until liberation. At the moment of the camp's liberation, the bodies of around 600 prisoners were found, who had either been shot or who had perished from disease, hunger, and exhaustion.

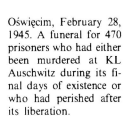

Oświęcim, February 28, 1945. A funeral for 470 prisoners who had either been murdered at KL Auschwitz during its final days of existence or who had perished after its liberation.

One of the wards of the Polish Red Cross hospital at the liberated camp.

The remnants of the plunder taken from the victims by the SS that were found on the grounds of the camp after liberation.

In the warehouses of the liberated camp, around seven tons of human hair from the victims were found. The SS had failed to ship it inside the Third Reich proper.

Session at Oświęcim of the Special State Commission for the USSR for the Investigation of German Crimes, chaired by Dr. Dimitri Kudriavtsev (1945).

The Commission for the Investigation of German Crimes in Poland examining Crematorium Nr. V and its gas chamber at Birkenau in 1945.

Nazi war criminals before the International Military Tribunal in Nuremberg.

Oswald Pohl, the former head of the Main Economic-Administrative Office of the SS, was condemned during Trial Nr. IV by the American Military Tribunal to death for the crimes he had committed at the concentration camps.

The first commandant of KL Auschwitz, *SS-Obersturmbannführer* Rudolf Höss being extradited to Poland, where he was condemned to death by Poland's Supreme National Tribunal in 1947.

The court chambers of the Supreme National Tribunal in Poland. In 1947, the trial against 40 SS staff members from KL Auschwitz was held here.

A few of the 40 defendants in the trial against the camp SS staff. In the first row are (l-r): Arthur Liebehenschel, the second commandant at the camp; Maria Mandel, *Lagerführerin* at the women's camp, and Hans Aumeier, *Lagerführer* at the main camp.

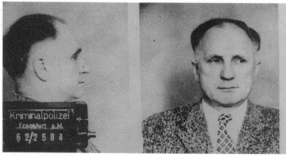

ichard Baer, the ird and last commandant at KL Auhwitz, died in prion in Germany dung preparations for trial against him efore the State ourt in Frankfurt n Main.

Some of the defendants at the trial of Robert Mulka and others in Frankfurt a. M. In the first row (in dark glasses) is SS pharmacist Victor Capesius and behind him, *Rapportführer* Oswald Kaduk.

On-site inspection at Auschwitz — in the first row (in the hat) is the presiding judge of the State Court in Frankfurt a. M., Walter Hotz.

SS doctor Horst Fischer during testimony at his trial in Berlin in 1966.

enemy threat, prisoners and POWs should be evacuated immediately on foot for at least the first portion of the evacuation route. The codename for the evacuation of prisoners, including those at Auschwitz, was "Karla", while the operations to evacuate POWs and slave laborers were dubbed *Krebs* ("Cancer") and *Amerika*.

The evacuation routes for Auschwitz prisoners were predetermined. For fear of potential rebellions, it was ordered that columns of prisoner-evacuees be given right-of way at all crossings where they met up with other evacuation columns. The guards that would be leading the columns of prisoners and the other Nazi functionaries responsible for the evacuation received an order that prisoners and POWs who tried to escape be treated like saboteurs — i.e., that they be killed on the spot. The final evacuation of prisoners from KL Auschwitz conformed for the most part to these instructions.

In mid-January 1945, the Supreme Commander of the SS and police in Wrocław (Breslau), *SS-Obergruppenführer* Schmauser, ordered the final evacuation of prisoners from KL Auschwitz. Theoretically, the columns of evacuees were supposed to be filled only with strong, healthy prisoners who could march a distance of several dozen kilometers, but, in practice, ailing and debilitated prisoners also reported for evacuation in the belief — which was not groundless — that those who remained at the camp would be murdered. Adolescents and children set out along with the adults.

From January 17-21, 1945, around 56,000 prisoners were led out of KL Auschwitz and its sub-camps on foot, in evacuation columns headed westward in the general direction of Upper and Lower Silesia. From two sub-camps, Eintrachthütte in Świętochłowice and Laurahütte in Siemianowice, around 2,200 prisoners were evacuated in railway transports on January 23. The earliest prisoners to be evacuated on foot — on January 17 — came from the Neu-Dachs (Jaworzno) and Sosnowitz II (Sosnowiec) sub-camps, and the last to be evacuated on foot, on January 21, were the prisoners of the Blechhammer sub-camp in Blachownia Śląska. Around 25,000 prisoners walked the route leading from Oświęcim through Pszczyna to Wodzisław Śląski, [9] while at least 14,000 were led along a route leading from Oświęcim through Tychy and Mikołów to Gliwice. In the end, a total of around 58,000 prisoners were evacuated.

The 3,200 prisoners of the Neu-Dachs sub-camp in Jaworzno had to walk one of the longest evacuation routes. It wound through the center of the Upper Silesian industrial region and through the foothills of the Sudeten Mountains to KL Gross-Rosen in Lower Silesia. The entire route was 250 km long.

As the prisoners marched along the various routes, the SS guards shot anybody who tried to escape, along with those who were unable to keep up with their comrades due to physical exhaustion. The cities of Wodzisław Śląski and Gliwice were the main centres at which the columns of marching prisoners

---

[9] Detailed descriptions of the evacuees' march along the road to Wodzisław Śląski can be found in: Halina Wróbel, "Die Liquidation des Konzentrationslager Auschwitz-Birkenau", *Hefte von Auschwitz* 6 (1962), pp. 16-49; A. Strzelecki, *Marsz śmierci*. In 1988, the Katowice chapter of a Polish organization, TOnO, placed markers along the path mentioned above that point out areas of particular significance.

were transferred onto rail transports. The prisoners who survived to make it to these cities were dispatched, among other places, through Bohemia and Moravia to the Mauthausen and Buchenwald concentration camps, located inside the *Reich* proper. Despite the cold, the prisoners were shipped to their final destinations in open freight cars. They also did not receive any rations. During the journey, the bodies of dead prisoners were thrown out of the freight cars.

The corpses of thousands of prisoners, either shot or dead from exhaustion and exposure, littered the evacuation routes both on foot and by train. For example, at least 450 prisoners were killed along the path to Wodzisław Śląski, while around 210 prisoners died on one of the other evacuation routes along a 20 km stretch of back roads between Płużnica Wielka (near Strzelce Opolskie) and Ujazd. During the evacuation, around 3,000 prisoners perished in Upper Silesia alone. It is estimated that in the course of the entire operation, at least 9,000 — and most likely up to 15,000 — prisoners from KL Auschwitz perished.

Massacres of prisoners occurred at several locations along the evacuation routes. One occurred in Leszczyny-Rzędówka, near Rybnik. On the night of January 21-22, 1945, a train carrying prisoner-evacuees from Gliwice was halted. On the afternoon of January 22, the prisoners were ordered to leave the cars. Some of the prisoners were too physically exhausted to carry out this order. The SS men who had accompanied the transport, along with local policemen, murdered the prisoners remaining inside the railway cars with blasts of machine-gun fire through the open doors. The prisoners who had made it out of the cars were driven on foot to the west. Once they left the immediate vicinity of the station, the corpses of 288 prisoners — shot along the way or dead from exposure and exhaustion — were gathered up. [10]

The large number of mass graves bears witness to the scale of the crimes committed against the prisoners in the course of the evacuation. The largest number of mass graves, around 60, can be found in Upper Silesia; and around 50, in what is today the Czech Republic. The local population devotes a great deal of care to these. Memorial tablets have been erected at the grave sites. Several tombstones bear inscriptions listing the camp numbers of prisoners buried at the site; the local population had written them down whenever they

---

[10] Around 2,200 prisoners were led in two separate groups from the station at Leszczyny-Rzędówka and to the west through Racibórz. Around 700 of them died during the march to Racibórz, and the largest number at one time — around 300 — during a stop in Rybnik. The first postwar estimates regarding these events appeared in Kazimierz Leszczyński, "Eksterminacja ludności polskiej na ziemiach polskich w latach 1939-1945. Opracowanie materiałów ankiety z 1945 r. (woj. śląsko-dąbrowskie i warszawskie)", *Biuletyn Głównej Komisji Badania Zbrodni Hitlerowskich* 11 (1960), pp. 220-22.

In 1986-90, in honor of Jan Delowicz from Żory below Rybnik, a social worker who is also an amateur historian assembled an extensive documentary work related to the route (accounts, memoirs and letters of former prisoner-escapees thanking several residents of the Rybnik area for saving their lives) and donated it to the archives of the State Museum at Oświęcim: APMO, Collection of Testimonies, vol. 120, 123; APMO, Collection of Photographs, vol. 127, photographs from the July 1945 memorial service in Leszczyny-Rzędówka at the mass grave of victims from the evacuation.

could be established on the basis of a tattoo or a patch on the prisoner's clothing.

The remains of younger prisoners, including children, rest in several of the graves. While they were working to unite three adjacent mass graves in Pszczyna in 1965, members of the work-crew conducting the exhumation found the remains of a small girl. Near her face was a tin mug that she had been holding in her hands. Her remains were re-buried in a new grave at the same site.

Few documents regarding the evacuaton of Auschwitz prisoners have survived the war. Besides the instructions of *Gauleiter* Bracht, mentioned above, two reports have survived, one written by Dr. Haffner, the District Attorney for Katowice, and the other by the President of the Katowice District Court in Nysa on February 1, 1945. The two reports describe the evacuation of different population groups from Upper Silesia, including Germans who had been living there. [11]

Another surviving form of documentation are reports from various German police outposts regarding prisoners' corpses found along the evacuation routes, including their camp numbers. Several such reports have survived. Other documents deserving of mention include the daily crematorium register for the cementery in Olomouc, Moravia. The register lists the camp numbers of fourteen prisoners who perished during the camp's evacuation. The logbook indicates that seven of the victims had been shot by the guards escorting the evacuation transports ("*Bordwaffen erschossen*"), while the remaininig prisoners had died from exposure ("*Erfroren*").

Documentation on the subject from after the war has proven to be much more extensive. One can list hundreds of accounts by participants and incidental witnesses to the evacuation. In addition to these accounts, reports based on the exhumation of prisoners' remains after the war, compiled by various judicial-investigative commissions, are of great importance.

One witness to the evacuation of the prisoners from Auschwitz was Teofil Balcarek, a farmer and resident of the small village of Branica, near Żory. In 1986, he presented the following account:

One night, we were awoken from our sleep by individual shots coming from the highway next to our house. This disturbed us, but we did not dare to leave the house. Nothing could be seen from the window. In the morning, at around 7:30 or 8:00, as a so-called carter, I left in my horse cart with containers of milk, mine and my neighbor's, in the direction of Kobielice, to deliver them to the designated locations around the crossroads. Not far from my house, I spotted on the shoulder of the road the corpse of a man dressed in concentration-camp clothes. It lay on the slope, you could see blood. Farther up, I saw several similar male corpses. Some of the ones who had been shot had been wearing camp uniforms, and others, workclothes. The sight of them horrified me, so I didn't stop. During my journey to Kobielice, I also came across colums of men going in the opposite direction, prisoners dressed in

[11] Originals of the reports can be found at the *Bundesarchiv* in Koblenz; they have also been published and discussed in: Andrzej Szefer, "Nieznany dokument hitlerowski z ostatnich dni Katowic", *Zaranie Śląskie* 1 (1973), pp. 151-52; A. Strzelecki, "Ewakuacja," pp. 155-56, 279, 280.

uniforms and workclothes. There were two or three groups of more than several dozen people. They were walking very slowly, 'barely moving their feet', under the escort of armed guards. At the edge of the woods, I personally became a witness to how a guard shot one of them. He had fallen behind the column. A guard quickly ran up behind him and shot him with a pistol (not with a rifle, but a sidearm). None of the other prisoners even looked back. This scene heightened my fears. After I delivered the milk, I went home.' [12]

A resident of Jastrzębie Zdrój, Maria Śleziona, stated in 1978:

I observed the tragic march of the prisoners along with other residents from the window of the house in which I have lived up to today. Women prisoners walked down Pszczyńska Street. On the left side of the street, a woman at an advanced stage of pregnancy fell out of line. She held herself up by the stomach against a transformer wall. The column went by and did not stop. An SS man came up and pushed the pregnant woman to the curb on the right side of the road. We ran to another window, from where we had a better view. The prisoner was lying on her back in the snow. The SS man shot her in the face with his pistol and a second time in the stomach. When the street had emptied out, we went out to see the prisoner who had been murdered. She was a young woman, around twenty-five years old. [13]

The residents of the towns and villages through which, or next to which, the evacuation route ran not only followed the drama that was playing out in the streets, but also offered assistance to the prisoners being evacuated. They helped despite threats of brutal retaliation by the Nazi authorities. It was mainly Poles in Silesia and Czechs in Bohemia and Moravia who rushed to assist the prisoners; Germans from these areas helped less often. Behind the backs of the SS guards or in front of their very eyes, they gave the prisoners water, bread and other food. They also helped escaped prisoners in various ways.

When people tried to help, the SS men would brutally drive them back from the columns of evacuees, threatening to use physical force or to shoot them. Thus, attempts to assist the prisoners with food were often ineffective. In his memoir, former prisoner Jan Wygas recounts a drastic case:

I remember that on one of the streets in the city of Gliwice, a woman came up to our column with a milk-can of water and told the SS men in German, 'Let them drink, they are people after all.' She gave the container of water to one of the prisoners. The SS men shouted at her, but she went back. While she was leaving, they shot her in the back of the head. The woman fell to the ground. I personally observed this scene. [14]

Thanks to the assistance of the local population in several parts of Upper Silesia, a number of escaped prisoners were able to make it to freedom. Certain villages harbored several escapees, while others hid ten or twenty; certain

---

[12] APMO, Collection of Testimonies, vol. 115, cards 204-5.

[13] APMO, IZ-27/3, 11, documents from the ZBoWiD circle in Jastrzębie Zdrój.

[14] APMO, Collection of Testimonies, vol. 89, p. 138. It is not known whether this resident of Gliwice was a German woman or a Pole.

towns hid several dozen. The former prisoners often had to be concealed for several weeks, until units of the Red Army arrived. Some of the escaped prisoners have kept in contact with their saviors to this day.

Three Polish veterans of the Silesian Uprisings after World War I residing in Jastrzębie Zdrój — Edward Marcol, Franciszek Parzych and Ludwik Pisarski — hid more than twenty prisoners, both men and women, in their homes. One of the former escapees, a Jewish woman, Helena Berman, wrote to Franciszek Parzych and his wife, Maria, about the help they had given her in a testimonial letter from January 1946: "I could write forever about those moments full of sacrifice and terror for us [former prisoner-escapees — AS] and the fate of my saviours, but I just want to say: let there be honour and God's blessing to our saviours, good-hearted Poles, fervent Polish patriots." [15] In 1964, the Polish government awarded Maria Parzych the Gold Service Cross for saving prisoners. Then, in 1984, for giving protection to Helena Berman, the Parzychs were recognized in Israel with the medal for the Righteous Among Nations. [16]

Numerous forms of documentation have survived in which former Auschwitz prisoners who escaped during the evacuation have expressed their gratitude to residents of Upper Silesia who assisted them, including, for example:

a) A declaration written in 1945 by a group of former Jewish prisoners in the village of Książenice-Lasoki (below Rybnik):

We, the undersigned, escapees from the camp at Auschwitz, attest that Jurytko Bruno from the village of Książenice kept us at the risk of his own life and that of his family for eight days, feeding us, giving us a room to stay and sleep in, and granting us every possible assistance. He did all of this at a time when German and SS units were searching for escapees throughout the entire area. In this way, he saved all our lives, without any material gain, as a good human-being.

The signatures of 14 former prisoners follow, from Poland, Austria, Holland, France and Germany. [17]

b) An October 1946 letter, written in German, by Friedel Gilsbach-Strauss in Amsterdam to Władysław Wuzik, a resident of the village of Brzeźce (near Pszczyna) and his family. The most important passage reads: "I will never forget you as long as I live, for I owe you my very life; if you had not been so good to me, I would have never seen my homeland again. [18]

---

[15] The text of the letter is contained in Józef Musioł, "Było to w styczniu", *Poglądy* 1:221 (1972), p. 6.

[16] The Institute for National Memory, Yad Vashem, recognizes individuals with this award who have distinguished themselves by saving Jews. In 1989, the Tender family in Pszczyna, who had originally lived in the nearby town of Radostowice, also received the award for their assistance to Eliezer Eisenschmidt, a former member of the *Sonderkommando* at Auschwitz.

[17] A copy of the declaration can be found in APMO. Mat./1623, Collection of Materials, vol. 211. Also see APMO, Collection of Testimonies, vol. 120, cards 41-43b, account of Bronisława Jurytko, and Łukasz Wyrzykowski, "Kamień by się zlitował," *Dziennik Zachodni* 77 (1988).

[18] APMO, Mat./1571, Collection of Materials, vol. 207, card 3.

c) The dedication by Olga Lengyel — the author of the well-known Holocaust memoir, Five Chimneys — in a folder on New York that she gave to the Paszek family in Brzeźce: "To the family Paszek in Brzeźce who had saved my life during the evacuation of the concentration camp Auschwitz, with love and gratitude. 19/20.04.1983." [19]

Nobody has ever added up all the escapees whom the people of Silesia saved, but, on the other hand, no one has ever added up all the escapees who — as a result of not having found assistance or a place to hide — perished in the hands of the Nazis. Evidence and traces of such tragedies have also been found.

When the evacuation transports from Auschwitz reached their destination at other camps, name lists were made of the new arrivals. Some of the surviving name lists from these other camps contain significant information. For example, a list of the 3,987 prisoners who arrived at KL Buchenwald on January 26, 1945, did not list 176 individuals who were unable to give their names because they were either unconscious or dead. The number dead totalled 143. [20]

Many of the prisoners who survived the evacuation from Auschwitz perished at concentration camps inside the Third Reich during the final months of its existence.

2.2. The Last Days of the Camp (January 18-27, 1945)

The evacuation of around 58,000 prisoners from KL Auschwitz in the second half of January 1945 represented the largest effort of its kind undertaken in the course of the camp's final liquidation. The camp staff at Auschwitz was also evacuated in a hurry, along with goods still stored at the camp (including, for example, a large quantity of foodstuffs and clothing). A number of last-minute efforts were also made to destroy evidence of the crimes committed at the camp.

A characteristic sight on the streets of the camp during its final evacuation were burning piles of camp documents. Oversight at the camp decreased; the SS men, working to leave the area as quickly as possible, only spot-checked to see whether prisoners were following their orders. So, the prisoners assigned to burn documents, aware of their future importance, managed to save some of them.

On January 20, 1945, Crematorium II and III were blown up (their internal mechanisms had already been removed at the end of 1944), and on January 26, Crematorium V, which had remained open for use up to that point, was demolished as well. On January 23, "Canada" II, the grouping of

---

[19] APMO, Mat./1650, Collection of Materials, vol. 214, correspondence of Olga Lengyel with the Paszek family from 1947-88.

[20] APMO, D-Bu-3/1/7, Document collection related to KL Buchenwald, vol. 7 ("Männer"), cards 82-85, 87 (copies). Part of the list has been reproduced in Strzelecki, "Ewakuacja", pp. 288-89.

warehouse barracks that had contained the possessions of victims, was burnt to the ground.

After the final columns of prisoner-evacuees had been marched out of KL Auschwitz, around 9,000 prisoners remained at the camp, most of whom were ill and emaciated, unfit for evacuation on foot. A number of sources indicate that the SS planned to liquidate them not only as witnesses to their crimes, but also as an unwanted burden, unexploitable for labor at camps inside the Third Reich. After the necessary orders were given, the SS men murdered around 700 prisoners in the final days of KL Auschwitz's existence — some from Birkenau, some from the sub-camps. At the Fürstengrube sub-camp, for example, more than 200 prisoners were burned alive inside their barracks. [21]

Most of the prisoners left at Auschwitz, however, were not murdered at the last minute and survived to be liberated by the Red Army. Undoubtedly, they were able to avoid extermination for two reasons: first, the decline in discipline among the SS men and second, the general disorganization, or even panic, within the ranks of the German troops retreating from Oświęcim and Upper Silesia.

After most of the SS guards had left the camp, the prisoners who could move spontaneously broke into warehouses and other camp buildings in search of food and clothing. They were so overwhelmed by the possibility of obtaining food and saving themselves from death through starvation that they did not even react when SS men began firing at them. Many prisoners were killed while they were removing food from the camp warehouses. Cases also occurred in which prisoners died from consuming excessive quantities of "organized" food.

Some of the prisoners, mainly from the camp hospital staff, made an effort to reorder life at the camp, particularly the conditions that confronted the severely ill, whom they sought to protect to the greatest extent possible.

They organized deliveries of food from the warehouses to the residential barracks and began rationing food. They also dealt with the problem of obtaining water and tried to clean up the rooms and prepare warm meals. In the infirmary at the men's camp, on the grounds of section BIIf at Birkenau, they even re-opened the kitchen, which had been closed since the beginning of the evacuation. To the extent that it was possible, they provided the ill with medicine and changed their dressings.

The self-help activities of the prisoners on the verge of liberation represented a natural continuation of the resistance movement that had developed at the camp. Naturally, the prisoners involved were unable to give the necessary assistance to everyone who needed it.

Up to the moment of the camp's liberation, the prisoners remaining at the camp continued to live with the feeling of complete uncertainty that they had

---

[21] The murder of these 700 prisoners was only a small link in a chain of massacres committed by the Nazis at the camps and other centers of confinement before the Allied onslaught into the Third Reich. Examples: Małyj Trostinec, near Minsk, at the end of June 1944, ca. 6,500 victims; KL Klooga in Estonia, 19 September 1944, ca. 2,200 victims; Łódź-Radogoszcz and Słońsk near Kostrzyn, second half of January 1945, more than 2,800 victims; the group of eleven "Kaufering" sub-camps (attached to KL Dachau), April 1945, hundreds of victims.

long known — i.e., with the knowledge that they could be exterminated at any given moment. At the same time, they lived with the hope of regaining their freedom, a feeling that grew stronger as they heard the front approaching.

On January 27, 1945, this hope became reality.

3. Liberation of the Camp

The task of liberating Auschwitz fell to the soldiers of the 60th Army of the First Ukrainian Front, advancing from the left bank of the Vistula from Cracow in the direction of the Upper Silesian industrial district. With the other Soviet armies, they were supposed to surround the industrial district and force a rapid retreat by the German army.

The 100th Lvov (Lviv) Infantry Division, led by Major General Fyodor Mikhailovich Krasavin, took direct part in the Auschwitz operation. On January 26, 1945, the infantry division crossed the Vistula. On Saturday morning, January 27, 1945, the first scouts from the division appeared in the eastern portion of Auschwitz, on the grounds of the Monowitz sub-camp (Monowice). Soviet soldiers reached the city center by mid day on January 27. In the afternoon, they entered the area of the main camp and the camp at Birkenau (Brzezinka), where they encountered resistance from retreating German units. They quickly overcame this resistance and liberated both the main camp, Auschwitz I, and the camp at Birkenau, Auschwitz II, at around 3 p.m. [22]

The atmosphere that prevailed at KL Auschwitz immediately upon its liberation has been recounted in the testimonies and memoirs of former prisoners. One of the women prisoners at the camp wrote as follows:

> We heard a grenade explode near the gate to the camp. We immediately looked out of the block and saw several Soviet scouts walking from the gates in our direction, with their guns ready to fire. We immediately hung out on poles sheets with red bands sewn on them in the form of a red cross. When they saw us, the scouts dropped their weapons. A spontaneous greeting took place. Since I knew Russian, I turned to one scout and said, *'Zdrastvi'tye pobyedit'eli i osvoboditl'eli!'* We heard the reply, 'Yzhe vy svobodny'e!' [23]

Two hundred thirty-one Soviet solidiers, including the commander of the 472nd Regiment, Lt. Col. Semon Lvovich B'ezsprozwannyj, fell in the struggle to liberate the general area of the camp at Monowice, the main camp and the

---

[22] The description of the operation to liberate Auschwitz presented here is based on the findings of Soviet researchers, in particular on the details contained in the brochure, "Oświęcim-Brzezinka. Państwowe Muzeum Oświęcim-Brzezinka. Ekspozycja radziecka," published in 1988 by the Vnyeshtorgizdal publishing house in Moscow. One of the Red Army Leaders who took direct part in the liberation of the Auschwitz camp was Lt. Gen. Wasily Jokowlewicz Petrenko. Also see: *The Liberation of the Nazi Concentration Camps 1945: Eyewitness Accounts of the Liberators* (Washington, 1987), pp. 181-2, 188-9, 195.

[23] Translator's note: The prisoners exclaimed in Russian, "Welcome, victors and liberators!" The reply: "You are free!" APMO, Collection of Testimonies, vol. 75, card 13, account of Anna Chomicz.

camp at Birkenau. Sixty-six, including second Lt. Col. Gilmudin Badry'evich Bashirov, perished during fighting immediately outside the camp.

A total of around 7,000 prisoners awaited liberation at the main camp, Birkenau and Monowitz. It has been difficult to establish the number of prisoners (probably around 500) whom the Soviets liberated around January 27 at the following sub-camps: Althammer in Stara Kuźnia, Blechhammer in Blachownia Śląska, Eintrachthütte in Świętochłowice, Fürstengrube in Wesoła, Janinagrube in Libiąż, Jawischowitz in Jawiszowice and Neu Dachs in Jaworzno.

Among the prisoners liberated at KL Auschwitz were well-known individuals who were respected both in Poland and abroad: Prof. Xawery Dunikowski, the Polish sculptor and artist; Bertold Epstein, Professor of Pediatrics at the Charles University in Prague and Director of the Prague Children's Clinic; Bruno Fischer, Professor of Psychiatry from Prague; the writer Dr. Alfred Fiderkiewicz, a Polish worker and peasant activist; Prof. Stanisław Kętrzyński, the Polish diplomat and historian of medieval history; Adam Kurcyłowicz, an activist in the Polish workers' movement; Prof. Henri Limousin, a professor of pathological anatomy at the University of Clermont-Ferrand; Geza Mansfeld, Professor of Pharmacology and Experimental Pathology in Pécs and member of the Hungarian Academy of Sciences; and Dr. Roman Łaba, the esteemed physician from Przemyśl in Poland.

The Soviet soldiers found the bodies of around 600 prisoners on the grounds of the Auschwitz and Birkenau camps, either shot by the retreating SS men or dead from malnutrition. The bodies were not the only evidence of crimes that they found, however.

Some of the prisoners liberated from Auschwitz who were in a relatively good state of health immediately made their way home.

4. Assistance for the Liberated Prisoners

Already in the first days after Auschwitz's liberation, the Red Army's medical staff, as well as Polish authorities and individual Poles, rushed to the former prisoners' assistance. The Polish Red Cross (PCK) chapters in Oświęcim, Brzeszcze and Cracow played a significant role. The largest contingent of PCK volunteers, from Cracow, also included Varsovians, former participants in the Warsaw Uprising, who had been evacuated from the capital by the Nazis. A PCK Camp Hospital arose alongside the Red Army field hospitals at the liberated camp. The Soviet hospitals were constantly changing as a result of reorganizations within the Red Army; at first, the hospitals were directed by Doctor-Commanders Wejtkov, Chitarorow and Mielai, and in a later period, by Drs. Żylińska and Grabovoi. Dr. Józef Bellert from Warsaw directed the PCK hospital.

Around 4,500 former prisoners came under the hospitals' care, citizens of over 20 countries, mainly Jews. Of the 960 who were Polish citizens, the largest grouping of 160-170 people were Polish women who had been deported to KL Auschwitz during the Warsaw Uprising. More than 200 children (up to 15 years of age) were housed at the hospitals, including many twins. Most of the former prisoners suffered from starvation diarrhea, a symptom of "hunger disease" (*distrophia alimentaris*), an affliction usually accompanied by complications — most often, tuberculosis.

In addition to Dr. Bellert, the following doctors worked on the staff of the PCK Camp Hospital: Jan Jodłowski, Jadwiga Magnuszewska and Bolesław Urbański from Cracow; and Jan Szcześniak from Oświęcim. Recognized individuals on the staff of the Soviet field hospitals included a Major Polakow and a surgical doctor, Major Jełtański, who served in the sections headed by Majors Mielai and Zhylińska.

Some resident-volunteers from Oświęcim, Brzeszcze and the general area worked for the Soviet field hospitals even before the PCK group arrived from Cracow on February 5-6, 1945. These volunteers included, among others, three residents of Brzeszcze — Tadeusz Mleko, Roman Pęcikiewicz and Wilhelm Wazdrąg — who came to Brzezinka (Birkenau) on their own and were the first Poles to assist the ill alongside the Soviet medical personnel. Other natives of Brzeszcze (e.g., Zdzisław Bosek and several of his friends) and a number of residents from Oświęcim (Józef Mroziński and several colleagues, and nuns from the Seraphim order) voluntarily assisted the Soviet medical staff at what had been the main camp. Residents of Poręba Wielka and Włosienica cooperated with Soviet doctors and sanitarians in caring for former prisoners at the Monowice sub-camp.

The successive Soviet field hospitals and the PCK Camp Hospital worked closely together. PCK nurses helped staff the blocks that were run exclusively by the Soviets. Eventually, consultations between Soviet and Polish doctors became more frequent, as did joint rounds inside the sick wards. The Polish and Soviet personnel began to work together, and the medical treatment at the hospitals became more standardized.

A number of conditions unique to the camp made the work of the Red Army medical staff and the PCK volunteers particularly difficult. The former Birkenau camp (Brzezinka) presented the greatest difficulties. Fires had to be kept burning day and night in order to heat the buildings sufficiently. Before the floors could be gradually washed, layers of excrement passed by patients suffering from starvation diarrhea first had to be scraped off with shovels. The water needed for — among other things — washing the patients and preparing their meals had to be carried in from distant fire barrels and wells. Sometimes, lumps of snow were melted. Due to the initial lack of sanitarians and other assistants, it was impossible to remove all the bodies left lying next to the barracks since liberation, let alone to clean up all the excrement and other excretions that could be seen all over the camp.

At first, besides several doctors and a few auxiliary staff, there were only twelve Polish Red Cross nurses working at Brzezinka (Birkenau) for the benefit of around 2,200 patients. Each nurse was thus responsible for around 200 patients. Striving to carry out their duties nevertheless, some members of the PCK team worked more than 12 hours each day, and at times, two to three days without a break.

Because the conditions at Brzezinka and Monowice did not permit the necessary care, all the patients at the two former camps were transferred to brick blocks at what had been the main camp in the course of several weeks. After an enormous effort, the personnel at the Soviet field hospitals and the Red Cross volunteers were able to adapt these buildings to the hospitals' needs. Hundreds of severely-ill prisoners were lifted off their existing pallets, covered with filth and excrement, and transferred to the freshly-cleaned rooms.

The medical staff progressively overcame the difficulties that they faced, including, for example, an insufficient number of medications and the lack of various types of food, bedding and water. With the passage of time, special wards were established at the PCK hospital: tuberculosis, internal diseases, surgery, and a section for women suffering from psychological and nervous disorders.

The statement of a former PCK volunteer, first assigned to a ward of 80 patients in February 1945, provides insight into the work carried out by PCK volunteers:

> Already during my first night-shift in the room, eleven women died. I had to lift the corpses off the pallets and carry them out into the corridor myself. Early the next morning, the sanitarians removed the bodies from the block. All night long, I heard calls from different corners of the room: *'Schwester, Schieber!'* (Nurse, a bed-pan!) The patients were suffering from *Durchfall*, or starvation diarrhea. So I was constantly handing out bed-pans. I did not have anyone to help. [24]

The patients were re-accustomed to eating by feeding them meals in medical doses — e.g., a tablespoon of strained potato soup three times a day, subsequently increased to several tablespoons. Weeks after the camps's liberation, the nurses would still find bread that the patients had hidden beneath their pallets or mattresses for the next day, due to their disbelief that they would soon receive a new ration. The constant fear that they had learned at the camp and the reflexes associated with it were stronger among the patients than their sense of reality. For the same reason, many patients sent to shower would run away at the word "bath". It took a long time to convince them that the bathhouse they were going to did not represent any threat. They still associated baths with the camp's "saunas", where — as we know — selections had been carried out among the prisoners and those found unfit for work had been sent to the gas chambers. A similar reaction confronted the nurses whenever they tried to administer intravenous and intramuscular injections. Some women patients did not like receiving injections and even defended themselves for fear of "phenol" — extermination by phenol injection, the fate of many of their comrades at KL Auschwitz.

Under the thoughtful care of the doctors and nurses, the patients slowly freed themselves from the reflexes that they had learned at KL Auschwitz. The impact on their psyches from their experiences at the camp, however, was irreversible.

For two to three months, the nurses, as well as the male nurse-sanitarians, assisted the patients in two shifts, one at day and one at night. Their

---

[24] APMO, Collection of Testimonies, vol. 74, card 175-76, account of nurse Maria Rogoż, a former Red Cross volunteer and participant in the PCK action in Oświęcim in 1945.

responsibilities surpassed their physical capabilities. As a result, patients only received partial care in many cases. A radical improvement came only in April-May, when the activities of the Soviet and PCK hospitals at the camp stabilized and the nursing staff began working eight-hour shifts.

We should stress the contribution made by several dozen former prisoners in helping cure their comrades lying in the PCK and Soviet field hospitals. Despite their own generally poor state of health, they worked as doctors, nurses, and sanitarians. Their assistance was in keeping with the self-help activity initiated among the prisoners before liberation. Former prisoners who volunteered at the hospitals included: Dr. Irena Konieczna from Poland, Dr. Tibor Villányi from Hungary, Dr. Otto Wolken from Austria, Terezie Jirová from Czechoslovakia and Aldo Ragazzi from Italy.

The former prisoners received assistance beyond medical care. The PCK, for example, served as an intermediary for correspondence between former prisoners and their families. The information-search activity conducted by the PCK hospital administration also deserves mention. It was taken over in subsequent years by the information offices of the PCK in Cracow and Warsaw, and then, in 1954, by a special information office at the State Museum in Oświęcim (*Państwowe Muzeum w Oświęcimiu*, PMO).

Of no small significance for many patients was the assistance rendered by the local Catholic clergy, including Father Jan Skarbek, the parish-priest in Oświęcim, and Father Stanisław Rokita, director of the Salesian monastery in the town of Oświęcim and the first chaplain to arrive at the camp after its liberation. The priests provided both moral and material aid.

Most of the former prisoners left the Soviet field hospitals and the PCK's Camp Hospital within three or four months after liberation. Some headed for their home country on their own, while others left in transports organized by the Soviet military authorities. Despite the shortage of vehicles between mid-February to July, several dozen transports were organized and sent off. Hundreds of former prisoners originating from outside Poland were dispatched to collective repatriation centers in Katowice, Bielsko and Cracow. A number of former prisoners released from the hospital, just like their comrades who had left Auschwitz immediately after its liberation, were received at feeding centers and shelters organized in Cracow and other localities by Polish charities and social organizations.

The residents of Oświęcim, Brzeszcze and the general area not only took part in activities to assist the prisoners hospitalized at the camp, but also admitted 100-200 former prisoners into small hospitals that they had organized in the town of Oświęcim and in Brzeszcze.

The PCK chapter formed in the town of Oświęcim on February 5, 1945, numbering around 70 members, worked in close cooperation with the PCK Camp Hospital and the Soviet military authorities in assisting former prisoners. The group's administrative director, Alojzy Etgens, and Antoni Leśniak, a member of the group's administration, coordinated matters with the Polish and Soviet hospitals at the former camp. Based on a joint agreement, the city group in Oświęcim sent volunteers to work as sanitation crews, to perform the dirtiest and most difficult tasks on the grounds of the liberated camp. They also admitted several dozen former prisoners into a hospital that they had founded. Two local doctors, Tadeusz Müller and Bogumił Pietrzyk, volunteered their medical services to these patients. Nuns from the Seraphim order in Oświęcim also housed and cared for a number of ill prisoners at their convent.

The PCK circle in Brzeszcze, reactivated after the area's liberation, played a similar role to helping former prisoners. The members of the Brzeszcze chapter organized a hospital, where they treated at least 23 former women prisoners from the camp, along with 24 children (including babies) and a group of prisoners suffering from tuberculosis. Dr. Józef Sierankiewicz, Jan Drzewiecki and Ernest Friebe directed the PCK hospital in Brzeszcze. One of the nurses, Anna Krotosz, fell victim to tuberculosis as a result of her work in the hospitals's TB ward and died shortly thereafter. Maria Bobrzecka, the owner of Brzeszcze's town pharmacy, provided the hospital with medications at no profit to herself. Before the camp's liberation, she had been extremely active in the underground movement outside the camp in assisting prisoners.

The Red Cross chapter in Brzeszcze also took in 66 former prisoners liberated from the Jawischowitz sub-camp (Jawiszowice) and gave professional medical assistance to seven or eight women liberated from Birkenau who had been taken in by residents of the nearby village of Wola. Several local families also began treating former prisoners in their home on the basis of an agreement with the organization.

Residents of Cracow, Oświęcim and other nearby areas (e.g., in Poręba Wielka) followed Brzeszcze's example and cared for former prisoners in their homes for periods of weeks at a time, or sometimes even months. Spontaneous and official food collections were also held for the sake of former prisoners. Particularly telling was the way in which residents of Oświęcim and Brzeszcze took in a large number of children from the camp and cared for them. In a number of cases, these guardians adopted the children after a period of time. Some of the children were able, after years of searching, to find their next of kin.

The dedication demonstrated by PCK volunteers in their work at the hospitals for liberated prisoners at Auschwitz won not only the recognition of the former prisoners, but also the praise of the Soviet doctors. The fact that most of the volunteers had actively participated in the resistance movement against the Nazis undoubtedly influenced the effectiveness of their work. They brought to the hospitals at the liberated camp and to the PCK hospitals in Oświęcim and Brzeszcze their acquired zeal for overcoming extreme difficulties. The Polish Red Cross units benefited from their five years of experience in assisting prisoners as part of the local resistance movement.

The hospitalization in January-February 1945 of several thousand prisoners liberated from KL Auschwitz was not the first such case in the history of the concentration camps. The prisoners who had been liberated earlier from Majdanek had also been hospitalized. At a later date, in the final weeks of the war, Allied military authorities and the Red Cross would organize hospitals for liberated prisoners from other concentration camps, including KL Bergen-
-Belsen, KL Buchenwald, and KL Mauthausen. In all these different hospitals,

medical science was confronted with a unique category of patients ailing to an extent unknown up to that time: the malnourished, physically- and mentally- -debilitated concentration-camp prisoners. Almost everywhere, the treatment of these patients was of a pioneering character. The situation confronted by the Soviet and Polish hospital staff on the grounds of the former Auschwitz camp and in the surrounding area, however, was unique in several respects. The difficult conditions near the front contributed to this, as did the significant size of the group of prisoners, which numbered several thousand. The difficulties faced by the Soviet doctors and PCK volunteers in January-March 1945 were undoubtedly significantly larger than at the hospitals organized during the last weeks of the war. It is in this light that we should evaluate the hard work and dedication of the 200-250 staff members of the hospitals at Oświęcim, Brzezinka and Brzeszcze, as well as the efforts of the local population, thanks to whom several thousand extremely ill former prisoners were able to regain their health after a relatively short period of treatment and return home to their countries of origin.

5. The First Investigations into the Crimes Committed at Auschwitz

In 1945, Soviet and Polish authorities conducted intensive investigations at the site of the former Auschwitz concentration camp into the crimes that had been committed there. The first body to begin investigating was the Prosecutor's Office for the First Ukrainian Front. It operated under the aegis and oversight of the Special Soviet State Commission for the Investigation of Crimes by the German-Fascist Aggressors. During the investigation, Dymitr Ivanovich Kudriawtsev and S.G. Kuzhmin represented the Special Soviet State Commission.

In February and March 1945, the Soviet experts inspected the grounds of the camp and its structures (including the ruins of the crematoria and the pits containing human remains), acquainted themselves with the facilities and methods used not long before in the extermination process, and examined the goods that the SS had plundered from their victims. The Soviet experts were assisted by Professor Jarosław Doliński and Professor Roman Dawidowski (a specialist in the area of construction and technology for heating and combustion from Cracow), six residents from Oświęcim, and five former prisoners. Among the items recognized as material evidence of the crimes committed at Auschwitz were the more than one million items of men's, women's and children's clothing that were found; more than 43,500 pairs of shoes and around 14,000 carpets left behind by the victims. [25] In the former tannery (*Lederfabrik*) warehouses, they found besides the shoes around seven metric tons of human hair. After establishing that an average person's hair weighs 40-50 grams, they determined that the hair they found belonged to at least around 140,000 people who had been exterminated at KL Auschwitz in its final stage of existence.

---

[25] APMO, IZ-1/5, Other Collections, cards 22-28, "Protokół oględzin magazynów z mieniem pomordowanych znajdujących się na terenie Oświęcimskiego obozu macierzystego", March 4, 1945 (photocopy).

The representatives of the Prosecutor for the First Ukrainian Front heard the testimony of more than 200 former prisoners, including two former members of the *Sonderkommando*, Szlama Dragon and Henryk Tauber. Moreover, representatives of the Soviet Medical-Judicial Commission, assisted by doctors from the Soviet field hospitals and several former prisoner-doctors, established that of 2,819 former prisoners they examined, including 180 children, the majority of them suffered from diseases acquired at the camp. The doctors also conducted autopsies on the corpses of 536 prisoners and established that exhaustion was the cause of death in 474 cases. The medical-judicial commission devoted a great deal of attention to former prisoners who had been victims of criminal experiments at KL Auschwitz. Statements and explanations by former prisoners, particularly by the doctors, helped the Soviet experts better understand the problems connected with the camp.

Szlama Dragon (Nr. 50359), who had escaped from an evacuation transport in January 1945 and returned to Oświęcim, was on hand for the work of the Soviet commission. In March, he had them dig up a note near Crematorium III that his colleague, Salmen Gradowski, had written while working in the *Sonderkommando*. Thanks to his efforts, the note, a unique document in the history of KL Auschwitz, was saved from destruction.

On May 8, 1945, the Special Soviet State Commission for the Investigation of Crimes by the German-Fascist Aggressors released a long communiqué in the newspaper *Krasnaya Zwiezda* (Nr. 106) entitled, "Regarding the Horrific Crimes of the German Government at Auschwitz", which contained the results of their investigations conducted on the grounds of the former camp.

Conducting investigations for the Polish authorities on the grounds of the camp in 1945-46 were the Supreme Commission for the Investigation of German Crimes in Poland (*Główna Komisja Badania Zbrodni Niemieckich w Polsce*) [26] and the District Commision for the Investigation of German Crimes (*Okręgowa Komisja Badania Zbrodni Niemieckich*) in Cracow. From March 1945, a number of commission members toured the grounds of the liberated camp, including: Minister of Justice Edmund Zalewski; the Cracow District Attorney, Dr. Wincenty Jarosiński; the writer, Zofia Nałkowska; the investigating magistrate for the district, Jan Sehn; and various experts, including former prisoner Adam Kuryłowicz and the court expert from Cracow, Professor Roman Dawidowski. Just like the Soviet experts, they spent a great deal of time acquainting themselves with the material traces of the crimes committed at KL Auschwitz. Samples of the human hair that the Nazis had taken from their victims, along with metal parts from the gas chambers, were sent for analysis to the crime laboratories of the Institute for Court Appraisals (*Instytut Ekspertyz Sądowych*) in Cracow. Thousands of camp documents found by the investigators were deposited at the headquarters of the District Commision in Cracow. The commission also questioned former

---

[26] Working at the time under the name of the main Commission for the Investigation of Crimes Against the Polish Nation — Institute for National Memory (*Główna Komisja Badania Zbrodni Przeciwko Narodowi Polskiemu — Instytut Pamięci Narodowej*).

prisoners. From May 11-25, representatives of the Supreme Commission toured the PCK Camp Hospital. A particularly active member of the commission was investigating magistrate Jan Sehn. He sought documents with a great deal of energy, even to the point of digging them out of heaps of garbage and latrines.

Two years after the war, the Supreme National Tribunal used the Polish experts' reports written and the documents that they had collected at the camp as the main evidence in the trials against the former commandant of KL Auschwitz, Rudolf Höss, and 40 former staff members from the camp. In the trial against the former staff members, the Soviet expert Kudriavtsev also testified to present the findings of the Soviet commission.

6. The Legacy of Auschwitz

Deserving of attention are the resolutions addressed by former prisoners residing at Oświęcim to the world in the first months after their liberation. In the resolutions, they condemned the Nazis' crimes, warned the world about the danger of their repetition, and called for opposition to the rebirth of Nazism. Three such resolutions are known. A group of around 100 Yugoslavs sent the first such resolution to the Yugoslav legation in Moscow, while the second was sent by French communists to the Central Committee of the French Communist Party. The third resolution was handed over to Soviet government representatives visiting Oświęcim at the beginning of March 1945. Signed by 27 former prisoners — professors, doctors, engineers, lawyers, students, and other members of the intelligentsia from various countries — it declared:

> We, the undersigned, freed by the Red Army from the bloody tyranny of the Nazis, accuse before the international community the German government, led by Adolf Hitler, of committing the largest mass murders and atrocities in the history of humanity....
>
> We turn to the international community with the request that the fate of the millions of vanished people of various nationalities be clarified and that the prisoners still being held in Nazi Germany be saved....
>
> In the name of humanity, we request that everything possible be done so that the crimes the Nazis committed will not be repeated in the future, so that the blood shed by innocent victims will not have been in vain.
>
> Along with around 10,000 prisoners of various nationalities, we request that the Nazis' crimes not go unpunished.
>
> We, the liberated prisoners, owe our lives to the heroic Red Army and request that the international community and all governments take this into account and express their gratitude in our name.
>
> The Prisoners of KL Auschwitz. [27]

---

[27] The signatures of 27 former prisoners at KL Auschwitz follow.
Resolution of a group of former prisoners from March 4, 1945, in APMO, Mat./459, Collection of Materials, vol. 23, cards 100-102.

The liberation of Oświęcim on January 27, 1945, put an end to KL Auschwitz, the largest Nazi concentration camp and extermination center, and freed the around 7,000 remaining prisoners at the camp.

The date January 27, 1945, did not, however, bring the history of the camp at Auschwitz to a close. Oświęcim-Auschwitz became a universal symbol for Nazi genocide. At the site of the former Auschwitz camp and wherever one can find former Auschwitz prisoners and other people moved by the history of the camp, a social movement has arisen that we may call the "Auschwitz movement". This movement began as a result of occurences on the grounds of the former camp in the months immediately following its liberation.

The campaign of assistance undertaken by the Red Army medical service, the Polish authorities, and PCK volunteers in January-February 1945 preceded acts of medical assistance organized for the former prisoners by other organizations. The state of health of former prisoners from Auschwitz and other concentration camps has become a subject of research for groups of doctors in different European countries. As a result of this research, a new group of diseases was added to the international taxonomy of diseases: "concentration-camp syndromes" (KZ-Syndrome). At the same time, the issue of reparations for former prisoners for their loss of property and loss of health took on great significance.

The efforts of the Polish Red Cross to save camp documents in 1945 represented the beginning of efforts to preserve the memory of Auschwitz. A significant development in this regard was the establishment in 1947 of the State Museum at Oświęcim (*Państwowe Muzeum w Oświęcimiu*) as a place of memory. Other institutions, established later, also memorialized the camp's victims, including, for example, the Institute for National Memory — Yad Vashem in Jerusalem; the United States Holocaust Memorial Museum in Washington, D.C., and such German organizations as *Aktion Sühnezeichen — Friedensdienste* (Campaign for Penance — Services for Peace). The history of the camp has also resonated in popular and scholarly literature and journalism around the world. The history of KL Auschwitz and its remains have also been a source of inspiration for artists seeking to create unique works of art in the fields sculpture, music and film.

Polish organizations have played no small role throughout the years in the world wide "Auschwitz movement", including groups of former prisoners (so-called *Kluby Oświęcimskie*); the Society for the Preservation of Auschwitz (*Towarzystwo Opieki nad Oświęcimiem*), and — at the international level — the International Auschwitz Comittee and the International Council for the State Museum at Auschwitz (*Międzynarodowa Rada Państwowego Muzeum w Oświęcimiu*).

The history of the "Auschwitz movement" stands as an integral part of the history of KL Auschwitz and bears witness to the extent to which the world has been touched by the existence of the camp and the enormity of the crimes committed there. It thus deserves all the attention that is being devoted to it by scholars.

THE PROSECUTION OF SS
MEN FROM THE STAFF
AT KL AUSCHWITZ

KAZIMIERZ SMOLEŃ

THE PUNISHMENT OF WAR CRIMINALS

1. The Pursuit and Punishment of War Criminals in Light of International Law

The issue of the international punishment of war criminals first appeared in the articles of the Treaty of Versailles, concluded after the end of World War I in 1919. In Part VII of the Treaty, entitled "Sanctions", Article 227 accused Kaiser Wilhelm II "of the utmost offence against international morality and the holy solemnity of treaties", and Article 228 demanded that proceedings be initiated against individuals accused of committing crimes "against the laws and customs of war", as stipulated by the IV Hague Convention of 1907. After the Paris Peace Conference in 1919, a special commission for war crime issues, known as the "Committee of Fifteen", began to work on interpreting the Conventions, including how to define war crimes and punish those who committed them. [1] On the basis of its findings, an inter-Allied "high tribunal" was supposed to be established.

In reality, however, these provisions were never carried out because the Germans, in order to hush up their war crimes, created tribunals of their own before the inter-Allied judicial body could be established. The *Reich*'s Supreme Tribunal in Leipzig, called to life in December 1919, dropped charges against 900 criminals — including such military leaders as Paul von Hindenburg, Erich Ludendorff, August von Mackensen, and Alfred von Tirpitz — and thus reduced the number of defendants to only 45 low-level and non-commissioned officers.

Of the 45 defendants, only nine were punished; there were no death sentences. Some of the criminals were never even apprehended, and Kaiser Wilhelm II, who was supposed to be tried before a special international tribunal of five judges (from the United States, Great Britain, France, Italy and Japan), escaped punishment by using the asylum granted him in the Netherlands.

The enormity of the crimes committed by the Third Reich during World War II increased the need for codifying new acts of international law on the basis of the existing and binding provisions of the IV Hague Convention of

---

[1] Alfons Klafkowski, *Ściganie zbrodniarzy wojennych w Niemieckiej Republice Federalnej w świetle prawa międzynarodowego* (Poznań, 1968), p. 49, fn. 20.

1907 (earlier ratified by all the warring nations, including the Axis powers) to allow for the rightful punishment of war criminals.

The Polish resistance movement informed the Polish Government-in-Exile in London about the crimes the Nazis were committing in Poland; this information sparked already during the war a number of international initiatives and diplomatic activities on the question of pursuing and punishing war criminals. Diplomatic notes, appeals, declarations, treaties and various scholarly works laid the groundwork for the rapid development of international law in the area of methods and procedures for pursuing suspect and punishing individuals guilty of war crimes.

The appeal, "To the World's Conscience", signed by the governments of Great Britain, France and Poland, already appeared in April 1940. "The three undersigned states", it declared, "are deeply horrified by the news of the crimes being committed in Poland by the German authorities and occupation forces". The declaration, born of Poland's initiative, reaffirmed Germany's responsibility for its crimes and affirmed that the wrongs being suffered upon the Polish people would not go unpunished.

The engagement of the United Nations in military operations explains why no significant initiatives appeared on the war-crimes issue during the subsequent year-and-a-half. Then, on October 25, 1941, two declarations were made at practically the same time — one by U.S. President Franklin Delano Roosevelt and the other by the British Prime Minister, Winston Churchill. The President of the United States declared that terror would never bring peace to Europe, that it would only sow hatred, which would one day grow into a terrible punishment. For his part, the Prime Minister of Great Britain declared that the atrocities the Nazis were committing in occupied countries — and particularly inside the theater of operations in the Soviet Union — surpassed all the deeds that had ever been committed in the darkest and most barbaric epochs of human history.

The Soviet Union's diplomatic notes from November 25, 1941, and January 6, 1942, "to all governments with whom the USSR maintains diplomatic relations", were even clearer on the issue of war crimes. They brought to the world's attention the crimes being committed against Soviet prisoners of war.

One of the earliest existing legal bodies to deal with the issue of how to go about punishing war crimes was the International Commission for the Reconstruction and Development of Criminal Law, founded in Cambridge in 1940. The main goal of the commission, which was composed of renowned legal experts, was to adopt a stance regarding the possibility of establishing principles for punishing war crimes, to develop a definition of these crimes, and to determine the way in which future courts should pass sentence. One of the principles adopted by the commission was that war criminals should be judged both in accordance with international law and in accordance with the local criminal code that applied to the area where the crimes were committed. Another legal body, the London International Assembly, also performed significant work in this area. Neither body, however, had an official character. They delivered their findings, including proposed laws, to the United Nations' War Crimes Commission, which held its first session on November 20, 1943.

THE PUNISHMENT OF WAR CRIMINALS

The UN commision was responsible for gathering evidence of war crimes, preparing lists of war criminals and developing principles that would assure their effective prosecution. The Commission, along with the so-called national administrations attached to it, began work in January 1944. One of the first national administrations established was the Polish one. [2]

The first United Nations documents to deal with the issue of criminal responsibility for war crimes was the Declaration of Allied Countries Occupied by Germany from January 13, 1942. The declaration was the result of a conference held in London on the initiative of the Polish and Czechoslovakian Governments-in-Exile; the polish premier, General Władysław Sikorski, had chaired the conference. The Declaration demanded the punishment of those individuals who had violated international law and announced the creation of a mechanism for extraditing war criminals.

The Declaration was not only of great diplomatic, but also great legal significance, because the governments of the occupied countries (Poland, Czechoslovakia, Belgium, France, Greece, Luxemburg, Holland, Norway and Yugoslavia), had adopted a united stance along with the representatives of the Great Powers that had been invited to the conference in London (Great Britain, the United States, the Soviet Union and China). Thereafter, one could observe these states undertaking a series of joint initiatives with the goal of establishing principles for pursuing and prosecuting war criminals and then ensuring that the respective sentences were carried out. A fruitful exchange of notes began, describing the Nazi German authorities' criminal acts committed in occupied. President Roosevelt made a new declaration on October 7, 1942, reaffirming the United States' commitment to prosecute Nazi war criminals.

The Moscow Declaration on war crimes, announced jointly by the Soviet Union, Great Britain and the United States on October 30, 1943, on behalf of the 32 states belonging to the United Nations, was an act of great international significance. It declared that

> (...) whenever an armistice is recognized by whatever government that might be created in Germany, those German officers and soldiers and members of the National Socialist party who are responsibile for the atrocities, massacres and executions that have been mentioned above, or who took part in them of their free will, will be sent to the country where they committed these horrible deeds so that they might be tried and punished in accordance with the laws of those liberated countries and the free governments that will be created there. A list of criminals will be assembled in all those countries with the greatest possible precision.

While, according to the Declaration, all war criminals would normally be extradited to those countries upon whose territory they had committed their crimes, it also stated that so-called leading war criminals, whose activities were not limited to one specific geographical area (i.e., who had been active on the territory of several countries or who had given orders that applied to several or all the occupied countries), would be punished on the basis of a joint decision

---

[2] Tadeusz Cyprian and Jerzy Sawicki, "Komisja Zjednoczonych Narodów do Spraw Zbrodni Wojennych", *Wojskowy Przegląd Prawniczy* 4 (1947), pp. 404-13.

by the United Nations. The Declaration further asserted that the three Allied powers would naturally pursue such criminals to the farthest corners of the globe and then hand them over for prosecution so that justice might be served.

The contents of the Moscow Declaration greatly influenced the decree of January 22, 1946, establishing a Supreme National Tribunal in Poland. It also affected the Polish Supreme Court's decision regarding whom to prosecute on the basis of a September 31, 1944, decree by the Polish authorities on the punishment of "Hitlerite-Fascist" war criminals and traitors to the Polish nation.

The Yalta Declaration on the German question, approved at the Crimean Conference of the Big Three on February 11, 1945, reaffirmed the Allies' resolve ".... to punish fairly and quickly all war criminals and to execute reparations in kind for the destruction wrought by the Germans". The Yalta Declaration also contained a passage on the need to extirpate National Socialism and German militarism in its entirety so that Germany would never again be a threat to world peace and security.

The Potsdam Accords of August 2, 1945, also dealt with the punishment of war criminals. Section VII, "War Criminals", was devoted to the issue. Article V, Part III of the accord contained the following passage:

> War criminals, as well as those individuals who took part in the formulation or execution of National-Socialist activities that led to or took the form of atrocities or war crimes, will be arrested and brought to justice. National Socialist leaders, influential sympathizers of Nazism and high functionaries of Nazi organizations and institutions will be arrested and interned just like everyone else.

2. The International Military Tribunal

Several days after the Potsdam Accords, the four Great Powers signed a new set of accords on the prosecution and punishment of leading war criminals from the European Axis states on August 8, 1945, in London. These accords were subsequently signed by 19 other member-states of the United Nations. A charter for an International Military Tribunal was attached to the Accords.

The charter was composed of thirty articles in seven sections, outlining the composition, competence and powers of the Tribunal. Part II, Article 6, listed three types of crimes that lay under the Tribunal's jurisdiction and dealt with the issue of individual responsiblity:

> a) Crimes against peace, namely: planning, preparing, beginning or conducting a war of aggression or a war in violation of treaties, agreements or international guarantees, or participating in a plot or conspiracy to carry out one of the goals named above;
> b) War crimes, namely: the violation of military laws and customs. Such crimes would encompass — but not be limited to — murders, mistreatment or deportation of civilians for forced labor or for other goals either within an occupied area or outside that area; murder or mistreatment of prisoners of war or individuals at sea; killing hostages; pillaging public or private property; wanton destruction of settlements, cities or villages or devastation unwarranted by military necessity;

c) Crimes against humanity, including: murders, extermination, enslavement, deportation and other inhuman acts, carried out against any civilian population before the war or during it; persecution on political, racial or religious grounds in committing any crime that falls within the competencies of the Tribunal or in connection with it, regardless of whether it was in accordance with or in opposition to the law of the country in which the crimes were committed.

The article ends with an explicit statement that

... leaders, organizers, and accomplices taking part in the formulation or execution of a common plan or plot with the goal of perpetrating one of the crimes named above will answer for all deeds that anyone committed in conjunction with the realization of such a plan.

Although the Tribunal's headquarters were in Berlin, Nuremberg was the location designated for its first session; subsequent sessions, it was added, would be held in locations to be established by the Tribunal. In the end, the International Military Tribunal held only one session, the so-called Nuremberg Trial of 1945-46. The International Military Tribunal conducted hearings from November 20, 1945, to August 31, 1946, and then began work on preparing its judgment, which was announced along with a justification on September 30 - October 1, 1946. On trial were 22 defendants — prominent political, military and industrial leaders in the Third Reich: Martin Bormann, Karl Dönitz, Hans Frank, Wilhelm Frick, Hans Fritzsche, Walter Funk, Hermann Göring, Rudolf Hess, Alfred Jodl, Ernest Kaltenbrunner, Wilhelm Keitel, Konstantin Freiherr von Neurath, Franz von Papen, Erich Raeder, Joachim von Ribbentrop, Alfred Rosenberg, Fritz Sauckel, Hjalmar Schacht, Baldur von Schirach, Artur Seyss-Inquart, Albert Speer and Julius Streicher. The International Military Tribunal sentenced twelve of the accused to death (Bormann was condemned *in absentia*), three received sentences of life imprisonment, and four — sentences of 10-20 years in prison. Three of the accused were found not guilty.

In keeping with the statutory provisions of the International Military Tribunal, it found the following Nazi organs to be criminal organizations: the political leadership of the *Nationalsozialistische Deutsche Arbeiterpartei* (NSDAP), the *Geheime Staatspolizei* (Gestapo) and *Sicherheitsdienst* (SD), the *Schutzstaffel* (SS), and, with certain limitations, the *Sturmabteilungen* (SA).

The question of crimes committed at the concentration camps appeared a number of times in the course of the proceedings at Nuremberg, particularly in connection with the Tribunal's designation of the SS as a criminal organization. The following statement also appeared in the text of the Nuremberg Judgment:

The evidence that has been presented demonstrates beyond any doubt that the constant, brutal treatment of prisoners in concentration camps was a result of the general policies of the SS, according to which the people held in the concentration camps were to be treated as people of a lower race, to be viewed with contempt ....

The Nuremberg Judgment recognized the concentration camps to be one "of the most ignominious measures of terror applied against the civilian population of occupied areas"; they were called "factories of death", at which starvation hunger and hunger rations, sadism, a lack of clothing, lack of medical attention, diseases, beatings, hangings, exposure, forced suicides, and executions played a central role in achieving their goal. The Judgment also included the finding that "a certain number of concentration camps were equipped with gas chambers for the mass annihilation of prisoners and ovens for burning corpses", along with the assertion that "it is simply impossible to point out even one SS unit that did not take part in criminal activity".

The legal norms established in the four powers' London Agreement of August 8, 1945 — to which the Charter for the International Military Tribunal had been attached — were repeated and justified in the Tribunal's judgment against the main war criminals, were ratified by the General Assembly of the United Nations, and became universally recognized as international law under the official name, the "Nuremberg Principles".

3. The Nuremberg Trials, 1947-49

In each zone of occupation in Germany, special military tribunals were in operation, called into existence by Statute Nr. 10 of the Allied Control Commission for Germany from December 20, 1945, on the punishment of war crimes, crimes against peace and crimes against humanity. In the American zone of occupation, at the International Military Tribunal's headquarters in Nuremberg, twelve large trials took place between 1947 and 1949. The legal principles of the Nuremberg Trial of 1945-46 provided sanction for these proceedings. Some of the trials dealt with the issue of crimes committed at the concentration camps:

1) At Trial Nr. I, around a dozen doctors from the *Wehrmacht* and SS were found guilty of conducting criminal, pseudo-medical experiments on prisoners at concentration camps and prisoners-of-war;

2) At Trial Nr. IV, against the leadership of the Main Economic-Administrative Office (WVHA) of the SS, the main defendant was the former director of that office, Oswald Pohl. The Tribunal found the accused guilty of war crimes and crimes against humanity, including the extermination of prisoners of war, the extermination of civilians in occupied countries, and crimes committed at concentration camps;

3) Trial Nr. V dealt with the deportation of civilians for forced labor, and in the case of concentration-camp prisoners, for slave labor;

4) At Trial Nr. VI, the directors of the German concern, IG Farbenindustrie, were put on trial for exploiting the unfree labor of civilians and concentration-camp prisoners and thus contributing to mass murder. At the trial, the firm was also found responsibile for pseudo-medical experiments conducted on concentration-camp prisoners, including prisoners at KL Auschwitz;

5) At Trial Nr. VII, the Main Office for Racial and Settlement Questions (RuSHA) was tried for having organized extermination campaigns against

Jews, Slavs and Gypsies, including their annihilation in concentration camps. During the trial, documentation was introduced and verified regarding the mass resettlement of Poles from the Zamość region and their deportation to concentration camps, especially to KL Auschwitz, along with evidence related to the kidnapping of more than 200,000 Polish children for Germanization;

6) Trial Nr. X, against the Krupp concern, disclosed the firm's criminal exploitation of prisoners of war and concentration-camp prisoners as a labor force. The trial verified that prisoners from the Auschwitz concentration camp had been forced to work for that firm's benefit;

7) At Trial Nr. XII, the main defendants were higher officers of the German High Command (*Oberkommando der Wehrmacht*, OKW). Among the many alleged crimes that were investigated was the extermination of 13,000 Soviet prisoners of war at Auschwitz.

The materials cited above — if only briefly — show that materials regarding war crimes and crimes against humanity at the concentration camps, along with documents on crimes against the peace, made up a significant portion of the evidence presented both to the International Military Tribunal and to the individual military tribunals operating in the zones of occupied Germany. The renewed disclosure at the trials of the Nazis' crimes appalled the world anew and brought the inhuman visage of German fascism into sharp relief. The resulting judgments reaffirmed the responsibility of the entire political, party, economic, and military apparatus of the Third Reich for the crimes committed.

4. The Legal Bases for the Punishment of War Criminals in Poland

Poland was among the countries that suffered the most from the activities of the German occupier during World War II. Given the magnitude of the crimes committed, the Polish authorities issued a "Decree on the Punishment of Hitlerite-Fascist Criminals" on August 31, 1944, only days after the establishment of the Polish Committee for National Liberation (*Polski Komitet Wyzwolenia Narodowego*). [3] The decree called for the punishment of all Nazi criminals guilty of murder and repression against the civilian population and prisoners of war, along with traitors to the Polish nation who had cooperated with the Nazi occupier. All crimes mentioned in the decree were to be punished in accordance with the provisions of the Criminal Code in force at the time.

---

[3] Translator's note: The PKWN was established on July 22, 1944, after Soviet troops had crossed the Bug River into what became postwar Poland. Dominated by Polish communists, it acted as a provisional government for those areas of (postwar) Poland liberated by Soviet forces. On December 31, 1944, the PKWN declared the establishment of a "Provisional Government for the Polish Republic" (*Rząd Tymczasowy Rzeczypospolitej Polskiej*), also known as the Lublin Government. Recognized by the Soviet Union, it stood as a rival to the Polish Government-in-Exile in London, which maintained relations with the United States and Great Britain. On the basis of an understanding among the "Big Three" (US, USSR and Great Britain) at the Yalta Conference (February 4-11, 1945), the Lublin Government was expanded — temporarily — to include non-communist politicians from the exile camp in a "Provisional Government of National Unity" (*Tymczasowy Rząd Jedności Narodowej*, TRJN).

A corollary to the PKWN's decree was a law of September 12, 1944, providing for the establishment of special criminal courts for trying Nazi criminals. Even while military operations continued, six SS men from the staff of the Majdanek concentration camp, captured at the scene of their crimes, were tried before a Special Court in Lublin from November 27 — December 2, 1944.

The August 31, 1944 decree was modified several times — e.g., following Poland's accession to the London Agreement. It provided a basis for the application of the Nuremberg Principles in Polish domestic law. Evidence of this is a February 23, 1948 decision by the Polish Supreme Court that declared: "The close jurisdictional link between national and international law in this area permits Polish courts to make use of the International Military Tribunal's judgment in applying Polish law based on that judgment." [4]

5. Auschwitz Criminals Before the Supreme National Tribunal

After military operations had ceased, several hundred war criminals were extradited to Poland in accordance with the provisions of the London Agreement (including such high-level figures as Arthur Greiser, Ludwig Fischer, Albert Forster, Josef Bühler, Rudolf Höss and others). It now became necessary to establish a Polish tribunal that — given the significance of the question — would become the national equivalent of the International Military Tribunal in Nuremberg. Thus a decree of January 22, 1946, established a Supreme National Tribunal to deal with these head war criminals. The Prosecutor for the Supreme National Tribunal and a special unit of the Ministry of Justice, the Main Commission for the Investigation of Nazi Crimes in Poland (established by decree on November 10, 1945), undertook all investigative and prosecutorial activities related to the Supreme National Tribunal's work.

The Main Commission for the Investigation of Nazi Crimes worked through district commissions. The Minister of Justice chaired the Main Commission and appointed the chairmen and members of the district commisions. The Main Commission was charged with investigating and collecting evidence on German crimes committed in Poland during the years 1939-45, along with crimes committed against Polish citizens or people of Polish descent beyond Poland's borders and crimes committed against foreigners in Poland during the same period. The decree establishing the Main Commission also foresaw the publication of the results of its investigations, along with documents related to its research. The Commission was supposed to make these materials available to judicial authorities, both in Poland and abroad.

The Supreme National Tribunal had the character of an assessor's court; the adjudicating body was composed of three qualified judges and four assessors, who had to be representatives from the National People's Council (*Krajowa Rada Narodowa*, KRN). The decree specified that the Supreme National

---

[4] E.S. Rappaport, "Z zagadnienia prawa międzynarodowego w orzecznictwie sądów polskich", *Rocznik Prawa Międzynarodowego* (1949), p. 233.

Tribunal was equal in rank to the Supreme Court. Defendants before the Tribunal were guaranteed counsel, to be chosen by the defendant or officially appointed. The chairman of the Tribunal appointed public defenders from among the attorneys residing in Poland. The decisions of the Supreme National Tribunal were final, although the accused had the right to petition the president of the National People's Council for a pardon.

Between 1946-48, the Supreme National Tribunal heard seven cases, two of which were connected with the Auschwitz concentration camp. The most famous was the trial of the first commandant of KL Auschwitz from March 11-29, 1947; the verdict was announced on April 2. The accused, Rudolf Franz Ferdinand Höss, camp commandant for many years, had been extradited to Poland by the British occupation authorities in Germany in May 1946. His trial was of great international importance. Because the trial was against the commandant of the largest concentration camp, it not only revealed how the entire system of Nazi concentration and death camps had functioned, but also served as an indictment of the ideology that had permitted the use of such camps for the realization of the Third Reich's criminal ethnic and racial policies.

The main issues addressed during Höss's trial included: the duties and goals that the Nazis had assigned to the concentration camps; the role of the camps in persecuting the Nazis' opponents; the type of training that SS men received before joining the staff at the camps; and the magnitude of the crimes committed — in particular, the extent to which the policy of exterminating Jews, Slavs and Gypsies had been carried out by using Zyklon B in the gas chambers. The Tribunal also dealt with the issue of experiments on human beings at the camp, whether for pseudo-scientific goals or for the development of methods for exterminating entire peoples.

The defendant Höss had already realized during the investigation against him that it would be senseless to hide the truth, given the amount of evidence, which was being constantly supplemented with new testimony, opinions and documents. He also realized what sentence he could expect for his crimes and calmly awaited it. Evidence of this are the memoirs that he wrote in his prison cell during the investigation, entitled, *My Soul, Evolution, Life and Ordeals.* [5] His horrifying descriptions of mass murder in the gas chambers, among other things, read like a factual account written by a completely disinterested observer. On the witness stand, Höss answered directly and categorically, without any hesitation.

Höss only demonstrated a certain liveliness when he testified about the mass exterminations. Höss spoke about it like a manufacturing process and

.... made at times the impression of some factory director explaining certain difficulties in how his factory works and striving to justify them in terms of objective difficulties: transports that were too large, the low productivity of the crematoria,

---

[5] The original manuscript of these memoirs can be found in the archives of the State Museum at Oświęcim (PMO) in the file, Reminiscences (Höss) 96, nr. inw. 49757. They were published as a book in Poland and several other countries, including the Federal Republic of Germany.

tie-ups caused by damage to the facilities. It was as if he wanted to explain to the Tribunal that he had done everything is his power to carry out the "special action" [what the Nazis called the mass extermination — KS] in the most effective way possible, and that if he had failed to do so, if the results did not reach the level that Himmler and Eichmann thought possible to achieve — then it was not his, Höss's, fault. .... What seemed particulary strange was the calmness with which he spoke about the extermination campaigns. Listening to him, one got the impression that he had sought to eliminate completely from his consciousness the issue of human life — which was playing the dominant role here — in carrying out his assignment. At times, one could sense in his voice a tone of gentle pride when he spoke about the obstacles that he had been able to overcome, and at other times, once again, a tone of guilt and shame that he had not been able to carry out his duties and had failed the trust placed in him by his superiors. [6]

The Supreme National Tribunal sentenced Höss to death by hanging. The sentence was carried out on April 16, 1947, at Auschwitz, outside the building that had housed the commandant's office, from where Höss had ruled the camp for many years.

A total of 40 defendants stood before the Supreme National Tribunal in the second trial, against former staff members at the camp, including: Höss's successor as commandant, Arthur Liebehenschel; Maximilian Grabner, the director of the camp Gestapo; *Lagerführer* Hans Aumeier; Karl Ernst Möckel, the director of the economic division; Maria Mandel, director of the women's camp at Birkenau; Franz Xawer Kraus, information officer; Dr. Johann Paul Kremer, camp doctor; Heinrich Josten, assistant *Lagerführer*; Dr. Hans Münch, an employee from the hygiene section; Erich Muhsfeldt, crematorium director; *Blockführers* Hermann Kirschner, Karl Seufert, August Reimond Bogusch, Kurt Hugo Müller, Paul Götze, Paul Szczurek, Richard Albert Schröder, and Herbert Paul Ludwig; SS overseers from the women's camp — Therese Brandl, Alice Orlowski, Luise Danz, and Hildegard Marthe Luise Lächert; sanitarian Hans Koch; overseer Wilhelm Gerhard Gehring; *Rapportführers* Ludwig Plagge, Otto Lätsch, and Fritz Wilhelm Buntrock; Eduard Lorenz, a driver; Hans Hoffman, an employee from the Political Division; and employees from the Economic-Administrative Division — Arthur Johann Breitweiser, Hans Schumacher, Adolf Medefind, and Franz Romeikat; Anton Lechner, an employee in the camp administration; Josef Kollmer, an overseer; Detlef Nebbe, company commander; Erich Dinges, a truck driver; and the guards Alexander Bülow, Joannes Weber and Karl Jeschke.

The defendants came from different personal and educational backgrounds. They included not only an assistant professor from the University of Münster (Johann Paul Kremer, M.D and PhD) and a master of law (Arthur Breitwieser), but also a baker's assistant (Erich Muhsfeldt) and a former waitress (Therese Brandl).

The trial was held from November 25 to December 16, 1947, in Cracow. Similar evidence was presented as at the Höss trial, but was supplemented by

---

[6] Janusz Gumkowski and Tadeusz Kułakowski, *Zbrodniarze hitlerowscy przed Najwyższym Trybunałem Narodowym* (Warszawa, 1961), pp. 141-2.

additional testimony from witnesses. The defendants adopted different tactics, however, than Höss had. They declared at the beginning of the trial that they did not feel themselves guilty, and only a few admitted to beating prisoners. The accused sought to place responsibility for the acts committed on their absent superiors, particularly Höss, and to justify their actions based on the orders that they had received. They often made arrogant and misleading statements. They stubbornly denied the facts presented and tried to dismiss the witnesses' testimony, even as they cringed before the Tribunal in the hope of receiving a light sentence.

A number of the defendants — particularly one of the most compromised individuals, Maximilian Grabner, the former director of the camp Gestapo — claimed to have had no authority at the camp. *Lagerführer* Aumeier asserted that if he died, he would be a "*Sündenbock* (scapegoat) for Germany". The accused Josef Kollmer bitterly and pretentiously asked where Hitler and Himmler were. The accused Liebehenschel tried to convince the Tribunal that conditions had improved at the camp after he became camp commandant.

During the three-week trial, the Tribunal analyzed the criminal activity and administration of the concentration camps and acquainted themselves with the prisoners' daily lives, the theft of property, slave labor and the entire mechanism for mass extermination. On December 22, 1947, the Tribunal handed down its judgment. Twenty-three defendants were sentenced to death; six others, to life in prison; seven, to sentences of more that 15 years; and three, to sentences of ten, five, and three years imprisonment. One defendant, Hans Münch from the Hygiene Office, was found not guilty.

In clarifying its judgment, the Supreme National Tribunal stated at the beginning of Section IV that the indictment had not only charged the accused with the commission of individual acts and of participation in either the NSDAP or SS — which the Nuremberg Judgment and the Polish decree on Nazi criminals had recognized as criminal organizations — but also of participation in a third criminal organization — namely, the leadership, administration, and staff of the Auschwitz concentration camp. In weighing its decision, the Tribunal had recognized that

> ... the Nuremberg Judgment is undoubtedly the first great step towards codifying international criminal law, but is not a criminal code in the sense that it does not preclude individual courts from recognizing activities that it does not deal with as crimes. Hence, from the viewpoint of international law, nothing prevents the extension of the legal principles contained in the Nuremberg Judgment to other legal principles not standing in contradiction to the contents of that judgment. .... The Nuremberg laws also find expression in Polish law. The decree cited regarding the sentencing of Nazi war criminals recognizes in Art. 4 Par. 2 such groups and organizations to be criminal organizations that have as their goal crimes against peace, war crimes and crimes against humanity, along with organizations that have other goals, but seek to achieve them through the crimes named above.

The Supreme National Tribunal then analyzed the provisions of Polish domestic law in the context of the Nuremberg Judgment. Point 14 of the judgment declared:

The German-concentration-camp organization was thus an organization having as its goal the commission of crimes against humanity, which are simultaneously criminal acts according to the laws of all civilized nations and war crimes, when it comes to the Soviet POWs.

In its conclusion, the Supreme National Tribunal declared the leadership, administration, and staff of the German concentration camps in Poland — especially at Auschwitz — to be a "criminal group", regardless of the names given to individual camps. (The Tribunal used the designation criminal "group", instead of "organization", because Article 4 of the Polish decree used both of these terms; the word "group" in this case is more accurate, given its etymology, than the term "organization".)

ALEKSANDER LASIK

TRIALS AGAINST THE SS STAFF FROM KL AUSCHWITZ

1. The Punishment of Staff Members from KL Auschwitz After World War II

The SS staff at KL Auschwitz, which turned over twice in statistical terms during the camp's existence — as was the case at other camps [1] — was a large, well-organized, coherent and efficient community. A total of around 7,000-7,200 SS men and female SS overseers passed through the camp.

These figures do not tell us, however, how many of these individuals, based on their various functions, would have been subject to prosecution for crimes against humanity. An analysis of the personal records of former SS staff members at Auschwitz shows that for the period 1940-44, around 50% of its members were transferred out of KL Auschwitz, with 37.1% ending up in front-line *Waffen-SS* formations. [2] In January and the beginning of February 1945, immediately before the camp's liquidation, around 12.5% of the remaining SS men at KL Auschwitz were transferred to front-line SS units. This information is of particular importance because it shows us that over the entire period of KL Auschwitz's existence, around 1,500 members of the camp's SS staff ended up on the front, so a portion of them fell in battle. Even if we assume that 50% of them perished, then around 6,300-6,500 SS men from the Auschwitz staff would have survived to the end of the war. On the basis of these estimates, we can safely assume that — taking into account desertions caused by the fear of ending up in Soviet captivity — from 5,500 — 6,000 SS men from the former camp at Auschwitz could have been found in the Western zones of occupation on May 8, 1945. This (certainly rounded-down) figure substantiates the assertion that around 6,000 members of the Auschwitz SS staff should have been prosecuted as potential war-criminals.

---

[1] The phenomenon of a twofold turnover of SS staff — in statistical terms — occurred, for example, at KL Stutthof, where a total of around 2,000 different SS men were assigned to its staff during the years 1942-45, but the daily population of SS staff members never surpassed 1,000. (The years 1942-45 mark the entire period of KL Stutthof's existence as a completely independent concentration camp, answering to the Inspector of Concentration Camps in Oranienburg.) The author has demonstrated this turnover in empirical studies that have not been published to date. It is likely that the same level of staff fluctuation occurred at all the Nazi concentration camps in existence in 1940 and thereafter.

[2] These figures are based on data contained in card files on the members of the KL Auschwitz staff assembled by the author.

The system for identifying potential war-crimes suspects, particularly in the American zones of occupation in Austria and Germany, usually went as follows: If a person with an unclear past appeared at a military-police control post — having been recognized, denounced, etc. — they were sent to the nearest internment center. There, the individual's identity was established, identifications papers were drawn up, and his or her wartime history was analyzed. Particularly sought-after were individuals whose names appeared in the lists of war criminals prepared by the United Nations War Crimes Commission (UNWCC). After a suspect was identified, the military authorities notified the appropriate intelligence organs and the military missions of the states formerly occupied by the Third Reich. Through the latter's mediation, the government that was interested in obtaining a particular suspect would initiate extradition proceedings. Once the necessary formalities were completed, the suspected war criminal was extradited to the country upon whose territory he or she was suspected of committing crimes. In the case of Poland, from 1946-48, almost every SS man who was caught and had been on the staff at KL Auschwitz was given over to the Polish courts. In the Soviet zone of occupation, such extraditions did not take place; the Russians applied the principle of limited collective responsibility to everyone who had taken part in the aggression against the Soviet Union — without investigating the backgrounds of individuals to see if they had been staff members at concentration camps and what deeds they might have committed there. Therefore, between 1945-49, Poland successfully extradited around 1,000 members of the Auschwitz staff from the Western zones of occupation, [3] while no extraditions took place at all from the Soviet zone. The extradition of war criminals was basically discontinued in 1949, when political and ideological factors began to influence the issue — i.e., the establishment of two German states and the Cold War.

2. The Question of Guilt and Responsibility

The assertion that all members of the SS staff at KL Auschwitz bore responsibility for the crimes committed at the camp is a generalization that tells us little about the guilt and responsibility of a given individual. If we did not differentiate between moral responsibility in a general sense (i.e., a certain type of collective responsibility) and the degree of actual guilt in a legal sense, we would not be able to evaluate the role of individual SS staff members in exterminating the hundreds of thousands of people killed at KL Auschwitz.

This question is significant because in many of the legal proceedings against SS men from Auschwitz, the prosecution did not have the necessary evidence to convict individual suspects. Furthermore, by differentiating between moral responsibility and legal guilt, we can evaluate from a historical and contem-

---

[3] This figure has been arrived at by adding up the individuals named in extradition lists from the Polish Military Mission in Berlin as having been sent to Poland. Documents from trials that were maintained at the Mission contain about 300 fewer names. Archiwum Głównej Komisji Badania Zbrodni przeciwko Narodowi Polskiemu — Instytut Pamięci Narodowej w Warszawie, syg. PMW/BZW, passim.

porary point of view how effective the international legal system was at distributing justice.

The thesis that all the members of the camp staff bore an equal amount of moral responsibility stands at variance with the fact that the internal structure of the camp administration was based on a hierarchy of competencies. For example, the authority that a normal camp guard held over prisoners was decidedly different from that held by a crematorium director. Furthermore, the camp administration was constructed in such a fashion that certain sub-units only served to keep the camp functioning in a technical sense (e.g., the technical section of the Economic-Administrative Division, Division IV), while others served to control and carry out annihilation from the very beginning.

The latter group of administrative units included, without a doubt: Division II — Political, whose functionaries had the authority to decide a prisoners' fate; Division III — Camp Administration, which was responsible, among other things, for the crimes committed in the prisoners' quarters; Division IIIa — Prisoner Employment, responsible for the murderous work conditions and prisoners' liquidation during work; and Division V — SS Health Service, which did not perform any medical services on the behalf of prisoners, but instead participated directly — *en bloc* — in the annihilation of prisoners.

In the case of Jews brought to the camp in RSHA transports for immediate extermination, the vehicular-transport column of Division I (Commandant's Office) also participated directly in the genocide. This section not only transported ill, weakened and deceased prisoners to the mass extermination facilities, but also delivered the poison used to kill them.

Summing up, it seems quite clear that functionaries from the divisions named above bore a significantly greater responsibility for the "Auschwitz hell" than other staff members who had only sporadic and brief contact with the prisoners or, as a result of the administrative duties of their particular organizational unit, did not have any regular or direct contact with the prisoners at all. Thus, the office that a given defendant held at the camp, as well as his or her length of stay, should have been considered by the various tribunals in establishing each individual staff member's guilt. The tribunals should not have been indifferent to the length of a given defendant's stay at the camp — whether several days or several years — at least in terms of their potential for committing crimes. [4]

Only based on these facts can we properly assess the work done by the various courts, which has influenced and continues to influence our notions of justice and civilization.

---

[4] The attitudes of the SS men towards the prisoners evolved in most cases according to the economic and military situation of the Third Reich. Besides such psychological factors, orders to the concentration-camp staff to preserve the prisoners for use as a potential labor force — i.e. in the context of Germany's declaration of "total war" — also had a certain significance. Thus, the length and time period of an SS man's service could have been of significance to the court, especially since the recruitment of the SS formations that staffed the concentration camps, the *SS-Totenkopfverbände* (Order of the Death's Head), changed dramatically. In mid-1944, for example, older soldiers from the *Wehrmacht* — unfit for duty at the front — were added to the guard staff at the camps. In some cases their numbers reached a significant percentage level in comparison to the permanent camp staff.

3. Statistics on the Punishment of SS Staff Members from KL Auschwitz

Most of the trials against former members of the Auschwitz camp staff took place in Poland after the war, from 1946-53. At least 673 people faced legal proceedings, including 21 women (who had served as SS overseers, radio operators and German Red Cross nurses at the camp). In the case of 23 individuals, the outcome cannot be established, due to a lack of documents; in 13 cases, the accused died while the trial was being prepared; and in one case, the prosecution was dropped.

The most famous trials to occur in Poland were the trial of the founder and first commandant of KL Auschwitz, Rudolf Höss, before the Supreme National Tribunal in Warsaw; and the trial of 40 camp staff members before the same court at a special session in Cracow (see p. 291). In the course of these proceedings, 24 defendants received death sentences, including the two former commandants, Rudolf Höss and Arthur Liebehenschel. Two of the condemned were granted reprieves: Dr. Johann Paul Kremer and Arthur Breitwieser, a functionary from Division IV. The severity of the sentences handed down (24 death sentences, six sentences of life in prison, ten shorter prison sentences, and one release) did not result merely from the attention devoted to the proceedings by the mass media, but also reflected the fact that most of the accused had held prominent posts in the camp administration. The accused included, besides the persons named above, the Directors of the Political Division (Maximilian Grabner) and the Economic-Administrative Division (Karl Ernst Möckel); the *Lagerführer* of the main camp, Hans Aumeier; the head *SS-Aufseherin* (overseer), Maria Mandel; the camp's information officer, Franz Xawer Kraus; the crematorium director, Erich Muhsfeldt; the *SS--Rapportführer* Ludwig Plagge, Otto Lätsch, and Fritz Buntrock; several *Blockführer*, overseers, functionaries from the various divisions, and guards. [5]

Other Polish tribunals also heard cases, including District Courts, Provincial (*Wojewódzki*) Courts and Special Criminal Courts in Cracow, Wadowice, Racibórz, Cieszyn, Sosnowiec, Gliwice, Bytom and Katowice. In several cases, former staff members from KL Auschwitz answered before the District Courts in Toruń and Lublin for crimes committed at other camps. (Their activities at Auschwitz were not, however, the main charge in their indictments.)

These judicial proceedings (a total of 636 established cases) resulted in the following judgments: a total of 32 death sentences (5.0%), some of which were never executed, due to reprieves; nine lifesentences of life in prison (1.4%), and in the remaining cases, prison terms from six months to fifteen years. Most of the accused were sentenced to three (31.9%) or four years (17.5%) in prison, and often to five (9.4%) or six years (8.8%). Eight defendants were found not guilty (1.3%).

---

[5] For more on the subject of the trials, see, for example, Janusz Gumkowski and Tadeusz Kułakowski, *Zbrodniarze hitlerowscy przed Najwyższym Trybunałem Narodowym* (Warszawa, 1967), pp. 81-173; Tadeusz Cyprian and Jerzy Sawicki, *Oskarżamy* (Kraków, 1949), pp. 161-212; Tadeusz Cyprian and Jerzy Sawicki, *Siedem procesów przed Najwyższym Trybunałem Narodowym* (Poznań, 1962), pp. 92-261.

To determine the effectiveness of the judicial apparatus, we should, it seems, establish the importance of the defendants tried in Poland in terms of their role within the camp administration. Of the 636 defendants[6], 426 had held exclusively guard functions at KL Auschwitz (67.0% of the judgments handed down), 174 had been employed in the camp administration (27.4%), and 34 (5.3%) had held lesser functions at the camp and had not been directly involved in exterminating prisoners. This distribution conforms to a large extent with the staff's statistical make-up in terms of their assignments at the camp.

A closer analysis of the sentences that defendants received shows, however, that the severity of the punishment only corresponded in part with the defendant's former post in the pyramidic administration of the camp. One indicator of this is the fact that while some guards and administrative officials were sentenced to three years in prison (34.0% and 28.3% respectively, according to our statistics), the distribution of four-year sentences was quite different (21.4% and 9.8% respectively). A greater disparity arises with regard to death sentences (0.9% of the guards and 9.8% of the administrators). Women from the camp SS staff received particularly harsh sentences. Of this group — 17 defendants in the 636 established cases — four received death sentences (23.5% of the entire group), while only two were sentenced to terms of three years in prison (11.8%).

From the information presented above we can conclude that before the Polish courts, no revenge was sought against the accused and that judgments were based on irrefutable evidence. On the other hand, we can state that in many cases, the defendant's former post within the camp administration was not taken into account; as a result, a number of controversial judgments were handed down, due to a lack of direct evidence. This occurred, for example, with the not-guilty verdict in the case of Otto Brossman, former commander of the First and Second Guard Companies at Monowice and former *Lagerführer* at the Blechhammer sub-camp in Blachownia Śląska; the five-year sentence given to Wilhelm Burger, director of the camp's Economic-Administrative Divison (IV); and the six-year sentence handed down to Alois Frey, director of the Günthergrube sub-camp in Lędziny and director of the Political Division's (II) Identification Office (*Erkennungsdienst*).

Another country to hold a dozen or more trials against former Auschwitz staff members was the Federal Republic of Germany. The most famous and spectacular trials took place from 1963-76 in Frankfurt am Main. In the first trial, which lasted from December 20, 1963, to August 20, 1965, 24 suspects were indicted (including one former prisoner-functionary, Emil Bednarek, the *Blockältester* from the punishment company). Two of the accused — Richard Baer, the last commandant at KL Auschwitz and Hans Nierzwicki, an SS sanitarian — were excluded from the trial due to their state of health. In the end, the follwing individuals had to answer for their crimes: Robert Mulka and Karl Höcker, adjutants to the commandant at the main camp; Franz Lucas,

---

[6] This figure includes the two commandants, along with the other 634 defendants listed by category.

Willi Frank, Willi Schatz, Victor Capesius, Josef Klehr, Herbert Scherpe, Emil Hantl and Gerhard Neubert — functionaries from the SS health service at the camp; *Lagerführer* Franz Hoffman from the main camp; and SS men formerly employed in the Political Division — Wilhelm Boger, Hans Stark, Klaus Dylewski, Pery Broad and Johann Schuberth. The remaining defendants had held various offices in the camp hierarchy: Oswald Kaduk, former *Rapportführer* at the main camp; the *Blockführer* Bruno Schlage, Stefan Baretzki and Heinrich Bischoff; and Arthur Breitwieser, a former functionary of the Economic-Administrative Division (IV), who had previously been tried in Poland and condemned to death, but had been granted a reprieve. In the course of the judicial proceedings, Gerhard Neubert and Karl Bischoff were also excluded on the basis of their health. In the end, six defendants received life sentences, the stiffest punishment allowed in the FRG, and the remaining defendants received sentences of anywhere between three to fourteen years in prison. [7]

The Second Frankfurt Trial was held from December 14, 1965 to September 16, 1966. Three defendants were put on trial: Wilhelm Burger, Director of the Economic-Administrative Divison (IV), once tried in Poland, as mentioned above; Josef Houstek-Erber; a functionary from the Political Division (II); and Gerhard Neubert, who had been dropped from the first trial due to his health. The three defendants received, respectively, terms of eight years, life, and three-and-a-half years in prison.

The Third Frankfurt Trial took place between August 30, 1967, and June 14, 1968. In the end, despite the prosecutor's plans to bring 32 defendants before the court, mainly drivers from Division I's vehicular-transport column, only two defendants — former prisoner-functionaries — were tried.

The last of the Frankfurt trials, Trial IV, lasted from December 18, 1973, to February 3, 1976. Indictments were handed down against two functionaries from Division III — Alois Frey, tried earlier in Poland, and Willi Sawatzki. The two defendants never went to trial, however. Frey was released, due to a lack of evidence for conviction, and the prosecutor dropped the case against Sawatzki. [8] Around a dozen other defendants were brought before the West German courts. No one from the Auschwitz guard staff was ever brought to trial, however, because it was universal practice in West Germany not to indict them.

Despite the efforts of several state prosecutors and the engagement of the *Zentralstelle der Landesjustizverwaltungen zur Aufklärung von NS-Gewaltverbrechen* [9] in Ludwigsburg, few members of the Auschwitz camp staff ever came before the (former) West German courts, although — as one might assume

---

[7] Hermann Langbein, *Der Auschwitz-Prozess. Eine Dokumentation* (Wien-Frankfurt a. M.-Zurich, 1965); Bert Naumann, *Auschwitz. Bericht über die Strafsache gegen Mulka u.a. vor dem Schwurgenicht Frankfurt* (Frankfurt a. M., 1965); Kazimierz Kąkol, *Sąd nierychliwy. Frankfurcki proces oprawców Oświęcimia* (Warszawa, 1966); Kazimierz Smoleń, "Karanie zbrodniarzy oświęcimskich" in *Oświęcim. Hitlerowski obóz masowej zagłady* (Warszawa, 1987), p. 183.

[8] K. Smoleń, p. 183.

[9] Literally, "Central Office of the State Judicial Authorities for the Investigation of Nazi Crimes".

— many of them were still living in the FRG. The Frankfurt trials themselves, as we can see from the statistics above, were mainly of a symbolic significance, given the number of defendants and the time passed since the end of the war. One should not, however, underestimate their importance, since they served to remind German public opinion and the world once more of the ignominy of the twentieth century that was KL Auschwitz.

In other European countries, even fewer former staff members from KL Auschwitz were ever brought to trial. This was particulary true of Austria, where only two trials took place, in Vienna in 1972 — one against two officers from the camp Construction Office, Fritz Ertl and Walter Dejaco, and the other against former functionaries of the Economic-Administrative Division (IV), Otto Graf and Franz Wunsch. It was assumed — quite correctly — that all of them had taken part in the mass-extermination process. All four cases ended, however, in a verdict of not guilty.

The former German Democratic Republic (GDR) achieved even less results in terms of prosecuting suspects. As one might expect, members of the camp SS staff also lived in East Germany after the war. Only one trial took place in the GDR, in 1966, against Horst Fischer, the former SS camp doctor, whose crimes were certainly of the same magnitude as the infamous Josef Mengele. He was condemned to death, but up to that point, he had had his own private practice — under his own name — in East Berlin.

Two other staff members — SS sanitarian Adolf Theuer and SS overseer Sophie Hanel — were both tried in Prague in the former Czechoslovakia and sentenced to death. In the Netherlands, an SS man from the Auschwitz-affiliated Deutsche Lebensmittel GmbH, Hans Lariviere, was convicted and sent to prison.

Other tribunals passed judgment on former staff members without considering their activities at Auschwitz. The American, British and French military tribunals put SS staff members from other concentration camps on trial, who — given the rotation of cadres throughout the camps — had also held posts at Auschwitz. In the trial against the staff from KL Bergen-Belsen, a British court-martial condemned the following former staff members from KL Auschwitz to death: Josef Kramer (Rudolf Höss's adjutant and later, commandant of KL Auschwitz II-Birkenau), Franz Hössler (one-time *Lagerführer* of the women's camp at Birkenau), Peter Weingärtner (*Blockführer* at Birkenau), Elisabeth Volkenrath (head SS overseer or *Oberaufseherin* at KL Auschwitz from 1944-45), and the SS overser Irma Grese. Another British military tribunal sentenced two former doctors from KL Auschwitz, Bruno Kitt and Alfred Trzebinski, to death in the trial of the camp staff from KL Neuengamme. American military courts subsequently tried, among others: Vinzenz Schöttl, former *Lagerführer* at KL Auschwitz III-Monowitz, and Otto Moll, the former head of the crematoria at Birkenau, in the trial against the staff at KL Dachau; Friedrich Entress and Helmuth Vetter, camp doctors, in the trial against the staff at KL Mauthausen; Hans Merbach, commander of the canine company, in the trial against the staff at KL Buchenwald; and Johann Schwarzhuber, former *Lagerführer* of the men's camp at KL Auschwitz II-Birkenau in the trial against the staff of KL Ravensbrück. The

Americans sentenced all the listed individuals to death and carried out the sentences. In its trial against the staff of KL Natzweiler, the French military tribunal sentenced to death Friedrich Hartjenstein, one-time commandant of KL Auschwitz II-Birkenau, and Heinrich Schwarz, commandant of KL Auschwitz III-Monowitz.

Based on our preceding evaluation of the international effort to dispense justice, we must conclude that it was not very impressive at all. Although at least 788 SS staff members from KL Auschwitz had to stand trial before various tribunals [10], this number represented only 12-15% of the former SS staff members at KL Auschwitz — by no means a significant figure. Many well-know criminals from the camp never had to face trial, including: Hans Schurz (Maximilian Grabner's successor as head of the camp's Political Division); Erich Wosnitza, Gerhard Lachmann, and Anton Brose — also employed in the Political Division; Johann Gorges, Hubert Busch, Ewald Kelm, Robert Seitz, Karl Steinberg and Peter Voss — crematoria directors at Birkenau; Anton Taube and Georg Sommerer from Division III — Camp Administration; and Richard Perschel from Division IIIa, Prisoner Employment. These are only a few examples. Several other major criminals escaped trial by perishing during military operations or committing suicide. Former staff members in this category included the infamous *Rapportführer-SS* Gerhard Palitzsch; the SS garrison doctor, Eduard Wirths; and the *Lagerfüher* at the main camp, Karl Fritzsch. In a number of cases, the dispensation of justice was hindered by problems with extradition (e.g., in the case of doctor-experimenter Horst Schumann) or a lack of effective pursuit (e.g., Josef Mengele).

It seems that after an initial — and to some extent, successful — period spent pursuing war-crimes suspects from KL Auschwitz in the 1950's, the international justice system decided to leave the judgment of war criminals to the historians. And at this point, the only judgment we can make is with regard to moral responsibility for the crimes committed.

This represents only one side of the issue. The other side is that in most cases, the adjudicating bodies treated the crimes committed by the guards at the camp in the same way as the crimes committed by functionaries in the camp administration. This mistake likely reflects the fact that the proposed changes in international law accepted during the war did not conform to the situation at the end of the war. On the basis of these regulations, war-crimes defendants were prosecuted on the same basis as common criminals. Legislators had not taken into account the way in which the camps had actually functioned and the role of individual staff members; as a result, courts wrongly interpreted the role of individual defendants in the camp's extermination mechanism. This was particulary true of the numerous cases in which no irrefutable evidence of guilt was available. Given the Nazis' systematic destruction of evidence related to their crimes and the lack of witnesses, courts had to make controversial decisions, particularly since their proceedings

---

[10] This figure is based on a list compiled by the author of former Auschwitz staff members who had to stand before various tribunals and is by no means final or definitive.

dragged out over a number of years for political and propaganda purposes. During the proceedings, many defendants died, and others were let go due to the state of their health.

As a result of this international conduct, we have to deal once more — at the end of the twentieth century — with the issue of genocide. Its initiators, undoubtedly aware of the results achieved in prosecuting Nazi war criminals, including those from KL Auschwitz, have been counting on — and will continue to count on — impunity.

BIBLIOGRAPHY

A d l e r, H. G. *Theresienstadt 1941-1945. Das Antlitz einer Zwangsgemeinschaft. Geschichte, Soziologie, Psychologie.* Tübingen, 1955.

L'Album d'Auschwitz. D'aprés un album déconvert par Lili Meier survivante du camp de concentration. Paris, 1983.

Amidst a Nightmare of Crime. Manuscripts of Members of Sonderkommando. Oświęcim, 1973.

A p o s t o ł - S t a n i s z e w s k a, Janina. *Nim zbudził się dzień.* Warszawa, 1979.

A r e n d t, Hannah. *Eichmann in Jerusalem. Ein Bericht von der Banalität des Bösen.* Reinbeck bei Hamburg, 1983.

Auschwitz. A History in Photographs. edit. Teresa Ś w i e b o c k a. Oświęcim, Bloomington, Warsaw, 1993.

Auschwitz. Anathomy of the Death Camp. edit. Michael B e r e n b a u m, Yisrael G u t m a n. Bloomington, Indianapolis, 1994.

Auschwitz 1940-1945. Węzłowe zagadnienia z dziejów obozu. t. I. Założenie i organizacja obozu. t. II. Więźniowie — życie i praca. t. III. Zagłada. t. IV. Ruch oporu. t. V. Epilog. edit. Wacław D ł u g o b o r s k i, Franciszek P i p e r. Oświęcim, 1995.

Auschwitz. Zeugnisse und Berichte. Herausgegeben von H. G. A d l e r, Hermann L a n g b e i n, Ella L i n g e n s R e i n e r. Köln, Frankfurt am Main, 1984.

B a u m, Bruno. *Widerstand in Auschwitz.* Berlin, 1957.

B i r e n b a u m, Halina. *Hope is the Last to Die. A Personal Documentation of Nazi Terror.* Oświęcim, 1994.

B r a h a m, Randolph L. *The Destruction of Hungarian Jewry.* New York, 1963.

B r a n d h u b e r, Jerzy. "Die sowjetischen Kriegsgefangenen im KL Auschwitz", *Hefte von Auschwitz* 4. Oświęcim, 1961.

B r i n g m a n n, Fritz. *Kindermord am Bullenhuserdamm. SS-Verbrechen in Hamburg 1945: Menschenversuche an Kindern.* Frankfurt am Main, 1978.

C e g ł o w s k a, Teresa. "Strafkompanien im KL Auschwitz", *Hefte von Auschwitz* 17. Oświęcim, 1985.

C i e s i e l s k i, Edward. *Wspomnienia oświęcimskie.* Kraków, 1968.

Commandant of Auschwitz. London, 1959.

C o n w a y, John S. "Fürhe Augenzeugenberichte aus Auschwitz. Glaubwürdigkeit und Wirkungsgeschichte", *Vieteljahrshefte für Zeitgeschichte.* Stuttgart, 1979 nr 2.

Criminal Experiments on Human Beings in Auschwitz and War Research Laboratories. Redaction Lore Shelley. San Francisco, 1992.

C z e c h, Danuta. "Deportation und Vernichtung der griechischen Juden im KL Auschwitz", *Hefte von Auschwitz* 11. Oświęcim, 1970.

C z e c h, Danuta. "Die Rolle des Häftlingskrankenbaulagers im KL Auschwitz II", *Hefte von Auschwitz* 15. Oświęcim, 1975.

C z e c h, Danuta. *Kalendarium der Ereignisse im Konzentrationslager Auschwitz-Birkenau 1939-1945.* Reinbeck bei Hamburg, 1989.

Death Books from Auschwitz. München, New Providence, London, Paris, 1995.

D u n i n - W ą s o w i c z, Krzysztof. *Resistance in the Concentration Camps 1933-1945.* Warsaw, 1982.

E i s e n b a c h, Artur. *Hitlerowska polityka zagłady Żydów.* Warszawa, 1961.

Erinnerungen Auschwitzer Häftlinge. Oświęcim, 1995.

F e j k i e l, Władysław. *Eksperymenty dokonywane przez personel sanitarny SS w głównym obozie koncentracyjnym w Oświęcimiu.* "Przegląd Lekarski — Oświęcim". Kraków, 1964.

F r a n k l, Viktor E. *Ein Psychologe erlebt das Konzentrationslager.* Wien, 1947.

F i d e r k i e w i c z, Alfred. *Brzezinka. Wspomnienia z obozu.* Warszawa, 1965.

G a r l i ń s k i, Józef. *Fighting Auschwitz. The Resistance Movement in the Concentration Camp.* London, 1994.

Gedenkbuch. Opfer der Verfolgung der Juden unter der nationalsozialistischen Gewaltherrschaft in Deutschland 1933-1945. Koblenz, 1986.

G i l b e r t, Martin. *Atlas of the Holocaust.* London, 1982.

G i l b e r t, Martin. *Auschwitz and the Allies.* New York, 1982.

G i l b e r t, Martin. *The Holocaust. The Jewish Tragedy.* Glasgow, 1990.

G l i ń s k a, Alicja. *Moralność więźniów Oświęcimia.* "Etyka", 1967 t. II.

G ł o w a c k i, Czesław. *Z dokumentacji zbrodniczych doświadczeń Carla Clauberga.* "Przegląd Lekarski — Oświęcim". Kraków, 1976 nr 1.

G r e i f, Gideon. *Wir weinten tränenlos... Augenzeugenberichte der jüdischen "Sonderkommandos" in Auschwitz.* Köln, Weimar, Wien, 1995.

G o d o r o w s k i, Kazimierz. *Psychologia i psychopatologia hitlerowskich obozów koncentracyjnych. Próba analizy postaw i zachowań w warunkach ekstremalnych obciążeń.* Warszawa, 1985.

Gumkowski, Janusz i Kułakowski, Tadeusz. *Zbrodniarze hitlerowscy przed Najwyższym Trybunałem Narodowym.* Warszawa, 1961.

Hart, Kitty. *Return to Auschwitz. The Remarkable Story of a Girl who survived the Holocaust.* London, 1981.

Hefte von Auschwitz. Verlag Staatliches Museum Auschwitz-Birkenau nr 1-19. Oświęcim, 1959-1995.

Hilberg, Raul. *The Destruction of the European Jews.* London, 1961.

Hrabar, Roman; Tokarz, Zofia; Wilczur, Jacek E. *The Fate of Polish Children during the Last War.* Warsaw, 1979.

Iwaszko, Tadeusz. "Häftlingsfluchten aus dem Konzentrationslager Auschwitz", *Hefte von Auschwitz* 7. Oświęcim, 1964.

Jagoda, Zenon; Kłodziński, Stanisław; Masłowski, Jan. *Więźniowie Oświęcimia.* Kraków-Wrocław, 1984.

Jagoda, Zenon; Kłodziński, Stanisław; Masłowski, Jan. *Przyjaźnie oświęcimskie. Przegląd Lekarski — Oświęcim.* Kraków, 1978 nr 1.

Jawischowitz une annexe d'Auschwitz. edit. Henri Morand. Paris, 1985.

Kautsky, Benedikt. *Teufel und Verdammte.* Wien, 1961.

Kielar, Wiesław. *Anus Mundi. Five Years in Auschwitz.* Harmondsworth, 1982.

KL Auschwitz seen by the SS. Rudolf Höss, Pery Broad, Johann Paul Kremer. Oświęcim, 1991.

Klafkowski, Alfons. *Ściganie zbrodniarzy wojennych w Niemieckiej Republice Federalnej w świetle prawa międzynarodowego.* Poznań, 1986.

Klarsfeld, Serge; Steinberg, Maxime. *Memorial de la Deportation des Juifs de Belgique.* (?), 1982.

Klarsfeld, Serge. *Memorial of the Deported from France 1942-1944.* New York, 1983.

Kłodziński, Stanisław. *Sterylizacja i kastracja promieniami Roentgena w obozie oświęcimskim. Dr Horst Schumann.* "Przegląd Lekarski — Oświęcim". Kraków, 1964 nr 1.

Kłodziński, Stanisław. *Zbiór szkieletów żydowskich dla uniwersytetu III Rzeszy w Strassburgu.* "Przegląd Lekarski — Oświęcim". Kraków, 1964 nr 1.

Kłodziński, Stanisław. *Zbrodnicze doświadczenia farmakologiczne na więźniach obozu koncentracyjnego w Oświęcimiu (Preparat 3582, rutenol, BE 1034, periston).* "Przegląd Lekarski — Oświęcim". Kraków, 1964 nr 1.

Kraus, Ota; Kulka, Erich. *Die Todesfabrik.* Berlin, 1958.

Kret, Józef. "Ein Tag in der Strafkompanie", *Hefte von Auschwitz* 1. Oświęcim, 1959.

K u b i c a, Helena. *Dr Josef Mengele i ślady jego działalności.* "Przegląd Lekarski — Oświęcim". Kraków, 1980 nr 1.

L a n g b e i n, Hermann. *Die Stärkeren. Ein Bericht aus Auschwitz und anderen Konzentrationslagern.* Köln, 1982.

L a n g b e i n, Hermann. *Menschen in Auschwitz.* Frankfurt am Main, Berlin, Wien, 1980.

L a n g b e i n, Hermann. *...nicht wie die Schafe zur Schlachtbank. Widerstand in den nazialsozialistischen Konzentrationslagern 1938-1945.* Frankfurt am Main, 1980.

L e n g y e l, Olga. *Five Chimneys — The Story of Auschwitz.* Chicago, New York, (?).

L e s c h, Franz Xawer. P. *Maximillian Kolbe.* Würzburg 1964.

L e v i, Primo. *If this is a Man.* Abacus, 1987.

L e v i, Primo. *Survival in Auschwitz. The Nazi Assault on Humanity.* New York, 1959.

L i p s t a d t, Deborah E. *Beyond Belief. The American Press and the Coming of the Holocaust 1933-1945.* New York, 1986.

L o r s k a, Dorota. *Blok X w Oświęcimiu.* "Przegląd Lekarski — Oświęcim". Kraków, 1965 nr 1.

M a k o w s k i, Antoni. "Organisation, Entwicklung und Tätigkeit des Häftlingskrankenbaus in Monowitz (KL Auschwitz III)", *Hefte von Auschwitz* 15. Oświęcim 1975.

Memorial Book. The Gypsies at Auschwitz-Birkenau. München, London, New York, Paris, 1993.

M a r k, Ber. *The Scrolls of Auschwitz.* Tel Aviv, 1985.

Medizin ohne Menschlichkeit. Dokumente des Nürnberger Prozesses. Herausgegeben und kommentiert von Aleksander M i t s c h e r l i c h und Fred M i e l k e. Frankfurt am Main, 1962.

M e r m e l s t e i n, Mel. *By Bread Alone. The Story of A-4685.* Los Angeles, 1979.

M e y e r, Alwin. *Die Kinder von Auschwitz.* Göttingen, 1990.

M i k u l s k i, Jan. "Pharmakologische Experimente im Konzentrationslager Auschwitz--Birkenau", *Hefte von Auschwitz* 10. Oświęcim, 1967.

M i k u l s k i, Jan. *Medycyna hitlerowska w służbie III Rzeszy.* Warszawa, 1981.

M ü l l e r, Filip. *Eyewitness Auschwitz — Three Years in the Gas Chambers.* New York, 1979.

Nationalsozialistische Massentötung durch Giftgas. edit. Eugen K o g o n, Hermann L a n g b e i n. Frankfurt am Main, 1983.

Nyiszli, Miklós. *Auschwitz. A doctor's Eyewitness Account*. New York, 1960.

"Obóz koncentracyjny Oświęcim w świetle akt Delegatury RP na kraj", *Zeszyty Oświęcimskie*, Special Edition 1. Oświęcim, 1968.

Numery mówią. Wspomnienia więźniów KL Auschwitz. Katowice, 1980.

Pankowicz, Andrzej. "Das KL Auschwitz in den Nürnberger Prozessen", *Hefte von Auschwitz* 18. Oświęcim, 1990.

Pawełczyńska, Anna. *Values and Violence in Auschwitz. A Sociological Analysis.* Berkeley, Los Angeles, London, 1979.

Piątkowska, Antonina. *Wspomnienia oświęcimskie*. Kraków, 1977.

Piper, Franciszek. *Arbeitseinsatz der Häftlinge aus dem KL Auschwitz*. Oświęcim, 1995.

Piper, Franciszek. *Die Zahl der Opfer von Auschwitz. Aufgrund der Quellen und der Erträge der Forschung 1945 bis 1990*. Oświęcim, 1993.

Posner, Gerald L.; Ware, John. *Mengele. The Complete Story*. New York, 1986.

Pressac, Jean-Claude. *Technique and Operation of the Gas Chambers*. New York, 1989.

Ptakowski, Jerzy. *Oświęcim bez cenzury i bez legend*. New York, 1985.

Righteous among Nations. How Poles helped the Jews. 1939-1945. edit. Władysław Bartoszewski, Zofia Lewinówna. London, 1969.

Reitlinger, Gerald. *The Final Solution*. London, 1971.

Schnabel, Raimund. *Macht ohne Moral. Eine Dokumentation über die SS*. Frankfurt am Main, 1957.

Schwarzberg, Günter. *Der SS Arzt und die Kinder. Bericht über den Mord vom Bullenhuser Damm*. Hamburg, 1979.

Sehn, Jan. "Carl Claubergs verbrecherische Unfruchtbarmachungsversuche an Häftlingsfrauen in den Nazi-Konzentrationslagern", *Hefte von Auschwitz* 2. Oświęcim, 1959.

Sehn, Jan. *Concentration Camp Oświęcim-Brzezinka (Auschwitz-Birkenau). Based on documentary Evidence and Sources*. Warsaw, 1957.

Sehn, Jan. *Sprawa oświęcimskiego lekarza SS J. P. Kremera*. "Przegląd Lekarski — Oświęcim". Kraków, 1962 nr 1.

Sobański, Tomasz. *Fluchtwege aus Auschwitz*. Warschau, 1980.

Sobolewicz, Tadeusz. *Aus dem Jenseits zurück*. Oświęcim, 1993.

Spritzer, Jenny. *Ich war Nr. 10 291. Tatsachenbericht einer Schreiberin der politischen Abteilung aus dem Konzentrationslager Auschwitz*. Darmstadt, 1980.

S t e r k o w i c z, Stanisław. *Zbrodnicze eksperymenty medyczne w obozach koncentracyj-nych Trzeciej Rzeszy.* Warszawa, 1981.

S t r z e l e c k a, Irena. "Das Männerlager in Birkenau (BIb) — März 1942 — Juli 1943", *Hefte von Auschwitz* 19. Oświęcim, 1995.

S t r z e l e c k a, Irena. "Die ersten Polen im KL Auschwitz", *Hefte von Auschwitz* 18. Oświęcim, 1990.

S t r z e l e c k i, Andrzej. *Endphase des KL Auschwitz. Evakuierung, Liquidierung und Befreiung des Lagers.* Oświęcim, 1995.

S t r z e l e c k i, Andrzej. "Das Nebenlager Jawischowitz", *Hefte von Auschwitz* 15. Oświęcim, 1975.

S t r z e l e c k i, Andrzej. *Marsz Śmierci — Przewodnik po trasie Oświęcim-Wodzisław Śląski.* Katowice, 1989.

S z m a g l e w s k a, Seweryna. *Smoke over Birkenau.* New York, 1947.

Ś w i e b o c k i, Henryk. "Auschwitz — czy w czasie wojny świat znał prawdę o obozie". *Zeszyty Oświęcimskie*, Special Edition IV. Oświęcim, 1992.

Ś w i e b o c k i, Henryk. "Die lagernahe Widerstandsbewegung und ihre Hilfsaktionen für die Häftlinge des KL Auschwitz", *Hefte von Auschwitz* 19. Oświęcim, 1995.

Š v a l b o v a, M. *Vyhasnuté oči.* Bratislava, 1964.

T e r n o n, Yves; H e l m a n, Socrate. *Histore de la médicine SS, on le mythe du racisme biologique.* Tournai, 1972.

Totenbuch — Theresienstadt. Wien, 1987.

W e l l e r s, Georges. *Essai de détermination du nombre de morts au camp d'Auschwitz.* "Le Monte Juif". Paris, 1983 nr 112.

W faszistowskich zastienkach. Mińsk, 1958.

W i e s e l, Elie. *Night.* London, 1960.

W r ó b e l, Halina. "Die Liquidation des Konzentrationslagers Auschwitz-Birkenau", *Hefte von Auschwitz* 6, Oświęcim 1962.

W y m a n, David S. *The Abandonment of the Jews. America and the Holocaust 1941-1945.* New York, 1984.

Ż y w u l s k a, Krystyna. *I came back.* London, 1951. lub. New York, 1951.

Abbreviations

AGKBZH	Archiwum Głównej Komisji Badania Zbrodni Hitlerowskich w Polsce (Archives of the Main Commission for the Investigation of Hitlerian Crimes in Poland)
AK	Armia Krajowa (Home Army)
APMO	Archiwum Państwowego Muzeum w Oświęcimiu (Archives of the State Museum at Oświęcim)
Aso	Asoziale
B	Bauabschnitt
BA Koblenz	Bundesarchiv Koblenz
BBC	British Broadcasting Corporation
BCh	Bataliony Chłopskie (Peasant Battalions)
BV	Berufsverbrecher
EH	Erziehungshäftling
E. Kdo	Einsatzkommando
FKL	Frauenkonzentrationslager
FL	Frauenlager
GBO	Grupa Bojowa Oświęcim (Kampfgruppe Auschwitz, or "Auschwitz Fighting Group")
Gestapo	Geheime Staatspolizei
GG	General Government
Greko	Grenzpolizeikommissariat
GU	Gesonderte Unterbringung
HKB	Häftlingskrankenbau
IBV	Internationale Bibelforschervereinigung
ISD Arolsen	Internationaler Suchdienst Arolsen
KGL	Kriegsgefangenenlager
KL	Konzentrationslager
Kripo	Kriminalpolizei
Mat RO	Materials from the camp resistance movement (pol. ruch oporu, resistance movement)
NN	Nacht und Nebel
OKH	Oberkommando des Heeres
OKW	Oberkommando der Wehrmacht
ONR	Obóz Narodowy Radykalny (National Radical Camp, prewar right-radical Polish political grouping)
Orpo	Ordnungspolizei
OT	Organisation Todt
PAP	Powiatowe Archiwum Państwowe (District Archive)
PH	Polizeihäftling
PPR	Polska Partia Robotnicza (Polish Workers' Party)
PPS	Polska Partia Socjalistyczna (Polish Socialist Party)
PSV	Polizeisicherungsverwahrte
PWOK	Pomoc Więźniom Obozów Koncentracyjnych (Polish group, Assistance to Concentration-Camp Prisoners)
RFSS	Reichsführer SS

RKG	Russische Kriegsgefangene (Russion Pow)
RKPA	Reichskriminalpolizeiamt
RSHA	Reichssicherheitshauptamt
RWO	Rada Wojskowa Oświęcim (pol., "Auschwitz Military Council")
RuSHA	Rasse- und Siedlungshauptamt (RuSHA) — Main Office for Racial and Settlement Questions
SA	Sturmabteilungen
SB	Sonderbehandlung
SD	Sicherheitsdienst
SS-WVHA	SS-Wirtschaftsverwaltunghauptamt
ZWZ	Związek Walki Zbrojnej ("Union of Armed Struggle", precursor to AK)

Glossary of Camp Terms

Arbeitseinsatz, division of the camp administration responsible for prisoner employment.

Arbeitseinsatzführer, the SS man who headed the camp's prisoner-employment division.

Asoziale (Aso), prisoner designation, "antisocial".

Aufseherin, female SS overseer for women prisoners.

Aufnahmegebäude, building where prisoners were received and registered at the camp.

Aussenlager, outside camp or sub-camp.

Bauabschnitt (B), building site at the camp (the camp at Birkenau was divided into the following building sites: BIa-b, BII-g and BIII, which themselves became individual camps of varying significance).

Bauhof, area where building materials were stored in warehouses.

Bauleitung, the camp construction office, responsible for the construction and expansion of the camp.

Bekleidungskammer, "dressing chamber", the camp warehouse for prisoner clothing.

Berufsverbrecher (BV), designation for prisoners who were professional criminals.

Blockältester, "block senior", the prisoner-functionary who oversaw prisoners in their residential block.

Blockführer, an SS man who oversaw a block of prisoners.

Blockführerstube, the guardhouse where the *Blockführer* resided.

"Blocksperre", a prohibition on prisoners leaving their blocks.

Briefaktion, the letter-writing campaign organized by the SS for Jews from Theresienstadt, who were forced before their annihilation to tell their relatives in Czechoslovakia that living conditions at the camp were good.

Bunkier, the cellar of Block 11, where the camp jail was located.

Depothäftlinge, prisoners temporarily "deposited" on the grounds of the camp at Birkenau. In original documents always referred to as "Durchgangsjuden".

Durchgangsjuden, Jewish prisoners temporarily held at the camp who were never registered.

Durchgangslager, transit camp.

Effektenkammer, the warehouse that held objects taken from prisoners upon their arrival at the camp.

Effektenlager, the area of the camp where warehouses containing objects taken from Jews upon their arrival were located (aka "Kanada").

Einsatzkommando (E.Kdo), a special operations group organized by the Nazis for conducting repressive activities against the civilian population in occupied areas outside the Third Reich.

Entwesungskammer, chamber in which disinfection and delousing were carried out.

Erkennungsdienst, the photographic facilities attached to the Gestapo's identification service at the camp.

Erziehungshäftling (EH), reformatory-work prisoner.

Erziehungskompanie, a company of reformatory-work prisoners.

Familienlager Theresienstadt, family camp at Birkenau where Jews from the Theresienstadt ghetto were held.

Familienzigeunerlager, family camp for Gypsies at the Birkenau camp.

Fluchtpunkt, a special designation for prisoners whom the camp authorities suspected of wanting to escape; the red point sewn on the uniform of such prisoners.

Frauenkonzentrationslager (FKL) women's concentration camp.

Frauenlager (FL) camp for women.

Führerheim, hotel and casino for the SS.

Geheime Staatspolizei (Gestapo), secret state police.

Geheimnisträger, "bearer of secrets" — designation written in the personal records of prisoners employed at locations where they could observe the mass extermination.

Gesonderte Unterbringung (GU), "separate chamber", codename used to designate the annihilation of prisoners.

Grenzpolizeikommissariat (Greko), commissioner's office for the German border police.

Grosse Postenkette, the "great cordon" of sentry posts surrounding the camp.

Häftling, prisoner.

Häftlingskrankenbau (HKB), the prisoner infirmary.

Häftlings-Personalbogen, the form containing the personal data of each prisoner.

Höhere SS- und Polizeiführer, Superior Commander of the SS and Police.

Hundestaffel, the canine company; the SS unit with specially-trained dogs.

Hygiene Institut der Waffen-SS und Polizei, the Hygienical Institute for the *Waffen-SS* and Police.

Interessengebiet, the camp's "area of interest" around the camp.

Internationale Bibelforschervereinigung (IBV), International Union for Study of the Scripture, or Jehovah's Witnesses; the abbreviation IBV was entered into the personal records of prisoners being held at the camp for membership in this religious group.

Kalfaktor, the prisoner-functionary who served as *Kapo* in the "Bunker" or camp jail.

"Kanada" the camp warehouses where the personal effects of Jews brought to the camp for annihilation were stored.

Kapo, a prisoner-functionary who oversaw prisoners in their work-details.

"Kiesgrube", the gravel-pit where prisoners were forced to work.

Kleine Postenkette, the "small cordon" of sentry posts surrounding the camp.

Kommando, work-detail for prisoners.

Kommandoführer, the SS man who directed and oversaw a given work-detail of prisoners.

Kommandanturbefehl, an order from the camp commandant's office.

Konzentrationslager, (KL), concentration camp.

"Königsgraben", "royal ditch", the main drainage ditch at Birkenau, excavated with the forced labor of prisoners.

Kriegsgefangenenlager, (KGL), prisoner of war camp.

Kriminalpolizei (kripo), criminal police

Lager, camp

Lagerarzt, camp doctor.

Lagerältester, the "camp senior", a prisoner-functionary.

Lagerführer, the SS man supervising the camp.

"Lagersperre", a prohibition on prisoners' leaving the camp.

Lagererweiterung, the camp extension; the additional blocks built for prisoners next to the main camp, Auschwitz I.

"Mexico", construction site BIII at Birkenau.

Muselman, prisoner in an extreme state of physical and psychological exhaustion.

Nationalsozialistische Deutsche Arbeiterpartei (NSDAP), National-Socialist German Workers' Party, the Nazis.

Nacht und Nebel, "Night and Fog"; codename for arrest campaigns carried out against individuals considered particularly dangerous, who were secretly delivered to the camp and isolated from the remaining prisoners.

Nebenlager, sub-camp.

Oberaufseherin, the SS-woman who worked as Head Overseer for the women's camp.

Oberkommando des Heeres, the High Command for German land armies.

Oberkommando der Wehrmacht, the German Armed Forces' High Command.

Ordnungspolizei (ORPO), German police responsible for public order.

Quarantänelager, the quarantine camp (BII) at Birkenau.

Politische Abteilung, the Political Division, or camp Gestapo.

Polizeihäftling (PH), a police prisoner.

Polizeisicherungsverwahrte (PSV), an individual placed under preventive arrest and held at a concentration camp.

Polizeistandgericht, police court-martial.

Postenkette, the security cordon around the camp.

Rapportführer, senlisted officers who answered to the *Lagerführer*.

Rapportschreiber, a prisoner-functionary responsible for writing reports.

Reichskriminalpolizeiamt (RKPA), Administration for the Criminal Police of the *Reich*.

Reichssicherheitshauptamt (RSHA), Main Office for Reich Security.

Revier, SS hospital at the camp.

Russische Kriegsgefangene (RKG), Russian prisoners of war.

Sammeltransport, collective transport of prisoners of various categories to the camp.

Sanitätsdienstgrad (SDG), SS-sanitarian.

Sauna, the camp showers.

Schreibstube, the camp writing office, where prisoners were employed.

Schutzhaft, protective custody.

Schutzhaftbefehl, warrant for protective custody.

Schutzhäftling, prisoner held in so-called "protective custody".

Schutzhaftlagerführung, Camp Administration, Division III.

Schutzhaftlagererweiterung, the camp extension.

Schutzstaffeln (SS), Nazi "security staff".

Sicherheitsdienst (SD), security service.

Sicherheitspolizei und Sicherheitsdienst (Sipo und SD), Security Police and Security Service.

Sonderaktion, special action.

Sonderbehandlung, "special treatment" — cryptonym used for the extermination of prisoners.

Sonderkommando, special work-detail made up of Jews whom the SS forced to remove corpses from the gas chambers and then burn them.

Staatspolizei (Stapo), the state police.

Stammlager, the main camp (Auschwitz I).

Standortarzt, doctor for the SS garrison.

Standortbefehl, order for the garrison.

Stärkebuch, the log book of the number of prisoners at the camp.

Stärkemeldung, the daily report on the number of prisoners at the camp.

Stehzellen, 90 × 90 cm cells, in which four prisoners were forced to stand together as a punishment.

Strafkompanie (SK), penal company, to which prisoners were assigned for various infractions.

Strafmeldung, report on the punishment of a prisoner.

Sturmabteilungen (SA), "storm" divisions.

Totenmeldung, report of an individual's death.

Transport RSHA, railway transports of Jews sent to the camp by the Jewish Section (IV B4) of RSHA.

Truppenbetreuung, the administration for SS divisions.

Truppenwirtschaftslager (TWL), economic warehouses of the SS.

Wirtschaftsverwaltungshauptamt der SS (SS WVHA) — the Main Economic-Administrative Office of the SS.

Verwaltung, the administration.

Zentralbauleitung der Waffen SS und Polizei, the Main Construction Office for the *Waffen-SS* and Police.

Zugangsliste, the list of newly-arrived prisoners at the camp.

Zigeuner (Z), Gypsy.

Zigeunerlager, camp for Gypsies.

SS Ranks

Rank in the SS	Wehrmacht Equivalent	Equivalent in English
SS-Bewerber	—	SS candidate
SS-Mann	Schütze	SS man, Private
SS-Sturmmann	Gefreiter	Private 1st-class
SS-Rottenführer	Obergefreiter	Private 1st-class
SS-Unterscharführer	Unteroffizier	Corporal
SS-Scharführer	Unterfeldwebel	Platoon Leader
SS-Oberscharführer	Feldwebel	Sergeant
SS-Hauptscharführer	Oberfeldwebel	Sergeant 1st-class
SS-Stabsscharführer	Stabsfeldwebel	Staff
—	Hauptfeldwebel	Sergeant
SS-Untersturmführer	Leutnant	Second Lieutenant
SS-Obersturmführer	Oberleutnant	Lieutenant
SS-Hauptsturmführer	Hauptmann	Captain
SS-Sturmbannführer	Major	Major
SS-Obertsturmbannführer	Oberleutnant	Lt. Colonel
SS-Standartenführer	Oberst	Colonel
SS-Oberführer		—
SS-Brigadeführer	Generalmajor	Brigadier General
SS-Gruppenführer	Generalleutnant	General (of a division)
SS-Obergruppenführer	General	General (Two-Star)
SS-Oberstgruppenführer	Generaloberst	General (Three-Star)
Reichsführer SS	Generalfeldmarschall	Supreme Commander

Index of names

Index of geographic names

Index of prisons, ghettos and camps

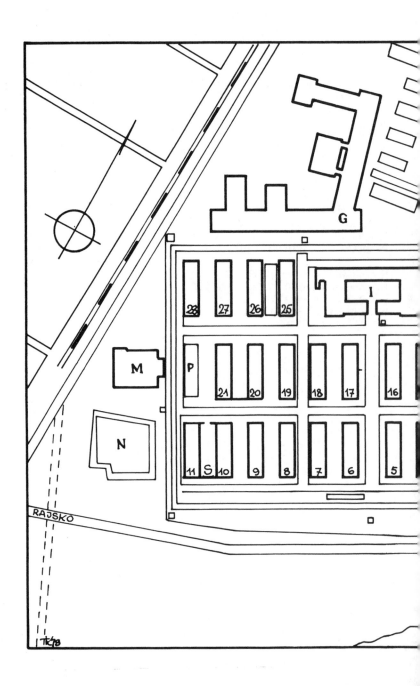

Map by Tadeusz Kinowski

KL Auschwitz I

A   Camp commandant's house
B   Main guardhouse
C   Offices of Division I,
      camp commandant's office
D   Offices of the Camp
      Administration
E   Hospital for the SS
F   Offices of the Political
      Division (camp *Gestapo*)
G   Building at which new
      prisoners were received
H   Entry gate with inscription
      Arbeit macht frei
I   Kitchen
KI   Gas Chamber and
      Crematorium I
L   Economic barracks
      and workshops
M   Warehouses for objects
      stolen from the victims
      ("Kanada I")
N   Gravel-pit; location where
      prisoners were executed
O   Area where the camp
      orchestra played
P   Barracks used as a laundry
      for the SS
R   *Blockführerstube*, guard
      house manned by the
      Blockführer
S   Execution Wall
1-28   Residential blocks for
      prisoners

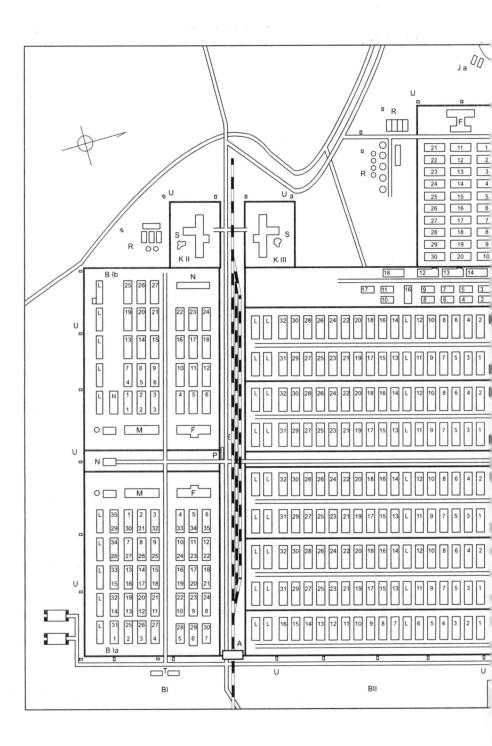

Map by Anna Strzelecka-Jasiewicz

KL Auschwitz II-Birkenau

A	Main gate guardhouse — the "gate of death"
BI	Sector of the Birkenau concentration camp
BIa	Aug. 1942 to Nov. 1944 — Camp for women (Jews and non-Jews) from different countries
BIb	March 1942 to July 1943 — Camp for men (Jews and non-Jews) from different countries July 1943 to Nov. 1944 — Camp for women (Jews and non-Jews) from different countries
BII	Sector II of the Birkenau concentration camp
BIIa	From Aug. 1943 — Quarantine area for men (Jews and non-Jews)
BIIb	Sep. 1943 to July 11/2, 1944 — "Family camp" for Jews from the Theresienstadt ghetto
BIIc	From June 1944 — Transit camp for Jewish women, mainly from Hungary
BIId	From July 1943 to Jan. 1945 — Camp for men (Jews and non--Jews) from different countries
BIIe	Feb. 1943 to Aug. 2,1944 — "Family camp" for Gypsies
BIIf	July 1943 to Jan. 1945 — Holding area for sick men prisoners ("infirmary")
BIII	Sector III of the Birkenau concentration camp ("Mexico"). Barracks marked according to an allied photograph from May 31, 1944.
C	Camp Headquarters and SS barracks
D	Warehouse for items plundered from the victims ("Kanada II")
E	Railway platform ("ramp") where transports of Jews were "unloaded" and selections were carried out
F	Shower barracks ("Sauna")
G	Sites where corpses were burned in the open air
H	Mass graves of Soviet prisoners of war
I	First temporary gas chamber
J	Second temporary gas chamber
I-a, J-a	Undressing barracks next to the temporary gas chambers.
KII	Gas Chamber and Crematorium II
KIII	Gas Chamber and Crematorium III
KIV	Gas Chamber and Crematorium IV
KV	Gas Chamber and Crematorium V
L	Latrines and washrooms
M	Kitchens
N	Warehouses
O	Barracks for peeling potatoes
P	SS guardrooms (Blockführerstuben)
R	Sewage plant
S	Locations used dumping the ashes of murdered victims
T	Barracks for the exit quarantine
U	Guard towers
W	Road built after the war

The barracks where prisoners were housed are marked with arabic numerals. In section BIa the numbers at the bottom of each strucure are barrack numbers, which were changed in mid-1944. In section BIb the numbers at the bottom are the first ones.

Compositior:
REPROTEKST — Kraków, phone (+ 48 12) 421-29-25

Printing:
DEKA — Kraków, phone (+ 48 12) 653-12-70